Lapland
p268

Oulu, Kainuu
& Koillismaa
p243

West Coast
p216

The Lakeland
p161

Karelia
p190

Tampere &
Häme
p136

Karelia
p190

Åland
Archipelago
p117

Turku & the
South Coast
p82

★ Helsinki
p42

PAGE
337
SURVIVAL
GUIDE

VITAL PRACTICAL INFORMATION TO
HELP YOU HAVE A SMOOTH TRIP

Language

THIS EDITION WRITTEN AND RESEARCHED BY
Andy Symington, Fran Parnell

welcome to
Finland

Call of the Wild

The Finland you encounter will depend on the season of your visit, but whatever the month, the call of the wilderness is a siren song not to be resisted. There's something pure in the Finnish air and spirit that's really vital and exciting; it's an invitation to get out and active year-round. With vast tracts of forest, speckled by picture-perfect lakes as if an artist had flicked a blue paintbrush at the map, Suomi offers some of Europe's best hiking, kayaking and canoeing. A fabulous network of national parks has well-marked routes and regularly spaced huts for overnighting. There are bears deep in the eastern forests, where you can watch them on nature-watching trips.

Summer Days

Finland's short but reliable sunny season sees the country burst into life. Finns seem to want to suck every last golden drop out of the summer in the hope that it will last them through the long dark winter months, and there's an explosion of good cheer and optimism. It's a time for music festivals, art exhibitions, lake cruises, midnight sunshine on convivial beer terraces, lazy days at remote waterside cottages and mouth-watering market produce.

After the Snowfall

Winter, too, has a special charm. The best way to banish those frosty subzero temperatures is to get out and active. For start-

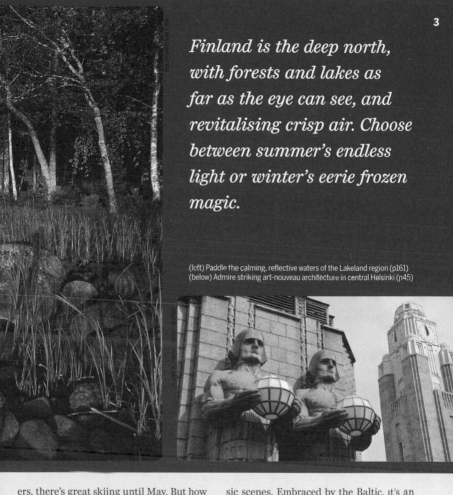

Finland is the deep north, with forests and lakes as far as the eye can see, and revitalising crisp air. Choose between summer's endless light or winter's eerie frozen magic.

(left) Paddle the calming, reflective waters of the Lakeland region (p161)
(below) Admire striking art-nouveau architecture in central Helsinki (p45)

ers, there's great skiing until May. But how about chartering a team of dogs, a posse of reindeer, or a snowmobile for a trek across the snowy wastes, lit by a beautiful, pale winter sun? Catch the aurora borealis (Northern Lights) after your wood-fired sauna and you'll feel blessed by the universe. Need to cool down? A night in an ice hotel or an ice-breaker cruise should do the trick.

City Lights

Don't get the idea that the country's just a backwoods emptiness, though. Vibrant cities stock the southern parts, headed by the capital, Helsinki, a cutting-edge urban space with world-famous design and mu-sic scenes. Embraced by the Baltic, it's an enticing ensemble of modern and stately architecture, island restaurants, and stylish and quirky bars. And complaints about Finnish food are so last-century: the 'new Suomi' restaurant scene is kicking.

Finns

The real bonus? The Finns, who tend to do their own thing and are much the better for it. Independent, loyal, warm and welcoming – a memorable people in an inspirational country. Make it your business to get to know some.

» Finland

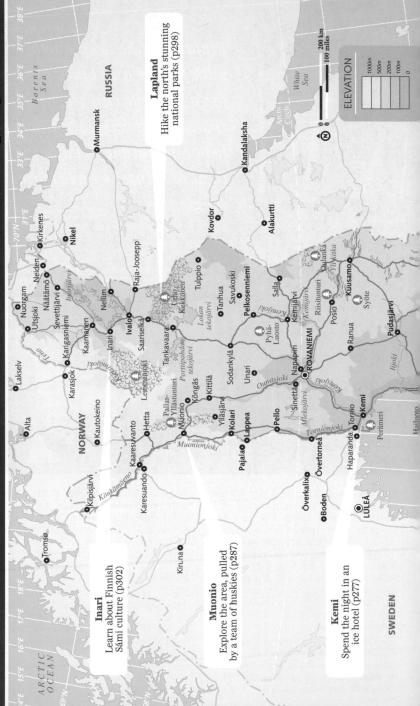

Inari
Learn about Finnish
Sámi culture (p302)

Muonio
Explore the area, pulled
by a team of huskies (p287)

Kemi
Spend the night in an
ice hotel (p277)

Lapland
Hike the north's stunning
national parks (p298)

ELEVATION

1000m
500m
200m
100m
0

200 km
100 miles

NORWAY

SWEDEN

RUSSIA

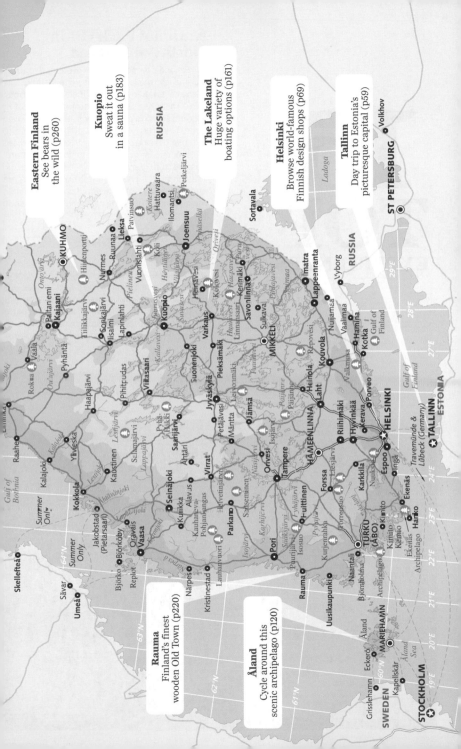

Eastern Finland
See bears in
the wild (p260)

Kuopio
Sweat it out
in a sauna (p183)

The Lakeland
Huge variety of
boating options (p161)

Helsinki
Browse world-famous
Finnish design shops (p69)

Tallinn
Day trip to Estonia's
picturesque capital (p59)

Rauma
Finland's finest
wooden Old Town (p220)

Åland
Cycle around this
scenic archipelago (p120)

RUSSIA

RUSSIA

ESTONIA

SWEDEN

Gulf of
Bothnia

Gulf of
Finland

Aland
Sea

ST PETERSBURG

TALLINN

HELSINKI

STOCKHOLM

MARIEHAMN

TURKU
(ÅBO)

PORI

VAASA

KOKKOLA

KAJAANI

KUHMO

JOENSUU

KUOPIO

MIKKELI

HÄMEENLINNA

Tampere

Summer
Only

Summer
Only

Travemünde &
Lübeck (Germany)

15 TOP EXPERIENCES

National Park Hiking, Northern Finland

1 Finland's great swaths of protected forests and fells make it one of Europe's prime hiking destinations. Head to the Karhunkierros (p262) near Kuusamo for a striking terrain of hills and sharp ravines, never prettier than in autumn. The Urho Kekkonen National Park (p298) in Lapland is one of Europe's great wildernesses; the spectacular gorge of the Kevo Strict Nature Reserve (p307) and the fell scenery of Pallas-Yllästunturi National Park (p289) are other great northern options. A network of camping huts make itinerary planning easy and are good spots to meet Finns. Oulanka National Park

Design Shopping in Helsinki

2 Functional, elegant, outrageous or wacky: the choice is yours. The capital's decidedly nonmainstream chic is best explored by browsing the vast variety of design shops that spatter its centre. Whether examining iconic 20th-century Finnish forms in the flagship emporia of brands like Iittala, Marimekko and Artek, or tracking down the cutting edge and just plain weird in the bohemian Punavuori district, you're sure to find something you didn't know you needed but just can't do without.

1

BLICKWINKEL / ALAMY ©

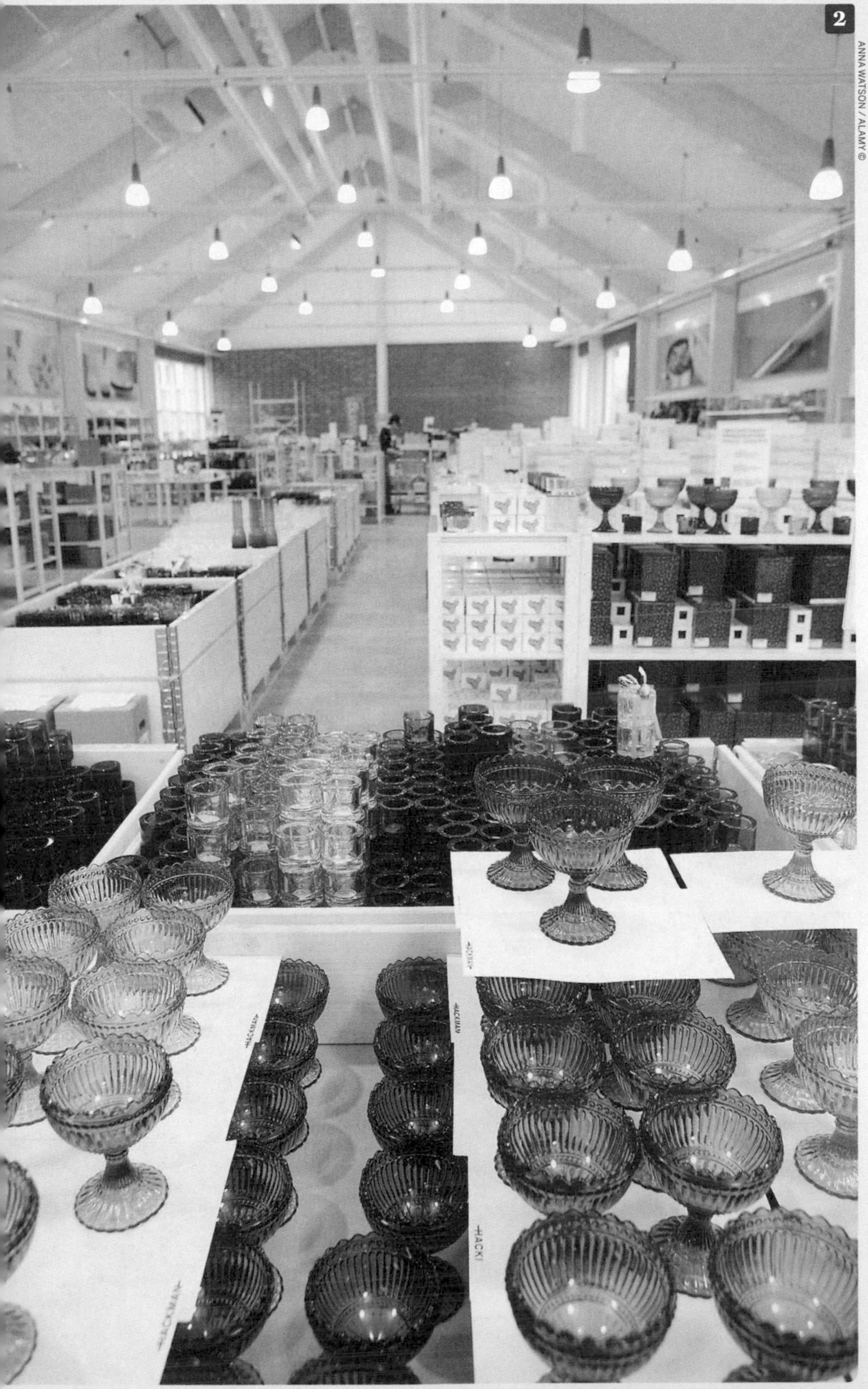

ANNA WATSON / ALAMY ©

Sledding & Snowmobiling, Lapland

3 Fizzing over the snow behind a team of huskies under the low winter sun is tough to beat. Short jaunts are great, but overnight safaris give you time to feed and bond with your lovable dogs and try out a wood-fired sauna in the middle of the winter wilderness. It's no fairy-tale ride though; expect to eat some snow before you learn to control your team. If you're more of a cat person, you can enjoy similar trips on a snowmobile or behind reindeer. Gulf of Bothnia, near Kemi

Music Festivals

4 Are you a chamber-music aficionado? Or do you like rock so raucous it makes your ears bleed? Whatever your pleasure, Finland has a music festival to suit. Savonlinna's fortress is the dramatic setting for a month-long opera festival; fiddlers gather at Kaustinen for full-scale folk; Pori, Espoo and Tampere attract thousands of jazz fans; workaday Seinäjoki flashes sequins and high heels during its five-day tango festival; temples to rock are raised in Seinäjoki, Tampere, Turku and Vantaa; and the Sibelius Festival ushers in autumn with classical grace. Savonlinna Opera Festival

Bear-Watching, Eastern Finland

5 Old Honeypaws, the brown bear *(Ursus arctos)*, is the national animal of Finland. Around a thousand of these powerful creatures live in the northeast, coming and going with impunity across the Finnish–Russian border. Several operators run bear hides close to the frontier, where you can sit a silent night's vigil as bruins snuffle out elk carcasses and carefully hidden chunks of salmon. The best time to see them is between mid-April and August – with a slight gap in July when the bears have mating rather than meals in mind.

Summer Cottages

6 The symbol of the Finnish summer is a cosy cottage perched on a placid blue lake, with a little rowing boat, a fishing pier, and perhaps its own swimming beach. The simplest rustic cabins have outside loos and water drawn from a well, while the most modern designer bungalows have every creature comfort, from state-of-the-art coffee machines to infrared saunas. Whether you're looking for a wilderness escape or somewhere for a big family party, you're bound to find the perfect place from the thousands of rental cottages on offer.

Food Markets

7 Counters selling speciality cheeses, rough black rye breads, handmade chocolates, Finnish sausages and smoked Baltic herring fill richly scented indoor market halls (kauppahalli) throughout Finland, while fleeting summer market squares (kauppatori) burst with straight-from-the-garden vegetables. Around Midsummer, fill your bags with tiny new potatoes, nutty and sweet. In July, meander with a mouthful of juicy red strawberries, or sit on a sunny bench to pop peas fresh from the pod. Autumn's approach is softened by tumbled piles of peppery chanterelles and glowing Lapland cloudberries, which appear through August like a magician's trick.

Sámi Culture, Inari

8 Finland's indigenous northerners have used technology to ease the arduous side of reindeer herding while maintaining an intimate knowledge of Lapland's natural world. Their capital, Inari, and the nearby Lemmenjoki National Park (p305) are the best places to begin to learn about Sámi culture and traditions, starting at the marvellous Siida museum (p302). Arrange wilderness excursions with Sámi guides, meet reindeer, and browse high-quality handicrafts and music, the sale of which benefits local communities.

Traditional Saunas

9 These days most Finns have saunas at home, but there are still a few of the old public ones left. They smell of old pine, tar shampoo and long tradition, with birch whisks and no-nonsense scrubdowns available as extras. Weathered Finnish faces cool down on the street outside, loins wrapped in a towel and hand wrapped around a cold beer. Helsinki and Tampere are the best places for this, while Kuopio's old-style smoke sauna (p183) takes a day to prepare and offers a more rural experience, with a lake to jump into right alongside.

PAUL HARDING / LONELY PLANET IMAGES ©

Watery Activities, Lakeland

10 This part of Finland seems to have more water than land, so it'd be a crime not to get out on it. You can take three days to paddle the family-friendly Oravareitti (Squirrel Route; p174) or head out into Kolovesi and Linnansaari national parks to meet freshwater seals (p171). Tired arms? Historic lake boats still ply what were once important transport arteries; head out from any town on short cruises, or make a day of it and head from Savonlinna right up to Kuopio or across Finland's largest lake, Saimaa, to Lappeenranta. Steamboat, Lake Saimaa

Finnish Barlife

11 Rumours about Finnish beer prices are a little exaggerated, and there's a big social drinking scene here that's great to take part in. Finns lose that famous reserve after a *tuoppi* (glass) or three of beer and are keen to chat to foreigners; it's the best way to meet local people. The main cities are full of original and offbeat bars, and you'll soon find a favourite Suomi tipple, whether it's the Finnish ciders, microbrewed beers, sweet-and-sour *lonkero*, or unusual shots such as salty liquorice vodka or cloudberry liqueur.

Icy Accommodation, Lapland

12 Even reading the words 'snow hotel' can shoot a shiver up your spine, but spending a night in one of these ethereally beautiful, extravagantly artistic icy buildings is a marvellous, though expensive, experience. There are several to choose from in Lapland (see p16); heavy-duty sleeping bags ensure a relatively cosy slumber, and a morning sauna banishes any lingering chills. Even if you don't fancy spending the night, you can visit the complexes, maybe pausing for a well-chilled vodka cocktail in the bar.

Day Trip to Tallinn

13 Estonia's capital, once an important Hanseatic port, is a short ferry ride across the Baltic from Helsinki and offers an intriguing contrast. Its majestic World Heritage–listed Old Town (p59) is one of Europe's best-preserved medieval jewel boxes, but take your time to wander away from the tourist beat, too. Estonia has a vibrant, up-and-coming energy that can be just as intoxicating as the cheap beer that draws the Finnish crowd.

Cycling, Åland Archipelago

14 Charming Åland is best explored by bicycle: you'll appreciate its understated attractions all the more if you've used pedal-power to reach them. Bridges and ferries link many of its 6000 islands, and well-signposted routes take you off 'main roads' down winding lanes and forestry tracks. Set aside your bicycle whenever the mood takes you, to pick wild strawberries, wander castle ruins, sunbathe on a slab of red granite, visit a medieval church, quench your thirst at a cider orchard, or climb a lookout tower to gaze at the glittering sea.

Rauma Old Town

15 The largest wooden Old Town in the Nordic countries, Vanha Rauma (p220) deserves its Unesco World Heritage status. Its 600 houses might be museum pieces, but they also form a living centre: residents tend their flower boxes and chat to neighbours, while visitors meander in and out of the low-key cafes, shops, museums and artisans' workshops. Rauman *giäl*, an old sailors' lingo that mixes up a host of languages, is still spoken here, and the town's medieval lacemaking heritage is celebrated during Pitsiviikko (Rauma Lace Week).

need to know

Currency
» Euro (€)

Language
» Finnish
» Swedish
» Sámi languages
» English is widely spoken

When to Go

Warm to hot summers, cold winters
Mild summers, cold winters

Rovaniemi
GO Dec–Apr, Jul–Sep

Oulu
GO Jun–Aug

Kuopio
GO Jun–Aug

Tampere
GO Jun–Aug, Dec

Helsinki
GO Jun–Aug, Dec

High Season (Jul)

» Attractions and lodgings are open

» Hotels are cheaper

» Winter-activity areas from December to March

» For northern hiking areas, it's September

» Numerous festivals

Shoulder Season (Jun & Aug)

» Long days with decent temperatures

» Most attractions are open

» Not as crowded as July

» Fewer insects up north

Low Season (Sep–May)

» Outside the cities, most attractions are closed

» Hotels charge top rates except at weekends

» December to April is busy for winter sports

» Short, cool or cold days

Your Daily Budget

Budget less than €100

» Dorm bed: €18–30

» Self-cater; take advantage of lunch specials

» Cheaper rooms in summer

» Cheap bike rental, good facilities

Midrange €100–200

» Standard hotel double room: €80–130

» Two-course meal for two with wine: €80–110

» Hotels cheaper during summer and weekends

» Week-long car hire: €40–50 per day

Top end over €200

» Room in boutique hotel: €120–200

» Gourmet meal for two with wine: €150–250

» Winter activities are biggest expense

» Two-hour husky sled ride: €80–120

Money

» ATMs are widespread.

» Credit/debit cards are accepted for any transaction.

Visas

» Generally not required for stays of up to 90 days; some nationalities will need a Schengen visa.

Mobile Phones

» Local SIM cards are cheap, widely available and will work with most unlocked phones.

» Roaming rates for international SIM cards.

» No public phones.

Driving

» Drive on the right.

» Steering wheel is on the left side of the car.

Websites

» **Metsähallitus** (www.outdoors.fi) Truly excellent resource, with detailed information on all Finland's national parks and protected areas.

» **Finnish Tourist Board** (www.visitfinland.com) Excellent official site.

» **Helsingin Sanomat** (www.hs.fi/english) Finland's best daily.

» **This is Finland** (virtual.finland.fi) Maintained by the Ministry of Foreign Affairs, excellent, informative and entertaining.

» **Lonely Planet** (www.lonelyplanet.com/finland) Destination information, bookings, travel forum and more.

Exchange Rates

Australia	A$1	€0.76
Canada	C$1	€0.74
Japan	¥100	€0.99
New Zealand	NZ$1	€0.58
Norway	NKr10	€1.28
Russia	R100	€2.42
Sweden	Skr10	€1.10
UK	£1	€1.19
USA	US$1	€0.77

For current exchange rates, see www.xe.com.

Important Numbers

Eliminate the initial zero from area/mobile codes if dialling from abroad.

Country code	☑358
International access code	☑00
General emergency	☑112
Police	☑122

Arriving in Finland

» **Helsinki-Vantaa airport**

Buses – Local buses and faster Finnair buses run into town from 5am to midnight; 30–45 minutes

Taxis – €40 to €50 to the centre; 30 minutes. Cheaper shared airport taxis from €27.

Train – Airport to city rail link opening in 2014

» **Tampere airport**

Buses – Meet all arriving flights; 30–40 minutes to the centre

Taxis – Shared taxis €17, standard taxis €30; 20 minutes to the centre

Seasonal Planning

The big swing between the seasons in Finland means that preparing for a trip depends greatly on when you want to go. Pack decent thermals and a warm top layer for winter visits, when even in Helsinki temperatures can easily be 20⁰ below, or less. A cosy hat and proper gloves, and eyewear if you're going out on the snow, are also essential.

In summer you can shed the long johns, but plan on protection of a different nature. The insect season is a short one, but the clouds of mosquitoes, gnats, black flies and horseflies make the most of it. This isn't the kind of blood donor you want to be so, especially in July, especially in Lapland, and especially if you're hiking or camping, a heavy-duty insect repellent will be your best friend.

if you like...

Wildlife

Finland's wild forests and unpopulated wildernesses harbour some impressive creatures. While there are some good zoos in Finland, there's nothing like catching a glimpse of these creatures in their natural habitat.

Bears Observe these magnificent carnivores through the long summer evenings from the comfort of a hide in Kuusamo (p260), among several other places

Elk These large beasts are widespread over Finland but harder to see now that increased fencing tends to keep them off the roads. Try an elk-watching safari out of Kuhmo for your best chance (p254)

Reindeer These domesticated animals are ubiquitous in Lapland, so much so that they are a real hazard on the roads. There are numerous places where you can meet and feed them, or take a sled safari with them in winter (p279)

Wolverines With luck, you'll spot this elusive predator on a trip out of Lieksa (p207)

Seals The rare Saimaa ringed seal is an inland variety, best seen by grabbing a canoe and exploring the lakes of the Kolovesi and Linnansaari national parks (p171)

Offbeat Accommodation

Are people suckers for paying top dollar to sleep in subzero temperatures or is a night in the icy splendour of a snow hotel a passport to frosty paradise? You decide; Finland has several places to try the ultimate in wintry sleeping.

Lumilinna, Kemi On the Lapland coast, this romantic snow castle offers stylish chateau sleeping in what is the most spectacular of Finland's snow hotels (p278)

Lainio Snow Village, Ylläs Down vodkas from icy glasses in the igloo bar, then snuggle up atop your icy mattress here in western Lapland (p281)

Hotel Kakslauttanen, near Saariselkä Here there are traditional ice igloos for a chilly Lapland sleep, or high-tech heated perspex ones for the chance of cracking aurora borealis views (p297)

Arctic Snow Hotel, near Rovaniemi In easy reach of Lapland's capital, this friendly place also boasts an ice restaurant (p274)

Art

Though comparatively little known outside the country, Finnish art, particularly the painters of its golden age in the late 19th and early 20th centuries, is well worth discovering.

Helsinki Several worthwhile galleries, headed up by the Ateneum (p49) – a real 'who's who' of Finnish art – and the contemporary Kiasma gallery (p49)

Espoo Adds two more to the picture: the Gallen-Kallelan Museo and EMMA, its impressive museum of modern art (p81)

Mänttä This small town's great gallery, the Gösta Serlachiuksen Taidemuseo, is the legacy of a pioneering industrial family (p151)

Tampere's cathedral Stunning frescoes by Hugo Simberg adorn the interior (p138)

Visavuori Visit the lakeside studio of sculptor Emil Wickström (p151)

Vaasa This west-coast city has several small galleries and styles itself as an art capital (p231)

Retretti Set among the famous Punkaharju landscapes, this spectacular underground gallery is a summer must-see (p170)

» Roaming reindeer are a common sight in Lapland (p268)

Traditional Architecture

Once upon a time, all towns in Finland were picturesque rows of painted wooden houses. Wars and a succession of great fires started by some unwary baker or smoker put paid to most of them, but some classic examples remain.

Porvoo The classic wooden warehouses and noble Old Town make this a great day trip from Helsinki (p77)

Rauma Vanha Rauma, the Old Town here, is the most extensive and intriguing wooden district left in Finland (p220)

Jakobstad An area of unspoiled wooden homes stretches north of the centre (p236)

Turku Luostarinmäki is a historic quarter of the city that has been preserved in situ as a museum (p85)

Naantali The quaint old cobbled streets here make for a very picturesque stroll (p93)

Hanko Opulent wooden villas built for Russian aristocracy line the streets of this coastal town (p106)

Kerimäki The enormous church here was planned by a churchman who overestimated the size and willingness of his congregation to attend his services (p170)

Traditional Dishes

Helsinki is full of modern Nordic restaurants, but classics and traditional ingredients are still found right across the country.

Smoked fish Head to any market in the country for a huge array of salmon and other fish; such as Hakaniemi in Helsinki (p65)

Lemin särä Majestic mutton roast, cooked on a birch tray, is a gastronomic highlight (p197)

Ålandspannkaka Hit the Åland archipelago for semolina pudding with stewed prunes (p124)

Kalakukko Tasty rye loaf stuffed with *muikku* (small freshwater fish), that's a speciality of Kuopio (p188)

Game Dine on bear, elk or grouse by the Ruka ski slopes (p262)

Comfort food Finnish staples like herring, meatballs and liver in the unchanged '30s atmosphere of Sea Horse in Helsinki (p64)

Mustamakkara This black sausage is a Tampere speciality and best eaten with a dollop of lingonberry jam (p144)

Karjalanpiirakka Rice-filled pastry that has its origins in Karelia and is best tried with traditional egg butter topping (p203)

Reindeer Staple meat of Lapland that's found right across the region, including Rovaniemi (p275)

Island-Hopping

Finland has tens of thousands of islands, ranging from population centres around Helsinki to rocky islets in the middle of nowhere.

Ukko Island In Lapland's enormous Lake Inari, this island has traditionally been a Sámi sacred spot and can be visited on a boat trip (p302)

Åland This archipelago between Finland and Sweden is ripe for exploration using local ferries or a sea kayak (p117)

Island dining Head out to one of the island restaurants in Helsinki harbour for a seafood dinner with great views (p65)

Kvarken This intriguing landscape of islands west of Vaasa is constantly changing (p237)

Hailuoto Grab the ferry out to this island near Oulu for a peaceful northerly beach break (p250)

Bengtskär Finland's southernmost inhabited island is famous for its staunch Baltic lighthouse (p110)

Turku archipelago Freewheel around this complex of islands south of Turku by bike (p98)

National parks There are five maritime national parks dotted along Finland's coast, and it's great to hire a boat and potter around the islands. One of these is near Ekenäs (p104)

If you like... the aurora borealis (Northern Lights), heading to Finnish Lapland in winter gives you a sporting chance of seeing something special. For more, see p295.

Music Festivals

Finland's passion for music of all varieties is reflected in its summer program of festivals: a continuous wall of sound right across the nation.

Tangomarkkinat The Pohjanmaa town of Seinäjoki packs out with four days of tango singing and dancing (p230)

Air Guitar World Championships Imaginary instruments are the order of the day as the highlight of a music video festival in Oulu (p247)

Ruisrock Finland's oldest and biggest rock festival descends upon the city of Turku in July (p88)

Kuhmon Kamarimusiikki Excellent chamber music festival in the remote northeastern forests (p255)

Savonlinna Opera Festival Finland's prettiest town hosts excellent opera in the incomparable setting of its majestic island castle (p166)

Sibelius Festival Lahti's famous orchestra tackles Finland's most famous composer (p158)

Pori Jazz Festival Finland's biggest jazz festival livens up the west coast port of Pori (p230)

Kaustinen Folk Music Festival This famous festival is one of Finland's summer highlights (p239)

Modern Architecture

Led by Alvar Aalto, Finnish architects were at the forefront of the discipline throughout the 20th century. The country has an enviable portfolio of modern buildings, which is a major draw for architecture lovers.

Jyväskylä This university town is central to Alvar Aalto's work; you can also visit his experimental summer house nearby (p177)

Musiikkitalo This cool, crisp music centre is the latest addition to Helsinki's stable of elegant buildings (p68)

Tampere Tampere's striking concert hall, built in 1990, glistens like a glacier (p146)

Temppeliaukion Kirkko Helsinki's most striking church is bored into a hill of solid rock (p53)

Seinäjoki Aalto was given licence to experiment as he redesigned the centre of this western Finnish town (p229)

Sibeliustalo By the waterside in Lahti, this spectacular wood and glass auditorium is the home of the city's garlanded symphony orchestra (p158)

Saunas

The sauna is where Finns go to sweat away their troubles, to socialise, or to contemplate the mysteries of life. While you'll come across electric saunas in hotels and apartments, it's worth seeking out some of the more traditional varieties.

Kuopio The sociable Jätkänkämppä smoke sauna is fired up here twice a week, a great chance to try this traditional type with its softer steam (p183)

Tampere Over a century old, the venerable Rajaportin sauna is a classic of its kind (p141)

Helsinki There are several offbeat saunas in bars and cafes, but the Kotiharjun Sauna in working-class Kallio is a winner for its traditional atmosphere and optional scrub-down (p55)

Cabin rentals The best sauna of them all is a wood-burning one that you've managed to light yourself. Rent a cabin by a lake somewhere and try it out. Add beer and sausages afterwards for the most classic Finnish experience (p339)

month by month

Top Events

1 **Sled Safaris & Skiing**, March

2 **Savonlinna Opera Festival**, July

3 **Ruisrock**, July

4 **Ruska Hiking**, September

5 **Aurora Watching**, November

January

It's cold. Very cold and very dark. But this is the beginning of the active winter; there's enough snow for ice hotels, and sledding, snowmobiling and skiing are reliable.

☆ Skábmagovat

In the third week of January, this is a film festival (www.skabmagovat.fi) with an indigenous theme held in the Sámi capital of Inari.

Ice Hotels

It's a memorable experience to spend a night in one of these ethereally beautiful places. See p16.

February

Skiing season really kicks off in northern Finland, with a peak holiday season around the middle of the month.

Runeberg Day

This day, on 5 February, commemorates Finland's national poet. Flags are at half mast and people eat 'Runeberg tarts' (p80).

Laskiainen

Seven weeks before Easter, and coinciding with Carnaval in other countries, people ski and toboggan down hills and enjoy other winter sports during this festival.

March

As the hours of light dramatically increase and temperatures begin to rise again, this is an excellent time to take advantage of the hefty snow cover and indulge in some winter activities.

Sled Safaris and Skiing

Whizzing across the snow pulled by a team of huskies or reindeer is a pretty spectacular way to see the northern wildernesses. Add snowmobiling or skiing to the mix and it's a top time to be at high latitude.

Oulu Winter

Oulu has two big outdoor events in the March snow. The Tervahiihto (Tar Ski Race; www.tervahiihto.fi) is a historic skiing race that's been running for over a century. The Ice-Fishing Marathon (www.oulutourism.fi) has contestants sitting by holes in the frozen sea for 48 hours straight.

Reindeer Racing

Held over the last weekend of March or first of April, the King's Cup in Inari is the grand finale of Finnish Lapland's reindeer-racing (www.paliskunnat.fi) season and a great spectacle.

April

Easter is celebrated in a traditional fashion. Spring begins in southern Finland, but there's still solid snow cover in the northern reaches. It's another great month for outdoor activities in Lapland.

Pääsiäinen (Easter)

On Easter Sunday people go to church, paint eggs and eat *mämmi* (pudding of rye and malt).

☆ Tampere Biennale

Festival featuring new Finnish music, held in even-numbered years only (www.tamperemusicfestivals.fi).

April Jazz

Held in Espoo on the outskirts of Helsinki, this has jazz with big-name artists and big crowds (www.apriljazz.fi).

May

A transitional month in the north, with snow beginning to disappear and signs of life emerging after the long winter. In the south, spring's in full flow. This is a quiet but rewarding time to visit.

Vappu

Traditionally a festival of students and workers, this also marks the beginning of summer, and is celebrated with plenty of alcohol and merrymaking. Held 1 May.

June

Midsummer weekend in late June is celebrated with great gusto, but it's typically a family event. Lapland's a little muddy, but the rest is warm and welcoming.

Praasniekka

These Orthodox celebrations are day-long religious and folk festivals held in North Karelia and other eastern provinces between May and September, most notably around the end of June.

Juhannus (Midsummer)

The most important annual event for Finns. The country completely shuts down as people head to summer cottages to celebrate the longest day of the year with bonfires, dancing and copi-

ous drinking. Ornate poles are decorated and raised in Åland. Seurasaari sees the best celebration around Helsinki. Held the weekend closest to 22 June.

Music Festivals

The glut of summer music festivals in Finland begins. Provinssirock (www.provinssirock.fi) is a big three-day rock fiesta in Seinäjoki, Kuopio Tanssii ja Soi is a major dance extravaganza in Kuopio (www.kuopiodancefestival.fi), and Mikkeli Music Festival (www.mikkelimusic.net) serenades that city with classical pieces.

Midnight Sun Film Festival

Round-the-clock screenings in Sodankylä (www.msfilmfestival.fi) while the never-setting sun circles around the sky outside. Great atmosphere in this small Lapland town.

Helsinki Day

Celebrations (www.hel.fi) of the capital's anniversary are a busy time to be in town, with lots of events and activities around the Esplanadi park on 12 June.

July

Peak season sees long, long days and sunshine. This is when the region really comes to life, with festivals throughout, boat trips, activities, cheaper hotels and a celebratory feel. Insects in Lapland are a nuisance.

Savonlinna Opera Festival

A month of excellent performances in the romantic

location of one of Europe's most picturesquely situated castles makes this Finland's biggest summer drawcard for casual and devoted lovers of opera (www.operafestival.fi).

Ruisrock

Finland's oldest and possibly best rock festival takes place in early July on an island just outside the southwestern city of Turku. Top Finnish and international acts take part (www.ruisrock.fi).

Wife-Carrying World Championships

Finland's, nay, the world's premier wife-carrying event is held in the village of Sonkajärvi in early July. Winning couples (marriage not required) win the woman's weight in beer as well as significant kudos (www.eukonkanto.fi).

Tangomarkkinat

Finnish tango is an institution, and the older generations converge on Seinäjoki in this massive celebration of singing and dancing it in early July (www.tangomarkkinat.com).

Sulkavan Suursoudut

This massive rowing festival in the Lakeland is all about participation...and downing lager in what turns into one of Finland's biggest parties. Second Sunday in July (www.suursoudut.fi).

Pori Jazz Festival

The nation's biggest jazz event packs out the port city of Pori on the west coast over a week in mid-July. More than a hundred concerts, free jam sessions, and dancing in the street make this hugely enjoyable (www.porijazz.fi).

Kaustinen Folk Music Festival

This tiny cereal-belt settlement hosts a massive folk music and dance knees-up in the third week of July. It's so emblematic that in Peanuts cartoons in Finland, Woodstock is called Kaustinen (www.kaustinen.net).

Kuhmon Kamarimusiikki

In remote Kuhmo, this is an excellent fortnight of chamber music, with concerts featuring a large bunch of young and talented performers from around Europe (www.kuhmofestival.fi).

Other Music Festivals

There are numerous others. Imatra draws international big bands (www.ibbf.fi), Tammerfest (www.tammerfest. fi) rocks the city of Tampere, Alandia Jazz brings performers to the Åland archipelago, while Kihaus Folk (www.kihaus.fi) is an acclaimed festival of modern and experimental Finnish folk music and dancing.

 Jyväskylän Kesä

This multifaceted festival makes sure the university town of Jyväskylä stays lively in the summer. It's one of Finland's oldest and most important arts festivals (www.jyvaskylankesa.fi).

Rauma Lace Week

A week in late July sees the old wooden centre of Rauma come alive with music and cultural events, as well as lace-making demonstrations and a carnival (www.rauma.fi).

Roviantti

Oulu loosens its belt for this culinary weekend, one day of which is completely given over to garlic, which makes its way into a number of surprising dishes (www.roviantti.info).

Kotkan Meripäivät

The port of Kotka celebrates this maritime festival at the end of the month. It features music, sailing races and cruises (www.meripaivat.com).

Unikeonpäivä

You don't want to be last out of bed on the 27th, 'Sleepyhead Day', as you'll traditionally be rudely awakened with water. In Naantali, the 'laziest person' (usually actually the mayor or someone important) is thrown into the sea in the morning, sparking a day of festivities (www.naantali.fi).

August

Most Finns are back at work, so this is quieter than July but still with decent weather across most of the region. It's a great time for hiking in Lapland or biking in Åland.

Air Guitar World Championships

Tune your imaginary instrument and get involved in this crazy rockstravaganza held in Oulu in late August as part of a music video festival. This surfeit of cheesy guitar classics and seemingly endless beer is all in the name of world peace (www.airguitarworldchampionships.com).

Neste Oil Rally Finland

Rallying is huge in Finland, and the local leg of the world championship, held around Jyväskylä, is a massive event that draws half a million spectators, normally in early August. The town packs out for a huge party (www.nesteoilrallyfinland.fi).

Savonlinna Ballet Festival

Hot on the heels of the opera festival, late July or early August sees a three- or four-day ballet festival held in the Olavinlinna castle (www.savonlinnaballet.net).

Ijahis Idja

Over a weekend usually in August in Inari, Lapland, is this excellent music festival that features groups from all spectra of Sámi music (www.ijahisidja.fi).

Hamina Tattoo

Hamina's parade of military music is held early in the month in even years only. The marches are backed up by evening concerts and a festive atmosphere (www.haminatattoo.com).

Mobile Phone Throwing World Championships

Savonlinna's quirkiest festival allows participants to indulge in a spot of Nokia-hurling (www.savonlinnafestivals.com).

Helsingin Juhlaviikot

Held over two weeks and three weekends from late August to early September, the all-arts Helsinki Festival keeps the capital pumping with loads of events, including plenty for kids (www.helsinginjuhlaviikot.fi).

September

The winter is fast approaching: pack something warm for those chilly nights. Autumn colours are spectacular in northern forests, making it another great hiking month. Many attractions and activities close down or go onto winter time.

 ### Ruska Hiking

Ruska is the Finnish word for the autumn colours, and there's a mini high season in Kainuu, Koillismaa and Lapland as hikers take to the trails to enjoy nature's brief, spectacular artistic flourish.

Ruska Swing

Combine your Lapland hiking with Kemijärvi's festival of swing music and dancing in early September (www.ruskaswing.fi).

 ### Sibelius Festival

Performances by the famous Lahti Symphony Orchestra, honouring composer Jean Sibelius, in the city's spectacular waterside auditorium (www.sinfonialahti.fi).

October

Snow is already beginning to carpet the north. It's generally a quiet time in Finland, as locals face the realities of yet another long winter approaching.

 ### Baltic Herring Market

Traditional outdoor herring market, held in Helsinki in the first week of October (www.portofhelsinki.fi).

November

Once the clocks change in late October, there's no denying the winter. November's bad for winter sports, as there's little light and not enough snow. It can be a good month to see the aurora borealis, though.

 ### Aurora Watching

Whether you are blessed with seeing the aurora borealis (Northern Lights) is largely a matter of luck, but the further north you are, the better the chances. Dark, cloudless nights, patience, and a viewing spot away from city lights are other key factors. See p295.

Tampere Jazz Happening

Finnish and international jazz musicians flock to Tampere in late October or early November (www.tamperemusicfestivals.fi).

December

The Christmas period is celebrated enthusiastically with cinnamon smells, warming mulled drinks, and festive traditions putting the meaning back into the event.

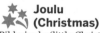 ### Itsenäisyyspäivä

Finland celebrates its independence day on the 6th with torchlight processions, fireworks and concerts.

Joulu (Christmas)

Pikkujoulu (little Christmas) parties, with plenty of *glögi* (hot punch) consumed, dot the lead-up to the main event, which features a family meal on Christmas Eve. Lapland sees Santas galore, reindeer, and plenty of kitschy but fun Christmas spirit.

itineraries

Whether you've got six days or 60, these itineraries provide a starting point for the trip of a lifetime. Want more inspiration? Head online to lonelyplanet.com/thorntree to chat with other travellers.

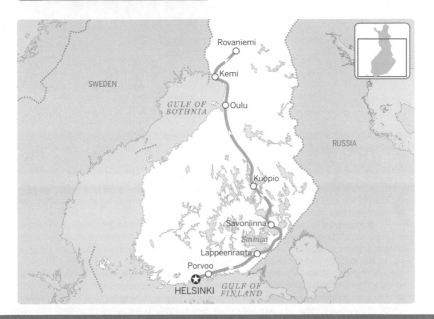

Two weeks
Essential Suomi

> Kick-off in capital **Helsinki**, prowling the buzzing design district and unwinding in excellent restaurants and bars. Hit Suomenlinna or an island restaurant to get a feel for the archipelago, and day trip to historic **Porvoo**'s enchanting wooden buildings.

Next head towards **Lappeenranta** on the shores of Finland's largest lake. Then – do this section by boat in summer – it's gorgeous **Savonlinna**, where the stunning castle hosts a top opera festival. Even if your trip doesn't coincide with the festival, it's a memorable place with plenty to do in the surrounding area: take your time.

Then to the heart of the Lakeland, **Kuopio**, another segment you can do on a lake boat. Try to time your visit to coincide with the convivial smoke sauna.

The high latitudes are in evidence once you get to **Oulu** – depending on the season, the sun barely sets or barely rises. It's one of Finland's liveliest towns, with a great summer marketplace.

In winter, stop in **Kemi** to see the snow castle and take an ice-breaker cruise. Finally, head to **Rovaniemi**, a great base for any number of activities. From there, explore Lapland or get the sleeper train back to Helsinki.

One to two weeks
Lapp Gold

Lapland's unique charms deserve plenty of time. It can be done in a week, but take two if you can, giving yourself time for some of the numerous activities on offer and national park hikes.

Rovaniemi is Lapland's capital and a logical place to start. It's also a good spot to hire a car. Santa Claus is the big crowd-puller here, but the real don't-miss attraction is the excellent Arktikum museum where you can learn about these northern latitudes. Further south in **Ranua**, you can see some of the region's fauna at its zoo.

Cut eastwards to **Ruka**, a lively winter ski resort and activity base. Here, there's walking to be done in the **Oulanka National Park**, including the Karhunkierros, one of Finland's best treks. You can also canoe some great river routes and go bear-watching from nearby **Kuusamo**.

From Ruka, head north via **Kemijärvi** to **Sodankylä**. Don't miss the wonderful old wooden church. Continue north through ever-more-sparsely populated territory; when you reach **Urho Kekkonen National Park**, you're in one of Europe's great wildernesses. Take some time out for a hike across the fells, or try gold-panning at **Tankavaara**. The best base for this region, **Saariselkä**, is a place to organise all sorts of summer and winter activities.

Inari, one of Lapland's most intriguing towns, is the capital of Finland's Sámi, a handi-crafts centre and home to the memorable Siida museum, where you'll learn a lot about the Sámi and the wildlife of these northern latitudes.

Next it's nearby **Lemmenjoki National Park**, where treks, river trips, gold-panning, and more Sámi culture await. With time, head up to the **Kevo Strict Nature Reserve** for a great three-to-four day trek.

Continue the loop towards northwest Finland, perhaps cutting through Norway, ending up at **Hetta**, another Sámi town, and trailhead for more excellent walking.

If you have time, take a detour up the 'arm' of Finland to remote **Kilpisjärvi**, in the shadow of fearsome Norwegian mountains and the smaller bulk of Saana Fell, a rewarding climb with some memorable views over three nations.

Then **Muonio**. In winter you go husky-sledding, but even in summer it's worth meeting the lovable dogs. Finally, return to Rovaniemi, stopping to ski or rent a summer cottage at busy **Levi** or peaceful **Pyhä**.

Legend:
- Baltic & Bothnian Coasts
- Contemporary Cityhopping

Map labels: SWEDEN, RUSSIA, Hailuoto, Oulu, Jakobstad, Kvarken Archipelago, Vaasa, Kristinestad, GULF OF BOTHNIA, Pori, Tampere, Rauma, Uusikaupunki, Iittala, Åland, Naantali, Turku, Turku Archipelago, Fiskars, Ekenäs, HELSINKI, Hanko, Fagervik, GULF OF FINLAND, TALLINN, ESTONIA

One to two weeks
Cityhopping

Finland's thriving design and music industries mean that its cities, though small, pack plenty of contemporary punch. Take a few days to get to know **Helsinki**, the capital. Check out the Design Museum, then snoop around Punavuori's small studios and shops. See what's cooking at Kaapelitehdas and Korjaamo cultural centres, and pay Kiasma a visit. Fine-dining restaurants and stylish, quirky or just plain weird bars make the evenings fly by.

Ferryboat across to **Tallinn**, the capital of Estonia. The traditional architecture of the old town meets the post-Soviet generation's creative energy in an always-intriguing mix.

Back in Helsinki, aim for **Tampere**, a model of post-industrial regeneration. Take in the city's bohemian vibe and stunning lakescapes, and head for a half-day trip down to **Iittala** to see the home of one of Finland's iconic design brands.

Cut southwest down to **Turku**. The country's stateliest city has plenty going on here, whether it's the Ruisrock festival or the latest exhibition in Ars Nova, the contemporary art centre that hosts the Turku Biennaali.

Head back to Helsinki along the coast. Thirsty for more? Sort out your visa and the city of St Petersburg is just a train ride away.

One to two weeks
Baltic & Bothnian Coasts

This trip takes you through Swedish- and Finnish-speaking communities and gives the chance to see picture-perfect wooden towns, sparkling blue water and more-than-decent beaches.

Heading west from Helsinki, stop at the pretty ironworks at **Fagervik** and **Fiskars**, near family-friendly seaside **Ekenäs**. Then on to the noble wooden villas of **Hanko**, where St Petersburg society once summered.

Turku has many drawcards, as does the surrounding **archipelago** and picturesque **Naantali**. Further offshore, **Åland** offers cycling opportunities and maritime history.

Turning north, **Uusikaupunki**'s museum deserves a prize for ironic humour, while **Rauma** features charming wooden buildings. **Pori** hosts a pumping jazz festival.

The next coastline is 'Parallel Sweden': **Kristinestad** with its Swedish-speaking majority. **Vaasa** has an excellent museum and kids' attractions. West of here, **Kvarken archipelago** is an ever-changing landscape of land rising from the seabed.

Jakobstad's old town rivals Rauma's for beauty. Beyond here, beautiful coastline runs north to **Oulu**. Stop off at **Hailuoto** island for a relaxing stay by the sandy beach; it's not often you can have a dip this far north.

The Great Outdoors

When to hike

June to September is the main hiking season in Finland.

Where to hike

There's a wide range of national parks with marked trails offering anything from short strolls to multiday treks.

What to take

Insect repellent There are literally clouds of biting insects, especially in July, and especially in Lapland.
Food You'll have to carry all food when you walk in wilderness areas.
Tent Though there are plenty of huts to overnight in, a tent gives more flexibility and protection from mosquitoes.

How to plan a hike

Finland's protected areas are comprehensively covered in English by the website www.outdoors.fi. It details walking routes, including all camping and other accommodation possibilities.

Finland's beauty and appeal lie in its fantastic natural environment, with vast forests, long waterways and numerous lakes to explore, as well as the harsh Arctic wilderness in the north. Getting outdoors is the best way to experience the country and Finland is remarkably well set up for any type of activity, from all-included safari-style packages to map-and-compass do-it-yourself adventures. There's almost unlimited scope in both summer and winter.

National Parks

Finland's excellent network of national parks and other protected areas is maintained by **Metsähallitus** (www.outdoors.fi). At last count, there were 37 national parks that made up a total area of over 8000 sq km. A similar amount of territory is protected under other categories, while further swaths of land are designated wilderness reserves. In total, over 30,000 sq km – some 9% of the total area – is in some way protected land.

The Metsähallitus website provides wonderful information on all these spots; the organisation also publishes individual leaflets on each park.

The largest and most pristine national parks are in northern Finland, particularly Lapland, where vast swaths of wilderness invite trekking, cross-country skiing, fishing and canoeing. See the Lapland chapter (p279) for more details.

Many of the national parks have excellent networks of wilderness huts that provide cosy

GREAT NATIONAL PARKS

NATIONAL PARK	FEATURES	ACTIVITIES	WHEN TO GO
Lemmenjoki (p305)	Broad rivers and old-growth forests; golden eagles, reindeer	Trekking, boating, gold-panning	Aug-Sep
Linnansaari & Kolovesi (p172)	Luscious lakes and fresh-water seals	Canoeing	May-Sep
Oulanka (p262)	Pine forests and river valleys; elk, white-tailed eagles; calypso flowers	Trekking the Bear's Ring, canoeing, rafting	late Jun-Sep
Urho Kekkonen (p298)	Fells, mires and old Sámi settlements; reindeer, flying squirrels	Trekking, cross-country skiing, fishing	Jul-Sep & Nov-Apr
Archipelago & Ekenäs Archipelago (p104)	Strings of islets and sker-ries; seals, eider ducks, greylag geese	Boating, fishing	May-Sep
Nuuksio (p77)	Forest within striking distance of Helsinki; woodpeckers, elk, divers	Nature trails	May-Oct
Patvinsuo (p208)	Broad boglands and old forest; bears, beavers, cranes	Hiking	Jun-Oct
Pallas-Yllästunturi (p289)	Undulating fells; bears, snow buntings, ptarmi-gans	Hiking, trekking, skiing	Jul-Sep & Nov-Apr

free places to overnight on hiking routes. See Hiking, below, for trail recommendations and more information about trekking.

Hiking

The superb system of national parks offers memorable trekking throughout Finland in the summer months. The routes are backed up by resources for camping and overnighting in huts, so it's easy to organise a multi-day wilderness adventure.

National parks offer excellent marked trails, and most forest and wilderness areas are criss crossed by locally used walking paths. Nights are short or nonexistent in summer, so you can walk for as long as your heart desires or your feet permit.

It's important to remember what the Finnish landscape does and doesn't offer. You will get scented pine and birch forest, low hills, jewel-like lakes and brisk, powerful rivers. Don't expect epic mountainscapes and fjords; that's not Finland.

The trekking season runs from late May to September in most parts of the country. In Lapland the ground is not dry enough for hiking until mid-June, and mosquitoes are an irritation during July. The first half of September is the *ruska* (autumn hiking) season, when the forests are alive with a glorious palette of autumn colours; it's a very popular time for hiking.

If heading off trekking on your own, always advise someone of your route and intended arrival date, or note these details in trekkers' books in huts and hostels.

Right of Public Access

The *jokamiehenoikeus* (literally 'everyman's right') is an ancient Finnish code that gives people the right to walk, ski or cycle anywhere they like in forests and other wilderness areas – even across private land – as long as they behave responsibly. Canoeing, rowing and kayaking on lakes and rivers is also unrestricted. You can rest and swim anywhere in the Finnish countryside, and camp for one night *almost* anywhere. Travel by motorboat or snowmobile, though, is heavily restricted.

Watch out for stricter regulations regarding access in nature reserves and national

parks where access might be confined to marked paths.

Camping

Everyman's right allows you to rest and camp temporarily in the countryside without permission, even on private property as long as you don't do so near homes. Try to camp on already-used sites to preserve the environment. Camping is not permitted in town parks or on beaches, and in national parks and reserves it may be restricted to certain designated areas.

Under the right of public access, you cannot make a campfire on private land unless you have the owner's permission. In national parks, look for a designated campfire area (*nuotiopaikka*), and watch for fire warning signs – *metsäpalovaroitus* means the fire risk is very high. Felling trees or cutting brush to make a campfire is forbidden; use fallen wood instead.

Huts & Shelters

Metsähallitus operates a huge network of free, properly maintained wilderness huts across its swath of national parks and protected areas. Huts typically have basic bunks, cooking facilities, a pile of dry firewood and a compost toilet. You are required to leave the hut as it was – ie replenish the firewood and carry away your rubbish. The Finns' 'wilderness rule' states that the last person to arrive will be given the best place to sleep, but, on busy treks in peak season, it's good to have a tent, because someone usually ends up sleeping outside. You may also sleep sounder in a tent, as the huts tend to fill with mosquitoes as the evening goes on.

Some huts require advance booking, or have a separate, lockable section that must be booked ahead (usually €10 per bed). This is called a *varaustupa*.

Various other structures, including day huts and tepee-style *kotas* (Sámi huts) in Lapland, are designed for cooking and for temporary or emergency shelter from the weather. In a *laavu* (simple log shelter), you can pitch your tent inside or just roll out your sleeping bag.

The website www.outdoors.fi has invaluable information on huts and hiking routes; a 1:50,000 trekking map is recommended for finding wilderness huts. These are published by Karttakeskus and cost €19.50 from tourist offices, national park visitor centres or map shops.

Where to Trek

You can hike anywhere in Finland, but national parks and reserves have marked routes, designated campfire places, well-maintained wilderness huts and boardwalks over the boggy bits.

Lapland is the main trekking region, with huge national parks that have well-equipped huts and good, long hiking routes. See p279 for details. There are other classic trekking areas in the Kainuu and Koillismaa regions, and in North Karelia.

Some recommended treks are described here. Excellent trekking maps are available in Finland for all of these routes.

Hetta-Pallastunturi (p289) One of western Lapland's best walks heads through light forest and up and down fells offering spectacular views for 55km through national park.

Karhunkierros (Bear's Ring; p262) The most famous of all Finnish trekking routes, this trail in northern Finland covers 80km of rugged cliffs, gorges and forest.

Karhunpolku (Bear's Trail; p210) This 133km marked hiking trail of medium difficulty leads

---

FOREST FOOD

Except in strict nature reserves, it's permissible to pick berries and mushrooms – but not other kinds of plants – under Finland's right of public access. Finns do so with gusto, filling pails with blueberries, which come into season in late July, and delicious little wild strawberries. But there are more. Bearberries, cowberries (lingonberries), crowberries, cranberries, whortleberries and more are there to look out for. But the prize is the cloudberry, so appreciated by Finns that you may not have a chance to sample this orange, slightly sour, creamy berry in the wild. Edible mushrooms are numerous in Finnish forests, as are poisonous ones; make sure you have a mushroom guide or know your stuff.

---

north from Lieksa through a string of stunning national parks and nature reserves.

Kevo Route (p307) A fabulous point-to-point or loop walk of 64km to 78km through a memorable gorge in far north Lapland.

UKK Route (p255) The nation's longest trekking route is this 240km route through northern Finland. It starts at Koli Hill, continues along the western side of Lake Pielinen and ends at Iso-Syöte Hill. Further east, there are more sections.

Cycling

Riding a bike in Finland is one of the best ways to explore parts of the country in summer. The country is flat, main roads are in good condition and traffic is light. Bicycle tours are further facilitated by the liberal camping regulations, excellent cabin accommodation at camping grounds, and the long hours of daylight in June and July.

The drawback is this: distances in Finland are vast. It's best to look at planning shorter explorations in particular areas, combining cycling with bus and train trips – Finnish buses and trains are very bike-friendly.

Even if your time is limited, don't skip a few quick jaunts in the countryside. There are very good networks of cycling paths in and around most major cities and holiday destinations (for instance, the networks around Oulu and Turku).

In most towns bicycles can be hired from sports shops, tourist offices, camping grounds or hostels for €10 to €20 per day, or €50 to €80 a week.

Bikes on Buses & Trains

Bikes can be carried on long-distance buses for €3 to €10 (often free in practice) if there is space available (and there usually is).

Bikes can accompany passengers on most normal train journeys, with a surcharge of €9 to €10. Inter-City (IC) trains have spaces for bikes, which should be booked in advance; you'll have to take your bike to the appropriate space in the double-decker wagon – you can lock it in with a 50-cent coin. You can take your bike on regional trains that have a suitcase symbol on the timetable; put it in the luggage van.

Where to Cycle

You can cycle on all public roads except motorways. Many public roads in southern Finland have a dedicated cycling track running alongside.

Åland

The Åland islands are the most bicycle-friendly region in Finland, and the most popular region for bicycle tours.

Southern Finland

Southern Finland has more traffic than other parts of the country, but with careful planning you can find quiet roads that offer pleasant scenery. Around Turku, the Archipelago route (p98) offers excellent coastal scenery and island-hopping.

Karelia & Northeastern Finland

Two theme routes cover the whole eastern frontier, from the south to Kuusamo in the north. *Runon ja rajan tie* (Road of the Poem and Frontier) consists of secondary sealed roads, and passes several typical Karelian villages before ending in Lieksa. Some of the smallest and most remote villages along the easternmost roads have been lumped together to create the *Korpikylien tie* (Road of Wilderness Villages). This route starts at Saramo village in northern Nurmes and ends at Hossa in the northeastern Kainuu region.

A recommended loop takes you around Lake Pielinen, and may include a ferry trip across the lake. Another good loop is around Viinijärvi, west of Joensuu.

Western Finland

This flat region, known as Pohjanmaa, is generally good for cycling, except that distances are long. The scenery is mostly agricultural, with picturesque wooden barns amid fields of grain in this breadbasket of Finland. The 'Swedish Coast' around Vaasa and north to Kokkola is the most scenic part of this region.

Winter Sports

Winter's a wonderful time to get active in Finland. For most activities, the best time is in March and April; you get a decent amount of light, and temperatures are more acceptable.

Sled Safaris & Snowmobiling

Whether you head out for an hour, or on an epic week-long adventure, being whisked across the snow by an enthusiastic team of huskies or reindeer is an experience like no other. Lapland (see p279) is the best place to do this, but it's also available further south in places like Nurmes (p214) and Lieksa (p207). Driving a sled takes a bit of practice, so expect sore arms and a few tumbles at first.

Similar excursions can be made on snowmobiles (skidoos). Operators in the same locations offer these trips. You'll need a valid driver's licence to use one.

NORDIC WALKING

Finland is proud of having invented the burgeoning sport of Nordic Walking, originally devised as a training method for cross-country skiers during the summer months. Basically, it involves using two specially designed handheld poles while briskly walking; it may look a little weird at first, but involves the upper body in the activity and results in a 20% to 45% increase in energy consumption, and an increase in heart rate, substantially adding to the exercise value of the walk. Nordic Blading is a speedier version, using poles while on in-line skates – some pretty scary velocities can be reached.

Prices for both sled safaris and snowmobiling are normally based on two sharing, taking it in turns to drive. If you want one to yourself, expect a hefty supplement.

Downhill Skiing & Snowboarding

Finnish slopes are generally quite low and so are well suited to beginners and families. The best resorts are in Lapland, where the fells allow for longer runs. In central and southern Finland, ski runs are much shorter, averaging about 1km in length.

The ski season in Finland runs from late November to early May and slightly longer in the north, where it's possible to ski from October to May. Beware of the busy Christmas, mid-February (or early March) and Easter holiday periods – they can get very crowded, and accommodation prices go through the roof.

You can rent all skiing or snowboarding equipment at major ski resorts for about €30/110 a day/week. A one-day lift pass costs around €35/170 a day/week (slightly less in the shoulder and off-peak seasons), although it is possible to pay separately for each ride. Skiing lessons are also available and start at around €60 for an hour's lesson for two.

The best resorts are Levi (p282), Ruka (p261), Pyhä-Luosto (p292) and Ylläs (p281), but Syöte, Koli, Pallas, Ounasvaara and Saariselkä are also good.

Cross-Country Skiing

Cross-country skiing is one of the simplest and most pleasant things to do outdoors in winter in Finland. It's the ideal way to explore the beautiful, silent winter countryside of lakes, fells, fields and forests, and is widely used by Finns for fitness and as a means of transport.

Practically every town and village has a network of ski tracks (*latu* or *ladut*) around the urban centre, in many cases illuminated (*valaistu*). The one drawback to using these tracks is that you'll need to bring your own equipment (or purchase some), as rentals often aren't possible.

Cross-country skiing at one of Finland's many ski resorts is an easier option. Tracks get much longer but also are better maintained. Ski resorts offer excellent instruction and rent out equipment. The best cross-country skiing is in Lapland, where resorts offer hundreds of kilometres of trails. Keep in mind that there

are only about five hours of daylight each day in northern Lapland during winter – if you're planning on a longer trek, spring is the best time. Cross-country skiing is best during January and February in southern Finland, and from December to April in the north.

Water Sports

Rowing, Canoeing & Rafting

With 10% water coverage, Finland has long been a boating country, and until relatively recently boats were an important form of transport on the lakes and rivers. Every waterside town has a place (most frequently the camp site) where you can rent a canoe, kayak or rowing boat by the hour or day. Rental cottages often have rowing boats that you can use free of charge to investigate the local lake and its islands.

Canoes and kayaks are suitable for longer adventures lasting several days or weeks. Route maps and guides may be purchased at local or regional tourist offices and at **Karttakeskus** (www.karttakauppa.fi), which takes orders via its website. Canoe and kayak rentals range in price from €20 to €40 per day, and €80 to €200 per week, more if you need overland transportation to the start or end point of your trip.

Where to Row & Paddle

The sheltered bays and islands around the Turku archipelago and Åland in southwest Finland are good for canoeing in summer.

Finland's system of rivers, canals and linked waterways means there are some extensive canoeing routes. In the Lakeland, the Kolovesi and Linnansaari national parks (p171) are excellent waters for canoeing, and offer plenty of exploration opportunities. North Karelia, particularly around Lieksa and Ruunaa, also offers good paddling. Rivers further north are fast-flowing, with tricky rapids, making many of them suitable for experienced paddlers only.

The website www.canoeinfinland.com has details of several Lakeland routes.

Ivalojoki Route (easy) A 70km route along the Ivalojoki, in northeast Lapland, that starts at the village of Kuttura and finishes in Ivalo, crossing 30 rapids along the way.

Lakeland Trail (easy to medium) This 350km route travels through the heart of the lake district

(Kangaslampi, Enonkoski, Savonranta, Kerimäki, Punkaharju, Savonlinna and Rantasalmi) and takes 14 to 18 days.

Oravareitti (easy to medium) In the heart of the Lakeland, the 'Squirrel Route' is a well-marked two- or three-day trip from Juva to Sulkava.

Oulankajoki and Kitkajoki (easy to difficult) A variety of choices on these neighbouring rivers in a spectacular wilderness area of northeast Finland.

Savonselkä Circuit (easy to difficult) The circuit, near Lahti, has three trails that are 360km, 220km and 180km in length. There are many sections that can be done as day trips and that are suitable for novice paddlers.

Seal Trail (easy) Explore the watery national parks of Kolovesi and Linnansaari, maybe spotting a rare ringed seal from your canoe.

Plenty of operators offer whitewater rafting expeditions in canoes or rubber rafts. The Ruunaa area (p209) is one of the best of many choices for this adrenalin-packed activity.

Fishing

Finnish waters are teeming with fish, and with people trying to catch them; Finns must be among the Earth's most enthusiastic anglers. Commonly caught fish include salmon, trout, grayling, perch, pike, zander (pike-perch), whitefish and Arctic char.

With so many bodies of water there is no shortage of places to cast a line, and not even the lakes freezing over stops the Finns (see this page). Lapland has the greatest concentration of quality fishing spots, but the number of designated places in southern Finland is also increasing. Some of the most popular fishing areas are the spectacular salmon-rich Tenojoki in the furthest north, the Tornionjoki, the Kainuu region around Kajaani, Ruovesi, Hossa, Ruunaa, Lake Saimaa around Mikkeli, Lake Inari, and the Kymijoki near Kotka.

Tourist offices can direct you to the best fishing spots in the area, and usually can provide some sort of regional fishing map and put you in touch with local guides. Fishing equipment of varying quality is widely available for hire from camp sites and other accommodation providers in fishy areas.

The website www.fishing.fi has plenty of useful information in English on fishing throughout the country.

ICE-FISHING

Nothing stops a Finn on a mission for fish. Not even when the winter closes in, the lakes freeze over, and the finny tribes below grow sluggish and hope for a breather from those pesky hooks.

No, the intrepid locals just walk or drive out to a likely spot on the ice, carve a hole using a hand-drill, unfold the campstool, and drop in a line. And wait, even if the temperature is around -30°C. Seriously warm clothes and your choice of a flask of coffee or a bottle of Koskenkorva complete the picture.

Many tour operators offering winter activities organise ice-fishing excursions.

Permits

Several permits are required of foreigners (between the ages of 18 and 64) who wish to go fishing in Finland, but they are very easy to arrange. The website www.mmm.fi has all the details. Simple angling with hook and line requires no permit; neither does ice-fishing, unless you are doing these at rapids or other salmon waterways.

For other types of fishing, first you will need a national fishing permit, known as a 'fishing management fee'. A permit is €7/22 per week/year; they're payable at any bank or post office. Second, fishing with a lure requires a regional permit (€7/29), also available at banks and post offices. In addition to this a local permit may be required. There are often automatic permit machines; tourist offices, sports shops and camping grounds can also supply permits. The waters in Åland are regulated separately and require a separate regional permit.

The Metsähallitus website (www.outdoors.fi) details fishing restrictions in protected areas.

Birdwatching

Birdwatching is increasingly popular in Finland, in no small part because many bird species migrate to northern Finland in summer to take advantage of the almost continuous daylight for breeding and rearing their young. The best months for watching birds are May to June or mid-July, and late August to September or early October.

Liminganlahti (Liminka Bay), near Oulu, is a wetlands bird sanctuary and probably the best birdwatching spot in Finland. Other good areas include Puurijärvi-Isosuo National Park in Western Finland, Siikalahti in the Lakeland, Oulanka National Park near Kuusamo, the Porvoo area east of Helsinki and the Kemiö Islands. Dave Gosney's *Finding Birds in South Finland* and *Finding Birds in Lapland* are field handbooks on birding sites with many practical tips.

Check out www.birdlife.fi for a good introduction and a few links for bird-watching in Finland. See also p16.

Travel with Children

Best Regions for Kids

Helsinki
Many attractions, with trams, boats, Suomenlinna fortress, Linnanmäki amusement park, and the Serena waterpark at Espoo. Most museums and galleries have child-friendly exhibits.

Åland Archipelago
Flat archipelago perfect for family cycling; also has forts and castles.

The Lakeland
The castle at Savonlinna and scope for watery activities make this region one of the best for children.

West Coast
Theme parks at Vaasa, sandy beaches at Kalajoki and tranquil shores.

Turku & the South Coast
Moominworld at Naantali is a magnet for the young, who drag their parents here from all over the northern lands.

Lapland
Winter wonderland with Kemi's snow castle, sled trips and children's ski runs. In summer, there's gold-panning, meeting reindeer or huskies, and national parks. The region's most famous resident, Santa, is at Napapiiri year-round.

Finland for Kids

Finland is incredibly child friendly, and is a terrific place to holiday with kids. Domestic tourism is largely dictated by children's needs, and child-friendly attractions abound in the height of summer. As it's such an outdoors-focused destination, planning a trip for kids could include plenty of splashing about on lakes and rivers, hikes in national parks, and cycling. In winter, the reliable snow opens up a world of outdoor possibilities, and there's also the Santa Claus angle in Lapland. There are several standout theme parks across the country, and enough in most cities to keep children of any age interested. Even potentially stuffy museums often make a real effort to engage kids, with simplified child-height information, hands-on activities, interactive displays or activity sheets in English.

All areas of Finland have plenty to offer, depending on what appeals. Activities like boat trips, canoeing and fishing are available almost everywhere, and large towns all have a swimming complex that includes water slides, jacuzzis, saunas and table tennis; excellent for all ages in both summer and winter.

Children's Highlights

Castles

» Suomenlinna, the fortress island in Helsinki's harbour.

» Raseborg, on its rocky perch near Ekenäs.

» Savonlinna's island castle is Finland's most impressive.

» Turun Linna lords it over the medieval city of Turku.

» Hämeenlinna's noble castle and the adjacent artillery museum both have appeal.

» Kastelholms Slott and Bomarsund are contrasting fortresses on Åland.

Animals

» Boat it over to the zoo in Helsinki, or learn about Arctic fauna at Ranua in Lapland.

» Horse-riding around the south coast town of Ingå.

» Admire the fish at aquariums in Kotka, Helsinki or Tampere.

» Meet the dogs at a Lapland husky kennel or feed the reindeer at a farm.

» See the tame orphaned bears near Kuusamo.

Winter

» Strap the skates on at Helsinki's outdoor rink, Jääpuisto.

» Tackle the family-friendly slopes at ski resorts like Levi, Ruka, Pyhä-Luosto or Jyväskylä.

» Get into the Christmas spirit around Rovaniemi, where Santa can be visited year-round.

» Visit the snow castles at Kemi or Hetta, or the snow village at Ylläs.

» Take a sledge ride pulled by huskies or reindeer in Lapland, or rev up a snowmobile and go for a spin.

» Take the brood ice-fishing on a frozen lake.

Theme Parks

» Linnanmäki, Helsinki.

» Serena Water Park, Espoo.

» Rauhalahti, Kuopio.

» Sarkanniemi, Tampere.

» Muumimaailma (Moominworld), Naantali.

» Wasalandia and Tropiclandia, Vaasa.

On the Water

» Head off on a boat cruise in Helsinki, Kuopio, Savonlinna, Tampere and more.

» Hire a boat and explore the Ekenäs Archipelago National Park.

» Take a trip out to the Bengtskär lighthouse from Hanko.

» Go fishing around Kotka, Tampere, Ruunaa or Nuorgam in Lapland.

» Paddle your way around the Linnansaari and Kolovesi national parks.

» Tackle the Oravareitti (Squirrel Route), a multi-day canoeing adventure.

» Shoot the rapids at Ruunaa, or on the Kitkajoki near Kuusamo.

» Pan for gold in the Lapland rivers at Tankavaara or Lemmenjoki.

Beaches

» Hietaranta is Helsinki's best city beach.

» The Hanko area has numerous beaches, ranging from paddleable to surfable.

» Check out the amazing Hiekkalinna sandcastle in Lappeenranta.

» Yyteri near Pori has a great variety.

» The resort of Kalajoki and Hailuoto Island near Oulu are excellent for families.

Museums

» Heureka science centre in Vantaa has the lot, with interactive exhibits, IMAX cinema and a planetarium. Tietomaa in Oulu is even more impressive.

» The sports museum in Helsinki and the ski museum in Lahti.

» Outdoor museums exhibit traditional buildings and have plenty of demonstrations and activities in summer. There are good ones in Helsinki, Turku, and at Turkansaari near Oulu.

» Enter the mad world of mechanical music at the Mekaanisen Musiikin Museo in Varkaus.

» Others guaranteed to please are the natural history museum in Helsinki, the spy museum in Tampere, Forum Marinum in Turku and the Kierikki Stone Age museum near Oulu.

Typical Finnish

» Take in the atmosphere of an ice hockey game in Helsinki.

» Sweat it out in the Jätkänkämppä smoke sauna in Kuopio, then fill up at the traditional buffet.

» Enjoy the action of Helsinki Day, or give the kids a go at the mobile-phone-throwing world championships in Savonlinna.

Planning
When to Go

Finnish children are on holidays from mid-June to early August, and many child-oriented activities are closed outside this period. This is when camp sites are buzzing with Finnish families – an instant social life for your kids – and temperatures are usually reliably warm.

Winter is also a great time to take the family to Finland, especially to the north. December sees all sorts of Christmassy things spring up in Lapland, with Santas, elves and reindeer galore. But if your kids are older and you want to get active in the snow, March or April are the months to go: there's plenty of daylight, better snow, and not such extreme negative temperatures.

Accommodation

Outside the big cities, self-catering is huge in Finland; the wide network of rental cabins, apartments and cottages – ranging from simple huts with bunks to luxurious bungalows with fully equipped kitchen and electric sauna – make excellent family bases. Camp sites are also particularly good, with cabins, boats and bikes available for hire, and often a lake beach. There are always things to do and other children in these places, and some of the larger ones offer child-minding services or activity programs.

Most Finnish hotels and hostels will put an extra bed in a room for little extra cost – and kids under 12 often sleep free. Many hotel rooms have sofas that can fold out into beds or family suites, and hostels often have connecting rooms. The **Holiday Club** (www.holidayclub.fi) and **Rantasipi** (www. rantasipi.fi) chains of spa hotels are especially child-friendly. These and other resort hotels always have family-friendly restaurants with a menu for the kids, or deals where children eat free if accompanied by adults.

Other Practicalities

Local tourist information booklets and websites usually highlight attractions with family appeal.

Car-hire firms have children's safety seats for hire at a nominal cost, but it is essential that you book them in advance.

The same goes for highchairs and cots (cribs); they're standard in many restaurants and hotels, but numbers may be limited.

Entrance fees and transport tickets for children tend to be around 60% of the adult charge in Finland.

Most museums in Helsinki are free for kids.

Nappies and baby food are very widely available.

Breast-feeding in public is normal practice in Finland.

See p56 for child-friendly Helsinki choices.

regions at a glance

Helsinki

Design ✓✓✓
Museums & Galleries ✓✓
Food & Drink ✓✓

Design
Finnish design is a byword for quality, but it's not just the reliable excellence of the big-name brands that impresses. Wander through the capital's back streets to discover a wealth of small ateliers and shops displaying the quirky, the innovative, the oh-dear, and the brilliant.

Museums & Galleries
Finns are very fond of museums, and Helsinki has an enviable selection. There are so many that you'll have to rigorously prune most of them, but there are enough must-see galleries and exhibitions to keep you busy for several days.

Food & Drink
Finnish food unfairly had a bad rap for years, but Helsinki's fine-dining restaurants turn heads all over the north. Ally that with traditional places serving heart-warming wintry fare and a wonderful array of offbeat drinking options, and you've got quite a package.

p42

Turku & the South Coast

Architecture ✓✓
Islands ✓✓
Beaches ✓

Architecture
This region holds the lion's share of Finland's historic buildings. Turku's castle and cathedral, old ironworks, Hanko's posh tsarist villas, and various fortresses and churches make this prime territory to explore the past.

Islands
Zoom in on a map and prepare to be astounded by the quantity of small islands speckling Finland's Baltic coastline. Some you can explore by bike, others will need boat hire.

Beaches
The sea might be a little chilly but there's plenty of sand and sun. The area around Hanko has many choices, but you can find decent strands right across the region.

p82

Åland Archipelago

Cycling ✓✓
Islands ✓✓
Historic Sights ✓

Cycling
Flat, comparatively sunny, light traffic: these islands are a paradise for cycling. Camp sites, farmstays, and bike-friendly inter island ferries make touring here a breeze.

Islands
If you love islands you'll love Åland. The main ones are already tranquil, but get out to the eastern archipelago and you'll virtually have a rock in the Baltic to yourself. Grab a kayak and you literally will.

Historic Sights
Åland has an intriguing history. As an important strategic point in the Baltic, it has a couple of major fortresses to explore, plus a grand post office. In the capital, Mariehamn, the museum-ship *Pommern* speaks of the islands' maritime heritage.

p117

Tampere & Häme

Galleries ✓✓✓
Beer ✓✓
Boat Trips ✓✓

The Lakeland

Canoeing ✓✓✓
Festivals ✓✓✓
Cruises ✓

Karelia

Hiking ✓✓✓
Festivals ✓
Food ✓

West Coast

Festivals ✓✓
Architecture ✓✓
Coastline ✓

Galleries
Finland's art has traditionally been linked with its nature, so it should be no surprise to find studios and galleries in small towns or by some lake in the middle of nowhere. The three main cities of the region back these up with a fistful of excellent museums.

Beer
Finland downs a lot of the stuff, but most Suomi beer is generic mass-produced lager. Small breweries and bars in this region buck the trend; sampling their ales and ciders is one of the area's highlights.

Boat Trips
Getting out on the water, whether for a short jaunt or town-to-town lake cruise, is one of the region's great summer pleasures.

p136

Canoeing
There's no better way to appreciate the lakes and rivers that form this watery land than by grabbing a canoe or kayak. Explore national parks hoping to spot an inland seal, or canoe the family-friendly Squirrel Route.

Festivals
Finland's festivals are a diverse bunch, and never more so than in the Lakeland, where glorious castle opera takes the stage alongside rowing boat regattas, car rallies, wife-carrying and mobile-phone throwing.

Cruises
Why jump on a bus to get to the next town when you can make the journey on the deck of a historic lake boat and appreciate the scenery at a stately pace?

p161

Hiking
Karelia has some excellent long-distance hiking routes that wind their way through some of Finland's deepest and most remote forests. There are hundreds of kilometres of marked trails to keep you busy.

Festivals
Karelia is the best place to go to explore Finnish Orthodox customs. Onion-domed churches and traditional festivals give the place a different feel from the predominantly Lutheran rest of the country.

Food
The savoury 'Karelian pie' is a rice-filled staple eaten widely across the country, but you'll find several intriguing variants here. Better yet is Lemi's speciality, birch-roasted mutton, a Finnish culinary highlight.

p190

Festivals
The west coast celebrates summer in style. Normally tranquil Seinäjoki kicks its heels up for contrasting tango and rock festivals, while Kaustinen becomes a folk-music mecca. Add Pori's jazz do and Rauma's bustling lace week and it's a busy season.

Architecture
Rauma, Jakobstad and Kokkola bring Finnish history alive with their rows of charming wooden buildings, some of the few to have survived the years and the fires.

Coastline
The Gulf of Bothnia isn't the likeliest of sun-and-sand destinations, but there are some great family beaches here. The weird rising landscapes of the Kvarken archipelago are another highlight.

p216

Oulu, Kainuu & Koillismaa

Activities ✓✓✓
Wildlife ✓✓
Festivals ✓

Activities
The area around Kuusamo and Ruka is fantastic for getting active. In summer, great hiking, canoeing and rafting is the draw; winter sees skiing, sled safaris and snowmobiling.

Wildlife
Around Kuhmo and Kuusamo there are all sorts of impressive beasts to see if you creep out into the forest with a guide. Elk, flying squirrels, wolverines and bears are all viewable from the comfort and safety of a hide.

Festivals
Oulu raises the weirdness stakes with its ice-fishing marathon, garlic ice-cream and air-guitar championships. A statelier counterpoint is Kuhmo's chamber music festival.

p243

Lapland

Hiking ✓✓✓
Activities ✓✓✓
Sámi Culture ✓✓

Hiking
The big skies, clear air, splendid landscapes and enormous national parks make Lapland one of Europe's best hiking destinations. Networks of wilderness huts and camp sites mean planning a walk is easy.

Activities
Winter doesn't get much more wintry than Lapland, but that's no invitation to huddle indoors: there's a fistful of things to do, like skiing, safaris with huskies or reindeer, ice-fishing and snowmobiling.

Sámi Culture
The northern part of Lapland is the homeland of various indigenous Sámi groups. Learning a little about their culture, art and reindeer-herding is a highlight of any visit.

p268

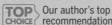

> Every listing is recommended by our authors, and their favourite places are listed first

> Look out for these icons:

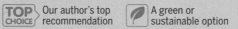

TOP CHOICE Our author's top recommendation   **🖉** A green or sustainable option   **FREE** No payment required

On the Road

Helsinki

📱 09 / POP 1.04 MILLION (GREATER METROPOLITAN AREA)

Includes »

Best Places to Eat

» Savoy (p62)
» Olo (p62)
» Demo (p62)
» Chez Dominique (p62)
» Zucchini (p62)

Best Places to Stay

» Hotelli Helka (p58)
» Hotelli Onni (p79)
» Hotel GLO (p58)
» Hotel Finn (p58)
» Hotel Fabian (p58)

Why Go?

It's fitting that harbourside Helsinki, capital of a country with such a watery geography, melds so graciously into the Baltic Sea. Half the city seems to be liquid, and the tortuous writhings of the complex coastline include any number of bays, inlets and a speckling of islands.

Though Helsinki can seem like a younger sibling to other Scandinavian capitals, it's the one that went to art school, scorns pop music, is working in a cutting-edge design studio and hangs out with friends who like black and plenty of piercings.

On the other hand, much of what is lovable in Helsinki is older. Its understated yet glorious art-nouveau buildings, the spacious elegance of its centenarian cafes, the careful preservation of Finnish heritage in its dozens of museums, restaurants that have changed neither menu nor furnishings since the 1930s – they are all part of the city's quirky charm.

When to Go
HELSINKI

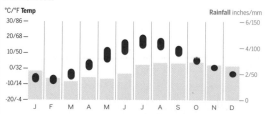

Jun Terraces are sprouting outside every cafe and the nights never seem to end.

Aug The city's functioning again after the July lull, but all the summer activities are still on.

Dec Skate on ice and absorb the Christmassy atmosphere before temperatures get too extreme.

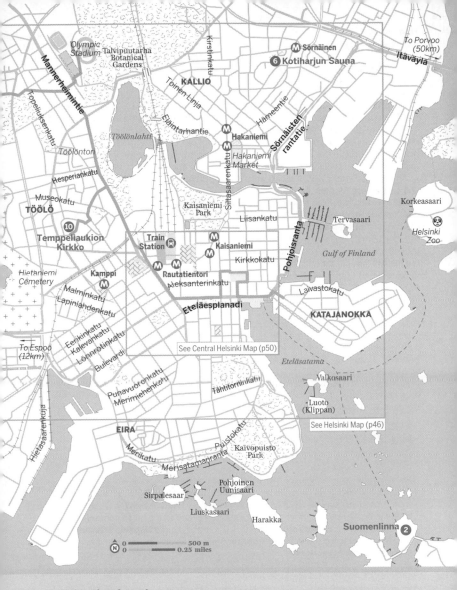

Helsinki Highlights

1 Descending into the weekend maelstrom in the roar of Helsinki's excellent variety of **pubs** and **clubs** (p66)

2 Grabbing a picnic and exploring the fortress island of **Suomenlinna** (p44) that guarded Helsinki harbour

3 Browsing exciting **design shops** (p69)

4 Selecting from the city's huge range of **museums** and **galleries** (p44)

5 Taking advantage of the great network of **bicycle paths** (p74) to explore on two wheels

6 Sweating out your cares in the traditional, atmospheric **Kotiharjun Sauna** (p55)

7 Taking a trip across to **Tallinn** (p59) to admire its unforgettable Old Town

8 Admiring wooden warehouses of **Porvoo** (p77)

9 **Dining** on traditional food like meatballs or liver, or avant-garde New Suomi cuisine (p62)

10 Nodding with respect to the **Temppeliaukion Kirkko** (p53)

History

Founded in 1550 by King Gustav Vasa, Helsinki was to be a rival to the Hansa trading town of Tallinn. Earlier trials at Ekenäs were fruitless, so by royal decree traders from there and a few other towns were shanghaied to the newly founded Helsingfors (the Swedish name for Helsinki).

For more than 200 years it remained a backwater market town on a windy, rocky peninsula. Nevertheless, the city was razed in 1713 to prevent the Russians occupying it. All the inhabitants fled or were captured, and only returned after the Peace of Nystad in 1721. Later, the Swedes built their fortress named Sveaborg in 1748 to protect this eastern part of their empire against further Russian attack. Following the war of 1808, however, the Russians succeeded in taking the fortress and a year later Russia annexed Finland as an autonomous grand duchy. A capital closer to St Petersburg was required to keep a closer inspection on Finland's domestic politics. Helsinki was chosen – in large part because of the sea fortress (now called Suomenlinna) just outside the harbour – and so in 1812 Turku lost its long-standing status as Finland's capital and premier town.

In the 19th and early 20th centuries, Helsinki grew rapidly in all directions. German architect CL Engel was called on to dignify the city centre, which resulted in the neoclassical Senaatintori (Senate Square). The city suffered heavy Russian bombing during WWII, but in the postwar period Helsinki recovered and went on to host the Summer Olympic Games in 1952.

In the 1970s and '80s, many new suburbs were built around Helsinki and residents celebrated their 'Helsinki Spirit', a term used for Cold War détente. These days, the capital is so much the centre of everything that goes on in Finland that its past as an obscure market town is totally forgotten.

⊙ Sights

Helsinki has over 50 museums and galleries but some are too obscure to interest any but enthusiasts. For a full list, pick up the *Museums* booklet (free) from the tourist office.

SUOMENLINNA

Just a 15-minute ferry ride from the Kauppatori (market square), a visit to **Suomenlinna** (www.suomenlinna.fi), the 'fortress of Finland', is a Helsinki must-do. Set on a tight cluster of four islands connected by bridges, the Unesco World Heritage Site was originally built by the Swedes as Sveaborg in the mid-eighteenth century.

From the main quay, a blue-signposted walking path connects the main attractions. By the bridge that connects Iso Mustasaari

---

HELSINKI IN...

One Day

Finns are the world's biggest coffee drinkers, so first up it's a caffeine shot with a cardamom *pulla* (pastry) at one of the centre's classic **cafes**. Then down to the **Kauppatori** (market square), and the fresh produce in the adjacent **kauppahalli** (covered market) building. Put a picnic together and boat out to the island fortress of **Suomenlinna**. Back in town, check out **Senaatintori** (Senate Square) and nearby **Uspenski Cathedral**. Then take the metro to the legendary **Kotiharjun Sauna** for a predinner sweat. Eat traditional Finnish at **Kuu** or **Sea Horse**.

Two Days

Investigate the art and design scene. Head to the **Ateneum** for a perspective on the golden age of Finnish painting, and then see contemporary works at still-iconic **Kiasma**. Feet tired? Catch the **number 3 tram** for a circular sightseeing trip around town, before browsing some of the **design shops** around Punavuori. In the evening, head up to the **Ateljee Bar** for great views, then on to **Tavastia** for a rock gig.

Four Days

With two more days, you can explore more of the region's jagged coastline. Familiarise yourself with traditional architecture at **Seurasaaren ulkomuseo**, and take a trip to **Porvoo** for its beautiful wooden buildings and gorgeous riverside. Dine in style on Modern Finnish cuisine at **Demo** or **Olo**.

and the main island, Susisaari, is **Suomenlinnakeskus** (Visitor Centre; www.suomenlinna.fi; walking tours €7, free with Helsinki Card; ☺10am-6pm May-Sep, 10.30am-4.30pm Oct-Apr, English walking tours depart 11am & 2pm Jun-Aug), which has tourist information, internet access, maps and guided walking tours, daily in summer and weekends only in winter. Within the centre is **Suomenlinna-museo** (admission €5, combined ticket with Ehrensvärd-museo & Lelumuseo €10), a two-level museum covering the history of the fortress. It's very information heavy, but the first part gives good background. There's also a 30-minute audiovisual display.

The most atmospheric part of Suomenlinna is at the end of the blue trail, the southern end of Susisaari. Exploring the old bunkers, crumbling fortress walls and cannons will give you an insight into this fortress, and there are plenty of grassy picnic spots. Monumental **King's Gate** was built in 1753–54 as a two-storey fortress wall, which had a double drawbridge and a stairway, the 'King's Steps', added. In summer you can get a boat back to Helsinki from here, saving you the walk back to the main quay.

Several other museums dot the islands. Perhaps the most interesting is **Ehrensvärd-museo** (admission adult/child €3/1; ☺11am-6pm Jun-Aug, to 4pm May & Sep), once the home of Augustin Ehrensvärd, the man responsible for designing and running the fortress. An attractive 18th-century house, it holds numerous portraits, prints and models giving an insight into daily life on the island. Ehrensvärd's tomb sits outside in the square, and opposite is a busy **shipyard** where sailmakers and other workers have been building ships since the 1750s. The dry dock holds up to two dozen boats being built or repaired.

Along the shore from here is another fish out of water. The **Vesikko** (admission €5; ☺11am-6pm mid-May–Aug) is the only WWII-era submarine remaining in Finland. It saw action against the Russians. It's fascinating to climb inside and see how it all worked. Needless to say, there's not much room to move.

Near the main quay, there's a supermarket, hostel, brewery pub and the distinctive pink **Galleria Rantakasarmi** (admission free; ☺Tue-Sun). One of the best-preserved remaining buildings of the Russian era, it now has various exhibitions.

Near here, the **church** was built by the Russians in 1854 and served as a Russian Orthodox place of worship until the 1920s when it became Lutheran. It's the only

HELSINKI CARD

The **Helsinki Card** (www.helsinkicard.fi; adult 24/48/72hr €35/45/55, child €14/17/20) gives you free travel, entry to more than 50 attractions in and around Helsinki, and discounts on day tours to Porvoo and Tallinn. It's cheaper to buy it online; otherwise, get it at the tourist office, hotels, R-kioskis and transport terminals. To get value for money, you'd need to pack a lot of sights into a short time.

church in the world to double as a lighthouse – the beacon was originally gaslight but is now electric and still in use.

Also on Iso Mustasaari is **Manege** (admission €5; ☺11am-6pm mid-May–Aug), which commemorates WWII and displays heavy artillery. Quite a contrast is the nearby **Lelumuseo** (Toy Museum; admission €5; ☺daily mid-May–Aug, weekends early May & Sep), a delightful private collection of hundreds of dolls and almost as many teddy bears. The cafe here serves delicious homemade apple pie.

Taking a picnic is a great way to make the most of Suomenlinna's grass, views and (hopefully) sunshine. There are also several cafes and restaurants (see p65). At around 5.15pm it's worth finding a spot to watch the enormous Baltic ferries pass through the narrow gap between islands.

Ferries to Suomenlinna depart from the passenger quay at Helsinki's Kauppatori, arriving at the main quay on Suomenlinna and stopping at other points on the islands in summer. Tickets (single/return €2/3.80, 15 minutes, three times hourly, 6.20am to 2.20am) are available at the pier. In addition, **JT-Lines** (www.jt-line.fi) runs a waterbus at least hourly from the Kauppatori, making two stops on Suomenlinna (single/return €4/6.50, 20 minutes, 8am to 7pm May to mid-September).

CENTRAL HELSINKI
The heart of central Helsinki is the Kauppatori on the harbour, where ferries leave for the archipelago islands and berries, fresh fish and souvenirs are sold in stalls.

Tuomiokirkko CHURCH
(Map p50; www.visithelsinki.fi; Unioninkatu 29; ☺9am-midnight Jun-Aug, to 6pm Sep-May) One of CL Engel's finest creations, the chalk-white neoclassical Lutheran cathedral presides over Senaatintori. Though as it was not completed

Helsinki

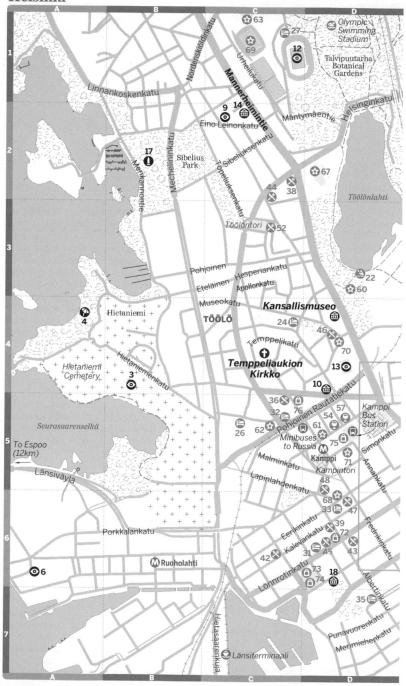

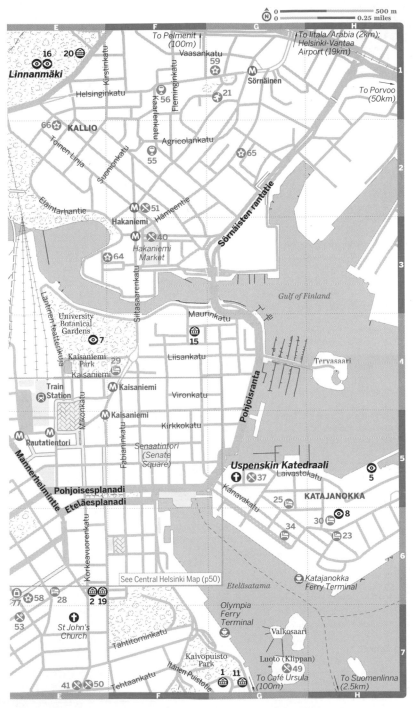

HELSINKI SIGHTS

Helsinki

until 1852, the architect, who died in 1840, never saw it. Though created to serve as a reminder of God's supremacy, its high flight of stairs has become a meeting place for canoodling couples, and a setting for New Year's revelry. The spartan interior has little ornamentation under the lofty dome beyond an altar painting of the Burial of Christ and three stern statues of the Reformation heroes Luther, Melanchthon and Mikael Agricola, looking like they've just marked your theology exam and taken rather a dim view of your prospects.

Uspenskin Katedraali   CHURCH
(Map p46; www.visithelsinki.fi; Kanavakatu 1; ☺9.30am-4pm Mon-Fri, to 2pm Sat, noon-3pm Sun, closed Mon Oct-Apr) Facing the Lutheran cathedral, the eye-catching red-brick Uspenski Cathedral is equally imposing on nearby Katajanokka Island. The two buildings face off high above the city like two queens on a theological chessboard. Built as a Russian Orthodox church in 1868, it features classic onion-topped domes and now serves the Finnish Orthodox congregation. The high, square interior has a lavish iconostasis with the Evangelists flanking panels depicting the Last Supper and the Ascension. Orthodox services held at 6pm on Saturday and 10am Sunday are worth attending for the fabulous chorals and candlelit atmosphere.

Kiasma   GALLERY
(Map p50; www.kiasma.fi; Mannerheiminaukio 2; adult/under 18yr €8/free; ☺10am-8.30pm Wed-Fri, to 6pm Sat & Sun, to 5pm Tue) Now just one of a series of elegant contemporary buildings in this part of town, curvaceous and quirky metallic Kiasma, designed by American architect Steven Holl and finished in 1998, is still a symbol of the city's modernisation. It exhibits an eclectic collection of Finnish and international modern art and keeps people on their toes with its striking contemporary exhibitions. Holl designed the unique structure to mimic the X-shaped Greek letter chi, representing an intersection.

As well as regular contemporary exhibitions in kinetic sculpture, cross media or installation, there's a rapidly growing collection of Finnish and international modern art from the 1960s to the present. Focusing on the left of field, there's a permanent collection on the 3rd floor and an experimental theatre with a changing program (tickets usually cost extra) on the ground floor, known for the handwritten clock outside the arty museum shop.

Kiasma's outstanding success is that it has been embraced by the people of Helsinki. Its sleek, glass-sided cafe and terrace are hugely popular, locals sunbathe on the grassy fringes, and skateboarders perform aerobatics under the stern gaze of the **CGE Mannerheim statue** outside.

Behind Kiasma, **Sanomatalo** is the HQ of the Helsinki daily, *Helsingin Sanomat*. A little further is the Musiikkitalo building, as cool and crisp as a gin and tonic on a glacier.

Ateneum   GALLERY
(Map p50; www.ateneum.fi; Kaivokatu 2; adult/child €8/free; ☺10am-6pm Tue & Fri, to 8pm Wed & Thu, 11am-5pm Sat & Sun) The top floor of Finland's premier art gallery is an ideal crash course in the nation's art. It houses

---

SUOMENLINNA: THE LION THAT SQUEAKED

In the mid-eighteenth century, Sweden was getting twitchy about the possibility of a Russian invasion, and decided to build a state-of-the-art offshore fortress near the eastern limits of its declining empire. At the time, Helsinki wasn't a particularly important town, and the bastion itself, named Sveaborg, became one of Finland's largest settlements and a thriving community.

Despite Suomenlinna's meticulous planning and impressive military hardware, its history in war has been rather less than glorious. When the Russians finally came calling in 1808, they besieged the islands. The commander, alarmed by Russian threats to bombard every last civilian to smithereens, tamely surrendered the fortress to spare the soldiers' families.

Once Finland was under Russian rule, the capital was moved from Turku to Helsinki, but the fortress was allowed to deteriorate. A wake-up call came with the Crimean War and rapid improvements were made. Or so they said. As it turned out, British ships pounded the islands with 21,000 shots in a two-day bombardment, but Suomenlinna's guns were so out of condition that they couldn't reach the range required to bother ships.

The fortress nevertheless remained in Russian hands until independence. During the Finnish Civil War it served as a prison for communist prisoners.

Central Helsinki

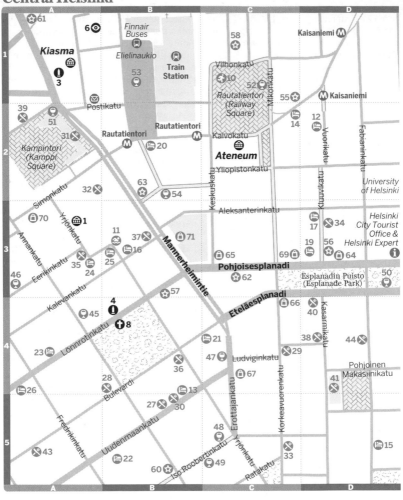

Finnish paintings and sculptures from the 'golden age' of the late 19th century through to the 1950s, including works by Albert Edelfelt, Hugo Simberg, Helene Schjerfbeck, the Von Wright brothers and Pekka Halonen. Pride of place goes to the prolific Akseli Gallen-Kallela's triptych from the *Kalevala* depicting Väinämöinen's pursuit of the maiden Aino. There's also a small but interesting collection of 19th- and early-20th-century foreign art. Downstairs is a cafe, good bookshop and reading room. The building itself dates from 1887.

Kansallismuseo   MUSEUM
(National Museum of Finland; Map p46; www.kansallismuseo.fi; Mannerheimintie 34; adult/child €7/free; ⏰11am-8pm Tue, to 6pm Wed-Sun) The impressive National Museum, built in National Romantic style in 1916, looks a bit like a Gothic church with its heavy stonework and tall square tower. This is Finland's premier historical museum and is divided into rooms covering different periods of Finnish history, including prehistory and archaeological finds, church relics, ethnography and changing cultural exhibitions. It's a very thorough, old-style museum – you might have trouble

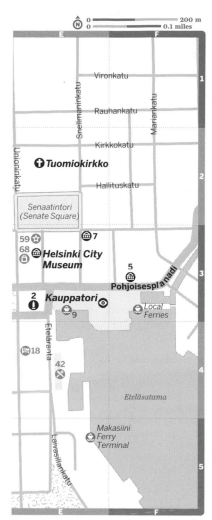

stroll. It's a paradise of upmarket Jugendstil (art nouveau) residential buildings with extravagant turrets and curious carvings galore. While the south side of the island has a major ferry terminal, the other side is more peaceful, with the Engel-designed Foreign Ministry looking out over the impressively functional **fleet of ice-breakers**. At the western end of the island, Uspenski Cathedral looks over a leisure harbour and a series of warehouses attractively converted into enticing restaurants and bars.

Luonnontieteellinen museo　　MUSEUM
(Natural History Museum; Map p46; www.luonnon tieteellinenmuseo.fi; Pohjoinen Rautatiekatu 13; adult/child €6/3; ⏰10am-6pm Tue-Fri, to 5pm Sat & Sun Jun-Aug, 9am-4pm Tue-Fri, to 6pm Thu, 10am-4pm Sat & Sun Sep-May) The city's natural history museum is known for its controversial weathervane of a sperm impregnating an ovum. Exhibitions like *Story of the Bones*, which puts skeletons in an evolutionary context, bring new life to the University of Helsinki's extensive collection of mammals, birds and other creatures, including all Finnish species. The dinosaur skeletons and the saggy African elephant in the foyer are hits with kids.

Designmuseo　　MUSEUM
(Design Museum; Map p46; www.designmuseum.fi; Korkeavuorenkatu 23; adult/child €7/free; ⏰11am-6pm daily Jun-Aug, 11am-8pm Tue, to 6pm Wed-Sun Sep-May) The Design Museum has a permanent collection that looks at the roots of Finnish design in the nation's traditions and nature. Changing exhibitions focus on contemporary design – everything from clothing to household furniture.

FREE **Helsingin Kaupunginmuseo**　MUSEUM
(Helsinki City Museum; www.helsinkicitymuseum.fi) A group of small museums scattered around the city centre constitute the kaupunginmuseo (city museum), which all have free entry. All buildings focus on an aspect of the city's past or present through permanent and temporary exhibitions.

The must-see of the bunch is **Helsinki City Museum** (Map p50; Sofiankatu 4; ⏰9am-5pm Mon-Fri, to 7pm Thu, 11am-5pm Sat & Sun), just off Senaatintori. Its excellent collection of historical artefacts and photos is backed up by entertaining information on the history of the city, piecing together Helsinki's transition from Swedish to Russian hands and into independence.

selling this one to the kids – but provides a comprehensive overview. Look for the imperial throne of Tsar Alexander I dating from 1809, and the basement treasury, gleaming with coins, medals, pewter and swords. From the 1st-floor balcony, crane your head up to see the superb frescoes on the ceiling arches, depicting scenes from the epic *Kalevala*, painted by Akseli Gallen-Kallela.

Katajanokka　　ISLAND
(Map p46) Just east of the Kauppatori, this island is divided from the mainland by a narrow canal and makes for an enjoyable

Central Helsinki

Other good museums in this group are **Sederholmin talo** (Map p50; Aleksanterinkatu 18; ⊙11am-5pm Wed-Sun, to 7pm Thu), Helsinki's oldest central building (dating from 1757 and built by a wealthy merchant), which holds temporary exhibitions; the delightful **Ratikkamuseo** (Tram Museum; Map p46; Töölönkatu 51A; ⊙11am-5pm), which displays vintage trams and depicts daily life in Helsinki's streets in past decades; **Ruiskumestarin talo** (Burgher's House; Map p46; Kristianinkatu 12; ⊙11am-5pm Wed-Sun Jun-Aug & Nov & Dec), central Helsinki's oldest wooden town house, built in 1818; and the **Työväenasuntomuseo** (Museum of Worker Housing; Map p46; Kirstinkuja 4; ⊙11am-5pm Wed-Sun May-Sep), showing how industrial workers lived in the early 20th century.

Vanha Kirkko   CHURCH
(Map p50; Lönnrotinkatu) Helsinki's most venerable church is this white wood beauty, designed by CL Engel. Opposite the church is a **memorial to Elias Lönnrot**, compiler of the *Kalevala* epic, depicting the author flanked by his most famous character, 'steady old Väinämöinen'.

Suomen Rakennustaiteen Museo   MUSEUM
(Map p46; www.mfa.fi; Kasarmikatu 24; admission €5; ⊙10am-4pm Tue & Thu-Fri, to 8pm Wed, 11am-4pm Sat & Sun) Just behind the Design Museum, the Museum of Finnish Architecture has mostly temporary exhibitions.

Amos Andersonin taidemuseo   GALLERY
(Map p50; www.amosanderson.fi; Yrjönkatu 27; adult/child €8/free; ⊙10am-6pm Mon-Fri, to 8pm Wed, 11am-5pm Sat & Sun) This gallery houses the collection of publishing magnate Amos Anderson, one of the wealthiest Finns of his time. It includes Finnish and European art from the 15th century to the present.

GREATER HELSINKI

Temppeliaukion Kirkko   CHURCH
(Map p46; Lutherinkatu 3; ⊙10am-8pm Mon-Tue & Thu-Fri, to 6.45pm Wed, to 6pm Sat, noon-1.45pm & 3.30-6pm Sun) The Temppeliaukio church, designed by Timo and Tuomo Suomalainen in 1969, remains one of Helsinki's foremost attractions. Hewn into solid stone, it feels close to a Finnish ideal of spirituality in nature – you could be in a rocky glade were it not for the stunning 24m-diameter roof covered in 22km of copper stripping. There are regular concerts, with great acoustics.

Linnanmäki & Sea Life   AMUSEMENT PARK, AQUARIUM
(Map p46; www.linnanmaki.fi; Tivolikuja 1; admission free, single ride €6.50; ⊙11am-10pm May–early Sep) Famous Linnanmäki is a real kid-pleaser with rides, roller coaster and nightly fireworks. Its profits are donated to child-welfare organisations. There are various day passes, some of which include nearby **Sea Life** (Map p46; www.sealife.fi; Tivolitie 10; adult/child €15/10; ⊙10am-7pm Jun-Sep, to 9pm Jul, 10am-5pm Oct-May), an aquarium complex with walk-through tunnels that let you spot sharks, rays and a myriad fish up close.

Discount tickets are available online. Bus 23 and trams 3B, 3T and 8 take you there.

Helsinki Zoo   ZOO
(www.korkeasaari.fi; adult/child €10/5, incl ferry ride €16/8; ⊙10am-8pm May-Aug, to 4pm Oct-Mar, to 6pm Sep & Apr) This spacious island zoo is located on Korkeasaari, best reached by ferry from the Kauppatori. Established in 1889, it has animals and birds from Finland and around the world housed in large natural enclosures, as well as a tropical house, a small farm and a good cafe and terrace.

Ferries leave from the Kauppatori and from Hakaniemi every 30 minutes or so during May to September, and zoo bus 11 goes from the railway station daily year-round.

Seurasaaren ulkomuseo   MUSEUM
(Seurasaari; www.seurasaari.fi; adult/child €6/free; ⊙11am-5pm daily Jun-Aug, 9am-3pm Mon-Fri, 11am-5pm Sat & Sun late May & early Sep) West of the centre, this excellent island museum has a collection of historic traditional houses, manors and outbuildings transferred here from around Finland. Wandering around the wooded island is a pleasure in itself; guides dressed in traditional costume demonstrate folk dancing and crafts such as spinning, embroidery and troll-making. While you'll see other museums like this across Finland, Seurasaari is the most complete. There are guided tours in English at 3pm in summer.

It's also a venue for Helsinki's biggest Midsummer bonfires and a popular area for picnicking. From central Helsinki, take bus 24 directly there, or tram 4 to its terminus and walk 700m west along the shoreline.

Urho Kekkosen Museo   MUSEUM
(Urho Kekkonen Museum; Seurasaarentie 15, Tamminiemi; adult/child €6/free; ⊙11am-5pm Mon, Tue & Thu-Sun, to 7pm Wed mid-May–mid-Aug) Near the bridge connecting Seurasaari with the mainland, this museum gives a

ⓘ HELSINKI ON A HANDSET

Packed your phone? Helsinki has a cut-down version of its tourism website designed to be delivered to your mobile at www.helsinki.mobi.

glimpse into the life of Finland's greatest president. A guided tour wanders through the magnificent villa and its surrounding park, and peeks into the traditional sauna that hosted diplomatic chinwags with Nikita Khrushchev. While here, don't miss a coffee at nearby Tamminiementien Kahvila. For the museum and Seurasaari, take bus 24 from central Helsinki, which takes you right there, or tram 4 to its terminus and walk 800m west. The museum reopened in 2012 after extensive renovation, so check opening hours and prices.

Mannerheim-museo   MUSEUM
(Map p46; www.mannerheim-museo.fi; Kalliolinnantie 14; adult/child €10/free; ⊙11am-4pm Fri-Sun) This fascinating museum in Kaivopuisto Park was the home of Baron Gustav Mannerheim, former president, commander in chief of the Finnish army and Finnish Civil War victor. The great field marshal never owned the building; he rented it from chocolate magnate, Karl Fazer, until his death. The house tells of Mannerheim's intrepid life with hundreds of military medals and photographs from his Asian expedition travelling 14,000km along the Silk Road from Samarkand to Beijing. Entry includes an informative one-hour guided tour in six languages, plus free plastic booties to keep the hallowed floor clean.

Suomen urheilumuseo   MUSEUM
(Finnish Sports Museum; Map p46; www.urheilumuseo.fi; Olympiastadion; admission €5; ⊙11am-5pm Mon-Fri, noon-4pm Sat & Sun) This sports museum, in the 1952 **Olympic Stadium**, houses Finland's sporting hall of fame including the triumph of runner Paavo Nurmi and Matti Nykänen, one of the most successful ski-jumpers of all time. There are good simulations that let you compete in the 200m race against champions and there's a novel exhibition about Pesäpallo, Finland's own baseball-like game. HI members get €2 off admission.

Also here, the stadium's **tower** (admission adult/child €5/2; ⊙9am-9pm Mon-Fri, 9am-6pm Sat & Sun) has a 72m-high viewing platform

that looks back to the city. Admission gives you a €2 discount to the sports museum. Trams 3B, 3T, 4, 7A, 7B and 10 from the city centre all run past it.

Kaapelitehdas   CULTURAL CENTRE
(Cable Factory; www.kaapelitehdas.fi; Tallberginkatu 1C) This sprawling site once manufactured sea cable and later became Nokia's main factory until the 1980s. It's now a bohemian cultural centre featuring studios, galleries, concerts, and theatre and dance performances. There's also a photography museum and a theatre museum here. Take tram 8, bus 15, 20, 21V, 65A or 66A, or the metro to the Ruoholahti stop; it's off Porkkalankatu.

Sinebrychoffin Taidemuseo   GALLERY
(Map p46; www.sinebrychoffintaidemuseo.fi; Bulevardi 40; admission €5; ⊙10am-6pm Tue & Fri, to 8pm Wed-Thu, 11am-5pm Sat & Sun) The largest collection of classic European paintings in Finland is in this former brewery. The main collection is Italian, Flemish and Swedish in origin. The Empire room is an impressive re-creation that drips with chandeliers and opulence.

Hietaranta   BEACH
(Map p46) Helsinki has several city beaches and this is the best. It's a likeable stretch of sand just west of the centre, and ideal in summer for either swimming or enjoying the terrace. The nicest way to get here is to stroll from Mechelininkatu west through the **Hietaniemi cemetery**.

Kaisaniemen Kasvitieteellinen Puutarha   GARDENS
(Map p46; www.luomus.fi; Unioninkatu 44; admission free; ⊙9am-8pm Apr-Sep, 9am-5pm Oct-Mar) Run by the university, this central spot comprises Finland's largest botanical collection, with classic 19th-century greenhouses (open shorter hours, adult/child €6/3), a cafe and a park.

Cygnaeuksen galleria   GALLERY
(Map p46; www.nba.fi; Kalliolinnantie 8; adult/child €5/free; ⊙11am-5pm May-Sep) Finnish art from the 19th century is showcased at this attractive wooden building in Kaivopuisto Park. It opened in 1882, which makes it Finland's oldest art gallery.

Korjaamo   CULTURAL CENTRE
(Map p46; www.korjaamo.fi; Töölönkatu 51) A diversity of cultural offerings by day and night in this renovated tram depot off Mannerheimintie.

Activities

Cycling is a great way to experience Helsinki's parks and sights. There's a free cycle route map at the city tourist office. For information on bike rental see p74.

Helsinki has several affordable public swimming pools. In summer there are good beaches at Hietaniemi, Seurasaari and Suomenlinna, though some don't let the winter chill stop them – ice-swimming is popular.

TOP CHOICE Kotiharjun Sauna SAUNA
(Map p46; www.kotiharjunsauna.fi; Harjutorinkatu 1; adult/child €10/5; ⊙2-8pm Tue-Fri, 1-7pm Sat, sauna to 10pm) This traditional public wood-fired sauna in Kallio dates back to 1928. This type of place largely disappeared with the advent of shared saunas in apartment buildings, but it's a classic experience, where you can also get a scrub-down and massage. There are separate saunas for men and women. It's a short stroll from Sörnäinen metro station.

Yrjönkadun Uimahalli SWIMMING, SAUNA
(Map p50; www.hel.fi; Yrjönkatu 21; swimming €5, swimming plus saunas €12; ⊙men Tue, Thu & Sat, women Mon, Wed, Fri & Sun, closed Jun-Aug) For a sauna and swim, these art-deco baths are a Helsinki institution – a fusion of soaring Nordic elegance and Roman tradition. There are separate hours for men and women. Nudity is compulsory in the saunas; bathing suits are optional in the pool.

Jääpuisto SKATING
(Ice Park; Map p50; www.jaapuisto.fi; admission €5, skate rental €5; ⊙noon-9pm Mon-Thu, 10am-10pm Fri & Sat, 10am-6pm Sun, late Nov–mid-Mar) In winter Rautatientori (Railway Square) becomes this outdoor ice-skating area where you can hire skates and get involved.

Töölönlahden Venevuokraamo BOATING
(Map p46; ☑041-540 9240; www.hesanpalvelut. com; per hr €10-13; ⊙noon-8pm May-Sep) You can hire rowing boats, pedalos and kayaks for a paddle on Töölönlahti from just behind Finlandia Talo.

HELSINKI ACTIVITIES

LOCAL KNOWLEDGE

ALEXIS KOUROS, FILMMAKER & FOUNDING EDITOR OF THE HELSINKI TIMES

Best cafe? In the wintertime one of my favourite places is Café Ursula, which is by the sea near Kaivopuisto. In the winter, when the days are short and light, you get the maximum amount of light when you sit there, and it's very nice scenery from the cafe.

What Finnish film would you recommend? People could watch a couple of the Kaurismäki brothers' movies. Aki has *Man Without a Past*, for example, which won a prize at the Cannes festival. His films are always a bit exaggerated, like a sort of caricature of Finnish society; but specifically through that they will give you a sort of exaggerated view that gives you an idea about the Finnish people's shyness.

Favourite building in Helsinki? My favourite building is the Temppeliaukion Kirkko, a round church built into the environment, which is basically a big hill with stones. It's a fantastic building and I really am amazed that the church authorities let it happen, because the roundness is pointing back to the pagan religions before Christianity.

For Finnish food? In the summertime, there are some tents in the Kauppatori which will give you an assortment of fish, potatoes, these kind of things. Those are really very typically Finnish. Then there is a newish restaurant called Juuri, with Finnish tapas: 'sapas'.

Helsinki in one word? One word! I would say 'fresh'. From the top of my head.

For design shopping? Well, there is a design district, which goes from the centre of the city towards Punavuori. It has evolved all the time, and there are always new shops. Lots of Finnish design.

Immigration is a hot topic in the EU at the moment. How well do Finns relate to immigrants? I would say that for the majority of cases, very well. Very well. You know, Finland has very few immigrants, and there are, as in all countries in Europe, some parts of society that are uncomfortable with immigrants being here. But I would say that the people I know, they are fantastic, they relate very well.

☞ Tours

An excellent budget alternative is to catch tram 3T/3B and pick up the free *Sightseeing on 3T/3B* brochure as your guide around the city centre and out to Kallio.

Helsinki Expert — BUS
(☎2288 1600; www.helsinkiexpert.fi; adult/child €27/15, with Helsinki Card free) Runs 90-minute sightseeing tours in its bright-orange bus. They depart from Pohjoisesplanadi, near the tourist office and include a taped commentary (in 12 languages) via a headset. A similar route runs daily from Katajanokka terminal (10.30am). The same company offers walking tours and tailored group tours.

Helsinki Cityride — WALKING, CYCLING
(☎044-955 8720; www.helsinkicityride.com) This outfit offers a variety of walking tours around various parts of the capital, year-round. Prices range from €25 to €40 but you get two people for the price of one. It also does a three-hour grand cycling tour that passes most of the major sights (€39 per person including bike rental). Book in advance.

Open Top Tours — BUS
(☎020-741 8210; www.stromma.fi) A hop-on, hop-off tour (adult/child €25/10) aboard a double-decker bus that leaves from Senaatintori, taking in some of the major sights. There are two discrete routes: for an extra €5, you get to travel both. If you're short on time, the 'Helsinki in a Nutshell' tour (adult/child €35/15) includes a quick boat tour.

Cruises

When strolling through the Kauppatori in summer, you won't have to look for cruises – the boat companies will find you. One-and-a-half hour cruises cost €17 to €20, while dinner cruises, bus-boat combinations and sunset cruises are also available. Most go past Suomenlinna and weave between other islands.

A visit to the zoo or Suomenlinna is a good way to combine a scenic boat ride with other sightseeing. There are also longer day cruises by ferry and steamer from Helsinki to the Finnish town of Porvoo and beyond; see p79.

Cruise operators:

IHA Lines (☎6874 5050; www.ihalines.fi)

Royal Line (☎020-711 8333; www.royalline.fi)

Sight Seaing Helsinki/Sun Lines (☎020-741 8210; www.stromma.fi) Also offers a 45-minute express cruise.

✯ Festivals & Events

Vappu — ACADEMIC
(1 May) This May Day student graduation festival is celebrated by gathering around the Havis Amanda statue, which receives a white graduation cap.

Maailma Kylässä — CULTURAL
(World Village; www.maailmakylassa.fi) World music, dance and art take the town in late May.

Ice Hockey World Championships — SPORT
(www.iihf.com) Televised on a big screen in Rautatientori in May, the atmosphere here is intense when Finland (the Leijonat) is doing well.

HELSINKI FOR CHILDREN

Helsinki has a lot to offer kids, with summer boat trips, amusement parks and outdoor events year-round. Finland is a child-friendly society and just about every hotel and restaurant will be keen to help out with cots or high chairs. Family rooms are available even in business hotels.

There's plenty to keep rug rats busy. Ferry destinations like the **zoo** and **Suomenlinna** can make for good excursions. **Linnanmäki amusement park** is as hard to resist as fairy floss, while Sea Life has a little more educational substance. The **Serena waterpark** in Espoo is great splashy fun.

The pick of the museums is the **Heureka science centre** at Vantaa. **Kiasma** has loads of interaction, though check that special exhibits won't raise any 'adult themes'. On Suomenlinna, visiting the **toy museum** and crawling through the **submarine** are always a hit, while the dinosaurs of the **Natural History Museum** and exhibits at the **Finnish Sports Museum** will also appeal to various age groups. Most museums are free to under-18s.

The **beaches** on Suomenlinna and at Hietaniemi are particularly safe, while there are **playgrounds** in both Kaivopuisto Park and Töölönlahti bay. In winter, the kids can tackle **ice skating** at Jääpuisto, while you stay snug in a nearby coffee shop.

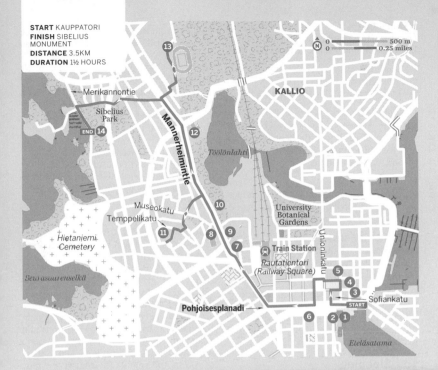

START KAUPPATORI
FINISH SIBELIUS MONUMENT
DISTANCE 3.5KM
DURATION 1½ HOURS

Walking Tour
Helsinki

The bustling **1 kauppatori** (square) is flanked by stately 19th-century buildings. The stone obelisk topped by a golden eagle is *The Stone of the Empress*, Helsinki's oldest monument, unveiled in 1835 in honour of a visit by Tsar Nicholas I and Tsarina Alexandra.

2 Havis Amanda, the female nude statue dipping in a fountain just west of the market, is regarded as the symbol of Helsinki. Across from the Kauppatori is the **3 Presidential Palace**, guarded by uniformed sentries.

Head up Sofiankatu to **4 Senaatintori** (Senate Square). Engel's stately **5 Tuomiokirkko** (Lutheran Cathedral) is the square's most prominent feature. The main University of Helsinki building is on the west side and the magnificent National Library is a little further north along Unioninkatu.

Walking back to Pohjoisesplanadi, stroll along **6 Esplanadin Puisto** (Esplanade Park), or browse the design shops and upmarket cafes along the pavement. Turn right onto Mannerheimintie, the main thoroughfare. An equestrian **7 statue of Marshal Manner-heim**, Finland's most revered military leader, dominates the square alongside Kiasma.

Continue walking northwest. The monolithic 1931 **8 Parliament House** dominates this stretch. Opposite it is the striking new **9 Musiikkitalo**, with concert halls and studios. Further up, on the right, is one of Alvar Aalto's most famous works, the angular **10 Finlandia Talo**, a concert hall built between 1967–72.

At this point you can detour west through backstreets to Temppelikatu, where you'll find **11 Temppeliaukion Kirkko**, a modern church hewn from solid rock.

A few blocks to the north, on Mannerheimintie, is the 1993 **12 Ooppertalo**, home of the Finnish National Opera. Stop at Carelia opposite for lunch or a glass of wine, then continue to the 1952 **13 Olympic Stadium**, with great city views from the top of the tower.

You can extend this walk westward to take in the **14 Sibelius monument**. This striking sculpture was created by artist Eila Hiltunen in 1967 to honour Finland's most famous composer. Bus 24 takes you back to the centre.

Helsinki Day CULTURAL
(www.hel.fi) Celebrating the city's anniversary brings many free events to Esplanade Park on 12 June.

Tuska Festival MUSIC
(www.tuska-festival.fi) A big metal festival in July.

Helsinki Festival ARTS
(Helsingin Juhlaviikot; www.helsinginjuhlaviikot.fi) From late August to early September, this arts festival features chamber music, jazz, theatre, opera and more.

Flow Festival MUSIC
(www.flowfestival.com) An August weekend festival that sees hip hop, electronic and experimental music rock the suburb of Suvilahti.

Baltic Herring Market FOOD
(www.portofhelsinki.fi) In the first week of October fisherfolk and chefs gather at the Kauppatori to sell and cook the time-honoured fish.

Lucia Parade RELIGIOUS
This pre-Christmas parade takes over Senaatintori on 13 December, with a procession of the Lucia maiden crowned with candles. A market is held the following day.

🛏 Sleeping

There's a dearth of cheap accommodation in Helsinki. From mid-May to mid-August, bookings are strongly advisable, although July's a quieter time for midrange and top-end hotels.

The **Sokos** (www.sokoshotels.fi) and **Scandic** (www.scandichotels.com) chains have several good business hotels in the centre, and other big multinationals are present.

CENTRAL HELSINKI

TOP CHOICE **Hotel GLO** HOTEL €€€•
(Map p50; ☑010-344 4400; www.palacekamp.fi; Kluuvikatu 4; r from €200; @) There are no starched suits at reception at this laid-back designer offshoot of Hotel Kämp, and the relaxed atmosphere continues through the comfortably modish public areas to the rooms. Beds: exceptionally inviting. Facilities: top-notch and mostly free. Location: On a pedestrian street in the heart of town. Cute extra: a stuffed tiger toy atop the covers. Online prices are the best; if there's not much difference between the standard and the standard XL, go for the latter as you get quite a bit more space. Service is friendly and excellent, and they'll stick an extra bed in free for under-15s.

TOP CHOICE **Hotelli Helka** HOTEL €€€
(Map p46; ☑613 580; www.helka.fi; Pohjoinen Rautatiekatu 23A; s/d €151/189, weekends & summer €100/124; P@) One of the centre's best midrange hotels – you can nearly always get a room cheaper than the listed price – the Helka has competent, friendly staff and excellent facilities, including free parking if you can bag one of the limited spots. Best are the rooms, which smell of pine with their Artek furniture, ice-block bedside lights and print of an autumn forest that hangs over the bed and is backlit to give rooms a moody glow. Hires bicycles to guests in summer.

Hotel Fabian HOTEL €€
(Map p50; ☑040-521 0356; www.hotelfabian.fi; Fabianinkatu 7; r from €150; P@) Central, but in a quiet part without the bustle of the other designer hotels, this place hasn't been open long but is getting everything right. Elegant standard rooms with whimsical lighting and chessboard tiles are extremely comfortable; they vary substantially in size. Higher-grade rooms add extra features and a kitchenette. There's no restaurant, but breakfast is cooked in front of you by the chef. Staff seem very happy to be there.

Hotel Finn HOTEL €€
(Map p50; ☑684 4360; www.hotellifinn.fi; Kalevankatu 3B; s/d with toilet from €69/79, with toilet & shower from €79/99) High in a central city building, this small, friendly hotel was under gradual refurbishment when we last passed by. The corridors were darkly done out in sexy chocolate and red, with art from young Finnish photographers on the walls, but the rooms were all bright white and blond parquet. Rates go up when it's nearly full, but if you bag one of the standard rates listed here, it's great value for Helsinki.

🏄 **Klaus K** HOTEL €€€
(Map p50; ☑020-770 4700; www.klauskhotel.com; Bulevardi 2; s/d from €120/155; @) Boasting excellent service and extremely comfortable beds, this central, independent design hotel has a theme of *Kalevala* quotes throughout, and easy-on-the-eye space-conscious architecture. Free fast wi-fi and other amenities ease the stay, but the best bit is the fabulous breakfasts, with all sorts of original and tasty morsels sourced from small Finnish producers.

TRIPPING TO TALLINN

Taking the boat over to Tallinn, the capital of Estonia, is the original booze cruise for Finns. Boats heave with drinkers and the city's pubs and clubs sometimes feel more like Kallio than another country. But Tallinn is so much more. It boasts a charming **Vanalinn** (Old Town), one of Europe's most evocative medieval districts, that's best enjoyed with an afternoon of ambling, particularly around **Raekoja plats** (Town Hall Square), which is dominated by its Gothic town hall complete with a minaret-like tower that you can climb to see the lie of the land. Wander a little further to **Saiakang** (White Bread Passage) with the 14th-century **Püha Vaimu Kirik** (Holy Spirit Church) at one end.

If you've worked up an appetite by now, head to **Ö** (☎661 6150; www.restoran-o.ee; Mere puiestee 6e; mains €17-25), an ethereal dining room that highlights Estonian produce. For heartier fare in a medieval atmosphere, **Olde Hansa** (www.oldehansa.ee; Vana turg 1; mains €10-24) is the go. There are plenty of good places to wet your whistle, such as comfy purveyor of local brews **Hell Hunt** (www.hellhunt.ee; Pikk 39). Don't worry about the name; it actually means 'gentle wolf'.

If you're looking to stay the night, check out **Tallinn Tourist Information Centre** (☎645 7777; www.tourism.tallinn.ee; cnr Kullassepa & Niguliste; ☉daily May-Sep, Mon-Sat Oct-Apr), which has a range of accommodation options.

Handily, euros are the currency here, and Estonia is a Schengen country so there are no entry requirements to visit from Finland.

The easiest way to Tallinn is by ferry; see p71. If you're looking at staying in Estonia for a while, you might like to head to shop.lonelyplanet.com to purchase a downloadable PDF of the Estonia chapter from Lonely Planet's *Estonia, Latvia & Lithuania* guide.

Hotel Haven
HOTEL €€€

(Map p50; ☎681 930; www.hotelhaven.fi; Unioninkatu 17, d from €165, P @) The closest hotel to the Kauppatori is an elegant and welcoming newcomer to the Helsinki scene. All room grades feature excellent beds and linen, soft colour combinations, classy toiletries, and thoughtful extras like sockets in the personal safes. 'Comfort' rooms face the street and are very spacious; higher grades give you a couple of add-ons – like a Nespresso machine in 'Lux' category – and the chance of a harbour view. Wi-fi's free, parking's expensive and limited, service is great.

Sokos Hotel Torni
HOTEL €€€

(Map p50; ☎020-123 4604; www.sokoshotels.fi; Yrjönkatu 26; d around €200; P @) In 1931 this building became Finland's Empire State Building and although no longer the country's tallest edifice, it still boasts excellent views, especially from Ateljee Bar (p66). Today, rooms have been stylishly renovated in keeping with the historic feel in art deco and nouveau styles, though modern rooms in rich red and black have hip decor. You pay a little extra for rooms with views, but they're worth it. Still a great Helsinki address.

Hotel Kämp
HOTEL €€€

(Map p50; ☎576 111; www.hotelkamp.fi; Pohjois-esplanadi 29; r from €295; P @) This grand and stylish hotel is one of the city's finest, and a Helsinki emblem, whose history includes plenty of long, animated piss-ups as the likes of Sibelius and Gallen-Kallela thrashed out their ideas. It romances with a stately marble lobby that seduces you back to historic inward-facing rooms furnished with antiques and then surprises in the marble bathrooms with their trademark rubber duck. Facilities include a plush day spa, saunas and restaurants. Book online for the best prices.

Hostel Erottajanpuisto
HOSTEL €

(Map p50; ☎642 169; www.erottajanpuisto.com; Uudenmaankatu 9; dm/s/d €26/53/72; @) Helsinki's smallest and most laid-back hostel occupies the top floor of a building in a lively street of bars and restaurants close to the heart of the city. Forget curfews, lockouts, schoolkids and bringing your own sleeping sheet – this is more like a guesthouse with (crowded) dormitories. Private rooms offer more peace. Great lounge and friendly folk.

Scandic Grand Marina
HOTEL €€€

(Map p46; ☎16661; www.scandic-hotels.com; Katajanokanlaituri 7, Katajanokka; s/d around €164/184; P @) On Katajanokka a very short stroll from the Viking Line ferries, this enormous hotel is a conversion from an early-20th-century brick warehouse. The never-ending corridors make it feel like you're on a ship, but the rooms, with their blond parquet, are typically Nordic. Bathrooms are a tad small for this price but it's a good package.

Hotelli Seurahuone
HOTEL €€€

(Map p50; ☎69141; www.hotelliseurahuone.fi; Kaivokatu 12; s/d €170/190; P @) This *seurahuone* (literally, 'club room') was a meeting place for high society, where visiting officers, gentlemen and ladies came to stay, and a venue for concerts and ballroom dances. The building remains a classic, with stately rooms in black and gold, and period fittings including the smoking cabinet and ballroom. Sadly there's no sauna, but Rautatientori views provide succour.

Omenahotelli
HOTEL €€

(☎060-018 018; www.omena.com; r €80-99) Eerikinkatu (Map p46; Eerikinkatu 24); Lönnrotinkatu (Map p50; Lönnrotinkatu 13); Yrjönkatu (Map p50; Yrjönkatu 30) This good-value staffless hotel chain has three handy Helsinki locations. As well as a double bed, rooms have fold-out chairs that can sleep two more, plus there's a microwave and minifridge. Book online or via a terminal in the lobby. Windows don't open, so rooms can be stuffy on hot days.

Hotel Carlton
HOTEL €€

(Map p50; ☎684 1320; www.carlton.fi; Kaisaniemenkatu 3; s/d €125/135; @) On a busy street near the station, this friendly small hotel has rooms in several shapes and sizes, all with decent-sized bathrooms and not too much street noise. It represents value for central Helsinki

and has a bit of soul. It can be difficult to spot from the street: enter via Roberts Coffee.

Hotel Arthur
HOTEL €€

(Map p46; ☎173 441; www.hotelarthur.fi; Vuorikatu 19; s/d €104/124, weekends €78/94; P) Close to the train station, Arthur is central but has a quiet, parkside location. It's a fairly standard Finnish hotel with a beer fridge at reception and comfortable rooms in light pastel colours. There's a huge range – it's worth upgrading if you value space – and there are good prices on the website.

Hotel Anna
HOTEL €€

(Map p46; ☎616 621; www.hotelanna.fi; Annankatu 1; s/d €130/170; @) Owned by the Finnish Free Church, this smallish hotel is good for family or business visitors looking for a bit of peace and quiet.

GREATER HELSINKI

Hostel Academica
HOSTEL €

(Map p46; ☎1311 4334; www.hostelacademica.fi; Hietaniemenkatu 14; dm/s/d €25/57/72; ☉Jun-Aug; P @ ≋) Finnish students live well, so in summer take advantage of this residence, a superclean spot packed with features (pool and sauna) and cheery staff. The modern rooms are great, and all come with bar fridges and their own bathrooms. Dorms have only two or three berths so there's no crowding. It's also environmentally sound, offsetting all of its carbon emissions, among other positive steps. HI discount.

Hellsten Helsinki Parliament
APARTMENT €€

(Map p46; ☎251 1050; www.hellstenhotels.fi; Museokatu 18; studio apt €140-180; ☉reception 8am-8pm Mon-Fri; @); Hellsten Helsinki Parliament

---

HOME IN HELSINKI

Renting an apartment can be a good way to see Helsinki. Options range from one-room studios with limited facilities, to expansive multiroom apartments that are like small homes. Often you'll get the use of an apartment building's sauna, parking area and other facilities. They're an ideal option for groups and families. The longer you stay the cheaper rates get, with deals for weekly and monthly stays.

We've listed their offices here so you can collect keys, but apartments are located throughout the city. Recommended agents for renting apartments:

City Apartments (Map p50; ☎612 6990; www.cityapartments.fi; Vuorikatu 18; studios from €115, 2-room apt from €140)

Kotihotelli (Map p50; ☎010-420 4700; www.kotihotelli.fi; Uudenmaankatu 26; studios from €74, 1-bedroom apt from €109)

Traveller's Home (Map p50; ☎044-211 9526; www.travellershome.fi; Lönnrotinkatu 16D; s/d €78/89) Some better than others. Office only open from 2pm to 6pm.

(Museokatu 18); Hellsten Helsinki Senate (Kauppi-aankatu 5) A step up in style and comfort from many hotels, the apartments here have sleek modern furnishings, kitchen-ette, internet connections and cable TV. Prices vary seasonally and there are dis-counts for longer stays. It's in a great loca-tion. They'll give you a keycode if you ar-rive outside hours. There's another branch on Katajanokka.

Rastila Camping CAMPGROUND, HOSTEL €
(Map p76; ☎031-078 517; www.rastilacamping.fi; Karavaanikatu 4; tent sites €13 plus €5 per person, modern/traditional 2-4 person cabins €77/50, cot-tages with/without sauna €187/139; hostel dm/s/d €20/35/60; P@) Only 20 minutes on the metro from the heart of town (Rastila sta-tion), in a pretty waterside location, this camping ground makes sense. As well as tent and van sites, there are wooden cabins and more-upmarket log cottages, as well as a summer hostel (open late June to early Au-gust). There are all sorts of facilities includ-ing saunas, and hire of bikes, rowing boats and canoes. Great for families.

Hotel Katajanokka HOTEL €€€
(Map p46; ☎686 450; www.bwkatajanokka.fi; Merikasarminkatu 1A; d €160-210; P@) Set in a refurbished prison, this characterful place offers so much more than proximity to the ferries. Double rooms stretch over two-and-a-half ex-cells, so they're anything but pokey, and it's possible to buy handcuffs at the front desk to share with your cell mate. While it doesn't miss a chance to have cheeky nudges at the former penal complex, it's not at the expense of luxury, with large flatscreen TVs and a sumptuous sauna. This jailhouse rocks.

Hostel Suomenlinna HOSTEL €
(☎684 7471; www.snk.fi/suomenlinna; Suomen-linna C9; dm/s/d/tr €26.50/58/66/95; ☺recep-tion 8am-9pm; @) This excellent alternative to staying in central Helsinki is on the for-tress island of Suomenlinna. The building was once a Russian primary school and later a barracks, which lends the place an institutional feel. Dormitories are bright high-ceilinged classrooms, while the pri-vate rooms upstairs have cosy sloping ceilings. There's a kitchen (supermarket opposite) and laundry. Note that you must check in during reception hours and re-member to get the key code. HI discount. It's very close to the main Suomenlinna ferry quay.

Eurohostel HOSTEL €
(Map p46; ☎622 0470; www.eurohostel.fi; Linnan-katu 9, Katajanokka; dm €23-26, s €43-49, d €52-59; @) On Katajanokka Island less than 500m from the Viking Line terminal, this HI-affili-ate is busy but a bit soulless and offers both backpacker and 'hotel' rooms. Both share common bathrooms. The small cafe/bar serves a breakfast buffet (€7.70) and other meals, and there's a morning sauna includ-ed. HI and online-booking discount. Tram 4 stops right alongside.

Hotel Linna HOTEL €€
(Map p46, ☎010-344 4100; www.palacekamp.fi; Lönnrotinkatu 29; s/d €139/159; P@) Linna is Finnish for 'castle' and the turreted facade and courtly service give you the royal treat-ment. Built in 1903 as the student club-house for the technical university opposite, the castle decor never feels cheesy, with rooms tastefully kitted out with extra-long beds, minibar and bathtubs in some rooms. There's a choice of three saunas.

Sokos Hotel Albert HOTEL €€
(Map p46; ☎020-123 4638; www.sokoshotels.fi; Albertinkatu 30; r €142, summer €93; @) A boutique-style hotel from this hotel chain that's well located for design shops and bars in Punavuori. Not to be confused with Sokos Hotel Aleksanteri in the same street.

Hostel Stadion HOSTEL €
(Map p46; ☎477 8480; www.stadionhostel.fi; Po-hjoinen Stadiontie 3; dm/s/d €20/38/47; P@) An easy tram ride from town, this well-equipped hostel is actually part of the Oly-mpic Stadium. There are no views though, and it feels old-style, with big dorms and not much light-heartedness. It's the cheapest bed in town, so sometimes there's the odd curious character about. HI discount.

AIRPORT HOTELS

GLO Airport
HOTEL €€€

(off Map p46; ☎010-344 4600; www.hotelglo.fi; s/d from €155/170; @) The most convenient spot for the airport is this small hotel in the terminal itself. The windowless rooms (no planespotting, folks) are small and a little claustrophobic, but the recent designer makeover has made them pretty comfortable, and a couple have a sauna. The day rate (€79 from 8am to 7pm) is decent value.

✗ Eating

Helsinki has by far the best range of restaurants in Finland, whether for Finnish classics, New Suomi cuisine or international dishes. Good budget options are in shorter supply: cafes offer good lunch options and there are plenty of self-catering opportunities.

Helsinki's famous love of coffee means there are always great places to grab a cup and maybe a *pulla*. Whether you choose one of the city's classic Esplanadi spots-to-be-seen or a bohemian backstreet hang-out, most also do sandwiches, lunch specials and other light meals.

Helsinki has no shortage of hamburger chains, pizza shops, kebab joints, hot-dog stands and grillis.

CENTRAL HELSINKI

TOP CHOICE Olo
MODERN FINNISH €€€

(Map p50; ☎665 565; www.olo-restaurant.com; Kasarmikatu 44; lunch menus from €29, 4-course dinners €59; ⊙lunch Mon-Fri, dinner Tue-Sat) Casual surveys on the street repeatedly flag this as one of the city's favourite current restaurants. It's one of ours too. Despite the quality, Olo is refreshingly unpretentious, with a dining room of muted greys and whites. All meals come with house-baked breads (try the fruity malt) and the wine list is broad enough to appeal to all palettes.

Savoy
FINNISH €€€

(Map p50; ☎6128 5300; www.savoy.fi; Eteläesplanadi 14; mains €40-45; ⊙lunch & dinner Mon-Fri, dinner Sat) Originally designed by Alvar and Aino Aalto, this is definitely a standout dining room, with some of the city's best views. The degustation menu is a modern Nordic tour de force, with the 'forage' ethos strewing flowers and berries across plates. À la carte sees more traditionally proportioned dishes displaying the finest Finnish game, fish and meat.

Chez Dominique
FRENCH €€€

(Map p50; ☎612 7393; www.chezdominique.fi; Rikhardinkatu 4; mains €55, set menus €99-136 plus wine; ⊙lunch & dinner Tue-Fri, dinner Sat, closed Jul) Helsinki's most renowned restaurant is still widely considered Finland's best. The focus these days is increasingly on its degustation menus, which present quality Finnish fare alongside French gourmet morsels and avant-garde combinations. The à la carte options have a more traditionally Gallic feel. There's an excellent wine list, with various matched suites available to accompany the set menus. Lunch is a comparative steal at €27 for two courses.

Demo
MODERN FINNISH €€€

(Map p50; ☎2289 0840; www.restaurantdemo.fi; Uudenmaankatu 9; mains €30-40; ⊙dinner Tue-Sat) Book to get a table at this chic spot, where young chefs wow a designer-y crowd with Modern Finnish cuisine. The quality is excellent, the combinations innovative, the presentation top notch and the slick contemporary decor appropriate. A place to be seen, not for quiet contemplation.

Zucchini
VEGETARIAN €

(Map p50; www.zucchini.fi; Fabianinkatu 4; lunches €7-11; ⊙lunch Mon-Fri) One of the city's few vegetarian cafes, this is a top-notch lunchtime spot; queues out the door are not unusual. Piping-hot soups banish winter chills, and fresh-baked quiche on the sunny terrace out the back is a summer treat.

Kitchen G18
FINNISH €€

(Map p50; ☎010-322 2940; www.kitcheng18.fi; Yrjönkatu 18; mains €19-27; ⊙lunch Mon-Fri, dinner Tue-Sat) The high ceilings in this stylish conversion of a noble old central building mean minimal noise, so it's a sound bet for a romantic dinner. Quality Finnish ingredients, including recommended organic beef, are presented with French-style sauces. Excellent, friendly service backs up an impressive new package.

Juuri
MODERN FINNISH €€

(Map p50, ☎635 732; www.juuri.fi; Korkeavuorenkatu 27; mains €24; ⊙lunch Mon-Sat, dinner daily) Creative takes on classic Finnish ingredients draw the crowds to this stylish modern restaurant, but the best way to eat is to sample the 'sapas', which are tapas with a Suomi twist (€4.30 a plate). You might graze on marinated fish, smoked beef or homemade sausages. There are cheap lunch specials here, but they're not as interesting.

Café Ekberg
CAFE €

(Map p50; www.cafeekberg.fi; Bulevardi 9; lunches €8-10; ⏰7.30am-7pm Mon-Fri, 8.30am-5pm Sat, 10am-5pm Sun) There's been a cafe of this name in Helsinki since 1861 and today it continues to be a family-run place renowned for pastries like the Napoleon cake. The buffet breakfasts and daily lunch specials are also popular, plus there's fresh bread to take away.

Karl Fazer
CAFE €

(Map p50; www.fazer.fi; Kluuvikatu 3; lunches €8-12; ⏰7.30am-10pm Mon-Fri, 9am-10pm Sat, plus 10am-6pm Sun summer) This classic cafe can feel a little cavernous, but it's the flagship for the mighty chocolate empire of the same name. The cupola famously reflects sound, so locals say it's a bad place to gossip. It is ideal, however, for buying Fazer confectionery or enjoying the towering sundaes or slabs of cake.

Café Bar 9
CAFE €

(Map p50; www.bar9.net; Uudenmaankatu 9; mains €8-10) It's tough to find low-priced food at dinnertime in Helsinki that's not shaved off a spinning stick, so this place stands out. It would anyway, with its retro red formica tables and unpretentious artsy air. Plates vary, with some solid Finnish fare backed up by big sandwiches, Thai-inspired stir-fries and pastas. Portions are generous so don't overdo it; you can always come back.

Kosmos
FINNISH €€

(Map p50; ☎647 255; www.ravintolakosmos.fi; Kalevankatu 3; mains €19-32; ⏰11.30am-1am Mon-Fri, 4pm-1am Sat, closed Jul) Designed by Alvar Aalto, and with a bohemian history, this place is a Helsinki classic. It combines a staid, very traditionally Finnish atmosphere with tasty not-very-modern dishes including reindeer.

Bar Tapasta
TAPAS €

(Map p50; www.marcante.fi; Uudenmaankatu 13; tapas €4-7; ⏰4.30pm-late Mon-Sat) An intimate and welcoming bar with quirky Mediterranean decor, an elegant young crowd and friendly staff. The tapas are cheap and generous; there is also a selection of wines and sangria. Get there early to ensure a table.

Ravintola Martta
FINNISH €

(Map p46; www.ravintolamartta.fi; Lapinlahdenkatu 3; lunches €7-10; ⏰lunch Mon-Sat, dinner Tue-Sat) One of the best-value lunch stops around, Martta is run by an historic women's organisation. The light, bright dining room is matched by the tasty, wholesome food.

EAT.FI

A good resource is the website www.eat.fi, which plots restaurants on a map of town: even if you can't read all the reviews (though there are usually some in English), you'll soon spot what are the latest favourites.

Orchid Thai Restaurant
THAI €

(Map p46; www.thaimaalainenravintola.com; Eerikinkatu 20; mains €10-16; ⏰lunch & dinner Mon-Sat, 2-9pm Sun) This cheap and cheerful little spot does tasty Thai with scrumptious stir-fried duck alongside classics such as green curry and cashew-nut chicken. There's a set dinner for €20.50 and very low-priced lunch deals.

Kitch
CAFE €

(Map p50; www.kitch.fi; Yrjönkatu 30; mains €12-15; ⏰Mon-Sat) Handily located in a central area, this offers good-value lunches as well as tapas portions, original salads and decent burgers. Most of the produce is sustainably sourced.

Bellevue
RUSSIAN €€€

(Map p46; ☎179 560; www.restaurantbellevue.com; Rahapajankatu 3; mains €20-30; ⏰lunch & dinner Tue-Sat) Helsinki's best Russian restaurant, complete with bear steak (€65). Closes Saturday lunch in summer.

GREATER HELSINKI

Tamminiementien Kahvila
TOP CHOICE
CAFE €

(www.villaangelica.fi; Tamminiementie 8; ⏰11am-7pm Apr-Oct) This memorable cafe is near the Urho Kekkonen Museum in lovely parkland. It's like a cross between a Chekhov play and a flower-loving granny's country cottage and is very charming indeed. Catch tram 4 or bus 24. Open until 10pm in high summer.

Sea Horse
FINNISH €€

(Map p46; ☎010-837 5700; www.seahorse.fi; Kapteeninkatu 11; mains €14-24; ⏰10.30am-midnight) Sea Horse dates back to the 1930s and is as traditional a Finnish restaurant as you'll find anywhere. Locals gather in the gloriously unchanged interior to meet and drink over hefty dishes of Baltic herring, Finnish meatballs and cabbage rolls.

Carelia
BISTRO €€

(Map p46; ☎2809 0976; www.carelia.info; Mannerheimintie 56; mains €15-29; ⏰lunch & dinner Mon-Fri, dinner Sat) Opposite the opera, this is a great spot for a pre- or post-show drink or meal. Glamorously decorated in period style, it offers smart bistro fare at very fair prices, and plenty of intriguing wines by the glass.

Kuu
FINNISH €€

(Map p46; ☑2709 0973; www.ravintolakuu.info; Töölönkatu 27; mains €14-26; ☺lunch & dinner) Tucked away on a corner behind the Crowne Plaza hotel on Mannerheimintie, this is an excellent choice for traditional Finnish fare given a confident modern touch and served in an upbeat bistro atmosphere. Salmon is smoked to order, the staff are eager to explain every dish, and there's a general ambience of good cheer. Prices are very reasonable for the quality on offer. Don't confuse this with another (good) place, Kuu Kuu, not far away.

Konstan Möljä
FINNISH €

(Map p46; ☑694 7504; www.konstanmolja.fi; Hietalahdenkatu 14; lunch/dinner buffets €8/18; ☺lunch & dinner Tue-Fri, dinner Sat) The maritime interior of this old sailors eatery hosts an impressive husband-and-wife team who turn out a great-value Finnish buffet for lunch and dinner. Though these days it sees plenty of tourists, it serves solid traditional fare, with salmon, soup, reindeer and friendly explanations of what goes in with what. There's also à la carte available. It tends to close for a month or so in summer, so ring ahead to check that it's open.

Tori
CAFE €

(Map p46; www.ravintolatori.fi; Punavuorenkatu 2; light meals €6-14; ☺10am-8pm Mon-Fri, noon-7pm Sat & Sun) Buzzing with a bohemian crowd, this 1950s revival has a menu including beetroot-and-blue-cheese pasta or a reinvention of meatballs with a brandy sauce. Breakfast is a build-your-own adventure, while sandwiches are good for those strapped for cash.

La Table
BISTRO €€€

(Map p46; ☑673 236; www.latable.fi; Lönnrotinkatu 27; 2/3 courses €34/39) The chef here changed the name of his restaurant so he'd lose his Michelin star: he was sick of pretentious customers. The French-style cuisine is still excellent though.

Koto
JAPANESE €

(Map p46; www.ravintola-koto.fi; Lönnrotinkatu 22; mains €10-16, lunches €9-15; ☺lunch & dinner Mon-Sat) It's blond-wood Zen at this Japanese joint that does sashimi, yakitori and brilliant sushi.

Ateljé Finne
MODERN FINNISH €€

(Map p46; ☑493 110; Arkadiankatu 14; 1/2/3 courses €24/33/39; ☺dinner Tue-Sat) Good-value modern cuisine at this elegant but relaxed spot. The menu changes regularly but the daily fish dish is always great.

Gran Delicato
CAFE €

(Map p46; cnr Kalevankatu & Albertinkatu; rolls €6-10; ☺8am-8pm Mon-Fri, 10am-6pm Sat, noon-6pm Sun) At the cornerstone of Helsinki's Little Italy (OK, it's really just this place and a restaurant across the road), this deli makes an ideal ciabatta grab. You have to make the tough choices between fresh fillings like olives, gravlax with spring onion and dill, or gutsy salami and Roma tomatoes, but otherwise there couldn't be a better Italian job in town. There's also authentic strong coffee plus a selection of slices.

Tin Tin Tango
CAFE €

(Map p46; www.tintintango.info; Töölöntorinkatu 7; light meals €7-10; ☺7am-midnight or later Mon-Fri, 9am-2am Sat, 10am-midnight Sun) This buzzy neighbourhood cafe decorated with prints from the quiffed Belgian's adventures has a bit of everything. There's a laundry and a sauna (handy if you need to wash your only pair of jeans), as well as cosy tables where you can sip a drink or get to grips with delicious rolls absolutely stuffed full. The welcoming, low-key bohemian vibe is the real draw though.

Silvoplee
VEGETARIAN €

(Map p46; www.silvoplee.com; Toinen linja 3; per kg €20; ☺11am-6pm Mon-Sat) Great vegan food, much of it organic. Near Hakaniemi market, it's a buffet and you pay by weight (the food's). Soups are cheaper.

Villa Thai
THAI €€

(Map p50; www.villathai.com; Bulevardi 28; mains €15-18; ☺lunch Mon-Fri, dinner Mon-Sat) It may not be the cheapest Thai food in Helsinki, but it's very tasty. Come for the decor; you could almost imagine you're in some Southeast Asian pleasure garden.

Kom
FINNISH €

(Map p46; www.kom-ravintola.fi; Kapteeninkatu 26; mains €12-20; ☺lunch Mon-Fri, dinner Mon-Sat) If Sea Horse is old bohemian, this place opposite, attached to a theatre, is the modern equivalent. Solid Finnish pub grub – including good vegetarian options – and the buzz of artsy chatter.

ISLAND DINING

There's no better way to appreciate Helsinki's seaside location than by heading out to the myriad island restaurants. Most are served by small boats ferrying to and from quays on the mainland opposite. Most famous is the stylish, spired **Saaristo** (Map p46; ☎7425 5505; www.asrestaurants.com; mains €20-33; ☺lunch & dinner Mon-Fri, dinner Sat, lunch Sun May-Aug, dinner Mon-Sat Sep), which is set in the Klippan villa on Luoto Island, and famous for society weddings and crayfish parties.

Suomenlinna has loads of eateries. Gourmet restaurant **Walhalla** (☎668 552; www.restaurantwalhalla.com; mains €26-30; ☺dinner Mon-Sat May–mid-Sep) is just above the King's Gate and serves Finnish classics like reindeer and Arctic char. It also runs adjacent **Pizzeria Nikolai** (pizzas €11-14; ☺noon-8pm Mon-Sat, noon-6pm Sun May–mid-Sep), which has a great sheltered outdoor terrace.

If you like a beer then **Suomenlinnan Panimo** (www.panimo.com; ☺noon-10pm Mon-Sat, noon-6pm Sun May-Aug, Tue-Sat noon-10pm Sep), by the main quay, brews several excellent beers including a hefty porter and offers good food to accompany it.

On the island of Liuskasaari, **Boathouse** (☎6227 1070; www.palacekamp.fi; Liuskasaari; mains €18-32; ☺dinner Mon-Sat May-Sep, plus lunch Mon-Fri early Jun–mid-Jul & dinner Sun mid-Jun–late Aug) is a circular two-deck restaurant, with ferries from the jetty at Merisataman-ranta. The restaurant does tasty seafood, which is best sampled with the seafood platter or a tuna steak. Instead of a guestbook, visitors pin notes to the lobby's chandelier.

Even if you're not dining at the restaurants, the islands can make a refreshing break and give a new perspective on the city. The boats are around €3 to €5 return for nondiners and run every 10 to 15 minutes during eating hours.

Manala FINNISH €€
(Map p46; www.botta.fi; Dagmarinkatu 4; mains €14-26; ☺11am-4am Mon-Fri, 2pm-4am Sat & Sun) For night owls. Decent sautéed reindeer and other Finnish comfort food at three in the morning in a proper restaurant.

Pelmenit EASTERN EUROPEAN €
(off Map p46; Kustaankatu 7; dishes €6-14; ☺11am-10pm) A real change from all the designer places in central Helsinki, this simple Kallio eatery serves cheap, tasty authentic home cooking, including the excellent dumplings it's named after.

Café Ursula CAFE €
(off Map p46; www.ursula.fi; Ehrenströmintie 3; lunches €8-10; ☺9am-10pm) Offering majestic sea views, this cafe looks out over the Helsinki archipelago and is a marvellous place to sit outside on a sunny day. In winter it's great too, as you can sit in the snug interior and watch the ice on the sea. It opens until midnight in summer.

Self-Catering

In summer there are food stalls, fresh produce and expensive berries at the Kauppatori, but the real picnic treats are in the **Vanha Kauppahalli** (Old Market Hall; Map p50; Eteläranta 1; ☺8am-6pm Mon-Fri, 8am-4pm Sat, plus 10am-4pm Sun summer only) nearby. Built in 1889, some of it's touristy these days (reindeer kebabs?), but it's still a traditional Finnish market, where you can get filled rolls, cheese, breads, fish and an array of typical snacks and delicacies. Similar **Hakaniemen kauppahalli** (Map p46; ☺8am-6pm Mon-Fri, 8am-4pm Sat), the traditional market hall by Hakaniemi metro station, is less visited by tourists. In both you'll find some great salmon-on-rye sandwiches. **Soppakeittiö** (soups €7-9; ☺lunch Mon-Fri, also Sat at Vanha Kauppahalli) is a great place to warm the cockles in winter; the boullabaisse is famous.

There are seven-day supermarkets and food courts in **Kamppi** (Map p50) and **Forum** (Map p50; Mannerheimintie 20) shopping centres. The nearest supermarket to the esplanade is **S-Market** (Map p50; Kasarmikatu; ☺Mon-Sun).

If you're after specialised supplies, **Ruohonjuuri** (Map p50; www.ruohonjuuri.fi; Salomonkatu 5; ☺10am-9pm Mon-Fri, 10am-6pm Sat) stocks food that's ethically sound, organic and often catering to special dietary needs. Nearby, **Eat & Joy Maatilatori** (Map p50; www.eatandjoy.com; Mannerheimintie 22; ☺Mon-Sat, plus Sun summer), in the Lasipalatsi building, is a small farmers market shop with an excellent selection of organic Finnish produce sourced from small producers. Great for unusual gifts.

HELSINKI DRINKING

THE CALL OF KALLIO

For the cheapest beer in Helsinki (under €3 a pint during the seemingly perpetual happy hours), hit working-class Kallio (near Sörnäinen metro station), north of the centre. Here, there's a string of dive bars along Helsinginkatu, but it, the parallel Vaasankatu, and cross-street Fleminginkatu are also home to several more characterful bohemian places: go for a wander and you'll soon find one you like.

 Drinking

Finns don't mind a drink and Helsinki has some of Scandinavia's most diverse nightlife. In winter, locals gather in cosy bars, while in summer, early-opening beer terraces sprout all over town.

The centre's full of bars and clubs, with the Punavuori area around Iso Roobertinkatu one of the most worthwhile for trendy alternative choices.

TOP CHOICE **Teerenpeli** PUB
(Map p46; www.teerenpeli.com; Olavinkatu 2) Get away from the Finnish lager mainstream with this excellent pub right by the bus station. It serves very tasty ales, stouts and berry ciders from a microbrewery in Lahti in a long, split-level place with romantic low lighting, intimate tables and an indoor smokers' patio. A top spot.

A21 Cocktail lounge BAR
(Map p50; www.a21.fi; Annankatu 21; ☻Tue-Sat) You'll need to ring the doorbell to get into this chic club but it's worth the intrigue to swing with Helsinki's arty set. The interior is sumptuous in gold, but the real lushness is in the cocktails, particularly the Finnish blends that toss cloudberry liqueur and rhubarb to create the city's most innovative tipples.

Corona Bar & Kafe Moskova BAR
(Map p50; www.andorra.fi; Eerikinkatu 11-15; ☻bar 11am-2am Mon-Sat, noon-2am Sun, cafe 6pm-2am Mon-Sat, Roska 10pm-4am daily) Those offbeat film-making Kaurismäki brothers are up to their old tricks with this pair of conjoined drinking dens. Corona plays the relative straight man with pool tables and cheap beer, while Moskova is back in the USSR with a bubbling samovar and Soviet vinyl. At closing they clear the place out by playing Brezhnev

speeches. But wait, there's more: Dubrovnik, in the same complex, does regular live jazz, and Roska ('rubbish'), downstairs, is completely decorated in recycled materials.

Bar Loose BAR
(Map p50; www.barloose.com; Annankatu 21; ☻4pm-2am Mon-Tue, to 4am Wed-Sat, 6pm-4am Sun) The opulent blood-red interior and comfortably cosy seating seem too stylish for a rock bar, but this is what this is, with portraits of guitar heroes lining one wall and an eclectic mix of people filling the upstairs, served by two bars. Downstairs is a club area, with live music more nights than not.

Ateljee Bar BAR
(Map p50; Sokos Hotel Torni, Yrjönkatu 26; ☻2pm-2am Mon-Thu, from noon Fri & Sat, to 1am Sun) It's worth heading up to this tiny perch on the roof of the Sokos Hotel Torni for the city panorama. Take the lift to the 12th floor, then there's a narrow spiral staircase to the top. Downstairs, the courtyard Tornin Piha is a cute little terrace with good wines by the glass.

Pub Tram Spårakoff PUB TRAM
(Map p50; www.koff.net; tickets €8; ☻departs hourly 2-3pm & 5-8pm, Tue-Sat late May–late Aug) Not sure whether to go sightseeing or booze the day away? Do both in this bright-red pub tram, the tipsy alternative to traditional tours around town. There are cheaper places to drink but the trundle of the tram past Helsinki's major landmarks makes for an enjoyable hour. Departs from Mikonkatu, east of the train station.

Zetor PUB
(Map p50; www.ravintolazetor.fi; Mannerheimintie 3-5; ☻11.30am-4am Tue-Sat, noon-midnight Sun & Mon) A fun Finnish restaurant and pub with deeply ironic tractor decor. It's owned by film-maker Aki Kaurismäki and designed by the Leningrad Cowboys. It's worth going in just for a drink and a ride on a tractor, but the food (mains €12 to €22) is decent value too, and served until very late.

Aussie Bar BAR
(Map p46; www.aussiebar.net; Salomonkatu 5) Run by descendants of convicts with plenty of 'G'days', this laid-back pub doesn't miss a cliché. Beneath the corrugated iron and faux-colonial fittings it makes for a good watering hole that's popular with locals.

mbar BAR

(Map p50; www.mbar.fi; Mannerheimintie 22) Not just a geek-bar with internet terminals, this cafe in the Lasipalatsi complex has a great terrace to soak up the sun, accompanied by DJs on weekends.

Cuba! Cafe BAR

(Map p50; www.cubacafe.fi; Erottajankatu 4) Certainly one of Helsinki's brighter bars, this place is done out in peach and mojito limes with a small stage that features a Havana-style taxi and DJs or salsa bands. Beers, cocktails and dancing are the order here.

Roskapankki PUB

(Map p46; www.kallioravintolat.fi; Helsinginkatu 20) A Kallio classic with cheap beer and ragged character.

Vltava PUB

(Map 50; www.vltava.fi; Elielinaukio 2) Right by the train station, this cheerful Czech pub has a sprawling terrace for meeting people, a menu of solid beer-hall-style comfort food, and a smarter upstairs lounge.

Kappeli BAR

(Map 50; www.kappeli.fi; Eteläesplanadi 1) This pleasant outdoor terrace has regular music in the nearby bandstand.

IsoRoba10 BAR

(Map 50; Iso Roobertinkatu 10) A new Punavuori arrival, this provides a typical welcome for this part of town, a bohemian vibe and moody dub spun by the house DJ at weekends.

☆ Entertainment

As the nation's big smoke, Helsinki has the hottest culture and nightlife. Music is particularly big here, from metal to opera. The latest events are publicised in *Helsinki This Week*. Tickets for big events can be purchased from **Lippupalvelu** (Map p50; ☑060-010 800; www.lippupalvelu.fi), with many central outlets including in Stockmann, **Lippu.fi** (☑060-090 0900; www.lippu.fi), **Tiketti.fi** (☑060-011 616; www.tiketti.fi) and **LiveNation** (www.livenation.fi).

Nightclubs

Helsinki has a dynamic scene that's always changing. Some club nights have age limits (often over 20), so check event details on websites before you arrive.

Tiger CLUB

(Map p46; www.thetiger.fi; Urho Kekkosen katu 1A; door charge €10; ☉10pm-4am Fri-Sun) Ascend into clubbing heaven at this super-slick club with stellar lighting and high-altitude cocktails.

HELSINKI ENTERTAINMENT

GAY & LESBIAN HELSINKI

Helsinki has an active scene, which may not be as massive as Copenhagen's or Stockholm's, but has several dedicated venues and a host of gay-friendly spots. Check out www.gayfinland.fi and www.guys.fi for more listings. There's also a list of gay-friendly places at www.visithelsinki.fi, following the 'For You' and 'Gay Visitors' links. The tourist office stocks a couple of brochures on gay Helsinki.

Every June, Helsinki's GLBT community gathers around **Helsinki Pride** (www.helsinkipride.fi), which includes balls, karaoke and picnics. The hyper-hip clubs are in Punavuori, while Kallio has more grungy venues.

Bars & Clubs

DTM (Map p46; www.dtm.fi; Iso Roobertinkatu 28; ☉9am-4am Mon-Sat, noon-4am Sun) Scandinavia's biggest gay club is a multilevel complex with an early-opening cafe-bar. There are a couple of club areas opening at 9pm (with cover charge and a minimum age of 22) and regular club nights, as well as drag shows and women-only sessions.

Hercules (Map p50; www.herculesgayclub.com; Lönnrotinkatu 4; ☉9pm-4am) A busy disco, aimed at men aged 30-plus, but dance-floor classics and campy karaoke attract everyone.

Hugo's Room (Map p50; www.hugosroom.fi; Iso Roobertinkatu 3; ☉noon-2am) A smart but laid-back gay lounge bar with a popular streetside terrace.

Bear Park Café (Map p46; www.bearparkcafe.net; Karhupuisto; ☉daylight May-Sep) Not just for the hairy, this is a relaxed outdoor spot for a cruise that sometimes features cabaret or jazz.

Fairytale (Map p46; www.fairytale.fi; Helsinginkatu 7; ☉4pm-2am Mon-Fri, 2pm-2am Sat & Sun) One of Kallio's dark drinking dens for men.

Music runs from chart hits to R&B; drinks are expensive but the view from the terrace is stunning. Entrance via Kamppi Square.

Kuudes Linja
CLUB

(Map p46; www.kuudeslinja.com; Hämeentie 13; tickets €8-12; ⊘9pm-3am Sun & Tue-Thu, 10pm-4am Fri & Sat) Between Hakaniemi and Sörnäinen metro stops, this is the place to find Helsinki's more experimental beats from top visiting DJs playing techno, industrial, post-rock and electro. There are also live gigs.

Teatteri
CLUB

(Map p50; www.royalravintolat.com; Pohjoisesplanadi 2; ⊘Mon-Sat) In a stylish former Swedish theatre, this club has three floors of fun, from the sophisticated Long bar, with its modernist paintings and web-spun light fixtures, to the summer-swelling terraces. It's got an older, more relaxed crowd and can be packed on weekends.

Lost & Found
CLUB

(Map p50; www.lostandfound.fi; Annankatu 6; ⊘to 4am) After having one in the characterful bar upstairs, head to the dark grotto-like dance floor downstairs that's decked out in luminescent designs. Still a gay venue (it styles itself as a 'hetero-friendly gay club'), the tunes are often chart-based, with a sign near the DJ booth 'Don't request. I'll play it eventually'. It's often the spot for after-parties for big gigs.

Heavy Corner
CLUB

(Map p46; www.heavycorner.com; Hietaniemenkatu 2; ⊘8pm-late Wed-Sat) This metal club virtually has an all-black dress code to hear the rockingest tunes and often metal karaoke, featuring super-serious patrons who believe they are auditioning for Children of Bodom.

Live Music

Major touring bands do gigs at **Hartwall Areena** (www.hartwall-areena.com) though Kaapelitehdas (p54) is attracting big-name bands with its unique ambience.

Tavastia & Semifinal
BAR, CONCERT VENUE

(Map p46; www.tavastiaklubi.fi; Urho Kekkosenkatu 4; tickets from €15; ⊘9pm-late) One of Helsinki's legendary rock venues, this attracts both up-and-coming local acts and bigger international groups. There's a band every night of the week. Also check out what's on at Semifinal, the smaller venue next door (tickets €6 to €8).

Storyville
JAZZ

(Map p46; www.storyville.fi; Museokatu 8; ⊘8pm-4am) Always smoking with trad, swing or Dixieland, this late-opener is the place for jazz most nights of the week.

Juttutupa
LIVE MUSIC

(Map p46; www.juttutupa.com; Säästöpankinranta 6; ⊘10am-late) A block from Hakaniemi metro station in an enormous granite building, Juttutupa is one of Helsinki's better music bars, focusing on contemporary jazz and rock fusion. Great beer terrace.

Virgin Oil Co
VENUE

(Map p50; www.virginoil.fi; Mannerheimintie 5) While it does pizzas and has a cosy front bar area and weekend nightclub, the big attraction of this central spot is the top-drawer Finnish bands it attracts on a regular basis.

Liberté
BAR, LIVE MUSIC

(Map p46; www.clubliberte.fi; Kolmas Linja 34) It's worth heading off to this slightly out-of-the-way place for the interesting live music it puts on every weekend. Underground beats, soul, jazz and non-mainstream rock are the order of the day.

Live Performances

For concerts and performances, see *Helsinki This Week*, enquire at the tourist office or check the website of ticket outlet **Lippupiste** (☑060-090 0900; www.lippu.fi). Opera (surtitles in Finnish) and ballet are held at the **Oopperatalo** (Opera House; Map p46; ☑4030 2211; www.opera.fi; Helsinginkatu 58; tickets from €14), while performances by the Finnish National Theatre are at the **Kansallisteatteri** (Map p50; ☑1733 1331; www.kansallisteatteri.fi; Läntinen teatterikuja 1), near the train station. The plays are in Finnish, but the lavish productions are worth a look even if you don't speak it. Next to Kiasma, the stunning new **Musiikkitalo** (Helsinki Music Centre; Map p50; www.musiikkitalo.fi; Mannerheimintie 13) has a main auditorium and several smaller ones: a fitting venue for the city's wonderful classical concerts.

Cinemas

There are several cinemas in Helsinki, all of which show original-version films with Finnish and Swedish subtitles.

Kino Engel
CINEMA

(Map p50; www.cinemamondo.fi; Sofiankatu 4; tickets €9) As well as the *kesäkino* (summer cinema) in the courtyard of Café Engel, in the warmer months, this independent theatre shows art-house and Finnish indie films.

Orion Theatre
CINEMA

(Map p46; www.kava.fi; Eerikinkatu 15; tickets €5.50; ☺screenings Tue-Sun) This art-house cinema shows classics from the Finnish Film Archive.

FinnKino
CINEMA

(☑060-000 7007; www.finnkino.fi; tickets €10.50) Operates several Helsinki cinemas, which screen big-name films:

Kinopalatsi (Map p50; Kaisaniemenkatu 2)

Maxim (Map p50; Kluuvikatu 1)

Tennispalatsi (Map p46; Salomonkatu 15)

Sport

Between September and April, ice hockey reigns supreme; going to a game is a good Helsinki experience.

Hartwall Areena
ICE HOCKEY

(www.hartwall-areena.com; tickets €15-35) The best place to see top-level hockey matches is at this arena, about 4km north of the city centre (take bus 23 or 69, or tram 7A or 7B). It's the home of local Super League side Jokerit Helsinki.

Helsingin Jäähalli
ICE HOCKEY

(Map p46; www.helsinginjaahalli.fi; Nordenskiöldinkatu 13) Ice hockey matches are also played at this indoor arena in the Olympic Stadium complex.

Sonera Stadium
FOOTBALL

(Map p46; www.sonerastadium.fi; tickets €8-15) Next to the Olympic Stadium, this is the home ground of local football team HJK Helsinki. The team's the closest thing Finland has to a Real Madrid or a Manchester United, having won 23 Finnish league titles at last count.

🛍 Shopping

Known for design and art, Helsinki is an epicentre of Nordic cool, from fashion to the latest furniture and homewares. The further you wander from Pohjoisesplanadi, the main tourist street in town, the lower prices become. The hippest area is definitely Punavuori, which has several good boutiques and art galleries to explore. The whole of that side of town is bristling with design shops and studios. A couple of hundred of these are part of **Design District Helsinki** (www.designdistrict.fi), whose invaluable map you can find at the tourist office. To get some pointers, stop by central **Design Forum Finland** (Map p50; www.designforum.fi; Erottajankatu 7; ☺10am-7pm Mon-Fri, to 6pm Sat, noon-5pm Sun), which operates a shop that hosts many designers' work. You're often better off price wise to hunt down your own bargains though.

Stockmann
DEPARTMENT STORE

(Map p50; www.stockmann.fi; Aleksanterinkatu 52) Helsinki's 'everything store' does a good line of Finnish souvenirs and Sámi handicrafts, as well as Finnish textiles, jewellery, clothes and lots more. It offers an export service.

Akateeminen Kirjakauppa
BOOKS

(Map p50; www.akateeminen.com; Pohjoisesplanadi 39; ☺9am-9pm Mon-Fri, to 6pm Sat, noon-6pm Sun) Finland's biggest bookshop, with a huge travel section, maps, Finnish literature and impressively large English section including magazines and newspapers.

Aarikka
DESIGN

(Map p50; ☑652 277; www.aarikka.fi; Pohjoisesplanadi 27) Specialising in wood, Aarikka is known for its distinctly Finnish jewellery.

Artek
DESIGN

(Map p50; www.artek.fi; Eteläesplanadi 18) Originally founded by Alvar Aalto and his wife Aino, this homewares, glassware and furniture store maintains the simple design principle of its founders.

Iittala/Arabia
GLASS, CERAMICS

(off Map p46; www.iittalaoutlet.fi; Hämeentie 135; ☺10am-8pm Mon-Fri, to 4pm Sat & Sun) The factory outlet of these legendary Finnish glassware and ceramics companies is worth the trip. Take tram 6 or 8 to the second-last stop. There's also an exhibition here.

Marimekko
CLOTHING

(Map p50; www.marimekko.fi; Pohjoisesplanadi 33) Finland's most celebrated designer fabrics, including warm florals and hipper new designs, are available here as shirts, dresses, bags, sheets and almost every other possible application.

Kalevala Koru
JEWELLERY

(Map p50; www.kalevalakoru.fi; Unioninkatu 25) Gold, silver and bronze jewellery with motifs based on Finnish and Nordic history and legend.

Fennica Records
MUSIC

(Map p46; www.fennicakeskus.fi; Albertinkatu 36; ☺Mon-Sat) This grungy store does a good range of secondhand and new CDs and vinyl from Suomi pop to jazz.

Moomin Shop
TROLLS

(Map p50; www.moominshop.fi; Forum, Mannerheimintie 20; ⊗9am-9pm Mon-Fri, 9am-6pm Sat, noon-6pm Sun) Stock up on all things Moomin, including books in English and Finnish.

Sauna Aitta
SAUNA

(Map p50; www.sauna-aitta.fi; Simonkatu 10) Gather sauna oils, back-scrubbers, water ladles and hundreds of other accoutrements for your own sauna.

Stupido Records
MUSIC

(Map p46; www.stupido.fi; Iso Roobertinkatu 23) Not so stupid when it comes to Finnish indie, rock and pop; staff are even happy to play something to see how smart it would sound on your stereo.

Levykauppa Äx
MUSIC

(Map p46; www.levykauppax.fi; Arkadiankatu 14B) Large record shop with a good attitude.

Markets
See p65 for details of food markets.

Hietalahden kauppahalli
ANTIQUES

(Map p46; ⊗9am-5pm Mon-Fri, to 3pm Sat) Renovated market at Hietalahti that includes craft and antique stalls. There's some outrageous Finnish retro to gawk at. Take tram 6.

Valtteri
MARKET

(www.kirpputori.com; Aleksis Kivenkatu 17; ⊗9am-3pm Wed, Sat & Sun) Indoor flea market in Kallio; trams 1 and 1A stop opposite.

Hietalahden kauppatori
MARKET

(Map p46; ⊗8am-3pm Mon-Sat, to 8pm daily Jun-Aug) Outdoor flea market close to central Helsinki, but it's pretty downmarket.

ⓘ Information

Emergency
Emergency (☑112)
Police (☑122)

Internet Access
Internet access at public libraries is free. Large parts of the city centre have free wi-fi, as do many bars and cafes – some also have terminals for customers' use.

Kirjasto 10 (Elielinkatu 2; ⊗10am-10pm Mon-Thu, to 6pm Fri, noon-6pm Sat & Sun, reduced hr in summer) On the 1st floor of the main post office. Several half-hour terminals and others bookable by phone.

mbar (www.mbar.fi; Mannerheimintie 22; per hr €5; ⊗9am-midnight, later at weekends) In the Lasipalatsi building. Heaps of terminals and proper drinks.

Rikhardinkatu Library (Rikhardinkatu 3; ⊗9am-8pm Mon-Thu, to 6pm Fri, 10am-4pm Sat) The most central of Helsinki's public libraries has a good English-language selection and free internet terminals.

Sidewalk Express (www.sidewalkexpress.com; per hr €2) There are several of these unstaffed stand-up access points around town. Buy your ticket from the machine; it's valid for all of them. Handy locations include the central railway station (far left as you look at the trains) and Kamppi bus station (outside the ticket office).

Medical Services
Haartman Hospital (☑3106 3231; Haartmaninkatu 4; ⊗24hr) For emergency medical assistance.

Töölö Health Station (☑3104 5500; Sibeliuksenkatu 14; ⊗8am-6pm Mon, to 4pm Tue-Fri) A medical centre for nonemergencies.

Yliopiston Apteekki Mannerheimintie (Mannerheimintie 96; ⊗24hr); city centre (Mannerheimintie 5; ⊗7am-midnight) The branch in the city centre is more convenient.

Money
There are currency-exchange counters at the airport and ferry terminals. ATMs ('Otto') are plentiful in the city.

Forex (www.forex.fi) Pohjoisesplanadi (Pohjoisesplanadi 23; ⊗10am-5pm Mon-Fri, to 4pm Sat) Train station (Pohjoisesplanadi 23; ⊗9am-8pm Mon-Fri, 9am-7pm Sat & Sun) One of many. OK rates, with a flat fee on travellers cheques. Opens longer hours in high summer.

Post
Main post office (Map p50; www.posti.fi; Mannerheiminaukio 1; ⊗7am-9pm Mon-Fri, 10am-6pm Sat & Sun) In the large building between the bus and train stations.

Telephone
Public telephones are nonexistent.

Tourist Information
In summer you'll probably see uniformed 'Helsinki Helpers' wandering around in their green bibs – collar these useful multilinguals for any tourist information.

Apart from the tourist office publications, free publications include *Helsinki This Week* (published monthly) and *We Are Helsinki*, which are available at tourist offices, bookshops and other points around the city.

Tourist office (Map p50; ☑3101 3300; www.visithelsinki.fi; Pohjoisesplanadi 19; ⊗9am-6pm Mon-Fri, to 5pm Sat & Sun Jun-Aug, 10am-4.30pm Mon-Fri, to 4pm Sat Sep-May) Busy multilingual office with a great quantity of information on the city. Also offices at the train station and the airport.

Helsinki Expert (Map p50; www.helsinkiexpert. fi; ⊙9am-4.30pm Mon-Fri, 10am-4pm Sat) Books hotel rooms (€8 commission) and sells tickets for train, bus and ferry travel around Finland and for travel to Tallinn and St Peters- burg; also sells Helsinki Card and is located in the tourist office, with another branch at the train station.

Travel Agencies

From Helsinki you can easily arrange trips to the Baltic countries, Russia and beyond.

Finnsov Tours (☑4366 9620; www.finnsov. fi; Annankatu 29) One of the more established operators, providing tours, travel arrangements and help with visas.

Kilroy Travels (☑020-354 5769; www. kilroytravels.com; Kaivokatu 10D) Specialises in student and budget travel.

Russian Expert (☑321 2009; www.russian expert.fi; Töölönkatu 7) One of the best spots for a Russian visa; charges €71 for most nation- alities including the 'invitation' – this becomes even cheaper if you book a hotel with them. Allow seven working days.

Rustravel (☑611 520; www.rustravel.fi; Tehtaankatu 12) Great for Russian visas, given its proximity to the Russian embassy, but also helpful with tours to Ukraine.

Traveller (☑660 002; www.traveller.fi, Kasarmikatu 26) Specialises in train routes from Helsinki to Russia and beyond on the Trans-Siberian and Trans-Mongolian.

Websites

City of Helsinki (www.hel.fi) Helsinki City website, with links to all the information you might need.

Helsinki Expert (www.helsinkiexpert.fi) Sight- seeing tours, accommodation bookings, tickets and events listings.

HSL/HRT (www.hsl.fi) Public-transport infor- mation and journey planner.

Visit Helsinki (www.visithelsinki.fi) Excellent tourist board website full of information.

❶ Getting There & Away

Small/large lockers cost €2/4 per 24 hours at the bus and train stations. There are similar lockers and left-luggage counters at the ferry terminals.

Air

There are direct flights to Helsinki, Finland's main air terminus, from many major European cities and several international ones. See p344 for details. The airport is at Vantaa, 19km north of Helsinki.

Between them, **Finnair** (☑060-014 0140; www.finnair.fi) and cheaper **FlyBe** (www.flybe. com) cover 20 Finnish cities, usually at least once per day. **Blue1** (☑060-002 5831; www. blue1.com) has budget flights to a handful of Finnish destinations.

Boat

International ferries travel to Stockholm (Swe- den), Tallinn (Estonia), St Petersburg (Russia) and destinations in Germany and Poland. There is also a regular catamaran and hydrofoil service to Tallinn. See p345 for more details.

There are five main terminals, three close to the centre: Katajanokka terminal is served by bus 13 and trams 2, 2V and 4, and Olympia and Makasiini terminals by trams 3B and 3T. Länsi- terminaali (West Terminal) is served by bus 15, while further-afield Hansaterminaali (Vuosaari) can be reached on bus 90A.

FERRIES TO TALLINN & ST PETERSBURG

Eckerö Line (☑060-004 300; www.eckeroline.fi; Mannerheimintie 10) Sails daily to Tallinn year-round (adult €19 to €25, car €17 to €25, three to 3½ hours) from Länsiterminaali (West Terminal).

Linda Line (☑0600-0668 970; www.lindaline.fi; Makasiini terminal) The fastest. Small passen- ger-only hydrofoil company ploughing the waters to Tallinn (from €26 to €46, day trips €35 to €45, 1½ hours) eight times daily when ice-free.

Tallink/Silja (☑060-015 700; www.tallinksilja.com; Erottajankatu 19) Runs at least six Tallinn services (one-way adult €26 to €44, vehicle from €25, two hours), from Länsiterminaali.

St Peter Line (☑010-346 7820; www.stpeterline.com; Makasiini terminal) Runs Monday, Thursday and Saturday evenings to St Petersburg (bunks €33 to €42, private cabins from €110, cars €30 to €35, 14 hours). Visa-free travel of up to 72 hours allowed. From Makasiini terminal. There's a mandatory shuttle bus (for visa-free requirements) from the harbour to the centre in St Petersburg. This costs an extra €15.

Viking Line (☑12351; www.vikingline.fi; Lönnrotinkatu 2) Operates car ferry (adult €21 to €39, vehicle plus 2 passengers €60 to €100, 2½ hours) from Katajanokka terminal.

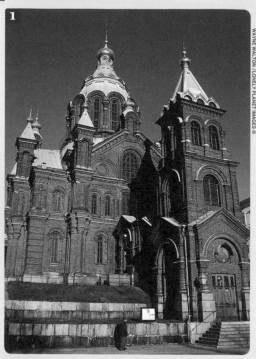

1

2

4

1. Architecture
Admire the impressive red-brick cathedral, Uspenskin Katedraali (p49)

2. Art
Enjoy cutting-edge art at Kiasma (p49), located within an iconic Steven Holl–designed building

3. Bars & Cafes
Join the locals for a drink at one of central Helsinki's many bars and cafes (p66)

4. Markets
Catch the sea breeze while picking up fresh produce on a stroll through the Kauppatori (p45)

BUSES TO RUSSIA

There are three daily services from Helsinki's bus station to St Petersburg (10½ hours, €40). Speedier, cheaper, but not necessarily safer are the minibuses that leave at 3pm daily from the corner of Fredrikinkatu and Pohjoinen Rautatiekatu (Map p46). These cost €25 and get into St Petersburg at around midnight Russian time.

Ferry tickets may be purchased at the terminal, from a ferry company's office (and often its website) or (in some cases) from the city tourist office. Book well in advance during the high season (late June to mid-August), and at weekends.

In summer there are daily ferries between Helsinki and Porvoo, through the southeast archipelago. See p79 for details.

Bus

Purchase long-distance and express bus tickets at **Kamppi Bus Station** (Map p46; Frederikinkatu; ⏱7am-7pm Mon-Fri, to 5pm Sat, 9am-6pm Sun) or on the bus itself. There's a terminal for local buses to Espoo in one wing, while longer-distance buses also depart from here to all of Finland.

There are direct services to/from nearby cities like Tampere and Lahti from Helsinki airport.

Some destinations with several daily departures:
Jyväskylä €46.90, 4½ hours
Kuopio €62, 6½ hours
Lappeenranta €38.10, four hours
Oulu €91.80, 11½ hours
Savonlinna €49.90, five to 5½ hours
Tampere €25.30, 2½ hours
Turku €29.50, 2½ hours.

Train

Helsinki's **train station** (rautatieasema; Map p50; www.vr.fi; ⏱tickets 6.30am-9pm Mon-Sat, 8am-9pm Sun) is central and easy to find your way around. It's linked by subway to the metro (Rautatientori stop) and is a short walk from the bus station.

The train is the fastest and cheapest way to get from Helsinki to major centres: express trains run daily to Turku, Tampere, Kuopio and Lappeenranta among others, and there's a choice of day and overnight trains to Oulu, Rovaniemi and Joensuu. There are also daily trains (buy tickets from the international counter) to the Russian cities of Vyborg, St Petersburg and Moscow.

 Getting Around

To/From the Airport

Bus 615 (€4, 30 to 45 minutes, 5am to midnight) shuttles between Helsinki-Vantaa airport (platform 21) and platform 5 at Rautatientori next to the main train station. Bus stops are marked with a blue sign featuring a plane.

Faster **Finnair buses** (Map p50) depart from Elielinaukio platform 30 on the other side of the train station, stopping once en route, by the top-end hotels further up Mannerheimintie (€6.20, 30 minutes, every 20 minutes 5am to midnight). The 415 bus departs from the adjacent stand but it's slower than the other two.

There are also door-to-door **airport taxis** (☎060-055 5555; www.airporttaxi.fi), which need to be booked the previous day before 6pm if you're leaving Helsinki (one to two people €27). A normal cab should cost €40 to €50.

There's a new airport–city rail link due to open in 2014.

Bicycle

With a flat inner city and well-marked cycling paths, Helsinki is ideal for cycling. Get hold of a copy of the Helsinki cycling map at the tourist office.

The city of Helsinki provides distinctive green 'City Bikes' at stands within a radius of 2km from the Kauppatori. The bikes are free: you deposit a €2 coin into the stand that locks them, then reclaim it when you return it to any stand.

For something more sophisticated, **Greenbike** (☎050-404 0400; www.greenbike.fi; Bulevardi 32; ⏱10am-6pm May-Sep) rents out quality bikes (per day/24 hours/week from €25/30/75) including 24-speed hybrid mountain bikes. Enter on Albertinkatu. **Ecobike** (☎040-084 4358; www.ecobike.fi; Savilankatu 1B; ⏱1-6pm, Mon-Thu) is another good option for bike rental, opposite Finnair Stadium. Call ahead to hire outside these hours.

Car & Motorcycle

Parking in Helsinki is strictly regulated and can be a big headache. Metered areas in the city centre cost up to €4 per hour during the week, but are free on weekends. There are several well-indicated underground car parks in the centre.

Car rental companies have offices in the city as well as at the airport:
Avis (www.avis.fi; Malminkatu 24)
Budget (www.budget.fi; Malminkatu 24)
Europcar (www.europcar.fi; Elielinaukio) By the train station.
Hertz (www.hertz.fi; Mannerheimintie 44)
Lacara (www.lacara.net; Hämeentie 12) A budget local option.
Sixt (www.sixt.com; Työpajankatu 2)

Public Transport

The city's public-transport system **HSL** (www. hsl.fi), operates buses, metro and local trains, trams and a ferry to Suomenlinna. A one-hour flat-fare ticket for any HSL transport costs €2.50 when purchased on board or €2 when purchased in advance. The ticket allows un-limited transfers but must be validated in the stamping machine on board when you first use it. A single tram ticket is €2 full fare. And be-cause it's Nokialand you can order any of these tickets for the same prices using your mobile: send an SMS to ☑16355 texting A1. Day or multiday tickets (24/48/72 hours €7/10.50/14, tickets up to seven days available) are the best option if you're in town for a short period of time. The Helsinki Card gives you free travel anywhere within Helsinki (see p45).

HKL offices (◷7.30am-7pm Mon-Thu, to 5pm Fri, 10am-3pm Sat) at the Kamppi bus station and the Rautatientori and Hakaniemi metro stations sell tickets and passes, as do many of the city's R-kioskis and the tourist office. The *Helsinki Route Map*, available at the city tourist office, is an easily understood map of the bus, metro and tram routes.

If you're heading to Vantaa or Espoo, you'll need a more expensive regional ticket.

Taxi

Hail cabs off the street or join a queue at one of the taxi stands located at the train station, bus station or Senaatintori. You can phone for a taxi on ☑0100 0700.

AROUND HELSINKI

Espoo

☑09 / POP 248,355

Officially the second-largest city in Fin-land, Espoo (Swedish: Esbo) is really part of greater Helsinki, with many residents commuting daily to their larger neighbour for work or vice versa. Nokia's headquar-ters is here and the city is known for its 'campus feel', with plenty of green space and spread-out environs. There are five distinct centres and many suburbs, includ-ing seaside Westend, known for its exclu-sive residences.

TO ST PETERSBURG & BEYOND!

One of Russia's most beautiful cities feels tantalisingly close to Helsinki, but for most visits, including on the new fast train, you'll need a Russian visa.

At the time of writing, the exception to this was the overnight Helsinki–St Peters-burg ferry run by St Peter Line, which allowed you a 72-hour visa-free stay in the city.

Applying in your home country for a Russian visa is easiest, and the process is constantly changing, with differences based on your nationality. If you want to apply in Finland, it's best to do it via a travel agent. Depending on nationality, it'll cost €60 to €100 for the normal seven to eight working days processing time, plus a hefty fee for express processing (three to four working days).

If you want to do it yourself, note the following:

» The processing of Russian tourist visas in Finland has been outsourced, and applica-tions in Helsinki should be submitted in person to the **Russian Visa Application Centre** (3rd fl, Urho Kekkosen katu 7B; ◷9am-3pm Mon-Fri). Save time by completing the form online first (www.vfsglobal.com/russia/finland/english/application.html) and printing it out.

» In all cases, you'll need a passport with more than six months' validity, two free pages, a couple of passport photos, and a 'visa support', namely an invitation docu-ment, typically either issued by accommodation you've booked in Russia (even hostels), or by an authorised tour agent. Travel agencies can also organise this for you, and there are reliable set-ups that organise visa support documents over the internet, such as **Way to Russia** (www.waytorussia.net) or **Visa to Russia** (www. visatorussia.com). These cost about US$30. Once you've got the paperwork, you're ready to get the visa itself.

Thankfully, once you've got the paperwork sorted, it's easy enough to jump on a train, bus or boat and head on east.

Around Helsinki

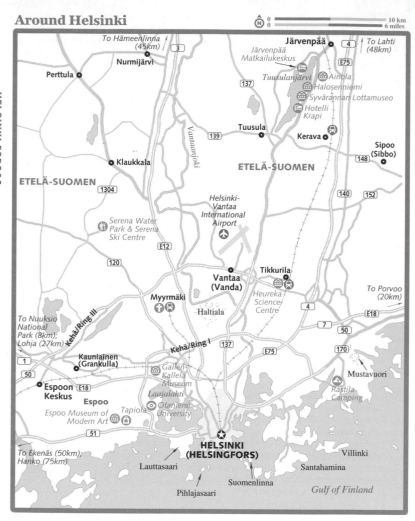

◉ Sights & Activities

Espoo Museum of Modern Art   GALLERY

(EMMA; Map p76, www.emma.museum; Ahertajantie 5, Tapiola; admission €10; ⊙11am-6pm Tue, Thu, Fri, to 8pm Wed, to 5pm Sat & Sun) The city's top sight has a huge collection of mostly Finnish modern art, ranging from the early 20th century to the present. It's definitely worth the trip from Helsinki. Sharing the same address and opening hours, and visitable with the same ticket, **Espoo City Museum** and **Finnish Toy Museum Leikkilinna** can round out a day trip. You can catch buses 106, 106T, 110, 110T or 110TA from Kamppi.

Gallen-Kallelan Museo   GALLERY

(Map p76; www.gallen-kallela.fi; Gallen Kallelantie 27; adult/child €8/free; ⊙11am-6pm daily mid-May–Aug, 11am-4pm Tue-Sat, 11am-5pm Sun Sep–mid-May) Part castle, part studio, this was the home of Akseli Gallen-Kallela, one of Finland's most significant artists. Many of his works are displayed here including his famed *Kalevala* illustrations. From Helsinki take tram 4 to Laajalahden aukio, then walk 2km or take bus 33 (Monday to Friday only).

Serena

WATERPARK

(Map p76; www.serena.fi; Tornimäentie 10; waterpark admission €24; ⊙11am-8pm Jun–late Aug, plus weekends Apr & May) Lots of fun, this waterpark is the largest in the Nordic countries, with a cavalcade of pools, jacuzzis and waterslides. There's also a ski centre here in winter that makes for a good day's skiing, close to Helsinki.

Nuuksio National Park

HIKING

No time to head into the wilderness? Nuuksio (www.outdoors.fi) is on the doorstep of Espoo and close enough to Helsinki to be a half-day trip. As well as marked walking trails through valleys chiselled out by the Ice Age melt, there's excellent cross-country skiing and camping. The park is a habitat for elk and nocturnal flying squirrels, which you'll see on most walks.

A flash new nature centre, Haltia, is due to open in early 2013. Meanwhile, there's an **Information hut** (⊙9am-5.30pm Mon-Fri, 10am-4pm Sat & Sun May-Sep, plus weekends only Oct) at the main Haukkalampi entrance to the park and an unstaffed nature exhibition in another cabin. There are also several free camp sites. You can book a couple of simple cabins through **Wild North** (☑020-344 122; www.villipohjola.fi).

To get to Nuuksio, catch bus 85 from central Espoo. In summer it goes all the way into the park to Kattila. Otherwise, it'll drop you about 2km from the Haukkalampi centre. Helsinki Expert (p71) also runs regular excursions out there in summer.

⚡ Festivals & Events

April Jazz Festival

MUSIC

(www.apriljazz.fi) Draws big crowds with international artists and the Espoo Top 20 concert, which features audience favourites.

ⓘ Getting There & Away

You can catch buses to various parts of Espoo from the dedicated Espoo wing in the bus terminal in Helsinki. Local trains from Helsinki will drop you off at several stations, including central Espoo.

Vantaa

☑09 / POP 200,410

Essentially Vantaa (Swedish: Vanda) is a satellite suburb of Helsinki and best known as the location of the Helsinki-Vantaa international airport. However it's also home to **Heureka** (Map p76; www.heureka.fi; adult/child exhibitions only €16/11, with planetarium film €20.50/14; ⊙10am-5pm Mon-Wed & Fri, to 6pm Sat & Sun, to 8pm Thu), a fantastic hands-on science centre, IMAX theatre and planetarium, next to the Tikkurila train station (15 minutes from Helsinki on a commuter train). In high summer it opens until 7pm every weeknight.

There is frequent local train and bus service between Helsinki and Vantaa, 19km to the north.

Porvoo

☑019 / POP 48,700

Finland's second-oldest town is an ever-popular day trip from Helsinki, but is also becoming a popular weekender. Porvoo (Swedish: Borgå) officially became a town in 1346, but even before that Porvoo was an important trading post.

The town is best known for the achingly beautiful brick-red former warehouses along the river that once stored goods bound for destinations across Europe. Today they're tipped to become a Unesco World Heritage Site and even the newer developments across the river are in reds and yellows to suit the town's aesthetic.

Three distinct districts make up the city: the Old Town, the new town and the 19th-century Empire quarter, which was built under the rule of Tsar Nicholas I. The Old Town, with its tightly clustered wooden houses, cobbled streets and riverfront setting, is the most popular, but the Empire quarter has its charms, including the home of Finland's national poet, JL Runeberg. During the day, Old Town craft shops are bustling with visitors, but staying on a weeknight will mean you could have the place more or less to yourself. The old painted buildings are spectacular in the setting sun.

Try not to visit Porvoo on a Monday, when all the museums are closed.

⊙ Sights & Activities

Vanha Porvoo (Old Town)

HISTORIC DISTRICT

Close your eyes in this tangle of cobbled alleys and wooden warehouses to hear the bustling market that the Old Town once was. The area north of Mannerheiminkatu was largely built after the Great Fire of 1760 but still throngs today with shoppers. Craft boutiques, art galleries, souvenir stores and

Porvoo

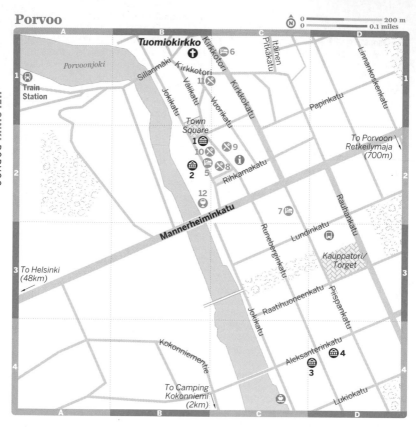

antique shops jostle for attention on the main roads, Välikatu and Kirkkokatu. The relatively less-touristed area is east of the cathedral; Itäinen Pitkäkatu is one of the nicest streets. The rows of rust-red **shore houses** along the Porvoonjoki were first painted with red ochre to impress the visiting king of Sweden in the late 18th century. They were originally used to store goods traded with German ships from the Hanseatic League. Cross the old bridge to the west bank of the Porvoonjoki for the best view of these photogenic buildings

Tuomiokirkko CHURCH
(⊙10am-6pm Mon-Fri, to 2pm Sat, 2-5pm Sun May-Sep, 10am-2pm Tue-Sat, 2-4pm Sun Oct-Apr) Porvoo's historic stone-and-timber cathedral sits atop a hill looking over the quaint Old Town. This is where the first Diet of Finland assembled in 1809, convened by Tsar Alexander I, giving Finland religious freedom. Vandalised by fire in 2006, the church has been completely restored, so you can admire the ornate pulpit and tiered galleries. The magnificent exterior, with free-standing bell tower, remains the highlight.

Porvoon Museo MUSEUM
(www.porvoonmuseo.fi; Vanha Raatihuoneentori; adult/child €6/3; ⊙10am-4pm Tue-Sat, from 11am Sun May-Aug, noon-4pm Wed-Sun Sep-Apr) Porvoo's town museum occupies two buildings on the beautiful cobbled square at the heart of the Old Town. The town hall building houses most of the collection, with a clutter of artefacts relating to the town's history, including work by painter Albert Edelfelt and sculptor Ville Vallgren, two of Porvoo's celebrated artists. The other building re-creates an 18th-century merchant's home.

Runebergin Koti MUSEUM
(Runeberg House; www.runeberg.net; Aleksanterinkatu 3; admission both museums €6; ⊙10am-4pm Tue-Sun, closed Tue Oct-Apr) National poet Johan Ludvig Runeberg's former home has become

Porvoo

Top Sights

Sights

Sleeping

Eating

Drinking

a museum, with a period interior including stuffed foxes and muskets portraying the poet's love of hunting. In an adjacent building, the **Walter Runeberg Sculpture Collection** (Aleksanterinkatu 5) has 150 sculptures by Walter Runeberg, JL Runeberg's eldest son, who produced the town's sculpture of his father. It's only open May to September.

Porvoon Nukke- ja Lelumuseo MUSEUM
(www.lelumuseo.com; Jokikatu 14; adult/child €2/1; ⊙11am-3pm Mon-Sat, from noon Sun Jun–early Aug) Houses over 800 dolls, tin toys and other childhood curiosities, making it Finland's largest toy museum.

Cruises

Cruises leave from Porvoo's passenger quays for the archipelago and other destinations in summer. Arriving by boat from Helsinki is the nicest way to reach Porvoo. Departure times vary, so check websites for the latest.

Saaristolinja Ky CRUISE
(☑523 1350; www.saaristolinja.com; Rantakatu; ⊙mid-Jun–mid-Aug) The little M/S *Borgå* runs 45-minute river jaunts past the Old Town hourly in summer from the passenger harbour (€8, hourly 11am to 4pm, Tuesday to Sunday). With more time you can take on an archipelago cruise aboard the *Fredrika* or *Sandra D* (€25, four hours, Saturday and Sunday), and stop off at islands en route.

JL Runeberg CRUISE
(☑524 3331; www.msjlruneberg.fi) This noble old steamship cruises from Helsinki to Porvoo (adult single/return €25/36, daily except Thursday) in summer and makes an excellent day trip, with various lunch options available. The trip takes 3½ hours each way, so you may prefer to return by bus.

Royal Line CRUISE
(☑020-711 8333; www.royalline.fi) Slightly speedier than the *Runeberg*, the M/S *Royal Cat* zips across to Porvoo from Helsinki's Kauppatori in just over three hours (Tuesday to Saturday late June to mid-August, return €36). It does a price for a boat-bus combination too.

🛏 Sleeping

There are plenty of choices in Porvoo itself, and if you've got a car, there are several other good options in the surrounding area, ranging from B&Bs to luxurious manor houses. Have a look online at www.porvoo.fi/tourism.

TOP CHOICE Hotelli Onni BOUTIQUE HOTEL €€€
(☑044-534 8110; www.hotelonni.fi; Kirkkotori 3; s/d/ste €150/180/250; P) Right opposite the cathedral, this gold-coloured wooden building couldn't be better placed. There's a real range here, from the four-poster bed and slick design of the Funk to the rustic single Peasant. Top of the line is the Honeymoon suite, a small self-contained apartment with bathtub and complimentary champagne. Breakfast is downstairs in the terraced cafe that serves as a popular coffee shop.

Hotelli Pariisin Ville BOUTIQUE HOTEL €€
(☑580 131; www.pariisinville.fi; Jokikatu 43; s/d €150/190, with sauna €290) This plush place in the heart of the Old Town combines modern luxury and heritage feel. Rooms named for former residents are tastefully decorated, with 2nd-floor rooms boasting their own minisaunas and views over the courtyard.

Porvoon Retkeilymaja HOSTEL €
(☑523 0012; www.porvoohostel.fi; Linnankoskenkatu 1-3; dm/s/d €20/35/48; P) Four blocks south and two east of the kauppatori, this historic wooden house holds a well-kept hostel in a grassy garden. It caters for groups, so you'll need to book ahead to ensure a spot, and linen is extra, so be prepared. There's a great indoor pool and sauna complex over the road. Check-in is from 4pm to 7pm. HI discount.

Gasthaus Werneri GUESTHOUSE €
(☑040-049 4876; www.werneri.net; Adlercreutzinkatu 29; s/d/tr €45/60/90; P) This cosy fam-

ily-run guesthouse in an apartment block a 10-minute walk from the Old Town (head east along the main road, then right down Adlercreutzinkatu) is decent value for Finland with five rooms (with shared bathrooms and kitchen) and a self-contained apartment.

Camping Kokonniemi CAMPGROUND €
(☏581 967; www.suncamping.fi; Uddaksentie 17; tent sites €14 plus per person €4, cabins from €59; ☉Jun–late Aug; ℗) On the western side of the river, this well-equipped family-friendly camping ground among the trees is 2km south of Porvoo.

Hotelli Sparre HOTEL €€
(☏584 455; www.avainhotellit.fi; Piispankatu 34; s/d €90/110) This serviceable hotel boasts friendly staff, a business sauna and a restaurant. Twenty euros off at weekends.

✕ Eating & Drinking

Although there are plenty of places to eat in the new part of town, especially around the kauppatori, Porvoo's most atmospheric cafes, restaurants and bars are in the Old Town and along the riverfront.

Porvoo is famous for its sweets; **Brunberg** (www.brunberg.fi; Välikatu 4) does legendary chocolate and liquorice, while the delicious Runeberg cake, a dense rum-and-almond-flavoured cylinder crowned with white icing and raspberry jam, is ubiquitous.

Wanha Laamanni FINNISH €€€
(☏020-752 8355; www.wanhalaamanni.fi; Vuorikatu 17; mains €25-35; ☉lunch & dinner) Top of the town in both geographic and culinary terms, this old Judges' Chambers serves up Finnish faves like reindeer and the unique tar-flavoured salmon. The building itself is a rambling late-18th-century conversion with a roaring fireplace and sprawling terrace that's ideal for people-watching.

Timbaali FINNISH €€
(☏523 1020; www.timbaali.com; Välikatu 8; mains €20-30; ☉11am-11pm) In the heart of the Old Town, this rustic restaurant specializes in slow food: locally farmed snails (€15 for a half-dozen) prepared in a variety of innovative ways. There's also a broad menu of gourmet Finnish cuisine, served in quaint dining rooms or the inner courtyard. At lunchtimes they do a fish buffet (€23).

Café Helmi CAFE
(www.cafehelmi.net; Välikatu 7; cakes €3-7) A kindly Russian grandmother would happily take tea from the distinctive lilac-and-white cups in the courtyard of this Tsarist teahouse. It does one of the best Runeberg tarts, but regular cakes and chocolates will also have you loosening your belt. Closed Mondays and Tuesdays in winter.

TOP CHOICE **Porvoon Paahtimo** CAFE, PUB
(www.porvoonpaahtimo.fi; Mannerheiminkatu 2; ☉10am-late) On the main bridge, this atmospheric red-brick former storehouse is a cosy, romantic spot for drinks of any kind: it roasts its own coffee and has tap beer and several wines. There's a terrace and boat deck, which come with blankets on cooler evenings. Open until 3am at weekends.

ℹ Information

Public library (Papinkatu 20; ☉10am-8pm Mon-Fri, 10am-5pm Sat; @) Free internet.

Tourist office (☏040-489 9801; www.porvoo.fi; Rihkamakatu 4; ☉9am-6pm Mon-Fri, 10am-4pm Sat & Sun early Jun–Aug, 9am-4.30pm Mon-Fri, 10am-2pm Sat Sep–early Jun) Free internet terminal. The gratis *Porvoo* booklet is a good resource.

PORVOO'S POET

Born near Jakobstad in 1804, JL Runeberg came to Porvoo in his 30s as a lecturer at Porvoo Gymnasium (or college). A bit of an overachiever, Runeberg founded the town's newspaper, *Borgå Tidning,* and served as its editor for several years.

The two jobs barely kept Runeberg busy, so he composed some of the epic poems of the period including *King Fjalar* and *The Songs of Ensign Stål,* the first part of which, *Vårt Land* (Our Land), became the Finnish national anthem. But all this couldn't keep Runeberg out of trouble as he had an affair with a pastor's daughter 20 years his junior.

The poet was a keen outdoorsman until a hunting accident in 1863 left him paralysed and he was unable to write during his final years.

Runeberg's work endured with the line 'Let not one devil cross the bridge!', which was used as a slogan in both the Finnish Civil War and WWII to inspire Finnish troops. His birthday is a national celebration on 5 February, but in Porvoo they make the cake that bears his name (see p80) in his honour.

❶ Getting There & Away

Boat See p79 for boats from Helsinki.

Bus Buses depart for Porvoo from Helsinki Kamppi every 30 minutes or so (€11, one hour) and there are frequent buses to/from towns further east. If coming from Helsinki, try not to catch an express bus: you pay a bit more, but they're no faster.

Tuusulan Rantatie

Just a 30-minute drive from Helsinki, the views from the narrow stretch of tar running along Tuusulanjärvi (Tuusula Lake) have inspired some of Finland's greatest artists. **Tuusulan Rantatie** (www.tuusulanrantatie.com; Tuusula Lake Rd) has hosted many heroes of the National Romantic movement including Sibelius, Nobel Prize-winning novelist FE Sillanpää and painter Pekka Halonen.

❍ Sights

The road has several museums as tributes to its artists. One of the most significant, **Halosenniemi** (www.halosenniemi.fi; Halosenniementie 4-6; admission €5.50; ☺11am-7pm Tue-Sun May-Aug, noon-5pm Tue-Sun Sep-Apr) is the Karelian-inspired log-built studio of Halonen, who had a deep love of Finnish nature, with a walking trail through his lakeside garden.

Another real highlight is **Syvärannan Lottamuseo** (www.lottamuseo.com; Rantatie 39; adult/child €5/1; ☺11am-6pm Tue-Sun May-Aug, to 5pm Wed-Sun Sep-Apr), commemorating the Lotta Svärd women's voluntary defence force. Named for a character in a JL Runeberg poem, these unarmed women took on military service during WWII to become one of the world's largest auxiliaries. Look out for the blue-and-white swastika and rose medals, which many Lottas wore among the military paraphernalia.

The most popular stop on the road is **Ainola** (www.ainola.fi; adult/child €5.50/1; ☺10am-5pm Tue-Sun May-Sep), Sibelius' home, east of the lake just south of Järvenpää. The family home, designed by Lars Sonck and built on this forested site in 1904, contains original furniture, paintings, books and a piano on which Sibelius plotted out tunes until his death. The graves of Jean Sibelius and his wife Aino are in the garden.

Järvenpää, the main town in the area, is a modern service centre with numerous restaurants and cafes but little to keep you there long.

🛏 Sleeping

Hotelli Krapi HOTEL €€

(☎274 841; www.krapi.fi; Rantatie 2; s/d €145/168; ℗) Unfortunately named, this historic estate, south of Halosenniemi, features an excellent independent hotel in what was once a cow-shed. It has great modern rooms, three restaurants, a traditional smoke sauna, summer theatre and, if you can believe it, its very own ghost. It also organises packages that can include cultural experiences like cooking classes, or activities such as cycling around the lake. It's a lot cheaper in summer and at weekends.

Järvenpään Matkailukeskus CAMPGROUND, HOSTEL €

(☎7425 5250; www.matkailukeskus.com; Stålhanentie; tent sites €10, s/q €20/45, cabins €25-50; ℗) Camping ground and hostel with a great lakeside location 2.5km from Järvenpää.

❶ Getting There & Away

Tuusulanjärvi is about 40km north of Helsinki. Take a local train or bus to Kerava (4km east of the lake) or Järvenpää (lake's northern end) or a bus to Hyrylä (lake's southern end) and proceed from there by bicylcle. The lake is about 8km long from north to south. Buses running between Helsinki and Järvenpää drop off at or near most of the museums.

Turku &
the South Coast

Best Places to Eat

» Mami (p90)

» Ada Café (p104)

» Makasiini (p109)

» Wanha Fiskari (p114)

Best Places to Stay

» Villa Maija (p108)

» Radisson Blu Marina Palace Hotel (p88)

» Naantalin Kylpylä (p96)

Why Go?

Beautiful Turku reclines along its grassy-banked river, flowing from Gothic cathedral to medieval castle. This seafaring city was once the capital of Finland, and its fascinating history is matched by an equally attractive present. Turku challenges Helsinki's cultural cred with excellent galleries, museums and restaurants, while rocking music festivals electrify the summer air. Historic Naantali, the home of Muumimaailma (Moominworld), makes a perfect side trip.

The south-coast towns, stretching to either side of Helsinki, share Turku's maritime heritage. Kotka's port remains a tough worker, while Hamina's fortress-town glory days make it a veteran with war stories to tell. Hanko, with its venerable villas and vibrant regatta, is a silver fox with immense powers of charm.

And everywhere there are islands, providing great yachting challenges or sea-salt retreats. The 20,000-strong Turku archipelago creates a sea-full of stepping stones across to Åland and Sweden.

When to Go

TURKU

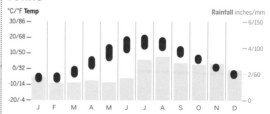

Mar Turku's venerable jazz festival keeps the winter blues at bay.

Jul Boats race in the Hanko Regatta, famous for its carnival atmosphere.

Aug Marching and military music at the weeklong Hamina Tattoo.

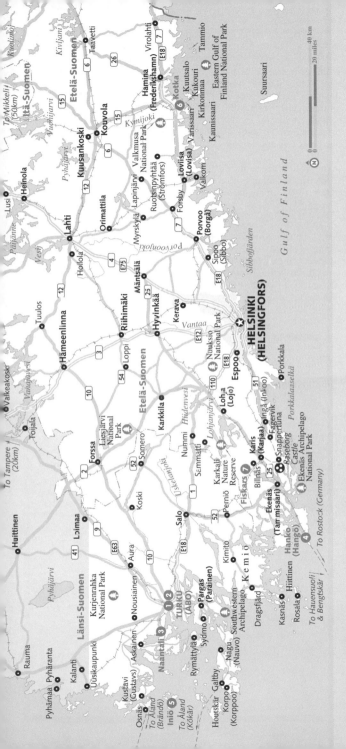

Turku & the South Coast Highlights

1 Getting medieval at massive **Turku Castle** (p84) or underground on the crooked streets of **Aboa Vetus** (p86)

2 Partying at the island festival **Ruisrock** (p88)

3 Cruising to Naantali aboard the **S/S Ukkopekka** (p87) and discovering your inner troll at delightful **Muumimaailma** (p93)

4 Watching the sun set at **Hanko** (p106), casting a golden glow over Russian villas, shining yachts and the prettiest beaches in Finland

5 Taking on the **Archipelago Trail** (p98), which meanders out through the Turku archipelago to remote Iniö

6 Setting sail for Kotka's **Maritime Centre Vellamo** (p112), an epic-scale retelling of the area's love of the sea

7 Balance on the cutting edge of industrial history and modern design at **Fiskars** (p105) ironworks

Turku

📱02 / POP 177,400

The historic castle and cathedral point to the city's rich cultural history when it was capital; but contemporary Turku, a European Capital of Culture in 2011, fizzes with museums, experimental art and a hectic festival calendar. It has its own TV station, and several of Finland's writers and artists call it home.

As the first city many visitors see as they get off ferries from Sweden and Åland, it's a splendid introduction to the mainland's delights.

History

A Catholic settlement began at Koroinen, near the present centre of Turku, in 1229. The consecration of a new church in 1300 and the construction of Turku Castle created an administrative and spiritual base for rulership. At points in history, Turku was the second-largest town in Sweden, though several fires, including the Great Fire of 1827, levelled much of the town.

Åbo was the original Swedish name because it's a settlement (*bo*) on a river (*å*). When the Russians took over, the long Swedish connection led them to make their new capital Helsinki, leaving Turku to concentrate on commerce. The Finnish name, Turku, is an archaic Russian word for 'marketplace'.

Turku's centre is its kauppatori (market square), 3km northeast of the harbour, where buses meet arriving ferries. The Aurajoki divides the city, most of which is within walking distance.

◎ Sights

Turku Castle   CASTLE
(Turun Linna; www.turunlinna.fi; adult/child €8/4.50, guided tours €2; ⊙10am-6pm Tue-Sun May–mid-Sep, 10am-6pm Tue &Thu-Sun, noon-8pm Wed mid-Sep–Apr) Mammoth Turku Castle, near

Turku

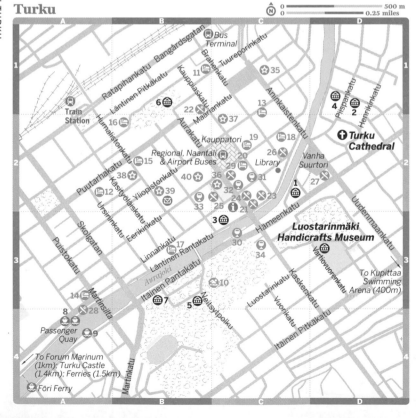

the ferry terminals, is easily Finland's largest; founded in 1280 at the mouth of the Aurajoki, the castle has been growing ever since. Swedish Count Per Brahe ruled Finland from here in the 17th century, while Sweden's deposed King Eric XIV was imprisoned in the castle's round tower in the late 16th century. He was moved to several prisons including Åland's Kastelholms Slott (see p128) to prevent his discovery by rebels.

The castle's highlights include two dungeons and sumptuous banqueting halls, as well as a fascinating **historical museum** of medieval Turku in the castle's Old Bailey. Models in the castle show its growth from a simple island fortress to a Renaissance palace. Most Finns recognise the castle's distinctive architecture as the logo for Turun Sinappi (Turku Mustard).

Guided tours in English are conducted daily from June to August, or you can download a free audio guide from www.turku.fi (follow the menus to the section on Turku Castle).

Luostarinmäki Handicrafts Museum
MUSEUM

(Vartiovuorenkatu 2; adult/child €6/4; ☉10am-6pm Tue-Sun May–mid-Sep, to 4pm Tue-Sun mid-Sep–Apr) When the savage Great Fire of 1827 swept through Turku, the lower-class quarter Luostarinmäki, on the edge of the city, escaped the flames. The 19th-century wooden workshops and houses, set along tiny lanes and around grassy yards, now form the outdoor handicrafts museum, a national treasure since 1940.

All of the buildings are in their original locations, unlike other open-air museums where the buildings are relocated or recreated. These include 30 workshops (including a silversmith, watchmaker, bakery,

TURKU & THE SOUTH COAST TURKU

Turku

pottery, shoemaker, printer and cigar shop), many of which spring to life in summer, when artisans in period costume practise their trades.

Guided tours in English are available in peak season – enquire at the ticket office. The gift shop sells goods produced in the museum's workshops.

Turku Cathedral
CHURCH

(◷cathedral & museum 9am-8pm mid-Apr–mid-Sep, to 7pm mid-Sep–mid-Apr) The 'mother church' of Finland's Lutheran faith, Turku Cathedral towers over the town in a square that makes ants of approaching worshippers. Consecrated in 1300, the brick Gothic building was rebuilt many times over the centuries after damaging fires.

Inside, the pulpit was designed by German architect CL Engel (who in the spirit of impartiality also built the Orthodox church on the market square). Romantic frescoes by RW Ekman depict the baptism of Finland's first bishop and Gustav Wasa presenting the nation with the first Finnish New Testament. The most famous tomb is that of Catherine Månsdotter (d 1613), Queen of Sweden and wife of the unfortunate Erik XIV. The small museum (admission €2) traces the stages of the cathedral's construction, and contains medieval sculptures and religious paraphernalia.

There are summer organ concerts (◷8pm Tue), and English-language services are held at 4pm most Sundays. Listen out for the cathedral's distinctive hourly bell, broadcast across the country at noon via the radio station YLE1 – a patriotic reminder of the Continuation War, when Finns were urged to pray together for victory at this designated hour.

Forum Marinum
MUSEUM

(www.forum-marinum.fi; Linnankatu 72; adult/7-15yr €7/4, incl museum ships €12/7; ◷11am-7pm daily May-Sep, to 6pm Tue-Sun Oct-Apr) Set back from the river, this excellent maritime museum has a permanent exhibition in an old granary and modern new extension. It's a comprehensive look at different aspects of ships and shipping, from scale models to full-sized vessels. Highlights include the hydrocopter, WWII torpedoes and multimedia displays, plus a cabin from a luxury cruise-liner, many of which were built in Turku.

Outside, anchored in the river, is a small fleet of museum ships (per ship adult/7-15yr €5/3, all ships & museum €12/7; ◷11am-7pm Jun-Aug), which you can climb aboard. The mine-layer *Keihässalmi* and the corvette *Karjala* take you back to WWII, while the graceful sweep of the full-rigger *Suomen Joutsen* hints at more-carefree prewar days. The beautiful three-masted barque *Sigyn* (moored 500m upstream) was originally launched from Göteborg in 1887 and has well-preserved cabins.

Inside the museum's cafe-restaurant, you'll find its namesake *Daphne,* a cute little boat that was home to author Göran Schild.

TOP CHOICE Aboa Vetus & Ars Nova
MUSEUM, GALLERY

(www.aboavetusarsnova.fi; Itäinen Rantakatu 4-6; adult/7-15yr €8/5.50; ◷11am-7pm, closed Mon mid-Sep–Mar, English-language tours 11.30am daily Jul & Aug) This pair of museums under one roof unite art and archaeology. The excellent Aboa Vetus ('Old Turku') draws you down underground to the city's medieval streets, dotted with engaging displays showcasing some of the 37,000 artefacts unearthed from

---

THE FLYING FINN

When Finnish champion runner Paavo Nurmi saw a sculpture of himself by Wäinö Aaltonen unveiled on Turku's Itäinen Rantakatu, he laconically remarked, 'I don't run naked.' It was typical of Finland's greatest athlete, who had won a total of 12 track and field medals for middle- and long-distance running during the 1920s. The press hailed him as the Flying Finn and there was much speculation about how saunas aided his phenomenal speed. He broke 22 world records and always ran with a stopwatch, which he was known to throw away when he knew he had enough of a lead.

His career was ended by bureaucracy when he was disallowed from competing at the 1932 Olympics as his paid running appearances and tours of the US were deemed to make him a professional athlete. He left the spotlight and quietly opened a haberdashery store in Helsinki. When he reappeared to light the flame at the 1952 Olympics in Helsinki, he was met with a very Finnish silence that burst into the sound of the 70,000-strong crowd cheering its champion.

the site – we particularly liked the sad story of the four little piggies, and hearing the music of the juniper-wood pochette (pocket violin). Digs continue in the museum and along the Aurajoki.

Back in the present, Ars Nova exhibits the best of contemporary art with changing exhibitions, which peak around the Turku Biennaali, a themed show in summer in odd years.

Turun Taidemuseo GALLERY
(Aurakatu 26; adult/under 16yr €10/free, admission free 4-7pm Fri; ☺11am-7pm Tue-Fri, to 5pm Sat & Sun) Turku Art Museum is housed in a striking granite building with elaborately carved pilasters and conical turrets. Much of the art is modern, though the Victor Westerholm room offers traditional Finnish landscapes; Gunnar Berndtson's *Kesä* (Summer) is an idyllic depiction of sunny Suomi; and Akseli Gallen-Kallela's depictions of the epic *Kalevala* are compelling – and we couldn't tear our eyes away from his *Akka ja kissa* (Old Woman and Cat).

Sibelius Museum MUSEUM
(Piispankatu 17; admission €3; ☺11am-4pm Tue-Sun, plus 6-8pm Wed) Near the cathedral, this is the most extensive musical museum in Finland, displaying some 350 instruments from accordions to Zimbabwean drums. A separate section is devoted to Finnish composer and bohemian carouser Jean Sibelius, displaying manuscripts and personal memorabilia. You can listen to Sibelius' music on scratchy record, or hear live jazz, folk and chamber music at Wednesday-evening concerts held in autumn and spring. For more on Sibelius, see p155.

Wäinö Aaltonen Museum GALLERY
(WAM; www.wam.fi; Itäinen Rantakatu 38; adult/child €6/4; ☺10am-6pm Tue-Sun May–mid-Sep, 10am-6pm Tue & Thu-Sun, noon-8pm Wed mid-Sep–Apr) This gallery displays naturalistic and cubist-tinged sculptures donated by the famous artist himself, along with temporary exhibitions of contemporary and experimental art.

Ett Hem Museum MUSEUM
(Piispankatu 14; admission €3; ☺noon-3pm Tue-Sun May-Sep) Preserves a wealthy turn-of-the-20th-century home designed by CL Engel, with furniture of various styles, and works by painters Albert Edelfelt and Helene Schjerfbeck.

TURKU CARD

The **Turku Card** (adult 24/48hr €21/28, family €40) gives free admission to most museums and attractions in the region, free travel on local buses, and discounts at some shops and restaurants. The 24-hour family card (two adults and three kids) is good value. The card is sold by the tourist office and at participating attractions. It may not be worthwhile on a Monday, when many attractions are closed.

Qwensel House MUSEUM
On the riverfront, Qwensel House is Turku's oldest surviving bourgeois home, built around 1700. It contains the small **Pharmacy Museum** (Läntinen Rantakatu 13; adult/child €4.50/3; ☺10am-6pm daily mid-Apr–mid-Sep, 10am-3pm Tue-Sun mid-Sep–mid-Apr), with an old laboratorium featuring medicinal herbs, 18th-century 'Gustavian' (Swedish) furnishings and an exhibition of bottles and other pharmacy supplies.

Turku Biological Museum MUSEUM
(Neitsytpolku 1; adult/child €4.50/3; ☺10am-6pm Tue-Sun) In a beautiful building, the Turku Biological Museum features much of Finland's wildlife represented in realistic dioramas.

🏃 Activities

Turku's coastal location means great sailing – catch a tour boat out into the archipelago; or get right into the water at one of the city's many pools.

See p92 for details of bicycle hire.

Cruises

Archipelago cruises are a popular activity in summer. Most departures are from the quay at Martinsilta bridge.

S/S Ukkopekka CRUISE
(☎515 3300; www.ukkopekka.fi) The historic steamship S/S *Ukkopekka* cruises to Naantali (one way/return €22/27, 10am and 2pm Tuesday to Saturday mid-June to mid-August), docking next to Muumimaailma (Moomin World) – Moomin packages are available. The trip takes 1¾ hours, and there's a cafe on board. To make a night of it, there's an evening dinner-dance cruise (€43 to €49, departs 7pm Tuesday to Saturday mid-May to mid-September), with meals served on the island of Loistokari.

M/S Rudolfina
CRUISE

(☑250 2995; www.rudolfina.fi) Ninety-minute lunch (1pm and 3pm) and dinner (5pm) cruises including a buffet meal (€25, Monday to Saturday from June to August), and a longer Sunday lunch cruise (€29, 1pm and 3.30pm).

Rosita
CRUISE

(☑213 1500; www.rosita.fi) *Rosita* does a one-hour cruise out to Vepsä Island (€12) three times daily from June to August, and occasional day-long adventures to the lighthouse island of Bengtskär (€65).

Swimming & Sauna

Jukupark Turku
WATERPARK

(www.jukupark.fi; Kurrapolku 1; admission €21; ⊙11am-5pm or 7pm early Jun–mid-Aug) Finland's biggest waterpark opened in Turku in 2010, and is packed with slides, plastic pirates and overexcited nippers. It's about 3km from the centre – take bus 13 or 28 from the kauppatori.

There are also two outdoor pools with saunas – the **Samppalinnan Swimming Stadium** (Volter Kilven katu 2; adult/5-16yr €5/2.50; ⊙6am-8pm Mon-Thu, to 7pm Fri, 8am-7pm Sat & Sun May-Sep), with an Olympic-sized pool and diving boards; and the family-oriented **Kupittaa Swimming Arena** (☑262 3581; Kupittaankatu 10; adult/5-16yr €5/2.50; ⊙10am-7pm Jun–mid-Aug). The indoor **Impivaara swimming hall**, north of the city centre, was closed for renovation/expansion at the time of writing – check with the tourist office to see if it has reopened.

There are good beaches at the 'recreation islands' of **Maisaari**, **Vepsä** and **Pähkinäinen**.

🎎 Festivals & Events

Turku Jazz
MUSIC

(www.turkujazz.fi; concert tickets €10-20) Has been warming the cockles in March with hot bebop and smoking sax for more than 40 years.

Medieval Market
CULTURAL

(www.keskiaikaisetmarkkinat.fi) Held over a variable long weekend in summer, this event brings a Middle Ages market back to the cathedral square.

Paavo Nurmi Marathon
SPORT

(www.paavonurmisports.fi) Named for the legendary distance runner, this marathon in late June/early July attracts an international field and runs from the town centre to Ruissalo Island.

Ruisrock
MUSIC

(www.ruisrock.fi; 1-/3-day tickets €80/110) Finland's oldest and largest annual rock festival, held since 1969. The festival takes place over three days in July at the recreational park on Ruissalo Island.

Down by the Laituri
MUSIC

(DBTL; www.dbtl.fi) By the river, this annual rock festival in late July/early August attracts mainly Finnish bands.

Turku Music Festival
MUSIC

(www.tmj.fi; tickets free-€35) From early August, this two-week extravaganza offers an eclectic mix of classical and contemporary music and opera with amazing venues including Turku Castle and the cathedral.

🛏 Sleeping

Because of Turku's proximity to Muumimaailma (p93), there's an emphasis on family accommodation, with some places offering Moomin packages.

TOP CHOICE Radisson Blu Marina Palace Hotel
HOTEL €€

(☑020-123 4710; www.radissonblu.com/hotel-turku; Linnankatu 32; d summer/winter from €99/129; P @) Far and away the best in town, this modern business hotel has pleasant, efficient staff, great amenities and stylish Scandinavian-style dark-wood rooms. It's worth paying extra for a superior room with one of the stunning river views; and couples who have grown weary of sleeping in pushed-together twin beds will be delighted to learn of real doubles on the 7th floor! Suites have extra luxuries like in-room espresso machines.

Centro Hotel
HOTEL €€

(☑211 8100; www.centrohotel.com; Yliopistonkatu 12; s/d incl breakfast €83/106; P @) One of Turku's best, the Centro Hotel is (as its name implies) central, but its courtyard location cuts out street noise (internal noise is another matter!). Attentive service always feels friendly, and blond-wood rooms are a good compromise between size and price. Superior ones have a more designer feel. The breakfast buffet has porridge, pastries and other delights worth getting out of bed for. Limited parking spaces.

Hostel Turku
HOSTEL €

(☑262 7680; www.turku.fi/hostelturku; Linnankatu 39; dm/tw/q €18/45/70; ⊙reception 6-10am & 3-9pm; P) Between the ferry and the city, this HI hostel is well situated for coming and going. It's a neat, quiet place with good lockers, spacious dorms (no more than four bunks) and a laundry room. There's also bike hire (€15 per day) and a coin-operated internet cafe. It's small and fills quite quickly: if you're stuck, **River Hostel Turku** (☑040-689 2541; riverhostel@turku.fi; Linnankatu 72; s/d from €43/62) aboard the S/S *Bore* at the Forum Marinum has tiny (stuffy!) cabins, but lots of them.

Bridgettine Convent Guesthouse B&B €

(☑250 1910; birgitta.turku@kolumbus.fi; Ursininkatu 15A; s/d incl breakfast €45/65; P) Glowing-white and dotted with nuns, this simple Catholic guesthouse is a haven of peace in the heart of the city: public areas are silent after 10pm, and the place has a general air of respectful hush. Rooms are small and plain, but cleanliness clearly goes along with the godliness. It's good value and handy for the train. Payment in cash only.

Scandic Julia HOTEL €€

(☑336 000; www.scandic-hotels.fi; Eerikinkatu 4; s/d €128/138; @) Renovated in 2011, rooms have a fresh, new feel and now come with air-conditioning (invaluable in summer). There are excellent views of the city and cathedral, particularly from the 6th-floor sauna. Service, however, can be a bit hit-and-miss, and parking is an extra €15 per day, making it a pricey option.

Park Hotel HOTEL €€

(☑273 2555; www.parkhotelturku.fi; Rauhankatu 1; s €100-115, d €135-155, ste €260; P@) This art nouveau house is a genuine character – an eccentric aunt – right down to Jaakko, the parrot that squawks a welcome when you check in. Rooms themselves are decorated in a lovably chintzy style, and other facilities like a pool table and a fireplace-warmed drawing room make this the antithesis of a chain hotel.

Omenahotelli HOTEL €

(www.omenahotelli.fi; Humalistonkatu 7; r from €50) This larger hotel on the 'apple hotels' chain (booked via the internet and without a reception desk) was actually designed by Alvar Aalto, but the plainness suggests that AA phoned it in. Still, it represents excellent value, with spaces that can sleep up to four people. Breakfast is extra. The nearest underground car park costs €16 per day.

Bed & Breakfast Tuure B&B €

(☑233 0230; www.tuure.fi; Tuureporinkatu 17C; s/d €38/54; P@) Upstairs in a homely building close to the city centre, this affordable option

is good for independent travellers. Rooms are small but sweet with shared bathrooms, and there's a little kitchen, laundry facilities, and good local tips from the friendly owners. Allergy sufferers note: Pörrö the cat lives here too!

Seaport Hotel HOTEL €€

(☑283 3000; www.hotelseaport.fi; Matkustajasatama; s/d/tr €78/95/120, f €99-119; P@) The bog-standard, orange-toned, slightly shabby rooms are not going to raise any pulses, but this restored warehouse is perfectly placed for an early ferry (it's right next to the Viking Line and Silja Line terminals), and the staff are fabulous. Facilities include restaurant and sauna, and frazzled parents can offload their kids at the large indoor playing area. Bus 1 shuttles to the city, or hire a bike for €15 per day.

Sokos Hamburger Börs & City Börs HOTEL €€

(☑337 381; www.sokoshotels.fi; Kauppiaskatu 6; Hamburger Börs s/d from €109/124, City Börs s/d from €88/103; P@⊠) Towering over the market square, this is the town's biggest hotel. The main hotel (where you check in for both options) comes with free sauna, flatscreen TVs and a restaurant, although rooms vary in quality from the old-and-tired to the recently renovated. Light sleepers should ask for a room at the back to avoid drunken noise from the kauppatori. The City Börs option is across the road and has simpler rooms that are more affordable.

Ruissalo Camping CAMPGROUND €

(☑262 5100; tent sites €12 plus per person €4, 2-/4-person r €40/65; ⊙Jun-Aug) On idyllic Ruissalo Island, 10km west of the city centre, this camping ground has lots of room for tents and a few cabins along with saunas, a cafeteria and nice beaches – including a nude option. It's the bunkhouse for the Ruisrock festival, so expect it to be booked out then and at Midsummer. Bus 8 runs from the kauppatori.

✖ Eating

Turku's dining scene is fairly sophisticated, with international options and some good chances to try Finnish food. The historic **kauppahalli** (covered market; Eerikinkatu; ⊙7am-5.30pm Mon-Fri, to 3pm Sat) is ideal for groceries and quick eats. The **kauppatori** (⊙8am-4pm Mon-Sat May-Sep) hosts a fruit and vegetable market, but there's no shortage of grillis (fast-food outlets) and kebab shops here. Turku is the home town of the ubiquitous Hesburger chain, Finland's answer to McDonald's.

Mami FINNISH, BISTRO €€
(☏231 1111; Linnankatu 3; lunches €8.50, mains around €22; ☉11am-10pm Tue-Fri, from 1pm Sat & Sun) One of a crop of riverside restaurants in the heart of town, this is the one that fills up first! Its summer terrace is perfect for people-watching, though you'll have to fight for a table with half of Turku – the restaurant is so popular that cynics have already placed bets as to when it will jump the shark. Seasonal ingredients from local, small-scale suppliers – goat's cheese, chanterelles, perch, salmon, duck – are prepared with care, and served with a twinkle.

TOP CHOICE Café Art CAFE €
(Läntinen Rantakatu 5; ☉10am-7pm Mon-Fri, to 4pm Sat) With freshly ground coffee, prize-winning baristas, a beautifully elegant interior, and artistic sensibility, there's no better place to get your caffeine fix. Cakes are pricey, but after tasting the blueberry cheesecake, it's unlikely you'll care. In summer, a terrace spills out onto the riverbank, perfectly shaded by linden trees.

Bossa BRAZILIAN €€
(☏251 5880; www.restaurantebossa.fi; Kauppiaskatu 12; mains €16-23; ☉4-10pm Tue-Fri, 2-11pm Sat, 3-9pm Sun) First-rate Brazilian food is the order of the day at this vibrant eatery, from hearty steaks to black-bean soups. Live music frequently jazzes up the joint.

Blanko FUSION €€
(☏233 3966; www.blanko.net; Aurakatu 1; mains €18-25; ☉lunch & dinner daily, bar to midnight or 3am) Look for the black-tile signage to locate this hip eatery. Inside it's all Scandi chic with periodic DJs, but the dining area is separate enough for you to enjoy the global menu of pastas, curries, a worthwhile lunch special and the best brunch in town.

Cafe Fontana CAFE, BISTRO €
(cnr Aurakatu & Linnankatu; pastries €3-6, salads & sandwiches €9; ☉10am-10pm Mon-Sat, noon-9pm Sun) Art nouveau Fontana, close to the city's heart, serves up delicious cakes toppling with glazed strawberries, and is a stylish spot for lunchtime salads, paninis or a full hot buffet. Also the perfect place to digest information from the tourist office, just across the road.

Tintå WINE BAR €€
(☏230 7023; www.tinta.fi; Läntinen Rantakatu 9; lunches €8.50; ☉11am-1am Mon-Thu, to 2am Fri, noon-2am Sat) Another central place on the river, this elegant wine bar, with a cosy red-brick interior, also offers much-loved lunches (Monday to Friday) and fabulous gourmet pizza slices (such as prosciutto and fig). Grab a glass of wine and watch the world walking along the shore.

Vaakahuoneen Paviljonki INTERNATIONAL €€
(☏515 3300; Linnankatu 38; mains €14-20, fish buffets €12; ☉11am-10pm May-Aug) A pleasant stroll away from the centre, this summer pavilion, right on the riverbank, has a big à la carte menu of snacks, pasta, pizzas and steak, and folk descend on the daily fish buffets like starving herring gulls. Best of all, evening live jazz accompanies the food and sunshine, giving it the happiest, most toe-tapping atmosphere of all Turku's restaurants.

Teini BARBECUE €€
(☏223 0203; Uudenmaankatu 1; lunches €11, mains €15-26; ☉lunch & dinner) Something of an institution with city workers for its lunch specials, this traditional grill house does great fish, lamb and steaks in an atmospheric little dining room. Dinner is a little pricey.

Viikinkiravintola Harald THEME €€€
(☏044-766 8204; www.ravintolaharald.fi; Aurakatu 3; set menus €30-50, mains €20-30; ☉lunch & dinner) Dust off your horned helmet for this Viking restaurant where subtlety is run through with a berserker's broadsword. Set menus (or Voyages as they're called here) are filling three-course samplers, but picking and mixing means you can indulge in barbarian ribs on a plank or tar ice cream with cognac. It's not exactly gourmet, but it is great fun.

Sininen Juna Aschan Café CAFE €
(kauppahalli; pastries €3-6) The 'Blue Train' cafe is right in the middle of the kauppahalli: its old railway-carriage seats make a good place to revive yourself after meandering round the market. Run by top-quality Turku bakery chain Aschan, it's a tasty destination.

Drinking

Turku's drinking crowds surge towards the river in summer. Evenings kick off on one of the 11 **boat bars** lining the south bank; popular ones include the upmarket *Donna*, and the down-to-earth *Papa Joe* and *Cindy* (the latter opens year-round). Most drinking spots serve until 2am (3am weekends).

TOP CHOICE Cosmic Comic Café
BAR

(www.cosmic.fi; Kauppiaskatu 4) This fab late-night haunt is a fanboy's dream – comics are papered to the walls and there's a huge collection (mostly in English) available to browse. There are 70 different kinds of beer and 25 ciders on its eclectic and ever-expanding menu, enjoyed by an arty, alternative crowd. Occasional live music.

Panimoravintola Koulu
BREWERY, PUB

(www.panimoravintolakoulu.fi; Eerikinkatu 18) Set in a former school, this brewery pub only serves its own brews – around five lager-style beers that change with the seasons, and a couple of interesting ciders flavoured with tart cranberries and blackcurrants. The exception is the whisky collection – there are around 75 to sample. As well as inkwells and school desks, there's a fantastic beer garden – the place to be on a summer evening.

Uusi Apteekki
BAR

(Kaskenkatu 1) South of the river, this bar is located in a converted historic pharmacy: the lovely old fittings are still in place, and some of the wooden dispensing drawers have been fashioned into tables where you can perch your pints. There's a good selection of beers, enjoyed by an older crowd.

Alvar
PUB

(Humalistonkatu 7) In a building that Aalto designed on a deadline, this low-key pub has a good beer list that's a magnet for local students and ale-fetishists alike. Artek-esque furniture is a nod to the designer of the building and free wi-fi makes it a lounge rather than a party.

Cow
COCKTAIL BAR

(www.thecow.fi; Aurakatu 3) If you were going to hold a hen's night in Turku, this would be the place to have it. The cocktails keep flowing and there's a good wine selection; but the atmosphere never gets too barnyard, with friendly staff and relaxed (cowlike) couches.

Old Bank
PUB

(www.oldbank.fi; Aurakatu 3) This former bank remains a grand monument, its cavernous interior attracting an older male crowd for a postwork drink or hockey game. It has the trappings of an Irish pub and a formidable roster of beers, including some real ales.

☆ Entertainment

Twenty-five thousand university students make Turku's nightlife young and fun, and the city has a strong reputation for its music and cultural events.

Nightclubs & Live Music

Most clubs open Wednesday to Saturday until 3am or 4am, with admission from €10 to €25, depending on the entertainment.

Klubi
CLUB, LIVE MUSIC

(www.klubi.net; Humalistonkatu 8A) This massive complex has several speeds from the casual drinking of Kolo ('cave') to the DJ-fuelled nightclub of Ilta, plus regular big Finnish bands at Live. It's part owned by a local record label, which means it snares its share of Finnish bands and visiting international acts.

Galax
CLUB, LIVE MUSIC

(www.galax.fi; Aurakatu 6) This monster venue holds Galax Dancing, with live Finnish pop acts; the Kooma nightclub, with regular DJs who spin danceable grooves; and Taivas Music Bar, a karaoke joint for punters who just love the limelight.

Monk
JAZZ

(www.monk.fi; Humalistonkatu 3; ☺9pm-4am Fri & Sat, to 1am Mon) Turku's best (OK, only) jazz club in town plays live jazz, funk and Latin.

Cinema

There is only one cinema in Turku – the **Kinopalatsi** (☐09-1311 9205; Kauppiaskatu 11; tickets €6.80-13) multiplex. It does have nine screens, though.

Classical Music & Theatre

Concert Hall
CONCERT VENUE

(☐262 0030; www.tfo.fi; Aninkaistenkatu 9; tickets €8-20; ☺Sep-May) Founded in the 1790s, the Turku Philharmonic Orchestra is one of the oldest in Europe; it performs here.

Svenska Teater
THEATRE

(☐277 7377; www.abosvenskateater.fi; tickets €20-40; Aurakatu 10) Next to the Hansa Shopping Arcade, Finland's oldest theatre hosts well-known musicals with performances in Swedish.

❶ Information

Internet Access

Most hotels have wi-fi, as do many Turku cafes and bars. The **library** (Linnankatu 2; ☺10am-8pm Mon-Fri, to 4pm Sat, plus noon-6pm Sun Sep-May) has several free internet terminals (maximum 15 minutes).

Money

Several banks on the market square have 24-hour ATMs.

Forex (Eerikinkatu 13; ⊘8.30am-7pm Mon-Fri, 10am-3pm Sat) The best place to change cash and travellers cheques.

Post

Main post office (Humalistonkatu 1; ⊘9am-8pm Mon-Fri)

Tourist Information

Turku City Tourist Office (☑262 7444; www.turkutouring.fi; Aurakatu 4; ⊘8.30am-6pm Mon-Fri, 9am-4pm Sat & Sun Apr-Sep, 10am-3pm Sat & Sun Oct-Mar) Busy, very helpful, information on entire region. Rents seven-gear bikes (€15/75 per day/week). Free internet for short periods; per hour €5.

Travel Agencies

Citytours (☑020-741 3590; www.citytours.fi; Eerikinkatu 4) Finnair agent.

Kilroy Travels (☑020-354 5769; www.kilroytravels.com; Eerikinkatu 2) Specialists in student and budget travel.

Getting There & Away

Air

Finnair (www.finnair.fi) flies to Turku from a number of Finnish cities daily along with several European capitals including Stockholm. Business airline **Turku Air** (www.turkuair.fi) flies to Mariehamn on weekdays.

Boat

Turku is a major gateway to Finland from Sweden and Åland, and smaller boats ply the waters up and down the coast.

The harbour, about 3km southwest of the centre, has terminals for **Silja Line** (www.tallinksilja.com) and **Viking Line** (www.vikingline.fi). Both companies sail to Stockholm (11 hours) and Mariehamn (six hours). Prices vary widely according to season and class, with deck-class one-way tickets ranging from €20 to €35. **Finnlink** (http://passenger.finnlines.com) sails to Sweden from nearby Naantali – see p97.

Tickets are available at the harbour, from Viking Line in the Hansa Shopping Arcade, or Silja Lines at Aurakatu 5. It's advisable to book ahead during high season, if you plan to take a car or if you're travelling on a weekend (or Friday night).

See p345 for more details about international ferry travel.

It's also possible to travel from the Turku archipelago – see that section (p98) for details.

Bus

From the bus terminal at Aninkaistentulli there are hourly express buses to Helsinki (€29.40,

2¾ hours), and frequent services to Tampere (€23.90, 2½ hours), Rauma (€20.50, 1½ hours), Pori (€26.90, 2¼ hours) and other points in southern Finland. Regional buses depart from the kauppatori.

Left Luggage

The train station, ferry terminal and Silja and Viking Line buildings have lockers (around €3).

Train

Turku is the terminus for the southeastern railway line. The train station is a short walk northwest of the centre; trains also stop at the ferry harbour and at Kupittaa train station east of the centre. Various buses shuttle between the centre and the main train station, but it's an easy walk. Express trains run frequently to and from Helsinki (€29.60, two hours), Tampere (€24.30, 1¾ hours), Oulu (€72.70, six to nine hours) and Rovaniemi (€83.60, 9½ to 14 hours). For Oulu and Rovaniemi there's usually a change in Tampere.

Getting Around

To/From the Airport

Bus 1 runs between the kauppatori and the airport, about 8km north of the city, every 15 minutes from around 5.30am to 11.30pm (€2.50, 25 minutes). This same bus also goes from the kauppatori to the harbour.

Bicycle

The city tourist office hires out bikes (per day/week €15/75), can suggest cycling routes, and publishes an excellent free *pyörätiekartta* (bike-route map) of the city and surrounding towns. Hostel Turku (p88) also offers hire services.

Bus

City and regional buses are frequent and you pay €2.50 for a two-hour ticket or €5.50 for a 24-hour ticket. The Turku Card (p87) allows for free bus transport. Important city bus routes include bus 1 (harbour–kauppatori–bus station–airport) and buses 32 and 42 (train station–kauppatori).

Car

There are several car-rental offices, among them **Avis** (☑020-799 1222) and **Budget** (☑020-746 6670), both at the railway station.

Ferry

There's a small **Föri ferry** (⊘6.15am-9pm, to 11pm May-Sep) that's free and crosses the river a few blocks downstream from the last bridge.

M/S Ruissalo (☑040-050 9523; www.merireitit.fi; ⊘Jul–mid-Aug) departs from the same spot as Föri to go to the island of Ruissalo (return €12).

Naantali

🗓02 / POP 18,800

For many Finns, Naantali (Swedish: Nådendal) means Moomins. Most visitors are day trippers from Turku, just 18km away, but some come from Sweden for a day out at the theme park or to wander the quaint Old Town. Even the president spends her time off here, leading many to call it the summer capital of Finland. Out of season Muumimaailma (Moomin World) closes its gates, and the Old Town acquires the melancholic air of an abandoned film set. But Naantali continues to work hard behind the scenes, with Finland's third most-trafficked port, an oil refinery and an electricity power plant.

🔘 Sights & Activities

Muumimaailma THEME PARK
(Moomin World; www.muumimaailma.fi; 1-/2-day pass 3yr & over €22/29; ⊙10am-6pm early Jun–mid-Aug, noon-6pm to end Aug) Crossing the bridge from town takes you into the downright delightful world of the Moomins, one of Finland's most famous families. Even if you've never read the books or seen the TV series or film, there's still something wonderful about these characters (see below).

Muumimaailma is based on Kailo Island, and has costumed characters wandering through the Moominhouse, Snork's Workshop (where kids help with inventions) and a host of places that leap to life from the books and cartoons. There's a swimming beach, and Emma's Theatre has different performances every year (some mimed, so the language barrier isn't a problem). Merchandising is limited, and the focus is on hands-on activities and exploration, not rides.

Older adventure-seekers will prefer **Väski** (🗓511 1111; www.vaski.fi; over 3yr €18, 2-day ticket incl Moominworld entry €32; ⊙11am-7pm early Jun–mid-Aug), the nearby pirate island that features rock climbing, obstacle courses, and shooting bows and arrows.

Old Town HISTORIC DISTRICT
Surrounding the harbour, 1km west of the bus terminal, Naantali's Old Town is a living museum with many townspeople living and working in the historic buildings. The town grew unplanned around its convent, with new buildings built on the sites of older ones. The photogenic district is made up of old narrow cobbled streets and wooden houses – many of which now house handicraft shops, art galleries, antiques shops and cafes. The main thoroughfare is Mannerheiminkatu and **Wanha Naantali Kauppa** (Mannerheiminkatu 13; ⊙11am-5pm daily Jun-Aug, Sat & Sun rest of year) is a popular shop selling old-fashioned Finnish sweets (brace yourself for liquorice and tar drops), bottled

---

MOOMINMANIA

When Tove Jansson's uncle tried to scare her from midnight snacking in the kitchen, he told her that Moomintroll lived there. It only heightened the young Finn's appetite for fiction as she began imagining what Moomins looked like. Her first Moomin drawing appeared as a signature on her political cartoons. Jansson wrote her first book, *Småtrollen och den stora översvämningen* (The Moomins and the Great Flood), to cheer herself up during WWII.

The Moomins, a family of white-snouted trolls, are nature-loving, eccentric and offer a heartfelt welcome to their many odd visitors. Moominpappa, Moominmamma and their loving but timid child Moomintroll are based closely on Jansson's own bohemian family. A host of other characters come and go: the eternal wanderer Snufkin; Little My, whose speciality is brutal honesty; the eerie Hattifatteners, who grow from seeds and are drawn to electrical storms; and the icy Groke, who leaves a frozen trail wherever she drifts.

Jansson wrote nine children's books and drew several cartoon books based on her characters; later adaptations included a Japanese cartoon series, a film and an album, and Moomintroll even appeared on Finnair planes. Her comic strips debuted in the *London Evening News* in 1954, before being syndicated around the world: Canadian publisher Drawn & Quarterly (www.drawnandquarterly.com) has recently republished them in six hardback editions. Moomin merchandise seems to be everywhere in Finland but the real deal is at the Moomin Shop (p70), which was set up by Jansson's heirs. Of course if you want to get even closer then there's Tampere's Muumilaakso (Moomin Valley Museum, p140) or Muumimaailma (see above).

1. Opera
Take in some high culture at the Savonlinna Opera Festival (p166)

2. Jazz
Swing by the huge Pori Jazz Festival (p225), held over nine days in July

3. Midsummer
Get involved in the festivities of Midsummer (p124) in Åland archipelago

soft drinks, postcards and souvenirs – it's a slightly pricey nostalgia trip.

Housed in three old wooden buildings dating from the 18th century, **Naantali Museum** (Katinhäntä 1; admission €2.50; ⊙11am-6pm Tue-Sun mid-May–Aug) casts a light on disappearing trades such as needlemaking and goldsmithing, as well as looking at how the town prospered from sock knitting.

Convent Church
CHURCH
(www.naantalinseurakunta.fi) Medieval Naantali grew up around the Catholic Convent of the Order of Saint Birgitta, which was dissolved after the 1527 Reformation. The only building that remains today is the massive Convent Church, which towers above the harbour. The church was completed in 1462, though its baroque stone tower dates from 1797. The interior is surprisingly wide, with elegant vaulting and a very handsome 17th-century pulpit depicting the apostles and evangelists in a blaze of colour. Also noteworthy is the carved 15th-century polychrome wood triptych behind the altar and an evocative wooden head of Christ below it. Archaeological digs around the church unearthed more than 2000 pieces of jewellery, coins and other relics now in the museum.

During summer there's a program of organ music; the tourist office can provide a schedule. At 8pm on summer evenings you'll hear 'vespers' (evensong) played by a trumpeter from the belfry of the church. The church was closed for repairs at the time of research: check the website for opening hours.

Naantalin Kylpylä
SPA
(☎445 5100; www.naantalispa.fi; pool entry per 3hr €23, day spa packages from €93) Naantali's spa traditions date from 1723, when people took health-giving waters from a spring in Viluluoto, and peaked in the 19th century when Turku's wealthy came to bathe. Today Naantalin Kylpylä, the town's top-class spa hotel, allows nonguests to use its fantastic facilities – including several pools and a Turkish bath – from 8am to 8pm. The huge range of spa, massage and beauty treatments are popular with mothers who don't want to go to Muumimaailma, so book ahead in summer.

Kultaranta
HISTORIC BUILDING
The president of Finland's summer residence is an elaborate stone castle on Luonnonmaa Island, with the flamboyant tower visible from Naantali harbour. The castle, designed by Lars Sonck, was built in 1916 and is surrounded by beautiful, extensive rose gardens.

Kultaranta grounds (☎435 9800; tours from gate/Naantali €10/14; ⊙Tue-Sun late Jun-late Aug) can only be visited by guided tours, which leave from the front gate (at 2pm and 3pm) or with a bus trip from Maariankatu (1.40pm). Tours are in Finnish, except at the end of August, when there are English tours from the gate at 2pm.

⚜ Festivals & Events

Naantali Music Festival
MUSIC
(www.naantalimusic.com; tickets €25-50) For over 30 years, this event featuring first-rate classical music has been held over two weeks from early June. Events in the Convent Church are a real highlight and performers come from around the globe.

Sleepyhead Day
CULTURAL
On 27 July Naantali celebrates this unusual Finnish festival by electing a 'Sleepyhead of the Year', who is woken early by being tossed into the sea. A carnival with music, dancing and games ensues.

🛏 Sleeping

Naantalin Kylpylä
SPA HOTEL €€€
(☎445 5100; www.naantalispa.fi; Matkailijantie 2; s/d from €152/200; P@☰) Indulgence is the call of the day at this upmarket spa hotel and its excellent restaurant, Le Soleil. The hotel is large but stylish with treatment rooms (massage and beauty) and pools downstairs. Rooms are spacious, with a lounge area and balcony or verandah; the sofa folds out to make a family room. The spa also owns the **Sunborn Princess Yacht Hotel** (singles/doubles €175/218), a stationary cruise ship with comfortable rooms; and has extended once again with the brand-new **Spa Residence**, which has deluxe hotel rooms (singles/doubles €185/238) and holiday apartments.

Harriet Homes
APARTMENT €
(☎040-910 4444; www.harriethomes.com; Katinhäntä 3; per person from €40) This collection of minihouses are all named after the owners' family members and make for an extremely central family stay. It's close enough to walk to Muumimaailma or the harbour. The buildings gather around a central courtyard, but vary somewhat in renovation/upkeep – Anna is probably the best. Parking €10 per day.

Naantali Camping CAMPGROUND €
(☑435 0855; Kuparivuori; tent sites €14 plus per adult €4, 2-/6-person cottages €40/140, 4-person cottages €50-110; ☺Jun-Aug) About 400m south of the harbour is this exceptional camping ground that's popular with holidaying Finns. It has great management and good facilities, including a beachside sauna. Four-person cabins have a huge range from basic to their own sauna, bathrooms and kitchens.

Naantalin Kylpylä Perhehotelli APARTMENT €
(☑445 5100; Opintie 3; 2-/3-room apt €118/177; ℗) Despite its institutional appearance, this family hotel is a decent option if you're looking for budget accommodation. It's not luxurious – apartments are hostel-standard, but they do include kitchens, and you can also use the neighbouring spa's swimming pools at a reduced rate (adult/child €9/7).

✖️ Eating

Naantali has a cluster of eating options around the harbour and you'll also find bites to eat at Muumimaailma.

Merisali BUFFET €€
(☑435 2451; Nunnakatu 1; breakfasts/lunches/dinners €8/13/17; ☺summer) This favourite spot is a restored spa pavilion that offers the best buffets in town, with plentiful hot and cold choices. The pierside terrace is the perfect place to enjoy your meal, and there's often live music.

Trappi FINNISH €€
(☑435 2477; www.ravintolatrappi.fi; Nunnakatu 3; mains €15-30; ☺lunch & dinner, closed Sun winter) This more gourmet option, in a fine wooden building, is perfect for a refined meal. Finnish influences – roast goose in apple sauce, whitefish, reindeer – rub shoulders with international dishes from chilli prawns to shashlik. Save room for the expertly chosen cheeses including deep-fried camembert with *lakka* (cloudberries).

Cafe Antonius CAFE €
(Mannerheiminkatu 9; cakes & pastries €4-7; ☺10am-6pm Mon-Sat, 11am-5pm Sun) Well placed for snack attacks ('If you're quiet until we get to Muumimaailma, Ulli, then you can have a gingerbread'), this cafe does pastries, sweets and other 'quieteners' for little ones. The convenience isn't cheap though.

❶ Information

Library (Tullikatu 11; ☺noon-7pm Mon-Thu, to 4pm Fri, plus 10am-2pm Sat winter) Free internet access on the 2nd floor of the post office building.

Tourist service (Naantalin Matkailu; ☑435 9800; www.naantalinmatkailu.fi; Kaivotori 2; ☺9am-6pm Mon-Fri, 10am-4pm Sat & Sun Jun-Aug, 9am-4.30pm Mon-Fri Sep-May) By the harbour. Internet access.

❶ Getting There & Away

Buses to Naantali (routes 11 and 110) run every 15 minutes from the market square (opposite Hansa Shopping Arcade) in Turku (€4.50, 20 minutes).

S/S *Ukkopekka* sails between Turku and Naantali in summer, arriving at the passenger quay on the south side of the harbour. For more information see p87.

Finnlink (http://passenger.finnlines.com) offers a fast service to Kapellskär (€45 plus car from €30, eight hours), 90km north of Stockholm in Sweden, up to three times daily. The ferry includes two meals, and berths are available. All passengers must board with a vehicle.

Askainen

The village of Askainen, 30km northwest of Turku, contains the palatial **Louhisaari Manor** (☑024-312 515; adult/under 18yr €5/free; ☺11am-5pm mid-May–Aug), built in 1655 by the influential Fleming family. When one of their number squandered the family fortune, the manor was sold to the Mannerheims, so becoming the birthplace of Finland's greatest military leader and president, Marshal CGE Mannerheim. Naturally it attracts lots of interested Finns – cameras flash and there's a definite hint of jostling at the Blue Bedchamber where the marshal was born. Entry is by a 45-minute tour only (every 30 minutes, in Finnish): follow the Finnish guide with an English brochure, or see if the obliging staff can arrange an English-language tour for you.

The village and manor are located just off Rd 193. Buses (with a change in Lemu) are rare.

Nousiainen

Nousiainen, 25km north of Turku, is noteworthy for its medieval **church** (☺noon-6pm Tue-Sun). It was the first resting place of St Henry, an Englishman and Swedish-consecrated bishop who was the first to bring Christianity to the Finns (with a little accompanying light war) in the mid 12th century.

His bones were taken to Turku Cathedral in the 13th century. The current church postdates this, having been largely built in the 14th century and restored in the 1960s.

Hourly buses (€5.70) from Turku to Mynämäki stop at Nousiainen.

Turku Archipelago

📷02

Twenty-thousand islands and skerries make up the Turku archipelago. The five largest inhabited islands – from east to west, Pargas, Nagu, Korpo, Houtskär and Iniö – are clustered in a tight crescent, and are known collectively as Väståboland (Länsi-Turunmaan). There are no 'big sights' as such, just quiet settlements, lots of birdlife, and ever-changing views of sea and land. It makes best sense to cycle so you can appreciate the details – picking wild strawberries in the verges, watching Arctic terns swoop, dabbling your toes in a silent inlet.

🛏 Sleeping

The tourist offices can help with accommodation bookings; and the brochure *Comfortable Accommodation in the Turku Archipelago*, available from tourist offices, has a good list of private cottages and B&Bs.

ℹ Information

Archipelago Booking (📷02-410 6600; www.archipelagobooking.com) Particularly useful for booking cottages.

Turku City Tourist Office (📷02-262 7444; www.turkutouring.fi) Also has useful information on the archipelago.

Turun Saaristo (📷040-011 7123; www.visitarchipelago.com) The best all-round source of information.

ℹ Getting There & Away

Out as far as Houtskär, the islands almost join, making them easy enough to explore by public transport, car or bicycle. From mid-May to September, you can complete the 250km circular **Archipelago Trail** from Turku by hopping between the main islands and islets, which are linked by eight ferries and a dozen bridges. More forward planning is required as you travel further round the crescent, particularly if you don't have your own transport.

It's possible to island-hop even further – all the way over to Åland by skipping from Galtby in Korpo out to Kökar (p132) and on to Mariehamn; or from Osnäs in Kustavi out to Brändö (p132) and on to Mariehamn.

Frequent, free ferries run continually between Pargas, Nagu and Korpo, with less frequent crossings from Korpo to Houtskär, and summer-only private ferries from Houtskär to Iniö. For details of all ferries and timetables, see **Ferryportal** (www.lautat.fi).

PARGAS

Hard-working Pargas (Finnish: Parainen), once a Hansa League port, is the de facto 'capital' of the archipelago. It still has a substantial port and its limestone quarry – Finland's largest – is a major employer. The archipelago's main **tourist office** (📷040-011 7123; www.visitarchipelago.com; Rantatie 28; ☉9am-5pm Mon-Fri, 10am-2pm Sat Jul–mid-Aug, 9am-4pm Mon-Fri mid-Aug–Jun) can help out with information on all the islands.

◉ Sights & Activities

When Lenin was on the lam from Russia to Stockholm in 1907, he stayed in Pargas under the pseudonym Mr Mueller. The outdoor **Local History Museum** (Storgårdsgatan 13; admission €2; ☉11am-4pm Tue-Sun Jun-Aug) contains the house where he hid, along with cottages, crofts and a restored schoolhouse; enthusiastic tour guides show visitors round. For more on Lenin in Finland, see p317.

The old town of **wooden houses** is behind **Pargas Church** (Kyrkoesplanaden 4), a beautiful early-14th-century building with whitewashed walls, medieval murals and brick-Gothic supports.

Just 10km on the Nagu–Pargas road, **Sattmark** (☉noon-7pm Jun-Aug) is a charming 18th-century red wooden sailor's cottage with a cafe and rustic handicrafts, plus a few nature trails and ski tracks.

The **M/S Autere** (📷040-052 4151; one way adult/4-11yr/bicycle €15/10/5) sails from Pargas to Nagu and back daily in July and early August.

🛏 Sleeping & Eating

Hotel Kalkstrand   HOTEL €€
(📷511 6200; www.strandbo.fi; Rantatie 1; s/d €78/96) A comfortable hotel on the edge of town, Kalkstrand is close to the harbour and many of its 38 rooms look out at the sea – try to get one of these, as the alternative is a view of the cement factory! A new sauna has recently been built, and there's a good restaurant.

Solliden Camping   CAMPGROUND €
(📷040-514 2354; www.solliden.fi; Norrby; tent sites €12.50 plus per person €4, 4-/8-person cottages €60/135; ☉May-Sep) Pargas' seaside camping ground, 1.5km north of the centre, with camping, a range of cottages that sleep up to eight, saunas and a laundry.

ℹ Getting There & Away

Numerous buses run to/from Turku (€5.70, 40 minutes). If you want to explore some of the more obscure islands, **Rosita** (☏213 1500; www.rosita.fi) island-hops out to Nötö Aspö and Utö.

NAGU

Nagu (Finnish: Nauvo) is an idyllic island nestling between Pargas and Korpo. Its guest harbour attracts yachties and cruise ships, so a lot of the action centres there – it's super-Swedish in feel, with a string of shoreside huts selling souvenirs and designer sailor-wear.

Lovely **Nagu church** (☉Jun-late Aug) dates from the 14th century and contains an impressive votive ship and the oldest Bible in Finland. There are some pleasant little walking trails in the area, and at the harbour in summer, **Skärgårdscykel** (per 4hr/day €7.50/15) hires bicycles. You can also hit the water with **MyKayak** (☏045-322 4555; www.mykayak.fi; per day/week €35/140).

🛏 Sleeping & Eating

Hotel Stranbo   HOTEL €€
(☏460 6200; Strandvägen 3; s/d from €87/115; ℗@) This is the sophisticated option at the guest harbour. Four buildings offer rooms in a variety of styles. The loveliest by far are the three light and airy bedrooms in the stately wooden seafront building, with balconies looking over the waves. A good restaurant offers a great lunch buffet and evening à la carte.

Västergård   B&D €€
(☏040-586 1317; www.nagu.net/vastergard; Gyttjavägen 29, Gyttja; s/d €55/90; ℗) In a super-peaceful spot, 12km from Nagu, this B&B is particularly sympathetic to cyclists. It has cosy rooms with private bathrooms, based in a beautifully converted barn. Bicycles (seven-/21-speed €15/20 per day, electric bikes €30 per day) and kayaks (€18 per day) are available, and dinner (€30) can be provided on request.

Hotel Stallbacken & Grännäs B&B   HOTEL, B&B €€
(☏0400-611 348; www.grannasgard.fi; Grännäsintie 14, Grännäs; B&B s/d €60/90, hotel s/d €80/120; ℗) Grännäs B&B guests get to share the hotel facilities – a private beach, summer à la carte restaurant, tennis court, sauna and boat, bike and canoe rental. The hamlet Grännäs is about 3km south of Nagu, just off the main road.

KORPO

Korpo (Finnish: Korppoo) is the perfect place to ship out to the Åland archipelago but is remote enough to be an intriguing destination in its own right. The friendly folk at **Restaurang Hjalmars** (☏463 1202; Köpmansvägen 2; ☉11am-9pm Mon-Thu, to 2am Fri & Sat, noon-8pm Sun) have tourist information in English. A highlight is the medieval **Korpo church** (☉10am-5pm Jun-Aug), built in the late 13th century and featuring naive ceiling frescoes and a statue of St George fighting a dragon. The main harbour is **Galtby** (3km east of Korpo village), which connects to Kökar (p132).

🛏 Sleeping & Eating

Faffas B&B   B&B €€
(☏464 6106; www.faffas.fi; s/d €45/70; ℗) A dignified old farmhouse, complete with corner stove in the downstairs bedroom, this four-roomed B&B looks out onto fields and has its own serene bathing pier a short walk away. In summer, there are also three simple cabins for rent from around €60. Payment by cash only. About 8km east of Korpo village.

Buffalo Ravintola   STEAKHOUSE €€
(www.restaurangbuffalo.com; Verkan guest harbour; mains €15-25; ☉11am-midnight Mon-Thu, to 3am Fri & Sat, to 10pm Sun late Jun–mid-Aug) Unsurprisingly, given its name, Buffalo specialises in steaks, but there are also fresh fish dishes and a couple of options to keep vegetarians content. Its sun-drenched waterside terrace is a prime spot for long lingering with a cold beer.

ℹ Getting There & Away

Regular buses go to Turku (€14.40, two hours). There's an hourly ferry from Galtby harbour to Houtskär (30 minutes). The trip from Galtby to Kökar takes 2¼ hours. It's free for passengers and bicycles, and €29 for cars.

Passenger ferries leave from nearby Verkan to outlying islands like Berghamn, Storpensar, Lillpensar, Käldersö and Elvsö.

HOUTSKÄR & INIÖ

Houtskär and its tiny neighbour Iniö are delightfully tranquil, if a little short of sights. Both islands have Swedish-speaking populations.

Houtskär's two ports are **Mossala** in the north and **Kittius** in the south, with **Näsby** between them. You can pitch camp or rent a cabin at Mossala's **Skärgårdens Fritidscenter** (☏463 3322; www.saaristo.com; tent sites

€15, cabins around €60 per person), which also has a restaurant and rents boats.

The modest **museum** (admission €2; ☉noon-4pm Mon, 1-7pm Tue-Fri, noon-4pm Sat & Sun Jun-early Aug) in Näsby includes a small windmill, restored dairy shed and period home, and can help with tourist information.

Iniö boasts the sweet stone **church of Sofia Wilhelmina**, built in the 18th century. You may also see **Midsummer poles** (see p124) if you're visiting in summer, but mostly the area is a good place for nature strolls.

The summer route between Houtskär (Mossala) and Iniö (adult/bicycle/car €6/3/15, one hour) is privately operated by **Arctia** (☏0400-320 049; www.arctia.fi).

KUSTAVI

The island village of Kustavi (Swedish: Gustavs) represents the final piece of the Archipelago Trail puzzle, offering scenic seascapes and a jumping-off point for the Åland islands.

Kustavi's wooden **church** (☉May–mid-Aug), built in 1783, features the cruciform shape and votive miniature ships common in coastal churches. It's possible to charter a boat from Kustavi to **Isokari lighthouse** and to **Katanpää Fort Island** – ask at the **tourist office** (☏842 6620; www.kustavi.fi; Keskustie 7; ☉8.30am-4pm Mon-Sat Jun-Aug). A great place to eat is **Peterzéns** (☏050-350 8346; www.peterzens.fi; Kustavi; ☉noon-10pm Jun-Aug), with outdoor tables on a picturesque wooden deck.

❶ Getting There & Away

A free ferry, the M/S *Aurora,* runs from Iniö to Kustavi (25 minutes). To complete the circle back to Turku, there are around four direct buses (€12.80, 1½ hours).

To hop across to the Åland archipelago, head for the port of Osnäs (Finnish: Vuosnainen) on the western tip of the island. From here, there are regular passenger ferries to Långö on northern Brändö (p132), with booking through **Ålandstrafiken** (☏018-525 100; www.alandstrafiken.ax; bicycle/car €5/12).

Kimito Island & Archipelago National Park

☏02

Kimito is the jumping-off point for the Archipelago National Park, a scattering of islands that stretches south of Korpo and west of Kasnäs. **Kasnäs**, the harbour on the southern extreme of Kimito Island, is the best place from which to explore the park, though it's worth breaking a journey at either **Dragsfjärd** or the township of Kimito. Swedish is the prominent language in this area and you'll hear it more if you journey into the islands of the archipelago such as Hittis or Bengtskär.

◉ Sights & Activities

Dragsfjärd, in the southwest of Kimito Island, is a quiet, rural village with a gold-coloured **church** dating back to 1755. The manor house of **Söderlångvik** (☏424 662; www.soderlangvik.fi; Amos Andersonvägen 2; adult/child €3.50/free; ☉11am-6pm mid-May–Aug) belonged to local newspaper magnate and art collector Amos Anderson. There are paintings, furniture and special exhibitions in this beautiful manor, as well as an extensive garden and a cafe.

Near Kimito village, **Sagalund Museum** (☏421 738; www.sagalund.fi; adult/under 7yr €5/free; ☉11am-6pm Jun-Aug) is an open-air museum with more than 20 old buildings including a traditional sauna and blacksmith. There are guided tours every hour.

If you're looking at exploring the national park, make for the **Visitor Centre Blåmussian** (☏020-564 4620; Kasnäs; ☉10am-5pm daily mid-May–Aug, 10am-3pm Tue-Fri, to 5pm Sat Sep–mid-Nov & Mar–mid-May, closed mid-Nov–Mar) for further information. The centre organises tours to some islands in June, July and August, depending on demand, and offers tips on nature trails in the area. There are also several films in English (most around 10 minutes long). It's on a small dirt road just away from the pier.

M/S Aura (☏0400-320 092) runs up to eight times daily to Hitis (Hiittinen), which is known for its wooden church. There's also a good one-day round trip (€55; 11am June to August) that goes to **Bengtskär's lighthouse** (www.bengtskar.fi; ☉10am-7pm Jun-Aug), Scandinavia's tallest, calling in on the way at the **Rosala Viking Centre** (www.rosala.fi; ☉10am-6pm Jun-Aug), which looks at Viking ships and daily life. The trip includes lunch at the centre.

🛏 Sleeping

Hostel Panget   HOSTEL €€

(☏424 553; www.panget.fi; Kulla; s/d €59/88) At the turn-off to Dragsfjärd, Hostel Panget is a pleasant spot, recently renovated and under fresh new management. Rooms are comfortable – all have a private toilet, and the four-person rooms also have a private shower. There are several common areas, including a pub downstairs and a well-stocked kitchen.

Hotel Kasnäs SPA HOTEL €€€
(☑521 0100; www.kasnas.com; Kasnäs; s/d/ste €88/126/210; ℗@⊠) At the end of the road, this sprawling hotel complex is perfect for pampering before heading further out. Facilities include a modern spa complex with a 25m pool. Rooms are spread over several buildings and there's an excellent restaurant and a terrace.

ⓘ Information

Tourist office (☑426 0170; www.visitkimitoon.fi; Villa Lande, Engelsbyntie 8, Kemiö; ☉10am-4pm Mon-Fri) Has bikes for hire.
Visitor Centre Blåmussian (☑020-564 4620; Kasnäs; ☉10am-5pm daily mid-May–Aug, 10am-3pm Tue Fri, to 5pm Sat Sep–mid-Nov & Mar–mid-May) Has good information on exploring the national park.

ⓘ Getting There & Around

There are several daily bus-and ferry connections from Dragsfjärd (Taalintehdas) to Turku (€16.20, 1¾ hours), less frequently to Helsinki (€30.60, three to four hours). To get here by car, turn off onto Rd 52, then Rd 183, from Salo, which will take you to Kimito village. Taxi boats are common – ask the tourist office for a list.

SOUTH COAST

The south coast is absolutely packed with characterful little towns. The great empires of Sweden and Russia fought for centuries over its juicy ports. Today they're commandeered by castles and fortresses that seem at total odds with the sunshine, smiles and sailing boats. Star-shaped Hamina, the Russian villas at Hanko, the tsar's fishing lodge near Kotka and Svartholma Sea Fortress off Loviisa's shore all show the unique influence of the Swedish–Russian tussle. Inland you'll find charming *bruk* (ironworks precinct) towns such as Fiskars; and Lohja, home to many of Helsinki's summer houses.

🏃 Activities

The south coast is a boaties' paradise, with numerous islets forming chains of archipelagos. Most towns offer summer cruises, guest harbour facilities, charter boats so you can discover your own island, and canoe and rowing boat hire.

Fishing is popular, with the Kymijoki just north of Kotka renowned as a great salmon water. The sizeable Lohjanjärvi, by the town of Lohja, is a good venue for ice-fishing in winter and lake sports in summer.

The region makes for brilliant cycling, with marked routes along the Kuninkaantie (tourist route from Bergen to St Petersburg) both west and east from Helsinki. There's also good horse riding to be had in the forests around Ingå.

West of Helsinki

To the west of Finland's capital are a scattering of pretty lakeside and coastal towns and villages. The holiday cottages in Lohja and the summery seaside towns of Ekenäs and Hanko are popular escapes for Helsinki's citizens.

LOHJA & AROUND
☑019 / POP 39,700
Lohjanjärvi is the biggest lake in these parts, and most of Helsinki's residents seem to have a summer cottage here. The woody environs were the stomping ground of Elias Lönnrot, compiler of the *Kalevala*. The town of Lohja (Swedish: Lojo) keeps the lake houses in beer and supplies, but has few actual sights.

LOHJA
Five hundred metres north of the town centre, **Tytyrin Kaivosmuseo** (Tytyri Mine Museum; adult/5-16yr €13/7; ☉tours noon & 2pm late Jun–mid-Jul, also 4pm mid-Jul–mid-Aug) is an authentic working limestone mine well worth a visit – book tours through the tourist office. A funicular takes you 80m down into the earth; good information panels in English explain the mine's traditions (here, as elsewhere in Finland, new mine shafts were painted with tar to keep out devils); and the visit culminates in a sound-and-light presentation looking into an awesomely large quarried cavern.

Lohja's church **Pyhän Laurin Kirkko** (St Lawrence Church; ☉9am-8pm Mon-Fri Jun-Aug, to 3pm Sep-May) has a great wooden bell tower and is renowned for its medieval murals. Rustic and naive in style, they depicted biblical stories for the illiterate population of the early 16th century.

Lohja Museum (Iso-Pappila; admission €4.50; ☉noon-4pm Tue-Sun, to 7pm Wed) re-creates a schoolhouse and a cowherd's cottage with an impressive range of horse-drawn carriages, including an old-style hearse. The main building is the former vicarage, and has innovative special exhibitions in summer.

You can wet your whistle at **Opus K** (Kauppakatu 6; ☺3pm-11pm Tue-Thu, 2pm-2am Fri, noon-2am Sat), which is one of Finland's best pubs, lined floor to ceiling with books and always with a new discovery from an obscure Finnish microbrewery.

The **tourist office** (☑369 1309; www.visitlohja .fi; Hossanmäentie 1; ☺9am-6pm Mon-Fri, 9.30am-2pm Sat Jun-Aug, 9am-4pm Mon-Fri Sep-May; @) has information on cottages around the lake, as well as information on canoeing and fishing in summer, and ice-fishing and cross-country skiing in winter.

Buses run hourly from Helsinki to Lohja (€11, one hour). There are also buses from Lohja to Salo and Turku, and to Ekenäs and Hanko on the south coast.

AROUND LOHJA

The limestone-rich soil around the lake is ideal for growing apples and you'll see orchards dotting the shores. The tourist office has a comprehensive booklet about local cider- and wine-producers. One of the largest is **Alitalo** (www.ciderberg.fi; Pietiläntie 138), on Lohjansaari, with thousands of apple trees, a cafe and gentle farm animals.

If you've got your own boat, or are passing through Virkkala (7km south of Lohja), the place for a summery drink is definitely **Kaljaasi** (☑040-522 6612; ☺noon-11pm Sun-Thu, to midnight Fri & Sat May–mid-Aug). The bar floats on a platform in the middle of the lake and makes for a scenic watering hole as pleasure boats dock right before you. They'll collect you from Virkkala (€14 each way).

Twenty-three kilometres northwest of Lohja, and 5km north of the village of Sammatti, just off Rd 104, is **Paikkari Cottage** (Torpantie 20; admission €3; ☺11am-5pm mid-May–Aug), the birthplace of Elias Lönnrot, compiler of the *Kalevala* (see p331). It's an endearing cottage set amid summer-flowering meadows that would have motivated Lönnrot's Arcadian vision but today inspire picnics. Inside there's a small museum to the man that includes his *kantele* (Karelian stringed instrument).

INGÅ
☑09 / POP 5560

The demure seaside village of Ingå (Finnish: Inkoo) is a predominantly Swedish-speaking town with a little marina that holds a library and cafe, a pottery workshop, and not much else. It makes a good day trip but you'd be twiddling your thumbs if you stayed the night here.

St Nicholas Church (☺8am-4pm Mon-Fri year-round, 9am-6pm Sat & Sun May-Aug) was founded in the 13th century. There are beautiful frescoes over the altar, but most striking is the Dance of Death frieze opposite the entrance door. In this frieze, grinning Reapers escort various members of society to the afterlife; all are equal in death. Across the river is **Ingå Gammelgård**, the local museum.

About 8km west of Ingå, **Fagervik Ironworks** (☑0400-673 664; Rd 105) was established in 1646 as a *bruk* and makes a quieter alternative to Fiskars. The Russian army razed the area during the Great Northern War in the 1720s, but the factory was rebuilt forging iron blades and ploughs until finally closing in 1902. It's a pleasant stroll to the 18th-century wooden church located by a lake, and the nearby privately owned manor that includes a resident ghost, the enigmatic Blue Lady.

Ingå is about 40km southwest of Helsinki on Rd 51, with several daily bus connections.

EKENÄS
☑019

Seaside Ekenäs (Finnish: Tammisaari) is a resort town, dozy in winter but brimming with holidaying Finns and Swedes when the sun comes out. The avenues of wooden buildings in its well-preserved Old Town are charming, though less spectacular than those at Rauma (p220). In 2009 the town combined with neighbours Karis and Pojo to become 'Raseborg' – tourist information about Ekenäs is often labelled with the new name.

Ekenäs is one of Finland's oldest towns – King Gustav Vasa conceived of it in 1546 as a trading port to rival Tallinn in Estonia. Its fortunes failed and many of its artisans were moved to Helsinki. Today it's a popular holiday destination (due to its proximity to both Helsinki and Turku) with a healthy fishing industry. It's the best base from which to explore the Ekenäs Archipelago National Park.

⊙ Sights & Activities

Gamla Stan   HISTORIC DISTRICT
Well-preserved Gamla Stan (Old Town) features wooden houses mostly from the 18th century, the result of the Swedish movement to create artisan centres for trade. So, narrow streets are named Hattmakaregatan (Hatters' St), Linvävaregatan (Linen Weavers' St) and after other types of artisans who worked in this precinct. Most

of the Old Town is residential, which gives it a deserted, untouristy air. The buildings themselves are named after types of fish, harking back to the area's fishing-village origins.

Gamla Stan's stone **church** (Stora Kyrkogatan; ⊗10am-6pm May-Aug) has a tower that can be seen from anywhere in town. It was constructed between 1651 and 1680, destroyed in the fire of 1821, and rebuilt in 1841 in the new classical style.

Ekenäs Museum   MUSEUM
(☑289 2512; Gustav Wasasgatan 11; admission €5; ⊗11am-5pm mid-May–Aug, closed Mon & reduced hours rest of year) Built in 1802, this is an interesting exhibit on Ekenäs through the ages, tracing its history back to the Stone Age using creative models and audio. The Lindblad building re-creates a 1950s photographer's studio, and a small row of 19th-century red-painted outbuildings contain agricultural implements and (brace yourselves) the alarming sound of invisible pigs.

BY THE SEA
The small family beach has a **water slide and diving board** where you swim just metres away from preening swans, plus there's minigolf. Bicycles (per day €10) can be hired at the marina from the **Guest Harbour Café** (☑241 1790; www.ekenasport.fi; Norra Strandgatan; ⊗8.30am-10pm Mon-Sat, from 10am Sun). You can also rent rowing boats and bikes at the camping ground.

Paddlingsfabriken (☑0400-411 992; www.paddlingsfabriken.fi) offers lessons and guided paddles, including an awesome one-day safari (€69) from Snappertuna's Raseborg Castle (p104) to Ekenäs – check the website for trip dates. If you want to go it alone, it will also rent kayaks to experienced paddlers.

☞ Tours

Saaristön Laivaristeilyt   BOAT
(☑241 1850; www.surfnet.fi/saaristoristeilyt; ⊗Sat & Sun May, Fri-Sun Jun, Wed-Sun Jul, Thu-Sun Aug) The company offers archipelago cruises aboard the 100-year-old former steamship M/S *Sunnan II*. Cruises last from two to four hours depending on the destination, and cost from €15 to €25 – see the website for the full timetable. All depart from the passenger harbour.

For cruises to Hanko, see p108.

⌂ Sleeping

There are three hotels and no large guesthouses in Ekenäs. The tourist office has details of homestays and cottage and apartment rentals.

Hotel Sea Front   HOTEL €€
(☑246 1500; www.hotelseafront.fi; Pojogatan 2; s/d from €80/100; P) Set a little way from the main harbour, this secluded spot feels like your own intimate yellow summer cottage, with a private pier if you need to park your yacht. It's well kept, and bayside rooms (prices a tad higher) have great little balconies.

Ekenäs Stadshotell   HOTEL €€
(☑241 3131; www.kaupunginhotelli.fi; Norra Strandgatan 1; s/d from €90/100; P) Showing its age a little, this large hotel, situated slap bang between the main square and the sea, does well with families and functions. Balcony rooms, with views over the park to the water, cost a smidge extra. The suites include a private sauna, DVD and bone-soaking bath.

Ormnäs Camping   CAMPGROUND €
(☑241 4434; www.ek-camping.com; tent sites €12 plus per person €4, 2-/4-person cottages €37/58; ⊗May-Sep) Within walking distance of town, this easygoing camping ground has its own slice of the beach and expertly caters to Finnish families, with a sauna included in the price, and bikes (€10 per day) and rowing boats (€20 per 24 hours) for hire.

HORSING AROUND INGÅ

The thick woods around Ingå make for some excellent horse riding and the stables around here have some interesting breeds. Prices are around €85 per half-day depending on your horse and need for lessons. Call ahead at any of the following stables:

Shetland Pony Rolle (☑045-651 5457, 050-651 5456; Södergårdsvägen 41, Solberg) Offers the chance to ride Shetlands with guides.

Taikatalli (☑044-9108217; www.taikatalli.fi; Ingarskilavägen 145, Täkter) Does activities on horses, or mules for beginners.

Violan talli (☑050-544 7018; www.violantalli.com; Västankvarnvägen 576) Has what the Finns call 'island horses', with lessons and guided rides.

✕ Eating

Several good cafes border the main square, Rådhustorget, including **Café Carl de Mumma** (⊙9am-5pm Mon-Fri, to 2pm Sat), an ever-popular bakery that does pastries, rolls and coffee; but be warned – its fabulous blueberry cheesecake sells out fast.

TOP CHOICE **Ada Café** BISTRO €

(☑040-801 4444; www.ada.fi; Norra Strandgatan 7; mains €20-26; ⊙dinner Wed-Sun, lunch Sat & Sun) Ada opened in 2009 and immediately seized the crown for 'best restaurant in town'. Just by the guest harbour, its cool, calm interior has large windows to let in the sea views. Dishes look absolutely magnificent, and taste just as good. The short, creative menu changes with the seasons – depending on when you visit, goodies on offer might include black pudding and lingonberry, fried perch or duck tagine.

Café Gamla Stan CAFE €

(www.cafegamlastan.fi, in Swedish; Bastugatan 5; cakes €3-6, lunches €6-13; ⊙11am-7pm May-Aug) This secluded garden cafe in the Old Town has tables under a shady apple orchard, which it uses to make its own juice. It's family run and there's plenty of home baking to sample, plus a craft shop and live music.

Knipan FINNISH €€

(☑241 1169; www.knipan.fi; Strandallén; mains €18-28; ⊙noon-10pm Mon-Sat, to 8pm Sun Jun-late Aug) This summer restaurant turned 100 in 2008, though the pier building has been here since 1867. It affords the best views in town, with a brief menu of Finnish favourites, particularly meat mains and seafood such as smoked pike with damsons.

Bossa Nova ITALIAN €€

(☑239 5000; www.bossanova.fi; Ormnäsvägen 1; pizzas €12, mains €20-25; ⊙lunch & dinner summer) Overlook the slow service, and you have here a pleasing summer restaurant, a 2km stroll from town, right next door to Ormnäs Camping. A spacious wooden terrace steps its way down towards the water, so you can watch the boats and jet-skiers while you're waiting for your food – cartwheel-sized pizzas and tasty meatballs, grilled salmon and pan-fried duck breast.

❶ Information

Naturum Visitor Centre (☑020-564 4613; ⊙10am-8pm Jul, to 3pm May, to 6pm Jun & Aug) If you're thinking of heading out to the Ekenäs Archipelago, a visit here is the place to start.

Public library (Raseborgsvägen 6-8; ⊙10am-7pm Mon-Fri Jun-Aug, 10am-8pm Mon-Fri, to 2pm Sat Sep-May) Free internet terminals.

Tourist office (☑289 2010; www.visitraseborg. com; Rådhustorget; ⊙8.30am-6pm Mon-Fri, 10am-2pm Sat summer, 8.30am-4pm Mon-Fri winter) Free internet terminal. Offers information for the entire southwest region.

❶ Getting There & Around

Ekenäs is 96km southwest of Helsinki on Rd 25. There are five to seven buses a day from Helsinki (€17.40, 1½ hours), Turku (with a transfer in Salo; €17.40, two hours) or Hanko (€7.70, 35 minutes).

Trains to Ekenäs coming from Helsinki and Turku go via Karis (Finnish: Karjaa), where a change is required. Seven to nine daily trains run from Helsinki (€17.90, 1½ hours) and Turku (€21, 1½ hours), both continuing on to Hanko (€4.80, 25 minutes). Some connections from Ekenäs to Karis involve a railbus.

The town is spread out and reasonably hilly: if you're puffed, get a **taxi** (☑106 9191) from the market square.

AROUND EKENÄS

EKENÄS ARCHIPELAGO NATIONAL PARK

Almost 90% of this 5200-hectare park is water, so to explore the 1300 islands you'll need to take a tour from Ekenäs harbour (p103) or charter your own boat – the tourist office keeps a list of charter craft. For information on the park and on where to stay, visit the Naturum Visitor Centre in Ekenäs.

The most popular island is **Älgö**, which has a 2km nature trail that takes in the island's observation tower. There's an old fisherman's home that's been converted to include a sauna and facilities for several camp sites, which can be booked through Naturum. There are also camping grounds on the islands of **Fladalandet** and **Modermagan**, but visits to many other islands are prohibited, particularly the ecologically fragile outer islands.

SNAPPERTUNA

☑019

The wonderfully named village of Snappertuna makes for a good stay away from it all. The small open-air folk **museum** (☑289 2500; admission €1; ☑noon-5pm Tue-Sun Jun-Aug) re-creates the life of farmers and fisherfolk in the village.

A 300m forest walk leads from the museum to **Raseborg Castle** (Finnish: Raasepori; ☑234 015; www.raseborg.org; admission €2;

⊙10am-8pm Jun–mid-Aug, to 5pm May & late Aug), the mightiest sight in the area. Dating from the late 14th century, the castle looms on a high rock overlooking a grassy sward. It was strategically crucial in the 15th century, when it protected the trading town of Tuna, and Karl Knutsson Bonde, the exiled king of Sweden, held his court here. By the mid-16th century, Raseborg's importance had declined, and it was deserted for more than 300 years. There's not a lot of explanatory material in English, but it's great to climb up and down the levels and patrol the ramparts. The castle is also the setting for various events, including a medieval market and tournament: contact Ekenäs tourist office (p104) for details.

There are a few good overnight options. **Snappertuna Youth Hostel** (☑044-941 9757, 234 180; Kyrkoväg 129; per person €20; ⊙May-Sep; Ⓟ) has 16 beds in four basic cabins, just a few hundred metres from the castle. Payment is in cash only. For a slightly more upmarket bed, **Norrby Gård** (☑040-742 2670; www.norrbygard. net; Norrbyvägen 277; per person €40; Ⓟ@) has rudimentary double rooms (breakfast extra) in a recently renovated building with shared bathrooms and a small sauna (€5).

There are a few Monday to Friday term-time buses (€5.70, 40 minutes) to Snappertuna from Ekenäs.

FISKARS
☑019 / POP 200

This historic village is best known outside Finland for the design company that produced iconic orange-handled scissors in the 1960s. It's the most attractive of several small *bruk* villages in this area, with its green river sidling between old brick buildings. Its ironworks, which began in 1649 with a single furnace, went on to make millions of horse-ploughs.

Today its quaint buildings, many of which display CL Engel's neoclassical flair, contain fabulous crafty shops, design studios and cafes (open from 11am to 5pm in summer, weekends only the rest of the year) – your credit card will be smoking by the end of the day. Those famous scissors – still made by Fiskars, but not here – are a particularly practical souvenir.

There's a **tourist information office** (☑277 7504; www.fiskarsvillage.fi; ⊙10am-6pm Mon-Sat May-end Aug) located in the workers' tenement buildings, near the distinctive clock-tower building.

⊙ Sights

Starting from the car park at the western (Pohja) end of Fiskars, with the river on your right, the first building on the left is the **Assembly Hall**, built in 1896 as a public hall. Just beyond is the 1902 **Granary**, which now hosts various exhibitions and is approached from the top via a bridge. Behind it is the **Copper Forge**, built in 1818, with more exhibition space, a glass studio and restaurant with a riverside terrace.

Continuing along the road, you pass the centrepiece of the village, **Stenhuset**, which was the mansion originally occupied by factory owner John Julin, and the old mill. The distinctive red-brick **clock-tower building** – originally a school – has characteristic CL Engel flourishes and now hosts houses, a cafe and the Fiskars shop itself, with a large free exhibition on the history of the company. Also in this row is **Onoma** (www.onoma.org; Fiskarsintie), one of the best design shops, selling unusual crafts and homewares produced by members of the Fiskars' Cooperative. Where the road forks is the marketplace with stalls and an outdoor cafe in summer. Continuing along the unpaved road towards Degersjojärvi, you pass more **workers' housing** and what remains of **Fiskars ironworks**.

Near the lake is **Fiskars Museum** (admission €3; ⊙11am-5pm Mon-Fri, to 4pm Sat & Sun May-Sep), which details the ironworks' evolution and the village that grew around it. Every season there is a different display of art and craft, with a special exhibition at Christmas.

🍽 Sleeping & Eating

Fiskars is best done as a day trip – the place becomes a ghost town on the stroke of 5pm – though there is (limited) accommodation if you want to extend your visit.

Fiskars Wärdshus   INN €€
(☑276 6510; www.wardshus.fi; s/d from €121/145; Ⓟ@) This refined inn was built in 1836 and offers upmarket rooms and eating. The neoclassical exterior is a disconnect from the swish Scandinavian chic of the rooms, but they use local timbers and include bathrooms and broadband. The restaurant serves up local game (mains around €28) and does a great three-course lunch (€37) on the scenic terrace.

Restaurant Kuparipaja   BISTRO €€
(www.kuparipaja.fi; mains €20-25; ⊙lunch & dinner summer, reduced hours winter) In the old copper

TURKU & THE SOUTH COAST WEST OF HELSINKI

forge, this is an excellent setting for a long lunch in the à la carte restaurant (sample elk and mutton sausages, if you're feeling carnivorous). The cafe-bar does quick filled rolls, pasta dishes and salad buffet, but it would be a shame not to enjoy the terrace overhanging the river.

In the clock-tower building, **Café Antique** (☉10am-6pm May-Sep) has books and makes for a browsing brunch.

HANKO
🎵 019 / POP 9500

On a long sandy peninsula, adorable little Hanko (Swedish: Hangö) retains the past grandeur of a Chekhov play. It blossomed as a well-to-do Russian spa town in the late 19th century, and its opulent seaside villas, built by wealthy summer visitors, are a star attraction. Locals refer to them as 'the old ladies', as many were named for Russian sweethearts (although newer ones have nautical names).

The population doubles in summer when Finns flock here for the sun and sand. While birdlife like the grey Canada goose summers here, and seals are regular visitors, human guests arrive for the huge Hanko Regatta, which is as famous for its 'spring break' wildness as for its feats of sailing.

History
Hanko, the southernmost town in Finland, was a strategic anchorage well before its foundation in 1874. The Russian Empire used it as a summer holiday destination, but Hanko was also a point of emigration from Finland. Between 1881 and 1931, about 250,000 Finns left for the USA, Canada and Australia via the Hanko docks, with many Finnish descendants tracing their families back to this port town.

At the end of the Winter War, the March 1940 peace treaty with Russia required the ceding of Hanko as a naval base. Its inhabitants evacuated, hauling their belongings on makeshift sledges, as the Russians moved in with a garrison of 30,000 and constructed a huge network of fortifications. After several bloody naval engagements, Hanko was eventually abandoned in December 1941, having been isolated from the Russian front lines. The citizens of Hanko returned to see their damaged town the following spring.

◉ Sights
The East Harbour (Finland's biggest guest harbour) is the centre of the town's activity in summer, the West Harbour handling only commercial traffic. Russian villas are on Appelgrenintie, east of East Harbour.

Take the lift to the top of the 50m **water tower** (adult/4-14yr €2/1; ☉noon-6pm Jun & Jul,

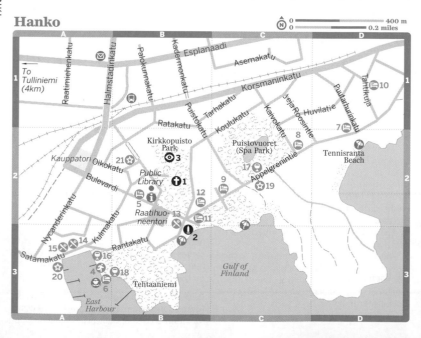

Hanko

1-3pm Aug) on Vartiovuori Hill for an excellent view across town and out to sea. The nearby neo-Gothic **Hanko Church** (☉noon-6pm Jul, 1-3pm to late Aug), built in 1892, was damaged in WWII but has been thoroughly renovated. Photographers love the challenge of aligning the church spire with the town hall and water tower in a single panorama.

Hanko is quite an artistic community, and there are half a dozen **art galleries** scattered around town, including changing exhibitions in the **town hall**. The tourist office has current details.

The Monument of Liberty is one of several impressive pieces of public art, but it's significant for its historical reinvention (see p109).

EAST OF HANKO

Neljän Tuulen Tupa HISTORIC BUILDING
(☉daily mid-May–mid-Aug, Sat & Sun Sep) On Little Pine Island, 1.5km east of the Hanko town centre, is the House of the Four Winds, where locals snuck swigs of 'hard tea' (alcohol) during the Finnish prohibition (1919–32). Field Marshal CGE Mannerheim, who had his summer cottage on the neighbouring island, wouldn't stand for it. Disturbed by the merrymaking, he bought the whole joint in 1927, fired the chef, imported teasets from France and personally ran the place until 1931. Little Pine Island is now connected to the mainland by a bridge and has a beautiful cafe (cakes €2 to €4) and summer terrace, with granite tables carved from the surrounding rocks.

Front Museum MUSEUM
(www.frontmuseum.fi; Lappohja; adult/child €4/2; ☉11.30am-6.30pm late May-early Sep) At the site of some of the worst fighting, 19km northeast of Hanko (on Rd 25), the Front Museum remembers Finland's WWII involvement. This area was occupied by Russia during the war and the people of Hanko were evacuated for a year. There are original trenches, bunkers, artillery guns and the indoor museum – unfortunately mostly in Finnish, but the knowledgeable guide can answer any questions.

🏃 Activities

Hanko is a great place for outdoor activities. With over 30km of beaches, swimming and sunbathing are two of the town's chief attractions. **Tennisranta** beach (Plagen) includes some sweet changing boxes and a fantastic water merry-go-round (move aside, kids).

There's some of Finland's best windsurfing, with good breaks southwest of the guest harbour at **Tulliniemi** and 3km northeast of town at **Silversand** (where natives also swear that you see the most exquisite sunsets). **Surfclub Hanko** (☎040-552 2822; www.surfclubhanko.com), based at Silversand, has surf equipment, kayaks and boats for rent.

SunFun Hanko (☎040-414 5681; www.sunfun.fi; East Harbour) has jet skis (€125 per hour) and motor boats (€105 per four hours) for hire. Its neighbour, **Hanko Diving** (☎040-530 1397; www.hankodiving.com; 2 dives €85; East Harbour), can take you underwater to dive Hanko's many wrecks.

The parklands and Russian villas east of the town centre are best visited by bicycle (see p110), though you can walk out to Neljän Tuulen Tupa on Little Pine Island in under an hour.

👉 Tours & Cruises

Private guided tours (€70 per 1½ hours), including history walks round the town or themed wildlife tours to spot the area's

Hanko

◉ Sights

⊕ Activities, Courses & Tours

🛏 Sleeping

🍽 Eating

☕ Drinking

🎭 Entertainment

elusive elks, can be arranged through the tourist office. There are two excellent cruise companies operating out of East Harbour.

Marine Lines
CRUISE

(☑040-053 6930; www.marinelines.fi) Runs a 5½-hour cruise (adult/four to 14 years €23/55) out to the lighthouse island of Bengtskär (departs 11am in summer), which includes lunch. Also runs a cruise (adult/four to 14 years €40/20 return) to/from Ekenäs (Tammisaari) every Wednesday in July, leaving Hanko at 10.30am and Ekenäs at 3pm.

SunFun Charter
CRUISE

(☑040-414 5681; www.sunfun.fi) Runs a two-hour seal safari (adult/four to 14 years €35/15) departing 11am Thursday and Sunday in July. At 11am on Tuesday and Saturday in July, it also runs two-hour tours (adult/four to 14 years €25/10) to the rock carvings in Hauensuoli (Pike's Gut) strait.

⭐ Festivals & Events

Hanko Regatta
SPORT

(www.hangoregattan.fi, in Swedish) Hanko's massive marina hosts the Hanko Regatta, with more than 200 competing boats. It takes place usually on the first (sometimes second) weekend of July, attracting thousands of spectators with a real carnival atmosphere.

Hanko Theatre Days
THEATRE

(☑050-338 5125, 248 6060; www.hangoteatertraff. org) June brings Finland's biggest festival of Swedish-language theatre and books out hotels throughout the town.

🛏 Sleeping

Accommodation can be tight in the summer months, so book ahead. Prices go up during the regatta. A unique feature of Hanko is its Empire-era Russian-style villas, four of which operate as B&Bs. Don't go expecting luxury, but do go with an open mind and a lively appreciation of history! You can book private accommodation (sometimes in unused villas) through the tourist office.

Hotel Regatta (www.hotelregatta.fi) will reopen in 2012 after a complete overhaul, and a controversial new seafront development containing a luxury hotel is due to open in 2014.

TOP CHOICE Villa Maija
RUSSIAN VILLA €€€

(☑248 2900; www.villamaija.fi; Appelgrenintie 7; s incl breakfast €90-120, d €95-200; ℗) Built in 1888, this is the best villa accommodation. Faultlessly restored rooms are so gosh-darned cosy and packed with character that it's difficult to prise yourself away. Prices vary according to the size of the room, and whether it has a private bathroom and balcony. Out the back are **Villa Janne** and **Villa Anke**, as light-filled and pleasant as the main building. An excellent breakfast is included.

TOP CHOICE Wild Viking Motel
MOTEL €€

(☑040-516 3837; www.wildvikingmotel.fi; Lasitehtaankatu 6; d/q €80/140, cottages €100) OK, this Viking-themed place isn't going to be for everyone and the fact that it's owned by a bikie club might dissuade some, but if you grab it by the horns it's a whole mess of party-flavoured fun. Public areas have a raw-wood pioneer feel that belies the bright, modern-looking rooms (with shared bathrooms). The grounds include a small amphitheatre that rocks out at the motel's summer festival. No longboats for rent, but you can hire a bicycle. The motel is 2km east of Hanko train station, and is well signposted from the main road (Rd 25).

Hotel B8
GUESTHOUSE €€

(☑040-485 1808; www.hotelb8.fi; Bulevardi 8; s €65-110, d €90-150, cells s/d €80/120) Central B8, built inside the former police station, is more guesthouse than hotel, and as such is a little overpriced. But it opened in 2010, so its simple rooms (some with private bathrooms) still feel sparkling new: each one is different, with walls and furnishings given splashes of pattern and colour influenced by iconic Finnish designers. And if you feel like indulging your bad blood, five of the former cells (with handles on both sides of the door) have been fitted out with beds.

Hotelboat Hanko
HOTEL €€

(☑050-061 0113; www.hotellilaivahanko.fi; East Harbour; d €80-200; ☺Jun-Aug) Left your yacht in another harbour? This purpose-built hotel boat gives you an ocean sleep with snug double rooms tricked out with flatscreen TVs and porthole views. The best room aboard features its own 'balcony' on the bow.

Villa Tellina
RUSSIAN VILLA €€

(☑248 6356; www.tellina.com; Appelgrenintie 2; s/d €70/90, d with bathroom €100; ☺Jun-late Aug; ℗) Right by the beach, Tellina is a rambling, paint-peeling villa that looks as though it's seen its share of hidden treasure and wild adventure – it's not for everyone, but we were charmed by the unbeatable sea views and cheerfully eccentric owners. TVs are banished from its basic but light-filled rooms. **Villa Eva** (Kaivokatu 2) and **Villa Thalatta** (Appelgrenintie 1) are owned by the same family, so they often have rooms during busy periods.

Villa Doris   RUSSIAN VILLA €€
(⚟248 1228; Appelgrenintie 23; d incl breakfast from €95; P) Done out in sky-blues and white, this charmer with blooming flower boxes in summer dates back to 1881. Rooms feature period furniture and a great breakfast is included, but it's a shame that service comes with a snarl.

Villa Solgärd   RUSSIAN VILLA €€
(⚟248 1481; Tähtikuja; s/d €50/80; ⊙Jun-Aug) Handy for the Spa Park and nearby beaches, this is a simple villa that makes a good family option, with larger rooms available.

Hanko Camping Silversand   CAMPGROUND €
(⚟248 5500; www.silversand.fi; Hopeahietikko; tent sites €12 plus per person €4, 6-person huts €83; ⊙Jun-Aug) About 3km northeast of the town centre, this camping ground is set on a long surfing beach with good shade, plus sauna and other facilities. Its funny little blue hexagonal huts were being supplemented at the time of writing by fancier cottages, to be completed by 2012.

✖ Eating

East Harbour has a row of red wooden buildings housing four restaurants – pasta, pizza, gourmet and family. It's a lovely spot to eat, but be warned – in summer you pay for the location with high prices, crowded terraces and slow service! During crayfish season (August to September) the flavoursome crustacean scurries over most menus.

Makasiini   SEAFOOD €€
(⚟248 4060; www.makasiini.fi; Satamakatu 9; mains €22-26; ⊙daily summer, dinner Tue-Sat winter) Specialising in tastes from the region, the emphasis falls on fish and seafood. Decor is a pleasing combination of rough wood, snowy napkins and sparkling candles. It's echoed by the food: simple cooking allows the high-quality ingredients to shine, and a long wine list enhances the experience. In summer, the archipelago buffet gives little tastes of crayfish, fish roe, shrimp and fried perch, and the small set menu is supplemented by a blackboard proclaiming the catches of the day.

REWRITING HISTORY?

Where Bulevardi meets the beach, the large obelisk-like **Monument of Liberty** marks an interesting passage in Hanko's history. The town was in Russian hands towards the end of WWI, and when Germany took the town in 1918 they were seen as liberators. The townsfolk collected money to create a monument honouring the Germans who 'assisted our country in the struggle for liberty', as the original inscription read.

In WWII Hanko was again occupied by the Russians, who – none too impressed by an edifice celebrating their military defeat – trashed the monument. After WWII, there was some debate about whether to replace it, since it was now difficult to see Germany as the bringers of liberty; but civic pride prevailed. The monument was remade with a new inscription that reads simply: 'For our liberty'.

🍴**Origo**   ORGANIC €€€
(⚟248 5023; www.restaurant-origo.com; Satamakatu 7; mains €20-30; ⊙lunch & dinner Easter-Dec) Another in the line-up of East Harbour eateries, this one distinguishes itself with a green slant (heating comes courtesy of geothermal energy), local, organic ingredients and a seasonal gourmet menu. Blackened perch is a treat, and even its crayfish soup comes with a croissant. Vegetarians are treated to unusual dishes, such as nettle crêpe with salsify.

Pâ Kroken   SEAFOOD €€
(⚟248 9101; www.pakroken.fi; Hangonkylä Harbour; mains €18-26; ⊙daily summer, Fri-Sun winter) Think you've had good Finnish seafood? With its own smokehouse and boat-fresh lobster and shellfish (it sells to Helsinki's Hakaniemi market), this place will make you think again. The yacht-shaped buffet teems with tasty choices, and its location at the northern harbour makes for great views. To get here, head along Halmstadinkatu and then follow the signs for the harbour.

Alan's Café   CAFE €
(Raatihuoneentori 4; ⊙11am-7pm Mon-Fri, 10am-4pm Sat, noon-4pm Sun May-Jul) Set in an old villa, this place features treats hand baked by the jolly owner; eat in the courtyard,

TURKU & THE SOUTH COAST WEST OF HELSINKI

shaded by a huge tree. With a gift shop and secondhand bookshop attached, it's the ideal place for a post-seaside-stroll cuppa.

Fyren   FISH €€
(☑040-776 2310; www.hangoncasino.fi/fyren; Itä-satama; mains €12-20; ☺lunch & dinner Jun-Aug) You'll need to catch a free ferry out to this little restaurant perched on a rugged granite island. The cane marine interior oozes comfort and the short menu is no-nonsense fish and pasta fare, including a rib-sticking 'lighthouse keeper's fry-up'.

🍷 Drinking & Entertainment

There are excellent summertime beer terraces in East Harbour, including Roxx (snacks €4-6), which is a hang-out for Hanko's youth, and the 2nd floor of HSF (www.ravintolakatu.fi; ☺summer), Hanko Yacht Club's top-notch restaurant.

Park Café   BAR
(www.restaurangpark.fi; Appelgrenintie 11; ☺from 4pm May-Sep) Opposite the Casino in Spa Park, this converted gymnastics hall makes for a brilliant evening's boozing, with barbecues and live bands. With a range of international beers including stout, it makes a good warm-up for the casino.

Casino   CASINO
(www.hangoncasino.fi; Appelgrenintie 10; ☺kitchen daily, casino 6pm-11pm Thu-Sat May-Aug) The imposing green-and-white casino has long been a celebrated nightspot in Hanko, with roulette and terrace drinking. Opening hours stretch to 4am on nights when there is live music and dancing.

Hangon Tivoli   BAR, CLUB
(www.hangontivoli.com; Satamakatu 4; ☺Fri & Sat 7pm-4am Jun-Aug) This hip spot has drinking and dancing in a deep-red building, with a massive fairylighted terrace and partying crowds.

Kino Olympia   CINEMA
(☑248 1811; Vuorikatu 11; ☺Thu-Sun) An independent cinema since 1919.

❶ Information

Public library (Vuorikatu 3-5; ☺11am-7pm Mon-Wed, to 5pm Thu, 9am-3pm Fri, plus 9am-3pm Sat winter) Several free internet terminals.
Tourist office (☑220 3411; www.hanko.fi; Raatihuoneentori 5; ☺10am-6pm Mon-Thu, to 8pm Fri, to 4pm Sat & Sun late Jun-Aug, 9am-4pm Mon-Fri Sep-late Jun). Super-helpful office with a large list of private accommodation.

❶ Getting There & Around

The bus and train stations are a little way from the town centre and beachside villas.

There are two to six daily express buses to/from Helsinki (€23.90, 2¼ hours) via Ekenäs (€7.70, 35 minutes).

Seven trains travel daily from Helsinki (€23.60, 1¼ hours) and Turku (€27.20, two hours) to Karis (Finnish: Karjaa), where they are met by connecting trains or buses to Hanko (via Ekenäs).

SunFun Hanko (p107) has the biggest selection of **bicycles** for hire, for €14 per day.

Call ☑106 910 for a **taxi**.

AROUND HANKO

PIKE'S GUT

The narrow strait between Tullisaari and Kobben, called Hauensuoli (Pike's Gut), is a protected natural harbour where sailing ships from countries around the Baltic Sea once waited out storms. The sailors killed time by carving their initials or tales of bravery on the rocks, earning the area the nickname 'Guest Book of the Archipelago'. Some 600 rock carvings dating back to the 17th century remain. Hauensuoli can be reached by charter taxi boat or on a cruise from Hanko – see p108.

BENGTSKÄR

Scandinavia's tallest **lighthouse** (www.bengtskar.fi), towering 52m above the waves, was built in 1906 to protect ships from the perilous waters of the archipelago. It was damaged extensively during the Continuation War by the departing Red Army, but remains a stunning spectacle thanks to substantial refurbishment. Today it also takes guests in simple rooms (one/two/four person/s €110/172/225) that have quite a view. There are exhibits explaining the historical significance of the island, and a shop.

This southernmost inhabited island of Finland is 25km from Hanko. Day cruises leave from Hanko in summer (see p108), or you can charter boats from Hanko or the village of Rosala on the island of Hiittinen.

East of Helsinki

Finland's fascinating past comes to life in the towns east of Helsinki. Strömfors is an intact ironworking village; Loviisa Hamina and Kotka are stuffed with defensive fortifications; and Kotka, a gritty working port, also contains the fabulous Maritime Centre Vellamo, where the country's seafaring history is explored.

LOVIISA

⊘019

Named for Swedish Queen Lovisa Ulrika in 1752, Loviisa (Swedish: Lovisa) is a sweet, sleepy port that had its glory days as a Russian spa town in the 19th century. Like many of the coastal towns, it was a pawn in Russo-Swede conflicts, most devastatingly in 1855 when much of it burnt down – only a small vestige of the Old Town survives. Today the town is a summer resort with little open out of season.

◉ Sights & Activities

The tiny **Old Town**, just south of Mannerheiminkatu, is all that remains of Loviisa's heritage of wooden buildings. The narrow streets around **Degerby Gille** restaurant are charming and the restaurant was built in 1662, making it the oldest building around.

The grand old market square is dominated by the red-brick neo-Gothic **Loviisa Church**, built in 1865 (and closed for renovation at the time of writing).

About 200m north of the square, **Loviisa Town Museum** (Puistokatu 2; admission €4; ⊙11am-4pm Tue-Sun Jun-Aug, noon-4pm Tue-Fri & Sun Sep-May) is set in an old manor house with three floors of interesting historical exhibits, particularly the exhibition on Jean Sibelius, who spent his childhood summer holidays at Sibeliuksenkatu 10.

In summer most of the action is at **Laivasilta Marina**, 500m southeast of the centre. A little cluster of old rust-coloured wooden storehouses now contains craft shops, cafes and a small maritime museum. You can also hire **bicycles** for €3/25 per hour/day.

The short trip to the **Svartholma Sea Fortress**, on an island 10km offshore, is a must when visiting Loviisa. A sister fortress to Suomenlinna, Svartholma was built in 1748 to protect against further Russian invasion after humiliating Swedish losses in eastern Finland. It lasted until the Crimean War (1853–56) when the British destroyed it, but has been reconstructed. Several ferries (€12 return, 45 minutes, June to mid-August) run each day from Laivasilta Marina, or you could sail in style on the yacht **Österstjernan** (⊘040-012 0929; www.osterstjernan.fi; return trip €35), a beautiful 19th-century replica that makes occasional trips in July and August. A free museum on the island details the fort's history, and there's a cafe.

Loviisa's biggest annual event is the **Sibelius Festival** (www.loviisansibeliuspaivat.fi; tickets €15-25) in mid- to late August, which features a weekend of chamber music.

🍴 Sleeping & Eating

Laivasilta Marina is a pleasant spot to while away a summer evening, with a fast-food/beer terrace, and the upmarket **Cafe-Restaurant Saltbodan** (Laivasilta 4; mains €18-25; ⊙May-Sep) serving great cakes, good evening mains and beer in the atmospheric old storehouses.

Hotel Degerby
HOTEL €€

(⊘50561; www.degerby.com; Brandensteininkatu 17; s/d/tr/ste incl breakfast €104/122/141/169; P@) By the main square, this is the only hotel in town. Rooms, decorated in staid blue checks, are comfortable (but hot in summer) and include a solid buffet breakfast in the restaurant. Prices drop at weekends. Wi-fi costs an extra €15 per 24 hours.

Gasthaus Loviisa
GUESTHOUSE €€

(⊘040-835 7997; www.majataloloviisa.fi; Sibeliuksenkatu 3; s/d €45/60; P) This guesthouse close to Sibelius' old house has small, clean, affordable rooms that are given pep and individuality with bold colours and 'retro' styling. Bathrooms are shared, but the ratio is good, with six showers to 14 rooms, all of which have washbasins. There's a self-catering kitchen with microwave.

Tamminiemi
CAMPGROUND €

(⊘530 244; www.tamminiemi.net; Kapteenintie 1; tent sites €15 plus per person €5, d €75-85, 4-person apt €153; ⊙camping early Jun-late Aug, other accommodation year-round) About 2km south of town, Tamminiemi is a tiny, peaceful and well-ordered camping ground whose grassy edges run right down to the sea. There are also simple rooms in two renovated wooden houses, most with bathrooms, and with access to a self-catering kitchen. Reception closes early: arrive in good time.

Degerby Gille
BUFFET €€

(Sepänkuja 4; ⊙noon-5pm Sat Midsummer-Aug) In the town's oldest building, this enchanting restaurant has Brigadoon-like opening hours, welcoming in diners only on summer Saturdays. The buffet (€24) is worth the wait, with a huge smorgasbord emphasising locally caught fish, which you can consume in one of five charmingly old-fashioned dining rooms.

ⓘ Information

Library (Kuningattarenkatu 24) Free internet access, just north of Mannerheiminkatu.

Tourist office (⊘555 234; www.loviisa.fi; Karlskronabulevardi 8; ⊙9am-6pm Mon-Fri, 10am-2pm Sat Jun-Aug, 9am-4pm Mon-Fri Sep-May)

ⓘ Getting There & Away

Loviisa is 90km east of Helsinki, reached by motorway E18 or Hwy 7. There are buses at least hourly to/from Helsinki (€20.50, 1½ hours), Kotka (€12.50, one hour) and Porvoo (€10.80, 40 minutes).

STRÖMFORS IRONWORKS

Good for a couple of hours' strolling, **Strömfors Ironworks** (⊘11am-5pm Jun-Aug), on the edge of tiny **Ruotsinpyhtää** village, is one of Finland's oldest *bruks*, dating back to 1698. Today its red-stained buildings are an open-air museum, nestled in a patchwork of forest, rivers and bridges. The **Forge Museum** has two sections: an old smith's workshop and the working millwheel. One ironworks building serves as an **art gallery**, and visitors also come to browse the little **craft shops**.

The 18th-century octagonal wooden **church** (⊘11am-4pm mid-Jun–mid-Aug), built after the old one was lost across yet another Sweden–Russia border change, boasts a fabulous altarpiece painted in 1898 by the young Helene Schjerfbeck.

Buses from Loviisa to Strömfors (20 minutes) are rare in summer, more frequent Monday to Friday term time.

KOTKA

☑05 / POP 54,800

The fortunes of Kotka have long been tied to the sea. The Vikings used the archipelago to launch themselves eastward into Russia, and the Kymijoki was once an important transport route for logging. Today Kotka is a major industrial port, and many of its attractions have saltwater at their heart: a large aquarium, the huge, wave-shaped Maritime Centre Vellamo, and the biannual **Kotkan Meripäivät** (www.meripaivat.com) maritime festival in late July, with boat racing, concerts, markets and a huge wooden boat show.

◉ Sights

Maritime Centre Vellamo   MUSEUM
(www.merlkeskusvellamo.fı; Iornatorintie 99; adult/under 18yr €8/free; ⊘11am-6pm Tue & Thu-Sat, to 8pm Wed) This spectacular new museum recounts Finland's seafaring life. The tanker-sized building, with its dockside location, walls of metal and printed glass, rooftop stage and wavelike design, is startling enough, and the glamour continues inside. The star exhibit is the *Tarmo*, the world's oldest ice-breaker (1908), which ploughed Finnish waters until it was retired in 1970.

There are also exhibitions on shipwrecks, navigation, fishing and logging, and a boat hall containing an Olympic-winning 49er and a boat that belonged to the Moomins' author, Tove Jansson.

Maretarium   AQUARIUM
(☑234 4030; www.maretarium.fi; Sapokankatu 2; adult/4-15yr €11/7.50; ⊘10am-8pm mid-May–mid-Aug, to 5pm mid-Aug–mid-May) The impressive Maretarium has over 20 giant fish tanks representing various bodies of water. The Baltic tank is the largest, with local sea life fed regularly by a diver. Water is piped in from the sea to keep the natural life cycle of fish going, so salmon spawn in autumn and in winter the freakish eelpout give birth. It's an absorbing insight; fish names are given in 17 different languages, and English guided tours can be arranged with advance notice.

PARKS & CHURCHES

Kotka is proud of its parks – pick up the free *Parks of Kotka* guide to learn more. Our favourite is the tiny **Sapokka Meripuisto** (Sapokka Waterpark), a verdant oasis with bridges, walking trails, a waterfall and the **Rose Terrace** garden, which is stunningly illuminated every evening.

In Isopuisto Park, soaring **St Nicholas Orthodox Church** (⊘noon-3pm Tue-Fri, to 6pm Sat & Sun Jun-Aug) was completed in 1801 and is Kotka's only building to survive the Crimean War. It is believed to have been designed by architect Yakov Perrini, who also designed the St Petersburg Admiralty.

Kotka Church (⊘noon-6pm Sun-Fri) is a neo-Gothic structure whose distinctive steeple is visible throughout town. Inside there's artful woodcarving, glowing rose windows, a baroque-style organ that can belt out a holy volume and a beautiful altarpiece painted by Pekka Halonen.

⚓ Activities

Archipelago cruises of all types depart from Sapokka Harbour (Sapokanlahti) in summer, along with scheduled ferries to the outlying islands (p114); the tourist office has timetables and details.

For rafting and fishing on the mighty Kymijoki, see p115.

⌂ Sleeping

Sokos Hotel Seurahuone   HOTEL €€
(☑010-782 1000; www.sokoshotels.fi; Keskuskatu 21; d from €129; ℗@) This dignified link in the hotel chain has the best bed in a town of restricted quality accommodation. Elegant

Kotka

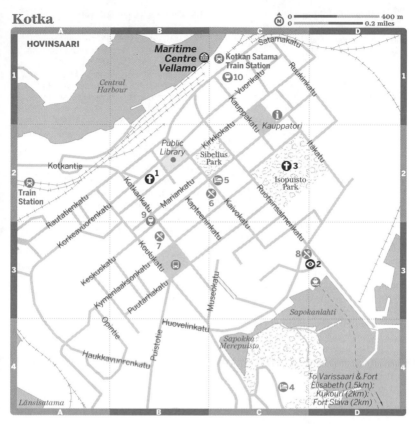

air-conditioned rooms exhibit Finnish cool, with birchwood headboards and furniture, and a Sibelius score woven into the curtains. It's very central, with a nightclub and restaurant, but few parking spaces.

Santalahti Holiday Resort   RESORT €€
(☑260 5055; www.santalahti.fi; tent sites €17, cottages from €66; ⊙May-late Sep) A sprawling resort on Mussalo, 5km west from central Kotka, with cottages, hotel rooms and camp sites.

Kesähotelli Katarina   HOTEL €€
(☑050-913 5763; www.kesahotellikatarina.net; Lehmustie 4; s/tw incl breakfast €50/70; ⊙early Jun-early Aug) Good-quality university accommodation. Rooms are clean and bright with a desk and TV (which may work, or not), and they connect with a large shared kitchen and bathroom. Prices include breakfast. The hilltop location can be a tough walk with a lot of baggage.

Kotka

✕ Eating & Drinking

Good restaurants are thin on the ground, and only the restaurant in the Sokos hotel is open on a Sunday night.

Wanha Fiskari
SEAFOOD €€€
(www.wanhafiskari.fi; Ruotsinsalmenkatu 1; mains €22-30; ⊙lunch & dinner Mon-Sat) Right by the Maretarium, this place specialises in seafood, smoking its own salmon and pan-frying a mean Baltic herring. You might not expect much on looks alone – the modest interior is filled with faintly tacky Captain Haddock nautical decor and is usually quite quiet – but it's first-rate food.

Vausti
FINNISH €€
(www.kotkankonserttitalo.fi/vausti; Keskuskatu 33; mains €16-22 ⊙lunch Mon-Fri, dinner Wed-Sat) Attached to Kotka's concert hall, Vausti is decorated in grown-up greys and fills with music-lovers making a night of it. The seasonal menu is traditional Finnish: fried perch, duck breast, *vorschmack* (a salty, meaty, fishy hash) just the way Mannerheim liked it... Throw in a good choice of salads, pizzas and pasta, and everyone's satisfied.

Canttiini
TEX-MEX €
(Kaivokatu 15; mains €11-18; ⊙10.30am-10pm Mon-Fri, noon-11pm Sat, noon-8pm Sun) A local favourite that dishes up a mixture of Tex-Mex, pasta and steaks in a relaxed pub-like atmosphere.

Blue
BAR
(Kotkankatu 9; ⊙4pm-2am Tue-Sun) The blue neon light might not be flattering for the 30-plus crowd, but this great little bar feels more comfy than cool. There are regular bands and DJs, usually with bluesy, R&B beats, but it also just makes for a good place to shoot the breeze over a few wines.

Kairo
PUB
(Satamakatu 7; ⊙from 11am Tue-Sat, to 4am Fri & Sat) A legendary old sailors' boozer right down to the ships' flags and saucy paintings, with live music and a great terrace. Ties are banned, and the rules state that if someone asks you to dance, you can't turn them down!

ℹ Information

Public library (Kirkkokatu 24; ⊙10am-7pm Mon-Fri year-round, plus 10am-3pm Sat Sep-May) Free short-term and paid long-term internet use.

Tourist office (☎234 4424; www.kotka.fi; Keskuskatu 6; ⊙9am-5pm Mon-Fri year-round, plus 10am-2pm Sat Jul–mid-Aug) Free internet access and a useful board of weekly events.

ℹ Getting There & Away

There are regular express buses from Helsinki (€26.90, 2½ hours), via Porvoo and Loviisa. Buses run roughly every half-hour to Hamina (€9.40, 45 minutes), 26km to the east.

There are between four and six local trains a day to Kouvola (€8.60, 45 minutes), which has connecting trains to all major Finnish cities. Trains stop both at Kotka Station, northwest of the city centre, and Kotkan Satama, at the handier main harbour.

AROUND KOTKA

ARCHIPELAGO ISLANDS

The islands around Kotka make good day trips during the summer months with daily boat connections from Sapokka Harbour.

Varissaari is famous for **Fort Elisabeth**, another Russian fortress built to defend the coast against the Swedes. A fierce naval battle was fought here in 1789, and the fortress was abandoned in the late 19th century. Today it's a popular picnic spot with a good restaurant. Ferries make the 10-minute trip (adult/four to 11 years return €10/5) from Kotka (hourly 9am to 8pm late May to mid-August).

On **Kukouri** is **Fort Slava**, also called the Fortress of Honour, with a stunning round structure that you'll spot from the jetty. It was built by the Russians in 1794 as part of a chain of fortresses in the Gulf of Finland, before the British destroyed it in 1855. Ferries (return ticket €10) run here on Mondays in July.

Kaunissaari has its own little community with a charming fishing village and a local museum, as well as a camping ground with cabins. There's a year-round boat service, increasing to several departures per day in July including an evening 'singalong cruise' (return ticket €20).

On Kaunissaari is a small information hut for the **Eastern Gulf of Finland National Park**, a 60km swath of over a hundred islets beginning just south of Kaunissaari. It's an important breeding ground for seabirds and a habitat for grey and ringed seals. Generally, you'll need your own boat to explore, but scheduled boats do run from Hamina to Ulko-Tammio Island, inside the park boundaries, on summer weekends.

LANGINKOSKI & KYMIJOKI

The **Langinkoski Imperial Fishing Lodge** (www.langinkoskimuseo.com; Koskenniskantie 5C; adult/6-14yr €5/2; ⊙10am-4pm daily May, to 6pm Jun-Aug, 10am-4pm Sat & Sun Sep), 5km north of Kotka on the salmon-heavy Kymijoki, is a surprisingly simple wooden lodge built in 1889 for Tsar Alexander III, who visited Langinkoski frequently. Most of the furniture is original and the rooms look much as they did at the end of the 19th century. The riverside forest setting (now a 28-hectare nature reserve) is beautiful and there are several walking trails around the area.

The Kymijoki is one of Finland's best fishing rivers – for detailed information, see the website www.lohikeskuskotka.fi. **Fly-fishing** is still allowed at Langinkoski: permits are sold at the Risto Rämä **petrol station** (☑05-218 000; Jylpyntie 39), about 1km from the lodge.

Groups can arrange rafting trips through **Erämys** (☑228 1244; www.eramys.fi) and **Keisarin Kosket** (☑040-561 0630; www.keisarinkosket.fi) for around €490 for two hours. Otherwise consult Kotka tourist office's program of events, as Erämys also runs occasional **rapids-shooting trips** (adult/child €50/30) in July that are open to individuals.

Very frequent buses stop at Langinkoski church, from where it's a 1.2km walk to the lodge.

HAMINA
☑05 / POP 21,400

Finnish ski-jumping champion and bad boy, Matti Nykänen, once quipped that 'Things are as mixed-up as the city of Hamina'. Given the strict octagonal street plan of this former fortress town, we assume he was being ironic. Hamina (Swedish: Fredrikshamn) has long been a military town, founded in 1653 as a Swedish outpost.

The town's incomplete fortifications were begun by panicky Swedes in 1722 after Vyborg fell to Russia. Their efforts were in vain, as the Russians marched in and captured Hamina. Today there's a modern military base in town and the whole town is on parade for the annual military tattoo (see this page). The only invasion today is by day trippers from across the Russian border, only 40km away.

◉ Sights & Activities

Old Town   HISTORIC DISTRICT

Just wandering the restored 19th-century town with its octagonal-wheel street plan will take you past many of Hamina's sights. The centre of the web is dominated by the 18th-century **town hall**, on either side of which is a church. The neoclassical **Hamina**

Church (☺11am-4pm Jun–mid-Aug) was built in 1843 and designed by CL Engel, while the 1837 **Orthodox Church of Saints Peter & Paul** (☺noon-4pm Tue-Sun Jun-Aug), with its classic onion dome, was designed by architect Louis Visconti, who designed Napoleon's mausoleum.

Housed in Hamina's oldest building, the **Town Museum** (Kaupunginmuseo; Kadettikoulunkatu 2; admission €2; ☺noon-4pm Wed-Sat, to 5pm Sun Sep-May, 10am-4pm Tue-Sun Jun-Aug) ruminates on local history. King Gustav III of Sweden and Catherine II (the Great) of Russia held negotiations here in 1783. The **Shopkeeper's Museum** (Kauppiaantalomuseo; Kasarminkatu 6; admission €2; ☺10am-4pm Tue-Sun Jun-Aug, noon-4pm Wed-Sat, noon-5pm Sun May & Sep) is a former merchant's store and residence, with staff dressing the part and serving customers.

Hamina Bastion   RUIN

Northwest of Old Hamina are the ruins of the 18th-century Hamina Bastion, including 3km of crumbling stone walls that would have made a star-shaped fortress. The bastion comes alive for the tattoo but you can get a deeper look by picking up a copy of *Walking in Old Hamina* from the tourist office.

Meriset   CRUISE

(☑228 5648; www.meriset.com) Meriset does summer cruises from Tervasaari guest harbour to the old fishing village on the island of Tammio (adult/four to 12 years €17/8, three to four hours). Departures are up to three times a week: check the website, as schedules vary significantly between mid-May and late August. Meriset also goes to Ulko-Tammio (adult/four to 12 years €20/10, five hours), an island further south and within the boundaries of the Eastern Gulf of Finland National Park (see p114), on weekends from early June to the end of July.

✿ Festivals & Events

Hamina Tattoo   MUSIC

(www.haminatattoo.fi) Every second (even) year in late July or early August, Hamina celebrates military music during the weeklong Hamina Tattoo, featuring not only Finnish and Russian military marching bands, but rock, jazz and dance music.

⌂ Sleeping

Homestays are the best option, with rooms costing around €35 per person. The tourist office can arrange these.

TURKU & THE SOUTH COAST EAST OF HELSINKI

Best Western Hotel Hamina HOTEL €€
(☑353 5555; www.hotellihamina.fi; Sibeliuskatu 32; s/d €110/130; ℗@) If you're in town on business, chances are you'll be staying in this standard chain hotel, done out in calming greens. Your heart won't be skipping any beats, but it's well located between the bus station and Old Town, and has everything necessary for a comfortable stay. Rates drop at weekends.

Hotel Seurahuone HOTEL €€
(☑010-763 5871; Pikkuympyräkatu 5; r €99; ℗) The other hotel in town is the small family-run Seurahuone, within the web of Hamina's old town. This friendly spot holds its own thanks to a hearty renovation in 2010, which gave rooms shining parquet floors and bathrooms, plus numbers 301 to 308 now have air-conditioning. If you're staying at the weekend, you might want to ask for a room away from the hotel's popular nightclub.

Hamina Camping
Pitkät Hiekat CAMPGROUND €
(☑/fax 345 9183; tent sites €12, 4-/6-person cottages €45/70; ☺May-Sep) In Vilniemi, 8km east of Hamina, this quiet spot offers free rowing boats and a sauna and laundry. It's well liked by visiting Russians.

✖ Eating

Hamina isn't blessed with restaurants, unless you count pizzerias: in summer, try your luck down at Tervasaari harbour. There are two great little cafes: **Konditoria A Huovila** (Fredrikinkatu 1; ☺8am-5pm Mon-Fri, to 1pm Sat) is in the old town; while **Café Varvara** (Puistokatu 2; ☺7am-5pm Mon-Fri, 7.30am-2pm Sat) is just off the market square.

Pursiravintola Vantti SEAFOOD, FINNISH €€
(☑040-140 2273; Pikku Vuohisaari; mains €18-30; ☺food 3-9pm Tue-Sat, noon-8pm Sun, bar to later Jun-Aug) On a small island, this yacht club has the best views in town. Dishes use local salmon and seafood, but also include traditional Finnish meatballs. A ferry collects you from Tervasaari harbour with the press of the buzzer.

Ruusu Rouva FINNISH €€
(www.ruusurouva.fi; Sibeliuskatu 28; lunches €7.50-10; ☺9am-3pm Mon-Fri) This excellent cafe/lunch restaurant is located in a historic building, where you can dine in a proper parlour or the atmospheric vaulted cellar. The two lunch options embrace Finnish fish and game dishes, backed up by a good salad bar...and who could resist a pudding called 'Elves' Dream'?

❶ Information

Monica Tours (☑344 0611; www.monicatours. fi; Raatihuoneentori 16; ☺9am-4pm Mon-Fri) Organises trips to St Petersburg as well as fishing excursions.

Public library (Rautatienkatu 8; ☺noon-7pm Mon-Fri, plus 10am-2pm Sat winter) Free internet terminals.

Tourist office (☑040-199 1330; www.visit hamina.fi; Raatihuoneentori 16; ☺9am-5pm Mon-Fri, 10am-3pm Sat & Sun early Jun-late Aug, 9am-4pm Mon-Fri late Aug-early Jun)

❶ Getting There & Away

You can reach Hamina by hourly bus from Kotka (€9.40, 45 minutes). There are express buses from Helsinki (€29.50, 2¾ hours). Buses pass through Hamina on the way to Vyborg and St Petersburg in Russia and, if you have a visa (see p75), you can organise a tour with Monica Tours (see above).

Åland Archipelago

Best Places to Eat

» Indigo (p124)

» ÅSS Paviljong (p125)

» Bagarstugan (p125)

Best Places to Stay

» Hotell Arkipelag (p123)

» Kvarnbo Gästhem (p131)

» Hotell Brudhäll (p133)

» Käringsund (p134)

Why Go?

The sweeping Åland archipelago is a kooky geopolitical entity: the islands belong to Finland, speak Swedish, but have their own parliament, fly their own blue-gold-and-red flag, issue their own stamps and have their own web suffix: 'dot ax'. Their 'special relationship' with the EU means they can sell duty free and make their own gambling laws.

The sunniest spot in northern Europe, in summer Åland attracts crowds of holidaying Swedes and Finns with its balmy weather and sandy beaches. The capital's bars, restaurants and ice-cream outlets teem with people; but once you get out of Mariehamn, a sleepy haze hangs over the islands' tiny villages. Finding your own remote beach among the 6500 skerries and islets is surprisingly easy. A lattice of bridges and free cable ferries connect the central islands, while larger car ferries run to the archipelago's outer reaches. Åland is also bicycle heaven, with flat, compact scenery and excellent cycle routes.

When to Go
ALAND ARCHIPELAGO

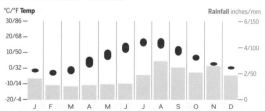

Feb & Mar Skate the frozen seas in the northern archipelago islands.

Jun Decorated poles are raised around the islands during Midsummer.

Jul Festivities at Kastelholms Slott on Gustav Wasa Days.

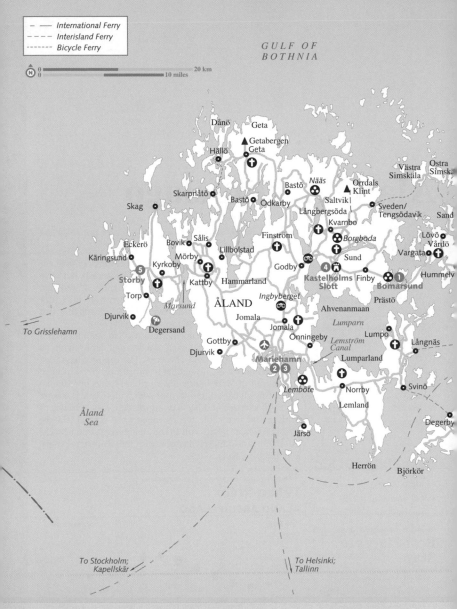

Åland Archipelago Highlights

❶ Running the ramparts and marvelling at the cannonball-scarred ruins at **Bomarsund** (p128)

❷ Climbing aboard the pride of Mariehamn, the four-masted barque **Pommern** (p121)

❸ Choosing your favourite church: is it the art nouveau glory of **Sankt Göran's Kyrka** (p122) or perhaps the quaint charm of **Sankta Maria Magdalena Kyrka** (p132)?

❹ Watching history come to life with jousting and feasting at **Kastelholms Slott** (p128)

on Gustav Vasa Dagarna
(Gustav Wasa Days)

5 Imagining the vain empire
that would construct the
majestically over-the-top post

office at **Post och Tullhuset**
(p133)

6 Cycling around the
fantastically flat landscape
along well-marked cycle
routes (p120)

7 Escaping to the outer
reaches of the archipelago and
experiencing a 'Wicker Man'
chill as the **Midsummer poles**
(p124) are raised

History

More than a hundred Bronze and Iron Age *fornminne* (burial sites) have been discovered across the Åland archipelago, attesting to more than 6000 years of human habitation. Though all are clearly signposted, most are in fairly nondescript fields. The archipelago was an important harbour and trading centre during the Viking era, with more than six fortress ruins discovered.

During the Great Northern War of 1700–21 (nicknamed the 'Great Wrath'), most Ålanders fled to Sweden to escape the Russians. Further Russian incursions took place in the 1740s and 1809. Unsurprisingly, when Finland gained independence in 1917, Ålanders feared occupation by Russian Bolsheviks. Many Ålanders lobbied to be incorporated into Sweden, but Finland refused to give up the island. The dispute concluded in 1921, when Åland was given its status as an autonomous, demilitarised and neutral municipality within Finland by a decision of the League of Nations.

Åland joined the EU in 1995, but was granted a number of exemptions, including duty-free tax laws that allow ferry services to mainland Finland and Sweden to operate profitably.

Today, peaceful Åland is divided into 16 municipalities, 10 on what is called 'Fasta Åland' (the main group of larger islands), while the other six municipalities cover the far-flung archipelago and its multitudes of tiny islands.

🏃 Activities

Åland is hugely popular as a cycling destination, with plenty of bike rental places and great facilities.

Sailing boats from all around the Baltic pull in at the archipelago's secluded islands in summer. You can do anything from chartering a luxury yacht to renting a kayak. Ice-fishing and fishing from boats and the shore are popular.

Self-Catering Accommodation

There are a wealth of cottages for rent across the islands. Both Eckerö and Viking ferry lines have a comprehensive list of bookable places, as does **Destination Åland** (☏0400-108 800; www.destinationaland.com; Östra Esplanadgatan 7, Mariehamn).

ⓘ Information

Åland shares Finland's time zone, an hour ahead of Sweden. While the euro is the currency, most places accept the Swedish krona.

Finnish telephone cards can be used across the Åland archipelago, but local cards are also available. Åland uses the Finnish mobile phone network but it can be sketchy, especially in the outer islands. Mail sent in Åland must have Åland postage stamps.

The website www.visitaland.com is very helpful, while www.alandsresor.fi lets you book accommodation online. The general EU-wide emergency number is ☏112; for the police call ☏10022, for medical services ☏10023.

ⓘ Getting There & Away

AIR

Åland's airport is 4km northwest of Mariehamn. There are no regular buses: a **taxi** (☏10066, 32000) to the centre costs about €20. **Air Åland** (☏17110; www.airaland.ax) is the main airline, with up to four flights daily (fewer weekends) to/from Helsinki and Stockholm, with one-way tickets costing from €80. In late 2011 **FlyBe** (www.flybe.com) set up in competition, flying to Helsinki for as little as €39. Business airline **Turku Air** (☏020-721 8800; www.turkuair.fi) flies to Turku Monday to Friday for €233 one way.

BOAT

Several car ferries head to Åland. Prices vary with season and web specials are common, but the prices listed here are all based on a one-way adult fare, with cars and cabins costing extra.

Eckerö Linjen (www.eckerolinjen.ax) Head office (☏28000; Torggatan 2, Mariehamn); Eckerö (☏28300; Berghamn, Eckerö) Sails from Eckerö to Grisslehamn, Sweden (€12, two hours). **Birka Line**, which runs luxury cruises from Stockholm to Mariehamn, is part of the same company.

Tallink & Silja Lines (☏060-015 700; www.tallinksilja.com; Torggatan 14, Mariehamn) Runs direct services to Mariehamn from Turku (€17, five hours), Helsinki (€40, 12 hours) and Stockholm (through Silja Lines; €30, six hours).

Viking Line (☏26211; www.vikingline.fi; Storagatan 3, Mariehamn) Runs to Turku (€8, five hours), Helsinki (€39, 11 hours) and Stockholm (€15, 5½ hours).

It's also possible to travel using the archipelago ferries to and from mainland Finland via Korpo (southern route, from Galtby harbour) or Kustavi (northern route, from Osnäs harbour), though it's cheaper to break your outward journey in the archipelago (see p121).

ⓘ Getting Around

BICYCLE

Cycling is a great way to tour these flat, rural islands. **Ro-No Rent** has bicycles available at Mariehamn and Eckerö harbours, and many camping grounds and guest harbours also have rental bikes. Green-and-white signs trace the excellent routes through the islands. Bicycle routes generally follow smaller, less busy roads, but special bicycle paths run parallel to main roads.

BUS

Five main bus lines depart from Mariehamn's regional bus terminal on Styrmansgatan, in front of the police station. Rte 1 goes to Hammarland and Eckerö; rte 2 to Godby and Geta; rte 3 to Godby and Saltvik; rte 4 to Godby, Sund and Vårdö (Hummelvik); and rte 5 to Lemland and Lumparland (Långnäs). Tickets from Mariehamn to the ferry ports cost around €4.40. Bicycles can be carried (space permitting) for €7.

FERRY

There are three kinds of interisland ferry. For short trips, free vehicle ferries sail nonstop. For longer routes, ferries run to a schedule, taking cars, bicycles and pedestrians. There are also two private bicycle ferries in summer, Hammarland–Geta and Vårdö–Saltvik. A ride is around €10/5 per adult/child.

Timetables for all interisland ferries are available at the main tourist office in Mariehamn and online at www.alandstrafiken.ax.

Mariehamn

🎵 018 / POP 11,200

Two out of every five Ålanders live in Mariehamn and, with the *lagting* (parliament) and the *landskapsstyrelse* (Åland's government) both located here, it's the biggest smoke in the islands.

The town was christened by Alexander II after the Empress Maria. Its broad tree-lined streets are indicative of its Russian heritage, and gave Mariehamn its nickname: town of a thousand linden trees.

Mariehamn's peninsula location has given it a unique strategic importance, with the ports on either side traditionally used for ship-building and repairs. Today the ports welcome regular ferries from both Finland and Sweden, whose residents take advantage of Åland's extra-EU status to buy duty-free goods – at least, in summer. Outside high season, you may have the place to yourself.

⊙ Sights

Pommern   MUSEUM
(☑531 421; adult/7-15yr €5/3; ☉9am-5pm May-Jun & Aug, to 7pm Jul, 10am-4pm Sep) The *Pommern* is the symbol of Mariehamn, a beautifully preserved four-masted merchant barque anchored by the western harbour.

Built in 1903 in Glasgow, Scotland, the ship once carried tonnes of cargo and a 26-man crew (plus numerous pigs, dogs, cats and rats!) on the trade route between Australia and England. Its record run was a speedy 110 days. There's a good audio guide (€3.50), and plenty of on-board information to bring the creaking timbers back to life, including photos, letters, cargo lists and subtitled interviews with the last men to sail her. You can explore Åland's marine heritage further at the nearby **Sjöfartsmuseum** (Maritime Museum; ☑19930; Hamngatan 2), due to reopen in 2012 after a major reconstruction.

Ålands Museum & Ålands Konstmuseum   MUSEUM
(Åland Museum & Art Museum; ☑25426; Stadshusparken; adult/7-15yr €4/3; ☉10am-5pm daily Jun-Aug, 10am-8pm Tue & Thu, 10am-4pm Wed & Fri, noon-4pm Sat & Sun Sep-May) In the centre of town, Åland's museum and art gallery are housed in the same large building. Permanent exhibits offer an insight into the islands' history, including a replica of a Stone Age boat made of sealskin, a reconstructed traditional pharmacy and a large illustration of Bomarsund (p128) in all its glory. It's a well-organised modern museum, but unfortunately there's little information available in English.

Luckily, art transcends language barriers: the adjoining gallery has changing exhibitions and a handful of paintings by local artists. Perhaps the best known is Karl Emanuel Jansson's *Åland Peasant Bride,* depicting a woman wearing an outfit that makes her look a little like a Midsummer pole.

Sjökvarteret   NEIGHBOURHOOD
(☑16033; www.sjokvarteret.com) At the northern end of Österhamn, Sjökvarteret has long been devoted to boat-building. You can stroll along the quay, admiring the traditional

Mariehamn

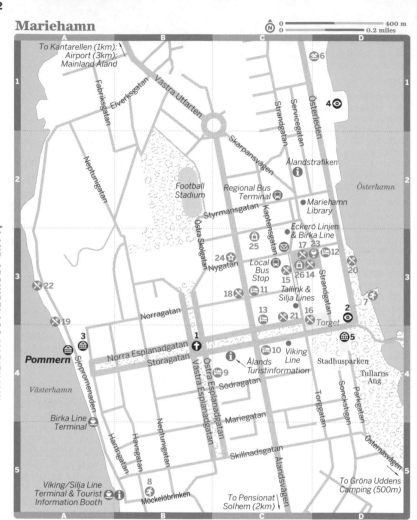

schooners moored here, and possibly even see boats under construction. The **museum** (adult/child €4/free; ⊙9am-6pm daily mid-Jun–mid-Aug, 9-11am Mon Fri mid-Aug–mid-Jun), with Finnish-only exhibitions on ship-building, is located in a small boatshed that still has the whiff of timber and sea salt. The quarter also has a good cafe, Café Bönan (p125), galleries, a shop and a reconstructed seafarers' chapel.

Sankt Göran's Kyrka   CHURCH
(⊙10am-6pm Mon-Fri, to 3pm Sat mid-Jun–Aug) The copper-roofed Sankt Göran's Kyrka, built in 1927, is one of the few modern churches on the islands. Its art nouveau style was conceived by Lars Sonck, who grew up in Åland. The glittering mosaic altarpiece is a real highlight.

FREE **Självstyrelsegården**   BUILDING
(Self-Government Bldg; ☑25000; cnr Österleden & Storagatan; ⊙tours 10am Fri mid-Jun–Aug) It may seem like a local council building, but Självstyrelsegården is actually the home of the Åland parliament. Free guided tours (available in English) explain the autonomous nature of Åland and the election of the

Mariehamn

Lantråd, the premier of Åland, and end with a slide show about the area.

🏃 Activities

Ro-No Rent　　　　BICYCLE RENTAL, WATER SPORTS
(☑12820, out of season 0400 529 315; www.visit aland.com/rono; bicycles per day/week €8/40, mopeds €80/200, kayaks €80/150, small boats per 4hr/day €50/100; ☺9am-6pm Jun-end Aug, call ahead rest of year) This company rents out a variety of bicycles, kayaks, small boats (that don't require a licence) and mopeds (which do) from its outlet at Österhamn. The smaller outlet at Västerhamn just has bicycles.

Mariebad　　　　SWIMMING
(☑531 650; www.mariebad.net; Österleden; adult/4-19yr €7.60/4.70; ☺noon-10pm Mon, from 10am Tue-Fri, to 6pm Sat & Sun) Mariebad is one of those fun northern European waterparks that are excellent for the whole family, with slides, sauna, indoor and outdoor pools with water jets, waterfalls etc, and a free sandy beach.

🎉 Festivals & Events

As well as the decorating and raising of the Midsummer poles (see p124), Mariehamn has a few other interesting events.

Organ Festival　　　　MUSIC
(www.alfest.org) Cleans out the organ pipes of some of the best churches on the islands in late June/early July, with Mariehamn as its centre.

Ålands Sjödagar　　　　CULTURAL
(www.sjokvarteret.com) Åland's biggest cultural festival: maritime history is celebrated in mid-July with boat races, folk music and short sailing tours on the schooner *Albanus*.

Rockoff　　　　MUSIC
(www.rockoff.nu; per day/9 days €30/80) Kicks off in late July and features Swedish pop and rock bands; it runs during the evenings for nine days.

🛏 Sleeping

Mariehamn's hotel rates are highest between mid-June and the end of August. Booking ahead is recommended, especially at weekends and/or when large ferries arrive. Mariehamn has no youth hostels.

TOP CHOICE 〉Hotell Arkipelag　　　　HOTEL €€€
(☑24020; www.hotellarkipelag.com; Strandgatan 35; s/d €130/160, with sea view €150/180, ste from €240; ▣@☒) One of the best hotels on the islands,

this high-class spot caters well to business visitors, though water views from the balconies are tempting for anyone. Rooms are large, with tasteful minimalist decoration and newly fitted air-conditioners, and bathrooms contain both baths and showers. Super facilities include indoor and outdoor pools, freshly refurbished sauna, nightclub, casino, two restaurants and several bars.

Hotell Pommern　　　　　　HOTEL €€
(☑15555; www.hotellpommern.ax; Norragatan 8-10; s/d €98/112) This family-owned hotel has plain but pleasantly proportioned older-style rooms done out in restful yellows and beiges, with minibars, TVs and space-saving fold-out shavers that are a marvel. Onsite restaurant. Handy for the town centre.

Park Alandia Hotelli　　　　　HOTEL €€
(☑14130; www.vikingline.fi/parkalandiahotel, in Finnish; Norra Esplanadgatan 3; s/d €94/112; 🅿🖭) This sophisticated spot is on the main boulevard and has good deals with Viking Lines. The spacious rooms are popular, though Sunday nights are cheaper. On sunny days its public terrace packs in the crowds.

Pensionat Solhem　　　　　GUESTHOUSE €
(☑16322; pensionat.solhem@aland.net; Lökskärsvägen 18; s/d €45/70; 🕙May-Oct; 🅿) Three kilometres south of the centre, this delightful seaside spot can feel like your very own villa. Rooms are basic with shared bathrooms, but cheerful staff keep the place running like clockwork. Guests also have use of the rowing boats and sauna. Local buses stop nearby.

Hotell Esplanad　　　　　　HOTEL €
(☑16444; Storagatan 5; s/d incl breakfast €60/65; 🅿) Mariehamn's best-value central accommodation is old style – think fritzing electri-

cal sockets, basket-weave wallpaper and tables that bow under the weight of huge retro TV sets. You might not want to spend the whole summer here, but it's OK for a cheap night or two. Rooms contain minifridges, and prices include a breakfast buffet.

Gröna Uddens Camping　　CAMPGROUND €
(☑21121; www.gronaudden.com; tent sites €8 plus per adult €8, 2-/4-person cabins €90/110, r €80; 🕙early May-Aug) By the seaside and 15 minutes' stroll south of the centre, this camping ground is a family favourite, which means you'll need to book its fully equipped spruce red cabins ahead in summer. There's plenty of outdoor fun including a safe swimming beach, minigolf course (admission €5), bike hire (€10) and sauna.

Eating

Mariehamn's many cafes serve the local speciality, *Ålandspannkaka* (Åland pancakes): the real deal is a fluffy square pudding made with semolina and served with stewed prunes (not strawberry jam). Look out in local markets for *Ålands svartbröd* (Åland dark bread), a malt-fruity loaf that takes four days to make and complements *sill* (pickled herring) or light local cheeses.

┌TOP┐
│CHOICE│ Indigo　　　　　　BISTRO €€
(☑16550; www.indigo.ax; Nygatan 1; mains €20-30; 🕙restaurant 11am-3pm & 5-10pm, closed Sun winter, bar to midnight or 3am) This slick spot has a warm interior of historic raw brickwork and an ever-buzzing summer courtyard. It's busy for a reason – the contemporary menu offers some of the most innovative dishes in Åland: try grilled swordfish served on roast sweet potato, or lemon-roasted salmon served with fennel salad. Vegetarians get a

---

MIDSUMMER POLES

If you're passing through the Åland archipelago during summer, you'll definitely notice the Midsummer poles. Up to 25m tall, the whitewashed spruce poles are a cross between a mast and a totem pole. Each village usually has at least one, decorated in a public gathering the day before Midsummer with leaves, ribbons, tissue paper, miniature flags and various trinkets, the nature and symbolism of which varies from place to place. Atop the poles is the Fäktargubbe, a figure representing toil and diligence. Other motifs include sailing boats, ears of corn representing the harvest, a wreath symbolising love, a sun facing east and other icons of community togetherness. Once raised, the pole then stands until the next Midsummer.

When the Midsummer pole came to Åland remains something of a mystery. Although some theorists believe that the pole is a manifestation of an ancient fertility rite, its origins on Åland itself are probably more recent. Others point to the resemblance to ships' masts, with cross-spars and cords, which suggests an appeal to a higher power for safe seas.

carefully considered (nonpasta!) option, and a bar menu offers lighter meals.

ÅSS Paviljong
SWEDISH, FINNISH €€

(☎19141; Västerhamn; lunch buffets €13, mains €20-27; ☺lunch & dinner May-Aug) The positioning could not be better for this upmarket yachtie favourite. Service can be a little erratic when the terrace gets swamped in summer, but the kitchen serves up some consistently good dishes, such as seafood pappardelle, white fish carpaccio or slow-baked organic pork. The lunch buffet is a good sampler for the budget conscious.

Bagarstugan
CAFE €

(Ekonomiegatan 2; light meals €5-12; ☺10am-6pm Mon-Fri, 11am-4pm Sat) This wonderful old tearoom looks *exactly* like a Carl Larsson drawing, with wood-panelled walls, scrubbed pine floor, and pink geraniums lining the windowsills. There's a light menu of homemade soup, salad, quiches, pies and cakes (scattered with flower petals and far too pretty to eat!), and nothing is too much trouble for the lovely staff.

Umbra
INTERNATIONAL €€

(www.umbra.ax, in Swedish; Norra Esplanadgatan 2; lunches €9.90, mains €18-21; ☺lunch Mon-Fri year-round, dinner Mon-Sat Jul & Aug) Primarily a lunch restaurant, Umbra has a cosy rustic interior that runs to bronzed fireplaces. Its daily specials vary from traditional Finnish dishes to curried chicken, and in high season there's a small à la carte evening menu: expect creamy fish stews and delicious desserts. Staff are swift, informed and down to earth.

Pub Niska
PUB €€

(Västerhamn; mains €19-25; ☺lunch & dinner Apr-Aug) This offshoot of ÅSS Paviljong is a cosy little boozer, named after a notorious local smuggler and decked out to look like the inside of a ship, complete with portholes and sailors' newspapers. It also does good *plåtbröd,* an Åland-style pizza.

Seapoint Restaurant & Bar
MODERN FINNISH €€

(☎15501; Österhamn; starters/mains €15/22; ☺11am-1am Mon-Fri, 1pm-1am Sat & Sun) This smart harbour pavilion contains a new upmarket Nordic restaurant (outdoor tables offer more-casual surroundings). Its portions won't suit the ravenous, but local ingredients are used to intriguing effect – grilled salsify, roe of whitefish, and ice cream

flavoured with local apple juice. Starters give diners little tastes of not one but three seafood, meat or vegetable dishes.

Café Bönan
VEGETARIAN €

(Sjökvarteret; www.cafebonan.ax; snacks €6; ☺10.30am-4pm) An oasis in a desert of meat and fish, this organic vegetarian place does healthy soups and salads such as fresh beans with couscous, washed down with elderflower cordial. All the food is sourced from ethical producers. It also hosts the occasional laid-back music event or themed food evening – check the website.

Eat
CAFE €

(Torget; meals €7-12; ☺10am-6pm Mon-Fri, 11am-4pm Sat) Located in the market square, the large roofed terrace (with sofas!) is always packed with drinkers and diners, particularly Åland's parliamentarians. The menu parades pizzas, ciabattas, enormous bowls of salad and an interesting range of designer fruit juices (blackberry and nettle, strawberry and yumberry).

Café La Strada
PIZZERIA, ICE CREAM €€

(Torggatan 6; mains €18-23, pizzas €10-12; ☺10am-8pm Mon-Thu, to 9pm Fri & Sat, plus 9am summer) Packed out in summer, this prime people-watching place on the pedestrianised shopping street suits all ages: holidaying dads sink frothy lagers while their kids gorge quietly on ice cream. The quality of its pizza and pastas is high, and daily specials are good value. It does great *Ålandspannkaka.*

Self-Catering

Some outer islands have limited general stores: Mariehamn may be your best chance to stock up. There are several minimarkets around town, but the most central supermarket is **K-Supermarket** (cnr Ålandsvägen & Norragatan; ☺9am-7pm Mon-Fri, to 4pm Sat, 11am-4pm Sun). Åland's biggest supermarket, **Kantarellen** (Nya Godbyvägen; ☺9am-9pm Mon-Fri, to 7pm Sat, 10am-7pm Sun), is 2km north of town on the road to Godby.

Drinking & Entertainment

Mariehamn has more or less the only nightlife in Åland. The hotel bars at Park Alandia Hotelli (p124) and Hotell Arkipelag (p123) are good options, and the latter also has a nightclub, **Arken** (admission up to midnight/2am/closing, €5/10/20; ☺10pm-4am Mon-Sat, plus Sun summer), with chart-conscious DJs.

ÅLAND ARCHIPELAGO MARIE-HAMN

SPARKLING SURPRISE

In 2010 there was great excitement when divers raised 162 bottles of champagne – the world's oldest – from a 19th-century wreck lying off the coast of Åland. Two bottles were auctioned in 2011 for the princely sum of €54,000. If that's beyond your budget, you can see a couple of the precious bottles in the Ålands Museum and imagine what the champagne tastes like – apparently it has 'tones of golden raisins and a clear aroma of tobacco'.

Dino's Bar & Grill   BAR
(www.dinosbar.com; Strandgatan 12; ☺bar to midnight Mon-Thu, to 4am Fri & Sat, to 10pm Sun) A good eating place (mains €18 to €22) for burgers, pastas and steaks, Dino's is also the best meeting place in town. It's particularly good fun in summer, when the outdoor tables and balcony overflow with happy people drinking beer and singing along to the nightly singers. As the evening progresses, the action heads inside as house band Made in Thailand starts roaring out rock covers.

Casino Paf   CASINO
(www.casinopaf.com; Strandgatan 35; ☺10am-2am) Because of its autonomous status Åland has been able to make its own rules about gambling, and punters can bet in this casino based inside Hotell Arkipelag.

Bio Savoy Cinema   CINEMA
(cnr Nygatan & Ålandsvägen) Razed to its foundations at the time of writing, the Savoy was due to reopen as a brand-new cinema and theatre complex in 2012.

🛍 Shopping

Åland has plenty of artists, many of whom have outlets in Mariehamn. The tourist office has maps of craft shops around Åland.

🖋 Salt   CRAFT
(www.salt.ax; Sjökvarteret; ☺10am-5pm Mon-Fri, to 2pm Sat) Features the work of 40 local artists and craftspeople working with textiles, ceramics, silverware and other jewellery. It also sells, well...salt.

Judy's Hantverk & Inredning   CERAMICS, HANDICRAFTS
(www.visitaland.com/judys; Köpmansgatan 11; ☺9am-7pm Mon-Fri, 10am-4pm Sat) This back-street find does hand-painted ceramics – if you're lucky you'll see them being painted and fired. It also stocks some tempting pieces of design from other local artists.

Guldviva   JEWELLERY
(www.guldviva.com; Sjökvarteret; ☺10am-5pm Mon-Fri, 11am-2pm Sat) Brooches, cufflinks and necklaces, based on the islands' flora and fauna. Some incorporate Åland's red rapakivi granite, making them good souvenirs.

Jussis Keramik   GLASS, CERAMICS
(www.jussiskeramik.fi, in Finnish; Nygatan 1) This outlet sells ceramics and glassware in a wide variety of bright colours, and you can also watch the glass-blowers at work.

ℹ Information

There are 24-hour luggage lockers at the ferry terminal.

Ålands Turistinformation (☏24000; www.visitaland.com; Storagatan 8; ☺9am-6pm daily Jul, to 5pm Mon-Fri, to 4pm Sat & Sun Jun & Aug, 9am-4pm Mon-Fri Sep-May; @) Useful information, plus tour booking and free internet.

Ålandsresor (☏28040; www.alandsresor.fi; Torggatan 2; ☺8.30am-5pm Mon-Fri year-round, 9am-2pm Sat Jun & Jul) Eckerö Linjen's travel-agent arm handles hotel, guesthouse and cottage bookings for the entire archipelago. Viking Line offers a similar service.

Ålandstrafiken (☏525100; www.alandstrafiken.ax; Strandgatan 25; ☺9am-5pm Mon-Fri year-round, 8am-5pm Mon-Fri, 9am-3pm Sat Jun & Jul) Information on buses and ferries around Åland. Will store backpacks for longer periods.

Cycle Info (☺11am-6pm mid-Jun–mid-Aug) Two-wheeled tourist information units during summer: flag them down and ask a question.

Main hospital emergency ward (☏5355; Norragatan 17)

Main post office (Torggatan 4; ☺9am-5pm Mon-Fri, 10.30am-1.30pm Sat) Sells ubercollectable Åland stamps, required to send mail from Åland.

Mariehamn library (☏531 411; Strandgatan 29; ☺10am-8pm Mon-Fri, to 4pm Sat, noon-4pm Sun) Wi-fi and several free internet terminals, available for 20 minutes maximum unless booked ahead.

ℹ Getting There & Away

See p120 for information on travelling to and from Mariehamn by air or boat. The **airport** is 4km northwest of the centre.

Most visitors to Mariehamn arrive via its two harbours: **Västerhamn** (West Harbour) and **Österhamn** (East Harbour). Ferries from Sweden and mainland Finland dock at Västerhamn; the guest harbour for small boats is at Österhamn. The harbours are linked by the long, tree-lined Storagatan.

Viking and Tallink/Silja ferries depart from the ferry terminal at Västerhamn. Just north of it is a smaller terminal used only by Birka Line.

All ferry lines have offices in Mariehamn:

Eckerö Linjen/Birka Line (☑28000; www. eckerolinjen.ax; Torggatan 2)

Tallink & Silja Lines (☑16711; www.tallinksilja. com; Torggatan 14)

Viking Line (☑26211; www.vikingline.fi; Storagatan 3)

Regional buses depart from the terminal near the library; for route and fare information see p121, or get a timetable from the tourist office or Ålandstrafiken office.

❶ Getting Around

The free local bus routes make for a cheap sightseeing tour. Buses depart from Nygatan, outside the post office, roughly every half-hour, with one set running north and the other south of the centre. **Röde Orm** (☑0457-548 3554; www.rodeorm. ax, in Swedish; tickets €3; ⊙11am-7pm Midsummer–mid-Aug) is a jeep with carriages that runs a circuit hourly of the major tourist attractions, including Sjöfartsmuseum and Sjökvarteret.

Hiring a car is a good way to see Åland. Friendly **RBS Biluthyrning** (☑525 505; www. rundbergs.com; Strandgatan 1) is based at the St1 petrol station opposite Mariebad. Rates for small cars start at around €70 per day, but there's often a 24-hour special for €60, plus it delivers free within Mariehamn.

Ro-No Rent hires out bicycles, mopeds and other recreation gear (see p135).

For a **taxi**, call ☑26000.

MAINLAND ÅLAND & AROUND

The archipelago has several large islands that form the core of Åland. Some of Finland's oldest historical landmarks are in this region, particularly around Saltvik and Sund. Eckerö in the west is a much-loved Swedish family destination, serviced by regular ferries to/from Grisslehamn.

Bicycle tours are very popular in summer. The islands are pretty flat, paths are well marked, distances comfortable, and bridges or ferries connect the various islands and make up an area large enough for an interesting week of touring.

Jomala

☑018 / POP 4100

You'll see Jomala's coat of arms, which features an enthroned St Olaf, Åland's patron saint, around its two main centres: **Kyrkby**, with a range of facilities, and smaller **Gottby**.

In 1886 landscape painter Victor Westerholm invited some of his artist friends to his summer house in **Önningeby**, a tiny village in eastern Jomala. For almost 30 years artists gathered here, with the house earning the name of the Önningeby Colony. There's an interesting **museum** (☑33710; admission €3; ⊙11am-4pm daily mid-Jun–mid-Aug, noon-3pm Sat Apr, May & Sep), which showcases the work of these artists (although there are none by Westerholm himself) alongside historical memorabilia from the era. Other exhibits follow the work of contemporary artists.

Jomala's **Sankt Olof's Kyrka** (⊙9.30am-3.30pm Tue-Fri, 12.30-3.30pm Sun Jun-Aug) dates back to the 12th century, having had several patch-ups in the meantime. In the worn stonework, carved by Italian stonemasons, it's still possible to make out a lion's jaw with a human head inside.

Two kilometres west of Gottby and 4km off the main road, the peaceful hamlet of **Djurvik** overlooks a gentle bay. Right by the water, **Djurviks Gästgård** (☑32433; www. djurvik.ax; s/d €40/50, 2-/4-person cabins €61/75; ⊙May-Oct; ℗) offers a choice of apartment with a kitchen, several cabins or simple rooms, and also has an endearing garden, plus a rowing boat and kayaks.

From Mariehamn, catch bus 5 to near Önningeby or bus 1 to Gottby.

Finström

☑018 / POP 2500

Finström is the central municipality in Åland, with **Godby** the island's second-biggest 'town' – but with 800 people, it's scarcely a metropolis. The friendly sports centre/youth hostel reception (see p128), 800m from the main crossroads, can help with local tourist information.

In Pålsböle, a small village just 5km north of Godby, **Sankt Mikael Kyrka** (⊙10am-4pm Mon-Fri May-Sep) features a well-preserved interior including a wealth of medieval frescoes and sculptures.

At the bridge across to Sund, the 30m-high **observation tower** (adult/child €1.50/1) at Café

ÅLAND ARCHIPELAGO JOMALA

Uffe på Berget (see below) affords superb views of the archipelago and is a popular photo stop. Across the road is **Godby Arboretum**, a small nature park with native and exotic trees along a short, marked nature trail.

🛏 Sleeping & Eating

Bastö Hotell & Stugby   HOTEL, COTTAGE €€
(☑42382; www.basto.aland.fi; s/d €78/98, cabins per week from €510; ☺mid-May–Aug; ℗) This holiday complex 12km northwest of Godby has short-term basic guesthouse rooms with ensuites, or longer stays (minimum one week) in your own waterside cabin. Family-friendly facilities include saunas, minigolf and a restaurant, and it has its own two-day country-music festival in early July.

Godby Vandrarhem   YOUTH HOSTEL €
(☑41555; www.idrottscenter.com; Skolvägen 2, Godby; dm/s/d €20/37/55; ℗🏊) Attached to Godby's sports centre/swimming pool, this hostel is basic – it's often used for putting up visiting youth sports teams and has that institutional vibe. But it's also one of Finland's newest hostels; it's never oversubscribed; and the super-helpful reception desk functions as a little tourist office. Consider bringing your own food; otherwise, there's a bar/restaurant and a supermarket 800m away at the main crossroads. Free laundry.

Café Uffe på Berget   CAFE €
(☺10am-8pm Jun-Aug, to 6pm May, 10am-6pm Sat & Sun Sep) One kilometre outside Godby, this laid-back cafe lords it over the bridge on the Mariehamn–Sund Rd. The espresso machine is busy, the pancakes are good and if the creaking wooden observation tower causes trepidation, the views from the cafe alone are gorgeous. The amiable staff will also make up a picnic bag for you.

🍺 Drinking

Stallhagen Brewery   BREWERY, PUB €
(☑48500; www.stallhagen.com; Getavägen 196, Godby) You'll see Stallhagen's brews being downed throughout Åland, but here's a chance to get it fresh. If you're interested in the brewing process, you can arrange a tour with the friendly owners.

ℹ Getting There & Away

Rd 2 from Mariehamn takes you to Godby. Buses 2, 3 and 4 from Mariehamn all go via Godby (€2.80), while bus 6 services other parts of Finström, leaving Godby three times a day, Monday to Friday.

Sund

☑018 / POP 1025

Sund, just east of the main island group and connected to Saltvik by bridge, is Åland's very own action hero. As well as having a muscular medieval castle and the big guns of the open-air museum, it's got its battle scars in the ruins of a Russian stronghold.

Sund is just 30km from Mariehamn, which makes it an easy half-day trip by car or, if you're cycling, an excellent place to stay overnight. Finby is the largest town, with all services.

◉ Sights & Activities

Kastelholms Slott   CASTLE
(adult/7-15yr €5/3.50; ☺10am-5pm daily May, Jun & Aug–mid-Sep, to 6pm Jul, English tours 2pm weekends late Jun-early Aug) One of Åland's premier sights is the medieval Kastelholms Slott, a breathtaking castle set alongside a picturesque little inlet. Construction began in the 14th century but several extensions have been made since, most notably by Gustav Wasa. The keep towers are 15m high in parts, with walls of 3m-thick red granite: it's easy to see how this castle would once have ruled over all of Åland.

Mad king Eric XIV, deposed by an uprising in 1569, was moved from prison to prison around the Swedish kingdom. He spent three months here, shut up (according to tradition at least) in a tiny chamber in the Kuretorn keep. A fire in 1745 reduced the castle to ruins: only the northern wing survived. Today it contains a good exhibition showing the castle's different phases, and archaeological finds including a medieval silver-coin hoard. The castle is clearly signposted off Rd 2.

The best time to visit is on **Gustav Vasa Dagarna** (Gustav Wasa Days; www.gustavvasadagarna.aland.fi; adult/6-12yr €10/5), actually a weekend in early July when the castle travels back to the 16th century, with dancing, feasting and jousting.

TOP CHOICE ⬦ Bomarsund   RUIN, FORTRESS
East of Sund, this is another mighty sight in Åland. Following the war of 1808–09, Russia began to build this major military structure and naval base as its westernmost defence against the Swedes. At its core was a huge fortress, built from brick and strengthened with distinctive octagonal blocks, containing a garrison town, and protected by ram-

parts and a planned 15 fortified towers. Over the bridge, Prästö became Bomarsund's island of the dead, with a **military hospital** and separate Greek Orthodox, Jewish, Muslim and Christian **graveyards**. The epic construction work took decades, drawing in masons, craftsmen and soldiers from across the Russian Empire.

In 1854 the fortress was still incomplete when the Crimean War began and a French-British naval force bombarded it heavily from the sea. The fortress had been a quarter of a century in the making; within two days the Russians were forced to surrender it.

The ruins stretch for a couple of kilometres, on both sides of the road. Only three of the defensive towers were completed and today, along with the **Huvudfästet** (Main Fort), they make the most impressive sights, particularly **Brännklint tower**, its walls scarred by cannon- and rifle-balls. The overgrown foundations of the garrison town **Nya Skarpans**, populated only by ants and butterflies, are also atmospheric.

Across the water on Prästö, the small **Bomarsund museum** (☑44032; admission by donation; ⊙10am-5pm Mon-Fri Jun & Aug, plus Sat & Sun Jul) displays bits and pieces excavated from the ruins.

FREE **Jan Karlsgårdens Friluftsmuseum**   MUSEUM
(⊙10am-5pm May–mid-Sep) Handily located next to Kastelholms Slott, Jan Karlsgårdens Friluftsmuseum is a sprawling open-air museum that really comes alive during Midsummer celebrations. You can stroll around traditional 18th- and 19th-century Ålandic buildings, including windmills and a smoke sauna. The guidebook (€2) from the museum shop is essential to get the background on each building.

Fängelsemuseet Vita Björn   MUSEUM
(☑432 156; admission €2; ⊙10am-5pm May–mid-Sep) By the entrance to the Jan Karlsgården Museum is this small but interesting prison museum. The building was a jail until 1975 and demonstrates how cells and conditions evolved over the two centuries it was in use. Although it looks like a cottage, the walls and floor are of thick stone, so there was no tunnelling out.

FREE **Sankt Johannes Kyrka**   CHURCH
(⊙9am-4pm Mon-Fri, noon-4pm Sun Jun-Aug) North of Kastelholm is the biggest church

CYCLING THE MAIL ROAD

Wherever you cycle in the Åland archipelago, you can be assured of flat, safe routes and picturesque views of green fields, red granite and sparkling seascapes. A good taster is the Mail Rd, a former postal route that crossed Åland on its way from Stockholm to Turku. Today it has been transformed into a 65km cycling route, marked by red poles, that takes you across nine municipalities, from Eckerö to Värdö – and beyond, if you're game. Handily, it also takes in some of the island's biggest sights including Kastelholms Slott and Bomarsund.

Allow a gentle two days – three if cycling with kids. There are accommodation and eating options along the way, and if you're curious about the history of this route, you can pick up a copy of 'Mail Road Across Åland' from the tourist office.

in Åland. The altarpiece is decorated with a dazzling triptych and a stone cross with the text 'Wenni E'. According to researchers, it was erected in memory of the Hamburg bishop Wenni, who died here while on a crusade in 936.

🍽 Sleeping & Eating

The cafe at Jan Karlsgårdens Friluftsmuseum (see above) serves light snacks and sandwiches that make it a good lunch stop. Local distillery **Tjudö Vingård** (☑0457-072 1192; tjudo.vingard@aland.net; tastings €15, incl lunch/dinner €25/50), which makes spirits from cherries, apples and other berries, can arrange a tasting session in the cafe with advance notice.

Kastelholms Gästhem   B&B €€
(☑43841; www.eckerolinjen.fi/kastelholmsgasthem; Tosarby; s/d €55/75; ⊙May–mid-Oct) The closest accommodation to Kastelholms Slott is this pleasant little guesthouse – very popular with golfers, thanks to its proximity to Åland's finest course. Most of its spotless rooms (with slightly old-fashioned floral decor) have private bathrooms, and there's access to a self-catering kitchen and laundry. The beautiful patios are perfect for evening lazing.

Puttes Camping CAMPGROUND €
(☑44040, 0457-313 4177; puttes.camping@aland.
net; tent sites €10 plus per person €3, cabins from
€35; ☺May-Aug; ℗) Right on the doorstep of
Bomarsund, this cheerful place has plenty
of grassy camp sites and well-priced simple
four-bed cabins. The beach sauna, bike hire,
rowing boats and a canoe jetty attract an out-
doorsy crowd. Its cafe does good pancakes.

❶ Getting There & Away

Rd 2 and bus 4 from Mariehamn to Vårdö will
take you to Sund. The bus goes via Kastelholm
(€3.20, 30 minutes), Bomarsund (€4.30, 40
minutes) and Prästö (€4.50, 45 minutes).

Vårdö

☑018 / POP 450

Vårdö is often skipped by tourists in favour
of the more remote, outer islands. But the
cluster of isles, connected by bridges and
ferries, stretches up to the two islands of
Simskäla (Västra and Östra; West and East,
respectively), with plenty of remote beaches
to discover. It's been a refuge for Finnish and
Swedish writers who have come for its rip-
pling bays, rustling silver birches and views
over the numerous islets of the archipelago.
Mountain-top bonfires were once lit here to
warn the rest of Åland's inhabitants of approaching danger: they're still burning on
the municipality's coat of arms.

Ferries to outer islands leave from Hummelvik, but **Vargata** is also a key settlement,
with a bank (but no ATM), shop and post
office; the library has free internet access.

The island's **church** (☺10am-6pm Jun-Aug),
parts of which date back to the 15th century, is recognisable by its curiously bulbous
tower. On the main road between Vargata
and Lövö, **Seffers Hembygdsgård** (Seffers Homestead; ☑040-0777 328; admission free;
☺10am-4pm Mon-Fri Jul) is an 18th-century
farmhouse that makes an easy if not essential break. It has a windmill, farm equipment and a Midsummer pole.

Sandösunds Camping (see opposite) rents
kayaks (from €30 per day) for exploring the
northern parts of the island.

🛏 Sleeping

Stormskärs Konferens &
Värdhus GUESTHOUSE €€
(☑47560; www.stormskar.ax; Västerövägen 176,
Västra Simskäla; d from €80) Set on the island
of Västra Simskäla, this family-run place has

excellent rooms in a traditional 19th-century
farmhouse (with broadband). Bathrooms
are shared but the house is small enough for
it not to be an issue. In peak season, the restaurant serves meat from the farm's organic
cattle and daily-caught fish. The guesthouse
also runs the bicycle ferry to the island.

Bomans Gästhem HOSTEL, B&B €€
(☑47821; www.visitaland.com/bomansgasthem;
Vårdöby; s/d from €40/75; ☺May-Aug; ℗) This
HI-affiliated hostel is signposted 500m off
the road between Vargata and Lövö. The
cheapest (smallest) rooms are in the main
building, with slightly nicer ones inside
a row of little bungalows. There's a guest
kitchen, sauna, rental bikes and a driving
range in the field out front.

Sandösunds Camping CAMPGROUND €
(☑47750; www.sandocamping.aland.fi; tent sites €2
plus per person/vehicle €2/2, 2-/4-person cabins
from €42/50; ☺May-Aug) This well-positioned
camping ground, just off the main road after
you cross the bridge from Vårdö to Sandö, offers several remarkably peaceful camp sites.
The beachside cabins are well kept, but the facilities here are the real bonus, and include a
range of kayaks and bicycles, plus the unique
'floating sauna' that lets you hop straight into
the water on the picture-perfect sound.

❶ Getting There & Away

Vårdö is connected to the island of Prästö by a
network of ferries. Bus 4 will take you to Vårdö
from Mariehamn (€4.50, one hour), crossing on
the short, free car ferry from Prästö.

Ferries on the northern archipelago route
depart from the village of Hummelvik on Vårdö;
the bus meets them. For more details see p132.
For information on the bicycle ferry between
Saltvik and Vårdö, see p131.

Saltvik

☑018 / POP 1800

Vikings have been sharpening their horned
helmets here for centuries: **Kvarnbo**, the
central village of Saltvik, is thought to have
been their capital on Åland. Many relics
have been unearthed around the municipality, though few signs of longhouses remain.

Southeast of Kvarnbo is the Iron Age fortress of **Borgboda**, built in the mid- to late
1st millennium. Some stone outcroppings
remain but the only structure is Ida's Stuga
(Ida's Cottage), the home of folk singer Ida
Jansson in the 20th century.

Kvarnbo also has the red-granite **Sankta Maria Kyrka** (☉10am-4pm Mon-Fri Jun-Aug), which dates from the 13th century and contains a fine clover-shaped baptismal font and fragmentary frescoes of the period. Around the church, it's possible to discern ruins of Vikings' homes.

At 129m above sea level, Åland's highest 'mountain' **Orrdals Klint** is really no more than a big hill. Two short, well-marked walking tracks (1km and 2.5km long, respectively) lead to the top, where there's a viewing tower and a simple four-bed camp hut.

The best chance to see Viking heritage is at Saltvik's annual **Viking Market** (☑0457-342 7500; www.fibula.ax; Kvarnbo; adult/6-10yr €10/5), a three-day festival of eating, drinking and costumed merrymaking in July.

TOP
CHOICE **Kvarnbo Gästhem** (☑44015; www. kvarnbogasthem.com; Kvarnbo; d incl breakfast €80) is a neat little guesthouse with eight top-notch rooms renovated – with love and attention to period style – to fit with the 19th-century building. All have private bathrooms, and a brilliant breakfast is included. You can also admire/dabble in the friendly owners' hobbies: Ella is a sommelier who runs wine-tasting courses in the guesthouse, and Martin restores old Indian motorbikes in the workshop out back!

ⓘ Getting There & Away

Bus 3 runs from Mariehamn to Kvarnbo (€3.40, 35 minutes) and other villages in Saltvik.

A private bicycle ferry, **Kajo** (☑040-078 3086; adult/child €10/5; ☉departs Tengsödavik 11.30am & Västra Simskäla 11am late Jun–mid-Aug by request), runs between Tengsödavik and Västra Simskäla in Vårdö with only one daily departure each way. You'll need to call ahead to confirm.

Geta

☑018 / POP 474

The quiet northern municipality of Geta is known as the apple basket of Åland. The main attraction is **Getabergen**, a formidable peak of 98m, with a nature trail (2km) aimed at kids (2km), and a longer trail (5.5km) leading to Djupviksgrottan, a spacious natural grotto.

Bus 2 runs from Mariehamn to the town of **Geta** (€4.50, 45 minutes) Monday to Friday via Godby.

The bicycle ferry **Silvana** (☑040-022 9149; ☉late Jun–mid-Aug) travels between Hällö in

Geta, and Skarpnåtö in Hammarland. There is one departure daily in early June (leaving Skarpnåtö at 11am and arriving at Hällö at 11.30pm) and two daily departures in July (the second leaves Skarpnåtö at 4.30pm and arrives at Hällö at 5pm). The one-way trip costs €9.

Hammarland

☑018 / POP 1500

Hammarland in the northwest has one of the largest populations of Swedish speakers in Finland, and is also one of the oldest inhabited areas in Åland. Although it's pleasant enough, there are few real sights, which makes it an ideal place to put your feet up. **Kattby** is the main village, with all facilities.

Sankta Catharina Kyrka (☉9am-4pm Mon-Fri summer) in Kattby was built in the 13th century, though a fire at the beginning of the 15th century led it to be rebuilt with fresh wall paintings. There's an **Iron Age burial site** to the west of the church, with more than 30 burial sites.

🛏 Sleeping & Eating

Kattnäs Camping   CAMPGROUND €
(☑37687; tent sites €3.50 plus per person/car €3.50/3.50, cabins €38-45; ☉May–mid-Sep) This well-equipped camping ground is delightfully distant from touristy Eckerö but still waterside. Cabins are comfy and there's a TV lounge and cafe in case you're missing civilisation. To get here, turn off the Eckerö–Mariehamn Rd and head 3km south to Kattby; the camping ground is to the west.

Holmgärds Stugor   COTTAGE €
(☑37848; holmgards@aland.net; per week cabins €75, cottages from €350) This reliable spot near Marsund has seven holiday cottages for weekly rent, and five sturdy timber cabins that come with fridges and kitchenettes. Handy communal facilities include a sauna, a laundry, and a smoke hut in case you catch any fish. And a family of tame hares hop about the place!

ⓘ Getting There & Away

Bus 1 from Mariehamn to Eckerö runs through Hammarland. For information on the bicycle ferry between Hammarland and Geta, see above.

Eckerö

🎣018 / POP 952

Let's face it: Eckerö is basically Sweden. This tiny island is a two-hour ferry ride from mainland Sweden, and vacationing Swedes have been outnumbering locals since Gustav Wasa decreed that an inn be built near Eckerö for his hunting pleasure. Even the red Viking longboat on the municipality's coat of arms seems to be setting sail for the west, possibly towing this little island back as a souvenir.

Eckerö is a picturesque spot with rusty red boatsheds and granite rocks looming from the water. There are plenty of little sandy beaches; **Degersand**, about 9km south of Storby beyond the village of Torp, is particularly good for swimming and sunning.

Storby (Big Village) is the main centre, with a petrol station and bank. The nearby ferry terminal has a year-round **tourist information desk** (🎣39462; www.eckero.ax); you can also get tourist information at the Post och Tullhuset, and the Jakt och Fiskemuseum.

NORTHERN & SOUTHERN ARCHIPELAGOS

Åland's tiny granite islets are strewn with silver birches and ripe for gentle exploration. Strap on a pair of stout walking boots, or hop onto a bicycle, and see where the archipelago tides take you. (But check return ferry times carefully to avoid getting stranded!)

Northern Archipelago

The scattered islands of Kumlinge (population 364) and Brändö (population 487) are little travelled – you may find yourself the only visitor on some islands.

Kumlinge (www.kumlinge.info) is a haven of peace. Its biggest attraction is a **walking path** from the Remmarina guest harbour to **Sankta Anna Kyrka** (⊙1-6pm Mon-Fri Jul–mid-Aug), an attractive church 2km north of Kumlinge village with 500-year-old Franciscan-style paintings. The best place to stay is **Hasslebo Gästhem** (🎣55418; www.hasslebo.com; tent sites €7, s/d €50/70; ⊚), 3km outside Kumlinge village. It has a green emphasis including bio-toilet, solar power and organic breakfast (with homemade jam), and massages (€40) are on offer for extra relaxation. Bike hire costs €9.

Ferries on the route between Hummelvik (Värdö) and Torsholma (Brändö) stop at Kumlinge (70 minutes).

Brändö (www.brando.ax) municipality is composed of over 1180 islands, but the core group of Brändö, Torsholma, Åva and Jurmo are connected by free ferries and bridges, with a signposted **bike route** running from Torsholma harbour north across the main island to Åva. Brändö, of course, has its church **Sankt Jakobs Kyrka** (⊙10am-9pm May-Aug), an example of the whitewashed style. In addition to admiring Åland's hallmark long-haired cattle, you can ride Icelandic horses at **Talli Perla** (🎣040-562 0488; www.talliperla.com, in Finnish; 2-day packages €210), which does a two-day ride-and-accommodation package.

There are various accommodation choices, whether you want to camp at **Brändö Stugby** (🎣56221; home.aland.net/lameta; tent sites €9 plus vehicle €3, cabins €60-80; ⊙May-mid-Oct), or stay at the modest **Hotell Gullvivan** (🎣56350; www.gullvivan.ax; d €96, cabins €88-96; 🅿), set near the pier on Björnholma island. All rooms have a view of the water, there's a restaurant, and you can hire boats and fishing gear. A summer **tourist office** (🎣040-189 2400; info@brando.ax; ⊙9.30am-6.30pm Mon-Fri, 12.45-6.15pm Sat, 10am-6pm Sun mid-Jun–early Aug) on Osnäs can help book cottages throughout the municipality.

Coming from Kustavi (passenger free, bicycle/car €5/15) on the Finnish mainland, you'll arrive at Långö in the north of Brändö. The ferry from Åland (passenger free, bicycle/car €5/25) departs from Hummelvik and takes about 2½ hours.

Southern Archipelago

KÖKAR

Today most of Kökar's 260 inhabitants live in the quaint little town of Karlby. The islands' appealingly barren landscape attracted earlier visitors, including Bronze Age seal hunters and Hanseatic traders, and **Sankta Anne Kyrka** (⊙9am-9pm May-Sep), with its unusual votive Turkish pirate ship, was built on top of a medieval Franciscan monastery – the

Post och Tullhuset HISTORIC BUILDING

Storby's Post & Customs House was designed by German architect CL Engel, famous for his classic architectural work in central Helsinki. It was completed in 1828, during the era of Tsar Alexander I of Russia, and has the hallmarks of that grand epoch. As Åland was the westernmost extremity of the Russian Empire, the building was built as a show of might to Sweden, which explains why this tiny town has such a majestic post office. It was also a crucial point in the Mail Rd that ran from Sweden to Finland.

The building has become a hub for local artists and craftspeople, with changing exhibitions and a small **craft shop** (☉10am-5pm Mon-Fri, 11am-3pm Sat & Sun Jun–mid-Aug). There's also the one-roomed **mailboat museum** (admission €3; ☉10am-3pm Tue-Sun Jun–mid-Aug), which tells the story (briefly!) of the dedicated people who sailed the Mail Rd, and a popular cafe (p135).

Käringsund Harbour HARBOUR

Just north of Storby is attractive Käringsund harbour. On summer evenings this peaceful little cove with its rustic old wooden

monks' chapel and ruined walls make for a pensive evening stroll. Nearby, **Otterböte**, where seal hunters set up camp 3000 years ago, is one of the archipelago's most important archaeological sites. Little remains, but a tangle of atmospheric **walking trails** crisscross the area – at times, you feel as though the hunters are only a turn of the path away. **Kökar Homestead Museum** (☎0457-524 4077; admission €2; ☉11am-5pm late Jun–mid-Aug) is a sweet little collection of local history in the village of Hellsö.

Hotell Brudhäll (☎55955; www.brudhall.com; Karlby; s/d/ste €103/126/225; ☉May-Aug; P) is one of the archipelago's best hotels, with stylish rooms (the nicest have dinky lofts) and a great terraced restaurant by the visitor marina. There's also a fabulous camping ground, **Sandvik Gästhamn & Camping** (☎55911; www.sandvik.ax; tent sites €10 plus per person €2.50; ☉May-Sep), 3.5km southwest of Karlby, with sheltered camping areas, kitchen facilities, a laundry, sauna, barbecue, shop, plenty of bikes for hire, and a good swimming beach.

Up to three ferries daily (passenger free, bicycle/car €5/25; 2¼ hours) come to Kökar from Galtby harbour, 75km from Turku. From Åland, there are up to five ferry connections (passenger free, bicycle/car €5/25; 2½ hours) from Långnäs (Lumparland; take bus 5 from Mariehamn).

FÖGLÖ

Föglö (population 582) island group is a short, easy hope from mainland Åland. Tiny **Degerby** is the main town, notable for its unusual architecture: historically, many Föglöites were civil servants rather than farmers, and chose to build in art nouveau or empire styles. Services here include a summer **tourist information kiosk** (☎045-7342 7274; www.foglo.ax/turism; ☉10am-5.30pm Mon-Sat, 12.30-4pm Sun mid-Jun–mid-Aug) and funny little local **museum** (☎50348; admission €2; ☉10am-1pm & 1.30-5pm Tue-Sun mid-Jun–mid-Aug), containing the islanders' personal collections of biros, bottle-tops and biscuit cutters.

A signposted **bike route** runs from Degerby to **Överö**; or you could pedal to the 14th-century **Sankta Maria Magdalena Kyrka** (☉11am-4pm Mon-Sat mid-Jun–mid-Aug), on an island south from Degerby, connected by a bridge and a scenic road. The conservation island of **Björkör** is close to Degerby harbour – **Coja Fishing** (☎040-094 7502; tours per hr €50; ☉Jun-Aug) can take you there.

Enighetens Gästhem (☎50310; tent sites €8, s/d €50/75; ☉May-Sep; P), a rustic former courthouse, is the best place to stay in Degerby. Creaky-floored rooms (with shared bathrooms) contain old stoves and period furniture, and a harmonium graces the sitting room. The cafe makes for a good bite, camping is possible, and there's a swimming pier. Hire bicycles (per four hours/day €5/8) from Degerby Mat & Café, near the harbour.

A dozen ferries make the one-hour trip between Svinö (Lumparland) and Degerby (bicycle/car €5/15), but only a couple link up with bus 5 from Mariehamn. Other ferries run from Långnäs to Överö (bicycle/car €5/15), some going on to Kumlinge, and others to Kökar. Advance booking is necessary with a car.

boathouses reflecting on the water is so scenic it's almost unreal. There's a nature trail and small beach here, and canoes and rowing boats can be hired from a kiosk nearby.

By the harbour is **Ålands Jakt och Fiskemuseum** (Åland Hunting & Fishing Museum; ☎38299; adult/child €4.20/1.70; ⏰10am-6pm mid-Jun–mid-Aug, to 5pm Mon-Sat late May & late Aug), which gets a little ghoulish after so much stuffed wildlife and gun-toting photographs. If you prefer your animals alive, just outside the museum is **Viltsafari** (☎38103; tours adult/7-14yr €8/5; ⏰departs noon, 1pm, 2pm & 3pm Mon-Sat mid-Jun–mid-Aug), a fenced-in nature park where you can get up close to Finnish fauna like red and fallow deer, swans and wild boar (plus the odd ostrich) on a 45-minute tour.

Sankt Lars Kyrka CHURCH
(admission by donation; ⏰10am-6pm Jun-Aug) The village of Kyrkoby, about 5km east of Storby on the road to Mariehamn, was named for the 13th-century Sankt Lars Kyrka. It's an attractive church with a 14th-century Madonna sculpture and rustic murals. The altar painting is a 19th-century work depicting a Magdalene penitent.

Nimix KAYAKING
(☎0506 6716; www.nimix.ax; per 2hr/day €17/35) Rents out kayaks. Based in Eckerö, but can deliver to locations all over Åland for a fee (€25 to €90).

Sleeping

Eckerö has more cabin and cottage rentals than any other Åland municipality – contact Ålandsresor (p126) in Mariehman for details.

Käringsund RESORT €€
(☎38000; www.karingsund.ax; tent sites €5-14, cabins €46-56, bungalows €82-250; ⏰closed Dec) A whistles-and-bells family resort set in green fields by the seashore, this place offers cabins and bungalows priced according to size (some sleep up to 10 people), cushiness and closeness to the beach. There's every conceivable form of child-friendly entertainment (air-football, minigolf, boules, pedal boats), plus a pizza restaurant, tennis court, sauna, and kayak, boat, bike and moped hire. The camping ground and cheap cabins are part of the resort's Alebo camp site, with separate reception desk.

Österängens Hotell HOTEL, COTTAGE €€
(☎38268; osterangen@aland.net; Torp; s/d €80/90, cottages from €75; ⏰Mar-Sep; P 🏊) There are just over 20 balconied rooms in this place, all of them looking out onto the quiet beach of Torp; or for more privacy, go for one of the little cottages. With a sweet little restaurant, an indoor pool, two saunas and fishing equipment, it's hard to find a reason to leave.

Hotel Elvira HOTEL €€
(☎38200; www.elvira.ax; Sandmovägen 85, Storby; s/d/tr €90/110/160) This idiosyncratic little spot, with its book-lined walls, quirky antiques and sea-monster murals, is the antithesis of the Käringsund resort: peace and civility reign. Twelve rooms have sea views; unlike many other places, they don't come with a higher price tag. Rooms vary in size, style (some are decorated with Marimekko prints, others with vintage sewing patterns) and datedness (those on the ground floor have new bathrooms). Upstairs is a brand-new sauna, and the à la carte restaurant opens for dinner year-round.

Eckerö Hotell & Restaurang HOTEL €€
(☎38447; www.eckerohotell.ax; Käringsundsvägen 53, Eckerö; s/d/f incl breakfast €99/120/156; ⏰Mar-Nov) Famous (some might say notorious) for its summer Saturday-night Elvis shows, this family-run hotel is a little gloomy, but the welcome is unfailingly warm. Its (mostly ground-floor) rooms are serviceable, with anti-allergen bedding and a good breakfast buffet thrown in. For the record, Presley pretender Ronald Karlsson might not have the look (he has a moustache) but sounds bang-on. This place is on the road to Käringsund, on the right just as you leave the village of Storby.

ISLAND OF WIDOWS

Dangerous dogs are the scourge of most modern posties, but the postmen who delivered mail along the Mail Rd, which ran from Stockholm to Turku via Åland, had far more formidable conditions to face. Between 1638 and 1895, local farmers were called upon to transport thousands of letters each week across the Åland sea. The most treacherous time was early spring when the sea ice broke, sending many of the small post boats to the bottom of the sea. During the years that the Mail Rd operated, 200 men from Eckerö died doing their postal duties, earning it the name 'the Island of Widows'.

✗ Eating & Drinking

All of the accommodation options listed have good licensed restaurants. Try the following for snacks and coffee while you're out and about.

Bara Bodegan   CAFE, BAR €
(Käringsund Harbour; snacks €9-13; ☺10am-11pm Jun-Aug) Set right on the pier, this atmospheric place is perfect for downing a few beers and watching the sun set over the red creaking boathouses. The menu runs to pasta and some good snacks fill the hole between drinks.

Café Lugn & Ro   CAFE €
(Post och Tullhuset, Storby; snacks €4-8; ☺10am-4pm May-Sep, to 6pm Jul) This friendly place serves sandwiches, but will particularly delight the sweet-toothed with cakes, pastries and handmade chocolates. Incidentally, the cafe sells some of the nicest postcards of Åland, with photos taken by local artists.

ℹ Getting There & Away

Rd 2 and bus 1 (€4.40, 35 minutes) run from Mariehamn to Eckerö. For information on ferries between Eckerö and Grisslehamn in Sweden, see p120.

Ferry passengers descend like starving locusts on the **Ro-No Rent** (☑0400 529 315; per day/week €12/60; ☺11am-2pm & 4-6pm Jun–mid-Aug) bicycle-rental hut at Eckerö harbour: book ahead to avoid disappointment. Bicycles can be dropped off at either of the Ro-No Rent outlets in Mariehamn (see p123). The distance from Mariehamn to Storby (40km) makes this a suitable day trip by bicycle.

Lemland

☑018 / POP 1820
When the occupying Russians needed a shipping route in the late 19th century, their prisoners of war dug the **Lemström Canal**.

Today it remains one of Lemland's defining sights. Lemland lies between Lumparland and the canal, 5km east of Mariehamn on Rd 3 (take bus 5), with **Norrby** village at its centre.

In Norrby, **Sankta Birgitta Kyrka** (☺noon-6pm Mon-Fri Jun-Aug) has 13th- and 14th-century wall paintings that tell the story of St Nicholas, the patron saint of seafarers. At **Lemböte**, on the western side of the island, is a restored 13th-century church and several ancient burial mounds. Near the crossing to Lumparland, **Skeppargården Pellas** (☑34420; adult/child €3/free; ☺11am-4pm late Jun-Aug) is the homestead museum of a local shipmaster.

Lumparland

☑018 / POP 392
Most travellers go straight to Lumparland's two ferry harbours, **Svinö** and **Långnäs**, but there are a few reasons to take a day trip here.

Sankt Andreas Kyrka (☺noon-6pm Mon-Fri Jun-Aug) was built in 1720 and is Åland's oldest surviving wooden church. The curious cross is actually a weathervane that was once attached to the steeple. The large altarpiece was painted by Victor Westerholm of the Önningeby colony (p127).

Lumparland is a good place to explore the wilderness. **Get Out Adventures** (www.get outadventures.ax), based at Svinö harbour, was unfortunately closed in 2011 due to flooding: check the website to see if its excellent guided kayak expeditions and nature hikes have resumed. If you're keen to do it yourself, the well-marked **Lumparlandsleden trail** from Svinö takes four hours through easy terrain and a few little villages.

From Mariehamn take bus 5 to Svinö and Långnäs (€3.80 and €4.30 respectively, 40 minutes); it meets the ferries from Sweden.

Tampere & Häme

Best Places to Eat

» Hella & Huone (p144)

» Tuulensuu (p144)

» Piparkakkutalo (p155)

» Ravintola Roux (p159)

Best Places to Stay

» Dream Hostel (p143)

» Haapasaaren Lomakylä (p149)

» Messilä (p160)

» Scandic Tampere City (p143)

Why Go?

Modern cities and traditional settlements exist side by side in this historic region, where you can explore Finland's rural past at ancient wooden churches, its unsettled history at Hämeenlinna's castle, and its industrial heritage at Tampere's textile factories. Lahti showcases two major 21st-century Finnish exports: technology and classical music.

A gateway to Finland for many travellers thanks to its budget flight connections, Tampere is Finland's second city. Its imposing red-brick factories, left derelict in the hangover of industrial decline, now hold a spicy mixture of restaurants and museums, and the infectious energy of the people makes this a favourite Suomi stop.

Every town in the region sits on a magical stretch of water. Boats were once the main form of transport, and one of Finland's essential summer experiences is to bring those slower-paced days back with a day-long lake cruise between towns.

When to Go
TAMPERE

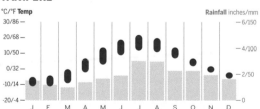

Jul Best time for lake cruises and long evenings on summer terraces.

Sep Great hiking in national parks, and the Sibelius festival in Lahti.

Dec Christmas atmosphere and spectacular lights in Tampere.

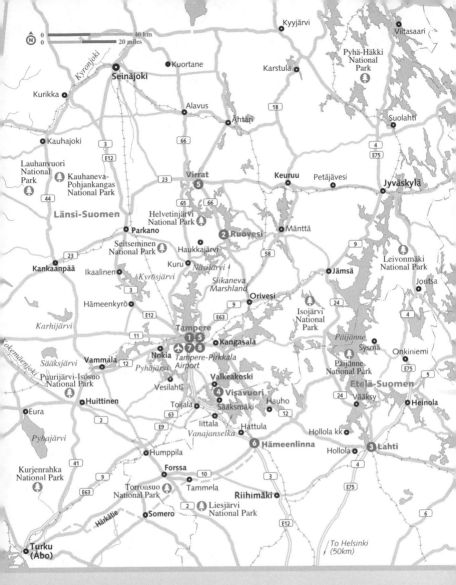

Tampere & Häme Highlights

1 Absorbing the laid-back but culturally engaged vibe in picturesque **Tampere** (p138)

2 Getting your kicks on Finland's Route 66, staying in peaceful **Ruovesi** (p149)

3 Luxuriating in the acoustics of a Sibelius performance at Lahti's **Sibeliustalo** (p158)

4 Admiring the work of Finland's greatest sculptor, Emil Wickström, at peaceful **Visavuori** (p151)

5 Cruising the **Poet's Way** (p142) from Tampere to Virrat, a memorable feast of Finnish lakescapes

6 Snooping from room to room in **Palanderin Talo**

(p154), one of Finland's most interesting house-museums

7 Perspiring like a racehorse in the soft steam of Tampere's traditional **public sauna** (p141)

8 Exploring the venerable churches throughout this region, contrasting the ancient artwork with that in Tampere's memorable **cathedral** (p138)

History

The region saw much of the earliest Swedish settlement in Finland's interior. In 1249 Earl Birger, on a Catholic crusade, founded Tavastehus (Hämeenlinna). The Swedish settlers who followed established large estates – causing irritation among locals. Tampere's rise to prominence was in the 19th century, and its important workers' movement was bolstered by Lenin himself. Finland's civil war erupted shortly after independence, and Tampere was the scene of the communist Reds' most decisive defeat at the hands of the progovernment Whites.

Tampere

📞 03 / POP 213,344

Scenic Tampere, set between two vast lakes, has a down-to-earth vitality that makes it a Finland favourite for many visitors. Through its centre, churn the Tammerkoski rapids, whose grassy banks contrast with the red brick of the imposing fabric mills that once gave the city the moniker 'Manchester of Finland'.

A popular weekend destination for Britons thanks to its budget flight connections, Tampere doesn't disappoint: its students ensure plenty of evening action, and its regenerated industrial buildings house quirky museums, enticing shops, pubs, cinemas and cafes. It's the launch pad for Finland's most romantic lake cruise, and a spot where there always seems to be something going on: its leap into the 21st century has given it an infectious energy.

Tampere is set between Näsijärvi and Pyhäjärvi, which are connected by the Tammerkoski. Just about everything is conveniently arranged along one street, Hämeenkatu, with the train station at its eastern end.

History

In the Middle Ages, the area around Tampere was inhabited by the Pirkka tribe, a devil-may-care guild of hunters and trappers who collected taxes as far north as Lapland. Modern Tampere was founded in 1779 during the reign of Sweden's Gustav III.

During the 19th century, the Tammerkoski rapids, which today supply abundant hydroelectric power, were a magnet for textile industries. The Russian Revolution in 1917 increased interest in socialism among Tampere's large working-class population. It be-

came the capital of the 'Reds' during the civil war that followed Finnish independence.

As many as 12,000 people were employed here in the textile industry in the 1950s, but as this dwindled, the city was forced to reinvent itself; its urban renewal is one of Finland's success stories.

◉ Sights

Tampereen Tuomiokirkko CHURCH
(Tuomiokirkonkatu 3; ⊘9am-6pm May-Aug, 11am-3pm Sep-Apr) Tampere's intriguing cathedral is one of the most notable examples of National Romantic architecture in Finland. It was designed by Lars Sonck and completed in 1907. The famous artist Hugo Simberg was responsible for the frescoes and stained glass; once you've seen them you'll appreciate that they were controversial at the time. A procession of ghostly childlike apostles holds the 'garland of life', the garden of death shows graves and plants tended by skeletal figures, while another image shows a wounded angel being stretchered off by two children. There's a solemn, almost mournful feel about it; the altarpiece, by Magnus Enckell, is a dreamlike Resurrection in similar style. The symbolist stonework and disturbing colours of the stained glass add to the haunting ambience.

Finlayson Centre CULTURAL CENTRE
Tampere's era as an industrial city began with the arrival of Scot James Finlayson, who established a small workshop by the Tammerkoski in 1820. He later erected a huge cotton mill; the massive red-brick building was the first in the Nordic countries to have electric lighting, which started operating in 1882. It has now been sensitively converted into a mall of cafes and shops; you'll also find a cinema here, as well as a great brewery pub and a couple of intriguing museums.

Vakoilumuseo MUSEUM
(Spy Museum; www.vakoilumuseo.fi; Satakunnankatu 18; adult/child €7/5.50; ⊘10am-6pm Mon-Sat, 11am-5pm Sun Jun-Aug, 11am-5pm daily Sep-May) The offbeat spy museum under the Finlayson Centre plays to the budding secret agent in all of us, with a large and well-assembled display of devices of international espionage, mainly from the Cold War era. As well as histories of famous Finnish and foreign spies, it has numerous Bond-style gadgets and some interactive displays – write your name in invisible ink, tap a telephone call, intercept an email or measure the micro-

wave emissions of your mobile. The folders with English translations are slightly unsatisfying though. For a little extra, the kids can take a suitability test for KGB cadet school.

Amurin Työläismuseokortteli
MUSEUM

(Amuri Museum of Workers' Housing; www.tampere.fi/amuri; Satakunnankatu 49; adult/child €6/1; ☺10am-6pm Tue-Sun mid-May–mid-Sep) An entire block of 19th-century wooden houses, including 32 apartments, a bakery, a shoemaker, two general shops and a cafe, is preserved here. It's one of the most realistic house-museums in Finland – many homes look as if the tenant has left just moments ago to go shopping. This area was built by the textile companies to house their workers.

Särkänniemi
AMUSEMENT PARK, GALLERY

(www.sarkanniemi.fi; day pass adult/child up to €34/29) On the northern edge of town, this promontory amusement park is a large complex with several attractions, including a good art gallery and an aquarium. There's a bewildering system of entry tickets and opening times depending on what your interest is, and it is cheaper to book online. A day pass is valid for all sights and unlimited rides, while €10 will get you up the observation tower, and into the gallery and farm zoo. To get to Särkänniemi, take bus 4 from the train station.

Inside the amusement park are dozens of **rides** (☺roughly 10am-7pm mid-May–Aug) including the 'Tornado super roller coaster', plus cafes and restaurants. The **aquarium** (☺noon-7pm mid-May–Aug, 11am-9pm winter) has limited information in English and isn't especially memorable, with the Finnish fish (including some rare sturgeon relatives) more interesting than the colourful hobby-tank favourites. The **planetarium**, with daily shows, is in the same complex, above which soars the 168m-high **Näsinneula Observation Tower** (☺11am-11.30pm). This is the tallest such tower in these northern lands and it alone is worth the visit, with spectacular views of the city and surrounding lakes. There's a revolving restaurant near the top.

Opposite, the **Dolphinarium** has cheerful bottlenoses who put on a show one to five times per day in summer. At other times of the year you can watch them training. Nearby is the **children's zoo**, with gentle domestic animals.

On a different note, the complex also contains the **Sara Hildén art museum** (www.tampere.fi/sarahilden; ☺11am-6pm Tue-Sun Sep–mid-May, noon-7pm daily mid-May–Aug), which has a collection of international and Finnish modern art and sculpture amassed by Sara Hildén, a local businessperson and art collector. The space is normally devoted to excellent exhibitions showcasing particular artists. There are good views from the cafe.

FREE Werstas
MUSEUM

(www.tyovaenmuseo.fi; Väinö Linnanaukio 8; admission charge for special exhibitions; ☺11am-6pm Tue-Sun) This labour museum is dedicated to the history of working and of workers' movements, with a variety of changing exhibitions covering social history and labour industries. The permanent exhibition consists of three parts: a reconstruction of various historically typical Finnish workplaces – a shop, a printing press; an in-depth focus on textiles and in particular Tampere's textile industry; and a hall holding the enormous steam engine and wheel that powered up the Finlayson factory in the 19th century.

Vapriikki
MUSEUM

(www.vapriikki.fi; Veturiaukio 4; adult/child €8/3; ☺10am-6pm Tue-Sun) Tampere's premier exhibition space is a bright, modern glass and steel gallery in the renovated Tampella textile mill. As well as regularly changing exhibitions on anything from bicycles to Buddhism, there's a permanent display on Tampere's history, a **natural history museum**, and a small but cluttered **ice-hockey museum**, with memorabilia of the players and teams that star in Finland's sporting passion. There's also a **museum of shoes** – Tampere was known for its footwear industry – and a pleasant cafe.

Lenin-Museo
MUSEUM

(www.lenin.fi; Hämeenpuisto 28; adult/child €5/3; ☺9am-6pm Mon-Fri, 11am-4pm Sat & Sun) Admirers of bearded revolutionaries won't want to miss the small Lenin museum, housed in the Workers' Hall where Lenin and Stalin first met at a conference in 1905 (see p317 for more on Lenin's time in Finland). His life is documented by way of photos and documents; it's a little dry but it's fascinating to see, for example, his old school report (Vladimir was a straight-A student) or a threadbare couch that the man slept on. There's a crazy gift shop where you can buy Lenin pens, badges, T-shirts and other souvenirs of the Soviet era.

Tampere

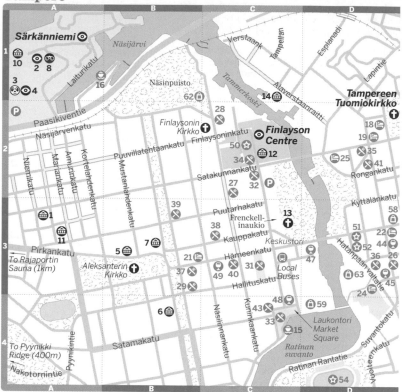

Muumilaakso MUSEUM

(Moomin Valley Museum; www.tampere.fi/muumi; Hämeenpuisto 20; adult/child €7/2; ☺9am-5pm Tue-Fri, 10am-6pm Sat & Sun) Explore the creation of Tove Jansson's enduringly popular Moomins in this museum in the basement of the public library building. It contains original drawings and elaborate models depicting stories from Moomin Valley (English explanations available), computer displays, toys and other memorabilia. Naturally, there's a gift shop.

Kivimuseo MUSEUM

(Mineral Museum; www.tampere.fi/kivimuseo; Hämeenpuisto 20; adult/child €4/1; ☺9am-5pm Tue-Fri, 10am-6pm Sat & Sun) Adjacent to the Moomins is this small museum, with a huge array of delicate, spectacular crystal formations and vivid colours, as well as fossils that include dinosaur eggs. Needless to say, although it has the same hours as Moomin Valley, it doesn't have the same crowds.

Hiekan Taidemuseo GALLERY

(www.hiekantaidemuseo.fi; Pirkankatu 6; adult/child €7/4; ☺3-6pm Tue-Thu, noon-3pm Sun) The collection of Kustaa Hiekka (1855–1937), a wealthy industrialist, is contained in this museum. There are paintings, furniture and fine old gold and silver items in the impressive building.

Tampereen Taidemuseo GALLERY

(www.tampere.fi/taidemuseo; Puutarhakatu 34; adult/child €6/2; ☺10am-6pm Tue-Sun) Tampere's city art gallery has good-quality changing exhibitions of mostly contemporary art.

Ortodoksinen Kirkko CHURCH

(www.ort.fi; Tuomiokirkonkatu 3; ☺10am-4pm Mon-Sat, from noon Sun Jun-Aug, Mon-Fri only May) Near the train station, the small, ornate, onion-domed orthodox church is also worth a visit. During the civil war, White troops besieged the church, which had been taken over by the Reds.

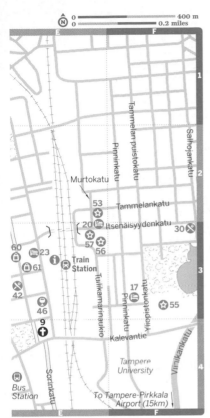

walk from the centre of town, west along Satamakatu, bearing left at a small park, then right up the hill.

Rajaportin Sauna
SAUNA
(www.rajaportinsauna.fi; Pispalan Valtatie 9; adult/ child €6/1; ☺6-10pm Mon & Wed, 3-9pm Fri, 2-10pm Sat) This traditional place is Finland's oldest operating public sauna. It's a great chance to experience the softer steam from a traditionally heated sauna rather than the harsher electric ones. It's a couple of kilometres west of the centre; buses 1, 13, and 22 among others head out there. There's a cafe on site, and massages can be arranged. Take a towel or rent one there.

Fishing
FISHING
To fish the Tammerkoski in the town centre, you will need a daily (€5) or weekly (€20) permit, available from the tourist office, among other places. The tourist office also has a list of operators who run guided fishing tours in the lakes and rivers in the area, which is known for pike and pike-perch (zander). The website www.zanderland.fi has useful information about fishing in the Tampere area.

☞ Tours
You can get an overview of Tampere's attractions on a (adult/child €16/4; ☺2pm mid-Jun–Aug). These depart from in front of the tourist office and cover the main sights, taking about two hours, with commentary in Finnish and English.

Cruises
Trips on Tampere's two magnificent lakes are extremely popular in summer and there are plenty of options. Trips on Näsijärvi leave from Mustalahti Quay, while Laukontori Quay serves Pyhäjärvi. All cruises can be booked at the tourist office.

Suomen Hopealinja
BOAT TOUR
(Finnish Silverline; ☏010-422 5600; www.hope alinja.fi) Runs a variety of cruises, including pirate cruises for kids. From Laukontori Quay, short cruises run on Pyhäjärvi from June to August, as well as a shuttle service (adult/child return €10/5) to nearby **Viikinsaari**, a pleasant picnic island with a beach, barbecues and a good restaurant. At Laukontori Quay, a vessel does lunch (€28) and dinner (€35) jaunts with live entertainment.

SS Tarjanne
BOAT TOUR
(☏010-422 5600; www.runoilijantie.fi) From Mustalahti Quay, this glorious steamship

Vanha Kirkko
CHURCH
(Keskustori; ☺11am-1pm Wed-Sun) A landmark on the central square, this is a lovely old wooden church.

✽ Activities
The www.gotampere.fi website has plenty more ideas for getting active in and around Tampere. See Getting Around, p148, for bike and boat rentals.

Pyynikki Ridge
PARK
Rising between Tampere's two lakes, this forested ridge of walking and cycling trails has fine views on both sides. It soars 85m above the lakeshores – this is an Everest by southern Finnish standards – and claims to be the highest gravel ridge in the world. There's a stone **observation tower** (Näkötorni; ☺9am-8pm; adult/child €2/0.50) on the ridge, with a cafe serving Tampere's best doughnuts (€1.50 each). The tower's a 1.5km

Tampere

does evening cruises on Näsijärvi, but is best boarded for the **Poet's Way**, one of the finest lake cruises in Finland. From June to mid-August, this departs Tampere on Wednesdays and Fridays, returning from Virrat on Thursdays and Saturdays. A one-way ticket costs €42 to Ruovesi (4¾ hours) and €53 to Virrat (8¼ hours). For €40 per person, you can sleep in this old boat before or after your trip. Day use of a cabin is also €40. Bicycles can be taken on board for a small fee. You can book a day trip to Virrat (€70) or Ruovesi (€59), with one of the legs made by bus.

The same company runs cruises south to Visavuori (one-way/return €44/66, five hours) at 9.30am Wednesday to Saturday from June to mid-August, continuing to Hämeenlinna (one-way €46, 8¼ hours).

✿ Festivals & Events

There are events in Tampere held throughout the year.

Tampere Film Festival   FILM
(www.tamperefilmfestival.fi) A respected international festival of short films usually held in early March.

Tampere Biennale   MUSIC
(www.tamperemusicfestivals.fi) A festival of new Finnish music, held in April of even-numbered years.

Tammerfest   MUSIC
(www.tammerfest.fi) The city's premier rock-music festival, held over four days in mid-July with concerts at various stages around town.

Tampere International Theatre Festival   THEATRE
(www.teatterikesa.fi) Held in early August, this is a showcase of international and Finnish theatre. **Off-Tampere** is a fringe festival held at the same time.

Tampere Jazz Happening   MUSIC
(www.tamperemusicfestivals.fi) An important event featuring Finnish and international jazz musicians in October or early November.

Tampere Illuminations   LIGHTS
(www.valoviikot.fi) The city streets are brightened by 40,000 coloured lights between late October and early January. The square becomes a Christmas market in December.

🛏 Sleeping

TOP CHOICE Dream Hostel   HOSTEL €
(045-236 0517; www.dreamhostel.fi; Åkerlundinkatu 2; dm €22-27.50, tw/q €65/110; @) Sparky, stylish and spacious, this recent arrival is just about Finland's best hostel. Helpful staff, super-comfortable wide-berth dorms (both unisex and female) in various sizes, a heap of facilities, original decor and the right attitude about everything make it a real winner. It's a short walk from the train station in a quiet area.

Scandic Tampere City   HOTEL €€€
(244 6111; www.scandichotels.com; Rautatienkatu 16; s/d €172/192; P@) Right opposite the train station, this hotel has modern Nordic lines and a fistful of facilities including a sauna, a gym, various restaurants and a cocktail bar. The rooms are spacious and spotless with a clean wooden feel. Superiors are almost

identical, but have a coffee tray and a comfier chair. The hotel has a family-friendly feel and you can borrow bikes or walking poles from reception.

Hostel Sofia   HOSTEL €
(254 4020; www.hostelsofia.fi; Tuomiokirkonkatu 12A; dm/s/d €28/58/75; P@) This comfortable hostel is right opposite the cathedral and fills up fast. A refit has left it looking very spruce, offering rooms with comfortable beds (no bunks), large windows and stepladder shelves, as well as good showers and a kitchenette on every floor. Two floors allow small groups to virtually have their own apartment, and breakfast and laundry are available. If you're going to arrive late, they'll text you a door code. HI discount and bike rental.

Hotelli Victoria   HOTEL €€
(242 5111; www.hotellivictoria.fi; Itsenä-isyydenkatu 1; s/d around €109/142, weekends & summer €89/99; P@) Just on the other side of the railway station from the centre, this friendly hotel offers sound summer value with its spruce rooms, free internet and commendable breakfast spread including waffles, sausage omelette and berry pudding options. Rooms are light and quiet despite the busy road and there's a good sauna. It's closed most of December. Bike hire available.

Sokos Hotel Ilves   HOTEL €€€
(020-1234 631; www.sokoshotels.fi; Hatanpään valtatie 1; s/d €148/168; P@) This huge tower hotel has over 300 rooms, bright with turquoise paint and light wood, and offering excellent views over the heart of town or the Tammerkoski below. Superiors have bigger beds and extras like bathrobes and bottled water, and there's a variety of excellent suites. It's a busy centre, with several restaurants, a popular nightclub and good business facilities. As well as the saunas, there's an enticing jacuzzi. As with all Sokos hotels, rates vary according to demand; above prices are a guide.

Omenahotelli   HOTELS €
(0600 18018; www.omena.com; Hämeenkatu 7 & Hämeenkatu 28; r €45-70) With two locations at the western and eastern ends of the main drag – the latter very handy for the station – this receptionless hotel offers the usual comfortable rooms with twin beds, a microwave, a kettle and a fold-out couch. There's free wi-fi, and the rooms are great value for a family of

four, for example. Book online or via the terminal at the entrance.

Camping Härmälä
CAMPGROUND €

(✆020-719 9777; www.suomicamping.fi; Leirintäkatu 8; tent sites €15 plus per person €5, 2-/5-person cabins €50-78; ☺mid-May–late Aug; P) Four-and-a-half kilometres south of the centre (take bus 1), this is a spacious camping ground on the Pyhäjärvi lakeshore. There's a cafe, saunas and rowing boats, as well as bike hire and an adjacent summer hotel with self-contained rooms (singles/doubles €47/61, open June to late August).

Mango Hotel
HOTEL €€

(www.mangohotel.fi; Hatanpään puistokuja 36; s/d incl breakfast €49/79; P) Unromantically set in a commercial district 2km south of the centre, this unstaffed hotel nevertheless represents value. The rooms – strange, with fake gilt baroque furnishings in pseudo-Asian style – are comfortable enough and share a bathroom between two. A simple breakfast is included, and there's free laundry. Book online or at the door. Buses 1, 3, 6, 7 and 21 get you there.

Sokos Hotel Tammer
HOTEL €€

(✆020-123 4632; www.sokoshotels.fi; Satakunnankatu 13; s/d incl breakfast €127/147; P@) Constructed in 1929, this is one of Finland's oldest hotels and enjoys a fine rapids-side location. After the gloriously old-fashioned elegance of the public areas, the rooms, behind ornate doors, are a little disappointing, though they have the expected facilities and Nordic comfort levels. Parking is very limited; a good breakfast buffet and sauna are included.

Hotel Cumulus Pinja
HOTEL €€

(✆241 5111; www.cumulus.fi; Satakunnankatu 10; s/d €128/153; P@) Around the corner from the cathedral, this elegant art nouveau choice features compact, renovated rooms and an intimate feel that's complemented by the quiet, appealing district and friendly, personal service. There are also suites with sauna and balcony.

✖ Eating

Tampere's speciality, *mustamakkara,* is a mild sausage made with cow's blood, black-pudding style. It's normally eaten with lingonberry jam and is tastier than it sounds. You can get it at the kauppahalli (covered market) or a kiosk at Laukontori market.

TOP CHOICE Tuulensuu
PUB €€

(www.gastropub.net/tuulensuu; Hämeenpuisto 23; mains €14-22; ☺food 3pm-midnight Mon-Fri, from noon Sat, from 5pm Sun) The best of a range of gastropubs that have recently sprouted, this corner spot has a fine range of beers and wines, as well as a lengthy port and cigar menu. The food is lovingly prepared and features staples such as liver and schnitzel, as well as more elaborate plates like duck confit and an excellent cassoulet (vegie version available too). Even the bar snacks are gourmet: fresh-roasted almonds. It's closed Sundays in summer.

Hella & Huone
FRENCH, FINNISH €€€

(✆253 2440; www.hellajahuone.fi; Salhojankatu 48; 1/2/3/6/8 courses €26/40/52/70/82; ☺dinner Tue-Sat) This smart spot serves exquisite French-influenced gourmet creations. There's a menu of eight courses: you choose how many you want to have and pay accordingly. Leave room for the fine Finnish cheeses and fresh berries. There are wines matched to every course.

Neljä Vuodenaikaa
BISTRO €

(4 Saisons; www.4vuodenaikaa.fi; Kauppahalli; dishes €9-18; ☺breakfast Tue-Fri, lunch Mon-Sat) Tucked into a corner of the kauppahalli, this recommended spot brings a Gallic flair to the Finnish lunch hour with delicious plates such as bouillabaisse and French country salad augmented by excellent daily specials and wines by the glass.

Wistub Alsace
FRENCH €€

(✆212 0260; www.wistubalsace.com; Laukontori 6B; mains €21-25; ☺lunch Tue-Fri, dinner Tue-Sat) This small, authentic spot specialises in Alsatian cuisine, offering a small selection of quality dishes, including an always-delicious fish of the day, as well as pizza-like *tartes flambées* (€14 to €16). Deliciously aromatic Alsatian white wines are available, as well as cheaper choices by the glass or jug. Desserts are original and scrumptious; a small terrace offers more-casual dining.

Tiiliholvi
FINNISH €€

(✆020-766 9061; www.tiiliholvi.fi; Kauppakatu 10; mains €21-28; ☺lunch & dinner Mon-Sat, 1-6pm Sun) Set in the brick vaulted cellar of a Jugendstil (art nouveau) building, Tiiliholvi is into its fifth decade. It's still old-fashioned in feel, but the food isn't, and there are some excellent flavour combinations, along with beautiful presentation and personal explanations by the chef if they're not too busy.

Panimoravintola Plevna   BEER HALL €€
(www.plevna.fi, Itäinenkatu 8; mains €10-19; ⊗food
served 11am-10pm) Inside the old Finlayson
textile mill, this big barn of a place offers
a wide range of delicious beer, cider and
perry brewed on the premises, including an
excellent strong stout. Meals are large and
designed to soak it all up: massive sausage
platters and enormous slabs of pork in classic beer-hall style as well as more Finnish
fish and steak dishes. Vegetables here mean
potatoes and onions, preferably fried, but it's
all tasty, and service is fast.

Frankly   BISTRO €€
(⌨212 0235; www.ravintolafrankly.fi; Hallituskatu
22; mains €20-27) This eatery offers a comfortable neighbourhood feel but some pretty
good food. The menu has meaty Finnish
classics like pepper steak alongside some
more-delicate dishes like breast of woodpi-
geon, all in a cosy atmosphere with solici-
tous service.

2h+k   BISTRO €
(www.2hk.fi; Aleksanterinkatu 33; mains €11-20)
Divided into a drinking side and an eating
side, this attractive brick space offers some
tempting, well-priced fare from its open
kitchen. A selection of huge toasted sandwiches, tasty salads as well as snails and an-
tipasti make for good bistro dining.

Finlaysonin Palatsi   FINNISH €€
(⌨040-021 9530; www.finlaysoninpalatsi.com;
Kuninkaankatu 1; mains €18-25) This grand
centenarian residence behind the Finlayson Centre has gardens and grounds and
houses a classy restaurant offering elaborate
dishes with classically Finnish ingredients
garnished with a variety of succulent sauces. The relaxing summer terrace has some
of the same meals plus a range of cheaper
snacks.

Runo   CAFE €
(www.kahvilaruno.fi; Ojakatu 3; sandwiches €3-
5; ⊗9am-8pm Mon-Sat, 10am-8pm Sun) With
an arty crowd and bohemian feel, Runo
('poem') is an elegant, almost baroque cafe
with books, paintings, decent coffee and
huge windows that allow you to keep tabs
on the weather. It's a top spot for either a
light lunch or a spot of quiet contemplation.

Thai Na Khon   THAI €
(www.thainakhon.fi; Hämeenkatu 29; lunch buffets
€7.80, mains €11-18) This Thai restaurant at
the centre's western end is soothingly and
tastefully decorated, with plush seats, var-
nished tables and a colonial-era feel.

Vohvelikahvila   CAFE €
(www.vohvelikahvila.com; Ojakatu 2; waffles €4-
6.50; ⊗10am-8pm Mon-Fri, to 7pm Sat, 11am-7pm
Sun) This cosy and quaint little place does
a range of sweet delights, but specialises in
fresh waffles, which come laden with cream
and chocolate. There's another branch on
Tuomiokirkonkatu.

Viikinkiravintola Harald   THEME €€
(www.ravintolaharald.fi; Hämeenkatu 23; mains
€14-26; ⊗11am-midnight Mon-Thu, to 1am Fri,
noon-1am Sat, 3-10pm Sun) This Viking-theme
restaurant isn't subtle but is plenty of fun.
Signature dishes are shared platters served
on a shield, or enormous vegetable or meat
kebabs speared on a sword.

Café Gopal   VEGETARIAN, CAFE €
(www.gopal.fi; Kuninkaankatu 15; per kg €17.50;
⊗lunch Mon-Sat) Tasty pay-by-weight vegetarian lunch buffet.

La Famille   CAFE €
(http://wanhawanilja.blogspot.com; Aleksis Kivenkatu
10; cakes €3-7; ⊗10am-7pm Mon-Fri, 11am-6pm
Sat) Airy and light, this friendly spot gets
many Tampere votes for the best cakes in
town. Good coffees and focaccia too.

Self-Catering

🛒**Kauppahalli**   MARKET
(Hämeenkatu 19; ⊗8am-6pm Mon-Fri, 8am-3pm
Sat) This intriguing indoor market is one
of Finland's best, with picturesque wooden
stalls serving a dazzling array of wonderful
meat, fruit, baked goodies and fish. There
are good places to eat here too; this is the
best place to try cheap *mustamakkara* with
berry jam.

🛒**Laukontori Market**   MARKET
(⊗6am-5.30pm Mon-Sat May–mid-Sep) This is a
produce and fish market at Laukontori, also
called *alaranta* (lower lakeside).

🛒**Ruohonjuuri**   ORGANIC
(Hatanpään valtatie 4; ⊗Mon-Sat) Great organic-
produce shop.

🍺 **Drinking**

Panimoravintola Plevna (p145) and Tuulensuu (p144) are also fine places for a beer or
two.

Café Europa
PUB, CAFE

(www.ravintola.fi/europa; Aleksanterinkatu 29; ☉noon-late) Furnished with 1930s-style horsehair couches and chairs, this is a romantic old-world European type of place complete with Belgian and German beers, board games, ornate mirrors and chandeliers, and an excellent summer terrace.

Teerenpeli
PUB

(www.teerenpeli.com; Hämeenkatu 25; ☉noon-late) On the main street, this is another good place with excellent microbrewery beer and cider. There's a relaxing, candlelit interior, heated terrace and heaps of choice at the taps. There's a huge downstairs space too, with comfy seating.

O'Connell's
PUB

(www.oconnells.fi; Rautatienkatu 24; ☉4pm-1am or 2am) Popular with both Finns and expats, this rambling Irish pub is handy for the train station and has plenty of time-worn, comfortable seating and an air of bonhomie. Its best feature is the range of interesting beers on tap and carefully selected bottled imports. There's regular free live music.

Nordic Gastropub
PUB

(www.gastropub.net/nordic; Otavalankatu 3; ☉3pm-2am Sun-Fri, noon-2am Sat) We're not sure about the 'gastro' part, but the range of perfectly poured microbrewed Finnish beers on tap, backed up by guest ales from around the Nordic lands, would tempt anybody in for a pint.

Suvi
BAR

(www.laivaravintolasuvi.fi; Laukontori; ☉10am-late May-Sep) Moored alongside the Laukontori Quay, this is a typical Finnish boat bar offering no-nonsense deck-top drinking. Prepare a boarding party and lap up the afternoon sun.

Ruby & Fellas
PUB

(www.rubyandfellas.fi; Hämeenkatu 15; ☉3pm-late Mon-Fri, 1pm-late Sat & Sun) Popular Irish pub with a range of beers on tap, best visited for its excellent riverside terrace.

☆ Entertainment
Nightclubs & Live Music
Tullikamari Klubi
BAR, LIVE MUSIC

(www.klubi.net; Tullikamarinaukio 2; ☉Mon-Sat, to 4am Wed-Sat) This cavernous place, near the train station, is Tampere's main indoor live-music venue; there are usually several bands playing every week, and big Finnish names regularly swing by for concerts.

Paapan Kapakka
JAZZ

(www.wanhaposti.fi; Koskikatu 9; ☉noon-late) A bit of a Tampere institution, this offers live jazz, blues or swing every night. The crowd are mostly 30-plus and really get into it; this can be a special place on a good night.

Telakka
LIVE MUSIC, PUB

(www.telakka.eu; Tullikamarinaukio 3) This is a bohemian bar-theatre-restaurant in another of Tampere's restored red-brick factories. There's live music regularly, theatre performances, art exhibitions and a brilliant summer terrace with colourful blocky wooden seats. The food – pastas, pepper steaks – isn't as good as the atmosphere.

Hämeensilta
CLUB

(www.hameensilta.fi; Hämeenkatu 13; ☉Tue-Sat 9pm-late) A restaurant, bar and nightclub popular with middle-aged Finns, with wonderful views over the rapids and the city from the top floor. There's live crooner music and plenty of traditional dancing going on.

Ruma
LIVE MUSIC

(www.ruma.fi; Murtokatu 1; ☉6pm-late Wed-Sat) A cool spot with offbeat decor, quirky lighting, friendly staff, and a mixture of Finnish and European pop and alternative rock every day of the week. There's a cover of €3 to €5 at weekends. It opens at 8pm in summer.

Classical Music, Theatre & Cinema
Tampere is a thriving performing-arts centre. There are several theatres and a program of what's on where is available from the tourist office.

Tampere-Talo
CONCERT VENUE

(Tampere Hall; ☎243 4111; www.tampere-talo.fi; Yliopistonkatu 55) Classical concerts are held in this spectacular modern hall. Performances by the Tampere Philharmonic Orchestra (www.tampere.fi/filharmonia) are on Fridays from September to May. In addition to this it puts on regular chamber-music concerts, and visiting opera and ballet performances.

Niagara
CINEMA

(www.elokuvakeskus.fi/niagara; Kehräsaari B-talo; tickets €5-8.50) In the Kehräsaari complex, this shows original-version art-house films daily.

Finnkino Plevna
CINEMA

(www.finnkino.fi; Itäinenkatu 4; tickets €6-12) In the Finlayson Centre, this is a cinema and the main venue for the film festival. There's another cinema in the Koskikeskus centre near the Sokos Hotel Ilves.

Sport

Ilves & Tappara   ICE HOCKEY
(www.ilves.com, www.tappara.fi) Tampere has two ice-hockey teams – Ilves and Tappara – both of which are among the best in the country, and the city is generally regarded as the Finnish home of the sport.

Hakametsä Ice Stadium, about 2km east of the train station, is the venue for matches on Thursdays, Saturdays and Sundays from September to March. Buy tickets (around €15 to €30) here, from the Stockmann or Sokos department stores in town, or from www.lippupalvelu.fi (for Tappara) or www.lippu.fi (for Ilves). It's off the Hervannan Valtaväylä fwy. Take eastbound bus 25 to get there.

Tampere United   FOOTBALL
(www.tampereunited.com) The local football team has been Finland's most successful in recent years but in 2011–12 served a year's ban for accepting money from dubious sources. It plays games in summer at Tampere (Ratina) Stadium; tickets cost €10 to €20 and are marginally cheaper if you buy them online at www.lippupalvelu.fi.

Teivo   HORSE RACING
(www.teivonravit.fi) Ten kilometres northwest of Tampere on Rd 3, this trotting track offers another popular, reader-recommended, Finnish experience. There are races nearly every Tuesday evening at 6pm, and entry is free, though you can bet as much as you like. Special buses from the bus station run to the track on race evenings. In winter the horses race on compacted snow under floodlights.

🔒 Shopping

Akateeminen Kirjakauppa   BOOKS
(www.akateeminenkirjakauppa.fi; Hämeenkatu 6; ☺9am-9pm Mon-Fri, 9am-6pm Sat, noon-6pm Sun) Big selection of English-language books.

Verkaranta   CRAFT
(www.taitopirkanmaa.fi; Verkatehtaankatu 2; admission €3.50; ☺10am-6pm Mon-Fri, noon-5pm Sat & Sun) This small former factory building by the river features exhibits and sells extraordinary textiles and handicrafts.

Kehräsaari   CRAFT
(☺10am-6pm Mon-Fri, to 4pm Sat) Across the footbridge from Verkaranta, just east of Laukontori Market Square, this converted brickfactory building has many boutiques selling authentic Finnish glassware, handicrafts, knitted clothing and T-shirts.

Tallipiha   CRAFT
(www.tallipiha.fi; Kuninkaankatu 4; ☺Tue-Sun Jun–mid-Aug) This restored collection of 19th-century stable yards and staff cottages houses artists and craftworkers who make handicrafts, chocolates, ceramics and shoes. The cafe and a shop or two are open in other months, but there's not much going on, except at Christmas time.

Swamp Music   MUSIC
(www.swampmusic.com, in Finnish; Tuomiokirkonkatu 32) A good place to pick up Finnish music, and it also has an online store. There's a good-value **secondhand outlet** (Verkatehtaankatu 11) around the corner.

ℹ Information

Emergency
Phone ☎112 in any emergency. To report a crime, phone ☎219 5111, or visit the police station at Sorinkatu 12.

Internet Access
In addition to the following, there are free terminals in the tourist office and at Vapriikki museum centre.

Internet Café Madi (Tuomiokirkonkatu 36; per hr €3; ☺10am-10pm Mon-Fri, 11am-10pm Sat & Sun) Free tea and coffee.

Tampere City library (Metso; Pirkankatu 2; ☺10am-8pm Mon-Fri, to 4pm Sat, 11am-5pm Sun, 10am-7pm weekdays only Jun-Aug) Has several free internet terminals, some first-come, first-served (15-minute time limit).

Medical Services
Dial ☎10023 between 7am and 10pm to get an on-call doctor.

Hatanpää Hospital (☎565 713; www.tampere.fi; Hatanpäänkatu 24) Main city hospital.

Yliopiston Apteekki (Hämeenkatu 16; ☺7am-midnight) Late-opening pharmacy just off the square.

Money
Forex (www.forex.fi; Hämeenkatu 4; ☺9am-9pm Mon-Fri, to 6pm Sat) Moneychangers in the Stockmann Building.

Tourist Information
GoTampere Oy (tourist office) (☎5656 6800; www.visittampere.fi; Rautatienkatu 25; ☺8.30am-4.30pm Mon-Fri Sep-May, 9am-6pm Mon-Fri, 11am-3pm Sat & Sun Jun-Aug) In the railway station. Has free internet terminals and a booking desk.

❶ Getting There & Away

There are lockers at the bus and train stations.

Air

Air Baltic Connects Tampere with Rovaniemi as well as Riga.

Blue 1 Flies direct to Copenhagen and Stockholm.

Finnair Flies to Helsinki – though it's more convenient on the train – and serves other major Finnish cities.

Ryanair From a dedicated terminal, has daily services to several European destinations including London Stansted, Edinburgh, 'Frankfurt' Hahn, Oslo and Rome.

Boat

Various lakeboats from Tampere can take you south to Hämeenlinna via Visavuori, or north to Virrat via Ruovesi; see p141 for details.

Bus

Regular express buses run from Helsinki (€25.30, 2¾ hours) and Turku (€23.90, two to three hours) and most other major towns in Finland are served from here.

Train

The train station is in the city centre at the eastern end of Hämeenkatu. Express trains run hourly to/from Helsinki (€29.60, 1½ hours). Intercity trains continue to Oulu (€61.40, five hours) and there are direct trains to Turku (€24.30, 1½ hours) and other cities.

❶ Getting Around

To/From the Airport

The Tampere-Pirkkala airport is 15km southwest of the city centre. Each arriving flight is met by a **bus** (☎010-029 400; www.paunu.fi), which takes 40 minutes to the city centre (€4.40).

Tokee (☎020-039 000; www.airpro.fi) serves Ryanair flights, leaving from the railway station forecourt about 2½ hours before take-off (€6). Note that there's no ATM at the Ryanair terminal, but you can buy bus tickets with a card if you're euro-less.

Shared **airport taxis** (☎10041; per person €17) carry up to eight passengers; these must be booked in advance from the city to the airport. A regular cab will cost around €30 between the airport and the centre.

Bus

The local bus service is extensive. A one-hour ticket costs €2.50. A 24-hour tourist ticket is €6. The tourist office has route maps; you can also check www.gotampere.fi.

Hire

There are several car-hire companies at the airport and in town, including **Hertz** (☎020-555 2400; www.hertz.fi; Rautatienkatu 28), behind the Orthodox Church, **Budget** (☎020-746 6630; www.budget.fi; Hatanpään valtatie 42) and **Sixt** (☎020-1122 530; www.sixt.fi; Hatanpään valtatie 24).

Bikes can be hired from about €15 a day from several places, including **Bike King** (☎050-553 0200; www.bikeking.fi; Suvantokatu 10; ◷Mon-Sat) and **Holiday Inn Tampere** (☎245 5111; Yliopistonkatu 44). The **Citybike** (www.tamperecitybike.fi) scheme requires a €10 fee and €40 deposit – do this online. Get the key from the tourist office and you have access to a whole network of bikes around town.

You can rent **rowing boats** and **canoes** from Camping Härmälä among other places.

Taxi

There are plenty of taxi ranks in town; otherwise call ☎0100 4131. For a wheelchair-friendly taxi, call ☎0100 4531.

Route 66

☎03

Route 66, starting northeast of Tampere and winding 75km north to Virrat, is one of Finland's oldest roads. When the famous song, first performed by Nat King Cole, was translated into Finnish, popular rock star Jussi Raittinen adapted the lyrics to this highway in his song 'Valtatie 66'. It's a good drive, through young pine forest and lakescapes. Cycling isn't such a great option, as the road is narrowish, and there are plenty of logging trucks hurtling by. Good hiking and fishing opportunities exist; Ruovesi is the best-equipped base. Outside the June to August high season, there's little going on.

ORIVESI

Route 66 begins in Orivesi, 40km northeast of Tampere. There's nothing spectacular in the village itself, but it is at a major crossroads. Its silo-like modern **church** (◷Mon-Fri Jun-Aug) was controversial when built, partly due to the Kain Tapper woodcarving in the altar. The old bell tower remains, with its *vaivaisukko* (pauper statue).

KALLENAUTION KIEVARI

Dating from 1757, this beautiful wooden **roadhouse** (www.kallenautio.fi; ◷10am-6pm late May–early Sep) is the oldest building along Route 66. Once very common, few of these historic spots now remain.

The complex has a beautiful cafe; sit at old long wooden tables and imagine winter travellers huddled around the blazing fire. There are handicraft exhibitions, including on the making of *päre,* thin wooden sheeting used for shingle roofs and also burned to provide light in houses. In times gone by this was often the cause of fires that destroyed entire towns.

SIIKANEVA

This large protected **marshland** accommodates some unusual bird species, including owls. It's a great place to walk, with duckboard paths across the peat bog alternating with stretches in peaceful pine forests. There are two loops: one of 3km, and one of about 10km. The entrance is on Route 66, 20km south of Ruovesi; you pass some sinister-looking military buildings on the way.

RUOVESI

Peaceful and pretty, Ruovesi's the main town on this stretch and the best place to stay along it. Apart from enjoying the nearby lakeside, there is not a huge amount to see or do in the village, but if you have a car it makes a good base for exploring the area's attractions.

Ruoveden Kotiseutumuseo (Museotie 2; adult/child €2/1; ⊙noon-6pm late Jun–mid-Aug) is the local museum, with a small history display and, more interestingly, a collection of 18th-century farm buildings including a picturesque wooden windmill.

The lakes around here are prime fishing country and teem with pike, perch, pike-perch and trout. Various fishing guides can take you out on trips in the area: www.ruovesi.fi has a list. The website www.zanderland.fi is another good resource.

Haapasaaren Lomakylä (☑044-080 0290; www.haapasaari.fi; Haapasaarentie 5; tents €14 plus per adult €4.50, cabins €39-69, 4-/8-person cottages €150/220; ℗) is a great place to stay on an islet north of the village, and is connected to town by a causeway. There's water all around, and fabulous self-contained cottages; they have a sauna, barbecue and kitchen. The cabins are simpler, but also have simple cooking facilities. It's great for kids, with a large play area. They discount heavily when things are quiet.

🖉**Ylä-Tuuhosen Maatila** (☑472 6426; www.yla-tuuhonen.fi; Tanhuantie 105; s/d €45/60, cabins d €56-70; ℗) is a rustic and historic organic farm run by generous-hearted owners, who offer three pretty rooms (sharing two bathrooms) and use of an excellent kitchen

and lounge. There's also a variety of cabins available, as well as evening meals. Head 9km north from Ruovesi on Route 66, then turn right onto Rd 3481 (signposted to Haapamäki). Continue 9km, and the farmhouse is 1km up a turn-off on the left.

Hotelli Liera (☑472 4600; Ruovedentie 11; s/d €50/75; ⊙Jun-Aug) is one of two hotels in the centre of town. It looks like a dive from the front but is a friendly spot operated out of a bar. The rooms are surprisingly good, with heaps of space, a sofa, and peaceful pastoral views over the fields below to the lake, plus there's a long shared balcony divided by privacy screens. You get breakfast on a tray in the morning, and the pub does no-nonsense pizzas, fish and steaks until 10pm.

There's summer **tourist information** (☑486 1388; www.ruovesi.fi; Ruovedentie 19; ⊙9am-5pm Mon-Fri Jun-Aug) on the main road.

Several daily buses connect Ruovesi with Tampere and other places in the region. The SS *Tarjanne,* travelling along the Poet's Way between Tampere and Virrat, stops at Ruovesi; see p141 for more information.

HELVETINJÄRVI NATIONAL PARK

Northwest of Ruovesi, this park's main attraction is narrow **Helvetinkolu Gorge,** gouged out by retreating glaciers at the end of the last Ice Age. There are numerous trails to follow, including a walk to **Haukanhieta,** a sandy beach and popular camping spot on the shores of Haukkajärvi. You can pitch a tent for the night at designated camp sites in the park and there's a free hut at Helvetinkolu, a couple of kilometres from the parking area, and signposted 8km west off Route 66 about 9km north of Ruovesi.

VIRRAT

The town of Virrat is the end point of Route 66, and of the Poet's Way cruise (p141) from

TAMPERE & HÄME ROUTE 66

ℹ️ **FARMSTAYS & COTTAGES**

As well as the nationwide operators mentioned in the Directory (p339), there are several options in the countryside around Tampere for seeking out that perfect cottage haven or warm and welcoming stay on an organic farm. Check www.gotampere.fi for ideas.

HIKING NORTH OF TAMPERE

The **Pirkan Taival** is a loose network of hiking trails totalling 330km in an area that stretches from Helvetinjärvi National Park westward to Seitseminen National Park and beyond. It's easy to work out your own route here; it's very well marked, and regular signboards show the distances involved. The scenery ranges from peaceful Finnish farmland to marshes, forests and gravel ridges. Huts and camping areas offer overnighting options. Easy trailheads to reach on a bus from Tampere are Virrat, Ruovesi and Kuru. Buy a map at Tampere bookshops or the Seitseminen park visitor centre.

Tampere, though itself not an especially romantic place.

The main sight is 4km northwest on the main road. **Virtain Perinnekylä** (Herrasentie 16; admission €5; ⊙noon-6pm mid-Jun–mid-Aug) is a sprawling open-air museum with several buildings including loggers' cabins and a windmill, handicraft shops, and an elegant cafe-restaurant with a lavish buffet lunch.

There's little in the way of accommodation, but **Domus Virrat** (☑475 5600; www.domusvirrat.fi; Sipiläntie 3; dm/s/d €25/43/64; ⊙Jun–mid-Aug; P) is a reliable summer hotel not far up from the harbour. The smart rooms have kitchens (though no utensils) and plenty of space; there's also a tennis court, bookable sauna, and bikes to rent. Breakfast is available for a small extra charge. HI discount.

Lakari (☑475 8639; www.virtainmatkailu.fi; Lakarintie; tent sites €13 plus per adult/child €3.50/1.50, cabins €49-68, cottages €95-125; ⊙May-Sep), 7km east of the town centre, is a beautifully situated camping ground between two lakes. It has tent sites, cabins and well-equipped cottages as well as a beach and plenty of trees.

There's **tourist information** (☑485 1276; www.virrat.org; Virtaintie 26; ⊙9am-3pm Mon-Fri) in the centre, and limited information is also available in the bar by the boat dock, 1km from town.

Several daily buses head from Virrat to Tampere and other towns in the region.

Keuruu

☑014

Sweet Keuruu sits in a lovely location on the northern shore of Keurusselkä and is definitely worth swinging by. Its major drawcard is its fascinating **wooden church** (admission €1; ⊙11am-5pm Jun-Aug, ask at museum rest of year), built in 1758, which has superb portraits of Bible characters (although the artist didn't complete the set, due to a pay dispute), and dark clouds all across the ceiling depicting the firmament, peopled by scattered beasts, angels and devils. There are also photos of the mummified corpses buried below the chancel, and a set of stocks for miscreants.

Across the road (and the railway) from the church, **Kamana** (☑040-572 5640; www.keuruu.fi; Kangasmannilantie 4; museum admission €3; ⊙11am-5pm daily mid-Jun–early Sep, Mon-Fri only rest of year) serves as local museum, exhibition centre and the tourist office. It's one of a clutch of historic buildings here (signposted Vanha Keuruu), which house craft shops and the like. The museum has an excellent cafe serving tasty buffet lunches.

There are lake cruises on historic **MS Elias Lönnrot** (☑010-422 5600; www.eliaksenristeilyt.fi) daily Wednesdays to Sundays from May to August. It also has a service to the town of Mänttä on Saturdays in July (one-way/return €20/30, 2¾ hours each way).

Another magnificent wooden church is only 28km east of here at Petäjävesi (p183).

Contact the tourist office for help booking lakeside cottages around Keuruu. There are also a couple of nearby camp sites and the **Hotelli Keurusselkä** (☑75100; www.keurusselka.com; Keurusseläntie 134; s/d €82/104; P@≋), a very Finnish holiday complex 8km south of town with a lake beach, spa complex and activities. As well as the comfortable hotel rooms, there are well-equipped cottages (€150) sleeping six, and cheaper rooms (singles/doubles €66/92) in a separate building near the lake. It's quite a bit cheaper outside high summer. You can also hire bikes and boats. The Elias Lönnrot lake cruises stop here, so you can arrive by boat one day, stay overnight, and sail back to Keuruu the next day.

Buses run to Keuruu from Tampere and Jyväskylä. Trains between Jyväskylä and Seinäjoki also stop here.

Mänttä
📖03

Mänttä, set on a narrow isthmus between fast-flowing rapids, grew around its paper mill, founded in the mid-19th century by the Serlachius dynasty. Progressive in outlook, the family endeavoured to build a model industrial community around their factory and endowed the town with noble buildings and art. After a merger in the 1980s, the company, Metsä-Serla, is now based in Espoo, but the paperworks still directly or indirectly employs much of the town.

The principal attraction was once the private home of Gösta Serlachius and is now the **Gösta Serlachiuksen Taidemuseo** (www.serlachius.fi; adult/child incl GA Serlachius Museo €8/1; ⊙10am-6pm daily Jun-Aug, noon-5pm Wed-Sun Sep-May), one of the nation's premier galleries. Situated 2km east of the town centre in elegant grounds, it houses an excellent collection of Finnish art: all the names from the golden age are here, including seemingly dozens of Gallen-Kallelas, plenty of Edelfelts and Schjerfbecks, as well as Wickström sculptures. Look out for a mischievous painting of Gallen-Kallela getting pissed with his mate Sibelius, and Hugo Simberg's whimsical *Entrance to Hades*. There's also a sizeable European collection, including a fine Deposition by Van der Weyden.

In the town centre, an elegant white 1930s modernist mansion, formerly the company HQ, is now the **GA Serlachius Museo** (www.serlachius.fi; Erik Serlachiuksenkatu 2; adult/child incl Gösta Serlachiuksen Taidemuseo €8/1; ⊙10am-6pm daily Jun-Aug, noon-5pm Wed-Sun Sep-May). There's a most comprehensive display on the history of the paperworks and old Gösta Serlachius himself, with audio exhibits on every conceivable aspect of the business – you'd be here a week if you listened to them all. Most information is in English. The attractive building also has two to three temporary exhibitions – of wonderful quality at our last visit. It also functions as the town's tourist office.

Nearby, the art nouveau **church** (⊙10am-4.30pm daily Jun-Aug, 10am-1pm Mon-Fri Sep-May) was, like most of the town, built (in 1928) by the company.

Honkahovi Taidekeskus (www.honkahovi.fi; Johtokunnantie 11; ⊙11am-6pm, to 8pm Thu early Jun & Jul, check website for exhibitions outside these months) is another mansion belonging to the Serlachius family. It's a 1938 art deco building containing temporary art exhibitions. Admission varies, but is usually around the €8 mark. You can walk between Honkahovi and the Göster Serlachiuksen Taidemuseo via a trail along the lakeside.

Around the corner from the church, **Hotelli Alexander** (📞474 9232; www.hotellialexander.fi; Kauppakatu 23; s/d €54/72; **P**) is much better inside than it looks from the scruffy exterior. You'll probably have to check in at Café Wilhelmiina, on Koskelankatu 8, across the main road and next to the Osuuspankki. The same people also run **Kesähotelli Mänttä** (📞488 6841; Koulukatu 6; dm/d €22/67; ⊙Jun–mid-Aug; **P**), a summer hostel in a student building; rooms have kitchen and bathroom. It's a short walk from the centre, crossing the main street.

❶ Getting There & Away

On Saturdays in July, you can catch the MS *Elias Lönnrot* from Keuruu. Otherwise, there are several weekday buses and a couple at weekends to Jyväskylä (€19.30, 1½ hours) via Keuruu, and Tampere (€19.30, 1½ to 1¾ hours). The town often appears as Mänttä-Vilppula on timetables.

Tampere to Hämeenlinna

Several interesting sights lie just off the main Tampere–Hämeenlinna highway. There's quite a diversity of attractions.

SÄÄKSMÄKI & VISAVUORI

This historic and scenic area is one of the region's highlights. It includes ridges, forest and great lake views. Some of the best vistas are from **Rapolan Linnavuori**, the outline of a large hill-fort that dominated the area for a long period around a thousand years ago. You can follow a marked trail that will take you to 100 burial mounds on the western side of the hill. You can get to Rapola following the signs from the main road, about 43km southeast of Tampere.

Nearby, also signposted off the main road and 4km from it, **Visavuori** (www.visavuori.com; adult/child €7/1; ⊙10am-6pm daily Jun-Aug, 10am-4pm Tue-Sun Sep-Nov & Feb-May, 10am-4pm Tue-Fri Dec-Jan) is the best-known sight in the region. Once the studio of Emil Wickström (1864–1942), a sculptor from the National Romantic era, it has a stunning situation on a ridge with water on both sides. It consists of three houses, the oldest of which was the home of Wickström, built in 1902 in Karelian and Finnish Romantic styles and containing fantastic art nouveau furniture; it really brings the man to life and is worth visiting first. Wickström was the curse of the local boatmen, who used to have to deliver huge slabs of marble. The beautiful studio next door, with dozens of models and sculptures, was built in 1903; the pervasive smell of baking will force you to stop for a *pulla* (cardamom-flavoured bun) in the brick-vaulted cafe downstairs. **Kari Paviljonki** is dedicated to Kari Suomalainen, Emil Wickström's grandson. The best known of Finland's political cartoonists, his long career spanned several decades and he was drawing up to his death in 1999. His cartoons are excellent; the ones that can be, are translated well. Even more amusing is the award from the US National Cartoonist Society in 1959 for his daring cartoons 'exposing the deceit of communism'.

Boats from Hämeenlinna and Tampere stop at Visavuori in summer (see those towns for details).

IITTALA

Little Iittala, 23km northwest of Hämeenlinna, is world-famous for the glass produced in its factory, and has been at the forefront of Finnish design for decades.

Behind the large **shop** (www.iittala.com; ⊙10am-6pm Sep-Apr, 10am-8pm May-Aug) and restaurant, a charming craft village includes chocolate shop, ceramics and gold studios, and the **Lasimuseo** (Glass Museum; www.iittalanlasimaki.fi; adult/child €4/2; ⊙11am-5pm daily May–mid-Sep, weekends only rest of year), whose two levels cover the history of the Iittala glassworks as well as the glass-making process, with pieces from most of the firm's famous ranges on display. Free tours of the nearby factory leave from here at noon from Monday to Friday; otherwise you can watch a glass-blower at work in an adjacent shop. The main shop, though sizeable, doesn't offer more than similar Iittala/Arabia/Hackman shops elsewhere in Finland.

Trains between Hämeenlinna (15 minutes) and Tampere (45 minutes) stop here, and buses also run here weekdays from Hämeenlinna. Tampere–Hämeenlinna express buses stop on the highway 2km from town.

HATTULA

Nine kilometres north of Hämeenlinna, this village has one of Finland's oldest and most memorable churches. **Pyhän Ristin Kirkko** (www.hattula-evl.fi; admission €3; ⊙11am-5pm mid-May–mid-Aug) dates from the early 1400s and has an interior filled with fabulous naive frescoes from the early 16th century. They tell the key stories of the Bible as you go around the nave; the Tree of Jesse in the sacristy is particularly fine. As this was the nearest that most of the parishioners of the time ever got to being able to read, it must have been an awe-inspiring place for them, and it still is. Nearby, the **old grain store** houses the information office and sells handicrafts.

The church is easy to reach from Hämeenlinna by public transport; take bus 5, 6 or 16. Take something warm to wear if you plan a lengthy look at the interior.

HÄME

Though no longer a province, this region of southern central Finland, also known as Tavastia, has historically been an important one. The castle at Hämeenlinna was the middle of the line of three imposing Swedish fortifications across the breadth of Finland. Today this ancient stronghold contrasts with the modernity of Lahti, the region's other main city.

Hämeenlinna

📞 03 / POP 66,854

Dominated by its namesake, majestic Häme Castle, Hämeenlinna (Swedish: Tavastehus) is the oldest inland town in Finland, founded in 1649, though a trading post had already existed here since the 9th century. The Swedes built the castle in the 13th century, and Hämeenlinna developed into an administrative, educational and garrison town around it. The town is quiet but picturesque, and its wealth of museums will keep you busy for a day or two. It makes a good stop between Helsinki and Tampere, and you could head on to the latter by lakeboat.

◉ Sights & Activities

Despite its small size, Hämeenlinna has a wealth of museums and other attractions.

Hämeenlinna   CASTLE
(Häme Castle; www.hameenlinna.fi; adult/child €6/3; ⊙10am-6pm Jun–mid-Aug, 10am-4pm Mon-Fri, 11am-4pm Sat & Sun mid-Aug–May) Hämeenlinna means Häme Castle, so it's no surprise that this bulky twin-towered red-brick fortress is the town's pride and most significant attraction. Construction of the castle

TAMPERE & HÄME HÄMEENLINNA

Hämeenlinna

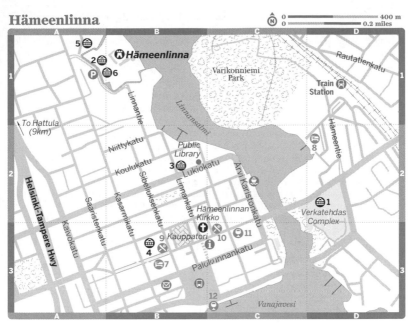

was begun by the Swedes during the 1260s, who wanted to establish a military redoubt against the power of Novgorod (p315). It was originally built on an island, but to the an-noyance of the defenders, the lake receded and necessitated the building of new walls. It never saw serious military action and, af-ter the Russian takeover of 1809 (p316), was converted into a jail. The last prisoners left in the 1980s and extensive renovations of the castle were finally completed in 1991.

The interior is a little disappointing, with a modern exhibition annexe, displaying peri-od costumes and furniture, tacked on to the original building (whose bare rooms don't really evoke its past). Free tours in English and German are given hourly from June to August; if you don't read Finnish/Swedish, a tour or the €5 guidebook is recommended, as there's little other information.

By the castle are three worthwhile muse-ums – Vankilamuseo, Historiallinen Museo and Tykistömuseo – that can be visited with the castle on a combined ticket (adult/child €15/6).

Vankilamuseo MUSEUM
(www.hameenlinna.fi; adult/child €5/1; ⊙11am-5pm Tue-Sun) The old prison block near the castle has been converted into a prison museum where you can visit a solitary con-finement cell or admire the graffiti left by former inmates. The most interesting bit is the three cells, left more or less as they were when the inmates departed, along with a

TAMPERE & HÄME HÄMEENLINNA

brief description of their occupants' crime and lifestyle. There's also a sauna, where prisoners would sometimes violently settle disputes. This particular building was last used as a prison in 1993.

Historiallinen Museo   MUSEUM
(www.hameenlinna.fi; adult/child €4/free; ⊙11am-5pm Tue-Sun) Next to the prison museum, the unassuming historical museum has displays labelled in English and covers the history of the town and the social history of the Häme region, with information on refugees from Karelia, the lynx, the town fire of 1831, and pop-culture memorabilia. While the reconstruction of a traditional savings bank might not get the pulse racing, it's the tangible respect for the everyday past that makes these Finnish museums lovable.

Tykistömuseo   MUSEUM
(www.tykistomuseo.fi; adult/child €6/3; ⊙11am-5pm Oct-Mar, 10am-6pm Apr-Sep) There are numerous museums devoted to Finnish involvement in WWII, but this artillery museum takes the cake. It's huge. There are three floors packed with war memorabilia, including good information in English on the beginnings of the Winter War. Outside, and in a separate hall, is a collection of phallic heavy artillery big enough to start a war on several fronts.

Hämeenlinnan Taidemuseo   GALLERY
(www.hameenlinna.fi; Viipurintie 2; admission €6-7; ⊙11am-6pm Tue-Thu, to 5pm Fri-Sun) The town's pleasing art museum is housed in a former grain store designed by CL Engel and has an interesting collection of Finnish art from the 19th and 20th centuries. Notable is Gallen-Kallela's painting of the *Kalevala*'s final scene, with the shaman Väinämöinen leaving Finland, which represents the conquest of Christianity in pagan Finland. Other scenes from the epic are painted on the ceiling. There are a couple of Schjerfbecks, including a *Rigoletto* painted when she was just 19, and a beautiful wooden lynx and cubs by Jussi Mäntynen. The building opposite houses temporary exhibitions that are invariably excellent.

Palanderin Talo   MUSEUM
(www.hameenlinna.fi; Linnankatu 16; adult/child €4/1; ⊙noon-3pm Tue-Sun Jun-Aug, noon-3pm Sat & Sun Sep-May) Finland loves its house-museums and this is among the best, offering a wonderful insight into well-off 19th-century Finnish life, thanks to excellent English-

speaking guided tours. There's splendid imperial and art nouveau furniture as well as delicate little touches like a double-sided mirror to spy on street fashion, and a set of authentic children's drawings from the period.

Sibeliuksen Syntymäkoti   MUSEUM
(www.hameenlinna.fi; Hallituskatu 11; adult/child €4/1; ⊙10am-4pm Tue-Sun May & Jun, 10am-4pm daily Jul & Aug, noon-4pm Tue-Sun Sep-Apr) Johan Julius Christian (Jean) Sibelius (p155) was born in Hämeenlinna in 1865 and went to school here, but surprisingly the town makes little fuss about this fact. His childhood home has been converted into a small museum that contains photographs, letters, his upright piano and some family furniture. It's a likeable place, although uninformative about his life; a pianist often accompanies your visit with some of the man's music. There are also regular concert performances, free with an entry ticket.

Aulanko   PARK
(www.aulanko.fi) This beautiful park, north of the town centre, was created early in the 20th century by Hugo Standertskjöld, who spent a fortune to create a central European-style park with ponds, swans, pavilions, a granite fortress, and exotic trees. Although the best way to explore it is on foot, the sealed one-way road loop is accessible by private car. A stone observation tower is open daily from May to September (free) and gives superb views. There's a nature trail in the park and a lakeside golf course.

Bus 2, 13 or 17 will take you to Aulanko from Hämeenlinna centre, but it's only 5km away (turn left on Aulangontie just east of the railway tracks) and makes a pleasant bike ride. Grab a map from the tourist office or at summer kiosks in the park itself.

🛏 Sleeping

Hotelli Emilia   HOTEL €€
(☑612 2106; www.hotelliemilia.fi; Raatihuoneenkatu 23; s/d €96/115; ℗) Located on the pedestrian street, this privately owned hotel is a good deal. Sizeable modern rooms, some of which can be connected for families, offer large windows, crisp white sheets and air-conditioning. There's a bar with terrace seating, a sauna, weekend nightclub and worthwhile buffet breakfast. Weekend prices (single/double €80/90) are also in place right through summer from June to August.

Rantasipi Aulanko SPA HOTEL €€€

(☏658 801; www.rantasipi.fi; Aulangontie 93; d €187; P@≋) This lakeside place in Aulanko Park, 5.5km from the centre, is enormous, with a huge range of facilities including a popular spa complex, numerous saunas and restaurants, and an adjacent golf course. It's very family friendly, with heaps to keep the young entertained, and large multibed rooms. Various much cheaper packages that include features such as meals or golf are available from travel agents or online. Nonguests can use the spa for €15.

Aulangon Lomakylä CAMPGROUND €

(☏675 9772; www.aulangonlomakyla.fi; Aulangon Heikkiläntie 168; tent sites €20, d/cabins/cottages €45/50/80; P) Located beyond the main body of Aulanko Park on the shores of a lake, this excellent camping ground offers cabins, cottages and simple bedrooms, as well as standard camping. It rents boats, bikes and fishing rods, and there's a restaurant and sauna.

Sokos Hotel Vaakuna HOTEL €€

(☏020-123 4636; www.sokoshotels.fi; Possentie 7; s/d/tw €105/115/130; P@) Across the river from the town centre and very near the train station, this attractive modern hotel has been designed to echo Häme Castle. Many of the rooms have great water views, as does the rounded restaurant, and the sunny bar terrace is particularly pleasant on a summer evening.

Eating

Piparkakkutalo FINNISH €€

(☏648 040; www.ravintolapiparkakkutalo.fi; Kirkkorinne 2; most mains €15-22; ☺lunch Mon-Sat, dinner Tue-Sat) Pleasing for both eye and stomach, the 'gingerbread house' is set in an historic 1906 shingled house that was once home to artist Albert Edelfeldt; the interior still has a warm, domestic feel. The food includes Finnish classics as well as more adventurous fare like quail in chocolate sauce; all are served in generous portions.

TAMPERE & HÄME HÄMEENLINNA

A MUSICAL GHOST

Leaving racing drivers out of the equation, Jean Sibelius, born in 1865 in Hämeenlinna, probably still takes the garland of most famous Finn. Apart from his towering musical legacy, the role he played in the cultural flowering that inspired Finnish independence makes him a legend in his homeland.

Like many artists of the time, Sibelius was fascinated by mythology and the forests at the heart of Finnishness. His first major works (*Kullervo, En Saga* and the *Karelia Suite*) were based on the *Kalevala* epic, but his overtly political 1899 *Finlandia* symphony became a powerful symbol of the Finnish independence struggle and is still his best-known work.

Sibelius experimented with tonality and rejected the classical sonata form, building movements from a variety of short phrases that grow together as they develop. His work, particularly the early symphonies, is notable for its economical orchestration and melancholic mood. His undeserved reputation for musical conservatism belies his genius, which lay in his ability to distil the essence of traditional forms into a tight modern product. The best example, his masterful seventh symphony, packs a powerful feeling of Finnish landscape and an epic Nordic quality into a very compact package.

Before his death in 1957, at the age of 92, he had produced very little in three decades. His missing eighth symphony is an El Dorado type legend of Finnish music, but evidence suggests that he consigned it to the fire at home in Ainola in the '40s.

There are Sibelius connections all over Finland. A trail could lead from his monument in Helsinki (p44) to Ainola (p81), the country home where he lived with his wife Aino Järnefelt (sister of the painter Eero), and their six daughters. Then his birthplace in Hämeenlinna (p154) and the excellent Sibelius Museum in Turku (p87), which frequently holds concerts. Festivals where you can hear his music include one in Loviisa (p111), where he had a summer home, and the Sibelius Festival in Lahti (p158), whose symphony orchestra is famed for its expertise in his works.

While Finland's current musical pre-eminence owes much to his legacy, there's also a feeling among younger musicians that it can be difficult to escape the shadow of Sibelius, whose lofty ghost still paces the forests and lakeshores of his beloved land.

Laurell CAFE €

(www.laurell.fi; Sibeliuksenkatu 7; pastries €2-3; ⊙8.30am-6pm Mon-Fri, to 8pm Wed, 8.30am-5pm Sat, 11am-5pm Sun) This spacious cafe on the kauppatori (market square) is a Hämeenlinna stalwart and popular meeting place. There's an appetising selection of squishy cakes, rolls, pastries and pies – including many options for special diets (ask) – and another branch in the same building as the tourist office.

Café Pannu CAFE €

(www.cafepannu.fi; Hallituskatu 13; lunches €6-8; ⊙lunch Mon-Sat) Tucked away behind Sibelius' birthplace, this typical Finnish lunching place has a Greek touch. Good-value soups, salads and hot dishes draw local workers daily, who take advantage of the outdoor seating on sunny days.

 Drinking & Entertainment

In summer two adjacent **boat bars** (Paasikivientie; ⊙from 11am Jun-Aug) offer relaxed lakeside drinking on floating wooden decks. Teemu is the earthier of the two, while Tyyne is more upmarket, with geranium boxes and beer served in a glass.

Birger PUB

(www.birger.fi; Raatihuoneenkatu 5; ⊙2pm-midnight Sun-Thu, to 2am Fri-Sat) The dark candlelit interior of this relaxing pub resembles a ship's saloon with low-hanging lamps and conspiratorial booth seating. It has an excellent range of bottled beer from around the world, plus interesting draught choices, and a few wines.

Albertin Kellari PUB

(www.ravintolapiparkakkutalo.fi; Kirkkorinne 2; ⊙from 4pm Mon-Sat) Underneath the Piparkakkutalo restaurant, this cosy pub is one for chilly nights, with a convivial hidden-away feel.

ⓘ Information

Library (Lukiokatu 2; ⊙Mon-Sat) Free internet terminals, can be prebooked.

Tourist office (☑621 3373; www.hameenlinna. fi; Raatihuoneenkatu 11; ⊙9am-5pm Mon-Fri, plus 10am-2pm Sat Jun-Aug) Plenty of information and free internet. Can book boats and hotels. Closes at 4.15pm Fridays.

ⓘ Getting There & Away

Boat

Departing from Hämeenlinna's passenger harbour, **Suomen Hopealinja** (Finnish Silverline; ☑010-422 5600; www.hopealinja.fi) cruises to Visavuori (one-way/return €38/57, 2¾ hours) at 11.30am, Wednesday to Saturday between June and mid-August. You can continue to Tampere (one-way €46, 8¼ hours).

Bus

Hourly buses between Helsinki (€15.90, 1½ hours) and Tampere (€11.80, one hour) stop in Hämeenlinna. From Turku, there are several buses daily (€27.90, two hours).

Train

The train station is 1km from the town centre, across the bridge. Hourly trains between Helsinki (€20.10, one hour) and Tampere (€17.20, 40 minutes) stop here. From Turku, change in Toijala.

Lahti

☑03 / POP 101,686

The region is steeped in history – indeed, some of Finland's oldest prehistoric sites are to be found not far away – but Lahti itself is basically a modern town, riding the wave of the technology boom and enjoying its proximity to Helsinki, 100km to the south. Its name is famous for winter sports – the frighteningly high ski jumps here have hosted several world championships – and classical music, with the city's symphony orchestra having gained worldwide recognition under former conductor Osmo Vänskä.

Lahti got its city charter in 1905 and lacks anything that could be called an old town: downtown consists of a series of linked shopping centres. However, architecture fans are amply provided for with the Aalto church and spectacular modern concert hall, and the city has a palpable energy, which was boosted after WWII with the arrival of thousands of refugees from occupied Karelia. Its lakeside location makes it a good activity base year-round.

◉ Sights

Lahden Urheilukeskus SPORTS CENTRE

At Lahti's Sports Centre, a 10-minute walk west of town, things are dominated by three imposing ski jumps, the biggest standing 73m high and stretching 116m. You'll often see high-level jumpers training here in summer. There's a whole complex here, including the football stadium, a summer swimming pool, ski tracks and the delightful **Ski Museum** (www.lahdenmuseot.fi; adult/child €6/2; ⊙10am-5pm Mon-Fri, 11am-5pm Sat & Sun). A history of skis includes excavated examples from 2000 years ago, and Lahti's proud record as a winter sports centre is

Lahti

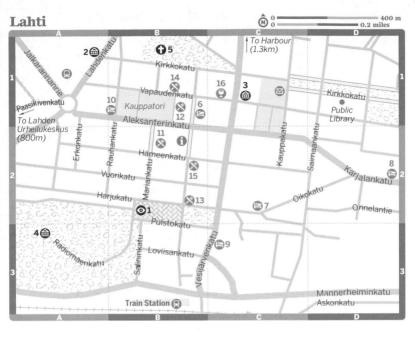

Lahti

◉ Sights

1 Kaupungintalo	B2
2 Lahden Historiallinen Museo	A1
3 Lahden Taidemuseo	C1
4 Radio- ja tv-museo	A3
5 Ristinkirkko	B1

🛌 Sleeping

6 Hotelli Musta Kissa	B1
7 Lahden Kansanopisto	C2
8 Lahden Koti	D2
9 Matkakoti Patria	C3
10 Omenahotelli	B1

🍴 Eating

11 Café Sinuhe	B2
12 Kauppahalli	B1
13 Ravintola Roux	B2
14 Spaghetteria Mamma Maria	B1
15 Taivaanranta	B2

🍷 Drinking

16 Teerenpeli	C1

given plenty of treatment. The fun starts in the next room: frustrate yourself on the ski-jump simulator, then try the biathlon and skiing on Velcro before nailing five bulls-eyes with your rifle. A combined ticket (€8) includes the chairlift up to the observation terrace at the top of the **ski jump** (⏰11am-4pm Fri-Sun May, 10am-5pm Mon-Fri, 11am-5pm Sat & Sun Jun-Aug); great if there's someone practising, and good for the views in any event.

Lahden Historiallinen Museo   MUSEUM
(www.lahdenmuseot.fi; Lahdenkatu 4; adult/child €6/2; ⏰10am-5pm Mon-Fri, 11am-5pm Sat & Sun) Lahti's historical museum is in a beautiful old manor house by the bus station. The ground and top floors hold changing exhibitions on aspects of Lahti's history (a little English information is usually available), while the middle floor is mostly devoted to the collection of Klaus Holma, a 20th-century Finnish diplomat. It's a treasury of French and Italian religious art, rococo furniture and fine porcelain, and an excellent series of interactive computer screens allows you to access detailed information (also in English) on every piece.

Radio- ja tv-museo   MUSEUM
(www.lahdenmuseot.fi; Radiomäki; adult/child €6/2; ⏰10am-5pm Mon-Fri, 11am-5pm Sat & Sun) This radio and television museum, on a hill by the radio mast just south of the centre, has an interesting history of those appliances in the basement. The entrance level has a feast

of interactive exhibits. Some, like classic '60s Finnish TV hits, won't keep you long, but the kids will love the chance to record their own radio show, or to find out why weather reporters can't wear blue.

Ristinkirkko CHURCH
(Church of the Cross; www.lahdenseurakuntay htyma.fi; Kirkkokatu 4; ☺10am-3pm) This striking church was designed by Alvar Aalto and finished in 1978. The brick exterior and concrete steeple give little clue as to the interior, a white and airy space with wooden benches echoing the organ's pipes. Structural lines angle towards the simple wooden cross behind the altar or perhaps emanating from it like rays.

Sibeliustalo CONCERT HALL
(Sibelius Hall; www.sibeliustalo.fi; Ankkurikatu 7) By the harbour on Vesijärvi, this spectacular concert hall in glass and wood is the home of the top-notch Lahti Symphony Orchestra, which is responsible for some of the best Sibelius recordings of recent years (there's a good selection in the shop here). The hall is wonderfully lit at night and has excellent acoustics.

Lahden Taidemuseo GALLERY
(www.lahdenmuseot.fi; Vesijärvenkatu 11A; adult/child €6/2; ☺10am-5pm Mon-Fri, 11am-5pm Sat & Sun) In the heart of town, this has temporary exhibitions of sculpture and paintings, usually featuring local artists.

Kaupungintalo TOWN HALL
(☎814 2224; Harjukatu 31) The art nouveau town hall was designed by the famous Finnish architect Eliel Saarinen. Phone ahead to arrange a guided tour.

 Activities

There's plenty to do at the Sports Centre. In winter, there is an ice-skating hall and a total of 145km of cross-country ski tracks, 35km of which are illuminated. Skiing and skating gear can be rented in the main building. In summer the centre offers bike trails and a large outdoor **swimming pool**. FC Lahti also play their home games at the stadium here, while the Pelicans, the local ice-hockey team, appear at the nearby Isku Areena.

You can rent **canoes** (☎752 0322; www. vesisamoilijat.fi) at the island of Kahvisaari near the harbour at Mukkula, 5km from the centre. A good day trip could take you out to Enonsaari island and back.

Cruises

As well as longer lake trips, in summer there are several daily 1½-hour return **cruises** from the passenger harbour, some including lunch (€16), as well as 3½-hour evening cruises to the Vääksy Canal and back on the **MS Suometar** (www.paijanne-risteilythilden.fi; adult/child return €22/11; ☺Jun-Aug). There are cruises to the Päijänne National Park on the **MS Elbatar** (☎040-035 1959; www.elbatar.fi; adult/child €15/7.50; ☺early Jul-early Aug) during summer. Contact the tourist office or see the website for times and bookings.

Festivals & Events

Lahti hosts several winter sports events including the **Ski Games** (www.lahtiskigames. com) in early March. There are also some good summer music festivals such as **Jazztori** (www.jazztori.com, in Finnish), a weeklong street festival in mid-August with jazz performances in the kauppatori, and the **Sibelius Festival** (www.sinfonialahti.fi) in mid-September, with the Lahti Symphony Orchestra.

WE HAVE LIFT-OFF!

Finland takes the apparently suicidal sport of ski-jumping pretty seriously, and Lahti is one of its main centres. You'll see competitors practising even in summer, with the frightening 'whoosh' as they descend the ramp sounding like a fighter aircraft on manoeuvres.

Pioneered in Norway in the mid-19th century, the sport has progressed in bounds with various technical leaps that have added significant distance improvements; these days all ski-jumpers lean forward and try to keep the skis in a 'V' as they sail towards, and hopefully beyond, the target line, usually set at 90m or 120m on competition pistes. Points are given for style as well as distance, so a slick, controlled flight and landing is preferable to risking life and limb in pursuit of extra metres. The 'extreme' version of ski-jumping is ski-flying, where special pistes produce extraordinary leaps of nearly 240m.

You can't really try it out as a visitor: you have to be a member of a local ski-jumping club, and start on gentle slopes before graduating to the serious jumps, but it's certainly worth watching these gravity-defying athletes perform.

🛏 Sleeping

There are Sokos and Scandic chain hotels in the centre of Lahti. See also nearby choices, p160.

Lahden Kansanopisto
HOSTEL €

(✆87810; www.lahdenkansanopisto.fi; Harjukatu 46; dm/s/d incl breakfast €25/35/60, s/d with bathroom €45/70; ❂Jun–mid-Aug; ℗) A standout budget option, the local folk college offers excellent summer accommodation in an enormous art nouveau building. The rooms feature comfortable beds, desks and bedside lamps, and there's a good kitchen on each floor. Shared facilities are spotless, and breakfast is included. Accommodation is often available outside summer, either in the building or in the nearby guesthouse. HI discount.

Hotelli Musta Kissa
HOTEL €€

(✆544 9000; www.mustakissa.com; Rautatienkatu 21, s/d €89/99; ℗@) The 'Black Cat' is a discreet place in a larger building right in the heart of town, and offers excellent value for money. The commodious carpeted rooms look over the centre of Lahti but are pretty quiet and have low but comfy-enough beds. An evening sauna is available from Monday to Thursday.

Matkakoti Patria
GUESTHOUSE €

(✆782 3783; www.matkakotipatria.com; Vesijärvenkatu 3; s/d €32.50/47.50) Very handy for the railway, this curious guesthouse has compact singles and twins with washbasin, TV, and cheery aquamarine sheets on the beds. Some rooms have bunks; the front rooms are airier but the street's pretty noisy. There's free tea, coffee and chocolate biscuits, and an HI discount. Phone ahead if you're going to arrive on Sunday as reception isn't open.

Lahden Koti
APARTMENT €€

(✆752 2173; www.lahdenkoti.fi; Karjalankatu 6; s/d studio apt €75/85, 4-person apt €155; ℗) A variety of attractive apartments are on offer in this building, and all come with tasteful furnishings and a well-equipped kitchen: a great option for families. Breakfast is left on a plate for you in your fridge, and you can use the sauna for an extra charge.

Omenahotelli
HOTEL €

(✆0600 18018; www.omena.com; Rauhankatu 14; r €45-70) With a great location on the central square, this staffless hotel makes a value-packed place to stay. Book online or via the terminal in the lobby. Rooms have a double bed, two fold-outs, and free wi-fi.

Mukkula Camping
CAMPGROUND

(✆753 5380; www.mukkulacamping.fi; Ritaniemenkatu 12; tent sites €9 plus per car/adult/child €5/3/1; ❂Jun-Aug, call ahead rest of year) Great lakeside location 5km north of Lahti. Has various upmarket cabins (per night €70 to €180).

🍴 Eating & Drinking

The place to enjoy the summer sunshine is down at the harbour where, benevolently overlooked by the Sibeliustalo, a number of beer terraces, boat bars, cute cafes in wooden warehouses and the old station building, and an historic lake-ship-turned-ice-cream kiosk draw the crowds.

The **kauppahalli** (❂8am-5pm Mon-Fri, 8am-2.30pm Sat) is a cosy spot for a coffee or snack; in fact it seems to have more cafes than stalls.

Ravintola Roux
FINNISH €€

(✆782 3377; www.roux.fi; Rautatienkatu 7; mains €23-33; ❂4-11pm Mon-Fri, 1-11pm Sat, 1-6pm Sun) In an atmosphere of quiet elegance, with well-spaced tables, this corner restaurant has brought a touch of culinary sophistication to the city. Local lakefish and crustaceans appear alongside hearty meat dishes, and the odd vegetarian option. The food's not as gourmet as it thinks it is, but it's easily Lahti's best.

Café Sinuhe
CAFE, BAKERY €

(www.sinuhe.fi; Mariankatu 21; light meals €5-9; ❂6.30am-8pm Mon-Fri, 9am-4pm Sat, 10am-4pm Sun) Half a block from the kauppatori, this is Lahti's best central cafe, with folk streaming in at all hours to sip mellow coffee, fork-up salads bursting with fresh things or buy a loaf of crusty bread.

Spaghetteria Mamma Maria
ITALIAN €

(http://koti.phnet.fi/mammam/; Vapaudenkatu 10; mains €9-22) With a range of risottos, chicken, pastas and pizzas as well as horse steaks, this Italian eatery on the kauppatori is a firm Lahti favourite. Quantities are generous and the food's tasty enough, particularly the homemade gelati.

Taivaanranta
FINNISH €€

(✆042-492 5230; www.taivaanranta.com; Rautatienkatu 13; mains €15-24; ❂lunch & dinner Mon-Sat, noon-6pm Sun) This good-natured place sits above the stills that produce Teerenpeli's single malt, so it's no surprise that whisky crops up in various sauces. It specialises in steaks and sausages, but also does fine pastas and fish dishes as well as Finnish favourites like liver and sautéed reindeer.

TAMPERE & HÄME LAHTI

Teerenpeli PUB

(www.teerenpeli.com; Vapaudenkatu 20; ☺noon-2am or 3am) A Lahti success story, this pub sells its own beers and ciders (try the blueberry one) and distils a single-malt whisky. It's got an upmarket interior, plush stools and an appreciative clientele, and is always humming with chatter or live jazz. There's a summer branch on a boat at the harbour.

ⓘ Information

Lahti has free wi-fi through much of the centre.

Public library (Kirkkokatu 31; ☺10am-7pm Mon-Fri, to 3pm Sat) Several free internet terminals. Opens Sundays outside summer.

Tourist office (☏020-728 1750; www.lahti travel.fi; Rautatienkatu 22; ☺9am-5pm Mon-Thu, to 4pm Fri, plus 10am-2pm Sat Jun-Aug) Can book cruises and hotels. Rent bikes. Free internet terminal.

ⓘ Getting There & Away

The Lahti tourist office rents **bikes** (per day/weekend €15/25), which you collect from a nearby sports store.

Boat

From early June to mid-August **Päijänne Risteilyt Hildén Oy** (☏014-263 447; www.paijanne-risteilyt hilden.fi) operates boats from Lahti's passenger harbour to Heinola at 10am (one-way/return €27/40.50, one-way 4½ hours, daily). The cruise goes via Vääksy and Kalkkinen Canals. It also has a weekly ferry to Jyväskylä at 9am on Tuesdays (€60, 10½ hours) from mid-June to early August, returning on Wednesdays.

Bus

There are regular buses along the motorway from Helsinki (€22.40, 1½ hours), and frequent services from other large cities. There are also hourly buses to Helsinki airport.

Train

There are at least 15 direct trains per day to/from Helsinki (€21.30, 1½ hours) and Riihimäki, where you can change for Tampere. It's substantially cheaper than this from Helsinki if you don't catch an Intercity train.

Around Lahti

HOLLOLA
☑03

Hollola (www.hollola.fi, in Finnish), west of Lahti, was the major settlement in the area until Lahti's rapid growth left the venerable parish as a pleasant rural backwater. There are two Hollolas – the modern town centre

is on the highway 7km west of Lahti, but the old village and most of the attractions are 15km to 18km northwest of Lahti on the southern shores of Vesijärvi. To get to the old village, either head north from the modern Hollola, or take Rd 2956 from Lahti and follow Vesijärvi. It's close enough to cycle.

Heading west along the lake from Lahti, the first place you'll reach is **Messilä** (www.messila.fi), a fine old estate with a golf course, craft shop, bakery, guest harbour and winter ski slopes; see also below. You can rent skis from €17 per day, and it has a ski school.

Pirunpesä (Devil's Nest) is a scenic rocky cleft near Messilä. A trail takes you there (1km from the car park), or you can walk the entire 7km *luontopolku* (nature trail) that goes via a series of hills with some good views. **Tiirismaa** is a skiing resort in winter.

On the shores of Vesijärvi, the large Hollola **church** (www.hollolanseurakunta.fi; admission free; ☺10am-6pm May-Aug), 17km northwest of Lahti, was once the heart of this parish, before Lahti grew up. It's an elegant late-15th-century structure with steep gables; the bell tower was designed by Carl Engel in the 19th century. Mounted above the double nave are polychrome wooden sculptures of saints; also noteworthy are the elaborate coats of arms, and the 14th-century baptismal font and Pietà that were from the earlier, wooden church. The church, and the village, are marked 'Hollola kk' on signs.

Nearby you'll find the local museum, with an indoor and outdoor section.

🍴 Sleeping & Eating

Messilä HOTEL, COTTAGE €€

(☏86011; www.messila.fi; Messiläntie 208; s/d €98/115, 3-/4-person cottages €150/185; P🏊) This estate offers modern hotel rooms, character-laden accommodation in the 'old storehouse', plus a holiday village with self-contained cottages. The several restaurants here serve everything from gourmet cuisine to burgers and beers, and this is a popular summer venue for music and dancing, and for après-ski socialising in winter.

Camping Messilä CAMPGROUND €

(☏876 290; www.campingmessila.fi; tent sites €16 plus per adult/child €4/1, cabins/apt €60/95; P) This beautifully equipped holiday park is next to the estate on Vesijärvi, 7km west of Lahti. There's a beach, cafe with beer terrace, and jetty for light fishing. It offers summer and winter activities. It even keeps a hole open in the ice for a hardy post-sauna dip!

The Lakeland

Best Places to Stay

» Lossiranta Lodge (p165)
» Mannila (p170)
» Lomakeskus Järvisydän (p172)
» Valamo monastery (p176)
» Hotel Yöpuu (p180)
» Oravi Outdoor Centre (p172)

Best Places to Eat

» Panimoravintola Huvila (p167)
» Musta Lammas (p188)
» Pöllöwaari (p181)
» Kummisetä (p188)

Why Go?

Most of Finland could be dubbed lakeland, but around here it seems there's more water than land. And what water: sublime, sparkling and clean. Reflecting sky and forests as clearly as a mirror, it leaves an indelible impression.

Get outdoors here, whether you rent a cottage and try your hand at kindling the perfect blaze in the sauna stove, grab a canoe and paddle the family-friendly Squirrel Route or go in search of rare inland seals.

Towns, too, have much to offer. Savonlinna hosts opera in the wonderful setting of its island castle, Jyväskylä's lively feel and architectural portfolio have obvious appeal, while Kuopio offers lake trips and a great smoke sauna.

Lakeland's people – the *savolaiset* – are among the most outspoken and friendly of Finns. They are often lampooned due to their distinctive Savo dialect, accent and humour. But they have the last laugh thanks to the unparalleled beauty of their region.

When to Go
THE LAKELAND

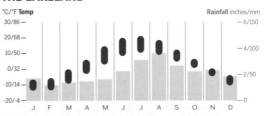

Feb Check out the ice sculptures in Savonlinna, and explore Linnansaari National Park on skates.

Jul Great weather for water activities, and the best festivals, including opera in Savonlinna's castle.

Aug See all the highlights in decent weather but without the July crowds.

The Lakeland Highlights

1 Soaring on the wing of an aria in the memorable castle setting of the **Savonlinna Opera Festival** (p166)

2 Paddling around the **Linnansaari and Kolovesi national parks** (p171 & 173) seeking a glimpse of the rare Saimaa ringed seal

3 Peering at the visionary buildings of Alvar Aalto in the lively university town of **Jyväskylä** (p178)

4 Sweating it out in Kuopio's sociable **smoke sauna** (p183)

5 Relaxing in a cottage by one of the region's thousands of lakes, including its largest, **Lake Saimaa** (p171)

6 Cruising the picturesque lakeland en route to a visit to the Orthodox monastery at **Valamo** (p176)

7 Entering a fantasy land at the seriously offbeat mechanical music museum in **Varkaus** (p175)

8 Descending to the arty underworld at **Retretti** (p170)

Savonlinna

📶 015 / POP 27,734

One of Finland's prettiest towns, Savonlinna shimmers on a sunny day as the water ripples around its centre. Set on two islands between Haapavesi and Pihlajavesi lakes, it's a classic Lakeland settlement with a major attraction: perched on a rocky islet, one of Europe's most visually dramatic castles, Olavinlinna, lords it over the picturesque town centre. The castle also plays host to July's world-famous opera festival in a spectacular setting.

Even if you're no ariaholic, the buzz of the festival makes this the most rewarding time to visit, with more restaurants and cafes open and animated post-show debriefs over dinner or bubbly going deep into the darkless night. But Savonlinna rewards a visit any time of year, and has other major drawcards like Kerimäki's church and the Retretti gallery within easy reach.

History

Savonlinna's slow growth began in 1475 with the building of Olavinlinna Castle, and in 1639 it received a municipal charter at the instigation of Count Per Brahe, the founder of many towns across Finland. Despite appearances, the castle didn't prove particularly defensible, and the Russians finally grabbed the town in 1743. It was returned to the Finnish grand duchy in 1812.

◉ Sights

Olavinlinna CASTLE
(www.olavinlinna.fi; adult/child €6/3, combined ticket with museum €8/3; ☺10am-6pm daily Jun–mid-Aug, 10am-4pm Mon-Fri, 11am-4pm Sat & Sun mid-Aug–May, last tour leaves 1hr before close) Standing haughtily on a rock in the lake, this castle is one of the most spectacular in northern Europe. As well as being an imposing fortification, it is also the spectacular venue for the month-long Savonlinna Opera Festival, comfortably seating 2300 within its sturdy walls.

The castle has been heavily restored after fire damage, but is still seriously impressive, not least in the way it's built directly on the rock in the middle of the lake. To visit the interior, including original towers, bastions and chambers, you must join a guided tour (around 45 minutes). Tours are multilingual and depart on the hour. Guides are good at bringing the castle to life and furnish you with some interesting stories: the soldiers, for instance, were partly paid in beer – five

litres a day and seven on Sundays, which makes the castle's frequent change-of-hands more understandable. During the opera festival, the last tour of each day includes a visit backstage.

Savonlinnan Maakuntamuseo MUSEUM
(www.savonlinna.fi/museo; Riihisaari; adult/child €5/2, with castle €8/3; ☺10am-5pm Tue-Sun, also Mon Jun-Aug) The town's provincial museum, in an old Russian warehouse near the castle, tells of local history and the importance of water transport to the area. There are plenty of old photographs and models and a changing art exhibition. Here also is **Nestori**, a national parks visitor and information centre for the Saimaa region.

Moored alongside is a selection of historic **museum ships**, all with exhibitions open from mid-May to mid-September during the same hours as the provincial museum (and accessible by the same ticket). The museum won't take your breath away like the castle, but is worthwhile and several orders of magnitude less touristy.

🏃 Activities & Tours

Numerous operators run tours allowing you to explore some of this Lakeland area. Savonlinna Travel runs many of them, from half-day to multiday trips.

The Savonlinna area, with its quiet country lanes and gently sloping hills, is terrific for **bicycle touring**. Bikes can be carried on board lakeboats for a small fee. To rent **canoes** and **rowing boats**, visit Vuohimäki Camping or the operators around the Seal Lakes detailed later in the chapter.

Lake Cruises

From June to August, Savonlinna **passenger harbour** is buzzing with dozens of daily scenic cruises that last about an hour and cost around €15. Boats include the **Ieva** and **Elviira** (www.ieva.fi), the **Lake Star** and **Lake Seal** (www.lakestar.info), and the **Paul Wahl** and **Punkaharju** (www.vipcruise.info). The boats anchor alongside the kauppatori (market square) and you can soon see which is the next departure. There are also many boats available for charter.

The **SS Heinävesi** (www.savonlinnanlaivat.fi) runs daily at 11am to Retretti art gallery in Punkaharju (adult/child one-way €25/10, return €33/15, two hours, July to mid-August), giving you 2½ hours there.

For cruises to Lappeenranta and Kuopio see Getting There & Away.

Savonlinna

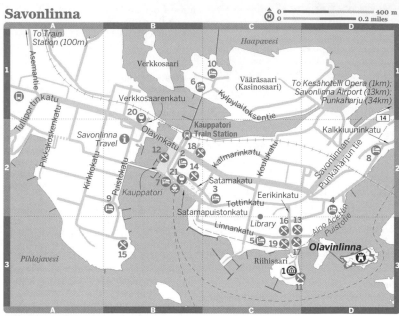

Savonlinna

🎊 Festivals & Events

When the opera's done, there's also an important **ballet festival** (www.savonlinnaballet.net), which runs for three to four days in late July or early August. Get tickets from **Lippu.fi** (☑060-090 0900; www.lippu.fi)

Less elegant, but keenly contested most years in late August, is the **Mobile Phone Throwing World Championships** (www.savonlinnafestivals.com).

In February, the castle hosts **Jäälinna** (www.jaalinna.fi), an ice-sculpture contest.

🛏 Sleeping

Prices rise sharply during the opera festival, when hotel beds are scarce. Fortunately, the students are out of town and their residences are converted to summer hotels and hostels. It goes without saying that you should book accommodation well in advance if you plan to visit during July. If you have a vehicle, staying in Punkaharju, Rantasalmi or Kerimäki is an option.

TOP **CHOICE** **Lossiranta Lodge** BOUTIQUE HOTEL €€€
(☑511 2323; www.lossiranta.net; Aino Acktén Puistotie; d €160-195; P) To get up close and personal with Olavinlinna Castle, this lakeside spot is the place to be: its impressive form looms just opposite. Offering five snug little nests in an outbuilding, this is one of Finland's most charming hotels. All are very different but decorated with love and style; they come with a small kitchen (yes, that's it in the cupboard) and numerous personal touches. The best has a wood sauna and jacuzzi – a honeymoon special. Breakfast is served on the lawn if weather allows; when the snows fall, an outdoor spa bath will keep the chills out. This is like a rural retreat but in the middle of town; warm personal service seals the experience.

Tavis Inn BOUTIQUE HOTEL €€€
(☑511 2323; www.lossiranta.net; Kalkkiuuninkatu 11; d €160-195; P) Tavis Inn, run by the same people as Lossiranta Lodge and further along the lakeshore, is in a secluded end-of-the-road spot, offering similar comfort minus the castle view. Rooms and suites are larger than at Lossiranta, and summer art exhibitions give it its own discrete ambience. Prices drop off-season. Check-in is at Lossiranta's reception.

Perhehotelli Hospitz HOTEL €€
(☑515 661; www.hospitz.com; Linnankatu 20; s/d €88/98; P@) This cosy place near the castle is a Savonlinna classic, built in the 1930s and redolent of that period's elegance, with striped wallpaper and ornate public areas. The rooms are also stylish, although beds are narrow and bathrooms small; there are larger rooms available for families. A balcony costs a little extra. The hotel has a pleasant terrace and orchard-garden with access to a small beach. Opera festival atmosphere

is great but rates rise accordingly (single/double €120/145), with midnight buffet laid on. Book eons in advance.

Hotel Seurahuone HOTEL €€
(☑020-757 1350; www.savonlinnanseurahuone.fi; Kauppatori 4-6; s/d €111/132; P@) Towering over the kauppatori, this friendly hotel offers a bit of everything; its rooms have views, big flatscreen TVs, sofas, sober but recently renovated decor, and decent little bathrooms. The top-floor bar has great views and fries up *muikku* (vendace, or whitefish); however the restaurant has disappointing food. There's also a nightclub onsite. Weekend prices are good but opera prices are substantially higher.

Spahotel Casino SPA HOTEL €€
(☑73950; www.spahotelcasino.fi; Kasinosaari; s/d €95/110, large d €135; P@≋) Charmingly situated on an island across a footbridge from the kauppatori, this is a good option. Nearly all rooms have a balcony; those that don't, have their own sauna. In the 'small' rooms, the beds are arranged toe-to-toe. The rooms aren't luxurious for the price, but guests have unlimited access to the excellent spa facilities, and the location is fantastic. Non-guests can use the spa for €9. Room prices fall at weekends and during winter and rise substantially during the opera festival, when it's a real favourite.

Vuorilinna HOTEL, HOSTEL €€
(☑73950; www.spahotelcasino.fi; Kylpylaitoksentie; dm/s/d €30/65/85; ☺Jun-Aug; P) Set in several buildings used by students during term time, this is run by the Spahotel Casino and has an appealing location across a beautiful footbridge from the town centre. Rooms are clean and comfortable; the cheaper ones share bathroom and kitchen (no utensils) between two. Happily, dorm rates get you the same deal, and there's a HI discount. Reception is most helpful, and there are free laundry

THE LAKELAND SAVONLINNA

LAKELAND: GETTING OUT ON THE WATER

With so many lakes, it's no wonder that the main summer activities involve getting out on them. One of the best ways to do so is to take a day-long lake cruise between Kuopio and Savonlinna; other cruises visit the Valamo Orthodox monastery.

The more active choice is to hire a canoe, whether for a short paddle or a longer trek. The Savonlinna area presents several choices, with two national parks, Linnansaari and Kolovesi, offering great rowing, canoeing and kayaking; there's also the popular two- or three-day 'Squirrel Route' from Juva to Sulkava.

SAVONLINNA OPERA FESTIVAL

The **Savonlinna Opera Festival** (www.operafestival.fi; Olavinkatu 27) is Finland's most famous festival, with an enviably dramatic setting: the covered courtyard of Olavinlinna Castle. It offers four weeks of top-class opera performances in July. The atmosphere in town during the festival is reason enough to come; it's buzzing, with restaurants serving post-show midnight feasts, and animated discussions and impromptu arias on all sides.

The first festival was held at Olavinlinna way back in 1912, the brainchild of Finnish soprano Aino Ackté. After a break of 39 years it was resurrected in 1967 and has grown in stature with each passing year. The festival's excellent website details the program: there are rotating performances of four or five operas by the Savonlinna company, as well as an international guest company performing, and concerts on the Sundays.

The performances themselves are magical: the muscular castle walls are a magnificent backdrop to the set and add great atmosphere. There are tickets in various price bands. The top grades (€110 plus) are fine, but the penultimate grade (€80 to €101) puts you in untiered seats, so it helps to be tall. The few cheap seats (€40) have a severely restricted view. Buy tickets up to a year in advance from **Lippupalvelu** (☎060-010 800; www.lippupalvelu.fi) or from Savonlinna Travel.

facilities. The spa hotel also runs Malakias, another summer lodging 2km west of town, with similar rooms and prices (open July only).

Kesähotelli Tott
HOTEL €€
(☎020-757 1356; www.savonlinnanseurahuone.fi; Satamakatu 1; s/d/f €88/106/110; ☺Jun-Aug; **P**) Run by the same people as the Seurahuone and not far from the kauppatori, this is another university residence that'll have you envying the Finnish student. Spacious rooms feature couches, comfortable beds, minibar, and some have great views. Apartment-style rooms are larger, a little more downmarket (lino floors) but have a fully equipped kitchen. Rates rise during July.

Villa Aria
HOTEL €€
(☎515 555; www.savocenter.fi; Puistokatu 15; s/d €108/158; ☺early Jun–mid-Aug; **P**) By the water in a quiet but central part of town, this stylish wooden former hospital has spacious high-ceilinged rooms, and runs as a summer hotel. The students who normally reside in it run reception in a haphazard manner, but it's still a fine, if expensive base. It's a bargain in June and in the week after the opera festival (singles/doubles €62/78).

Kesähotelli Opera
HOTEL €€
(☎521 116; www.savocenter.fi; Kyrönniemenkuja 9; d/q €102/176; ☺early Jun–mid-Aug; **P**) Operating as a summer hotel, this student residence is across the bridge from the main part of town, about 1.5km east of the centre. Some of the clean, spacious rooms share a bathroom and kitchen, while others have their own facilities. A double's only €55 outside July.

Vuohimäki Camping
CAMPGROUND €
(☎537 353; www.suncamping.fi; Vuohimäentie 60; tent sites €14, 4-person r €75-80, cottages €65-90; ☺early Jun-late Aug; **P**) Located 7km southwest of town, this camp ground has good facilities but fills up quickly during July. You can hire canoes, bikes and rowing boats here. Prices for rooms and cabins are cheaper in June and August.

SS Heinävesi
BOAT €
(☎050-065 3774; www.savonlinnanlaivat.fi; cabins upper/lower deck d €68/58; ☺Jul-early Aug) After the last cruise every afternoon/evening during high summer, this steamer offers cramped but cute two-bunk cabins. There's a good chance of getting a bed here, even during the opera festival, and it's moored right in the centre of things.

Lake Star
BOAT €
(☎040-020 0117; www.lakestar.info; d €40) The Lake Star offers cabins during the festival.

Panimoravintola Huvila
B&B €€
(☎555 0555; www.panimoravintolahuvila.fi; Puistokatu 4; tw €75; **P**) Above this brewery restaurant are two cosy, compact attic rooms (€120 during opera festival).

SKO
HOSTEL €
(☎572 910; www.sko.fi; Opistokatu 1; s/d basic €42/65, superior €65/80; **P**@) Six kilometres southwest of town, in the same direction as the camp site, this Christian college offers hostel rooms in a variety of buildings in a peaceful location near a lake. Excellent facilities on offer. Get close on bus number 3. Follow signs for Kristillinen Opisto. HI discount.

✗ Eating & Drinking

The lively lakeside **kauppatori** is the place for casual snacking. A *lörtsy* (turnover) is typical and comes savoury with meat *(lihalörtsy)* or sweet with apple *(omenalörtsy)* or cloudberry *(lakkalörtsy)*. Savonlinna is also famous for fried *muikku*; try these at Kalastajan Koju on the kauppatori, or the Muikkubaari on the top floor of the Seurahuone hotel. The opera festival peps up Savonlinna's nightlife, with restaurants open late and pubs thronged with post-performance merriment.

TOP CHOICE Panimoravintola

Huvila FINNISH, BREWERY €€

(✆555 0555; www.panimoravintolahuvila.fi; Puistokatu 4; mains €15-26; ⊗lunch & dinner Jul, dinner Mon-Fri May & Sep, dinner Mon-Fri, lunch & dinner Sat & Sun Jun & Aug) This noble wooden building was formerly a fever hospital then a mental asylum, but these days writes happier stories as an excellent microbrewery and restaurant just across the harbour from the town centre. The food focuses on fresh local ingredients and might feature unusual fare like goose or wild boar, all expertly prepared and served in generous quantities. The staff will recommend a beer match, whether it be fresh, hoppy Joutsen, traditional sweet *sahti* (ale flavoured with juniper berries), or the deliciously rich dessert stout. The terrace is a wonderful place on a sunny afternoon, with live music some weekends.

Majakka FINNISH €€

(✆206 2825; www.ravintolamajakka.fi; Satamakatu 11; mains €12-20) This restaurant has a deck-like terrace, fitting the nautical theme (the name means 'lighthouse'). Local meat and fish specialities are tasty, generously sized and fairly priced, and the select-your-own appetiser plate is a nice touch. It's child-friendly too, and opens late during the opera festival, when it buzzes with good cheer.

Hilpeä Munkki THEME €€

(✆515 330; Riihisaari; dishes €15-30; ⊗2pm-1am Jul) Alongside the museum in a delightfully ramshackle wooden building, this terraced restaurant gets back to basics in medieval style. Waiters dressed as monks bring out beer in tankards and meat on skewers. Views of the castle are superb.

Liekkilohi SEAFOOD €€

(www.liekkilohi.fi; Kauppatori; fish buffet per kilo €39; ⊗Jun–mid-Aug) This bright-red pontoon, anchored just off the kauppatori, specialises in 'flamed' salmon, a delicious plate that forms part of an excellent pay-by-weight fish buffet.

Valo FINNISH €

(✆514 425; www.savocenter.fi; Linnankatu 12; burgers €11-14; mains €10-22; ⊗noon-late Jun-Aug) A great terrace near the water makes this an opera favourite. They do a nice line in gourmet burgers (think reindeer, smoked salmon), and the main menu features several Finnish favourites.

Olutravintola Sillansuu PUB

(Verkkosaarenkatu 1; ⊗2pm-late) Savonlinna's best pub by some distance is compact and cosy, offering an excellent variety of international bottled beers, a decent whisky selection and friendly service. There's a downstairs area with a pool table; during the festival amateur arias are sometimes sung as the beer kegs empty.

Sinikka CAFE €

(www.cafesinikka.fi; Olavinkatu 35; salads €6; ⊗7am-5pm Mon-Fri, 9am-3pm Sat, also 9am-3pm Sun Jul) Run with a motherly air, this local cafe does quiches and salady lunches as well as decent coffee and excellent cakes.

Oopperalerassi BAR

(www.savonmafia.fi; Satamapuisto; ⊗from 2pm Mon-Fri, noon Sat & Sun May-Sep) Near the kauppatori, this flat wooden deck is one of Savonlinna's most popular spots for a summertime drink.

Near the castle, several handsome Linnankatu cafe-bars compete for the pre- and post-opera crowd with mini bottles of fizz and traditional, if priccy, Finnish plates.

Sarastro CAFE, ITALIAN €€

(www.savocenter.fi; Linnankatu 10; mains €13-23; ⊗noon-1am late Jun-early Aug) Lovely back garden. Salads, tapas and pasta.

Linnakrouvi FINNISH €€

(www.linnakrouvi.fi; Linnankatu 7; mains €15-28; ⊗Jun-Aug) Tiered outdoor seating and a short menu of tasty stuff like smoked salmon, *muikku* and filet mignon.

Saima CAFE €

(www.kahvilasaima.net; Linnankatu 11; meals €7-17; ⊗10am-5pm Mon-Fri, 10am-4pm Sat, noon-4pm Sun Aug-May, 10am-6pm daily Jun, 10am-1am Jul) Friendly owner, cosy interior, licensed and open year-round.

THE LAKELAND SAVONLINNA

ⓘ Information

Public library (Tottinkatu 6; ◷11am-7pm Mon-Thu, 10am-4pm Fri) Free internet. Also opens Saturday mornings outside summer.

Savonlinna Travel (✆060-030 007; www.savonlinna.travel; Puistokatu 1; ◷9am-5pm Mon-Fri Aug-Jun, 10am-6pm Mon-Sat, 10am-2pm Sun Jul) Tourist information including accommodation reservations, cottage booking, farmstays, festival tickets and tours. Free internet.

ⓘ Getting There & Away

Air

FlyBe fly daily between Helsinki and Savonlinna in summer, and more seldom in winter. They also connect Savonlinna with Seinäjoki and several other Finnish cities, as well as Gdansk in Poland. During the opera festival, a concert greets arriving passengers and night flights return punters to the capital after the show.

Boat

From mid-June to mid-August, century-old **MS Puijo** (✆250 250; www.mspuijo.fi) travels to Kuopio on Mondays, Wednesdays and Fridays at 9am (one-way €88, 10½ hours), returning on Tuesdays, Thursdays and Saturdays. The boat passes through scenic waterways, canals and locks, and stops en route at Oravi, Heinävesi, Karvio canal and Palokki, among others. Meals are available onboard. You can book a return from Savonlinna with overnight cabin accommodation for €175. Look for the downloadable English pdf file on the Finnish-language website.

MS Brahe (✆055-410 140; www.saimaatravel.fi) heads to/from Lappeenranta (€75-85, 8½ hours) twice weekly from early June to mid-August; the fare includes lunch and return bus transfer to Savonlinna.

The *Brahe* also sails from Helsinki to Lappeenranta, so you could combine all these routes into a Helsinki-Kotka-Lappeenranta-Savonlinna-Kuopio extravaganza.

Bus

Savonlinna is not on major bus routes, but there are several express buses a day from **Helsinki** (€49.90, 5 to 5½ hours), and buses run regularly from **Mikkeli** (€22.40, 1½ hours). There are also services to **Joensuu** (€24.50, 2¾ hours), **Kuopio** (€30,60, three hours) and **Jyväskylä** (€41, 3½ hours).

Train

Trains from **Helsinki** (€57, 4½ hours) and **Joensuu** (€29.60, 2¼ hours) both require a change in Parikkala.

For Kuopio, Jyväskylä and Tampere, railbuses (stop at both the main train station and the bus station) run the two hours to Pieksämäki and connect with trains there. The main train station, (buy tickets at an R-kioski or onboard) is a walk from the centre of Savonlinna; board and alight at the Kauppatori station instead.

ⓘ Getting Around

Savonlinna airport is 13km northeast of town. A taxi shuttle (✆044-025 2471; €14) meets arriving flights in July and August; it picks up at hotels on demand and leaves from the taxi rank by the bus station one hour before the flight departs. A regular cab costs around €30.

Three car rental agencies have central offices: **Sixt** (✆020-112 2557; www.sixt.fi; Olavinkatu 15), **Europcar** (✆040-306 2855; www.europcar.fi; Puistokatu 1) in the tourist office, and **Hertz** (✆020-555 2750; www.hertz.fi; Rantakatu 2). Hertz, Sixt and **Avis** (✆013-122076; www.avis.com) share a desk at the airport. Rates are expensive and cars should be booked well ahead.

Several places in town rent bikes in summer, including Café Seepra in front of the tourist office, and **InterSport** (✆517 680; Olavinkatu 52; ◷Mon-Sat).

Around Savonlinna

KERIMÄKI
✆015

Kerimäki is a small farming community, yet it's dominated by the world's largest wooden church (see p170), which towers over the village. It's a memorable sight, and close to Savonlinna.

The nearby protected island of **Hytermä** celebrates one of the weirdest human achievements: it has a grandiose stone staircase and monument to Romu-Heikki (Junk Heikki), a man who built large structures with millstones. The island is also quite beautiful, and is easily visited by hiring a rowing boat at the tourist office.

🛏 Sleeping & Eating

Herttua   HOTEL €€

(✆769 900; www.herttua.fi; Veneenniementie 64; s/d €79/89; 🅿@🛊) A kilometre and a half east of Kerimäki centre, this relaxing lakeside place is a good base for activities and has a spa complex. The neat little rooms, with varying colour schemes, all have relaxing perspectives: grab an odd-numbered one for lake views. There are numerous facilities, and also a weapon and artillery exhibition – this was once a frontline in the Winter War. Prices rise to €99/137 in July.

Around Savonlinna

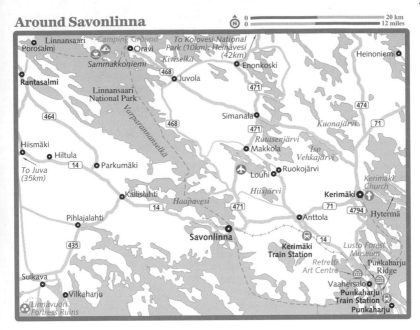

Gasthaus Kerihovi · GUESTHOUSE €€
(☑541 225; www.kerihovi.com; Puruvedentie 28; s/d/q €40/75/116; P) An attractive old wooden house not far from the church, this friendly guesthouse has simple, colourful rooms with creaky floors and washbasins above a pub/restaurant. Breakfast and sauna included, and there are good rooms for families/groups.

ⓘ Information
Tourist office (☑044-417 5002; www.kerimaki. fi; Puruvedentie 59; ☉10am-5pm Mon-Fri, 10am-1pm Sat Aug-late Jun, daily late Jun-Jul) Across from the church in a craft shop.

ⓘ Getting There & Away
Hourly buses run Monday to Friday between Savonlinna and Kerimäki (€5.70, 30 minutes). Don't catch a train: Kerimäki station is miles away from the village.

PUNKAHARJU
☑015
Punkaharju, the famous pine-covered sand esker (sand or gravel ridge) east of Savonlinna, is a popular summer destination and touted as 'Finland's national landscape'. The region was first declared a protected area by Tsar Alexander way back in 1803 and became a favoured summering spot for the tsars and St Petersburg gentry. The area is very picturesque and great for walking or cycling; there's also an innovative gallery and a forestry museum. It's an easy day trip from Savonlinna on the train but also an appealing place to stay.

Punkaharju village has services including a guesthouse and a large supermarket.

⊙ Sights & Activities
Punkaharju · OUTDOORS
During the Ice Age, formations similar to this 7km-long sand ridge were created all over the country. Because it crosses a large lake, it's always been an important travel route. Short sections of the original unsealed road along the ridge top remain – once part of a route to Russia connecting the Olavinlinna and Vyborg (Viipuri) castles. To stroll on the ridge, get off at the Retretti train station and walk east towards Punkaharju village, either shadowing the main road, or along the quieter and equally spectacular by-road signposted Harjualue. It is a spectacular walk, particularly on a sunny day, with water on both sides. Other labelled trails explore the forested areas from the Arboretum car park, which is located between Lusto and Retretti.

Boat cruises exploring the area leave from Retretti train station at 2pm in summer (adult/child €18/7).

TOP CHOICE Retretti GALLERY

(www.retretti.fi; adult/child €16/5, with Lusto €24/9; ⊙10am-6pm Jun-Aug) This is one of the world's most unusual galleries. An innovative annual exhibition of contemporary art is displayed inside an enormous subterranean cavern complex, artificial but authentic in atmosphere. The intriguing combination of craggy walls, watery pools and semi-darkness allows for startling, elaborate installations. There's also a vast subterranean auditorium. More conventional exhibition spaces have high-profile annual exhibitions of more mainstream art; upstairs is a workshop, gallery for kids and a good cafe-restaurant. Entrance is steep, but it's unique, and the descent into the arty underworld is memorable. It's wheelchair accessible throughout.

Lusto MUSEUM

(www.lusto.fi; adult/child €10/5, with Retretti €24/9; ⊙10am-7pm Jun-Aug, 10am-5pm May & Sep, 10am-5pm Tue-Sun Oct-Apr) The Finnish Forest Museum is dedicated to Finnish forests and forestry and is a good visit, with plenty of information in English. Displays cover hunting, cottage culture, and world global forest resources; a new section has a kid-pleasing range of machinery and chainsaws. More peaceable is the lakescape room from the Expo 2000 pavilion – a spot to relax for five minutes. The building itself is an interesting timber structure with the main display hall designed to represent the trunk of a tree, while the attractive cafe does a summer lunch buffet. There's a free internet terminal.

Kesämaa AMUSEMENT PARK

(www.kesamaa.fi; admission €16; ⊙mid-Jun–mid-Aug) Most reasonable children will allow you the Retretti gallery in exchange for this waterpark, very close at hand and featuring waterslides, bouncy castles and pirate ships. It's cheaper after 4pm.

🛏 Sleeping & Eating

The best places to eat are the Valtionhotelli and the cafes at Retretti and Lusto, which all have a good lunch buffet.

Mannila HOTEL, FARMSTAY €€

(☑644 265; www.maatilamatkailumannila.com; Koskelonniementie 127, Vaahersalo; d main/outbuilding €110/90, tent €6 plus per person €3, farm d €60-80; ⊙May-Sep plus winter if prebooked; P) This farm complex is in one of Punkaharju's most picturesque areas. The wonderful lakeside is the highlight: here you'll find a camp site and the welcoming Rantakatti hotel. The main building has attractive rooms, some with an enormous balcony. Rooms in the secondary building are smaller but share a large common area. There are cheaper but cosy rooms in converted farm buildings, separate family apartments, bikes, saunas, pony rides and a restaurant. It's remote enough to be a great Finnish retreat but handy enough to make a top Lakeland base.

Punkaharjun Valtionhotelli HOTEL €€

(☑020-752 9100; www.punkaharjunvaltionhotelli.fi; Tuunaansaarentie 4; s/d €90/120, tw without bathroom €60, superior r €150; ⊙Jun-Aug; P @) Right on the old walled ridge-road to Russia between Lusto and Retretti, this romantic

KERIMÄKI CHURCH

Finland has many notable churches, but few impose like Kerimäki's – the largest **wooden church** (www.kerimaenseurakunta.fi; admission free; ⊙10am-6pm Jun & early Aug, 10am-7pm Jul, 10am-4pm late Aug) in the world. Built in 1847, it was designed to accommodate 5000 churchgoers.

The oversized church was no mistake, but was deliberately inflated from original plans by overexcited locals. At the time the church was built, the population of Kerimäki parish was around 12,000, and the reverend felt that half of the residents should be attending church on any given Sunday. Worshippers arrived by water, crossing the lakes in a *kirkkovene* (church longboat).

As stunning as the yellow-and-white church appears from outside (dominating the tiny township), the scale isn't apparent until you survey the massive interior – the height of the nave is 27m. Heating it was impossible: the original eight stoves weren't enough, and a smaller winter chapel was built at the rear. The main church is still used for services in summer. It's largely unadorned apart from an altarpiece by Aleksandra Såltin.

There's a cafe and gift shop in the separate bell tower in front of the church (proceeds go to the maintenance, an onerous burden for a small parish), and for €2 you can climb the tower on steep wooden steps for a better view.

A COTTAGE BY A LAKE

The Lakeland is a particularly enticing place to search out a waterside cottage retreat or cosy rural farmstay for a true Finnish holiday. Around 100,000 rental cabins and cottages are dotted around the myriad lakes.

A good first point of investigation is the nationwide operators (p339) – **Lomarengas** has heaps of options in this area and also has links to farmstays and rural B&Bs. A local operator with a decent portfolio is **Saimaa Tours** (www.saimaatours.fi). Local tourist offices and websites also have extensive lists of accommodation options. Savonlinna's travel website, www.savonlinna.travel, and Mikkeli's, www.visitmikkeli.fi, both link to farmstay and cottage-rental providers. **Ready to Go** (www.readytogo.fi) is another worth checking out; other local providers are mentioned throughout this chapter.

Cabins normally provide at least a rowing boat and wood-fired sauna, though you may need your own bedding; cottages come with fully equipped kitchens; and farmstays often offer all manner of summer and winter activities such as horse riding, fishing and snowmobiling.

wooden hotel dating from 1845, was once the gamekeeper's lodge for the royal Russian hunting estates, and includes a villa built for the tsarina. There's a variety of room types and prices, including cabins (€50 plus €10 if you need linen). The doubles have a cramped sleeping space but an extra sitting area; the superiors are huge and beautiful, with views down the hill. It's wonderfully peaceful up here among the pines, and there's also a fine restaurant. Prices rise about 25% in July.

Gasthaus Punkaharju   GUESTHOUSE €€
(☑050-340 0867; www.naaranlahti.com; Palomäentie 18; s/d €55/75; P⛵) This guesthouse, in Punkaharju village 2km south of the bus station, has simple but comfortable rooms; there's a sauna and pool and you can also rent bikes, boats and snowmobiles. The owners also run the farm-estate Naaranlahti.

Naaranlahti   FARMSTAY €€
(☑473 123; www.naaranlahti.com; Kesälahdentie 1614; s/d €60/85; P⛵) This farmstay, run by the owners of Gasthaus Punkaharju, has good apartment rooms. You can relax and take part in rural activities, including canoeing, fishing or gathering berries. It's 15km from Punkaharju but transport to and from the town is provided from the guesthouse.

Punkaharjun Lomakeskus   CAMPGROUND €
(☑029-007 4050; www.punkaharjunlomakeskus. fi; tent sites €13.50 plus per adult/child €4/2, 2-/4-person cabins €40/60, self-contained cottages €95-159; P) Very handy for Retretti, this enormous lakeside camp site has a whole town's worth of solid cabins and cottages, and a raft of facilities. Good for kids, who'll

soon find a posse of Finnish playmates; there's also a reindeer to feed and the popular waterpark next door.

Kruunupuisto   SPA HOTEL €€
(☑775 091; www.kruunupuisto.fi; Vaahersalontie 44; s/d €83/96, superior s/d €96/122; P@⛵) Off the main road in a pretty part between Retretti and Punkaharju village, this spa and rehabilitation centre can understandably sometimes have a hospital-like feel, but it offers great facilities – pool, gym, massages, bike hire – at good prices. The superior rooms are huge. It's 25% more from mid-June to the end of July.

❶ Information
Tourist Information (☑527 5400; www. punkaharju.fi; Kauppatie 20; ⏰Mon-Fri) There's information here in the town hall in Punkaharju village, but you can also get info at the Lusto train station and at the petrol station by Retretti train station, the latter open long summer hours (9am to 8pm Monday to Friday, 10am to 8pm Saturday & Sunday).

❶ Getting There & Away
Trains between Savonlinna and Parikkala stop at Retretti, Lusto and Punkaharju train stations (€4, 30 minutes, five to six daily). You can also get here on less regular buses from Savonlinna or by boat (see Savonlinna).

The Seal Lakes
☑015

Enticing Linnansaari and Kolovesi, two primarily water-based national parks in the Savonlinna area, offer fabulous lakescapes dotted with islands, all best explored by hiring a canoe or rowing boat. Several

THE LAKELAND THE SEAL LAKES

outfitters offer these services, and free camping spots dot the lakes' shores. This is perhaps the best part of the Lakeland to really get up close and personal with this region's natural beauty.

This is the habitat of the freshwater Saimaa ringed seal. This endangered species was separated from its Baltic cousins at the end of the last Ice Age, and after being in imminent danger of extinction during the 20th century due to hunting and human interference, its population levels have stabilised and are on the increase, although there remain only a precarious 300-odd of the noble greyish beasts.

Late May is the most likely time to see seals, as they are moulting and spend much time on rocks. As well as information points detailed below, the Nestori centre in the Savonlinna museum is a good source of national park information.

There are numerous cabin and cottage rentals available around the two parks. Check www.savonlinna.travel for starters.

LINNANSAARI NATIONAL PARK

This scenic national park (www.outdoors.fi) consists of Haukivesi lake and hundreds of uninhabited islands; the main activity centres around the largest island, Linnansaari, which has marked hiking (5km to 7km) and nature trails (2km). As well as the seal population, rare birds, including ospreys, can also be seen.

The best way to experience the park is to pack camping gear and food, rent a kayak and spend a few days exploring. Rowing boats, motorboats, kayaks, canoes and camping equipment can be hired from the offices of **Saimaaholiday** (www.saimaaholiday.net) Oravi (☑647 290; Kiramontie 15); Porosalmi (☑020-729 1760; Porosalmentie 313). This is an excellent set-up with a comprehensive range of hiring, guiding and advice, as well as great accommodation options at the two main access points for the park (see below). It can book the huts on Linnansaari island and organise activities too; this region is also a good winter destination, with a marked skating track right across the lake, ice-fishing and snowshoe walks.

Oskari (☑020-564 5916; www.outdoors.fi; ☺9am-4pm Mon-Fri late Feb–mid-Jun & mid-Aug–Oct, 10am-6pm mid-Jun–mid-Aug) in Rantasalmi is the visitor information centre for the park and village and also has an environmental display and a film about a Saimaa seal pup (adult/child €3/1.50). It rents canoes too.

If you haven't rented your own, there are scheduled boat services to Linnansaari island from Oravi (adult/child €8.50/4, three daily mid-June to August, 15 minutes), and Porosalmi (adult/child €14/5, two daily, 30 minutes). These are run by Saimaaholiday, who can also arrange on-demand watertaxi departures from May to October at a higher rate.

Buses run to Oravi and Rantasalmi from Savonlinna. From Rantasalmi, it's an extra 7km to the turn-off for Porosalmi (Varkaus-bound buses can drop you here), and a further 3km walk down to the boat dock and accommodation complex. The Savonlinna–Kuopio ferry stops at Oravi.

🛏 Sleeping & Eating

TOP CHOICE Oravi Outdoor Centre   HOTEL, HOSTEL €€

(☑647 290; www.saimaaholiday.net/oravi; Kiramontie 15, Oravi; hostel s/d €30/45, hotel s/d €75/90; ᴘ@) Beautifully set by the river in Oravi, the eastern access point for Linnansaari National Park, this excellent facility, as well as providing everything you could possibly need to get on the water (or ice), offers a variety of comfortable accommodation. As well as various self-catering cottages in the vicinity, it has simple summer-only hostel rooms and a cracking modern hotel. The great rooms have a kitchen, drying cabinet and free sauna use; it's more expensive in July, and cheaper outside summer. There's an attractive waterside restaurant in summer and a year-round cafe-shop. They may let you camp here.

Lomakeskus Järvisydän   COTTAGE, HOTEL €€

(☑020-729 1760; www.jarvisydan.com; Porosalmentie 313, Porosalmi; s/d/ste €85/105/200, cottages from €125, villas from €250; ᴘ@) This rather impressive medieval-themed holiday village is at the Porosalmi embarkation point for the Linnansaari National Park. There's a big variety of accommodation, mostly in log cottages which, despite the old-time look, feature plenty of modern comforts inside. Good meals are available in the highly atmospheric restaurant and hall – get a look at the unusual wine cellar – and it runs activities and rent out all sorts of equipment so you can get canoeing in summer or skate across the lake in winter.

Sammakkoniemi   CAMPGROUND, CABIN €

(☑050-027 5458; www.outdoors.fi; tent sites €7, cabins €45) On the island of Linnansaari in the park, this camping ground offers a wood sauna, cooking places and (in summer) a kiosk-cafe. Several smaller islands also have designated camping areas.

Rinssi-Eversti HOTEL €€
(②440 761; www.rinssieversti.fi; Ohitustie 5; s/d €55/75; P) In Rantasalmi itself, this hotel-restaurant near the water offers bright simple rooms with bathroom that are a decent deal.

KOLOVESI NATIONAL PARK
Northeast of Linnansaari, less-trafficked Kolovesi (www.outdoors.fi) covers several islands, which feature well-preserved pine forests. There are high hills, rocky cliffs and caves, and prehistoric rock paintings dating back 5000 years. Saimaa seals, as well as otters and eagle owls, call Kolovesi home.

The park's a paradise for canoeing, the best way to explore the fantastic scenery. Motorboats are prohibited. There are several restricted areas, and the islands are out-of-bounds all winter to protect the seals, whose pups are born in February.

The gateway town to the park is pleasant Enonkoski, with a bright stream and rapids dividing it in two. There's a **park information cabin** here. The park starts a further 12km north. A free ferry north of Enonkoski crosses the narrows between two lakes on Rd 471.

Nahkiaissalo walking trail (3.3km) is in the south of the park, signposted 17km north of Enonkoski, and accessible without a boat. Mäntysalo, an island in the north, has another trail (3.8km). Just north of the park, **Vierunvuori hill** has prehistoric rock paintings depicting stick figures and elk.

Kolovesi Retkeily (②040-558 9163; www.sealtrail.com) is the best and most experienced tour operator, specialising in canoe rental, outfitting and multiday journeys for all abilities. The office is located east of the park at Leipämäki, north of Enonkoski by the junction with the Savonranta road. The website www.norppateam.com lists other operators.

You can head from Kolovesi National Park to Oravi and thence Linnansaari National Park by canoe; Saimaaholiday (see Linnansaari above) will deliver canoes to Kolovesi for you if you want to do this.

🛏 Sleeping & Eating
Inside the national park are 12 simple camping grounds and a cabin on Mäntysalo. You can book this via Oskari (see Linnansaari above) in Rantasalmi or the Wild North website www.villipohjola.fi.

Kievari Enonhovi GUESTHOUSE €
(②479 431; www.norppateam.com/enonhovi; Urheilukentäntie 1, Enonkoski; s/d €40/70, d with shower €90; P) This curious spot is the heart of Enonkoski village and handy for Kolovesi National Park. It's pleasant, with a terrace, parkland leading down to the river and occasional live music in summer. There are two grades of rooms, all simple and likeable. The better ones have their own shower and kitchenette. HI discount.

Sulkava
②015
Scenic Sulkava, 39km southwest of Savonlinna, is quiet for most of the year but leaps into life in July when it hosts an enormous rowing festival that's an equally enormous party. Sulkava is the finishing point for the Squirrel Route (see p174).

There's tourist information in **Alina** (②044-417 5215; www.sulkava.fi; Alanteentie 28; ⊙9am-4pm Mon-Fri), a cafe that can provide details of the numerous rental cottages in the area. It opens until 6pm and weekends too in July.

Sulkavan Suursoudut (www.suursoudut.fi) is a massive rowing festival that attracts big crowds and some 7000 competitors over its four days in mid-July. Competitors row wooden boats around Partalansaari over a 70km two-day course or a 60km one-day course, then get thoroughly hammered. The highlights are races between large longboats – *kirkkovenettä* – traditionally used to get to church across the lakes. There are competitions for all abilities, and you might be able to find an oar for yourself in one of the teams.

There are various camp sites in and around Sulkava. In the centre, **Muikkukukko** (②471 651; www.muikkukukko.fi; Alanteentie 4; s/d €45/70; P) is a small motel behind a restaurant/bar. The 10 doubles are simply decorated and comfortable; go for an upstairs one, which have balconies.

Sulkava is served by daily buses from Savonlinna and weekday ones from Mikkeli. There are two buses from Sulkava to Juva each weekday, leaving at 7am and 12.25pm.

Mikkeli

♪015 / POP 48,824

Mikkeli is a sizeable provincial town on the shores of Saimaa, Finland's largest lake. It's an important transport hub and was the headquarters of the Finnish army during WWII; museums relating to those years are the main sights in town. It's still an important military base, and soldiers sometimes seem to outnumber civilians. It's a friendly place though, and although there's little to see, it often makes a convenient stopover between the northern and southern parts of the country.

Päämajamuseo (Headquarters Museum; www.mikkeli.fi/museot; Päämajankatu 1-3; adult/child €5/free; ⊙10am-5pm Fri-Sun Sep-Apr, 10am-5pm daily May-Aug) was Gustav Mannerheim's command centre during the war; and **Jalkaväkimuseo** (Infantry Museum; www.jalkavakimuseo.fi; Jääkärinkatu 6-8; adult/child €6/free; ⊙10am-6pm May-Sep, 11am-4pm Wed-Sun Oct-Apr) is one of the largest military museums in Finland. You can also visit Mannerheim's wartime railway carriage at the train station.

CANOEING THE SQUIRREL ROUTE

The 57km Juva to Sulkava canoeing route, known as **Oravareitti** (Squirrel Route; www.oravareitti.net) is a Lakeland highlight. The beginner- and family-friendly route starts at Juva on Jukajärvi and traverses lakes, rivers and gentle rapids on the way to Sulkava. It's a very pretty journey – you feel miles away from the stresses of everyday life; information boards along the route describe the local nature.

You can do the trip in two fairly strenuous days; there's a good camp site midway. But this means 6-8 hours of paddling each day, so you may want to take it easier and do it in three, or even four days. This would mean taking a tent, which you can hire at Juva Camping. Another option is to get dropped off a little further along the route, making for an easier first day.

Early summer sees the highest water levels, which means little portage. The rapids are fairly simple, although you might want to carry the canoe round Kuhakoski, depending on conditions.

Getting Started

The best starting point, **Juva Camping** (☑015-451 930; www.juvacamping.com), provides everything you need: it rents two-person Canadian canoes (per day €38) or single kayaks (per day €28), supplies a good waterproof route map, rents tents and camping gear, and can arrange to pick you (or just the canoe) up at Sulkava. It's just off the north-south highway between Mikkeli and Varkaus, 3km west of the town of Juva and 63km west of Savonlinna. Buses will drop you nearby. There are tent sites and cottages here.

The Route

There are regular rest stops with fireplaces and toilets, as well as a camping area midway. From Juva Camping it's an easy 8km paddle across Jukajärvi to the first resting place and beginning of the river section, Polvijoki, where you must carry your canoe around the dam to the right. Passing through the small lakes Riemiö (where there's a resting place) and Souru, you come to the first rapids, gentle 200m Voikoski, followed by a rest area to the left of a small island. Continue along the canal, carrying the canoe across the road at the end, before negotiating the Karijoki.

There's a friendly camping ground on the 2km long Kaitajärvi, **Sulkavan Oravanpesät** (☑040-093 8076; www.oravanpesat.fi), with tent sites, cottages and a much-appreciated sauna. These folk can also rent you canoes and kayaks and arrange transport along the route. This is more or less the halfway point. Next comes a series of rapids including Kissakoski and the strong currents of the Kyrsyänjoki. You continue through the Rasakanjoki and Tikanjoki before coming to the large Halmejärvi, where there is another resting place at the end. The route continues on the western shore of Lohnajärvi to the Lohnankoski. From here it's a leisurely paddle down the Kuhajärvi, past a final set of rapids and into Sulkava, where you pull in at the Kulkemus Boat Centre on the right after the bridge. There's a camping ground and a cafe here.

The Mikkeli area is excellent for fishing – the lakes teem with perch, salmon and trout, and ice-fishing is popular in winter. The tourist office can help with permits, guides and equipment rental.

Mikkeli Music Festival (www.mikkelimusic. net), held here in late June/early July, is a week-long classical music event featuring top Finnish and Russian conductors. Balancing it out is **Jurassic Rock** (www.jurassicrock. fi), a two-day festival in early August that features plenty of Finnish and Scandinavian bands.

🛏 Sleeping & Eating

Hotelli Uusikuu   HOTEL €
(☑221 5420; www.uusikuu.fi; Raviradantie 13; s/d €49/59; P) This staffless hotel is quite a bargain. Rooms are clean, comfortable, modern and spacious. There's a free internet jack, and some rooms also have a fold-out bed so can sleep up to four. Book online. It's about 15 minutes' walk from the centre; turn right out of the train or bus station, then left on Savilahdenkatu; Raviradantie is on your right after crossing the small river.

Sokos Hotel Vaakuna   HOTEL €€
(☑20201; www.sokoshotels.fi; Porrassalmenkatu 9; s/d around €99/107; P @) Mikkeli's most central hotel is just a block south of the kauppatori. It's been designed more with the business traveller in mind, but it's in a handy location and the rooms are attractive enough if a little short on space.

Kenkävero   FINNISH €€
(www.kenkavero.fi; Pursialankatu; lunch €25; ⊙10am-6pm Sun-Fri, to 4pm Sat) This design shop and art centre is picturesquely set in a lovely vicarage building a short walk southeast of town (cross the railway tracks away from the centre and turn right, cross a roundabout and you'll be there in ten minutes). The cafe still feels like an elegant drawing room and you half expect the vicar himself to bring in tea and cucumber sandwiches. Instead there's a reader-praised lunch buffet (11am to 4pm daily) that pulls out all the stops.

Hilla   FINNISH €€
(www.ravintolahilla.com; Hallituskatu 7; mains €18-24; ⊙lunch & dinner Mon-Sat, noon-7pm Sun) This elegant basement restaurant on the pedestrian street has a few typical Finnish dishes, along with some rather-far-south reindeer offerings. Perch fillets are good, as is the short menu of choices obtained from local producers.

❶ Information

Tourist office (☑044-794 5669; www.visit mikkeli.fi; Maaherrankatu 16; ⊙9am-5pm Mon-Fri, also 10am-3pm Sat Jun-Aug) On the western side of the kauppatori. Staff can help find you a cottage to rent – there are hundreds around the area.

❶ Getting There & Away

Mikkeli is a transport hub served by many trains and buses that run between Helsinki and the eastern Lakeland or Kuopio. Train and bus stations are adjacent, a block east (downhill) from the kauppatori.

Bus destinations include Helsinki (€38.10, 3½ hours) and Savonlinna (€22.40, 1½ hours). Trains run to Helsinki (€41.30, 2¾ hours), Kuopio (€25.80, 1½ hours) and further north around five times daily. For other cities, change at Pieksämäki or Kouvola.

Around Mikkeli

Twenty kilometres south of Mikkeli, **Ristiina** is one of the region's most historic villages, founded by Count Per Brahe in 1649 and named after his wife. Little remains of the village's glorious past, though it has a pleasant enough lakeside location.

It's a further 19km (along Rd 4323 to Puumala) to the region's main attraction, the **rock paintings** of Astuvansalmi (Astuvansalmen Kalliomaalaukset). Estimated to be 5000 years old, they cover a 15m stretch of steep cliffs, and include elk, human and animal tracks. Amber artefacts have been found in the lake. From the car park, it's a 2.5km walk to the paintings.

Varkaus

☑017 / POP 22,757

Spread-out Varkaus is surrounded by water and covers several islands cut by canals. The location is appealing to the timber-pulp industry, whose factory complex is in the heart of the town. Varkaus is a transport hub, and you might find yourself changing buses here, especially to visit the monastery of Valamo. The town's name means 'theft' in Finnish.

TOP CHOICE **Mekaanisen Musiikin Muse**   MUSEUM OF MECHANICAL MUSIC
(www.mekaanisenmusiikinmuseo.fi; Pelimannin-katu 8; adult/child €14/7; ⊙11am-6pm Tue-Sat, 11am-5pm Sun Mar–mid-Dec, 11am-6pm daily Jul) is Varkaus's stand-out attraction. 'You must

understand', says the personable owner, 'it's not a normal museum; more a madhouse'. A truly astonishing collection of musical instruments ranges from a ghostly keyboard-tinkling Steinway piano to a robotic violinist to a full-scale orchestra emanating from a large cabinet. This is just the beginning; political cabaret in several languages and an overwhelming sense of good humour and imagination make it a cross between a Victorian theatre and Wonka's chocolate factory. Having a coffee outside under the steely gaze of sizeable macaws seems like a return to normality. The museum is signposted 1km west of the main north–south highway and also provides tourist information.

Varkaus has a few places to stay. Turn left out of the bus and train station, then left again across the bridge to reach **Hotelli Joutsenkulma** (☑366 9797; www.joutsenkulma. fi; Käärmeniementie 20; s/d €66/89; P). Reception is up the back of a low-key local drinking den, but the modern rooms have zippy silver sheets and a big comfy armchair as well as plenty of space.

Most eateries are around the kauppatori, 1km east of the station (head for the factory chimneys). The best is **Kaks Ruusua** (www. kaksruusua.fi; Ahlströminkatu 25; mains €17-26; ☺lunch Mon-Sat, dinner Tue-Sat) in a fine old building across the street from the pulp complex. It does all-day service as a popular cafe and offers a cheap lunch buffet and tasty dinners in the early evening.

Daily FlyBe flights connect Helsinki with Varkaus except in high summer. Keskusliikenneasema is the central station, which includes the train and bus terminals. Frequent trains run east to Joensuu (€17.10, 1½ hours), and west to Pieksämäki (€6.60, 30 minutes), where you can change for westbound, southbound or northbound services.

Heinävesi & Around

☑017

Heinävesi village lies amid hills north of Kolovesi National Park and among some of the most scenic lakeland in Finland. The Savonlinna to Kuopio boat route passes through here and canals provide a means of local transport. The town itself isn't a beauty, but waterscapes and nearby monasteries are the drawcard.

A huge yellow wooden **church** perches on a hill at the end of Kirkkokatu, a kilometre from the centre. It was built in 1890, seats 2000 people, and offers good views over Kermajärvi. Just below is the local **museum** (admission by donation; ☺11am-6pm Jul) in a former grain store.

🛏 Sleeping

There's also accommodation at Valamo and Lintula.

Gasthaus-Hotelli Heinävesi GUESTHOUSE €€ (☑562 411; www.gasthausheinavesi.fi; Askeltie 2; s/d €65/85; P) This well-cared-for spot in the bustling heart of Heinävesi makes a good base for exploring the region. The rooms offer value – some have a balcony – and the kindly owners run a decent cheap restaurant downstairs.

❶ Information

Tourist information (☑040-710 1919; www. heinavesi.fi; Kermanrannantie 7; ☺Mon-Fri) In the town hall on the main street.

❶ Getting There & Around

Heinävesi is easily reached by bus from Varkaus and Kuopio. Trains between Varkaus and Joensuu stop at Heinävesi station, but it's several kilometres south of the town.

In summer, the lakeboat MS *Puijo*, which runs between Kuopio and Savonlinna, calls at the Heinävesi jetty just south of the village. For a short trip, you can do one leg by boat and return by bus, or vice versa (€19).

Valamo

Finland's only Orthodox **monastery** (☑017-570 111; www.valamo.fi) is one of Savo's most popular attractions and, although it's only been at this location for 70 years, it has a long prior history on a Karelian island (which is now part of Russia).

One of the great, ancient Russian monasteries, old Valamo, set on an island in gigantic Lake Ladoga, survived the aftermath of the Russian Revolution because it fell just within the territory of newly independent Finland, but was soon after under grave threat during the Winter War of 1939. Ladoga froze (a rare occurrence), allowing a hurried evacuation from Russia of monks, icons and treasures. Those men that survived the journey resettled here in a beautiful lakeside estate. Monks and novices, almost a thousand strong a century ago, can now be counted on one hand, but the complex in general is thriving.

The first church was made by connecting two sheds; the rustic architecture contrasts curiously with the fine gilded icons.

The new church, completed in 1977, has an onion-shaped dome, icons, and is redolent with incense.

Visitors are free to roam and enter the churches; from June to August there's a **service** at 1pm. A **guided tour** (€5), which lasts an hour, is recommended for an insight into the monastery and Orthodox beliefs and symbolism; they are available in English and German. Take time to stroll to the peaceful **cemetery**, with a *tsasouna* (chapel) dedicated to Herman, a Valamo missionary monk who took Christianity to Alaska. There's also a museum and summer boat cruises to fill out the day, or you could take a walk to the Pilgrims' Cross or to Lintula convent, 18km away.

Aware of the need to redefine a monastery's place in 21st-century Europe, the community openly encourages visitors, whether they just want a coffee, or to browse the icons and chant-CDs in the shop. The monastery also offers visitors peace and relaxation in the beautiful surrounds, or the opportunity to engage further in Orthodox culture by attending a service or doing a course in theology, philosophy or icon-painting.

Valamo makes an excellent place to stay, and is even more peaceful once evening descends. Two **guesthouses** (s/d €32/54; P) in picturesque wooden buildings provide comfortable, no-frills sleeping with shared bathroom; there are also two grades of **hotel room** (s/d €60/70 or €75/120; P) offering a higher standard of accommodation. The complex's eatery, **Trapesa** (◔breakfast, lunch & dinner) has high-quality buffet spreads (€12 to €15), Russian-style high tea (€8), and evening meals with not a hint of monastic frugality; try the monastery's own range of berry wines.

ⓘ Getting There & Away

Valamo is clearly signposted 4km north of the main Varkaus–Joensuu road. A couple of daily buses run to Valamo from Joensuu and from Helsinki via Mikkeli and Varkaus. From Heinävesi change at Karvio.

The most pleasant way to get to Valamo (and Lintula, below) in summer is on a **Monastery Cruise** (☑015-250 250; www.mspuijo.fi) from Kuopio. The cruise uses a combination of the regular Kuopio to Savonlinna ferry and road transport. The ferry departs Kuopio at 9am Tuesday, Thursday and Saturday, then there's car transport from Palokki to Lintula and Valamo, then a bus back to Kuopio (adult €79). On Mondays, Wednesdays and Fridays, transport is reversed with a bus to Valamo at noon and a ferry back from Palokki (adult €60); you don't get to see Lintula.

Lintula

Not far from Valamo, the nation's only Orthodox **convent** (☑017-563 106; http://sites.google.com/site/lintulanluostari; ◔9am-6pm Jun-Aug) is much quieter. It's a serene contrast that is worth the short detour.

Lintula was founded in Karelia in 1895 and transferred to Savo and then Häme during WWII. A convent was founded at the present location in 1946; it's now at more or less full capacity, home to 15 nuns. A souvenir shop on the premises sells wool and candles hand-made here (the nuns supply all the Orthodox churches in Finland with candles), and there's a pleasant coffee shop. The highlight is the lovely grounds, which are perfect for strolling. In the garden is a beautifully simple log chapel, whose icons glint in the candlelight.

Lintulan Vierasmaja (☑017-563 225; s/d €24/40; P) is a small red house at the back of the convent. There are simple but clean rooms, with separate bathrooms, and it's open to men and women.

ⓘ Getting There & Away

A daily bus from Kuopio stops in the nearby village of Palokki. The convent is an 18km walk from Valamo monastery. See Valamo for details of cruises.

Jyväskylä

☑014 / POP 130,974

Vivacious and young-at-heart, western Lakeland's main town has a wonderful waterside location and an optimistic feel that makes it a real drawcard. Jyväskylä (pronounced *yoo*-vah-skoo-lah) was founded in 1837 and, in the mid-19th century, was the site of the country's first Finnish-language school and teacher-training college. The city's reputation for scholarship was boosted with the 1966 inauguration of its university. Thanks to the work of Alvar Aalto, the city also has a global reputation for its architecture, and petrolheads know it as the legendary venue for the Finnish leg of the World Rally Championships.

The 16,000 students and lively academic and arts scenes give the town plenty of energy and nightlife. In summer you can't

Jyväskylä

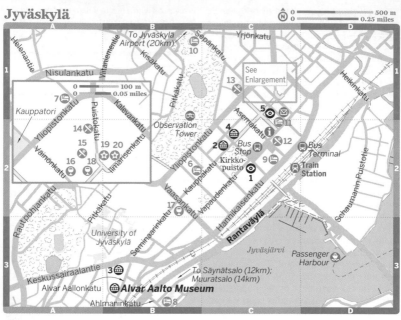

Jyväskylä

beat arriving by lakeboat from Lahti, while in winter there are plenty of winter sports on offer.

◉ Sights

Many people come to Jyväskylä for its modern architecture; at times the whole city centre is full of folk curiously pointing wide-angled lenses at every Aalto building. If you're coming for that, the best time is from Tuesday to Friday, as many buildings are closed at weekends and the Aalto Museum is closed on Mondays. Jyväskylä's other museums are all free on Fridays outside summer and closed on Mondays.

Alvar Aalto Buildings ARCHITECTURE

Alvar Aalto (see p327) was a giant of 20th-century architecture. He was schooled in Jyväskylä, opened his first offices here and spent his summers in nearby Muuratsalo.

The city has dozens of Aalto buildings, but stop first at one of his last creations, the **Alvar Aalto Museo** (www.alvaraalto.fi; Alvar Aallonkatu 7; adult/child €6/free, free Fri Oct-May; ☺11am-6pm Tue-Sun, from 10am Tue-Fri Jul; @), near the university to the southwest of the city centre. It chronicles his life and work, with a detailed focus on a number of his major buildings, as well as a section on his furniture design and a display of his glassware. It's very engaging, and you get a real feel for the man and his philosophy. The cafe does awful espresso but decent lunch, and the museum also has a free internet terminal.

The museum stocks the free pamphlet *Alvar Aalto's Jyväskylä,* which plots some of the significant buildings in and around Jyväskylä, designed by Aalto. It also has simple bikes for hire (per day/two days €10/15) to help you explore them.

Aalto's list includes the university's main buildings and the **City Theatre** (Vapaudenkatu 36). On the corner of Kauppakatu and Väinönkatu is the old **Workers' Club Building** (1925), an early work with Renaissance-inspired features such as columns and a Palladian balcony; there's a pub and restaurant downstairs.

Also see Säynätsalo and Muuratsalo under Around Jyväskylä p182.

Keski-Suomen Museo · MUSEUM
(www.jyvaskyla.fi/keskisuomenmuseo; Alvar Aallonkatu 7; adult/child €6/free; ☺11am-6pm Tue-Sun) The Museum of Central Finland is adjacent to the Alvar Aalto Museum and designed by him, but sees a fraction of the visitors. A pity, for it's a well-presented display. The main exhibition is an attractive overview of rural life in central Finland from prehistoric times onwards. There's an ancient sledgerunner dated to 4000 BC, and displays on hunting, fishing and logging, with English translations. It gives a good feel for traditional Finnish life and finishes in a typical old grocery. Upstairs is a history of Jyväskylä itself, with great scale models; the top floor holds temporary art exhibitions, often associated with the arts festival.

Jyväskylän Taidemuseo · GALLERY
(www.jyvaskyla.fi/taidemuseo; Kauppakatu 23; adult/child €6/free; ☺11am-6pm Tue-Sun) Opposite the church, this houses temporary exhibitions of modern art and sculpture, often arranged by the active local artists' association. Don't miss the astonishingly grand toilets.

Suomen Käsityön Museo · MUSEUM
(www.craftmuseum.fi; Kauppakatu 25; adult/child €5/free; ☺11am-6pm Tue-Sun) This craft museum is all about Finnish handicrafts and their history, and incorporates the National Costume Centre, which displays regional dress from around Finland. The permanent collection is small, and most space is taken up with temporary exhibitions. It's an enjoyable insight into activities that, partly due to the long Finnish winters, have always been an important part of life here. There's also a good shop attached.

🏃 Activities

It's a nice walk or cycle around the lake on a sunny day; it's about 12km, which you can cut in half using the road bridge.

Laajavuori · SKIING
(www.laajavuori.com; Laajavuorentie) Very handy for town, this has five modest slopes plus a kids' run and 62km of cross-country trails, as well as a number of scary ski jumps. There's a good ski area for children and the resort is popular with families; there's a **hotel** (www.rantasipi.fi) here that offers packages as well as a hostel (see below). It's 4km from the centre of Jyväskylä; catch bus 25.

Lake Cruises
There are numerous boating options – check www.jyvaskyla.fi for more choices.

Päijänne Risteilyt Hilden · CRUISE
(☎263 447; www.paijanne-risteilythilden.fi; ☺early Jun–mid-Aug) The main cruise operator runs several routes on several different boats, including the SS *Suomi,* one of the oldest steamers plying the Finnish lakes.

Short cruises on Lake Päijänne depart daily from the passenger harbour (some are lunch or dinner cruises) and cost €17 to €24, half-price for kids. Longer trips include trips northwards to the Keitele canal.

For the Jyväskylä to Lahti route see Getting There & Away.

✪ Festivals & Events
Jyväskylän Kesä · ART
(Jyväskylä Arts Festival; www.jyvaskylankesa.fi) In mid-July, this has an international program of concerts, exhibitions, theatre and dance. Over 50 years old, it has a strong liberal and radical tradition and is one of Finland's most important arts festivals.

THE LAKELAND JYVÄSKYLÄ

Neste Oil Rally Finland RALLY
(www.nesteoilrallyfinland.fi) In early August, Jyväskylä is the centre of what many Finns regard as the most important event of the summer calendar. Formerly called the Thousand Lakes, this is the Finnish leg of the World Rally Championship, which Finns follow closely and have traditionally been very successful at. It's perhaps the most spectacular of all the stages, and draws half a million spectators. The event goes for four days, with big concerts and parties on the Thursday, Friday and Saturday nights. Book tickets (€60) through **Jyväskylä Booking** (☎020-748 1830; www.jyvaskylabooking.fi; Piippukatu 7). Staff here can also find you accommodation, which should be booked well in advance.

🛏 Sleeping

As well as the following options, Sokos (www.sokoshotels.fi) and Scandic (www.scandichotels.com) have chain hotels right in the centre.

⬆ TOP CHOICE Hotel Yöpuu HOTEL €€
(☎333 900; www.hotelliyopuu.fi; Yliopistonkatu 23; s/d/ste €105/146/175, weekend s/d €88/125; P@) Among Finland's most enchanting boutique hotels, this exquisite spot has lavishly decorated rooms, all individually designed in markedly different styles (the Africa room is really something to behold). Service is warm and welcoming with an assured personal touch – including a welcome drink – that makes for a delightful stay. They're always renovating and improving here so standards are kept high. Suites offer excellent value.

Hotelli Milton HOTEL €€
(☎337 7900; www.hotellimilton.com; Hannikaisenkatu 29; s/d €80/110; P@) Right in the thick of things, this family-run hotel has an old-fashioned dark foyer, but the modern rooms offer plenty of natural light, space and attractive wooden floors; most have a balcony. An evening sauna on weekdays is included and it's very handy for the bus and train stations. Weekend prices are great (s/d €60/80).

Kesähotelli Harju/Amis HOTEL €
(☎443 0100; www.hotelliamis.com; Sepänkatu 3; s/d/tr €49/60/72; ☺Jun-early Aug; P@) Five minutes uphill from the city centre, this excellent summer hotel has modern, light, spacious student rooms each with a kitchenette (no utensils, but there's an equipped kitchen downstairs) and good bathrooms. It's a real

bargain, especially given that breakfast and an evening sauna are included.

Kesähotelli Rentukka HOTEL €
(☎010-279 2006; www.hotelrentukka.fi; Taitoniekantie 9; s/d/tr €42/54/66; ☺mid-May–Aug; P) A half-hour walk from the centre (pleasant if you cut across parkland), or a short trip on bus 18, this student accommodation offers light, no-frills rooms which are particularly good for families, in a campus with restaurant, shops and a bar. Rooms have bathroom and kitchen facilities but no utensils. Breakfast is included.

Retkeilyhotelli Laajari HOSTEL €
(☎266 7053; www.laajavuori.com; Laajavuorentie 15; dm/s/d €29/45/64; P) Part of Laajavuori sports complex 4km from town, this hostel is often booked out in winter by ski groups. It's easily accessed by bus 25 (get off when you see the caravan park on your left) and has institutional rooms with whitewashed brick walls, OK beds, and shared bathrooms and kitchen. There's also a burger cafe. HI discount, and it's a little cheaper in summer and at weekends.

Hotelli Alba HOTEL €€
(☎636 311; www.hotellialba.fi; Ahlmaninkatu 4; s/d €88/118; P@) Within the university, and very handy for the Aalto museum, this hotel is right by the water, and the terrace of its restaurant and bar takes full advantage. The telescopic corridors lead onto mediocre rooms with narrow beds and parquet floors, but the view from those facing the water compensates for this; you could fish out of the windows.

Hotel Pension Kampus GUESTHOUSE €€
(☎010-279 2002; www.hotelkampus.fi; Kauppakatu 11A; s/d €62/76; P) Central, spotless 3rd-floor option with kitchen facilities in rooms. Breakfast included. Price drops a little at weekends.

Omenahotelli HOTEL €€
(☎060-018 018; www.omena.com; Vapaudenkatu 57; r usually €70-90, P@) Central reception-less hotel. One of the best, with comfortable beds and endless corridors. Book online or via the lobby terminal.

🍴 Eating

Jyväskylä's kauppahalli isn't Finland's most intriguing, but it's still a place to go to grab fresh produce or a quick snack.

Pöllöwaari FINNISH €€
(📞333 900; www.hotelliyopuu.fi; Yliopistonkatu 23; mains €22-27; ⏰11am-midnight Mon-Fri, 1pm-midnight Sat, Sundays by prior reservation) The Yöpuu hotel's fine-dining restaurant makes a very tempting meal stop. There are various set menus, including an eight-course degustation special, but à la carte dining is rewarding here too, with main courses very fairly priced for the exceptional quality on offer. Wines are pricey, but there's a good selection including some great Burgundy, and the welcoming staff are keen to explain the matching possibilities.

Figaro FINNISH €€
(📞212 255; www.figaro-restaurant.com; Asemakatu 4; mains €21-27; ⏰11am-midnight Mon-Fri, noon-midnight Sat, 1-9pm Sun) With a warm drawing-room feel and cordial service, this backs up the atmosphere with excellent food served in generous portions. The fish is especially good, served with creamy sauces and inventive garnishes. Sizeable steaks are a given, and reindeer and bear make occasional appearances. There are good vegetarian mains too, and it's youngster-friendly.

Kissanviikset FINNISH €€
(📞010-666 5150; www.kissanviikset.fi; Puistokatu 3; mains €16-24; ⏰lunch & dinner) Quiet, romantic and welcoming, the 'cat's whiskers' is an enticing choice. The genteel upstairs dining room is complemented by an atmospheric cellar space when busy. Dishes are thoughtfully prepared and feature delicious combinations of flavours such as salmon with baked fennel, or meat dishes with sinfully creamy wild mushroom sauces.

Soppabaari SOUP €
(www.soppabaari.fi; Väinönkeskus; soup & pasta €7.50; ⏰lunch & dinner Mon-Sat) This cute wee spot is situated in a little arcade out the back of Ye Old Brick's Inn. They do three daily soups and pastas, either of which is €7.50 and pretty much guaranteed to be delicious.

Katriinan Kasvisravintola VEGETARIAN €
(www.maijasilvennoinen.fi; Kauppakatu 11; lunch €6-9; ⏰lunch Mon-Fri) A couple of blocks west of the pedestrian zone, this vegetarian lunch restaurant is an excellent bet. Six euros gets you soup and salad bar, seven buys a hot dish instead of the soup, and nine gets you the lot. It changes daily – you might get pasta, ratatouille or curry – but it's always tasty.

🍷 Drinking & Entertainment

Jyväskylä's students ensure a lively nightlife when they're not on holidays.

Ye Old Brick's Inn PUB €€
(www.oldbricksinn.fi; Kauppakatu 41; most mains €13-20; ⏰11am-2am or 3am, food until 11pm) In the liveliest part of the pedestrian zone, this warm and welcoming pub has several excellent beers on tap, a cosy interior and an outdoor terrace screened by plastic plants – the place to be on a summer evening. It also has a good upmarket bar menu. The kitchen shuts at 9pm on Mondays.

Sohwi PUB
(www.sohwi.fi; Vaasankatu 21; ⏰2pm-midnight Mon, 2pm-1am Tue-Thu, 2pm-2am Fri, noon-2am Sat, 2-10pm Sun) A short walk from the city centre is this excellent bar with a spacious wooden terrace, a good menu of snacks and soak-it-all up bar meals, and plenty of lively student and academic discussion lubricated by a range of good bottled and draught beers. There's an internet terminal too. A great place.

Katse NIGHTCLUB
(www.pubkatse.fi; Väinönkatu 26; ⏰3pm-3am) This looks like a constricted dive from outside, but actually has an enormous, popular upstairs bar playing alternative and heavier music to Finns in their 20s and 30s.

Poppari JAZZ
(www.jazz-bar.com; Puistokatu 2; ⏰3pm-late) This downstairs venue is the place for relaxing live music, with regular jazz slots and jam sessions, particularly on weekends (cover usually €2 to €5).

London NIGHTCLUB
(www.london.fi; Puistokatu 2; entry €5-8; ⏰nightly until 4am) This massive space has several areas with live music, disco, Suomi-pop and rock.

ℹ Information

Public library (Vapaudenkatu 39-41; ⏰11am-8pm Mon-Fri, 11am-3pm Sat) Free internet.

Tourist office (📞266 0113; www.jyvaskyla region.fi; Asemakatu 6; ⏰9am-5pm Mon-Fri, plus 9am-2pm Sat Jun-Aug) Has comprehensive information on the whole of Finland, ticket sales and a free internet terminal.

❶ Getting There & Away

Air

Finnair operates daily flights from Helsinki to Jyväskylä. The airport is 21km north of the centre; a bus leaves the Matkakeskus (bus and train station building) an hour before departures and meets arriving flights (€5). Shared taxis make the journey for €21. A normal cab is around €35. Both taxi types can be reserved on ☎100 6900.

Boat

There is a regular boat service on Lake Päijänne between Jyväskylä and Lahti, operated by **Päijänne Risteilyt Hildén** (☎263 447; www. paijanne-risteilythilden.fi). Boats leave Lahti at 9am on Tuesdays from mid-June to mid-August and return from Jyväskylä on Wednesdays at 9am (one-way €60, 10½ hours).

Bus

The bus terminal shares the Matkakeskus building with the train station and has many daily express buses connecting Jyväskylä to southern Finnish towns, including hourly departures to Helsinki (€46.90, 4½ hours). Some services require a change.

Train

The train station is in the Matkakeskus building. There are regular trains from Helsinki (€46.90, 3½ hours) via Tampere, and some quicker direct trains.

❶ Getting Around

Bicycle

Jyväskylä is a good spot to explore by bike. The tourist office also has maps of suggested circular routes in central Lakeland of three to five days. You can rent a 3-gear hybrid at **Rent@Bike** (☎050-443 3820; Humppakuja 2; per day/week €15/50); they'll deliver anywhere in town for €5. The tourist office has a list of other operators.

Bus

For reaching Aalto buildings or the ski centre, you'll find the network of local buses useful. Local buses all leave from Vapaudenkatu, near the tourist office. Tickets cost €3.10 to €6.30 depending on distance. Day tickets can be bought at the tourist office – value if you'll be making three or more journeys.

Around Jyväskylä

SÄYNÄTSALO

FREE **Säynätsalon Kunnantalo**　　ARCHITECTURE
(☎266 1522; www.jyvaskyla.fi/saynatsalo; Parviaisentie 9, Säynätsalo; voluntary donation; ☺8.30am–3.30pm Mon-Fri) Säynätsalo town hall is on an island 10km southeast of Jyväskylä. It's one of Alvar Aalto's most famous works, the architect having won a competition in 1949 to design it. The sturdy brick tower of this 'fortress of democracy' recalls a castle, but the grassy patio bathes the interior with light and reflects a relationship with nature that is present in much of Aalto's work. The classroom-like council chamber is on the top floor.

Two **rooms** (r €50) are available here; they are furnished with Aalto chairs and stools and named after the man and his second wife, who often slept here while supervising construction. They are singles (although extra beds can be put in), share a bathroom, and have simple kitchen facilities.

Säynätsalo can be reached from central Jyväskylä on bus 16 or 21 (€4.40, 30 minutes); get off at the SS-*Kunnantalo* stop.

MUURATSALO

Muuratsalon Koetalo　　ARCHITECTURE
(☎266 7113; www.alvaraalto.fi; adult/student/child €17/7/free; ☺1.30-3.30pm Mon, Wed & Fri Jun–mid-Sep) The peaceful wooded islet of Muuratsalo is connected to Säynätsalo by bridges and was Alvar Aalto's summer retreat from the early 1950s onwards. On Päijänne's shores he built his **Experimental House**, a must-see for Aalto lovers, but pricey if you're not. Entrance is by guided tour, and must be pre-arranged by phone or email (the Aalto Museum or tourist office in Jyväskylä can do this). You first see his beloved boat, *Nemo Propheta in Patria* ('nobody is a prophet in their own land') on dry land, never having been particularly seaworthy. Then it's the lakeside sauna and house itself. It's often called the 'experimental house', because Aalto used the charming patio to try out various types and patterns of bricks and tiles to see how they looked in different seasons and how they weathered.

The interior is surprisingly small; it's cool and colourful, but doesn't particularly evoke the man's spirit. A guest wing is perched on timber and stones (another playful experiment), but is deemed too precarious to enter.

The setting's very Finnish, and you can well imagine Aalto looking out over the beautiful lake and pondering his designs. It's a quiet, peaceful place (apart from the mosquitoes).

To get here, take bus 16 from central Jyväskylä and ride it to the end, where there's a small cafe. The house is 500m further along this road on the right. For the 1.30pm tour, get the bus at 12.15pm (€4.40, 40 minutes).

PETÄJÄVESI

Thirty-five kilometres west of Jyväskylä, pause at Petäjävesi to see the wonderfully gnarled Unesco-listed wooden **church** (☑040-582 2461; Vanhankirkontie; adult/child €5/3; ☺10am-6pm Jun-Aug, call for winter visits). Finished in 1765, it's a marvellous example of 18th-century rustic Finnish architecture with crooked wooden pews and a fairy-tale shingle roof. Burials took place under the floorboards, and there's also a spooky wine cellar under the nave – ask the guide to show you.

Buses from Jyväskylä to Keuruu stop in Petäjävesi. If coming by car, walk across a road bridge to the church from the car park.

Kuopio

☑017 / POP 96,830

Most things a reasonable person could desire from a summery lakeside town are in Kuopio, with pleasure cruises on the azure water, spruce forests to stroll in, wooden waterside pubs, and local fish specialities to taste. And what better than a traditional smoke sauna to give necessary impetus to jump into the chilly waters?

But Kuopio has year-round appeal, with its fistful of interesting museums, student-driven cultural scene and nightlife, and winter activities like ice-fishing and snowmobiling on offer.

Kuopio has good transport connections but there's no better way to arrive than by leisurely lakeboat from Savonlinna.

◉ Sights

Kuopio has several worthwhile museums; if you're going to visit a few, grab the Museum Card from the Kuopio Tourist Service or any museum, which gives discounted entry (€12).

Jätkänkämppä   SAUNA
(www.rauhalahti.com; adult/child €12/6; ☺4-10pm Tue, also Thu Jun-Aug) There are different types of saunas, but the *savusauna* (smoke sauna) is the original and, some say, the best. This, by the lakeside near Rauhalahti hotel south of town, is a memorable and sociable experience that draws locals and visitors.

The 60-person, mixed sauna is heated 24 hours in advance with a large wood fire (ie there's no sauna stove). Guests are given towels to wear, but bring a swimsuit for a dip in the lake. Sweat it out for a while, cool off in the lake, then repeat the process sev-

---

SHE AIN'T HEAVY, SHE'S MY WIFE

What began as a heathenish medieval habit of pillaging neighbouring villages in search of nubile women has become one of Finland's oddest – and most publicised – events. Get to Sonkajärvi, in the northern Lakeland, for the **Wife-Carrying World Championships** (www.eukonkanto.fi) in early July.

The championship is a race over a 253.5m obstacle course, where competitors must carry their 'wives' through water traps and over hurdles to achieve the fastest time. Dropping your cargo means a 15-second penalty. The winner gets the wife's weight in beer and, of course, the prestigious title of World Wife-Carrying Champion. To enter, men need only €50 and a consenting female. There's also a sprint and a team competition.

The championship is accompanied by a weekend of drinking, dancing and typical Finnish frivolity.

---

eral times – devoted sauna-goers do so even when the lake is covered with ice. Then buy a beer and relax, looking over the lake in Nordic peace.

There's a **restaurant** (adult/child buffet plus hot plate €20/10; ☺4-8pm) in the adjacent loggers' cabin serving traditional Finnish dinners when the sauna's on, with accordion entertainment and a lumberjack show. Bus 7 departs every half-hour from the kauppatori to the Rauhalahti hotel complex, from which it's a 600m walk to the sauna, or take the lakeboat from the passenger harbour in summer.

Puijo   HILL
Even small hills have cachet in flat Finland, and Kuopio was so proud of Puijo that it was crowned with a tower. The views from the top of the **Puijon Torni** (www.puijo.com; adult/child €6/3; ☺10am-9pm Mon-Sat, 10am-7pm Sun Jun-Aug, 10am-7pm Mon-Thu, 10am-9pm Fri, 11am-9pm Sat, 11am-4pm Sun Sep-May) are very impressive; the vast perspectives of (yes, you guessed correctly) lakes and forests represent a sort of idealised Finnish vista. Atop the structure is a revolving restaurant, cafe and open-air viewing deck.

Kuopio

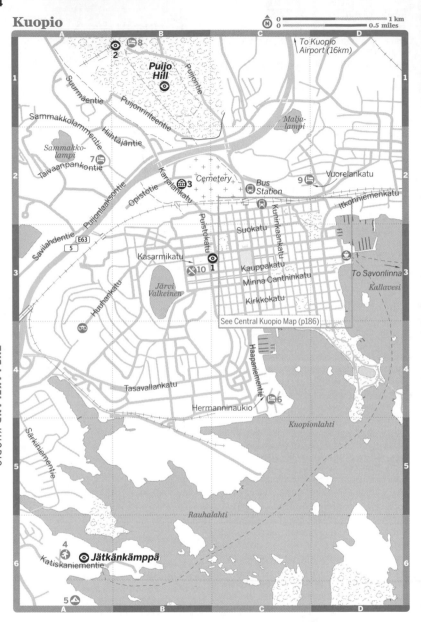

To Kuopio Airport (16km)

Puijo Hill

Puijontie

Puijonrinteentie

Sammakkolammentie

Hiihtäjäntie

Sammakko-lampi

Malja-lampi

Taivaanpankontie

7

Opistotie

Cemetery

Bus Station

Vuorelankatu

9

Karjalankatu

3

Puijonlaaksontie

Itkonniemenkatu

Savilahdentie

E63
5

Puistokatu

Suokatu

Kuninkaankatu

Kasarmikatu

10 1

Kauppakatu

To Savonlinna

Järvi Valkeinen

Minna Canthinkatu

Kallavesi

Kirkkokatu

Huuhankatu

See Central Kuopio Map (p186)

Haapaniementie

Tasavallankatu

Hermanninaukio

6

Kuopionlahti

Sarkiniementie

Rauhalahti

4

Jätkänkämppä

Katiskaniementie

5

THE LAKELAND KUOPIO

Surrounding it is one of the region's best-preserved **spruce forests**, popular for walks and picnics. Also here is a ski jump and chairlift. Even in summer you can see ski jumpers in training; the whoosh as they descend the ramp sounds like a small fighter plane. There are no public buses to Puijo, but it's a nice walk through the trees, or a short drive or cab ride.

Puijo Hill has mountain-bike and walking tracks; in winter there are cross-country ski trails and equipment rentals.

Kuopio

Kuopion Museo　　　　　　　MUSEUM
(www.kuopionmuseo.fi; Kauppakatu 23; adult/child €6/4; ⊙10am–5pm Tue, Thu & Fri, 10am–7pm Wed, 11am–5pm Sat & Sun) Kuopio's city museum, in a castlelike art-nouveau mansion, has wide scope. The top two floors are devoted to cultural history, with household objects, a boat builder's workshop, coffee shop and a re-created wooden house among the attractions. But the real highlight is the natural history display, with a wide variety of beautifully presented Finnish wildlife, including a mammoth and an ostrich wearing snowboots. The ground floor is devoted to temporary exhibitions.

There's little information in English, but tours in English are sometimes scheduled during summer.

Kuopion Korttelimuseo　　　　MUSEUM
(www.korttelimuseo.kuopio.fi; Kirkkokatu 22; adult/child €4/free; ⊙10am-5pm Tue-Sun mid-May–Aug, 10am-3pm Tue-Fri, 10am-4pm Sat & Sun Sep–mid-May) This block of old town houses forms another of Kuopio's delightful museums. Several homes – all with period furniture and decor – are very detailed and thorough and the level of information (in English) is excellent. **Apteekkimuseo** in building 11 contains old pharmacy paraphernalia, while

in another building it's fascinating to compare photos of Kuopio from different decades. There's also a cafe serving a delicious *rahkapiirakka* (a local sweet pastry).

Suomen Ortodoksinen Kirkkomuseo　　　　　　　MUSEUM
(Orthodox Church Museum; www.ortodoksinen kirkkomuseo.fi; Karjalankatu 1; adult/child €5/1; ⊙10am-4pm Tue & Thu-Sun, to 6pm Wed May-Aug, noon-3pm Mon-Fri, noon-5pm Sat & Sun Sep-Apr) This museum holds an excellent collection of items brought here from monasteries, churches and *tsasounas* (chapels) that are now in Russian-occupied Karelia. It was being renovated at last visit, but will be opening as this book goes to press.

Kuopion Taidemuseo　　　　　　GALLERY
(www.taidemuseo.kuopio.fi; Kauppakatu 35; adult/child €4/free; ⊙10am-5pm Tue-Fri, to 7pm Wed, 11am-5pm Sat & Sun) This features mostly modern art in temporary exhibitions, but also displays permanent works. Look out for paintings by the local artist Juho Rissanen (1873–1950), whose realistic portraits of Finnish working people were a contrast to the prevalent Romanticism of the time.

VB Valokuvakeskus　　　MUSEUM, GALLERY
(www.vb.kuopio.fi; Kuninkaankatu 14; admission €5; ⊙11am-5pm Tue-Fri, to 7pm Wed, 11am-3pm Sat & Sun Sep-May, 10am-6pm Mon-Fri, 11am-4pm Sat & Sun Jun-Aug) Excellent summer exhibitions grace this photographic centre, devoted to Victor Barsokevitsch, one of the pioneers of Finnish photography. His studio is now a gallery, but there are enough old cameras and photos to call this a museum. In the garden you can enjoy a coffee in summer and check out the camera obscura.

Pikku-Pietarin Torikuja　　　　　MARKET
(www.pikkupietarintorikuja.net; ⊙10am-5pm Mon-Fri, to 3pm Sat Jun-Aug) Pikku-Pietarin Torikuja is an atmospheric narrow lane of renovated red wooden houses converted into quirky shops stocking jewellery, clothing, handicrafts and other items. Halfway along is an excellent cafe (open from 8am) with cosy upstairs seating and a great little back deck for the summer sun.

Activities

Rauhalahti　　　　　　　　　OUTDOORS
(✆473 000; www.rauhalahti.com; Katiskaniementie 8) This estate is converted into a year-round family park. The whole area is full of activities for families including boating, cycling,

THE LAKELAND KUOPIO

Central Kuopio

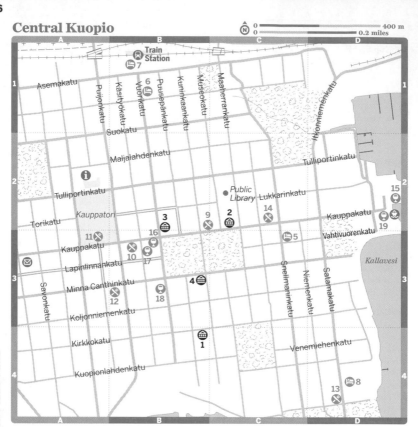

tennis and minigolf in summer, and skating, ice-fishing, snowmobile safaris and a snow castle in winter. You can rent bikes (per day from €20), rowing boats, canoes, in-line skates and even Icelandic ponies for gentle trail rides. Take bus 7 from the town centre or a ferry from the passenger harbour in summer (see Cruises). There's also a variety of accommodation here.

Tours

Several different cruises depart from the town's passenger harbour daily during summer. Ninety-minute jaunts from the harbour cost €13/7 for adults/children and depart hourly from 11am to 6pm from late May to late August. There are also cruises to Rauhalahti (www.koskilaiva.com; €13 return) Monday to Saturday from mid-June to early August; a good way to get to the smoke sauna. Special theme cruises include dinner and dancing, wine tasting or a trip to a local berry farm. There are also canal cruises and a monastery cruise to Valamo and Lintula, with return bus transport (adult €79).

Tickets for all cruises are available at the tourist office or directly on the boat. Most are run by **Roll** (277 2466; www.roll.fi), whose website has schedules. The tourist office does too; otherwise just stroll the harbour area to see when the next departure is.

A **tourist train** (adult/child €6/4; Mon-Sat Jun-late Aug) does the city circuit, with departures on the hour from the kauppatori. It has commentary in English.

Festivals & Events

Kuopion Tanssii ja Soi　　　　　　DANCE
(www.kuopiodancefestival.fi) In mid-June, this is the most international and the most interesting of Kuopio's annual events. There are open-air classical and modern dance performances, comedy and theatre gigs, and the town is generally buzzing at this time.

Central Kuopio

◉ Sights

🛏 Sleeping

✕ Eating

◉ Drinking

Kuopio Rock Cock　　　　　　　MUSIC
(www.kuopiorock.fi) This is a two-day rock festival in late July which features heaps of concerts by local acts and a couple of big-name headliners.

🛏 Sleeping

Hotelli Jahtihovi　　　　　　HOTEL €€
(☏264 4400; www.jahtihovi.fi; Snellmaninkatu 23; s/d €89/109, superior s/d €99/109; P@) Well-located near the harbour on a quiet street, this cordial independent hotel makes a good address. Regular rooms are good-sized and pleasant; the superiors, in a modern wing, add big windows, extra mod cons and a stylish look. A session in the smart new sauna is included, and parking's free. Prices drop €20 at weekends.

Matkustajakoti Rautatie　　GUESTHOUSE €
(☏580 0569; www.kuopionasemagrilli.com; Asemakatu 1 & Vuorikatu 35; s/d without bathroom €45/60, with bathroom €55/79; P) Let's get one thing straight: sleeping as close as you can to transport options isn't lazy, it's practical. True. This friendly place, operating out of the grilli (fast-food outlet) in the railway station, actually offers ensuite rooms in the building itself – very comfortable, exceedingly spa-cious and surprisingly peaceful. There are more rooms, with shared bathrooms, across the road on Vuorikatu. No wi-fi.

Spa Hotel Rauhalahti　　　SPA HOTEL €€
(☏030 60830; www.rauhalahti.com; Katiskaniementie 8; s/d €106/140; P@) Though it feels a bit faded in parts, this still makes a great place to stay, largely because of the huge scope for activities here. The spa complex is good (available to non-guests for €12), and the rooms are spacious, with low beds and decent in-room facilities. In the same complex is the cheaper **Hostelli Rauhalahti** (single/doubles €77/92), with simple Nordic rooms and full use of the hotel's facilities, as well as **Apartment Hotel Rauhalahti** (2-/4-person apartment from €140/212) which has excellent modern pads with all the trimmings, including (for not much extra dough) a sauna. There are some excellent family packages offered on their website. It's 5km south of town; take bus 7, or it's €20 in a cab.

Scandic Hotel Kuopio　　　HOTEL €€
(☏195 111; www.scandichotels.com; Satamakatu 1; s/d €113/133; P@) Down from the busy part of the harbour, this unobtrusive but large hotel has an appealing, quiet lakeside location, professional service, and fine facilities that include a gym, sauna and jacuzzi, as well as a couple of bikes able to be borrowed by guests. Rooms have plenty of natural light and crisscross parquet floors. The superior rooms are worth the extra €10 to €15, as they have king-sized beds and balconies with lake views. The above rates are approximate, as supply-and-demand pricing operates. There can be good summer rates.

Camping Rauhalahti　　CAMPGROUND €
(☏473 000; www.rauhalahti.com; Kiviniementie; sites €13 plus per person €4, cabins €30-57, cottages €110-239; ☉late May-late Aug; P) Next to the Rauhalahti complex, this place has a great location, plenty of facilities and is well set up for families. Bus 16 will get you here. The upmarket cottages are open all year.

Hotelli Savonia　　　　　　HOTEL €€
(☏255 5100; www.savonia.com; Sammakkolammentie 2; s/d/ste €91/110/190; P@) Not far from Puijo Hill, this offers easy access from the main road and decent value. The spotless rooms are rather nice, with plenty of space and headroom; the new wing offers even better ones, including suites with huge comfy beds and a tiny jacuzzi. There are also cheaper economy rooms (s/d €80/96).

There's a restaurant and cafe; breakfast, sauna and swimming are included. Buses 5 and 14 stop outside.

Hostelli Hermanni
HOSTEL €

([✆]040-910 9083; www.hostellihermanni.fi; Hermanninaukio 3E; dm/s/d €25/45/50; [P][@]) Tucked away in a quiet area 1.5km south of the kauppatori (follow Haapaniemenkatu and bear left when you can: the hostel's in the Metsähallitus building), this is a decent hostel with comfy wooden bunks and beds, high ceilings and reasonable shared bathrooms and kitchen. Check-in is between 2pm and 9pm; if you are going to arrive later, call ahead. Bus 1 from the centre makes occasional appearances nearby.

Puijon Maja
GUESTHOUSE €

([✆]255 5253; www.puijo.com; Puijontornintie; s/d €49/65; [P]) Right by the tower on top of Puijo Hill, this has simple but neat rooms, complete with fridges. Get one backing onto the forest if you can, so you can take advantage of the wide windows. Rates include sauna and admission to the tower, where you have to check in. There's no public transport from the town centre except for a summer bus at 10.50am Mondays to Fridays from the kauppatori.

Retkeilymaja Virkkula
HOSTEL €

([✆]040-418 2178; www.kuopionsteinerkoulu.fi; Vuorelankatu 5; dm €19; ⊙early Jun-Jul) This school converts to a simple hostel in summer. Bedding is €6 extra. Fridge and microwave but no kitchen.

✕ Eating

[TOP CHOICE] Kummisetä
FINNISH €€

(www.kummiseta.com; Minna Canthinkatu 44; mains €14-22; ⊙dinner daily, lunch Sat) The sober brown colours of the 'Godfather' restaurant give it a traditional and romantic feel that's replicated on the menu, with a variety of excellent sauces featuring fennel, berries and morel mushrooms garnishing prime cuts of beef, tender-as-young-love lamb, and succulent pike-perch. Food and service are both excellent. There's also a popular back terrace and an attractive bar that is open longer hours.

Musta Lammas
FINNISH €€€

([✆]581 0458; www.mustalammas.net; Satamakatu 4; mains €25-32; ⊙dinner Mon-Sat) The 'black sheep' is resting on its laurels a bit these days, but it's still Kuopio's best gourmet meal. Set in an enchantingly romantic vaulted space, it offers delicious mains with Finnish ingredients and French flair. Various set menus include a vegetarian one (€32).

[✎] Kauppahalli
MARKET HALL

(Kauppatori; ⊙8am-5pm Mon-Fri, 8am-3pm Sat) At the southern end of the kauppatori is a classic Finnish indoor market hall. Here stalls sell local speciality *kalakukko,* a large rye loaf stuffed with whitefish and then baked. It's delicious hot or cold. A whole one – a substantial thing – costs around €20, but the bakery by the western door sells mini ones for €2 if you just want a bite.

Kaneli
CAFE €

(www.kahvilakaneli.net; Kauppakatu 22; ⊙noon-6pm Mon-Fri, 11am-4pm Sat, noon-4pm Sun) This cracking cafe just off the kauppatori evokes a bygone age with much of its decor, but offers modern comfort in its shiny espresso machine, as well as many other flavoured coffees to accompany your toothsome and sticky *pulla* (cardamom-flavoured bun). Opens longer hours in summer.

Lounas-Salonki
FINNISH €

(www.lounassalonki.fi; Kasarmikatu 12; lunches €6-9, mains €11-22; ⊙9am-9pm Mon-Sat, noon-9pm Sun) This charming wooden building west of the city centre is warm and friendly, with little rooms sporting elegant imperial furniture. They do a salad buffet and daily hot lunch featuring traditional Finnish fare (eg sausage soup and liver 'n' onions) as well as coffee and à la carte options including vegetarian choices like crêpes filled with blue cheese and vegetables.

Vapaasatama Sampo
FINNISH €

(www.wanhamestari.fi; Kauppakatu 13; muikku dishes €11-15) Have it stewed, fried, smoked or in a soup, but it's all about *muikku* here. This is one of Finland's most famous spots to try the small lakefish that drive Savo stomachs. The 70-year-old restaurant is cosy, and classically Finnish.

Isä Camillo
FINNISH €€

(www.isacamillo.net; Kauppakatu 25; mains €16-23; ⊙lunch & dinner Mon-Sat) Set in a beautifully renovated former bank – look out for the old strongroom – this is an elegant but informal spot for a meal, offering fair prices for Finnish specialities. There's a good enclosed terrace at the side and a decent pub downstairs.

🍷 Drinking & Entertainment

Kuopio's nightlife is conveniently strung along Kauppakatu, running east from the market square to the harbour. Here, grungy, popular and likeable **Ale Pupi** (Sale Pub; www.alepupi.fi; Kauppakatu 16; ⊙9am-midnight or later) has a huge interior, surprisingly classy decor and big drawcards of cheap beer and karaoke, but there are many other options in this block, some with summer terraces.

TOP CHOICE Henry's Pub LIVE MUSIC
(www.henryspub.net; Käsityökatu 17; ⊙9pm-4am) One of Lakeland's best rock and metal venues, this atmospheric cellar has bands playing several times a week, including big Finnish and international names, but it's a good spot for a drink even if there's nothing on.

Wanha Satama PUB
(www.wanhasatama.net; Matkustajasatama; mains €13-19; ⊙from 11am late Apr-Aug) In a noble blue building by the harbour, this has one of Lakeland's best terraces, definitely the place to be on a sunny day to watch the boats come and go. There's Finnish fish and meat dishes and regular live music.

Albatrossi PUB
(www.ravintolaalbatrossi.fi; Makasiininkatu 1; ⊙11am-late May-Sep) This old wooden warehouse conversion is an atmospheric place to see some live music or grab a drink, particularly when you can sit outside and look at the lake. Drinks are served in plastic, but the atmosphere's great.

K Klubi BAR
(www.k-klubi.com; Vuorikatu 14; ⊙8pm-late) This bohemian bar is so bad it's good. Ingrained dirt, armchairs held together by staples, a wiring system that'll turn electricians pale, toilet doors with chunks kicked out of them, seedy red-lit ambience: it's definitely one of Kuopio's best.

LUSCIOUS LIQUEURS

One of Kuopio's signature companies is Lignell & Piispanen, a traditional liqueur maker that has been in business for 230 years. Try some while you're here; their cloudberry (*lakka*) drink is a classic, but the newer strawberry-flavoured Pople has conquered a younger crowd.

ℹ️ Information

Kuopio Info (☎182 585; www.kuopioinfo.fi; Haapaniemenkatu 17; ⊙9.30am-4.30pm Mon-Fri Sep-May, to 5pm Jun-Aug, also 9.30am-3pm Sat Jul) By the kauppatori. Information on regional attractions and accommodation.

Public library (Maaherrankatu 12; ⊙10am-7pm Mon-Fri, 10am-3pm Sat) Free internet.

ℹ️ Getting There & Away

Air
Finnair and Blue1 both fly daily to Helsinki, while Air Baltic serves Riga in Latvia.

Boat
From mid-June to mid-August, **MS Puijo** (☎015-250 250; www.mspuijo.fi) travels to Savonlinna (€88 one-way, 10½ hours) on Tuesdays, Thursdays and Saturdays at 9am, returning on Mondays, Wednesdays and Fridays. It passes through scenic waterways, canals and locks, stopping at Heinävesi and Karvio canal, among other places. You can book a return with overnight cabin accommodation for €175. Look for the English PDF on their Finnish-only website.

Bus
Express services to/from Kuopio:
Helsinki (€62, 6½ hours)
Jyväskylä (€23.90, 2¼ hours)
Savonlinna (€30,60, three hours)

Train
Five daily trains run to Kuopio from Helsinki (€59.10, 4½ hours). Trains run north to Kajaani (€24.30, 1¾ hours) and Oulu (€46.10, four hours). Change at Pieksämäki or Kouvola for other destinations.

ℹ️ Getting Around

To/From the Airport
Kuopio airport is 14km north of town. Bus service was down at last visit, but check when you get there. Airport **taxis** (☎106 400, one-way €20) must be booked two hours in advance. A boat service from the terminal to the centre is being planned.

Bike & Car Hire
You can hire bikes for €15 a day at **Hertz** (☎020-555 2670; www.hertz.fi; Asemakatu 1) and **Asemagrilli** (☎580 0569; www.kuopionasemagrilli.com; Asemakatu 1), both in the railway station building. Both also hire cars.

Karelia

Includes »

Best Places to Eat

» Bomban Talo (p215)

» Café Wolkoff (p195)

» Buttenhoff (p200)

Best Places to Stay

» Imatran Valtionhotelli (p199)

» Sokos Hotel Vaakuna (p202)

» Sokos Hotel Bomba (p215)

Why Go?

The forests in Karelia are...*deeper* somehow. Visit Karelia and you'll experience the truth of this wistful statement. If you're looking for wilderness, powerful history and perhaps even the Finnish soul, your search starts here.

Koli National Park is close to every Finnish heart, but the whole region is a blessing for nature lovers. Hiking routes thread through the area, Ruunaa is renowned for rafting, lovely Lake Pielinen is a kayaker's dream, and there's great winter skiing. Bears, wolverines and even wolves roam freely across the Russian frontier and animal hides allow visitors a close encounter.

Karelia is a region of contradictions, with its culture, language, religion, cuisine and music all heavily influenced by its eastern neighbour. The fierce battles of WWII are raw and close; you can feel the weight of history in Lappeenranta, pining for its sister cities lost to Russia, while battle-scarred Joensuu has reinvented itself as a lively young university town.

When to Go

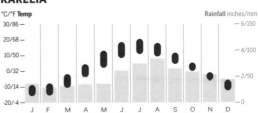

KARELIA

Mid-Apr The bear-watching season begins, when brown bears wake from their winter sleep.

Jul Folk in Joensuu have a blast at the international Ilosaari Rock Festival.

Dec Finland's most accessible ski resort at Koli National Park opens for business.

Karelia Highlights

1 Be inspired by the views at **Koli National Park** (p213) before skiing down the country's highest slope

2 Visit the lost Karelian town of Vyborg on a **cruise to Russia** (p197)

3 Fall in love with the woodland chapel at **Paateri** (p212), carved by a single artist

4 Shoot **Ruunaa's rapids** (p209) on a rubber raft

5 Dangle upside-down over torrents of water at the **Imatra Rapids Show** (p198)

6 Spend the night in an animal hide near Lieksa, awaiting **wolverines** and **bears** (p207)

7 See how the pros build a sandcastle at Lappeenranta's immense **Hiekkalinna** (p193)

8 Hike the peaceful walking trail **Karhunpolku** (p210), scattered with WWII remains

SOUTH KARELIA

South Karelia has almost drowned beneath the waves of Russian and Swedish empire building. Over the centuries the border has shuttled backwards and forwards – the once-busy South Karelian trade town of Vyborg (Finnish: Viipuri) and the Karelian Isthmus reaching to St Petersburg are now part of Russia. Wars have haunted this troubled region, apparent in the remains of Russian fortifications and a common culture, particularly in the former garrison town of Lappeenranta.

Lappeenranta

☑ 05 / POP 72,000

Sunning itself on the banks of Finland's largest lake, Lappeenranta is the veteran soldier who has endured and enjoyed the wild swings of fortune familiar to all Karelians. Much of the town was destroyed during the Winter and Continuation Wars, but its massive fortress lends it historical weight. Today it's a popular (shopping) destination for Russians, particularly those with Karelian heritage, and is famous for its summer sandcastle, the largest in Scandinavia.

Lappeenranta

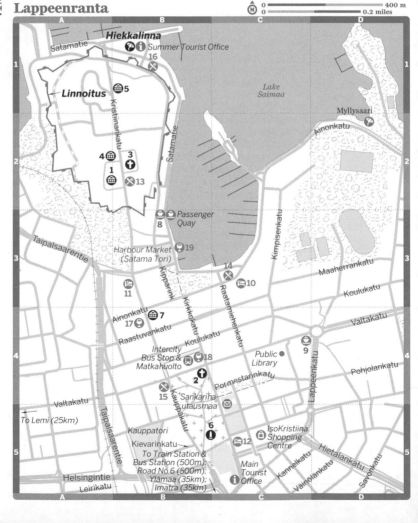

Once famous for its scarlet-clad garrison, the 17th-century 'Cavalry City' was a humming trade port at the edge of the Swedish empire. In 1743, it fell under Russian control where it remained for the next 68 years, becoming a spa town and playground for Russia's wealthy.

Russian still owns half of the 43km Saimaa Canal, Finland's most important waterway, which links Lappeenranta to the Gulf of Finland. It's currently 'on loan' to Finland until 2063 – popular day trips run through its eight locks and on to Lappeenranta's lost sister town, Vyborg.

◉ Sights

Linnoitus FORTRESS
(www3.lappeenranta.fi/linnoitus) This hulking fortification, standing guard above the harbour, was begun by the Swedes and finished by the Russians in the late 18th century. Today it has a quaint village vibe, with buildings transformed into galleries, craft workshops and fascinating museums.

There are **walking tours** (€5, one hour) of the fortress on Friday, Saturday and Sunday in July and August, leaving from the harbour (in front of S/S *Suvi-Saimaa*). To go your own way, grab a copy of the walking guide *The Fortress of Lappeenranta* (free), available from the tourist offices.

South Karelian Museum
(Etelä-Karjalan Museo; adult/child €6.50/free) Focusing on the history of Lappeenranta - and of its two sister towns, Käkisalmi (Priozersk) and Vyborg, lost across the Russian border

in 1939, this museum is a source of much wistful nostalgia, with older Finns sometimes moved to tears by how effectively its exhibits bring Vyborg back to life.

Cavalry Museum
(Ratsuväkimuseo; adult/child €3/free; ◎10am-6pm Mon-Fri, 11am-5pm Sat & Sun) The cavalry are honoured as Lappeenranta's greatest heroes and the former garrison (the town's oldest building) now houses this museum in their honour. It tells how this band of red-trousered forces began as the finest mounted forces in the Russian Empire and throughout the 1920s and '30s became Finland's national heroes. The skeleton jackets, weapons and implements for castrating horses give a small but intriguing glimpse into that lost world.

South Karelia Art Museum
(Etelä-Karjalan Taidemuseo; adult/child €6.50/free) This art museum has a permanent collection of modern paintings by Karelian and other Finnish artists. A large part of the space is devoted to temporary exhibitions, often featuring local artists.

Orthodox Church
(◎10am-4pm Tue-Sun early Jun–mid-Aug) This is Finland's oldest church. It was completed in 1785 by Russian soldiers and features a glittering iconostasis and other saintly portraits.

Hiekkalinna SAND SCULPTURE
(◎10am-8pm mid-Jun–Aug) In summer, around 30 sand artists from Finland and

---

Lappeenranta

SELF-CATERING ACCOMMODATION

In North Karelia, the tourist service **Karelia Expert** (☑0400-239 619; www.visitkarelia.fi) has a dedicated accommodation booking service for cottage, cabin and apartment rental. For South Karelia, **GoSaimaa** (www.gosaimaa.com) has a good selection of lakeside cottages around Imatra (p197) and Lappeenranta (p192).

abroad gather to build the Hiekkalinna, a giant themed 'sandcastle' that uses about 180 truckloads of sand. Previous incarnations have included a Wild West scene, incorporating a gigantic steam train, and an outer space theme that brought together ET and Darth Vader. There's plenty of entertainment here for kids too.

Wolkoff Home Museum MUSEUM
(Wolkoffin Talomuseo; ☑616 2258; Kauppakatu 26; adult/child €5.50/free; ☉10am-6pm Mon-Fri, 11am-5pm Sat & Sun early Jun–mid-Aug) The home of a Russian family is lovingly preserved at this museum. Built in 1826, the house was owned by the merchant clan Wolkoff from 1872 to 1986, and the 10 rooms have been maintained as they were in the late 1800s. Join the hourly guided tours (40 minutes; departing at quarter past the hour) to view them.

Lappee Church CHURCH
(☉10am-6pm early Jun-late Aug) The adorable wooden Lappee Church was built in 1794 to an unusual 'double cruciform' floor plan, the only one of its kind in Finland. It's barely on speaking terms with its bell tower, situated diagonally across the park. South of the church stretches the graveyard, with an evocative **war memorial**, which features cubist and modernist sculptures commemorating Finns who died in the Winter and Continuation Wars. The most striking depicts a mother mourning her soldier son lost in battle, by Kauko Räsänen.

Myllysaari BEACH
East of the harbour, this beach is perfect for a sunny afternoon, with its sandy shore full of sunbathers, an outdoor swimming pool, beach volleyball and a **beach sauna** (admission €6; ☉women 4-8pm Wed & Fri, men 4-8pm Tue & Thu).

Activities
Many big hotels offer packages including a night's accommodation and a cruise: check websites or ask at the tourist office.

Saimaan Risteilyt CRUISE
(☑020-787 0620; www.saimaanristeilyt.fi; adult/child 4-12yr €15/8; ☉departs 11am, 3pm & 6pm mid-May-Aug) Offers popular two-hour trips on Lake Saimaa and the Saimaa Canal aboard the M/S El Faro, departing from the passenger quay at the harbour.

Karelia Lines CRUISE
(☑453 0380; www.karelialines.fi; adult/child 4-14yr €15/7; ☉noon & 6pm Mon-Sat Jun & Aug, plus 3pm Sat, 2pm Sun Jul) Offers similar cruises aboard the larger M/S Camilla, which also departs from the passenger quay at the harbour.

Saimaan Matkaverkko CRUISE
(Saimaa Travel; ☑541 0100; www.saimaatravel.fi; Valtakatu 49; from €75 per person; ☉departs Thu & Sat Jun–Aug) Longer day cruises across Lake Saimaa to Savonlinna aboard M/S Brahe, returning by bus.

Festivals & Events
Lemin Musiikkijuhlat CHAMBER MUSIC
(www.leminmusiikkijuhlat.fi, in Finnish; tickets free-€20) This four-day chamber-music festival takes place in late July or early August, mainly in churches throughout Lappeenranta, Imatra and Lemi.

Sleeping
Scandic Hotel Patria HOTEL €€
(☑677 511; www.scandichotels.com; Kauppakatu 21; s/d €116/136; P@☀) Definitely one of the best places to stay in Lappeenranta since its recent revamp, the Scandic is also close to the harbour and fortress. The better doubles feature balconies with park views, but all rooms are fitted out with minimalist Scandic chic. Service is super helpful, especially with the advice on sightseeing around town.

Sokos Hotel Lappee HOTEL €€
(☑010-762 1000; www.sokoshotels.fi; Brahenkatu 1; r from €117; P@☀) Another contemporary option with decent standards, this is a huge, efficiently-run if somewhat impersonal business hotel. It's some distance from the harbour and fortress, but close to the IsoKristiina, the region's largest shopping centre. Some rooms could do with pepping up.

Lappeenrannan Kylpylä
SPA HOTEL €€

(✆616 7201; www.kylpyla.info; Ainonkatu 17; s/d/tr from €99/138/189; P@≋❄) If you're after a healthy stay, then this compact little hotel is your place. Rooms are decked out in appealing bronzes and golds, and some have great balconies (costing a tad extra) that look across the park to the water. There are saunas, a gym, a couple of pools and a waterfall that delivers a pounding shoulder massage. It's a popular spot with wealthy Russian tourists.

Huhtiniemi Tourist Resort
HOSTEL, CAMPGROUND €

(✆451 5555; www.huhtiniemi.com; Kuusimäenkatu 18; tent sites €12 plus per person €4.50, 2-/4-person cottages €35/45, apt €75-90; ⊙mid-May–Sep) Located 2km east of the town centre, this large complex has a bed for every taste, although it fills to the gills in summer – reservations are a must. There's the expansive camping ground by the lake (pack mosquito repellent), as well as neat cottages with bunks and fridges, and self-contained apartments. There are also two HI hostels: **Huhtiniemi Hostel** (dm €15; ⊙Jun-Aug; P), with two simple six-bed dorms, and **Finnhostel Lappeenranta** (s/d/tr €60/75/95; P≋) offering good hotel-style rooms with bathrooms and breakfast. The South Carelia Sports Centre is nearby and hostel room prices include a morning swim at its pool. Buses 1 and 5 run past here, as do most incoming intercity buses.

Karelia Park
HOTEL €

(✆453 0405; www.karelia-park.fi; Korpraalinkuja 1; dm from €25, s/tw €55/70; ⊙Jun-Aug; P) For most of the year this tidy HI hostel 300m west of Huhtiniemi is student accommodation. In summer it still has an institutional feel but rents out rooms to travellers. Each of the two-bed rooms has a shared kitchen and bathroom, and breakfast is included.

Eating

Café Wolkoff
FINNISH €€€

(✆415 0320; Kauppakatu 26; lunch €12, mains €21-29; ⊙11am-10pm Mon-Fri, 4.30-10pm Sat) The bustling cafe arm of the Wolkoff Museum, this grand old-world restaurant specialises in Finnish cuisine, such as reindeer, elk and cloudberry soup. Using organic produce and seasonal ingredients, Café Wolkoff is the town's gourmet dining choice.

Kahvila Majurska
TEAHOUSE €

(www.majurska.com; Kristiinankatu 1; pastries €3-5; ⊙10am-7pm) If you can't hop the border to a genuine Russian teahouse then this is as close as you'll get in Finland. A former officer's club (note the august portrait of Mannerheim and relic furniture), they still serve tea from the samovar and do a range of homemade pastries. The traditional serving maids' outfits are a little kinky.

Wanha Makasiini
PIZZERIA €€

(✆010-666 8611; Satamatie 4; pizzas €9-14, mains €22; ⊙11am-11pm) A wonderfully cosy atmosphere and friendly service provide a good backdrop for the high-quality grub served here. There's a good selection, from fresh fish to pasta dishes, horse steaks and seasonal delicacies like chanterelle soup. The thin, crispy pizzas are super, and come with traditional toppings as well as more unusual ones, such as smoked *muikku* (vendace, or whitefish), pickled cucumber and blue cheese.

Kasino
RUSSIAN, EUROPEAN €€

(Ainonkatu 10; lunch €12.50, mains €15-22; ⊙11am-3pm) Acclaimed as a favourite of Catherine the Great, this refurbished casino house has excellent Russian options like salmon *blini* (pancakes) and *zakuska* (light buffet), but also does more traditional European fare such as steak and pork schnitzel.

Tassos
GREEK €€

(✆010-762 1452; Valtakatu 33; mains €15-30; ⊙11am-11pm Mon-Fri, noon-midnight Sat, noon-8pm Sun) This long-standing family restaurant, based in the stately old Nordea bank building, lacks a little in atmosphere but you can't fault the food. Greek favourites are supplemented with the odd Finnish fish. Ensure you have stomach space for a plateful of the excellent mixed starters.

🍷 Drinking

On the harbour, **S/S Suvi-Saimaa** and **Prinsessa Armaada** both make for good booze boats in summer, especially above decks on a sunny day.

Birra
BAR

(Kauppakatu 19; ⊙2pm-1am) This is one of the swankier bars in town with a shaded terrace and a great beer and cider selection. On weekends it gets frantic but you can usually cosy up in a booth.

DIY: FARMHOUSES

If you're looking to get off the beaten track, meet locals and experience rural life, try a farmstay in the countryside around Lappeenranta. Your double room, costing around €70, could be in a traditional 19th-century farmhouse, a former granary or perhaps a cosy log cabin in the grounds. Some places have domestic animals for children to pet, and almost all offer outdoor activities, such as smoke saunas, rowing, fishing, snowshoeing, snowmobiling or even horse-drawn sleigh-riding.

One option is **Asko & Maija's Farmhouse** (📞040-507 5842; www.rantatupa.net; Suolahdentie 461; ☺mid-May–late Sep; P). 30km northwest of Lappeenranta. Contact the town tourist office to find others.

Old Park   IRISH PUB
(Valtakatu 36; ☺noon-1am Sun-Thu, noon-3am Fri & Sat) This is the best pick in a compact central complex that runs over two floors. It's a gently Irish-themed place (no shamrocks but plenty of hard rock), with a popular terrace.

ℹ Information

Main tourist office (📞667 788; Kauppakatu 40d; ☺9am-5pm Mon-Fri, 10am-4pm Sat Jun-Aug, 10am-4.30pm Mon-Fri Sep-May; @) On a little plaza just outside the Galleria shopping centre. Accommodation booking service for €3.50.

Public library (📞616 2341; Valtakatu 47; ☺10am-7pm Mon & Tue, 10am-6pm Wed-Fri Jun-Aug, 10am-8pm Mon-Fri Sep-May) Free bookable internet terminals.

Summer tourist office (📞040-352 2178; ☺10am-6pm Jun & late Aug, 10am-8pm Jul & early Aug) Located at Hiekkalinna (the Sandcastle).

ℹ Getting There & Away

Air

Air Baltic flies to Riga and Ryanair flies to several European destinations from Lappeenranta airport.

Bus

All buses along Finland's eastern route, between Helsinki and Joensuu, stop in Lappeenranta. The train and bus stations are located about 1km south of the town centre, but most intercity buses stop on Valtakatu in the middle of town.

Bus 9 (€6.10) runs between the bus and train stations and the centre of town.

Bus and train tickets can be booked at the central office of **Matkahuolto** (📞0200 4000; www.matkahuolto.fi; Valtakatu 36B; ☺9am-5pm Mon-Fri),opposite the church park on Valtakatu, where many intercity buses stop. Regular services include Joensuu (€41, 4½ hours), Helsinki (€38, 4¼ hours), Savonlinna (€27.30, four hours, via Parikkala), Mikkeli (€22.40, 1¾ hours) and Imatra (€11.80, 45 minutes).

Train

Seven to eight trains per day run via Lappeenranta (Vainikkala) on their way between Helsinki and Joensuu. There are also frequent direct trains to/from Helsinki (standard train €41.30, Pendolino €47, 2¼ hours). For travel to Russia, the new high-speed Allegro service from Helsinki passes through Lappeenranta on its way to Vyborg (1½ hours, €31) and St Petersburg (2½ hours, €46.60), as does the daily Tolstoi service to Moscow (10 hours, from €85). Book through **VR** (Finnish Railways; 📞060-041 902; www.vr.fi).

ℹ Getting Around

To/From the Airport

Bus 4 (€3.10) travels the 2.5km between the city centre and the airport.

Bicycle

The best way to explore this large town is to hire a bike from **Pyörä-Expert** (📞411 8710; Valtakatu 64; 1-day hire €7; ☺9am-6pm Mon-Fri, 9am-2pm Sat) or from **Karelia Lines** (📞453 0380; 3hr/1-day hire €15/25; ☺10am-6pm Mon-Sat summer) at the passenger harbour.

Public Transport

In summer, you can give your feet a rest on the hourly **Street Train** (day ticket adult/child €10/5; ☺10am-5pm), which links the market square, IsoKristiina shopping centre, the fortress, Hiekkalinna and the beach at Myllysaari.

Around Lappeenranta

YLÄMAA
📞05

Ylämaa, 35km south of Lappeenranta, is a rural municipality best known for the gemstone spectrolite, a rare labradorite feldspar that glitters from red to blue. Also mined in Russia, Norway and Madagascar, the stone was first found in Finland during excavations for WWII fortifications.

The **Jewel Village and Museum** (📞040-821 4379, 0500-459156; www.ylamaa.fi; Rd 387; admission €2; ☺10am-4pm Jun-Aug) located on the

Lappeenranta–Vaalimaa road is Ylämaa's main attraction. As well as a tourist information office, you'll find stone grinderies, quarries, a goldsmith's workshop and a collection of spectrolite, precious minerals and fossils. Many gemstones are backlit while others provide their own fluorescence. The **Gem Fair** in early July draws plenty of international rockheads; and **Ylämaa Mystique** (☑045-878 3855; www.ylamaamystique.fi; per person €195; ☉Jul & early Aug) offers the truly hypnotised a chance to unearth their own stone and create a piece of iridescent jewellery.

Ylämaa Church (Koskentie; ☉10am-3pm Jun–mid-Aug) was built in 1931 and has an unusual spectrolite font.

A limited Monday–Friday bus service runs from Lappeenranta (45 minutes) during term-time only.

LEMI

Like Champagne and Burgundy, the tiny village of Lemi, 25km west of Lappeenranta, is more famous for its signature dish – *lemin särä* (roast mutton) – than any of its sights. Cooked in a birch trough to add a sweet, woody flavour to the meat, it has been hailed as one of the seven wonders of Finland. As it takes nine hours to prepare, you'll need to book your meal at least two days in advance. **Säräpirtti Kippurasarvi** (☑414 6470; www.sarapirtti.fi; Rantatie 1; adult/4-12yrs €28/14; ☉see website for serving times), on the lakeshore, is a specialty restaurant in the truest sense and the best place to sample the dish. It serves nothing but *lemin särä*, accompanied by thick rye bread and homemade *kalja* (beer).

Imatra

☑05 / POP 29,155

Once the darling of Russian aristocracy, Imatra's rapids were harnessed for hydroelectricity in 1929, but the water pours forth again during dramatic summer shows. Imatra is currently rebuilding itself as a spa town; but unless you're here for pampering a weekend is ample time for a visit.

Imatra has a number of dispersed 'centres', mostly brassy and modern and all separated by kilometres of highway. Imatrankoski, the site of the rapids, is of most interest to travellers. It's where you'll find the tourist office and most restaurants and hotels. Boaties, beach bums and spa babes may feel more at home in the Imatran Leisure Centre area, 7km northwest of Imatrankoski.

TRAVELLING TO RUSSIA

For Finns a boat cruise over the border to Vyborg (60km away, in Russia) along the Saimaa Canal is almost a spiritual journey to reunite Karelia. For the rest of us this trip can be a good chance to sample Russia or head further on to St Petersburg, but it does require advance planning and can be very difficult for non-EU visitors (see p75).

Saimaan Matkaverkko (Saimaa Travel; ☑541 0100; fax 541 0140; www.saimaatravel.fi; Valtakatu 49; ☉9am-5pm Mon-Fri) runs quick-and-easy 'visa-free' day cruises to Vyborg aboard the M/S *Carelia* (from €58, departs 7.45am four to six times weekly from late May to mid-September) that allow you around 3½ hours to sightsee and shop. It's also possible to stay overnight in Vyborg, with prices varying by season and usually costing more on weekends. You must provide the company with a copy of your passport at least three days before departure (and passports must be valid for at least a further six months from the end date of your trip). Book well in advance, as these cruises are heavily subscribed. This company can also organise a package (from €300, meals and excursions extra, departing July to August) to St Petersburg that includes the cruise to Vyborg and a bus on to St Petersburg, with two nights' accommodation in Russia.

If you want to travel independently (and you have a visa), several train and bus services pass through Lappeenranta on the way to St Petersburg and Moscow. See p196 for details.

If you aren't an EU citizen and you haven't organised a Russian tourist visa before leaving your country of origin, then God help you. If you can endure a long wait and difficult bureaucracy then you could try the embassy in Helsinki (see p75) or the **Russian Consulate** (☑872 0722; Kievarinkatu 1A; ☉9am-noon Mon, Wed & Fri) in Lappeenranta.

Saimaan Matkaverkko can also help EU residents apply for a visa through its **visa service** (☑541 0123; viisumit@saimaatravel.fi; Valtakatu 49). Visas take at least a week to process, and cost from €90.

Imatra

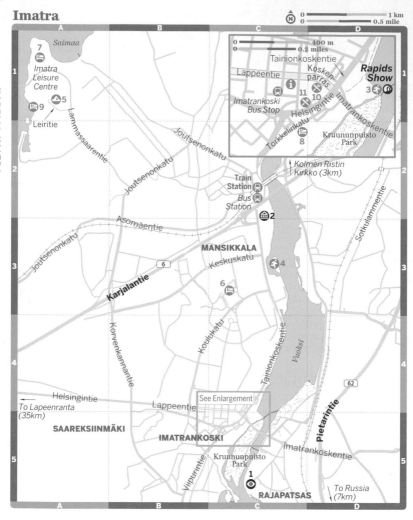

◉ Sights & Activities

Imatra Rapids   RIVER

One of the first tourists to the area was Catherine the Great who in 1772 gathered her entourage to view Imatra's thundering rapids. The building of the hydroelectric complex (Finland's largest) in 1929 dammed the river, but the watery wonder lives on with the 20-minute **Rapids Show** (⊙6pm Jun-late Aug), when the dam is opened to a rousing *son et lumière*. It's still a spectacle, with locals showing up half an hour early with beer and chips to make an evening of this artificial Niagara.

If your inner daredevil wants to get involved, **Imatra Express** (☑044-016 1096; www.imatraexpress.fi, in Finnish; basic/inverted €35/50; ⊙5-7pm Mon-Fri & Sun, noon-7pm Sat Jun-late Aug, or by arrangement) runs a flying fox over the gushing waters with an upside-down option to really make you lose your lunch.

The **Imatra Power Plant Exhibition Room** (adult/child €3/1.50; ⊙11am-5pm late Jun–mid-Aug) has several slick displays on how the dam works.

Imatra

Imatran Taidemuseo   ART GALLERY
(Virastokatu 1; admission free; ◷10am-7pm Mon-Thu, to 4pm Fri Jun-Aug, 10am-7pm Mon-Fri, 11am-3pm Sat Sep-May) Imatran Taidemuseo in the public library has temporary exhibitions and a strong collection of Finnish modernism, including works by Wäinö Aaltonen. If you're visiting outside of the rapids show season, there's a Gallen-Kallela watercolour here of the rapids during their heyday in 1893.

Vuoksen Kalastuspuisto   FISHING
(☏432 3123; www.vuoksenkalastuspuisto.com; Kotipolku 4; ◷9am-10pm May-Sep) A stocked salmon pond on Varpasaari in Mansikkala, where you can also purchase licences (per day/week €7/12) here for the surrounding waters, as fish suitable for smoking can be caught in the river. They also rent bikes (per day €12), rowing boats and kayaks (per day €30), and offer comfy camping (tent sites €14 plus per person €2) and good-sized cabins (€40) for fisherfolk, and is the closest camping ground to the rapids.

Kolmen Ristin Kirkko   CHURCH
(Ruokolahdentie 27; ◷10am-6pm Jun-Aug, 9am-3pm Sep-May) Architecture aficionados will be able to tell by the clean white lines and soaring narrow tower that the Church of the Three Crosses (1957) was designed by Alvar Aalto. Its spire echoes both the silver birches and the factory chimneys in the area, the building being located in the industrial suburb of Vuoksenniska, about 7km northeast of the falls. Local buses run here Monday to Friday.

⚜ Festivals & Events

Imatra Big Band Festival   MUSIC
(☏020-747 9400; www.ibbf.fi; tickets €35-49) Since 1982, jazz, swing and blues players have been blowing their own trumpets around Imatrankoski in late June–early July.

🛏 Sleeping

Imatran
Valtionhotelli   HISTORIC HOTEL, SPA HOTEL €€€
(☏625 2000; www.rantasipi.fi; Torkkelinkatu 2; castle s/d €154/175, spa centre s €150, d €160-180; P@☀) With art-nouveau furnishings and flamboyant turrets, this is definitely the top of the town – some rooms even afford views of the rapids. It was a favourite of the Russian aristocracy and now attracts their nouveau-riche equivalent with its opulent style. The spa centre next door has modern Scandinavian rooms in chocolate and cream. It is pleasant enough but lacks its neighbour's historical might and amazing views.

Imatran Kylpylä Spa   SPA HOTEL €€
(☏020-7100 500; www.imatrankylpyla.fi; Purjekuja 1; s €90-106, d €120-152, ste 2 nights from €460; P@☀) A whopping complex in Imatra's leisure area, it incorporates the family-oriented Promenade Hotel (with lake views), the Spa Hotel (newly renovated but with rather tight rooms), and gorgeous two- to four-person luxury suites, aloof from the rest of the complex on their own little hill. There are cafes and bars, a bowling alley (€20 per lane), bike rental, a badminton court, and of course the spa itself, with several pools, jacuzzis, and all kinds of health and beauty treatments. There's no real reason to set foot outside.

Hostel Mansikkala   HOSTEL €
(☏044-7975 452; www.hostelmansikkala.com; Pilvikuja 1; dm €18, s/d €38/55; ◷Jun–mid-Aug) This summer hostel, in excellent Finnish student accommodation, is like a pleasant stay in a suburban housing estate. Two or three spacious bedrooms share a well-equipped kitchen and bathroom, and there's access to a laundry and a sauna. It's a little way from the action; you'll need private transport or to hire a hostel bicycle (€10 per day).

Ukonlinna Hostel
HOSTEL €

(📞432 1270; ukonlinna@elisanet.fi; Leiritie 8; r per person €25; 🅿) This little HI hostel, with its prime position on the beach in Imatra's leisure area, is popular with families and books out quickly.

Camping Ukonniemi
CAMPGROUND €

(📞040-5151 310; Leiritie; tent sites €10 plus per person €5, 3-/4-/5-person cabins €40/50/58; ⊗Jun-Aug) Operated by Imatra Kylpylä Spa, this place offers camping and cabins in a huge recreation area in Imatra's leisure zone.

✕ Eating & Drinking

Most of Imatra's eating options are on the pedestrianised area of Imatrankoski.

Buttenhoff
FRENCH, RUSSIAN €€

(📞476 1433; www.buttenhoff.fi; Koskenparras 4; mains €18-28, set menu €40; ⊗lunch & dinner Mon-Sat) Serving up Burgundy escargot and *blini* (pancakes) with caviar, this is definitely the best place in town. The menu wanders across the border with Russian favourites given a decidedly French treatment, such as the pan-fried *perch à la Russe*. Daytime **Cafe Julia**, on the ground floor, has tempting cakes.

Café Prego
CAFE €

(Napinkuja 2; snacks €3-8; ⊗8am-5pm Mon-Fri, 10am-4pm Sat) This excellent Italian coffee spot also does good salads, rolls and light meals, and has a lovely little terrace out the front. It has the best java in town, as well as cakes and cookies that will have you lingering.

ℹ Information

Public library (📞020-617 6600; Virastokatu 1, Mansikkala; ⊗10am-7pm Mon-Thu, 10am-4pm Fri Jun-Aug, plus 10am-3pm Sat Sep-May) In the Kaupungintalo near the bus and train stations. Has free internet access.

Tourist office (📞235 2330; www.gosaimaa.com; Lappeentie 12; ⊗9am-5.30pm Mon-Fri Jun–mid-Aug, plus noon-4pm Sat mid-Jul–Aug, 9am-4.30pm Mon–Fri mid-Aug–May) Helpful and friendly; extended opening hours for the Big Band Festival (p199).

ℹ Getting There & Away

Imatra is served by trains (€45.50, 2¾ hours, eight daily) and buses (€41, five hours) from Helsinki, some of which continue to Joensuu (trains €30, 2 hours; buses €38, 3¾ hours). There are a similar number of trains (€8, 25 minutes) and buses (€9, one hour) from Lappeenranta.

The bus and train stations are 3km north in Mansikkala and frequent local buses connect it with the centre (€3.10). Buses also pick up and drop off at Imatrankoski near the rapids on Olavinkatu, a handier option. Otherwise you'll need a **taxi** (📞020-016 464).

NORTH KARELIA

Even today, Finland's wild frontier has many southerners imagining wolves and Russian border raids. True, the sparsely populated area does have some of Finland's best wildlife, but you'd be lucky to see a wolf or a bear on even the most rugged treks. And you will see Russian influence too – in stunning Orthodox cathedrals and old towns.

North Karelia has had more than its share of strife, fought over for centuries by Sweden and Russia, and having seen fierce fighting during the Winter and Continuation Wars. Its towns are modern – older incarnations were razed by the Russians during WWII – and you'll often stumble across trenches, old battlegrounds and memorials to the fallen inside the quiet forests.

Just beyond North Karelia, Kuhmo (p253) also has a Karelian heritage though it's not strictly part of this province.

Joensuu

📞013 / POP 73,300

The capital of North Karelia is a bubbly young university town, with students making up almost a third of the population. Today Joensuu looks pretty modern – 23 bombing raids during the Winter and Continuation Wars flattened many of its older buildings – and it's a lively little place to hang out. It's also the gateway to the deep, quiet depths of the Karelian wilderness.

At the mouth of the Pielisjoki, the town (Joensuu meaning 'river mouth' in Finnish) was founded by Tsar Nikolai I and grew to importance as a trading port with the completion of the Saimaa Canal in the 1850s.

◉ Sights

Carelicum
MUSEUM

(📞267 5222; Koskikatu 5; admission €5; ⊗10am-5pm Mon-Fri, to 3pm Sat & Sun) If you want to know more about Karelian history or culture, the Carelicum, which reopened in January 2011 after a long refurbishment, should be your first stop. It's a conceptual museum, with themed displays – on the re-

Joensuu

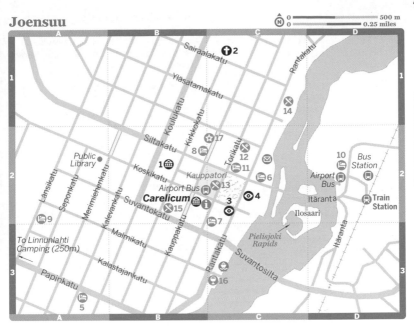

Joensuu

◎ Top Sights
Carelicum................................ B2

◎ Sights
1 Joensuu Taidemuseo............................ B2
2 Orthodox Church of St Nicholas............C1
3 Taitokortteli... C2
4 Town Hall C2

🛏 Sleeping
5 Finnhostel Joensuu A3
6 Hotel Atrium C2
7 Hotel GreenStar.................................... C2
8 Hotelli Karelia...................................... B2
9 Kesähotelli Joensuun Elli...................... A2
10 Sokos Hotel Kimmel.............................. D2

11 Sokos Hotel Vaakuna.............................. C2

🍴 Eating
12 Kahvila & Konditoria Houkutus C2
13 Kauppatori Food Stalls..........................C2
14 Ravintola Astoria C1
15 Ravintola Kielo B2
    Teatteri ....(see 4)

🍷 Drinking
    Palaveri ....(see 6)
16 Tuulaaki C3

🎭 Entertainment
17 Multiplex Tapio C2
    Night..(see 10)

gion's prehistory, its war-torn past, the Karelian evacuation, the importance of the sauna etc – that cover both sides of the present-day border. Temporary exhibitions (Karelian pop music and cartoons at the time of research) are interesting, but in Finnish only.

Taitokortteli   ARTS CENTRE
(☏220 140; www.taitokortteli.fi; Koskikatu 1; ☉10am-5pm Mon-Fri, to 3pm Sat year-round, also noon-4pm Sun in Jul) A chubby cherub perches

on the balcony of Taitokortteli, a pocket of town where local craftsfolk make clothing, toys and homewares. It's a chance to see weavers at work, browse contemporary art and purchase local designers' work, plus there's a sweet cafe and gallery space.

Joensuu Taidemuseo   ART GALLERY
(☏267 5388; http://taidemuseo.jns.fi; Kirkkokatu 23; admission €4.50; ☉11am-4pm Tue & Thu-Sun, 11am-8pm Wed) Near the kauppatori,

Joensuu's art museum boasts an impressive collection including Chinese pieces, examples of Finnish modernism and an intriguing selection of Orthodox icons swiped from the Soviets.

Town Hall   BUILDING
(Rantakatu 20) The art deco town hall dominates the centre, between the kauppatori (market square)and river. It was designed by Eliel Saarinen, the architect most famous for Helsinki's train station, and was built in 1914. It now houses the local theatre and Teatteri restaurant.

Orthodox Church of St Nicholas   CHURCH
(☎266 000; Kirkkokatu; ☉10am-4pm Mon-Fri mid-Jun–mid-Aug) Joensuu's most intriguing church is the wooden Orthodox church, built in 1887 with icons painted in St Petersburg during the late 1880s. There are services at 6pm on Saturday and 10am on Sunday.

Activites

For ferry cruises to Koli and Lieksa, see p206.

Pielisjoki Cruise   BOAT TOUR
(☎050-566 0815; www.satumaaristeilyt.fi, in Finnish; tours from €15) From June to mid-August, there are two-hour scenic cruises on the Pielisjoki, a centuries-old trading route, aboard the M/S *Vinkeri II* and M/S *Satumaa*. They leave from the passenger harbour south of Suvantosilta bridge. For further information and bookings, call Juha Mustonen on the number above or contact the city tourist office.

Carriage Ride   TOUR
(☎0400-239 549; www.kareliaexpert.com; Koskikatu 5; tours from €20) From the park by the kaup-

---

patori you can take a carriage tour in a 19th-century Victorian buggy from June to mid-August. In winter the operator switches to sled tours, both bookable through Karelia Expert.

🎆 Festivals & Events

Ilosaari Rock Festival   MUSIC
(www.ilosaarirock.fi; 2-day ticket €75) Held over a weekend in mid-July, this massive rock festival attracts Finnish and international acts. It has received awards for its environmental record.

🛏 Sleeping

Sokos Hotel Vaakuna   HOTEL €€
(☎010-782 3100; www.sokoshotels.fi; Torikatu 20; s €80-90, d €130; P@❋) A respectable and central member of Joensuu's busy hotel scene, with excellent staff, the Sokos went through a massive revamp in 2010 and doubled in size. Be sure to ask for accommodation in the new section, as its slick, spacious air-conditioned rooms knock spots off the slightly threadbare older half of the hotel. It's also worth spending the extra €20 on a superior room, for extra space, tea-and-coffee facilities, bathtub and a thicker, comfier mattress. Parking is €8 per day.

🌿 Hotel GreenStar   ECO-HOTEL €
(☎010-423 9390; www.greenstar.fi; Torikatu 16; r €59; P) This recently built low-energy hotel keeps environmental guilt at bay, with water heating rather than air-con blaring away and small communal areas to reduce heating. It's great value; clean, comfortable rooms sleep up to three for the same price (a pull-out armchair converts into a third bed). Breakfast (€6) is an optional extra. There's an automatic check-in kiosk in the lobby, but we recommend arriving during the (short) hours when the reception desk is staffed, as the automatic system can be temperamental.

Hotel Atrium   HOTEL €€
(☎225 888; www.hotelliatrium.fi; Siltakatu 4; s/d €83/112; P) One of the more character-filled stays in town, comfortable Atrium is guarded by Jaakko, the wolf-whistling parrot. Many of its rooms look out over concrete rooftops – for aesthetic reasons, ask for one with a river view, balcony or private sauna. Some rooms are showing signs of wear but it's still good value, especially as prices fall in summer.

SHARING A CAB

In North Karelia the set-route *kimppakyyti* (shared taxi) system is a particularly useful service given the scarcity of buses. There's a different telephone number for each route (see town Getting There & Away sections), which connects directly to the driver. As English levels vary, it may be easier to ask a Finnish speaker to phone for you. You need to book a day in advance, and fares are about the same price as the bus.

Finnhostel Joensuu
HOSTEL €

(☎267 5076; www.islo.fi; Kalevankatu 8; s/d from €46/70; P) Recently renovated, this smart HI-affiliated establishment is run by a sports institute. It was once student halls, and some bathrooms and kitchens are still shared (one for every two rooms), but half the rooms do have private facilities. The accommodation is spacious, with flatscreen TVs and mini-balconies. Separate buildings contain a gym and sauna, and healthy breakfasts (€6) are available in Restaurant Sportti.

Kesähotelli Joensuun Elli
HOTEL €

(☎010-421 5600; www.summerhotelelli.fi; Länsikatu 18; s/d/tr €47/57/77, apt from €97; ☉mid-May–mid-Aug; P) You may consider enrolling in a Finnish university after seeing these quality student apartments, which open to the public in summer. Facilities include a sauna, a laundry and shared kitchens and bathrooms (one for every two rooms). The simple four-bed apartment is handy for families. There's also the Gaude pub which does excellent pizzas and snacks on the lower floors.

Linnunlahti Camping
CAMPSITE €

(☎010-666 5520; www.linnunlahti.fi; Linnunlahdentie 1; tent sites €7 plus per person €2, apt €150; ☉Jun-Aug) Surely the cheapest big-town accommodation in the Scandic countries, this bargain lakeside camping ground is mobbed during the rock festival (p202), but has sites to spare at other times.

Sokos Hotel Kimmel
HOTEL €€

(☎020-123 4663; www.sokoshotels.fi; Itäranta 1; s/d around €100/122; P@☎) Joensuu's largest hotel is clean if a little characterless. Handy for the train station, it also has amazing river views and a popular nightclub.

Hotelli Karelia
HOTEL €€

(☎252 6200; Kauppakatu 25; www.hotellikarelia.fi; s/d €89/105; P) Mature but pleasant rooms have been given a recent boost with new bathrooms. Weekend prices are cheaper, although light sleepers should request rooms at a distance from the Friday and Saturday cabaret/dance nights.

✖ Eating

At the busy **kauppatori food stalls**, look for Karelian specialities such as the classic *karjalanpiirakka* (a rice-filled savoury pastry) and *kotiruoka* (homemade) soups. Joensuu's restaurant scene is overrun by fast-food chains but there are a couple of standouts.

Ravintola Astoria
HUNGARIAN €€

(☎229 766; Rantakatu 32; mains €20-30; ☉lunch & dinner Jun-Aug, dinner Mon-Fri, lunch & dinner Sat & Sun Sep-May) In an unusual building – a former girls' school built in brick-Gothic style – this wood-panelled restaurant is a stylish affair with a Hungarian influence. Expect a menu with plenty of paprika and garlic in goulashes and hefty steaks. Hungarian wines complement the food and chilled *slivovitz* (plum brandy) makes a strong finisher.

Teatteri
KARELIAN €€

(☎256 6900; www.jns.fi/teatteriravintola; Rantakatu 20; lunch €8.60, mains €14-24; ☉lunch & dinner Mon-Sat year round, plus noon-8pm Sun Jun-Aug) You'll have trouble keeping an eye on your plate amid the swanky surroundings of this art-deco town hall building, which is decked out in Karelian maroons and blacks. The menu is representative of the region, with *muikku* from nearby lakes and border-crossing borscht.

🖋 Ravintola Kielo
KARELIAN €€€

(☎227 874; www.ravintolakielo.fi; Suvantokatu 12; mains €25-30; ☉dinner Mon-Fri, lunch & dinner Sat) A relative newcomer to Joensuu's restaurant scene, this gourmet restaurant specialises in Karelian treats. Dishes seem a little fussy at times, but when they work they are superb. The menu changes with the seasons, but the five-portion tasting starter is always a beautiful-looking introduction to the region's specialities. We also recommend the braised wild duck and the salmon, when available.

Kahvila & Konditoria Houkutus
CAFE €

(Torikatu 24; cakes €4-7; ☉7.30am-7pm Mon-Fri, 8.30am-5pm Sat) Decent coffee shops are thin on the ground in Joensuu. Luckily, this smart bakery does great coffee and even better cakes. The mint blackcurrant cake is a treat.

🍷 Drinking & Entertainment

The pedestrianised area of Kauppakatu has several late-night bars, which turn the volume up to 11 on weekends. The town's biggest nightclub, imaginatively named **Night**, is in the basement of the Sokos Hotel Kimmel.

Tuulaaki
BAR

(Rantakatu 2; ☉to 2am daily May-Aug) This summer terrace is sweetly placed right on the river and features live rock at weekends. At other times it's often quieter, as it's away from the city centre.

Palaveri   PUB
(Siltakatu 4) Beer-lovers should head straight for the Palaveri, a bar-restaurant with the best selection of beers in town – offered at a discount to lucky students.

Multiplex Tapio   CINEMA
(☑122 238; www.savonkinot.fi, in Finnish; Kauppakatu 27; tickets €9.50) This large four-screen cinema on the main shopping street brings the big movies to town.

ℹ Information
Karelia Expert (☑0400-239 549; www.karelia expert.com; Koskikatu 5; ⊙10am-5pm Mon-Fri year round, plus 10am-3pm Sat mid-May–mid-Sep & 10am-3pm Sun Jul; @) Located in the Carelicum, Karelia Expert handles tourism information and bookings for the region. Free internet access (15 minutes).

Public library (☑267 6200; Koskikatu 25; ⊙11am-8pm Mon-Fri year-round, plus 10am-3pm Sat Sep-May) Several free internet terminals.

ℹ Getting There & Around
To/From the Airport
The airport is 11km west of Joensuu. A bus service (one-way €5) departs from the bus station (50 minutes before plane departures) and a stop on the corner of Koskikatu and Kauppakatu (45 minutes before departures). There's also an **airport taxi** (☑060-090 100; one-way €20).

Air
Finnair (www.finnair.com) and **Flybe** (www.flybe.com) operate several flights a day between Helsinki and Joensuu.

Bus
Joensuu is a transport hub for North Karelia. Services include links with Kuopio (€27.90, 2½ hours), Oulu (€68, seven hours), Jyväskylä (€41, four hours), Helsinki (€56.10, 7½ hours), Lappeenranta (€41, 4½ hours), Ilomantsi (€14.40, 1¼ hours) and Nurmes (€27, two hours). For Kuhmo, change buses at Nurmes or Sotkamo.

Car
Most big car-hire operators have offices at the airport, with the following branches in town:
Avis (☑122 222; www.avis.fi; Kauppakatu 33)
Europcar (☑040-306 2852; www.europcar.com; Merimiehenkatu 37)
Hertz (☑020-555 2690; www.hertz.fi; Itäranta 12, train station)

Shared Taxi
A *kimppakyyti* route runs from Joensuu to Koli in the Lake Pielinen area. See p214 for details.

Train
Direct trains run six times daily to/from Helsinki (€62.20, 4½ hours), as well as north to Lieksa (€13.60, 1¼ hours) and Nurmes (€19.30, two hours, twice daily). For Savonlinna you'll have to change at Parikkala.

Ilomantsi
☑013 / POP 5900
Like Ålanders and Sámi in northern Lapland, Karelians see themselves as a distinct cultural group. You'll see that on the streets of this small town, which refers to itself by the Russian *pogost* (village) rather than Finnish *kylä* (village). Ilomantsi is the closest town to the border, has an Orthodox religion and even speaks its own dialect. The town itself has some unusual and worthwhile sights, but with no worthwhile accommodation and few eating options it makes a poor base. Better to head for the farmhouses, national parks and scenic areas round about once you've ticked off the town.

◎ Sights
Parppeinvaara   MUSEUM
(☑881 248; adult/child €5/3; ⊙10am-6pm Jul, to 4pm Jun & Aug) Karelian traditions are brought to life at the little Bardic Village. The hill is named for Jaakko Parppei (1792–1885), a bard and *kantele* player, whose songs inspired the *Kalevala* epic. The folked-up harpsichord-like sounds of this local stringed instrument can be heard at the small cultural museum, on the hour from noon to closing time.

The **Border General's Cabin**, tucked away down an overgrown pathway, contains a fascinating exhibition relating to the war years. The cabin served as headquarters for Major General Erkki Raappana, a local hero who was decorated by Mannerheim for his achievements, and contains many of his personal effects, plus a case of Finnish and Russian weaponry from Uzis to homemade bombs.

The new **Mesikkä Animal Museum** is a small but beautifully presented attraction that uses natural-history exhibits to explore the relationship between Karelians and nature.

Hermanni Wine Tower (Viintorni) TOWER

(☎0207-789 233; Kappalaisentie; ⊙10am-10pm Jun–mid-Aug) Finnish wine isn't necessarily an oxymoron. Blackcurrants, crowberries and white currants from the fields and bogs around Ilomantsi are blended here to create some intriguing flavours. Abandon your car and head for the Viinitorni at the top of the local water tower, where you can sample local Hermanni berry wines and liqueurs by the glass or tasting tray (€12 for five wines and one liqueur). The views from the panoramic balcony are fabulous even without alcoholic enhancement.

Hermanni Winery WINERY

(☎0207-789 230; www.hermanninviinitila.fi; Käymiskuja 1; ⊙9am-5pm Mon-Fri, 10am-5pm Sat, noon-5pm Sun Jul, 9am-5pm Mon-Fri, 10am-5pm Sat Jun & Aug, 9am-4pm Mon-Fri Sep-May) Once you've discovered your favourite wines at the Hermanni Wine Tower, visit the winery itself to buy bottles and chat about the fascinating wine-making process. (You'll need to track down an Alko liquor shop if you want the strongest apple and honey brandy).

Pyhän Elian Kirkko CHURCH

(Kirkkotie 15; ⊙11.30am-5.30pm mid-Jun–mid-Aug) One of two fabulous churches in Ilomantsi, this beautiful wooden Orthodox church has an obvious Russian influence. Follow the *kalmisto* (graveyard) sign to the waterfront **Kokonniemi Cemetery**, where trees shade the graves of those lost in the many conflicts the town has endured.

Lutheran Church CHURCH

(Henrikintie 1; ⊙11.30am-5.30pm Mon-Sat late Jun–mid-Aug) When the Swedes took the area they sought to convert the Orthodox population by building this gigantic Lutheran church in 1796. It's also known as the Church of a Hundred Angels for its colourful and comprehensive wall paintings, completed in 1832 by Samuel Elmgren – vivid images that must have done much to sway illiterate locals towards the Western faith.

Piirola Piha MARKET

(☎050-315 6950; Kauppatie 26; ⊙10am-5pm Mon-Fri, plus 10am-2pm Sat Jul) This little place sells authentic souvenirs, including locally made *terva* (tar) soaps. On Wednesdays in July, crafty types demonstrate their skills on looms and spinning wheels.

✨ Festivals & Events

As an Orthodox centre, Ilomantsi has several Praasniekka events. Originally these were strictly religious events, but these days they also attract tourists, with dancing afterwards. Ilomantsi village celebrates **Petru Praasniekka** on 28 and 29 June and **Ilja Praasniekka** on 19 and 20 July every year.

🛏 Sleeping & Eating

Accommodation in town is exceptionally limited – the town's central **Hotel Pääskynpesä** (☎682 1400; www.paaskynpesa.fi; Henrikintie 4; s/d €83/124) is also a rehabilitation centre, which does not make for a holiday atmosphere. You really need your own transport to access farms and holiday villages in the surrounding area (see also p206). Eating options are equally poor; check that your accommodation can provide evening meals or self-catering facilities.

Anssilan Farm FARMSTAY €

(☎040-088 1181; www.ilomantsi.com/anssila; Anssilantie; s/d/tr/q €30/60/90/120; 🅿) Originally built in 1751, this former dairy farm is on a hill 4km south of Ilomantsi. It's family friendly with rides on horses and sleds for kids, and rooms are available in a range of converted farmhouse buildings with breakfast and linen included. You can also camp in the garden here for €7 per person.

Ruhkaranta Lomakeskus CAMPGROUND €

(☎045-138 9077; www.ruhkaranta.fi; Ruhkarannantie 21; tent sites €12 plus per person €3, cottages €44 99) Secluded in a thick pine forest 9km east of Ilomantsi, this camping ground and collection of neat cottages has amazing lake views and free-to-hire rowing boats. There's also a traditional smoke sauna here for groups and a cafe-bar. Out of high season,book at least two days in advance.

🔝 TOP CHOICE Parppeinpirtti BUFFET €€

(☎010-239 9950; www.parppeinpirtti.fi; lunch €20; ⊙10am-7pm Jul, to 5pm Jun & early Aug, to 3pm Mon-Fri other times) The one foodie highlight in Ilomantsi is this cafe-restaurant in the Parppeinvaara village, which does a real-deal *pitopöytä* (Karelian buffet) in summer in a traditional house complete with a *kantele* soundtrack. Here you can heap your plate high with *vatruskoita* (salmon-stuffed pastry), swill down the nonalcoholic *kotikalja* (which tastes like a home-brewed beer) and finish with sticky berry soup.

KARELIA ILOMANTSI

ℹ️ Information

Karelia Expert (☑0400-240 072; www.visit karelia.fi; Kalevalantie 13; ⊙9am-5pm Mon-Fri Jun-Aug, 8am-4pm Mon-Fri Sep-May) Reservations and information.

Library (Mantsintie; ⊙10am-7pm Mon & Tue, 1-7pm Wed & Thu, 10am-5pm Fri) Free internet access.

ℹ️ Getting There & Away

There are several buses between Joensuu and Ilomantsi (€14.40, 1½ hours) on weekdays and fewer on weekends; buses stop in the centre of town. During the school term there are weekday buses from here to surrounding villages, but in summer you'll have to rely on **taxis** (☑881 111).

Around Ilomantsi

From Ilomantsi, Rd 5004 heads east towards the Russian border, through a patchwork of lakes and into the wild trekking country.

PETKELJÄRVI NATIONAL PARK

The track to one of Finland's smallest (6.3 sq km) national parks is about 14km east of the main highway, off Rd 5004. The park's birch and pine forests, eskers (gravel ridges) and ruined fortifications of the Continuation War are threaded with nature trails. The marked 35km **Taitajan Taival** (Master's Trail) starts here and runs northeast to the village of Mekrijärvi, about 13km north of Ilomantsi. More than one-third of the park is water, with two sizeable lakes dominating.

Petkeljärvi Nature Centre (☑013-844 199; tent sites €12 plus per person €7, lodge s/d/ tr/q €40/50/69/84; ⊙May-Aug), in the heart of the park, is a real end-of-the-line retreat. As well as tent and caravan sites, there's a lodge building with hostel-style accommodation – basic bunks and none-too-thick walls, but hedgehogs and beavers on the doorstep as compensation. There are self-catering facilities, plus a daytime cafe, lakeside sauna, and boats and canoes for use on the lake. You'll find park information and maps, and the Harjupolku Nature Trail (3.5km) and Kuikan Kierros Nature Trail (6.5km) also begin here.

Hattuvaara

☑013

About 40km northeast of Ilomantsi, you'll know you're in the wilds by the dirt roads and logging trucks passing through this last outpost – Finland's most easterly set-tlement. The village was famous for poem-singers, such as Arhippa Buruskainen who is thought to have inspired tales in the *Kalevala*. The *runon ja rajan tie* ('Poem and Border Rte') runs through Hattuvaara as a tribute.

The main attraction is the striking wooden **Taistelijan Talo** (Heroes' House; ☑0400-273 671; www.taistelijantalo.fi; ⊙10am-8pm Jul, 10am-6pm Jun, 10am-4pm Aug-early Sep, 10am-3pm Mon-Fri May), designed by Joensuu architect Erkki Helasvuo to symbolise the meeting of East and West. The **WWII museum** (admission €5) downstairs shows a short film in several languages with multimedia, photo exhibitions and weaponry displays relating chiefly to the Winter and Continuation Wars fought along the nearby border. You'll see artillery and vehicles surrounding the building as well as a **Big Hat sculpture**, a nod to the meaning of the town's name – literally 'Hat Mountain'.

Taistelijan Talo offers an excellent all-day Karelian buffet (€14), heavy with meat, fish and *karjalanpiirakka*. You can also ask here about accommodation in the village and hunting trips into the surrounding wilds.

Hattuvaara has Finland's oldest **Orthodox tsasouna**, a sweet white wooden chapel by the side of the main road. Built in 1790, it has several original Russian icons and its small tower became a watchtower during WWII. On 29 June each year the colourful **Praasniekka festival** takes place here, complete with a *ristinsaatto* (Orthodox procession).

A **shared taxi** (☑0500-675 542; €6) runs here from Lieksa, twice daily on Mondays and Thursdays only.

LAKE PIELINEN REGION

At the heart of northern Karelia is Pielinen, Finland's sixth-largest lake, which offers plenty of water-sports action. Finns flock to Koli National Park for epic views and winter skiing, while Lieksa and Nurmes equip intrepid travellers to head out into wilds such as Ruunaa for whitewater rafting. Bring your hiking boots because this is a place to be active; towns here are really just bases for getting into the great outdoors. A main road loops the lake while ferries cross it from Lieksa to Koli. When the lake freezes solid during winter, take the thrilling short cut on a snowmobile or cross-country skis.

Lieksa

🕿 013 / POP 12,700

Situated on the banks of Lake Pielinen, Lieksa is unlovely in itself, but makes a good base for nearby activities. From here, you can easily explore Koli or go whitewater-rafting, riding, canoeing and bear-watching.

⊙ Sights

Pielisen Museo MUSEUM

(🕿040-104 4151; www.lieksa.fi/museo; Pappilantie 2; adult/child €5/1.50; ⊙10am-6pm mid-May–mid-Sep) Even those jaded by outdoor museums will be impressed by the sprawling complex of North Karelia's largest museum. It consists of an indoor section, and more than 70 Karelian buildings and open-air exhibits, organised by century or trade (such as farming, milling, fire-fighting). It gives a fascinating insight into the forestry industry, which was once crucial to the region, including a look at a logging camp and floating rafts and machinery used for harvest and transport.

In winter, only the **indoor museum** (admission winter adult/child €3/1; ⊙10am-3pm Tue-Fri mid-Sep–mid-May) section is open. This features photographs and displays on Karelian folk history.

🏃 Activities

Most trips and activities can be booked through Karelia Expert (p208), which can also provide detailed driving instructions for out-of-the-way operators. It's also possible to arrange a pick-up from Lieksa to go whitewater rafting in the Ruunaa Recreation Area (p209).

Fishing is good in Lake Pielinen, Pudasjoki River and the Ruunaa and Änäkäinen recreational fishing areas. They each require separate permits, available from local sports shops or Karelia Expert.

Ratsastustalli Ahaa HORSEBACK RIDING

(🕿040-525 7742; www.ahaatalli.fi, in Finnish) Offers lessons and cross-country treks.

Kuivalan Islanninhevostalli HORSEBACK RIDING

(🕿0400-579113; www.kuivala.fi) This company has gentle-natured Icelandic ponies to ride. Horse riding costs about €25 per hour.

Bear Hill Husky DOG-SLEDDING

(🕿040-779 0898; www.bearhillhusky.com) In winter, husky-dog sleds, cross-country skiing and snowmobile expeditions along the Russian border are popular and can be tai-

---

EASTERNMOST POINT

Collectors of coldest places, deepest mines and tallest towers may be interested in a trip to the **Easternmost Point of the EU**. Tight border restrictions were relaxed a little in 2010, allowing visitors to cross the Finnish-Russian border at Virmajärvi without a permit, then drive a further 15km down a rough gravel road to the furthest flung part of the EU. There's not much to see, and nothing to do there...apart from add another tick to your 'superlative places' list. Taistelijan Talo in Hattuvaara can arrange trips and provide a 'diploma' to mark the occasion.

---

lored to your needs. The tourist office has a long list of tour operators but Bear Hill Husky, based near Hattuvaara, is one of the best.

Erä Eero BEAR-WATCHING

(🕿040-015 9452; www.eraeero.com; per person €160; ⊙4pm-6am) Looking to go bearwatching? Erä Eero runs overnight trips to its observation cabin, where you may see bear between April and October, as well as birds of prey, wolverines, and the odd lynx.

⚒ Festivals & Events

Lieksa Brass Week (🕿045-132 4000; www.lieksabrass.com; Koski-Jaakonkatu 4; admission varies), during the last week of July, attracts a number of international musicians and has a few free events.

⛺ Sleeping & Eating

There are a few places to stay in Lieksa, but it's also worth considering surrounding options in Vuonislahti (p212), Koli (p213) and Ruunaa (p210). Most places to eat and drink are on Lieksa's main street, Pielisentie.

Timitran Linna HOSTEL €

(🕿044-333 4044; www.timitra.fi, in Finnish; Timitrantie 3; per person from €25) Once the national training centre for the Finnish border guard, this HI-affiliated hostel is a little way from the main street but makes for a quieter stay. Its 1st-floor rooms (singles, doubles, quads and five-bed rooms) are standard fare but the smaller ones have been freshened up recently. Sea kayaks are available for exploring the nearby river.

Hotelli Puustelli
HOTEL €€

(☑511 5500; www.puustelliravintolat.fi; Hovileir-inkatu 3; s/d €90/105; P) This lo-fi building by the riverside has good-sized rooms (if a little musty), with affordable rates that include breakfast and sauna. There's also a restaurant serving no-fuss fish, steak and pizza – though vegetarians will struggle.

Timitraniemi Camping
CAMPGROUND €

(☑045-123 7166; www.timitra.com; Timitrantie 25; tent sites €14, cabins €48-105; ⊘mid-May–mid-Sep) This well-equipped family-oriented camping ground at the mouth of the river has 45 log cabins of varying sizes and plushness, plenty of camp sites and facilities like lakeside cafe, saunas, and bikes and boats for hire. They're also great for organising additional activities like rafting and fishing.

Lieksan Leipomo
BAKERY €

(☑729 9152; Pielisentie 31; soup €7; ⊘6am-5pm Mon-Fri, 9am-2pm Sat) This endearing weatherboard bakery is famous with locals for its homemade treats and filling soup lunches.

Tinatähti
PUB €

(☑222 131; Pielisentie 28; ⊘) There are very few places to grab an evening meal in Lieksa but this lively pub is one of them. It serves straight-up meals and has a pleasant terrace.

❶ Information

Karelia Expert (☑0400-175 323; www.visitkarelia.fi; Pielisentie 19; ⊘9am-5pm Mon-Fri Jun-Aug, plus 9am-2pm Sat Jul, 8am-4pm Mon-Fri Sep-May) Books tours and accommodation.

Library (☑040-104 4125; Urheilukatu 4) Free internet access.

❶ Getting There & Away

BUS There are around seven weekday buses (€17.40, 1¾ hours) from Joensuu, with fewer on weekends.

FERRY The car ferry **MF Pielinen** (☑040-022 8435; www.pielis-laivat.fi; adult/child/car/bicycle €15/8/10/2) makes the 1¾-hour trip from Lieksa to Koli twice daily from mid-June to mid-August, departing from Lieksa at 10am and 3pm, and returning from Koli at noon and 5pm. In winter, when the ice is thick enough, there is an ice road crossing the lake from Vuonislahti to Koli, a substantial short cut.

SHARED TAXI Contact Karelia Expert for information on and bookings of shared taxis.

TRAIN There are daily trains from Helsinki to Lieksa (€75.10, 6½ hours), via Joensuu (€13.60, 1¼ hours).

Patvinsuo National Park

This large marshland area between Lieksa and Ilomantsi is a habitat for swans and cranes, and if you're exceedingly lucky you might see bears. Using the *pitkospuu* (boardwalk) network, you can easily hike around.

It's an easy 3.5km stroll to the southern shore of Suomunjärvi from the main road, where you'll find a **birdwatching tower** at

A WILD LIFE

I was born on a little farm near Lake Pielinen, and have lived in Karelia all my life, serving 28.5 years in the Finnish Frontier Guard. I have always been interested in nature. My favourite mammals are bear, wolverine, wolf and lynx – the best place for seeing large predators here is Erä Eero's (p207) hide in Lieksa. Of the birds, I like capercaillie, black grouse, hawks, owls, cranes, and listening to the song thrush as it sings through the summer nights – Patvinsuo National Park (see above) contains many rare bird species.

Beyond the border lies Europe's biggest wilderness, and the animals from that wilderness sometimes visit Finland. I have a special permit to guide people in the eastern frontier zone, which has the wildest nature as human activity is usually limited to border patrols. Here you can see, for example, wild forest reindeer. This is a very arresting area.

Nature tours are becoming more popular, as foreign visitors want to see truly wild wildlife. Most come in summer, but tracking animals is easier in the winter snow, and winter photographs are more unusual...although the cold can cause difficulty with electrical devices. Commercial forestry has affected areas of old woodland – flying squirrels and wolverines are particularly under threat – but luckily in Finland, we have legal protection of many endangered habitats. Not to mention friendly people and pure food!

Esa Muikku, Wildlife Caravan Safaris Guide, www.caret.fi

Teretinniemi. The walk weaves through forests and wetlands, with sightings of waterfowl guaranteed if you're quiet.

There are three marked nature trails (between 3km and 4.5km long), and several challenging hiking routes (mostly half-day walks) along the boardwalk path. You can walk around Suomunjärvi or follow *pitkospuu* trails through the wetlands. In winter there's cross-country skiing on the unmaintained **Mäntypolku** and **Nämänpuro Trails**, which both start from Suomu car park.

Suomu Information Hut (☏548 506; ☺11am-3pm mid-May–mid-Sep) has a summer warden who can help with advice, fishing permits and maps, and point you towards the eight camping areas. You can hire canoes and rowing boats here (per hour/day €5/20; cash only), and make bookings for accommodation; there are nine beds (per night €12) in the information hut itself and two cabins in the park. There's also Lake Hopealampi's **loggers' cabin** (per night €163), which sleeps 30; and the smaller **Väärälampi cabin** (per night €86), which sleeps four. Facilities are basic at both cabins, but include dry toilets, cooking facilities and, of course, saunas. They can also be booked via **Wild North** (☏020-344 122; www.villipohjola.fi). The Susitaival (Wolf's Trail) and Karhunpolku (Bear's Trail; see p210) trailheads begin here.

❶ Getting There & Away

The only way to get to the national park is to drive. Or walk – if you are trekking, the Karhunpolku and Susitaival trails both meet at the park.

Ruunaa Recreation Area

☏013

Ruunaa, just 30km northeast of Lieksa, is an outdoor activities hub east of Lake Pielinen. It boasts 38km of waterways with six whitewater rapids, unpolluted wilderness, excellent trekking paths and good fishing. Designated camp sites (with fire rings) are also provided and maintained. Keep your eyes peeled as the area is home to otters, deer and sometimes bears.

There's an observation tower situated at Huuhkajavaara. Set atop a hill, it offers a magnificent panorama over Neitijärvi. **Ruunaa Visitor Centre** (☏020-564 5757; ☺10am-5pm late May-Jun & Aug-Sep, 9am-6pm Jul) is near the bridge over the Naarajoki, where most boat trips start. There are exhibitions, maps,

a library and a short film about the area. It's a good place to read up on Ruunaa's plantlife, birds and beasts, and to research hiking trails.

❧ Activities

Ruunaa is busy all year, hosting snow sports in winter, and rafting in summer.

Rafting

There are six rapids (class II-III) that you can shoot in wooden or rubber boats, the latter being more thrilling (and sometimes more spilling). There are several launches daily from May to October, departing from either the Ruunaa Visitor Centre area, or from the wilderness camps belonging to the three rafting operators. Prices are around €45/30 with/without lunch for a three-hour trip. Book directly with the companies or through Karelia Expert in Lieksa (p208) – advance reservations are definitely recommended. Transport can also be arranged from Lieksa if you book a tour, and there are packages that offer camp meals, smoke saunas or overnight accommodation too.

Koski-Jaakko RAFTING
(☏050-036 6033; www.koski-jaakko.fi; Yläviekintie 50) This place is a smidge cheaper than the other two rafting operators. Rubber rafts leave from the Koski-Jaakko HQ around 7km along Siikakoskentie (turn right immediately after the Naarajoki bridge). Trips in wooden boats (made by Jaakko himself) leave from the parking place at Naarajoki.

Lieksan Matkakaverit RAFTING
(☏040-708 5726; www.lieksanmatkakaverit.fi; Siikakoskentie 65) Offers rafting and canoeing trips, as well as a smoke sauna. Rubber rafts launch from Rannin Maja, about 8km along Siikakoskentie (turn right immediately after the Naarajoki bridge). Wooden boats depart from the Ruunaa Visitor Centre.

Ruunaan Matkailu RAFTING
(☏533 130, 040-035 2207; www.ruunaanmatkailu.fi) Offers rafting and can organise cottages in the area, plus skiing, snowmobile safaris and ice-fishing during the winter. Trips depart from Cafe Ruunaan Tupa, opposite the Ruunaa Visitor Centre.

Canoeing

Although 'rafting' and 'Ruunaa' are almost synonymous in these parts, another way to shoot the rapids is by canoe.

Erästely

CANOEING

(☎040-027 1581; www.erastely.fi) Organises guided trips down the rapids (per person €65), and gentler canoeing expeditions on the surrounding lakes and rivers. Erästely also offers equipment hire and excellent information on self-guided routes, and can arrange winter sled rides and husky tours.

Fishing

Ruunaa is one of the most popular fishing spots in North Karelia. Trout and salmon fishing is exhilarating in the numerous rapids, with quieter spots accessible along a long wooden walkway. Two prized spots are Haapavitja and Siikakoski, where fly-fisher folk have long snagged bites.

One-week fishing permits (€35) are available in Lieksa and at the Ruunaa Visitor Centre (p209). There is also a fishing-permit machine near the Neitikoski rapids. Fishing is permitted from June to early September and again from mid-November to late December.

Trekking

The **Karhunpolku** (Bear's Trail) passes through Ruunaa. You can pick it up just 50m north of the Naarajoki bridge – the path is marked with round orange symbols on trees. See below for details.

Around the river system and over two beautiful suspension bridges runs **Ruunaan Koskikierros**, a marked 29km loop along good *pitkospuu* (boardwalk) paths. If you have more time, there are another 20km of side trips you can take. Starting at the Naarajoki bridge, walk 5km along Karhunpolku to reach the trail. Another 3.3km brings you to the Ruunaa Hiking Centre (p210) where you'll find camping, cabins and a restaurant, as well as boat-, bike- and fishing-equipment hire.

🛏 Sleeping & Eating

There are 12 *laavu* (basic lean-to shelters) in the hiking area. Campers are encouraged to pitch their tents by the shelters, or at one of the 19 dedicated campfire sites. Camping

KARELIAN TREKS

North Karelia's best trekking routes form the **Karjalan Kierros** (Karelian Circuit; www.vaellus.info), a loop of 14 marked hiking trails (plus some canoe and cycling variants) with a total length of more than 1000km between Ilomantsi and Lake Pielinen. The best known are the Bear's Trail (not to be confused with the more famous Bear's Ring in Oulanka National Park) and Wolf's Trail, which link up in Patvinsuo National Park (see p208). You can walk in either direction but we've described them here from south to north. You'll need to arrange transport to the trailheads, including Patvinsuo National Park, in advance, although there is a bus service to and from Möhkö village, a former ironworks with a cheerful lakeside camping ground where the Wolf's Trail commences.

There are wilderness huts and lean-to shelters along the way, but it's advisable to carry a tent. Hire of hiking equipment can be arranged at Karelia Expert. Much of the Ilomantsi region is boggy marshland, so waterproof footwear is essential. For more information on these and other routes contact the Lieksa (p208) or Ilomantsi (p206) offices of Karelia Expert, or **Metsähallitus** (☎020-564 120; www.metsa.fi, www.outdoors.fi), the information office for the Forest & Park Service. You can book huts and cabins along the trail with **Wild North** (☎020-344 122; www.villipohjola.fi).

See also www.outdoors.fi for bags of information on hiking in Finland, and turn to the Great Outdoors chapter (p27) for general trekking tips.

Susilaival (Wolf's Trail)

The 97km Wolf's Trail is a marked four- to six-day trek running north from Möhkö village to the marshlands of Patvinsuo National Park. The terrain consists mostly of dry heath, pine forest and swampy marshland, which can be wet underfoot – in places, you'll need to haul yourself over water courses on a pulley-operated raft. This trail skirts the Russian border in areas where many of the battles in the Winter and Continuation Wars were fought. Early in the trek, at Lake Sysmä, you'll see a memorial and antitank gun. There are five lean-to shelters and three wilderness cabins along the route, and farm or camping accommodation is available in the village of Naarva. In the Ilomantsi wilderness area there are around 100 bears and 50 wolves – the chances of running into one are slim but not impossible.

and sleeping in a *laavu* is free of charge. You can book national park accommodation at **Wild North** (☏020-344 122; www.villipohjola.fi), Karelia Expert (p208) and Ruunaa Visitor Centre (p209).

Ruunaa Hiking Centre   CAMPGROUND €
(☏533 170, 040-579 5684; www.ruunaa.fi; tent sites €12 plus per person €3, cabins/cottages €35/100; **P**) Near the Neitikoski rapids is this centre, which incorporates a large cafe, camping area, kitchen, sauna, luxurious four- to six-bed cottages, and simple cabins. There are mountain bikes, canoes and rowing boats for hire and the *pitkospuu* (boardwalk) to the rapids starts near here.

Ruunaan Matkailu   COTTAGES €-€€
(☏533 130; www.ruunaanmatkailu.fi; Siikakoskentie 47; d from €30, cabins €40-100; **P**) Five kilometres east of Naarajoki bridge, this place has self-contained cabins, as well as accommodation upstairs from its cafe. It also offers a traditional smoke sauna, boats and various snowmobile, rafting and boating tours.

❶ Getting There & Away

There is a **shared taxi** (☏0500-675 542; €6) from Lieksa to Ruunaa, running twice daily on Mondays and Fridays only.

Nurmijärvi District
☏013

Known for its canoeing routes on the Jongunjoki, the Nurmijärvi area is wild and remote. **Nurmijärvi village** (www.nurmijarvi.fi) has enough services to get you to the Jongunjoki or Lieksajoki, or to the Änäkäinen area for fishing and trekking.

⚡ Activities

Canoeing
You can tell the waters are great round these parts, as canoe experts **Erästely** (☏040-027 1581; www.erastely.fi) are based here. It offers all manner of guided trips (from around €40), or you can hire canoes and kayaks (from per hour/day/week €10/40/110) and

---

If you do happen to meet a bear or wolf in the wild, back away slowly in the direction you came from.

Karhunpolku (Bear's Trail)

The Bear's Trail is a 133km marked trail of medium difficulty leading north from Patvinsuo National Park near Lieksa, through a string of national parks and nature reserves along the Russian border, including through the Ruunaa Recreation Area. Because of this accessibility, the trail can be walked, or even mountain-biked, in relatively short stages. The trail ends at Teljo, about 50km south of Kuhmo. You'll need to arrange transport from either end.

From Patvinsuo, the trail crosses heathland and boardwalks for 17km to the first lean-to shelter at Ahokoski, then runs another 9km to a wilderness hut at Pitkäjärvi. Four kilometres further, a short trail detours to the WWII battleline of Kitsi. The trail then heads northwest to the Ruunaa Recreation Area, where there are several accommodation choices and opportunities for fishing, canoeing and rafting.

Beyond Ruunaa it's around 30km to Änäkäinen, once a WWII battlefield but today a tranquil recreational fishing area. The trail follows the Jongunjoki through a peatland nature reserve on its final leg to the Ostroskoski wilderness hut, about 6km from Teljo. If you still have energy to burn, you might like to head back south to Nurmijärvi by canoe – if so, call canoe-rental outfit **Erästely** (see p211), which may also be able to help with transport from the trail end.

Tapion Taival (Fighter's Trail)

The easternmost trekking route in Finland, Tapion Taival gives you the choice of a 13km wilderness track along the Koitajoki, or an 8km northern extension across the Koivusuo Nature Reserve, or yet another extension north of Koivusuo to Kivivaara. The Koitajoki section is certainly the highlight – a stunning walk through epic wilderness. The path is marked by orange paint on tree trunks. You'll need a car and good local map to reach the trekking area, or you can negotiate at Taistelijan Talo (p206) in Hattuvaara about transport.

arrange transport to and from the beginning or end of a route.

The circular **Pankasaari Route** from Nurmijärvi village can easily be done with a free route guide, available from Karelia Expert (p208). It follows the Lieksajoki downstream to Pankajärvi, then rounds Pankasaari before returning to Nurmijärvi. There's almost no gradient and it's suitable for beginners. Only the Käpykoski might present a challenge.

The beautiful wilderness river **Jongunjoki** has nearly 40 small rapids, none of them very tricky. Karelia Expert in Lieksa (p208) has a good guide to the route. You can start at either Jonkeri up north (in the municipality of Kuhmo), further south at Teljo bridge, at Aittokoski, or even at Lake Kaksinkantaja. Allow four days if you start at Jonkeri and one day from Lake Kaksinkantaja.

Fishing

The Forest and Park Service controls fish quantities in three lakes in the Änäkäinen fishing area, 8km northeast of Nurmijärvi village, including some stocking of the waters. Fishing is allowed year-round, except in the first three weeks of May. **Kahvila Annukka** (②546 503; Nurmijärventie 154) has fishing permits (per day/week in summer €10/30). Permits are also available from the **Lieksan Retkiaitta** (②040-017 2226; Pielisentie 33, Lieksa) outdoor shop in Lieksa.

🛏 Sleeping & Eating

Jongunjoen Matkailu B&B €
(②040-094 9215; Kivivaarantie 21, Jongunjoki; beds per person from €35; P) This place is 2km from the main road towards Änäkäinen and the Russian border. There are four doubles and two four-person rooms, all decked out in clean, spare style. Prices include breakfast. You can borrow canoes and boat, as well as fishing or skiing equipment.

Erästelyn Melontakeskus HOSTEL €
(②040-027 1581; www.erastely.fi, in Finnish; Kivivaarantie 1, Jongunjoki; dm €28; P) The main canoe rental company, Erästely, also offers bed-and-breakfast at its headquarters – a former schoolhouse – with rooms sleeping four to 25 people. There's a cafe and it's a good place to hire equipment. It's also possible to pitch a tent.

Vuonislahti
☑013

The excellent countryside inn at this rural lakeside hamlet (little more than a train station in a field) makes it a good place to break a trip. A **war memorial** on a small hill across the road from the train station commemorates where the Finns halted a Russian advance in 1808.

The inn, **Kestikievari Herranniemi** (②542 110; www.herranniemi.com; Vuonislahdentie 185; dm €15, s/d €56/78, cabins €30-70, cottage €135; P) is about 2km south of the train station. It's a quaint 200-year-old farm with a restaurant and various accommodation (cheap dormitories, doubles, basic cabins and comfortable cottages), plus two lakeside saunas and rowing boats. There's even a range of treatment therapies such as massages, herbal baths (€12) and *turvesauna* (a sauna-cum-mud bath; per hour €25). To get to Herranniemi, walk straight from the Vuonislahti train station to the main road, turn left and proceed 500m.

Hotelli Pielinen (②045-264 0303; www.hotellipielinen.com; Läpikäytäväntie 54; hostel s/d €40/64, hotel s/d €60/88; P🐾) in Vuonislahti is a modern hotel in a peaceful location, with hostel and hotel room styles, both of reasonable value. It has plenty of facilities and can arrange activities including mushroom picking, fishing and snowmobile trips. In winter, the ice road across to Koli's slopes makes this a handy base for skiers.

There are two daily trains to Vuonislahti from Joensuu (€11.30, one hour) and Lieksa (€4, 20 minutes). If you're driving, take Rd 5871 to get there.

PAATERI

Don't miss **Paateri** (②040-017 5323, 044-331 1411; Paateri 21, Vuonisjärvi; adult/4-12yrs €4/2.50; ⊙10am-6pm mid-May–mid-Sep), a fascinating spot between Vuonislahti and Vuonisjärvi. Here you'll find the home and workshop of Eva Ryynänen (1915–2001), Finland's most respected wood sculptor – as well as her greatest work, **Paateri Wilderness Church** (1991). Carved flowers and animals adorn the beams, but the eye is constantly drawn to the great tree-root altar and the glass window behind it, which pulls the living pine trees outside into the building. Every bit of wood in Eva's home is embellished, and some beautiful sculptures are displayed in her workshop. The free guided tour gives insights and on the way out you can buy a birchwood postcard or stop for coffee at the carved cafe.

It's possible to drive to Paateri, but the trip across the lake makes for an adventure. In summer the country inn Kestikievari Herranniemi rents out boats (per day €30), which will take approximately 1½ hours to row across the lake. It also offers motorboat trips (per person €19) if there are enough takers.

Koli National Park

🖉013

The magnificent sweep of islands strewn through Lake Pielinen is the landscape equivalent of the Finnish national anthem. Though relatively small, the 347m-high Koli National Park inspired Finland's artistic National Romantic era (p331) with artists including Pekka Halonen and Eero Järnefelt setting up their easels here.

Accessible by ferry from Lieksa, Koli was dubbed Finland's first-ever tourist attraction and continues to draw holidaymakers year round. It is a winter sports resort but boasts hiking, boating and of course that impressive scenery in summer. While the lake views are panoramic and nature trails are enjoyable leg-stretchers, without the Finnish cultural context it could just be a pleasant pine- and birch-covered hill.

Koli was declared a national park in 1991 after hot debate between environmentalists and landowners, mainly about the placement of the hulking Hotel Koli on the hill. The area remains relatively pristine with over 90km of marked walking tracks.

The hill has road access with a short **funicular** (free; ☺8am-10pm) ride from the lower car park up to the hotel and there's also a longer **summer ski lift** (one-way/return €4/6; ☺10am-5.45pm Jul, 11am-5.45pm late Jun & early Aug) that sweeps you from the shore of Lake Pielinen up the east side of the hill to the same point. From here it's a brief walk to **Ukko-Koli**, the highest point and 200m further is **Akka-Koli**, another peak. On the western slope of Akka-Koli is a 'Temple of Silence', an open space for contemplation, complete with a stone altar and wooden cross mounted in the rock. Further south is **Mäkrävaara**, a hill that offers great views. For a slightly longer walk, it's 2.6km from Ukko to Koli village or a steep 1.9km walk to Satama.

Also at the car park, **Luontokeskus Ukko** (☎020-564 5654; www.ukko-kolinystavat.fi; exhibitions adult/child €5/2; ☺9am-7pm Jul, 10am-5pm Feb-Jun & Aug-Sep, 10am-5pm Mon-Sat, 10am-3pm Sun Oct-Jan) is a modern visitor centre with exhibitions on the history, nature and geology of the park, and information on hiking.

🏃 Activities

Koli is one of the closest ski resorts to southern Finland. Its two skiing areas open from 6 December until Easter, and basic hours are 10am to 5pm daily; book through **Koli Info** (☎020-123 4662; www.koli.fi; ski/snowboard hire per day €22, lift ticket per hr/day €20/33). **Loma-Koli** (☎010-762 3631), with four slopes, is more suitable for snowboarders and families; whereas **Ukko-Koli** (☎010-762 3630), with six slopes, provides a steeper challenge. There are more than 60km of cross-country trails, including 22km of lit track.

Koli Activ   WALKING TOUR
(☎688 7250; www.koliactiv.fi; two-hr guided walks from €16) Offers guided walks and skiing and snowshoe excursions for groups of over six, with saunas and meals as optional extras.

Koli Husky   DOG-SLEDDING
(☎040-712 0366; www.kolihusky.com) Offer winter husky trips; rates vary.

Matkailutila Paimentupa   HORSEBACK RIDING
(☎672 175; www.paimentupa.fi; Kotaniementie 1; 4hr rides €70, 1hr lesson from €30) Offers treks and lessons on Icelandic horses, catering to all levels of experience.

🛏 Sleeping & Eating

There are eight basic **cabins** (www.vaara varaukset.fi, in Finnish; 2-/4-/6-person €35/60/90) in the national park that can be booked through the heritage centre or via the website. To book other holiday cottages in the area, use Karelia Expert's **Koli accommodation service** (☎050-408 1051; koli@visitkarelia.fi).

🖉**Vanhan Koulun Majatalo**   HOSTEL €
(☎050-343 7881; Niinilahdentie 47; www.vanhankou lunmajatalo.fi; 1/2/3/4 people from €30/45/65/75, apt €80-120; 🅿) This environmentally conscious hostel set in the countryside 6km from Koli village is based in an old schoolhouse. There are eight rooms and two apartments – simply decorated, but nevertheless, you feel as though they're taken good care of. Facilities include a kitchen and smoke sauna.

Sokos Hotel Koli HOTEL €€

(📞020-123 4662; www.sokoshotels.fi; Ylä-Kolintie 39; s/d €109/129; 🅿@) Yep, this is the controversial place at the top of Koli Hill. Some rooms were in need of a touch of TLC when we visited, but with Finland's finest views, you won't be paying much attention to the decor. It sells out in winter when skiers pay higher rates for the comfort of four saunas and a hot tub.

Kahvila Kolin Ryynänen CAFE €

(Kolintie 1C; meals €8-16; ☉10am-5pm) Opposite the supermarket in Koli village, this pleasant cafe serves as an exhibition space and even has an artist-in-residence.

ℹ Information

In Koli village, **Karelia Expert** (📞045-138 7429; www.visitkarelia.fi; Ylä-Kolintie 4; ☉10am-6pm Jun-Aug, 9am-5pm Sep-May) is the tourist office and has a comprehensive range of information and maps plus internet. The village also has a post office and a supermarket, but the last stop for banks and fuel is Kolinportti.

ℹ Getting There & Away

BUS There are a couple of bus connections to Koli *kylä* (village) from Joensuu (€19.30, 1½ hours), changing in Ahmovaara (9km from Koli).

CAR If you're coming by car follow Rd 6 and turn off at Rd 504.

FERRY In summer the best way to arrive is by lake ferry from Lieksa (p208).

SHARED TAXI A **shared taxi service** (📞0100 9986; www.koli.fi; adult/child €25/12) operates year-round between Joensuu and Koli, with three taxis Monday to Friday and two at weekends.

Paalasmaa Island

📞013

Noted for its scenery, this is the largest island in Lake Pielinen and the highest in Finland at 225m above sea level. It's linked to the mainland by a free ferry, and bridges continue the journey through two smaller islands tucked behind it. The best view is from the 18m-high wooden **observation tower** 3km from the island's camping ground via a marked trail.

The ferry terminal is 15km east of the main road and the turn-off is about 2km north of Juuka. **Paalasmaan Lomamajat** (📞040-088 2008; tent sites €10, cabins €35-45; ☉Jun–mid-Aug) is the camping ground at the eastern end of the island. It's a nice lakeside spot from which to explore with a rowing boat (per day €10) or canoe (per hour €5).

Nurmes

📞013 / POP 8500

With wide birched streets and a small terraced Puu-Nurmes (Old Town), the Russian heritage of this town, founded in 1876 by Tsar Alexander II, is clear. Oddly, the biggest sight in town is a Sokos hotel restaurant. The imposing **Bomba House** (2.5km southeast of the centre), with high roof and ornate wooden trim, is a 1970s replica of a Karelian family house originally built in 1855 by Jegor Bombin, a farmer from Suojärvi, now in Russian Karelia. Surrounding it is **Bomba Village** (📞678 200; Tuulentie 10), a kitsch reconstruction of a Karelian settlement that has a cafe and craft shops.

Back in town the massive brick **Lutheran Church** (Kirkkokatu 17; ☉11am-5pm early Jun-early Aug) dates from 1897 and is the largest in North Karelia, with around 2300 seats. Inside are several models of Nurmes' previous wooden churches that burnt down, earning this part of town the name 'Ash Village'.

Nurmes' location at the northern tip of Lake Pielinen makes it an excellent base for dog-sledding, snowmobiling, ice-fishing and cross-country skiing from January to the end of March, and canoeing, rapids-shooting (at Ruunaa) and farmhouse tours from June to the end of August. Karelia Expert (p215) takes bookings (at least 24 hours in advance)

FINNISH STONE CENTRE

Learn everything you ever wanted to know about stone, and more besides, at **Suomen Kivikeskus** (Finnish Stone Centre; 📞020-763 6600; www.kivikyla. fi; Kuhnustantie 10; admission incl special exhibition €13; ☉9am-6pm Mon-Fri, to 4pm Sat, to 6pm Sun mid-Jun–Aug, to 5pm Mon-Fri mid-May–mid-Jun & Sep-Oct, closed Nov–mid-May). There's a permanent geological exhibition, plus temporary exhibits (glittering displays of diamonds and emeralds at the time of research), shops and showrooms, a small soapstone museum and an excellent cafe. Getting a photo in the sculpture garden's giant stone armchairs is almost compulsory.

The centre lies halfway between Nurmes and Koli. You can't miss it – it's a glaringly huge boxy building in the middle of this peaceful countryside.

for most services and has the latest details. You can hire a bike to explore town from **Kesport Konesola** (☑480 180; Kirkkokatu 16A; per hr/day €5/8), and this place can also arrange fishing permits for Pielinen and fishing trips. There's a good chance you'll hook salmon at **Lokinlampi** (☑040-573 5751; www.lokinlampi.fi; Lokinvaarantie 3; 3hr licence €10, 3hr boat rental €10), a stocked pond north of town.

Hyvärilä Holiday Centre and Sokos Hotel Bomba offer a huge list of high-energy activities.

🛏 Sleeping & Eating

The best places to stay are a few kilometres southeast of the centre.

Sokos Hotel Bomba SPA HOTEL €€
(☑687 200; www.sokoshotels.fi; Suojärvenkatu 1; s €100-140, d €125-165, apt from €160; P@🏊) Resembling an ocean liner, complete with portholes, this indulgent spa hotel contains a wellness centre, several saunas and chic rooms. The massive indoor pool is a feature of the breakfast lounge and other spa facilities can be used by nonguests (from €20). Set 200m from the main complex is a group of Karelian-style cabins refurbished as apartments, several with their own saunas. If you prefer adventure to pampering, onsite tour company **Metsänväki Oy** (☑687 2229, 040-096 6524; www.metsanvaki.fi, in Finnish) can arrange quad bike trips, canoeing expeditions and snowmobile safaris.

Hyvärilä Holiday & Youth Centre HOSTEL, CAMPGROUND €€
(☑020-746 6780; www.hyvarila.com; Lomatie 12; tent sites €10 plus per person €4, cottages from €42, hostel dm/s €11.50/21, hotel s/d/ste €74/92/107) There's something for everyone at this lakeside resort next door to the golf club – camping ground, hostel accommodation, a decent hotel and a restaurant, all managed by cheerful, helpful reception staff. Activities include a small swimming beach, tennis courts, golf, and canoe and boat rentals. The hostel is small but pleasant, with the bonus of access to resort facilities. The hotel has large, well-proportioned rooms... although some of the creaky furniture could do with replacing!

Loma Sirmakka APARTMENTS €€
(☑480 455; www.lomasirmakka.com; Tavintie 6; apt from €102) Each furnished apartment in this cluster has a full kitchen and laundry and makes a great option for larger families. Rates are cheaper for longer stays, and you can hire bikes, boats and canoes.

Nurmeshovi HOTEL €€
(☑256 2600; www.nurmeshovi.com, in Finnish; Kirkkokatu 21; s/d without bathroom €39/67, with bathroom €55/79; P) This central hotel offers some of the cheapest rooms in town and has a decent restaurant and a sauna. Staff are friendly, and the shared bathrooms have recently been renovated, but it's still rather fusty and in need of refreshment.

TOP CHOICE Bomban Talo KARELIAN €€
(☑678 200; Bomba Village, Suojärvenkatu 1; lunch buffet €18.50, mains €12-25; ⊙11am-11pm) This mammoth wood cabin contains the Sokos Hotel's famed restaurant – it's the place to sample a Karelian buffet. Try the variety of *karjalanpiirakka* (rice-filled savoury pastry) ingeniously designed to swab up *karjalanpaisti* (stew). The buffet is served until 7pm in summer, and the à la carte options (think rainbow trout and rosehips) are just as authentic.

ℹ Information

Karelia Expert (☑050-336 0707; www.visitkarelia.fi; Kauppatori 3; ⊙9am-5pm Mon-Fri Jun-Aug, 9am-4pm Mon-Fri Sep-May) Local information and bookings.

Post office (☑020-071 000; Torikatu 5) In Siwa supermarket.

Public library (☑040-531 4816; Kötsintie 2; ⊙noon-7pm Mon-Fri, 10am-3pm Sat Jun-Aug, longer hrs winter) Free internet access and a *Kalevala* collection in various languages.

ℹ Getting There & Away

Buses run regularly to/from Joensuu (€23.50, two hours), Kajaani (€21.90, two hours) and Lieksa (€11, one hour).

Trains run to Joensuu (€19.30, two hours, twice daily) via Lieksa (€7.80, 45 minutes). Buses and trains depart from just by the main square (near the tourist office); the train station is unmanned, so you'll have to buy tickets online before you travel or on the train.

West Coast

Includes »

Best Places to Eat

» Gustav Wasa (p234)

» Athens Palace (p231)

» Bucco (p225)

» Vanhankaupingin Ravintola (p240)

Best Places to Stay

» Hotel Kantarellis (p234)

» Hotel Astor (p234)

» Spa Hotel SaniFani (p241)

» Sokos Hotel Vaakuna (p225)

Why Go?

The West Coast offers 500km of charming seashore, along with historic towns and fantastic summer festivals. Tiny Kaustinen hosts the north's biggest folk-music affair, and hardworking Seinäjoki and Pori let their hair down at huge rock, tango and jazz festivals.

Heading north from Turku, the coast is lined with venerable old wooden towns like Uusikaupunki, Kristinestad and Unesco-recognised Rauma, founded at the height of the Swedish empire. The western shore still shares more with neighbouring Sverige (Sweden) than Suomi. Newsstands are packed with Swedish gossip magazines, Stockholm's radio and TV fill the airwaves, and you'll hear Swedish spoken almost everywhere.

Seaside Vaasa, known for its arty atmosphere and an island-full of kids' theme parks, is super-accessible by budget airline. The area is popular with families, boasting expansive sandy beaches at Kalajoki, and cosy holiday cottages dotting the dunes and woods.

When to Go
WEST COAST

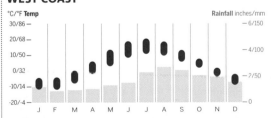

May Windsurfing season starts at Finland's most popular beach, Yteri.

Jun Water babies delight as outdoor waterparks open their slides and turn on the wave machines.

Jul Some of Finland's biggest festivals – Pori Jazz, Seinäjoki's Tangomarkkinat and Vaasa Rock.

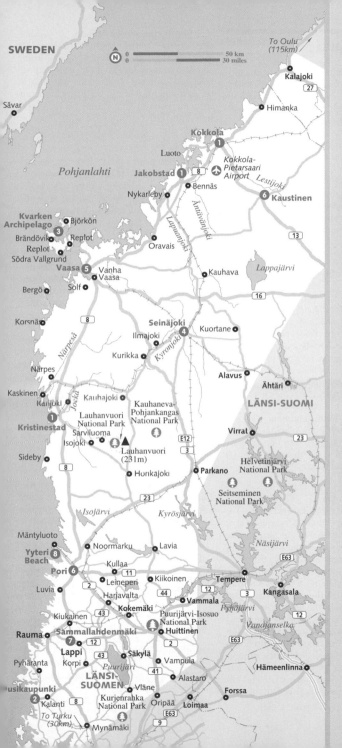

West Coast Highlights

1 Wandering the picturesque wooden Old Towns of **Rauma** (p220), **Jakobstad** (p236), **Kokkola** (p239) and **Kristinestad** (p227)

2 Paying your respects to genius inventor Per Bonk at Uusikaupunki's **Bonk Dynamo Centre** (p218)

3 Exploring the scattered **Kvarken Archipelago** (p237) by bike or canoe

4 Seeing a city as a symphony with Alvar Aalto's masterful town centre in **Seinäjoki** (p229)

5 Viewing modern art at Vaasa's impressive **Kuntsi museum** (p232)

6 Joining jolly crowds at Pori's fabulous **Jazz Festival** (p225), or pitching a tent at the fiddletastic **Kaustinen Folk Music Festival** (p239)

7 Letting the forest whisper you back to the Bronze Age at **Sammallahdenmäki burial site** (p223)

8 Paddling, windsurfing or flashing your bits in the naturist section – Finland's favourite beach **Yyteri** (p226) has space for everyone

Uusikaupunki

02 / POP 15,800

Sweet Uusikaupunki (*oo-see-cow-poonki*) has a name that means 'New Town', which is ironic for a town founded way back in 1617 and filled with historic wooden buildings. It's famous for the treaty of 1721, which quelled hostilities between Sweden and Russia after the gruelling Great Northern War.

Built either side of an inlet, the town's port was once a popular destination for smugglers...until the customs house was built in 1760. Today it draws a buzzing yachtie crowd in summer, while the local car-manufacturing industry brings in suited visitors all year-round.

◉ Sights

TOP CHOICE **Bonk Dynamo Centre** MUSEUM

(841 8404; www.bonkcentre.fi; Siltakatu 2; adult/3-14yr €6.50/3; 10am-3pm Mon-Fri Jun, 10am-6pm daily Jul, 11am-4pm Mon-Fri to mid-Aug) One of Finland's kookiest attractions, the Bonk Dynamo Centre traces the rise of the exceptional Bonk dynasty, who rose from humble beginnings to become the owners of a multiglobal industrial empire producing 'fully defunctioned machinery'. The creation of local artist Alvar Gullichsen, this spoof museum/art installation is a classic display of oddball Finnish humour. Kids can construct their own Bonk machines in the lethal-looking workshop – they don't receive wages, 'but neither are they charged for swallowed nuts and bolts'.

Vanha Kirkko CHURCH

(Old Church; Kirkkokatu 2; 11am-5pm Mon-Sat, noon-4pm Sun mid-Jun–mid-Aug) The lovely 17th-century Vanha Kirkko is one of Uusikaupunki's highlights: a pleasure to look at, and at the same time tremendously moving. Its star-speckled, barrel-vaulted roof was built to resemble a ship's hull – perfect for a town so reliant on the sea – and its interior has retained the original rustic furniture, right down to the coarse black biers along the north wall. Outside are the neatly tended graves of young Finns who died during the Winter War. The new church was built when architects suspected the original was unstable, and its construction practically bankrupted both the parish and the widow who commissioned RW Ekman's vast altarpieces.

Kulttuurihistoriallinen Museo MUSEUM

(Museum of Cultural History; 8451 5447; Ylinenkatu 11; adult/under 18yr €2/free; 10am-5pm Mon-Fri, noon-3pm Sat & Sun early Jun-Aug, noon-3pm Tue-Fri rest of year) This museum is set in a delightful house built by a shipping magnate. Ground-floor rooms are furnished in wealthy 19th-century style, while the attic is given over to the story of Uusikaupunki's maritime history.

Merimiehen Koti MUSEUM

(Seaman's Home; 044-351 5413; Myllykatu 18; adult/under 18yr €1/free; 11am-4pm Tue-Fri, noon-3pm Sat & Sun mid-Jun–mid-Aug, weekends only late Aug) Once a local sailor's home, this museum evokes family life in the early 20th century.

Luotsimuseo MUSEUM

(Pilot Museum; 044-351 5450; Vallimäki; adult/under 18yr €1/free; same hours) Ships sailing into town once summoned pilots from the tiny Luotsimuseo to guide them safely into port.

🏃 Activities

In July and early August at 11am, two boats run **day cruises** from Uusikaupunki to **Isokari Lighthouse**, one of Finland's oldest. The waterbus **Diana** (044-515 2502; adult/4-12yr €30/15) heads there on Tuesdays, Wednesdays and Saturdays, and the brigantine **Mary Ann** (040-010 2111; www.mary-ann.fi; adult/child €40/20) sets sail on Fridays and Sundays. Speedier 1½-hour rides to the lighthouse and back (adult/five to 15years €7.50/5) can be booked through the tourist office from June to mid-August.

A popular weekend cruise runs to **Katanpää Fort Island** (adult/four to 12 years €40/20). The *Mary Ann* sails at 11am on Saturday and *Diana* at 11am on Sunday.

FINNISH OR SWEDISH?

Just when you thought you'd got the hang of the double vowels of Finnish, you're in a part of the country that often prefers Swedish. You'll generally need to know both place names: Jakobstad, for example, generally sticks to its Swedish name, but if you look on the VR website (www.vr.fi) you'll have to know its Finnish alias, Pietarsaari. When you're in the area, a few basic Swedish phrases will help you connect with locals.

Charter boats and water taxis are also available for private exploration of the archipelago; contact the tourist office for details.

🛏 Sleeping

Hotelli Aquarius　　　　　　　HOTEL €€
(☑841 3123; www.hotelliaquarius.fi; Kullervontie 11; s/d/ste incl breakfast & sauna €99/119/175; P@☀) This large hotel is the choice for business travellers, with a fantastic setting in a park on the edge of town. Most rooms have sea views, and some were being spruced up with new beds at the time of research. Good facilities include tennis courts and a pool. Prices fall a little at weekends.

Gasthaus Pooki　　　　　GUESTHOUSE €€
(☑847 7100; www.gasthauspooki.com; Ylinenkatu 21; s/d incl breakfast €75/100; P) A good thing in a small package, this endearing granite building has only four rooms and feels like an old-fashioned inn. Rooms have a nautical theme in clean ocean blue, and come with private bathrooms. The twin is plainer and more businesslike, but still winning.

Santtioranta Camping　　　CAMPGROUND €
(☑842 3862; www.santtionranta-camping.fi; Kalalokkikuja 14; tent sites €13 plus per person €3, 2-/4-person cabins €45/60; ☉late May–early Sep) This picturesque seaside camp site with a beach is 1.5km northwest of the town centre. Simple cabins (linen not included) have kitchens with hotplates and fridge. You can rent bikes (per hour/day €3/15), rowing boats and canoes to explore the area.

Hotel Lännentie　　　　　HOTEL, MOTEL €€
(☑845 6100; www.lannentie.fi; Levysepänkatu 1; motel s/d €55/65, hotel s/d €75/89; P) Blank-eyed gamblers feed fruit machines in the lobby and carpets in communal areas are trodden grey: this hotel-motel on the road to Rauma has a downbeat feel, but it is the cheapest option in town. Rooms themselves are tired but serviceable and come equipped with a small fridge and fans for hot nights.

🍴 Eating & Drinking

The **kauppatori** (market square; ☉10am-6pm Mon-Fri May-Sep) is good for snacks and produce.

Juhla Pooki　　　　　　INTERNATIONAL €€
(☑847 7100; Ylinenkatu 21; lunch €9.80, mains €15-26; ☉buffet noon-6pm Jun-Aug, other areas lunch & dinner daily) Attached to the Gasthaus Pooki, this multilevel courtyard and indoor dining

SWEDISH ROOTS

The first sizeable party of Swedish crusaders arrived in 1155 at the village of **Kalanti**, about 7km east of Uusikaupunki. This wasn't a mere bunch of know-nothing knights. Led by King Erik himself, the party also contained Henry, bishop of Uppsala, who began the process of Christianising Finland. Kalanti's **St Olaf's Church** dates from the late 14th century and has sumptuous interior paintings, one of which records the historic occasion of Bishop Henry meeting a devilish pagan on the Finnish coast. This early medieval incursion marks the beginning of our knowledge of Swedish influence and rule over Finland.

A limited Monday to Friday bus service runs from Uusikaupunki to Kalanti (€3.70, 10 minutes); buses are marked 'Laitila'.

room has something for everyone. There's terrace dining, casual burgers outside and an à la carte menu. It's been given Slow Food Awards (the service can match sometimes!), and around a quarter of the dishes on offer are vegetarian-friendly.

Captain's Makasiini　　　INTERNATIONAL €€
(☑841 3600; Aittaranta 12; pizzas €8-12, steaks €18-24; ☉from 11am daily summer, evenings only winter) The converted red shop-houses just over the bridge contain four riverside restaurants. We've cited Captain's Makasiini here, but all four are decent places to sit back with a beer when the sun is out, and all do passable pizzas, burgers, steaks, nachos and other filling bar food – wander along the water's edge and see which one takes your fancy.

Pakkahuone Café　　　　　　CAFE €
(☑044-712 3500; snacks €4-9; ☉9am-8pm summer) The guest-harbour cafe offers coffee, cakes, ice cream and a small salad bar to its customers as they gaze covetously at all the shiny-shiny boats. The quayside terraced bar around the corner serves beer until late and sometimes has live music.

ℹ Information

Tourist office (☑8451 5443; http://uusikau punki.fi; Rauhankatu 10; ☉9am-5pm Mon-Fri, to 3pm Sat late Jun-early Aug, 9am-4pm

Mon-Fri rest of year) Free internet terminal and rents bikes (€3/15 per hour/day).

ℹ Getting There & Away

Uusikaupunki is 70km north of Turku and 50km south of Rauma. Buses to Turku (€12.80, 1½ hours) run from behind the kauppatori in the centre of town once per hour on weekdays, less frequently on weekends. There are five to eight buses per day from Rauma (€9.40, 1½ hours), some with a change in Laitila. Buses from Helsinki run via Turku.

Rauma

📞 02 / POP 39,700

Rauma's old town district, Vanha Rauma, is the big draw here – it's the largest wooden town preserved in the Nordic countries, and bears Unesco World Heritage status. It swarms with day trippers, but at night you'll have its cobbled streets to yourself.

The inhabitants of Rauma (Swedish: Raumo) are a distinctive bunch. As far back as the Middle Ages, Rauma's lace-makers ignored King Gustav Wasa's order to move to Helsinki to boost the capital's industry. Their stubbornness paid off: by the 18th century Rauma was a thriving trade centre, thanks to the European fashion for lace-trimmed bonnets. Locals still turn out the delicate material, and celebrate their lace-making heritage with an annual festival.

You might hear snatches of Rauman *giäl*, the local dialect that mixes English, Estonian, German and other languages that worked their way into the lingo from Rauma's intrepid sailors. Rauma remains an important shipping centre, transporting Finnish paper around the world.

◉ Sights

Vanha Rauma HISTORIC DISTRICT
(📞834 4750; www.oldrauma.fi) The World Heritage–listed Old Town in the heart of modern Rauma remains a living centre, with low-key cafes, shops, residences and a few artisans and lace-makers working in small studios. The biggest pleasure is wandering and browsing, so try to get here Tuesday to Friday when everything is open and the town thrums with life.

The area boasts over 600 wooden buildings, built in the 18th and 19th centuries, and each introduces itself by name – look for the small oval nameplate near the door. The two main streets are Kuninkaankatu and Kauppakatu, but meander away from them and you'll find several serendipitous spots. For a detailed history, pick up a copy of *A Walking Tour in the Old Town* from the tourist office.

Rauma

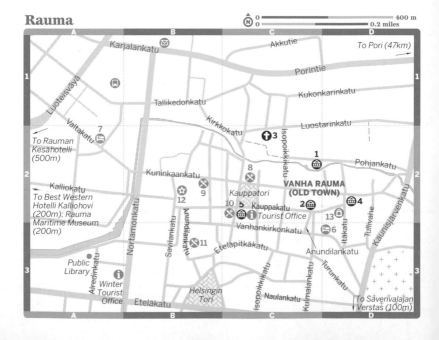

As with much of Finland, the **kauppatori** is the heart of old Rauma. Although there was recently a controversy about creating a covered area of the market, it remains a lively market square.

Rauma Museum   MUSEUM
(combined entry to 4 museums €7, single entry €3) Rauma Museum is divided over four sites. On the southern side of the kauppatori is Rauma's most impressive building, **Vanha Raatihuone** (Old Town Hall; ☑834 3532; Kauppakatu 13; ⏰10am-5pm daily Jun & Aug, 10am-5pm Tue-Sun Jun & Aug, noon-5pm Tue-Fri, 10am-2pm Sat, 11am-5pm Sun Sep-May), built in 1776. It now houses the summer tourist office and exhibits a few choice lace pieces and changing local history displays.

Down the road, **Marela** (☑834 3528; Kauppakatu 24; ⏰as per Vanha Raatihuone) is the preserved home of a wealthy 19th-century merchant family, furnished with antiques, wall paintings and Swedish ceramic stoves.

Towards the other end of the social scale, **Kirsti** (☑834 3529; Pohjankatu 3; ⏰10am-5pm daily Jul, 10am-5pm Tue-Sun Jun & Aug) is a lovable collection of lopsided wooden buildings, circling a little yard by the river. Inside, rooms represent different periods of the home's life right through to the 1970s.

Located outside the Old Town due to the fire risk, **Savenvalajan Verstas** (Pot-ter's Workshop; ☑044-793 3529; Nummenkatu 2; ⏰11am-4pm Jul) is a tiny museum that once made distinctive stove tiles. It provides an insight into this fascinating trade, and you can have a go yourself.

Pyhän Ristin Kirkko   CHURCH
(Luostarinkatu 1; ⏰May-Sep) North of the kauppatori is the bold stone Church of the Holy Cross, a 15th-century Franciscan monastery church much favoured for summer weddings. It has early-16th-century frescoes and several beautiful painted panels, a fine Prussian triptych from the 15th century and an ornate pulpit. On the north wall is Finland's oldest votive painting, an image of Margareta, a former mayor's daughter who died of the plague.

Rauman Taidemuseo   ART GALLERY
(☑822 4346; www.raumantaidemuseo.fi; Kuninkaankatu 37; admission €5; ⏰11am-5pm Mon-Thu, to 4pm Fri-Sun Jun-Aug, closed Mon Sep-May) Rauma Art Museum is larger than you think: its changing exhibitions of traditional and modern art stretch over two sides of a courtyard and two storeys. Allow an hour or two for a good look around.

Rauma Maritime Museum   MUSEUM
(☑822 4911; www.rmm.fi; Kalliokatu 34; adult/child 00/5, ⏰11am-5pm daily Jun–mid-Aug, noon-4pm Sun Sep-May) Wandering around the Old Town, it's easy to forget that Rauma is a port, so the Rauma Maritime Museum is a good reminder of the town's seafaring livelihood. As well as old photos and displays, there's a thrilling navigation simulator.

Torni   TOWER
(☑040-502 4351; www.taidekahvilatorni.fi; Vesitorni; adult/under 15yr €2/0.50; ⏰10am-8pm May–mid-Sep) The spectacular 360-degree panorama from the summit of Torni, a 70m-high water tower, would sooth the most savage breast. It's worth every step – although there's also a lift – and there's even a laidback little art cafe at the top.

Kiikartorni   TOWER
(☑834 3532; www.rauma.fi/museo; Suvitie; ⏰11am-6pm Jul) If you're view-hungry, Kiikartorni at the port is a pretty wooden copy of the observation tower that gave weather reports and shipping news to the town until the 1940s. It's a vision in itself, but it also affords a fresh perspective on the archipelago.

Rauma

◉ **Sights**

🛏 **Sleeping**

🍴 **Eating**

🎭 **Entertainment**

🛍 **Shopping**

✖ Festivals & Events

Rauma Rock
MUSIC

(www.raumarock.fi) June's predominantly Finnish rock festival.

Rauma Blues Festival
MUSIC

(www.raumablues.com) Draws in Finland's best blues musicians and a few international visitors for a weekend in mid-July.

Pitsiviikko
CULTURAL

(Rauma Lace Week; www.pitsiviikko.fi) Rauma's biggest event is Pitsiviikko, beginning in the last week in July, and celebrating the town's lace-making history. From the turning of the first bobbin to the crowning of Miss Lace, the whole town comes to life, particularly for Black Lace Night.

Festivo
CLASSICAL

(www.raumanfestivo.fi) A week of classical and choral music at various venues held in early August.

⌖ Sleeping

Best Western Hotelli Kalliohovi
HOTEL €€

(✐83881; Kalliokatu 25; s/d €89/139; P@) This modern hotel does well with business visitors. Simple rooms are furnished in dark woods, and have well-stocked minibars – and air-conditioning puts them to the top of the list on hot summer days! The restaurant has a subtle nautical theme, including portholes and plenty of seafood.

Hotelli Vanha Rauma
HOTEL €€

(✐8376 2200; www.hotelvanharauma.fi; Vanhankirkonkatu 26; s/d incl breakfast €125/150; P) Once a warehouse in the old fish market, this is now the Old Town's only hotel. Its 20 rooms embrace modern Scandinavian design with lino flooring, leatherette chairs, flatscreen TVs and views onto the park or courtyard. The service is lovely, and the restaurant is one of the best in Rauma.

Poroholma Holiday Resort
CAMPGROUND €

(✐533 5522; www.poroholma.fi; Poroholmantie; tent sites €10 plus per person €5, cottages €75-100; ☺May-Aug) On Otanlahti bay, 2km northwest of the city, this five-star seaside holiday resort bursts at the seams with sun-browned families, here for paddling, ice cream, theatre performances, handy boat trips and the onsite restaurant. Campers benefit from a brand-new shower block and great facilities (sauna, laundry, kitchen, and bike and canoe hire). The cottages are spick and span: the more expensive ones were built in 2010.

Maffi
B&B €€

(✐533 0857; www.hotelliravintolamaffi.fi; Valtakatu 3; s/d incl breakfast €50/75) The iron-shuttered sports bar downstairs looks off-putting, but don't be too dissuaded: rooms are private and double-glazed. At this price, the budget furniture and feel is to be expected, but rooms do come with small fridges, TV and some have private showers.

Rauman Kesähotelli
SUMMER HOTEL €

(✐511 8855; Satamakatu 20; s/d/tr incl breakfast €47/62/72; ☺Jun-Aug; P) Ten minutes' walk from the bus station, this summer hostel, based in an ugly concrete block straight from Stalinist Russia, actually offers spotless student-style accommodation. Pairs of rooms share a bathroom, TV and kitchen.

✖ Eating

Look out in restaurants and bars for Rauma's signature drink, Puksprööt – a juniper-rowan liqueur mixed with white wine and served with tar-infused rope!

Cafe Sali
CAFE, BISTRO €€

(✐010-423 3161; Kuninkaankatu 22; salads €9-12, mains €18-24; ☺9am-9pm) Step from Vanha Rauma's 18th-century surroundings straight into a loud, brash white space filled with giant photos of New York skyscrapers! Once you get over the shock, it's a real buzz – crowds of all ages, enthusiastic staff, salads and antipasto, a fine bistro menu in the cosy lounge next door, and a popular terrace on the square. English newspapers available.

Rosmariini
BUFFET €

(✐822 0550; www.rosmariini.fi; Kauppakatu 11; lunch €8-10; ☺8am-7pm Mon-Fri, noon-7pm Sat & Sun summer, 8am-4pm Mon-Fri winter) This winning lunchroom is decked out in traditional woods and throws on good old-fashioned belly-busting buffets that include salads, sweet grandmotherly pastries, house-baked breads and fruity pot roasts. The terrace out the back is relaxed given its closeness to the bustling kauppatori.

Wanhan Rauman Kellari
FINNISH €€

(✐866 6700; Anundilankatu 8; mains €16-22; ☺11am-11pm Mon-Thu, to midnight Fri & Sat, 1-11pm Sun) Looking for atmospheric dining? This ever-busy, good-value cellar restaurant also has a sun-drenched rooftop terrace in summer. Meals run to top-notch salads and the tastiest grilled salmon, with meat choices prevailing (poor vegetarians get only a single dull pasta option).

Kontion Leipomo CAFE €
(Kuninkaankatu 9; pastries €4-8, mains €8-14; ⏱7.30am-5.30pm Mon-Fri, 8am-3pm Sat, 11am-4pm Sun) A 50-year-old bakery bakes all the breads, cakes and pastries for this old-school place, which is so well known that it even has its own cookbook. Light lunches – soups, stews – are available, too. Enjoy them in the secluded summer courtyard or wrestle a teddy bear for a seat in the main cafe.

☆ Entertainment

Iso Hannu CINEMA
(☎822 5054; www.isohannu.fi; Savilankatu 4) This delightful independent cinema hosts its own mini film festival (www.blueseafilmfestival.com) in August.

Shopping

Pits-Priia LACE
(Kauppakatu 29; ⏱11am-3pm Mon-Fri, 10am-1pm Sat Jun-Aug, 10am-1pm Sat Sep-May) The venerable lace-making workshop, Pits-Priia, is the place to buy the town's distinctive bobbin lace. You can also watch it being made.

Information

Tourist office (☎834 3512; www.visitrauma.fi; ⏱10am-5pm daily Jul, 10am-5pm Tue-Sun Jun & Aug, noon-5pm Tue-Fri, 8am-4pm Mon-Fri Sep-May) Based in Vanha Raatihuone (the Old Town Hall) on the kauppatori in summer and at the Cultural and Leisure Centre, Nortamonkatu 5, in winter.

Getting There & Away

Between Rauma and Pori (€12.50, one hour), there are around two buses every hour Monday to Saturday, fewer on Sunday. From the south, Turku (€17.40, 1¾ hours) and Uusikaupunki (€9.40, 1½ hours) are connected by buses every two hours or so (fewer on Sunday). There are also direct services to Helsinki and Tampere.

Around Rauma

SAMMALLAHDENMÄKI

Vanha Rauma is not the only Unesco World Heritage site in the area. There's also the Bronze Age burial complex **Sammallahdenmäki** (close to Lappi village, 20km from Rauma), which dates back more than 3500 years. Thirty-six stone burial cairns of different shapes and sizes are spread over a kilometre of forest. The two biggest are **Kirkonlattia** (Church Floor), a monumental quadrangle measuring 16m by 19m, and the **Huilun pitkä raunio** (Long Cairn of Huilu), both of which continue to challenge archaeologists. The piles of stones themselves aren't much to look at, but the size of the site, the setting, and the absence of visitors create an eerie atmosphere that is hard to dispel.

The site is well signposted from Hwy 12 (which heads east from Rauma). You really need your own transport; buses to Lappi from Rauma run infrequently and on school days only.

Puurijärvi-Isosuo National Park

Puurijärvi, 65km due east of Rauma, is one of the best **birdwatching** lakes in Western Finland. The lake and surrounding marshlands have been protected since 1993 and are a favourite nesting site for migrating waterfowl of many varieties, totalling about 500 pairs in season. The lake itself can be reached by an 800m nature trail from the main road. A boardwalk makes a loop of the open marshland, where there's an observation tower. The *näköalapaikka* (viewing cliff) also offers a good general view. Visitors are required to stay on marked paths during breeding season, and camping is not allowed in the park at any time.

Pori

☎02 / POP 83,000

Try to get to Pori (Swedish: Björneborg, or 'Bear Castle') during the renowned annual jazz festival, which attracts 150,000 visitors and has the streets scatting for a week in July. The whole town buzzes with holiday joy, and the mood is infectious even if you don't know bebop from your own bottom.

After its burst of frivolity, hardworking Pori settles back down to business. The town is known across Finland for the Porin Olut brewery, which produces the Karhu (bear) brand. Domestically it's one of the most important deep-water harbours in Finland, as well as being a big exporter of lightning conductors, combine harvesters and oil rigs.

Sights

Despite being one of Finland's oldest towns, devastating fires (the last in 1852) mean that Pori has few historic buildings. The neo-Renaissance **Old Courthouse** (designed by CL Engel), the neo-Gothic **Keski-Pori**

Pori

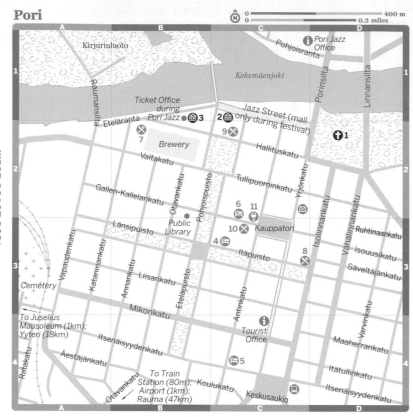

WEST COAST PORI

---

church with its cast-iron steeple, and the impressive red-brick **factories** over the water are the town's most distinctive pieces of architecture. Many holidaymakers come to bask on 'Finland's Riviera', Yteri, a fabulous stretch of beach 15km from Pori (see p226).

Satakunta Museum   MUSEUM
(☑621 1063; Hallituskatu 11; adult/7-17yr €4/1.50; ⊙11am-6pm Tue-Sun, to 8pm Wed) This excellent museum is laid out with care and imagination over three floors, with the omnipresent river and sea showing how water has shaped Pori's history. There are some fascinating exhibits, from intact Viking skis to a display showing how a handbag's contents have changed over the centuries. The upper floor explores regional customs and traditions by tracing a poignant journey from birth to death. Each floor has comprehensive English information in a box by the stairs.

Porin Taidemuseo   ART GALLERY
(Pori Art Museum; ☑621 1080; www.poriartmuseum. fi; Eteläranta; adult/child €5/2.50, 6-8pm Wed free; ⊙11am-6pm Tue-Sun, to 8pm Wed) The large white spaces of this modern art gallery house changing exhibitions by international artists – Andy Goldsworthy had just created a site-specific installation at the time of writing, for example. One room holds a small, permanent collection.

FREE **Juselius Mausoleum**   MEMORIAL
(Käppänä Cemetery; ☑040-030 9778; Maantiekatu; ⊙noon-3pm May-Aug) Very much a family affair, this place was built by FA Juselius, a wealthy businessman, as a memorial to his daughter who died of tuberculosis at the age of 11. The original frescoes were painted in 1898 by Finnish artist Akseli Gallen-Kallela (who had just lost his own daughter). After they decayed, Akseli's son, Jorma Gallen-Kallela, repainted them after his father's death.

Pori

◎ Sights

🛏 Sleeping

During the Jazz Festival accommodation books out up to a year in advance, and hoteliers send rates higher than the church steeple and just as sharp. The tourist office has a list of festival-only accommodation. Check the Yyteri beach options, which are not far from town.

Sokos Hotel Vaakuna   HOTEL €€
(☏020-123 4626; www.sokoshotels.fi; Gallen-Kallelankatu 7; r from €115; P@) It's easy to get lost in this labyrinthine place! But the town's grandest hotel is well placed, with reliable rooms (all with air-con) from this always-chic chain. Superior rooms have a few extras like bathrobes, and tea and coffee facilities. The restaurants and club make it a centre for local nightlife.

Scandic Hotel Pori   HOTEL €€
(☏624 900; www.scandichotels.com; Itsenäisyyden katu 41; s/d from €104/124; P@) Within walking distance of the bus and train stations, this place has older-style rooms that are fine, if a mite tired. It's definitely worth paying extra for the newly renovated superior versions, with flatscreen TVs, sleek bathrooms, jazzy halogen reading lights, and all-important air-conditioning for hot summer nights. Free bike hire.

Hostel Buisto   HOSTEL €
(☏044-333 0646; www.hostelbuisto.net; Itäpuisto 13; s/d/tr €38/50/72; P) Once one of the best beds in town, Buisto has been neglected and is starting to show its age. It still, however, provides decent value for money, with a modern kitchen and bright rooms that include washbasins.

✕ Eating & Drinking

Pori has few good dining options but plenty of bad ones – grillis and the usual fast-food suspects crowd out the kauppatori. The hotel restaurants are reliable.

Bucco   MEDITERRANEAN €€€
(☏622 6185; www.bucco.fi; Hallituskatu 22; mains €20-29, 3-/4-/6-course set menus €42/52/62; ☺lunch & dinner Tue-Fri, dinner only Sat) You won't find any overalls in this dashing Italian place, once an old brewery workers' canteen

WEST COAST PORI

PORI JAZZ FESTIVAL

Running over nine days in mid-July, **Pori Jazz Festival** (☏office 010-391 6000, advance tickets 010-522 3200; www.porijazz.fi; Pohjoisranta 11D; tickets free-€65; ☺8.30am-4.30pm Mon-Fri) is one of Finland's biggest summer events. The festival began in 1966 when local jazzsters ran a two-day event, with an audience of only 1000 people. These days the jazz festival has well over 100 concerts held in tents, outdoors, clubs or old warehouses – and over half of them are free. Performers – and thousands of visitors – pour in from around the globe, and hotels are fully booked up to a year in advance. Even the local football team is now called FC Jazz.

Although the emphasis is on jazz, other musical styles are included, so previous line-ups have included Carlos Santana, James Brown, Tom Jones and Seasick Steve. There are 10 venues, with the main arena being Kirjurinluoto Concert Park, on the north side of the river, where an open-air stage is set up for an audience of up to 25,000. Jazz Street, the closed-off section of Eteläranta along the riverfront, is where a lot of the action happens, with stalls, free concerts, makeshift bars and street dancing. A **ticket office** (☺8.30am-10pm) opens up inside Satakunta Museum during the festival – pop in to pick up last-minute tickets.

and now Pori's top restaurant. While it's decidedly Mediterranean, there's good use of local specialities like grilled whitefish served on risotto with a snap of pear.

Steak & Whisky House Galle   STEAK €€€
(☑648 2170; www.ravintolagalle.fi; Gallen-Kallelankatu 6; mains €22-30; ☺11am-midnight Mon-Thu, to 1am Fri, noon-1am Sat, 1-10pm Sun) The menu here is built around fillet steaks – topped with pastry, oozing with goat's cheese, braised in cream, pounded with peppercorns or nestled in a warm mushroom sauce. No one can claim that the restaurant's name is misleading. Did we mention there's a huge whisky selection, too?

Raatihuoneen Kellari   FINNISH €€
(☑633 4804; Hallituskatu 9; lunch from €10, mains €18-27; ☺lunch & dinner Mon-Sat) A little on the expensive side, but the location in the vaulted cellar of the town hall is atmospheric. The weekday buffet luncheon impresses, and there are solid standards (salmon with lemon butter) with a few international taste twists (chicken with coconut-and-chilli sauce) in the evenings.

Kauppahalli   MARKET €
(Isolinnankatu; ☺9am-5pm Mon-Fri, 8am-2pm Sat) This is a good source of pastries and picnic victuals. Look out for the local speciality, smoked river lamprey, an eel-like fish that killed England's Henry I when he gorged too many.

Beer Hunter's   BREWERY PUB €
(cnr Gallen-Kallelankatu & Antinkatu; www.beerhunters.fi; ☺11am-2am) An ale-lovers' paradise, this place has its own distillery and microbrewery. As well as selling its own beers, cider and whisky, there's a vast list of brews from other countries, and meals are available.

❶ Information
There are 24-hour luggage lockers at the train and bus stations.
Tourist office (☑621 7900; www.pori.fi, www.maisa.fi; Yrjönkatu 17; ☺9am-6pm Mon-Fri, 10am-3pm Sat Jun-Aug, 9am-4.30pm Mon-Fri Sep-Apr)

❶ Getting There & Away
Air
There are two to four daily Finnair flights between Pori and Helsinki (from €90, 40 minutes). The airport is a couple of kilometres southeast of the centre.

Bus
There are frequent direct daily buses between Pori and Helsinki (€39, four hours), Rauma (€12.50, one hour), Turku (€26.90, 2¼ hours), Tampere (€19.30, 1¾ hours) and Vaasa (€35.60, 3¼ hours). Some Tampere-bound buses require a change at Huittinen and take considerably longer.

Train
All trains to Pori go via Tampere, where you usually have to change. There are frequent daily trains (regional and Intercity) between Tampere and Pori (€17.10, 1½ hours), all of which have good connections with trains from Helsinki (€36.30, three to four hours).

❶ Getting Around
Local buses run from the kauppatori; route maps are available from the tourist office. These are handy for reaching Yyteri beach, but aren't necessary within the compact town.

If you're cycling, the excellent *Pori Pyöräilykartta* gives details of bike paths around town. Hire bikes from **Porin Kaupungin Vapaa-aikavirastosta** (☑044-701 1421; valinevuokraus@pori.fi; Isolinnankatu 12; per day €6; ☺8.30am-4.30pm Mon-Fri) or in the summer from **Luontotalo Arkki Nature Centre** (☑621 1176; Pohjoispuisto 7; ☺11am-5pm Tue-Sun).

Around Pori
☑02

YYTERI BEACH
The most popular beach in Finland, Yyteri beach (18km northwest of Pori) is a classic resort and very accessible from town. Six kilometres of yellow sand offer something for everyone. It's the nation's best beach for windsurfing, and the venue for the 2012 Raceboard World Championships; equipment is available for hire in summer. There are also lots of good stretches for family swimming, and even a naturist beach.

Beyond Yyteri, **Reposaari**, linked by a causeway to the mainland, has a pretty, wooden harbour village, which is a great place to wander around or enjoy a drink.

❏ Sleeping
The tourist office in Pori has privately owned villas that can be rented for short periods.

Top Camping Yyteri   CAMPGROUND €
(☑634 5700; www.yyteri.fi/camping; tent sites €11 plus per adult €4, 2-/4-person cottages €60/115) This large family camp site is on Yyteri beach, with great facilities including year-

round cottages, a restaurant, playground, minigolf, tennis, bicycle hire (€12 per day) and a laundry.

Yyterin Kylpylähotelli SPA HOTEL €€
(☏628 5300; www.yyterinkylpyla.fi; Sipintie 1, Yyteri; s/d €103/144; P🖭) Situated on Yyteri beach, the spa itself is good. Rooms are a mixed bag – newly renovated ones are pleasant, old ones are not worth these prices.

LEINEPERI

This venerable village was first developed in 1771 by the Swedish as a *bruk* (ironworks precinct) for making household items, and was in operation for about a century. Today it is a lively place, particularly on summer weekends. Attractions along the scenic Kullaanjoki riverside include the renovated **Masuuni ironworks**, a blacksmith's shop and some artisans' workshops. There's also the two-roomed **Museo Kangasniemi** (☏559 1551; Pitkäjärventie 8; admission €2; ◐10am-4pm Tue-Sun summer), devoted to Kaarlo Kangasniemi, the 1968 Olympic weightlifting champion.

Leineperi is on an unpaved road that runs parallel to the Tampere–Pori Rd 11. Buses between Pori and Kullaa stop at Leineperi; there are usually a couple daily.

Kristinestad

☏06 / POP 7160

Named for Queen Kristina of Sweden, this seaside town (Finnish: Kristiinankaupunki) is dominated by Swedish speakers and was founded in the mid-17th century by the maverick count Per Brahe. The town was once a booming ship-building centre and a port for shipping tar and timber out of Pohjanmaa, but these days it's a sloopy little spot, sustained by potato farming. Fittingly, in 2011 it became Finland's first 'Cittaslow' town, a movement that attempts to improve life by eliminating all traces of hectic pace.

◉ Sights

Old Town HISTORIC DISTRICT
The town itself is the biggest attraction – it's currently trying to gain Unesco World Heritage Site recognition for its rows of colourful wooden houses. In its heyday as a key port, travellers had to pay customs duty, collected at the **Old Customs House** (Staketgatan), a smallish rust-wood building dating from 1720, just along from the imposing town hall.

One of Finland's loveliest churches, behind the customs house, is the striking redwood **Ulrika Eleonora Kyrkan** (◐9am-4pm Mon-Sat mid-May–Aug), with its crooked shingled steeple. Built in 1700, it retains much of its original detail. The red-brick **New Church** (Nya Kirka; Parmansgatan; ◐9am-4pm Mon-Sat mid-May–Aug) has a high wooden ceiling and an archetypal church-ship dedicated by mariners.

Sjöfartsmuseum MUSEUM
(☏221 2859; Salutorget 1; admission €4; ◐noon-4pm Tue-Sun mid-Jun–mid-Aug) Sjöfartsmuseum was originally built in 1837 as a merchant's home to dominate the market square. Today it showcases Kristinestad's maritime heritage, especially ship-building, with reconstructions of a captain's cabin and a ship's helm.

Lebellska Köpmansgården MUSEUM
(Lebell House; ☏221 2159; Strandgatan 51; admission €4; ◐11am-5pm Mon-Fri, to 2pm Sat & Sun mid-May–Aug) Another affluent merchant built Lebell House, a block south of the market square. Dating from the mid-19th century, the museum gives an insight into upper-class life, including a baroque-styled salon with original linen wallpaper.

Carlsro Museum MUSEUM
(☏221 6343; Carlsrovägen 181; admission €4; ◐11am-5pm Tue-Sun Jun-Aug) About 5km north of town, the summer villa of yet another cashed-up merchant has become Carlsro Museum. If the collection of over 11,000 toys, bric-a-brac and other items from around the area doesn't impress, then there's always a wander in the idyllic gardens from the tsarist era.

Susiluola ARCHAEOLOGICAL SITE
(Wolf Cave; www.susiluola.fi) Heading east on Rd 663, you'll find Wolf Cave just before the village of Karijoki. This small cave is one of the most significant archaeological finds in Finland, with evidence to suggest that humans occupied this area more than 120,000 years ago, before the ice age. It's badly signposted – contact Kristinestad's tourist office for maps and information before heading off.

🛏 Sleeping & Eating

Hotel Leila HOTEL €€
(☏221 1164, 040-418 5185; www.hotelleila.fi; Västra Långgatan 39; s/d incl breakfast €95/125; P) Of the two hotels Café Alma runs in town, Leila is the newer of the two with bigger rooms;

WEST COAST KRISTINESTAD

it hosts the reception for both. Breakfast is served at a nearby cafe in summertime, and in guest rooms in winter.

Hotel Alma
HOTEL €€

(☏221 1164, 040-418 5185; www.hotelleila.fi; Parmansgatan; s/d incl breakfast €90/110; P) Sister hotel to Leila, this property contains the splendid tower suite (€155), a crow's nest with four-way views across the wooden rooftops and over the water.

Houneistomajoitus Krepelin
B&B €€

(☏040-066 1434; www.krepelin.fi; Östra Långgatan 47; d €80, d incl breakfast & sheets €100; P) This former sailor's residence does refurbished double rooms that include kitchenette and cable TV. They're tiny but ever so sweet: if you're curious about how it would feel to live in one of Kristinestad's little wooden houses, these will give you a taster.

Bockholmens Camping
CAMPGROUND €

(☏050-527 3356; Salavägen 32; tent sites €12, cabins €40-75; ⊘mid-May–early Sep) Just 1.5km southwest of the town centre, this small camping ground boasts its own beach and has bikes for rent. Cabins (shared bathrooms and limited linen) vary based on location and extras, but all have kitchenettes.

Café Alma
CAFE, RESTAURANT €

(☏221 3455; Sjögatan; ⊘7am-9pm Mon & Tue, to 11pm Wed & Thu, to 2am Fri, 9am-2am Sat, 9am-7pm Sun) Glass, wood and airy space epitomise this waterside pavilion cafe – that, and the amazing 8ft-long model of the barque *Alma* that dominates the dining room. There's an excellent summertime lunch buffet and à la carte dinner.

Vinkel
CAFE €

(☏221 1711; Salutorget; ⊘10am-5pm Mon-Fri, to 3pm Sat, plus noon-3pm Sun Jul) If it's cake you're after, Vinkel, diagonally opposite Café Alma, does homemade masterpieces.

Crazy Cat
PIZZA €

(☏221 3100; Östralånggatan 53-55; lunches €8.50, mains €11-18; ⊘11am-9pm Mon-Fri, noon-9pm Sat & Sun) This frisky feline is a cut above the other pizzerias, adding filling pastas and a generous lunch spread to make you feel like the cat who got the cream.

❶ Information

Tourist office (☏221 2311; www.kristinestad.fi; Östralånggatan 53-5; ⊘8am-4pm Mon-Fri, plus 10am-2pm Sat & Sun Jul) Free internet access as well as bike hire (€5/10 per three hours/day).

❶ Getting There & Away

Kristinestad is on Rd 662 off Hwy 8, 100km south of Vaasa. Buses between Pori (€20.50, 1½ hours) and Vaasa (€22.40, 1¾ hours) stop at Kristinestad.

Kaskinen

☏06 / POP 1430

Built on a strict grid system, Kaskinen (Swedish: Kaskö) is technically Finland's smallest town. It's also the westernmost town on the Finnish coast, with a large pulp factory and fish-processing plant to keep the economy going.

The main pleasure lies in wandering the silent streets of this sweet little town, puzzling over where the 1430 people are hiding. To help you, pick up the excellent brochure *Town Walk Through Squares and Parks of Kaskinen,* available at the guest harbour **tourist office** (☏0400-868 781; www.kaskinen. fi; ⊘9am-3pm Mon-Fri, 8am-2pm Sat early Jun–mid-Aug, plus 8am-3pm Sun Jul).

There are a few small sights, with limited opening hours. Restored **Bladh House** (☏220 7211; cnr Cneiffinpolku & Satamakatu), built by an 18th-century burgher, is solid and impressive with a trapezoid roof characteristic of the period – it's sometimes used as a concert venue. The **local museum** (☏222 7358; Raatihuoneenkatu 48; admission €2; ⊘2-5pm Wed-Sun Jun-Aug) re-creates a wealthy Finnish home from the 19th century, as well as a fisherman's cottage. At the northern end of the island, near Kalaranta boat dock, is a small **fishing museum** (☏040-504 2535; Sjöbobacken; admission €2; ⊘noon-4pm Thu Jul, plus 2-4pm Sat & Sun early Jul-early Aug), which includes smokers and other gear used to snag catches in the surrounding waters.

Mariestrand Beach makes for good swimming.

Kaskinen Music Summer (☏045-263 9011; www.musicsummer.info; concerts €15-30) draws in visitors over four days in mid-July, with classical concerts at Bladh House.

⬛ Sleeping & Eating

Options are limited.

Björnträ Vandrarhem
HOSTEL €

(☏222 7007, 040-541 7027; bjorntra@co.inet.fi; Raatihuoneenkatu 22; per person €20-25; ⊘Jun–mid-Aug) The chirpy owner was celebrating his 80th birthday when we visited, and had finally decided to retire! He hoped to sell the business as a going concern, and we hope he succeeds: its six twin rooms in a low wooden building are clean and peaceful, plus there's a self-catering kitchen.

Hotelli Kaske HOTEL €€
(📞222 7771; www.hotelkaske.com; Raatihuoneenkatu 41; s/d €79/95; 🅿) The village's only hotel is reasonably comfy with rooms that have large recessed windows. There's no restaurant, although the bar menu runs to seven snacks, including stir-fry, pasta, salad and toast.

Mariestrands Camping CAMPGROUND €
(📞050-595 6296; tent sites €12 plus per person €2, cabins €25-45; ☺May-Oct) Set on the tranquil northern edge of town, this small camping ground is right by Mariestrand Beach. There are a few well-maintained cottages, good plots to pitch a tent, and bike and boat hire.

Sininen Hetki PIZZA €
(Blue Swan; 📞040-583 2247; www.sininenhetki.com; Satamakatu 37; pizzas €8-11, mains €18-26; ☺11am-8pm Sun-Thu, noon-10pm Fri & Sat May-Sep, 11am-2pm Mon-Thu, 1-8pm Fri & Sat, 1-6pm Sun Oct-Apr) The Blue Swan is the liveliest spot in Kaskinen on a summer's evening, when birds of a feather flock to its waterside terrace for fine wood-fired pizzas and a pint of beer. There are also a couple of guest rooms here (double €30, with sauna €100).

Närpes

📞06 / POP 9430

Known as the tomato capital of Finland, Närpes (Finnish: Närpiö) has one of the highest populations of Swedish speakers in the country (93% Swedophone), with a local accent that has evolved into a peculiar dialect that wouldn't be understood in Sweden.

It's worth stopping for the impressive 15th-century *kyrkstallar* (church stables), built for parishioners who rode in from rural farms to worship at the medieval **Närpes Church**, a well-preserved wooden building with an atmospheric graveyard filled with Swedish names. There are over 150 stables, and they make a memorable sight, clustered together on a quiet hillside. Just 100m down the same road, **Öjskogparken** (📞050-350 6797; www.ojskogsparken.fi; Kyrkvägen 23; ☺11am-4pm Mon-Fri Jun–mid-Aug) is a collection of historic buildings, the marooned locomotive Kasköbässin, and an incredible outdoor revolving theatre, which gives summer performances in the local dialect.

Seinäjoki

📞06 / POP 57,930

Hardworking Seinäjoki (Swedish: Östermyra) is a commercial hub, with everyday tourism low on its list of priorities. Visitors are instead concentrated at three huge events – the Tango Fair, Provinssirock and Vauhtiajot – which bring in tens of thousands each summer. Seinäjoki is often overlooked by visitors hugging the coast, but anyone interested in unusual buildings should drop in to check out its town centre, designed by Alvar Aalto.

◎ Sights & Activities

Aalto Centre ARCHITECTURE
In 1951 Alvar Aalto won a competition to design Seinäjoki's civic and cultural heart from scratch, down to the last light fitting and door handle. The Aalto Centre, completed in the 1960s, is one of his most important works – a collection of icy white structures and green spaces that exemplify his modernist style.

You'll need to walk around the buildings to appreciate the space, balance and attention to detail. The fan-shaped **public library** is characteristic of Aalto's multilevel approach; the **theatre** foyer contains a series of his famous wooden reliefs; and the glittering blue tiled **town hall** curves like a wave (as 'aalto' means wave, it was almost a signature for the architect).

Over the road is Aalto's crowning achievement, **Lakeuden Risti Church** (☺10am-8pm mid-May–mid-Aug, noon-6pm mid-Aug–mid-May), recognisable by its oddly secular steeple-clock tower. You'll get a great perspective of the whole project by taking the **lift** (admission €1; ☺10am-8pm mid-May–mid-Aug) – the best bargain in Finland – to the top.

Civil Guard & Lotta Svärd Museum MUSEUM
(📞416 2734; Kauppakatu 17; admission €4; ☺noon-6pm Wed, to 4pm Thu-Sun mid-May–Aug, closed Sat Sep–mid-May) Also designed by Alvar Aalto, this museum houses a collection based around the Lotta Svärd women's voluntary defence force. Named for a fictional character in a JL Runeberg poem, these unarmed women took on military service during WWII and became one of the world's largest auxiliaries.

Provincial Museum South Ostrobothnia MUSEUM
(📞416 2649; Törnäväntie 23; admission €4; ☺noon-6pm Wed, to 4pm Thu-Sun mid-May–Aug, closed Sat Sep–mid-May) Five kilometres south of town

in the leafy suburb of Törnävä, the Provincial Museum South Ostrobothnia is an open-air museum based around the mansion of the wealthy Wasastjerna family. Local bus 1 runs from Seinäjoki bus station.

✯✯ Festivals & Events

Provinssirock   MUSIC
(✆421 2700; www.provinssirock.fi; 1-/3-day pass €65/112) This open-air international rock concert is held 4km south of town, near Törnävä, over three days in mid-June. International acts duel guitars with top Finnish bands from across the musical spectrum (David Bowie and the Black Eyed Peas have held the same stage as HIM and The Rasmus). There are four stages and connecting buses both from Seinäjoki and Helsinki.

Tangomarkkinat   DANCE
(✆420 1111; www.tangomarkkinat.fi; 5-day pass €95) Enormous crowds spangle their way to the international Tangomarkkinat. Held in early July, the first heels are kicked up at a huge open-air dance party in 'Tango Street'. Five days of dance competitions, tango classes and other festivities culminate with the crowning of the best tango singer as the Tango King or Queen.

Vauhtiajot   MOTORSPORTS, MUSIC
(✆487 2800; www.vauhtiajot.fi; 2-day racing/rock ticket €20/60) Bringing together revheads and rockers, Vauhtiajot features street racing and two rocking stages in mid-July. Past bands have included Iggy and the Stooges, and Thin Lizzy.

🛏 Sleeping

Book accommodation well in advance for Seinäjoki's major summer festivals; at any other time of the year it's easy to get a bed here.

Sokos Hotel Vaakuna   HOTEL €€
(✆010-764 7000; www.sokoshotels.fi; Kauppatori 1-3; s/d €129/149; ℗@) The reliable Sokos chain has two hotels in the city centre. Vaakuna is the better of the two, with peaceful top-grade rooms and smiling service.

Sokos Hotel Lakeus   HOTEL €€
(✆010-764 8000; www.sokoshotels.fi; Torikatu 2; s/d €115/139; ℗@) Also a member of the Sokos chain, Lakeus has stunning views across to the Aalto Centre, although the rooms themselves are due for a freshen-up.

Hotel Alma   HOTEL €€
(✆421 5200; www.hotelalma.info; Ruukintie 4; s/d/ ste from €79/89/120; ℗@) This well-appointed boutique spot has traditional wood decor and generously spaced (if rather dark) rooms with plenty of luxuries. It's popular with visiting business folk who enjoy the restaurant and terrace area for a post-deal tipple. Prices rise at weekends.

Omenahotelli Seinäjoki   HOTEL €
(✆055-520 7716; www.omenahotels.com; Kalevankatu 2; r from €45) Right opposite the train and bus stations, this reliable 'lobby hotel' has tight rooms favoured by people overnighting and getting early trains. Book online or on the booking computer in the doorway.

Törnävän Leirintäalue   CAMPGROUND €
(✆784 4120, 585 4146; Törnäväntie 29; tent sites €12, cabins €50-60; ☺Jun-Aug) South of the city centre, this camping ground is one of the most affordable. There are also temporary camping areas set up near the festival during Provinssirock, which cost €35 per person for the weekend or €15 for one night.

Kotikolo Jatta   B&B €
(✆040-559 3500; www.kotikolojatta.com; Pikkukuja 2; per person €30) A simple B&B offering homey comfort, just off Valtionkatu, 4.5km north of the centre. Eclectically decorated rooms (with shared bathroom) are full of odd knickknacks;

TANGO

Seinäjoki is the undisputed tango capital of a country that is certifiably tango-mad. In the rest of the world the tango craze was swept away by Elvis, but in Finland it never died.

Argentinean musicians and dancers brought tango to Europe around 1910. A Finnish version of tango developed soon after, championed by the composer Unto Mononen and Olavi Virta, the Finnish king of tango dancing.

No other music could better epitomise the melancholic Finn. If Finns lack the electrifying tension that Latin Americans bring to the tango, they lack none of the enthusiasm. Finnish tango music is usually performed with a live band and the lyrics deal with loneliness, unrequited love and desperation. It's fair to say that it's not as popular with the younger generations.

you can use the kitchen, lounge and washing machine (€2.50); and rare-breed hens strut in the garden. Breakfast is extra.

Perhehotelli Nurmela HOTEL €€
(📞414 1771; www.netikka.net/nurmela; Kalevankatu 29; s/d incl breakfast from €50/70; P) This good-value family-run hotel won't blow you away with its small sauna and modest rooms, but it won't blow the budget either.

✖ Eating

Aside from the pizzerias and kebab shops along Kauppakatu and Kalevankatu, and the reliable hotel restaurants, Seinäjoki has limited dining options, with a couple of notable exceptions.

TOP CHOICE **Athens Palace** GREEK €€
(📞5709 8070; Kauppakatu 1; mains €16-25; ☺lunch & dinner) The Athens Palace, serves Greek dishes with nods and winks at the Med. It opened in 2011 and became the instant darling of the town. Service is fast and friendly, the moussaka is rich and authentic, and the fab meze meal (€60 for two) makes hard-and-fast dish decisions unnecessary with its selection of 14 hot and cold starters, mains and puds.

Thai Ravintola Satang THAI €
(📞414 2144; Maamiehenkatu; mains €10-15; ☺lunch & dinner) Look out for the flower-filled window of this side-street place for a very meat-based (this is Finnish Thai after all) menu that includes favourites such as green chicken curry and fried pork with bamboo. This place is a spicy antidote to the winter blues.

❶ Information

Tourist office (📞420 9090; matkailu@ep-matkailu.fi; ☺9am-5pm Mon-Fri) In the bus and train station complex; book accommodation here in private homes during the festivals.

❶ Getting There & Away

The bus and train stations are adjacent and very central. There are buses to towns and villages throughout Western Finland.

Seinäjoki is a rail hub and has the fastest intercity trains from Helsinki (€48.50, three hours), with connections to Vaasa (€10.70, one hour), Jyväskylä (€20, three hours) and cities further north.

There are direct commuter flights Sunday to Friday to/from Helsinki (from €50 to €120 one way) with Flybe.

Vaasa

📞06 / POP 59,670

We're beyond the 63rd parallel here, so southern Finns class Vaasa (Swedish: Vasa) as 'The North'. But the city has three universities, a thriving art scene and has long been a popular family destination – it's anything but a one-reindeer town.

Just 45 nautical miles from Sweden, Vaasa embraces the culture of the country that's visible across the Gulf of Bothnia. A quarter of the population speak Swedish as a first language and you'll hear conversations in restaurants and bars switching deftly between Finnish and Swedish, often in the same sentence.

The 17th-century town was named after Swedish royalty, the noble Wasa family, although a mere 200 years later it had fallen into Russian hands. The old town burned down in Vaasa's Great Fire of 1852 – caused by a careless drunk trying to light his pipe – and the new city was built from scratch, 7km away from the cinders.

◉ Sights & Activities

Vaasa has a thriving art scene. Look out for public art as you wander the streets, especially Finland's 'Statue of Liberty' (1938) by Yrjö Liipola in the kauppatori. Two older works of art are Vaasa's impressive churches, the neo-Gothic **Vaasa Church** (Kirkkopuistikko; ☺10am-6pm Tue-Fri Jun–mid-Aug, 1-3pm Tue-Fri rest of year) and the icon-filled **Orthodox Church** (Barracks Sq; ☺2.15-4.15pm Mon-Fri Jul), both worth a look if you're passing.

Vaskiluoto ISLAND
The island of Vaskiluoto is a big holiday destination for Finnish families, with beaches, boating, a popular camping ground and **Wasalandia Amusement Park** (📞020-796 1200; www.wasalandia.fi; day pass €18, with Tropiclandia €35; ☺11am to 5pm or 7pm mid-Jun–mid-Aug), a great one for preteens.

Nearby is **Tropiclandia** (📞020-796 1300; www.tropiclandia.fi; admission €21, with Wasalandia €35; ☺outdoor waterpark 10am-7pm mid-Jun–mid-Aug, indoor spa & pools 10am-8pm Mon-Thu, to 9pm Fri & Sat, to 3pm Sun year-round), with enough water slides, wave machines, jacuzzis, saunas and spa treatments to keep both kids and adults happy.

The **Lilliputilla** (per person €5, family €15; ☺10.30am to 4.30pm) street train runs hourly from the market square to this island of delights from late June to early August.

Vaasa

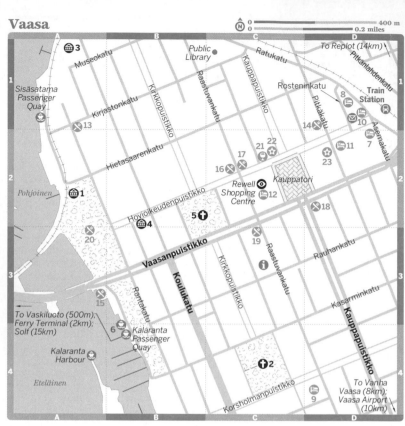

Pohjanmaan Museo and
Terranova
MUSEUM

(☑325 3800; www.museo.vaasa.fi; Museokatu 3; admission €5, Wed free; ◷noon-5pm Tue & Thu-Sun, to 8pm Wed) Vaasa's dynamic, modern museum is divided into three sections. Downstairs in the **Terranova** section there's a brilliant evocation of the region's natural history – complete with dioramas and storm-and-lightning effects – that includes information on the Kvarken Archipelago (see p237). On the ground floor, yesteryear Vaasa is brought to life with artefacts and audio in the **Pohjanmaan Museo** (Ostrobothnian Museum): particularly interesting are the sections on its violent past – in the 17th century, Vaasa was the most lawless town in Finland. The 2nd floor contains the **Hedman collection** (◷2-3pm Tue-Sat), with 300 works of art, including a Tintoretto, a Botticelli Madonna,

works from all the Finnish masters, and a huge number of ceramics.

Kuntsi
ART GALLERY

(☑325 3920; http://kuntsi.vaasa.fi; Sisäsatama; admission €6, Fri free; ◷11am-5pm Tue, Wed & Fri-Sun, to 8pm Thu) The fantastic Kuntsi houses changing exhibitions of pop art, kinetic art, surrealism and postmodernism in a beautiful gallery space that was once the customs house. At the root of the gallery is the collection of Simo Kuntsi, who gathered almost a thousand modern Finnish works from the 1950s onwards.

Tikanojan Taidekoti
ART GALLERY

(Tikanoja Art Gallery; ☑325 3916; www.tikanojan taidekoti.fi; Hovioikeudenpuistikko 4; adult/under 18yr €6/free; ◷11am-4pm Tue-Sat, noon-5pm Sun) This gallery features a strong international collection, including work by Degas, Gauguin, Matisse and Picasso.

Vaasa

Stundars Handicraft Village   MUSEUM
(☑344 2200; www.stundars.fi; adult/child €5/2; ◷11am-5pm Jul–mid-Aug) In the attractive village of Solf (Finnish: Sulva), about 15km outside Vaasa, is a fine open-air museum and crafts centre. It boasts 60 traditional wooden buildings that were moved here from surrounding villages, including crofts, cottages and cowsheds, a pottery, windmills and a schoolhouse. There's a humming calendar of events in summer, from markets to craft demonstrations. The entrance fee includes a guided tour. Buses are a pain: you really need your own transport or a taxi.

Vanha Vaasa   HISTORIC DISTRICT
Vaasa's Old Town developed around the harbour, 7km southeast of the modern centre, but was abandoned after the 1852 fire. Today it's a quiet suburb with little to see, although the grand **Court of Appeal** (built in 1776) is an impressive piece of architecture: it now serves as **Korsholm Church** (◷9am-4pm Mon-Fri Jun-Aug). There's also a ruined **medieval church** and **Vanhan Vaasan museo** (☑356 7087; Kauppiaankatu 10; admission €3; ◷11am-5pm Thu-Sun mid-May–mid-Aug), a former merchant's home with rooms decor-ated in 18th-century bourgeois style.

Buses 7 and 9 run hourly between Vanha Vaasa and the town centre weekdays (less frequently on weekends).

Tours

M/S Tiira   BOAT
(☑050-553 1236; www.jannensaluuna.com; adult/under 12yr €15/7; ◷departs noon & 3.30pm late Jun–mid-Aug) M/S *Tiira* cruises the Vaasa archipelago to Kuusisaari, departing from Kalaranta passenger quay. The cruise lasts about 3½ hours, with a lunch stop (food not included) at **Janne's Saloon** (light lunch €10, mains €20-28), a restaurant owned by the same outfit.

✦✦ Festivals & Events

Vaasa Choirfestival   MUSIC
(☑325 3745; www1.vaasa.fi/choirfestival) Showcases Finland's best choirs in atmospheric venues for five days in May.

Vaasa Rock Festival   MUSIC
(www.rocknrollcircus.fi; 2-day pass €60) The Vaskiluoto shoreline reverberates to Vaasa Rock Festival, a two-day festival held in mid-July and attracting mostly Finnish and Swedish bands.

Korsholm Music Festival   MUSIC
(☑322 2390; www.korsholmmusicfestival.fi) This international chamber music festival is held in early August.

🛏 Sleeping

Many families opt for packages with Wasalandia Amusement Park (see p231).

TOP CHOICE **Hotel Kantarellis** HOTEL €€

(☑357 8100; www.hotelkantarellis.fi; Rosteninkatu 6; s/d €120/140; @) A relief from the big, bland chain hotels, this place has style and superb facilities – every room has a private sauna, and most have jacuzzis and air-conditioning. The decor is dramatically dark, with spotlit nature-themed photos above the bed – it might not appeal to everyone, but we liked the tongue-in-cheek noir. Solid soundproofing means you won't hear your neighbours' giant flatscreen TV set. Parking extra.

Hotel Astor HOTEL €€

(☑326 9111; www.astorvaasa.fi; Asemakatu 4; s €85-124, d €100-143, d with private sauna €121-164; P @) This great little business hotel (the handiest for trains and buses) has a personal feel, from the fresh-baked cakes at breakfast to the cheery staff. It's traditional in style with a historic interior, and rooms in the older wing feature polished floors and dark-wood furnishings. Better rooms have their own microsauna. Three parking spaces.

Sokos Vaakuna HOTEL €€

(☑020-123 4671; Rewell Centre; s/d €120/140; P @) This property has well-appointed, spacious rooms with clever Scandinavian design. It's right in the middle of the action, and the excellent rooftop bar and attached restaurants make it a good place for a metro minibreak. On the flipside, the nightclub noise can bother early sleepers.

Omenahotelli HOTEL €

(020-771 6555; www.omenahotelli.fi; Hovioikeuden-puistikko 23; r €60-90) With only 34 rooms, this is one of the smaller hotels in this internet-booking chain (you can also book using the terminal in the foyer). Rooms are newish, with a twin bed and fold-out couch that can accommodate a couple for the same price. Internet access and breakfast at a nearby cafe are optional extras.

Radisson Blu Royal Hotel HOTEL €€

(☑020-123 4720; www.radissonsas.com; Hovioikeudenpuistikko 18; s/d/ste €120/140/225; P @ ☒) The biggest and boldest hotel in Vaasa traverses the road between with an underground tunnel in a complex that includes an Irish pub, restaurants, a nightclub and a rooftop pool. Rooms are functional and unsurprising – some are definitely showing their age – but contain everything you need, and suites come with their own cosy saunas and coffee machines. Parking extra.

Kenraali Wasa Hostel HOSTEL €

(☑040-066 8521; www.kenraaliwasahostel.com; Korsholmanpuistikko 6-8; s/d/tr €50/60/65; P) This former military base, now a hostel, is guarded by quirky rusted soldiers. It's in a quiet spot, with most rooms looking onto a grassy courtyard hopping with bunnies – internal noise can be disturbing, though, as rooms are not too well soundproofed. There's a self-catering kitchen and a couple of free bikes.

Top Camping Vaasa CAMPGROUND €

(☑020-796 1255; www.topcamping.fi/vaasa; Niemeläntie; tent sites €12 plus per person €7, 4-person cabins €68; ☉late Jun–mid-Aug) This good family getaway is 2km from town on the green edge of Vaskiluoto. It rents bicycles and boats, with packages that include discounts for Tropiclandia and Wasalandia Amusement Park. Cabins must be booked for a minimum two-night stay.

✖ Eating

Cheap grillis (fast-food outlets) encircle the kauppatori and Rewell Shopping Centre, with quick snacks and market goodies available at the **kauppahalli** (Kauppapuistikko; ☉8am-5pm Mon-Fri, 9am-4pm Sat).

TOP CHOICE **Gustav Wasa** FINNISH €€€

(☑466 3208; Raastuvankatu 24; mains €28-34; ☉dinner Mon-Sat) This underground restaurant is one of Finland's best, with a concise gourmet menu that blends classic Finnish with modern cuisine such as reindeer on tangy risotto. Once a coal cellar, the transformation to suave restaurant is achieved through low lighting and attentive service. The seven-course tasting menu lets you experience the very best of the restaurant's dishes.

Bacchus FINNISH €€€

(☑010-470 6200; www.bacchus.fi; Rantakatu 4; mains €24-32; ☉dinner Tue-Sat) In a golden wooden building not far from the water, Bacchus has a well-chosen menu that could include slow-baked hare with potato terrine or fillet of reindeer with juniper-and-apple gravy, according to the season. The rustic brickwork interior is warmed by animal skins. As you'd expect from a place named for the Greek god of boozing, the wine cellar is exceptional.

Strampen INTERNATIONAL €€

(☑041-451 4512; Rantakatu 6, Sisäsatama; mains €16-26, lunch buffets €8.50-11.50; ☉lunch & dinner daily May-Aug, lunch & dinner Mon-Fri, dinner

Sat Sep-Dec) This favourite in a 19th-century waterside pavilion manages to do top-end meals inside and affordable burgers and pastas for drinkers on its harbourside terrace. Both clienteles are happy, and staff keep the outdoor bar pumping until late.

Loftet CAFE €
(☑318 5314; www.loftet.fi; Raastuvankatu 28; cakes €3-6, lunches €6-12; ☺10am-5pm Mon-Fri, to 3pm Sat) This cafe-cum-craft shop has a beautiful oak-panelled dining room, where you can sample cakes and coffee in 19th-century style. It's a relaxed lunch spot that does good vegetarian-friendly soups and salads. The adjoining craft shop has great jewellery and linen gifts.

Faros FINNISH €€
(☑312 6411; Kalaranta; snacks €9-12, mains €20-28; ☺dinner Mon-Fri, lunch & dinner Sat & Sun summer) Moored in Kalaranta Harbour south of the bridge, Faros makes for an atmospheric bite: try the salmon soup with a dollop of mousse or the beef steak and reindeer tournedos. Once your dinner's settled down, there is frequent live music and dancing on the pier.

Don Abbe Deli DELI €
(☑312 3323; Pitkäkatu 34; lunches €5-7; ☺10am-3pm Mon-Fri) This likeable little Mediterranean lunch spot does good paella, salads and lasagne. Look out for the panini and salad deal (€6.50), a healthy alternative to the grillis and pizzerias.

Kaffehuset August CAFE €€
(☑320 0555; www.kaffehusetaugust.fi; Hovioikeudenpuistikko 13; mains €17-24; ☺9am-11pm Mon-Fri, 11am-11pm Sat) This wonderfully central spot attracts an older crowd with Swedish pastries and sandwiches for lunch, and more substantial dinners such as plank-grilled salmon on a bed of horseradish and mussels. Thanks to its summer terrace, it's ideal if you like your coffee served with a side of people-watching.

🍷 Drinking & Entertainment

Sky NIGHTCLUB
(Sokos Vaakuna, Rewell Centre; ☺Wed, Fri & Sat 10pm-4am) Great views of the city are a big part of this popular bar's appeal. Friday and Saturday feature DJs (entrance €7) and the terraces are always relaxing. Don't drink too much, though, as the zippy lift could leave your stomach on the 9th floor.

Fontana NIGHTCLUB
(www.fontanaclub.com; Hovioikeudenpuistikko 15; ☺10am-4pm Wed-Sat) With six bars and two dance floors, this dressy place is one of the biggest clubs in town. The main room features current dance hits, while things get retro in the Bank Club. A large summer terrace lets you get a gulp of air between bouts of boogieing.

Doo-bop Club JAZZ CLUB
(www.doobop.fi; Kauppapuistikko 12; admission €8; ☺9pm-2am Fri & Sat) This joint swings with live jazz, funk and soul in a suitably dark bar that attracts a 30-plus crowd. Periodic jam sessions are not unheard of – join in, if you've packed your clarinet.

Kino City Gloria CINEMA
(☑312 7113; Hovioikeudenpuistikko 16; tickets €9.90) A swish five-screen cinema showing all the latest releases.

❶ Information

There are left-luggage lockers (€3) at the bus/train station.

Main post office (Hovioikeudenpuistikko 23A; ☺8am-7pm Mon-Fri)

Tourist office (☑325 1145; www.visitvaasa.fi; Raastuvankatu 30; ☺9am-6pm Mon-Fri, 10am-6pm Sat & Sun Jun Aug, 9am 4pm Mon Fri Sep-May; @) Books accommodation, rents bikes and has internet access.

❶ Getting There & Away

Air
Finnair (www.finnair.com), **SAS** (www.flysas.com) and budget operator **Blue1** (www.blue1.com) all have frequent daily flights from Vaasa to Helsinki and Stockholm.

Boat
From late June to early August there are daily ferries (adult/car/bicycle €65/70/6, 4½ hours) between Vaasa and the Swedish town of Umeå (Finnish: Uumaja) with **RG Lines** (☑0207-716 810; www.rgline.com). Check the website for departure times; online bookings are also cheaper. The ferry terminal is on the western side of Vaskiluoto.

Bus
There are frequent buses from Helsinki (€46.90, 7½ hours) and Turku (€56.10, six hours), most with changes in Pori or Tampere. Buses run up and down the west coast pretty much hourly from Monday to Friday.

Train

Vaasa trains connect via Seinäjoki (€10.70, 50 minutes, up to eight daily) to main-line destinations such as Tampere (€35.10, 2½ hours) and Helsinki (€54.90, four to five hours).

❶ Getting Around

The airport is situated 12km southeast of the centre; local buses pass by Monday to Friday (one way €2.90). A **taxi** (☑100 411) costs about €25.

Avis (☑0500-864 835; www.avis.fi) and **Budget** (☑050-563 9944; www.budget.fi) both have offices at the train station.

Bicycles can be rented at the tourist office, Top Camping Vaasa (see p234) or **Bikes A Viertola** (☑317 1423; Kauppapuistikko 28; ⊙10am-5pm Mon-Fri, to 1pm Sat) for around €5 to €10 per day.

Jakobstad

☑06 / POP 19,660

Over half the population are Swedish-speaking in Jakobstad (Finnish: Pietarsaari), making it the unofficial capital of *Parallelsverige* (Parallel Sweden). Give yourself a day or two to investigate the well-preserved historic Skata area and the town's interesting museums (including one devoted to chicory coffee), and to make the most of the old harbour and pretty beaches further west.

The town's name comes from Swedish war hero Jacob de la Gardie, whose widow Ebba Braha founded Jakobstad in 1652, naming it in her husband's memory. Jakobstad is also the birthplace of Finland's national poet, JL Runeberg, though surprisingly little fuss is made of the fact.

◎ Sights & Activities

Skata HISTORIC DISTRICT

Stretching for several blocks north of the new town, Skata, the old town of Jakobstad, has around 300 of the best-preserved wooden houses in Finland. Most were built in the 19th century and were originally occupied by sailors. While the 18th-century houses along Hamngatan are the oldest, the prettiest street is Norrmalmsgatan. You enter through an ornamental entranceway, with a stunning clock tower bridging the street. Most of the old town remains residential so it feels refreshingly untouristy.

Aspegrens Trädgård Rosenlund GARDENS

(Aspegren's Gardens; ☑724 3101, 0400-541 073; www.aspegrenstradgard.net; Masaholmsvägen 1; admission €3; ⊙11am-5pm Tue-Sat Jun-Aug) A

Jakobstad Ⓝ 0 —— 300 m / 0 —— 0.15 miles

Jakobstad

◎ Sights
1 Jakobstadsmuseum............................A3

⊜ Sleeping
2 Hostel Lilja.......................................A3
3 Hotel Epoque....................................B2
4 Jugend Home Hotel & Guest
    Home..B2
5 Stadshotellet...................................B2
6 Westerlund Resandehem..................B1

⊗ Eating
    After Eight...................................(see 2)
7 Café Konditori Frederika...................A2

little walled oasis lies 1km southeast of the kauppatori. Aspegren's Gardens was created by priest Gabriel Aspegren in the 1700s, and is one of the oldest rectory gardens in Finland. Butterflies and winged berry thieves flit around the formal flower beds, a tiny rose garden bursts with scent, and horses and sheep chomp grass in the paddock. The rectory outbuildings hold the **hembygdsmuseum** (☑050-378 4242), which is crammed with sleighs, agricultural equipment and hunting traps. The orangery cafe uses produce from the gardens.

Gamla Hamn HARBOUR

The old harbour has a child-friendly swimming beach and a small waterpark **Fanta-Sea** (☎040-042 3204; www.fantasp.fi; admission €7; ☺11am-6pm Jun-Aug), with outdoor swimming pool and water slides.

The harbour also boasts the pride of Jakobstad, **Jacobstads Wapen**, a modern replica of a beautiful 18th-century galleon. Unfortunately, the ship has been beset by problems over the last five years, from rotten timbers to a leaking propeller, but should be out of the repair yard and sailing from the harbour again by 2012.

FREE Chicory Museum MUSEUM

(☎040-585 2152; Alholmen; ☺noon-5pm Tue-Sat Jun & Jul) Of Jakobstad's eclectic collection of small private museums, our favourite is the Chicory Museum, based in a 19th-century chicory factory 3km north of town, where the herb was processed into the coffee substitute 'Kaffino'. The factory was built by local entrepreneur/maverick Wilhelm Schauman, who designed most of the machinery himself. Tours of the factory are fascinating, and guides can chat about the contemporary art exhibitions that are staged here every year.

Motormuseum MUSEUM

(☎724 4500; Alholmsvägen 71; adult/under 12yr €5/3; ☺noon-5pm Tue-Fri, to 4pm Sat & Sun late Jun–mid-Aug) A huge collection of engines and around 500 motorcycles and mopeds – from old Harley-Davidsons and Nortons to homemade, motor-powered bicycles.

Jakobstads Museum MUSEUM

(☎785 1373; Storgatan 2; admission €2; ☺noon-4pm) Finland's richest man, shipping magnate Otto Malm, was the last person to live in Malm House. On his death in 1898, the house became Jakobstads Museum, with local-history displays on the shipping industry and Jakobstad itself. The museum also runs a tobacco exhibition and two historic buildings associated with poet JL Runeberg.

Pedersöre Church CHURCH

(☎040-310 0440; Vasavägen 118; ☺9am-4pm mid-May–mid-Aug) Dating back to the 1400s, this is one of the region's oldest churches. King Gustav III of Sweden personally signed off on the plans to expand the church into the cruciform, though builders ignored his instruction to demolish the towering spire, which was later destroyed by fire, before being restored in its dazzling original form.

🛏 Sleeping

Hotel Epoque HOTEL €€€

(☎788 7100; www.hotelepoque.fi; Jakobsgatan 10; s €102-125, d €122-187; @) This restored customs house is the best place in town – service is great (although reception hours are limited), and with just 16 rooms, it feels quiet, private and exclusive. The restaurant downstairs does a blend of Finnish and modern European that will have you dining in.

WORTH A TRIP

KVARKEN ARCHIPELAGO

Listed as a Unesco World Heritage site in 2006, **Kvarken** (www.kvarken.fi) stretches across to the Umeå region of Sweden and includes the sea and islands between the two countries. Kvarken is unique for the way in which the land is actually rising at a surprising rate – around 8mm per year. New islands are appearing, and it's estimated that by the year 4500, a land bridge will join Sweden and Finland. The best place to learn more is Vaasa's **Terranova** (see p232), which has details of the nature trails and hiking huts in the area. There's also good canoeing around many of the islands.

Thanks to Finland's longest bridge, Kvarken's most accessible point is **Replot** (Finnish: Raippaluoto), a large island just off the Vaasa coast. A new information centre at the bridge, **Havets Hus** (☎050-378 5988; ☺10am-5pm Jun-Aug), can supply on-the-spot maps and information. It's a great cycle out here with bridges linking smaller islands. **Södra Vallgrund** is a small village on the island's southwest, some 10km from the main village, which is also called Replot. **Klobbskat** village, at the western end of the island, is in a barren, Lappishlike setting. **Björkön** (Swedish: Björköby) is a fishing village on a smaller, northern island, accessible from Replot by bridge.

Further afield, smaller islands like **Rönnskären** are good for intrepid explorers with their own boats. You can even explore across to Swedish islands such as **Holmöarna**, which is known for hiking, camping and birdwatching.

Jugend Home Hotel & Guest Home
HOTEL €€

(☑781 4300; Skolgatan 11; www.visitjugend.fi; guest home s/d €39/52, hotel s/d/ste incl breakfast €72/95/119; P) The lovely new rooms at the Jugend Home Hotel, just on the edge of Skata, are light, peaceful and filled with understated pieces of Finnish design; they include tea-and-coffee-making facilities. The smaller 'guest home' rooms for budget travellers are also pleasant.

Westerlund Resandehem
B&B €

(☑723 0440; www.multi.fi/westerlund; Norrmalmsgatan 8; s/d/tr €29/45/55) You'll forgive the minute rooms (with shared bathroom) in this charming spot thanks to its location in the peaceful heart of Skata. Rooms still manage to cram in a tiny table and washbasin, there's a microsauna, and the people here are very helpful. Breakfast is €5.

Stadshotellet
HOTEL €€

(☑788 8111; www.cfhotel.fi; Kanalesplanaden 13; d €84-110; P) Well placed on the main pedestrian boulevard, the Stadshotellet is a characterful building offering comfortable but ageing rooms. It has a first-rate sauna and nightclub (to 4am Wednesday, Friday and Saturday).

Hostel Lilja
HOSTEL €

(☑781 6500, 050-516 7301; www.aftereight.fi/hostellilja; Storgatan 6; s/d/tr/ste €40/50/60/80) Eight thoroughly restored rooms are dotted over two storeys of a 19th-century barn. Rooms are sweet but teeny, with narrow bunk beds and shared toilet facilities (although the honeymoon suite includes a small bathroom). Extras include cheap bike rental (€5 per day), a sauna and the excellent After Eight cafe. Breakfast is €6.50.

Svanen-Joutsen Camping
CAMPGROUND €

(☑723 0660; www.multi.fi/svanen; Larsmovägen 50; tent €14, 2-person cabins €21-28, 4-person cabins €38-65; ☼Jun–mid-Aug) Definitely aiming for the family market, this camping ground includes comfy cabins, minigolf, and canoe and bike hire. It's located 6km north of town in Nissasörn, accessible via the Larsmo–Kokkola bus from the bus station.

✗ Eating

Jakobstad has a couple of lovely daytime cafes, but a dearth of evening options. Hotel Epoque has a good restaurant, otherwise you'll probably end up in O'Leary's Sports Bar.

After Eight
CAFE €

(☑781 6500; www.aftereight.fi; Storgatan 6; lunch €8.50; ☼10am-7pm Mon-Fri) This smashing cafe-cum-cultural centre is the best hangout in town, with a relaxed atmosphere, friendly service, well-spaced tables, a book swap, chilled-out music and a grassy courtyard garden. The lunch option features simple but tasty choices, such as pea-and-bacon soup or chicken stir-fry, and big slabs of homemade cake are on offer at all times.

Café Konditori Frederika
CAFE €

(☑723 3533; Storgatan 13; cakes €3-6, lunch buffets €8; ☼9am-9pm Mon-Fri, to 5pm Sat, 1-6pm Sun) Everyone crowds into this central cafe for the indulgent cakes and well-priced lunches. The terrace is irresistible when the sun's shining and the beer's flowing.

❶ Information

Tourist office (☑723 1796; www.jakobstad.fi; Salutorget 1; ☼8am-6pm Mon-Fri, 9am-3pm Sat Jun-Aug, 8am-5pm Mon-Fri Sep-May)

❶ Getting There & Away

There are regular buses to Jakobstad from Vaasa (€20.50, 1¾ hours), Kokkola (€7.70, 50 minutes) and other towns along the west coast.

Bennäs (Finnish: Pännäinen), 11km away, is the closest railway station to Jakobstad. A shuttle bus (€3.70, 15 minutes) meets arriving trains.

Kokkola-Pietarsaari airport (see p241) is 30km from Jakobstad and buses (€5.70, 25 minutes) meet arriving flights.

Your own wheels can be handy for exploring further afield – try **Avis** (☑050-309 4586; www.avis.fi; Skolgatan 1) for rental cars.

Around Jakobstad

FÄBODA

About 8km west of Jakobstad, Fäboda is a recreational area on the Gulf of Bothnia. Small sandy beaches make for top swimming, sunbathing, surfing and windsurfing, while rocky inlets and thick forests are favoured for walking and mountain biking. Cycling to Fäboda is easy, but use caution as the country road is narrow and winding.

While not strictly accurate (the Arctic Circle is, after all, several hundred kilometres to the north), **Nanoq Arctic Museum** (☑729 3679; www.nanoq.fi; Pörkenäsvägen 60; adult/under 15yr €8/4; ☼noon-6pm Jun-Aug) is a surprisingly good little museum that's worth a detour. Housed in a model of a Greenlandic peat house, the collection is the private achievement of Pentti Kronqvist, who has made several expeditions to the Arctic. There are Inuit tools, fossils, authentic Arctic huts from Greenland and elsewhere, and various other Arctic souvenirs.

Café Fäboda (☑729 3510; Lillsandvägen; mains €16-23; ☺10am-11pm May-Aug), near the beach, has a small international menu. On summer evenings the terrace throbs with live music.

Kokkola

☑06 / POP 46,300

The biggest draw in Kokkola (Swedish: Karleby) is its charming old town Neristan, which was once the home of the town's fisherfolk. Locals say that until the 1960s fishing boats could sail up the coffee-coloured river to sell fish in the kauppatori, but you wouldn't believe it to look at the shallow water today. The land around Kokkola is rising, which means Kokkola is chasing its port as the sea gets further from the town.

◉ Sights & Activities

There are several good family beaches including around the camping ground, and the paddling water around **Elba** and **Laajalahti**, where volleyball is popular in summer.

Neristan   HISTORIC DISTRICT
(www.neristan.fi) Once the working-class area of Kokkola (Neristan means 'Lower Town') where the sailors and fishermen lived, this collection of 19th-century wooden houses makes for a pleasant afternoon's wander. Strolling along the struggling river from the kauppatori, past the Baltija Fountain, one of the first buildings you'll spot is the well-preserved gold-coloured **Rantakatu 27**, the childhood home of Finnish statesman, JV Snellman. At the other end of the economic scale are **Läntinen kirkkokatu 57 and 59**, two tiny sailors' cottages. On the same street there's the **Home of Anna and Fredrik Drake** (Läntinen kirkkokatu 20), originally built in the 1830s and one of the few that's open to the public. To explore further, pick up the *Neristan/Oppistan Step by Step* brochure at the tourist office.

If you follow the Suntti stream beyond Neristan, you'll come to **Halkokari**, the beach that was once another retreating harbour. A British attack was repelled here during the Crimean War, and the captured gunboat at the English Park just north of Neristan is one of few trophies ever taken from the mighty British navy.

Tankar Island   ISLAND
(www.tankar.fi) This lighthouse island, 18km northwest of Kokkola, once offered safe passage through tangled waters. Now it makes a popular day trip (adult/child €17/7) for birdwatching, nature walks and a leisurely lunch at the pierside **Café Tankar** (☑044-780 9139; meals €10-14; ☺lunch & dinner Jun-Aug).

M/S *Jenny* makes the 1½-hour sailing in summer, departing from the camping ground: book with the tourist office or directly with **Kokko Line** (☑828 9716; www.kokkoline.fi; ☺noon Tue-Sun, also 6pm Sat mid-June–mid-Aug, noon Wed, Sat & Sun early Jun & late Aug).

Museum Quarter   MUSEUMS
(☑828 9474; combined ticket €4; ☺11am-4pm Tue-Sun Jun-Aug, noon 3pm Tue-Fri, noon-5pm Sat & Sun Sep-May) Pitkänsillankatu near the town centre is the museum quarter, where the museums share opening hours and ticketing.

FIDDLING FUN IN KAUSTINEN

In the Finnish translation of the *Peanuts* cartoon, the character of Woodstock is called 'Kaustinen', which indicates how closely this little Finnish village is associated with its beloved music festival.

Kaustinen Folk Music Festival (☑020-72911; www.kaustinen.net; Jyväskyläntie 3; daily pass €30), the biggest gathering of folkies in the Nordic countries, kicks off in mid-July. More than 300 Finnish bands and international acts perform over six days, with a theme country chosen to showcase its music and dance. And dance they do, at official concerts, bar gigs and endless impromptu jam sessions.

The festival has an **accommodation office** (☑068-229 811; myynti@ saleskeskusvaraamo.fi) that can assist with enquiries and reservations. There are several buses to Kaustinen on weekdays (patchier at weekends) from Kokkola (€12.50, 50 minutes), which has a railway station. During the festival season there are express buses from other cities; check the festival website.

The **Mineraalikokoelma** (mineral collection; Pitkänsillankatu 28; admission free) will surprise with its assembly of natural beauty, including stunning but fragile crystals and meteorite fragments. In the same building, the **Luontomuseo** (natural history collection) has a collection of stuffed mammals and birds.

Across the courtyard, the **Pedagogio** (schoolhouse) dates from 1696, making it the country's oldest secular building in a town. After 200 years of education, it currently houses a fantastic collection of folk and outsider art – angels carved with chainsaws and ships made from bones. Nearby **Lassander House** is preserved as an 18th-century merchant's home. There's also a small cafe here that specialises in waffles.

A block up the street, **KH Renlund Museo** (Pitkänsillankatu 39) is in a large 19th-century mansion. It contains the collection of Karl Herman Renlund, a shopkeeper who left his art collection for the benefit of 'students and the working class'.

Vesi Veijari
SWIMMING

(☏823 4650; www.kokkola.fi; Kaarlelankatu 55; admission €5.20, infrared sauna per 30min €7; ◷roughly 8am-8pm) In winter or if you need a sauna, the remodelled Vesi Veijari swimming centre has indoor and outdoor pools, water slides, jacuzzi and three different kinds of sauna.

🛏 Sleeping

Town-centre accommodation is dominated by big hotels.

Sokos Hotel Kaarle
HOTEL €€

(☏826 6111; www.hotelkaarle.fi; Kauppatori 4; s/d €135/160; P@⊛) Right on the central square, this is Kokkola's best hotel, with smallish but respectable air-conditioned rooms. Staff are immensely helpful, and facilities – including a swimming pool – are good. Anyone bothered by noise should ask for a room away from the restaurant/nightclub.

Hotel Seurahuone
HOTEL €€

(☏795 9600; www.seurahuone.com; Torikatu 24; s/d €99/119; P) One of Finland's oldest continuous hotels (since 1894), this place has a dark and off-putting foyer, but contrastingly light and well-appointed rooms, some with views onto the square and/or tubs in the bathrooms. Don't skimp on price – economy-class rooms are a definite step downwards and directly over the nightclub.

Camping Suntinsuu
CAMPGROUND €€

(☏831 4006; www.kokkola-camping.fi; Pikiruukki; tents €10 plus per person €4, cabins €47-92, apts €150; ◷Jun-Aug; P) This small, super-friendly riverside camping ground is 2km northwest of the centre, following the river from the kauppatori. The cabins and service block were refitted in 2010, and look fantastic (the nicest kitchens we've seen on a camp site), and the brand-new apartments have terraces looking onto the water. If only the camping area were larger than a postcard.

🍴 Eating & Drinking

Vanhankaupingin Ravintola
FINNISH €€€

(☏834 9030; www.vkr.kpnet.com; Isokatu 28; mains €26-32; ◷dinner Tue-Fri Jun-Aug, also Sat Sep-May) Set in a Neristan town house, this elegant spot does great Finnish cuisine. Try the reindeer starter that's set off with Lappish cheese or sample local Arctic char with scallops.

Kaavya Kitchen
INDIAN €€

(☏822 0900; www.kaavyakitchen.com; Pitkänsillankatu 23; lunch €8.80, mains €15-20; ◷lunch & dinner) Opened in 2010, Kokkola's first Indian restaurant has quickly become a town favourite. Service is warm and helpful, and once you get stuck into the menu and the mango milkshakes start flowing, it feels like the finest place to be. Tandoori dishes are cooked in a proper clay oven, and there's an excellent vegetarian selection.

Wanha Lyhty & Kellari
STEAK €€

(☏868 0188; www.kpnet.com/wanhalyhty; Pitkänsillankatu 24; mains €18-26; ◷dinner Tue-Sun) This old-fashioned cellar restaurant is a testament to nautical history, bedecked with model ships and ropes – although strangely there's barely a fish to be seen on the menu. Instead, meaty traditional Finnish food features heavily, with an emphasis on steaks.

English Pub
PUB

(☏831 9969; www.englishpub.fi; Isokatu 12; ◷tn 2am or 3am) Thirsting for the British Isles? This boozer slakes with UK beers that have made it a hit with a local cross-section of young and old, suits and Goths.

ℹ Information

Tourist office (☏828 9402; www.kokkola.fi; kauppatori; ◷8am-5pm Mon-Fri, 9am-1pm Sat Jun-Aug, 8am-4pm Mon-Fri Sep-May) Extremely helpful office in the main square.

❶ Getting There & Around

Kokkola-Pietarsaari airport is 20km southeast of Kokkola and served by a regional bus service to Kokkola (€7.50, 15 minutes) and Jakobstad (€5.70, 25 minutes). There are several flights a day to/from Helsinki, run by Flybe.

Regular buses run to/from all coastal towns, especially Vaasa (€26.90, three hours) and Jakobstad (€7.70, 50 minutes). The bus station is one block northwest of the train station.

Kokkola's train station is a main western-line stop. The journey from Helsinki (€60, up to nine daily) takes less than five hours.

You can hail a **taxi** (🗐010-085 111) around the kauppatori.

Kalajoki

🗐08 / POP 12,600

Red-brown holiday houses snuggling into white sand dunes – it's easy to see why Finnish families flock here for their summer holidays. Cosy rather than stunning, there's swimming for beginners with sandbars to catch your breath on, golf for executive stress relief, and Nordic walking was invented here so you'll see people toting ski poles in summer. The tourist industry is thriving, with big new beachside resorts springing up (something of a shock after the region's quiet coastal towns and countryside) and winter visitors attracted by cross-country skiing.

Kalajoki village is just off the highway, with most of the facilities (bus terminal, banks, post office and travel agency), but the resort area, with the beach, airfield and most of the accommodation, is 6km south of the village along Hwy 8 in Hiekkasärkät.

The hectic **summer tourist office** (🗐466 655; www.kalajoki.fi; Jukupolku 3; ⊙9am-8pm Mon-Fri, 11am-8pm Sat & Sun Jun-Aug) is inside the SaniFani spa at Hiekkasärkät. In **winter** (🗐469 4449; ⊙9am-5pm Mon-Fri Sep-May) it's based at Pohjankläntie 1 . Both of the offices and the website have a list of all the rental cottages hereabouts.

🏃 Activities

Hiekkasärkät   BEACH

This stretch of sand is one of the country's most popular family-holiday beaches.

Nordic walking was born in the 1930s in Kalajoki, when world-championship skier Jussi Kurikkala decided to keep up his form in summer by working out on the dunes. A 44km network of walking routes was

marked out around Hiekkasärkät in his honour in 2011, and you can hire Nordic walking sticks from Fontana Hotelli Rantakalla.

Kylpylä SaniFani   SPA, AMUSEMENT PARK

(🗐469 2400; Jukupolku 3; adult/4-15yr €13.50/8.50; ⊙2-9pm Mon-Fri, 11am-8pm Sat & Sun) This spa and waterpark offers slippery slides and a flowing 'river' for the kids, massages and manicures, and a bowling alley. The spa also owns **JukuPark** (🗐469 2308; www.jukupark.fi; Hiekkasärkät; admission €21; ⊙11am-5pm late Jun, 11am-7pm Jul–mid-Aug), an outdoor waterpark that has recently been given a massive facelift, with loads of water slides, rides for little 'uns and paddle boats. A combination ticket (€28) covers both.

Kalajoki Golf   GOLF

(🗐466 666; www.kalajokigolf.fi; Hiekkasärkät; admission & green fee €55; ⊙year-round, snow permitting) This 18-hole golf course wanders pleasantly between the forest and beach.

🛏 Sleeping & Eating

Hiekkasärkät is ideal for beachside accommodation with dozens of summer cottages and some resortlike options. The best place to book is through the tourist office, which can also hunt out package deals.

Spa Hotel SaniFani   SPA HOTEL €€

(🗐466 642; Matkailutie 150; standard s/d/f from €99/122/142, superior from €115/154/174; P 🔞 🐾) Built in 2007, this whopper is Kalajoki's newest hotel. The dramatic exterior hints at something out of the ordinary, but the modern rooms, although they have huge windows and amazing sea views, are very conventional. It's still the best place to stay in Kalajoki, particularly for families, with entrance to the spa and waterparks included in the price.

Tapion Tupa   B&B, COTTAGE €€

(🗐466 622; www.tapiontupa.com; Hiekkasärkät; r/apt from €45/120; P 🐾) Just off the main road and close to the beach, this rambling complex has red cottages set in the forest. There's a range of options, from rooms in an Ostrobothnian house to basic log cabins to brand-new self-contained holiday apartments, though some require you to book for at least three nights.

Fontana Hotelli Rantakalla   HOTEL, COTTAGE €€

(🗐466 642; Matkailutie 150; hotel s/d from €80/105; P 🐾) Hotel rooms here vary in quality: those in the main building are comfortable, while the annexe is looking tired and dated. The welcome is lovely, though, and there are good family-holiday facilities, with saunas, karaoke and live music in summer. Rantakalla's cottages – 120 of them, from basic to swanky – are reliable year-round options.

Hostel Retkeilijä HOSTEL €

(☑040-150 8470; Opintie 2, Kalajoki; s/d €25/34; ☺mid-Jun–early Aug) Fairly handy for the bus station in Kalajoki village, this hostel has basic though spacious rooms and includes a sauna and two self-catering kitchens. It was empty when we visited in the height of summer – clearly Hiekkasärkät is the only place to be! – but that makes it a peaceful alternative to the resort madness further down the coast.

Hotelli-Ravintola Lokkilinna PIZZA €

(☑469 6700; lunch buffets €12, pizzas €10-12; ☺lunch & dinner) This well-positioned yet secluded spot overlooks the dunes, and has an excellent summer terrace perfect for a beer, filling lunch buffet or evening pizza. It's a small place with a charming family feel.

❶ Getting There & Away

Several daily buses running between Oulu (€26.90, 2½ hours) and Kokkola (€15.90, 40 minutes express) stop at Kalajoki and the beach.

Oulu, Kainuu & Koillismaa

Includes »

Best Places to Eat

» Hella (p248)

» Riipisen Riistaravintola (p262)

Best Places to Stay

» Hotel Lasaretti (p247)

» Luotsi Hotelli (p250)

» Kierikki (p251)

» Kartanohotelli Karolineb-urg (p251)

» Royal Hotel Ruka (p261)

» Hotelli Kalevala (p255)

» Basecamp Oulanka (p267)

Why Go?

Stretching across Finland's waist from the Gulf of Bothnia to the long Russian border, this broad swath of territory takes in the boffins of Oulu's booming technology sector and the brown bears raising their shaggy heads as they patrol the eastern forests. It offers some of the nation's most memorable outdoor experiences, from birdwatching and beach-combing in the west to skiing, canoeing and trekking in the east.

The further you get from Oulu, the more remote things become. Kainuu is a heavily wooded wilderness and important animal habitat traversed by the famed UKK trekking route. Koillismaa, near the Russian border, is the transitional region between the south and Lapland, and includes Oulanka National Park, one of Finland's natural highlights. It is an area of tumbling rivers, isolated lakes and dense forests. This is perhaps Finland's best destination for getting active in the great outdoors, whether in summer or winter.

When to Go

OULU

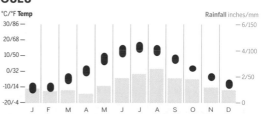

Apr Still good snow cover for skiing, but acceptable temperatures and plenty of light.

Jul Bear-watching in Kuusamo, ca-noeing in Oulanka National Park and chamber music in Kuhmo.

Sep The most beautiful time for hiking, with autumn *ruska* colours filling the forests.

History

The region's geography reflects its tar-producing history. In the 19th century the remote Kainuu and Koillismaa areas began producing tar from the numerous pines, and sent it on the precarious journey downriver to Oulu, whence it was shipped to the boatbuilding nations of Europe. The merchants prospered, and Oulu still has a sleek, cosmopolitan feel compared with the backwoodsy feel of the rest of its province.

Oulu

📞 08 / POP 141,671

Prosperous Oulu (Swedish: Uleåborg) is one of Finland's most enjoyable cities to visit. In summer, the angled sun bathes the kauppa-

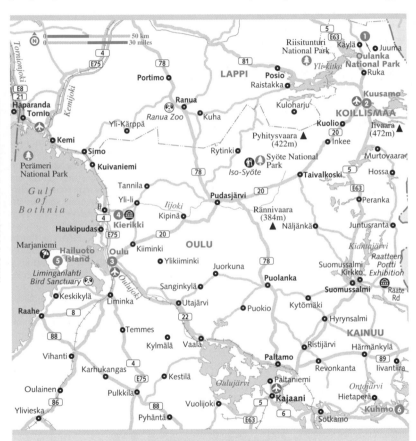

Oulu, Kainuu & Koillismaa Highlights

❶ Canoeing the varying river routes or trekking the Karhunkierros trail in **Oulanka National Park** (p262), through some of the best wilderness scenery in Finland

❷ Creeping into the evening forests to spot brown bears or meeting their boisterous orphaned cousins near **Kuusamo** (p256)

❸ Chilling out in the evening sunshine that kisses the kauppatori in **Oulu** (p245), or getting involved in one of the city's weird festivals (p247)

❹ Getting back to Finland's Stone Age at the informative **Kierikki** (p251) museum

❺ Braving the Bothnian waters on relaxing **Hailuoto Island** (p250)

❻ Letting the young musicians string you along at Kuhmo's excellent **chamber music festival** (p255)

tori (market square) in light and all seems well with the world. Locals, who appreciate daylight when they get it, crowd the terraces, and stalls groan under the weight of Arctic berries.

The centre is spread across several islands, elegantly connected by pedestrian bridges, and water never seems far away. This layout has made it very convenient for cycling, and Oulu's network of bike paths is one of Europe's best.

Oulu is also one of the world's foremost technology cities; the university turns out top-notch IT graduates and the corporate parks on the city's outskirts employ people from all over the globe.

But it's not all laptops and cycle lanes; this is Finland after all, and there's a good dollop of weirdness, particularly when the Air Guitar World Championships come to town.

⊙ Sights

Kauppatori   SQUARE
Oulu has the liveliest market square of all Finnish towns, and its position at the waterfront makes it all the more appealing. The square is bordered by several old wooden storehouses now serving as restaurants, bars and craft shops. The squat *Toripolliisi* statue, a humorous representation of the local police, is a local landmark. On the square is the **kauppahalli** (covered market), with freshly filleted salmon glistening in the market stalls and plenty of spots to snack on anything from cloudberries to sushi.

Tietomaa   MUSEUM
(www.tietomaa.fi; Nahkatehtaankatu 6; adult/child €15/11; ⊙10am-5pm or 6pm, to 8pm Wed) This huge, excellent science museum can occupy kids for the best part of a day with a giant IMAX screen, hands-on interactive exhibits on planets and the human body, and an observation tower. There's a yearly mega-exhibition that's the focal point.

Pohjois Pohjanmaan Museo   MUSEUM
(www.ouka.fi/ppm; Ainolanpuisto; adult/child €3/free, admission free Fri; ⊙10am-6pm Mon-Fri, 11am-6pm Sat & Sun Jun-Aug, 10am-5pm Tue-Sun Sep-May) The Museum of Northern Ostrobothnia in the city park merits exploration but has almost too much information to take in at first bite. It covers the earliest habitation of the region through to the 20th century, including plenty of information on the tar trade. Cameras allow you to zoom in on the

impressive scale model of 1938 Oulu; a traditional pharmacy, paintings of the Great Fire of 1822, and a schoolroom are included in the wide-ranging display.

Oulun Tuomiokirkko   CHURCH
(Kirkkokatu 36; ⊙11am-8pm Jun & Aug, to 9pm Jul, noon-1pm Sep-May) Oulu's imposing main church was built in 1777 but then came the great fire of 1822, which severely damaged the structure. Tireless architect CL Engel rebuilt it in empire style, adding a dome and Renaissance-style vaulting, which impart a powerful airiness to the fairly unadorned interior.

FREE Merimiehen Kotimuseo   MUSEUM
(www.ouka.fi/ppm; Pikisaarentie 6; ⊙noon-6pm late May-early Sep) This house-museum on Pikisaari belonged to a local sailor. Built in 1737, it is the oldest house in Oulu and was transferred here from the town centre in 1983. The wallpaper and extendable bed are typical of 19th-century Finnish homes.

Oulun Taidemuseo   GALLERY
(www.ouka.fi/taidemuseo; Kasarmintie 7; adult/child €3/1, admission free Fri; ⊙10am-5pm Tue-Thu & Sat-Sun, noon-7pm Fri) Oulu's art museum is a bright spacious gallery with excellent temporary exhibitions of both international and Finnish contemporary art, and a cafe.

FREE Oulunlinna   CASTLE
There's not much left of Oulu Castle, although you can clearly see the remaining fortlike structure dominating the small park near the bridge. The observation tower, rebuilt in 1873, houses a cafe.

Hupisaaret   PARK
Just north of the town centre and connected by small bridges, this great park has bike paths, museums, greenhouses and a summer cafe, as well as a fishway built so that salmon can bypass the hydroelectric dam to get to the spawning grounds.

🏃 Activities

One of Oulu's best features is the extensive network of **bicycle paths** crossing bridges, waterways and islands all the way out to surrounding villages. Grab a cycle map from the tourist office. A good short ride is from the kauppatori, across the bridge to Pikisaari and across another bridge to Nallikari, where there's a beach facing the Gulf of Bothnia. For details of bicycle hire, see, p250.

OULU, KAINUU & KOILLISMAA OULU

Oulu

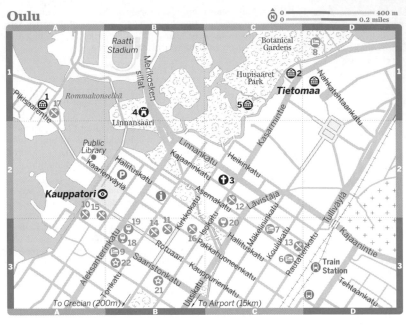

☞ Tours

From late June to late August, free English bus (3pm Saturday, two hours) and walking (6pm Thursday, two hours) tours leave from the town hall.

The 'Potnapekka' – a tourist train – travels from around late June to mid-August, from the pedestrian zone to Hupisaaret or Nallikari beach. The fare is €6/3 per adult/child to either destination.

Go Arctic! SUMMER, WINTER

(☑044-022 4060; www.goarctic.fi) Runs a week-ly program of activities in summer (and winter), including tar-boat cruises to Tur-kansaari, cycling tours, sea canoeing, guided walks, and excursions to Kierikki.

✦ Festivals & Events

In a country that wrote the book on oddball festivals, Oulu hosts more than its fair share. Take the **Air Guitar World Championships** (www.airguitarworldchampionships.com), which are part of the **Oulu Music Video Festival** (www.omvf.net) in late August. Contestants from all over the world take the stage to show what they can do with their imaginary instruments.

There are two unusual winter events, both the largest of their kind anywhere in the world. The **Tervahiihto** (Oulu Tar Ski Race; www.tervahiihto.fi), held in early March, is a 70km skiing race (40km for women) that is entering its 113th year. The **Ice-Fishing Marathon** (www.oulutourism.fi) is a 48-hour contest held on the open sea in late March (when the ice is still thick) and draws more than 400 participants.

Pack the breath-mints for the **Roviantti** (www.roviantti.info), a culinary festival held over a weekend in mid-July, one day of which is devoted wholly to garlic.

Elojazz (www.elojazz.com) is a two-day jazz and blues festival in early August, **Oulun salo Soi** (www.oulunsalosoi.fi) is a chamber music festival around the same time, while **Qstock** (www.qstock.org) is a high profile rock festival in late July.

🛏 Sleeping

There's little budget accommodation in Oulu.

TOP CHOICE **Hotel Lasaretti** HOTEL **€€**

(☑020-757 4700; www.lasaretti.com; Kasarmintie 13; s/d €128/150, summer €72/84; **P@🏊**) Bright, modern and optimistic, this invit-ing hotel sits in a group of renovated brick buildings, once a hospital. It's close to town but the parkside location by the bubbling-bright stream makes it feel rural. The artis-tically modern rooms have floorboards and flatscreen TVs; some have fold-out sofa bed for families. Facilities and staff are excellent and there's also a busy restaurant with sun-kissed terrace.

Sokos Hotel Eden SPA HOTEL **€€€**

(☑020-1234 905; www.sokoshotels.fi; Holsten-salmentie 29, Nallikari; s/d €151/171, superior €171/191; **P@🏊**) This excellent spa hotel by the beach on Hietasaari offers great watery facilities – slides, intricate indoor pools, saunas – and massage treatments. Superior rooms on the new side of the building are bigger and have air-conditioning (handier than you may think) as well as a sea-view balcony. Nonguests can use the whole spa facilities for the day for a pretty reasonable €15 (€9 for kids). Prices are usually lower than listed above; check online. It's a half-hour walk or faster cycle west of the centre; by car you have to head north out of town and loop around. Bus 17 gets you there from Linnankatu (€3.10), as does the tourist train.

Nallikari CAMPGROUND **€**

(☑044-703 1353; www.nallikari.fi; Hietasaari; tent sites €13-16 plus per adult/child €4/2, cabins €36-42, cottages €98-139; **P@**) This excellent camping ground offers all sorts of options in a location close to the beach on Hietasaari, a 40-minute walk to town via pedestrian bridges. Both summer and winter activities are on offer, plus a large variety of cabins and cottages, substantially cheaper outside of high season. It's very child-friendly. Bus 17 gets you there from Linnankatu (€3.10), as does the tourist train.

Forenom Hotel Oulu HOTEL, APARTMENT **€**

(☑020-198 3420; www.forenom.fi; Rautatienkatu 9; s/d €80/95, weekends & summer €55/65; **P**) You can't beat this spot for convenience: it's bang opposite the train station. Bright, modern rooms have plenty of space; there's a range of them, sleeping up to five. Book online or via the terminal in the lobby. It also offers good-value apartments elsewhere in Oulu on the same webpage, so make sure you get the address right if you want to stay here. Reception is staffed Monday to Friday dur-ing working hours.

Hotel Scandic Oulu HOTEL **€€€**

(☑543 1000; www.scandic-hotels.com; Saaris-tonkatu 4; s/d €148/165, summer €84/94; **P@**) This sleek hotel occupies half a city block right in the middle of town. From the space-opera lights in its spacious foyer to the high-ceilinged rooms with clean Nordic decor and flatscreen TV, it's a temple to efficiency, hygiene and modern design (art, individual-ity: look elsewhere).

Pohto Hotel Kortteeri
HOTEL €

(☏010-843 4500; www.pohto.fi; Vellamontie 12; r €70; ☉daily late Jun–mid-Aug, Mon-Fri rest of year; P@≋) Near the Nallikari camping ground, this congress complex consists of low brick buildings tranquilly set among mature pines. Facilities are good for this price, and there's a kitchen and common room for guests to use, as well as a 12m pool. It's basically a summer hotel, but rooms are available during the week at other times if it's not booked out for a conference. Family rooms put your kids in easy reach of the beach and the facilities of the Sokos Hotel Eden.

Hotel Apollo
HOTEL €€

(☏52211; www.hotelapollo.fi; Asemakatu 31; s/d €122/140, weekends & summer r €82; P@) Handy for the station, this spot boasts warm and efficient service and three types of room. Standard rooms are compact, with ultracompact bathrooms, but comfortable enough; the top-floor rooms have sloping ceiling windows and more space; while the sauna rooms are classier, with dark furniture and flatscreen TVs. Check for good-value packages on the website.

Kesähotelli Välkkylätalo
HOTEL €

(☏010-272 2987; www.valkkylatalo.fi; Ylioppilaantie 4; s/d €40/45; ☉8am-8pm mid-Jun–Jul; P) Next to the Ouluhalli sports stadium, a few blocks east of the bus station, this converted student accommodation offers summer value.

✕ Eating

Snacks and local specialities can be found in the kauppatori and **kauppahalli** (☉8am-5pm Mon-Thu, to 6pm Fri, to 3pm Sat). In summer, stalls sell salmon, paella and Oulu specialities, such as *rieska* (flat bread), *leipäjuusto* (baked cheese) and *lohikeitto* (salmon soup).

Hella
BISTRO €€

(☏371 180; www.hellaravintola.fi; Isokatu 13; mains €18-28; ☉lunch & dinner Mon-Fri, 3-11pm Sat, noon-6pm Sun) This sweet little corner spot is a welcoming two-person show that offers excellent Italian-inspired fare. Attentive service is backed up by the food, which changes seasonally but features great salads, cannelloni stuffed with goat's cheese, and tender, well-treated meat dishes.

Café Bisketti
CAFE €

(www.cafebisketti.fi; Kirkkokatu 8; lunches €5.50-8.50) This top double-sided spot transforms itself throughout the day. Think twice before getting that pastry with your morning coffee; they're enormous and might not leave room for lunch, with cheap deals on soup, salad, coffee and a pastry, and hot dishes for not much extra. In the evenings, the terrace is a decent spot for a people-watching beer.

Puistola
BISTRO, RESTAURANT €€

(☏020-792 8210; www.ravintolapuistola.fi; Pakkahuoneenkatu 15; bistro mains €15-23, restaurant mains €20-32) This ambitious new arrival offers a deli-cafe and two restaurant areas. The entry-level bistro is a comfortable space, and turns out tasty, imaginative dishes from its open kitchen with plenty of flair, and also does good-value lunches (€9 to €11) – try for a seat out on the terrace. Downstairs is a more formal restaurant (open dinner only, Tuesday to Saturday), with somewhat higher prices. Service throughout is excellent. Be sure to check out the toilets – highly original.

Crecian
GREEK €€

(www.crecian.fi; Kirkkokatu 55; mains €20-27) It's worth the short stroll from the centre to this popular neighbourhood restaurant, predictably decked out in blue and white, though the owner's actually Cypriot. The dishes are tasty and generously proportioned, and service is welcoming.

Sokeri-Jussin Kievari
FINNISH €€

(☏376 628; www.sokerijussi.fi; Pikisaarentie 2; mains €14-30) An Oulu classic, this timbered inn on Pikisaari was once a sugar warehouse and has outdoor tables that have good views of the centre. Although the renovated interior has lost a bit of the original character, it's still an attractive spot to eat, with no-frills traditional dishes, including reindeer, and a selection of much more upmarket plates. It's also a nice place to go for a few beers away from the bustle of the city but just a few steps from it.

Istanbul Oriental
TURKISH €€€

(☏311 2922; www.istanbuloriental.fi; Kauppurienkatu 11; mains €22-34; ☉dinner Tue-Fri, lunch & dinner Sat) This stylishly decorated place in the heart of things is a rather good Turkish restaurant with plenty of vegetarian options and succulent chargrilled meat. Service is excellent, though the food's somewhat overpriced.

1881 Uleåborg
FINNISH €€€

(☏881 1188; www.uleaborg.fi; Aittatori 4; mains €30; ☉dinner Mon-Sat) In an old warehouse near the kauppatori, this classy spot combines chic Finnish style with a traditional setting. The terrace by the water is one of Oulu's loveliest summer spots.

Indian Cuisine INDIAN €
(www.indiancuisine.fi; Kajaaninkatu 38; mains €13-15) Opposite the station, this is the best Indian in town, and probably for quite a few hundred kilometres. Excellent service. There's a lunch buffet for €8.90.

🍷 Drinking

There's plenty going on in Oulu at night. The kauppatori is the spot to start in summer: bars set in traditional wooden warehouses have terraces that lick up every last drop of the evening sun.

Never Grow Old BAR
(www.ngo.fi; Hallituskatu 17; ⊙6pm-2am or 3am) This enduringly popular bar hits its stride after 10pm, with plenty of dancing, DJs and revelry in the tightly packed interior. The goofy decor includes some seriously comfortable and extremely uncomfortable places to sit, and a log-palisade bar that seems designed to get you to wear your drink. It opens earlier in summer.

Kaarlenholvi Jumpru Pub PUB
(www.jumpru.fi; Kauppurienkatu 6; ⊙11am-2am Mon-Tue, to 4am Wed-Sat, noon-2am Sun) This Oulu institution is a great place for meeting locals and its enclosed outdoor area always seems to be humming with cheerfully sauced-up folk. There's a warren of cosy rooms inside, as well as a nightclub opening from 10pm Wednesday to Saturday.

Oluthuone Leskinen PUB
(www.leskinen.fi; Kirkkokatu 10; ⊙noon-2am) This bar on the central pedestrian zone has a popular terrace that complements the dark, cosy interior with its wide range of Finnish and international beers, as well as malt whiskies. There's notably friendly service and a good atmosphere.

Graali PUB
(www.graali.fi; Saaristonkatu 5; ⊙2pm-2am) When it's cold and snowy outside, there's nowhere cosier than this pub, decorated with suits of armour and sporting trophies. Sink into a leather armchair by the open fire and feel the warmth return to your bones. A good whisky selection will help you along.

Sarkka BAR
(Hallituskatu 13; ⊙9am-3am Thu-Sun, to 2am Mon-Wed) This old-time Finnish bar is worth it for

the downbeat traditional atmosphere and heroic opening hours.

☆ Entertainment

45 Special CLUB
(www.45special.com; Saaristonkatu 12; ⊙8pm-4am) This grungy three-level club pulls a youngish crowd for its downstairs rock and chartier top floor. There's a €7 cover at weekends and regular live gigs.

Finnkino Plaza CINEMA
(☑060-000 7007; www.finnkino.fi; Torikatu 32) An enormous central cinema complex, with eight screens.

Sport
Oulu loves its ice-hockey team, the Kärpät (Stoats), who have been successful in recent years. They play at **Oulun Energia Areena** (☑club 815 5700, ticketline 060-010 800; www.oulunkarpat.fi; tickets €10-30) in Kaksila east of the centre.

ℹ Information
Wireless internet is available throughout the city centre on the PanOulu network.

Forex (www.forex.fi; Kauppurienkatu 13; ⊙Mon-Sat) Currency exchange.

Public library (Kaarlenväylä; ⊙10am-8pm Mon-Fri, to 5pm Sat, noon-4pm Sun) On the waterfront opposite the Oulu Theatre. Several internet terminals.

Tourist office (☑5584 1330; www.oulutourism.fi; Torikatu 10; ⊙9am-5pm Mon-Thu, to 4pm Fri) Good range of information on Oulu and other Finnish destinations.

ℹ Getting There & Away
Air
There are several daily direct flights from Helsinki with Finnair. Norwegian flies to Rovaniemi, Helsinki, Scandinavian capitals and other European cities. Blue1 services Helsinki, FlyBe goes to Tallinn, and Air Baltic links Oulu with Turku and Riga.

Bus
Kajaani €29.40, three hours
Helsinki €91.80, 11½ hours
Rovaniemi €41, 3½ hours
Tornio €23.50, 2½ hours

Train
Several direct trains run daily to Helsinki (€72 to €79, six to seven hours). There are also trains via Kajaani and trains north to Rovaniemi.

ⓘ Getting Around

Bus 19 runs between the centre and the **airport** (€3.10, 25 minutes, every 20 minutes). There's a good network of local buses (www.koskilinjat.fi). Each ride costs €3.10; check route maps online and at bus stops.

Bicycles can be hired from **Pyörä-Suvala** (☑338 175; www.pyorasuvala.fi; Saaristonkatu 27; per hr/day/week €5/12/15/42; ⊙9am-5pm Mon-Fri) – ask for a better one if you don't like the yellow hire ones – and from the Nallikari camping ground (per day/24hr €10/15), which also hires out skis in winter.

The various car-hire operators in town, including **Sixt** (☑050-049 8875; www.sixt.fi) at the airport and **Budget** (☑020-746 6640; www.budget.fi; Kaarnatie 10), do cheap weekend deals. Call ☑060-030 081 for a **taxi**.

Around Oulu

The zoo at Ranua (p277) is an easy day trip from Oulu.

TURKANSAARI

Set across two river islands on the scenic Oulujoki, this **open-air museum** (www.ouka.fi/ppm; Turkansaarentie 165, Oulu; adult/child €3/1; ⊙10am-6pm late May–mid-Aug, to 4pm mid-Aug–mid-Sep) is a collection of wooden buildings of various traditional types, from loggers' cabins to stables, and includes a handsome traditional farmhouse. The 1694 church is an original from this former trading settlement; look for the faded date carved above the inside doorway. A working tar pit at the far end of the complex comes to the fore during **Tar-Burning Week**, a festival in late June.

Turkansaari is 14km east of Oulu off Rd 22; catch bus 3 or 4 from Oulu. You can also get there by boat from town in summer: the Oulu tourist office has the timetable. Entry is free with the Pohjois Pohjanmaan Museo ticket (see p245).

HAILUOTO

☑08 / POP 1003

A favourite Oulu beach escape, Hailuoto is a sizeable island of traditional red farmhouses, venerable wooden windmills, modern wind farms, and Scotch pines growing tall from the sandy soil.

A free car ferry crosses the 7km from the mainland, dropping you at Hailuoto's easternmost point, from where the road winds 30km to the beach at **Marjaniemi** at the opposite end of the island. There's **tour-**ist information (☑044-497 3500; www.hailuototourism.fi) at the cafes at both ferry docks, in Marjaniemi, and in the middle of the island at Hailuoto village, which has shops, a bank and a striking A-frame church. Here also is **Kniivilä** (☑044-497 3565; Marjaniementie 20; admission €2; ⊙11am-5pm late Jun-Aug), an open-air museum of old wooden buildings.

At Marjaniemi, there's a shallow-water beach perfect for kids, looked over by a **lighthouse** (adult/child €5/3; ⊙noon-2pm Sat & Sun early Jun-Aug). At the base of the lighthouse is Luototalo, which contains a free **nature exhibition** (⊙9am-6pm daily) on the dune ecosystem, a wooden-tabled restaurant/cafe with lunch buffet and great sea views.

ⓣ**Luotsi Hotelli** (☑772 5500; www.luotokeskus.fi; Marjaniementie 783; s/d/ste €65/90/120; ⊙Mar-Nov; Ⓟ@) is an excellent modern facility with spacious rooms airily kitted out in light wood and a vague nautical feel. It's worth upgrading to the suites: wonderful spaces with curving picture-windows. Excellent rates are available for longer stays.

The **RantaSumppu camp site** (tent sites €20, small/large cabins €85/100; Ⓟ@) is a 10-minute walk down the beach, with cabins within striking distance of the sea and good facilities including a cafe/lunch restaurant. Reception is open here in summer until 8pm; otherwise, check in at the hotel.

Bus 66 travels two to three times daily from Oulu, crossing on the ferry and running the length of the island to Marjaniemi. Free **ferries** (www.finferries.fi) run half-hourly at busy times, and hourly at other times. Rides are 30 minutes. The ferry is 28km southwest of Oulu via Rd 816.

LIMINGANLAHTI BIRD SANCTUARY

The bird sanctuary at Liminka Bay attracts numerous avian species, with several rare waders nesting here during summer, and many species of waterfowl and birds of prey also visible. Prominent species include the yellow-breasted bunting, black-tailed godwit, Ural owl, bittern, marsh harrier and tern. There are several observation towers, boardwalks and a couple of designated camp sites.

Head first for **Liminganlahden Luontokeskus** (☑562 0000; www.liminganlahti.fi; Rantakurvi 6; ⊙10am-5pm Apr-May, weekdays only Jun-early Aug), a well-equipped nature centre 6km west of Liminka village. Accommodation is available: call ☏040-0494 609 outside of centre opening hours.

Several daily Raahe-bound buses make the 30km trip from Oulu to Liminka and on to Lumijoki, and will stop at the turn-off to the nature centre.

HAUKIPUDAS
☏08

Haukipudas, 21km north of Oulu at a scenic spot along the Kiiminkijoki, is known for its beige **church** (admission free; ☉10am-6pm Mon-Fri early Jun-late Aug), one of Finland's most notable 'picture churches'. The interior is decorated with striking naive scenes painted in the 18th century and depicting biblical events, including a scary Day of Judgment. Outside, by the separate belfry, stands a wooden moustachioed *vaivaisukko* (pauper statue).

From Oulu town centre, buses 15 and 20 run to Haukipudas.

KIERIKKI

This excellent **museum** (www.kierikki.fi; adult/child €8/4; ☉10am-5pm daily Jun-Aug, to 4pm Mon-Fri, noon-4pm Sat Sep-May) is set by the Iijoki, whose banks are riddled with Stone Age settlements that have provided archaeologists with valuable information about this period in the Nordic lands. The communities made a comfortable living fishing and sealing, using surplus production for trade. Settlements in the Kierikki area date from about 4000 BC to 2000 BC and were coastal, moving gradually west as the land rose.

The display is most informative, and sensibly only includes a handful of artefacts, including fortunately preserved wooden fences to trap fish. A ponderous video gives excavation histories, and there's a cafe-restaurant. A short boardwalk takes you down to the picturesque riverbank, where they've re-created some buildings from the period and you can take potshots at a deer using a primitive bow and arrow, or send the kids out for a paddle in a Stone Age canoe. In winter this isn't available, but admission is slightly cheaper.

There's also a **hotel** (☏817 0492; www.kierikki.nl; s/d €68/95; ☉year-round; ℗) here, consisting of wooden buildings surrounding a little pond; the attractive, spacious rooms have balconies over it. Rates include museum entry.

Kierikki is 5km south of Yli-Ii, itself 27km east of Ii, on the main road north of Oulu. Buses run from Oulu on school days only and you have to change in Ii.

Kajaani
☏08 / POP 38.137

Essentially a one-street town, Kajaani, capital of the Kainuu region, is nevertheless the major settlement in these parts. Apart from its pretty riverside and fabulous rural church at nearby Paltaniemi, there's little to keep you, though it makes a handy stopover between Lakeland and the north.

Kajaani was long an important station on the Kainuu tar transportation route – until the 19th century, this region produced more tar than anywhere else in the world. Other claims to fame are that Elias Lönnrot, creator of the *Kalevala* (see p331), worked here for a period, using it as a base for his travels, and long-reigning president Urho Kekkonen lived here as a student (at Kalliokatu 7).

You'll find most services along the main street, Kauppakatu.

⊙ Sights & Activities

Facing the small raatihuoneentori (town square) is the old **town hall**, designed by CL Engel.

FREE **Kajaanin Linna** CASTLE
(www.kajaaninlinna.fi) Picturesquely set on a river island in the town centre, these ruins show all the signs of damage by war, time and more-recent mischief. It's a fine spot to bask on the grass on a sunny day, but there isn't much more to it than what you can see.

Near the castle there's a **tar-boat channel** with a lock built in 1846 to enable the boats laden with tar barrels to pass the Ämmäkoski rapids. The replica boat moored by the lock features in demonstrations at 11am on Saturdays in July.

Kainuun Museo MUSEUM
(www.kainuunmuseo.fi; Asemakatu 4; adult/child €4/free; ☉noon-4pm Sun-Fri, to 7pm Wed-Thu) The town museum, near the railway station, has a good permanent exhibition on Kajaani's history, including info on the castle, tar boats and Elias Lönnrot. There are also regular temporary exhibitions.

🛏 Sleeping

Kartanohotelli Karolineburg HOTEL €€
(☏613 1291; www.karolineburg.com; Karoliinantie 4; s/d from €70/90, d with sauna from €100, ste from €130; ℗) Set in a wooden manor house and various outbuildings across the river from town, this makes an intriguing place to stay;

HEAD FOR THE FELLS

Syöte, the southernmost fell in Finland, is a popular winter-sports escape from Oulu, with both downhill and cross-country available. The **Syöte National Park** (www.outdoors.fi) covers discrete areas of old-growth spruce forest and is great for skiing or hiking treks. There's a visitors centre and plenty of accommodation, including a couple of good hotels with great views, and rentals managed by **Pudasjärven Matkailu** (🖉823 400; www.syote.net; Kauppatie 3, Pudasjärvi; ☺9am-5pm Mon-Fri), based in Pudasjärvi between Syöte and Oulu. There's a bus service from Oulu to Syöte (€24.50, 2¼ hours) leaving once daily Monday to Friday. Another option is to change in Pudasjärvi.

it's a refreshing change from sterile business hotels. Run somewhat airily by a friendly family, it offers a wide range of chambers, from suites with their own sauna and terrace to simpler modern rooms. Elegant furnishings, bosky grounds and classy restaurant fare make it a romantic choice. Cross the bridge past the castle and you'll see it signposted to your left.

Hotelli Kainuu   HOTEL €€
(🖉030-608 6100; www.hotellikajaani.fi; Onnelantie 1; s/d €72/90; P@) This unassuming hotel has neat, spotless rooms in a nice location among pines near the pretty riverside a kilometre east of town. From the train station, turn right and go along Niskantie for 10 minutes and you'll see it on your left. You can usually bag it a bit cheaper than the above rates.

Sokos Hotel Valjus   HOTEL €€
(🖉615 0200; www.sokoshotels.fi; Kauppakatu 20; s/d €106/122, weekends & summer from €71/82; P@) Right in the centre of town on the main street, this is one of two Sokos hotels almost opposite each other. There's a mixture of rooms in its labyrinthine interior; some have a staircase down from the door, while superiors have their own balcony.

Kainuunportti   HOTEL, CAMPGROUND €
(🖉613 3000; www.kainuunportti.fi; Mainuantie 350; tent sites €9.50, s/d €49/60; ☺camping May-Oct; P) The cheapest accommodation choice is

this hotel and camping ground by a service station 4km from town down the Iisalmi road. It's not a romantic location, but the rooms are decent value and include sauna and breakfast.

🍴 Eating & Drinking

As you head north, Finland's restaurant scene starts to worsen somewhere around Kajaani.

Sirius   FINNISH €
(🖉612 2087; www.ravintolasirius.fi; Brahenkatu 5; lunches €6.50-13; ☺lunch Mon-Fri) Located above the rapids, this restaurant is set in a characterful 1940s villa built as a residence for the local paper company. Choices range from salad table to a full buffet (€29), and there are also delicious, classy daily fish or meat specials. There's a great terrace out the back. It opens in the evenings for group bookings only.

Ranch   TEX-MEX €€
(www.ranch.fi; Kauppakatu 26; mains €13-25; ☺lunch Mon, lunch & dinner Tue-Sat, 2-8pm Sun) In an alley off the main street, the painted windows here defy casual stickybeaking but conceal a pleasant interior. The food's for meat-eating people with an appetite; big burgers and choose-your-weight steaks smothered in sauce, alongside some Mexican options. Good service and free corn chips add points.

ℹ Information

Kajaani Info (🖉6155 2555; www.visitkajaani. fi; Kauppakatu 21; ☺9am-5pm Mon-Fri, to 2pm Sat Jun-Aug, to 4.30pm Mon-Fri Sep-May) Helpful tourist office, just off the tiny town square. Free internet.

Public library (Kauppakatu 35; ☺10am-8pm Mon-Fri, to 3pm Sat) Free internet.

ℹ Getting There & Away

Finnair flies daily from Helsinki. The **airport** is 8km northwest; a **bus** (www.akyllonen.fi; ticket €4.50) runs from the kauppatori via the Kajanus hotel to coincide with flights. It's about €20 in a cab.

Kajaani is Kainuu's travel hub. There are up to eight daily bus departures for Kuhmo (€19, 1¾ hours) and other towns in the region during the week, but few departures on weekends. There are daily trains from Helsinki (€71.10, 6½ hours), via Kuopio, and services on to Oulu.

Around Kajaani

PALTANIEMI

Paltaniemi village is 9km northwest of Kajaani and has its own distinctive history as a separate and significant parish. Its enchantingly weathered wooden **church** (Paltaniementie 851; admission free; ☺10am-6pm mid-May–mid-Aug) was built in 1726, and has some of Finland's most interesting church paintings; rustic 18th-century works full of life and colour that enliven the roof and walls. Above the entrance, symbolically representing the dangers of life outside the church's protective bosom, is a vivid scene of hell, complete with a queen riding a scary beast, and numerous serpents and tormented souls. It was covered for many years to avoid offending parish sensibilities. There's someone on hand to explain or answer any questions.

Alongside the church, what looks like a woodshed is the **Keisarintalli**, an old stable that was actually used as a boarding house for Tsar Alexander I when he toured Finland in 1819. This simple building (moved from Vuolijoki) was the best available.

Nearby, the **Eino Leino-Talo** (Sutelantie 28; admission free; ☺10am-6pm Sun-Fri mid-Jun–mid-Aug) is a re-creation of the place where Leino, one of Finland's foremost independence-era poets, was born in 1878. It's a lovely lakeside spot, with a cafe as well as photos and memorabilia. You can rent bikes here to explore the area.

Take local bus 4 from Pohjolankatu in Kajaani to Paltaniemi; there are hourly departures on weekdays only. Otherwise, it's 9km or a €20 cab.

Kuhmo

📞08 / POP 9478

Kuhmo, once a major tar producer, is a good launch pad for the wilderness; it makes a natural base for hiking the UKK route, Finland's longest marked trek. The vast taiga forests run from here right across Siberia and harbour 'respect' animals like wolves, bears and lynx; you can learn about these creatures in the nature centre.

It's also the unofficial capital of Vienan Karjala, the Karelian heartland that is now in Russia. This was the region that artists explored in the Karelian movement, such a crucial part of the development of Finnish national identity. Most of their expeditions set off from Kuhmo, as did one of Elias Lönnrot's, when he headed into 'Songland' to record the verses of bards that he later wove into the *Kalevala* epic. There's a fine *Kalevala* resource centre in town, as well as a theme park.

This likeable little town also has a great chamber music festival in July, when there's a real buzz about the place, and quality concerts at accessible prices.

◉ Sights

Juminkeko　　　　MUSEUM, CULTURAL CENTRE
(www.juminkeko.fi; Kontionkatu 25; adult/child €4/free; ☺noon-6pm Mon-Thu, daily Jul) If you are interested in the *Kalevala* or Karelian culture, pay a visit to this excellent resource centre, a beautiful building made using traditional methods and modern styling. The fantastic staff can tell you anything you wish to know; there are also three to four detailed exhibitions here yearly.

Tuupalan Museo　　　　　　MUSEUM
(www.kuhmo.fi; Tervatie 1; adult/child €2/1; ☺10am-4pm Mon-Fri, 11am-4pm Sat & Sun Jun & Jul) This house-museum consists of various traditional Karelian red-painted wooden farm buildings that have been fitted out to depict traditional Kuhmo life at the turn of the 20th century for wealthy families and their servants. It's a gentle, charming display of everyday objects from the past. There's also a traditional tar boat. The optional guided visit (English available) is worthwhile.

Kalevalakylä　　　　　THEME PARK
(Kalevala Village; ☎0440-755 500; www.kalevalaspirit.fi; ☺early Jun–mid-Aug & Christmas) Four kilometres from the centre, this theme park is actually less about the *Kalevala* epic than traditional Karelian life. Part of the village, by the camping ground, is free to enter. It has a number of Karelian wooden buildings with characteristic overlapping corners, including a sauna, craft shops and Pohjolantalo, a large hall that functions as cafe, restaurant and gallery.

The rest of the area, which includes a smoke sauna, tar-making, fishing etc, is basically designed for group visits: ask if there are any tours scheduled that you can join.

Kuhmon Talvisotamuseo　　　MUSEUM
(www.kuhmo.fi/talvisotamuseo; Väinämöinen 11; adult/child €3/2; ☺9am-6pm Mon-Fri, 11am-4pm Sat & Sun Jun–mid-Aug) Opposite the Kalevalakylä, this Winter War museum covers that bitter conflict in the Kuhmo area, mostly through maps and excellent photographs

Kuhmo

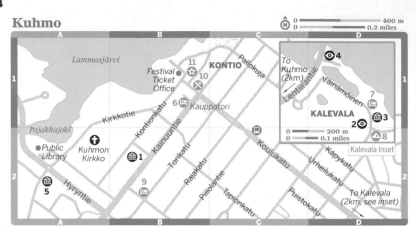

(descriptions available in English). The Finns were very successful on this front, inflicting enormous casualties on the Russian divisions in frighteningly low temperatures. It sometimes opens for reduced hours in winter.

FREE **Petola Luontokeskus** NATURE CENTRE (www.outdoors.fi; Lentiirantie 342; ☺9am-5pm daily Jun-Aug, to 4pm Mon-Fri Sep-May) This is on the main road near Kalevalakylä and has an informative exhibition in various languages on Finland's quartet of large carnivores,

known hereabouts as *karhu* (bear), *ilves* (lynx), *ahma* (wolverine) and *susi* (wolf), as well as wild reindeer, present in the region in small numbers, and the golden eagle. There are various audiovisuals, as well as a summer cafe, information sheets on most of Finland's national parks, and a cute gift shop.

🏃 Activities

Hiking is the big drawcard in Kuhmo – the eastern 'branch line' of the UKK route passes through here then turns north near the Russian border and heads up to Suomussalmi – but there are plenty of other ways to get active; the tourist office can help organise things like **whitewater rafting**, while the Petola nature centre has more **walking** information and can arrange **fishing** permits.

The website www.wildtaiga.fi has details of activities offered in the region. There are bears, elk, flying squirrels, beavers, wolverines and wild reindeer around here: safaris and bear-viewing from hides are organised by **Wild Brown Bear** (☎040-546 9008; www.wbb.fi) and **Taiga Spirit** (☎040-746 8243; www.taigaspirit.com) for €130 to €150 a time. Bears can be seen from May to early October. Both these companies take you out to hides near the Russian border, where you spend the whole night (sleeping places available). **Erämatkailu Piirainen** (☎0400-219 197; www.erapiira.fi) offers watching of wolverines, beavers and flying squirrels, as well as canoeing. **Ultima Taiga** (☎040-557 1977; www.ultimataiga.fi) can sort you out with canoeing and trips to Russian Karelia in summer, as well as husky-sledding in winter.

Festivals & Events

TOP CHOICE **Kuhmon Kamarimusiikki** MUSIC
(Kuhmo Chamber Music Festival; www.kuhmofestival
.fi; most events €15-22) This festival runs for
two weeks in mid- to late July and has a full
program of about 80 top-quality concerts
performed by a variety of Finnish and international musicians. Most concerts, usually
five or six short pieces bound by a tenuous
theme, are held in the **Kuhmo-Talo**, a beautiful hall that looks like one of those hobby
models made out of matchsticks. Other
concerts are in the adjacent school and in
the church; ask about late-night informal
events. Get tickets via the website or the
ticket office in the school.

🛏 Sleeping

Book well ahead during the festival, when
prices are up a little. The **town hall** (☏6155
5291; neuvonta@kuhmo.fi) can help you find accommodation in private homes at this time.

TOP CHOICE **Hotelli Kalevala** HOTEL €€
(☏655 4100; www.hotellikalevala.fi; Väinämöinen 9;
s/d €87/124; P@) Four kilometres from the
centre, by Kalevalakylä, this striking building of wood and concrete is a great place
to stay. The pretty rooms in pastel colours
mostly have tantalising lake views with
sounds of the lapping water. It's the facilities
that win you over here, though, with rentals of boats, bikes, snowmobiles and more; a
gym and spa complex; peat sauna; and various tailored trips on foot or skis, or to land a
fish or two. It's about €10 from the centre in
a cab. Ring ahead in spring and autumn, as
it will only open if there's a booking.

Matkakoti Parkki GUESTHOUSE €
(☏655 0271; matkakoti.parkki@elisanet.fi; Vienantie
3; s/d/tr €30/50/70; P) Run in a most kindly
manner, this quiet and handsome little family guesthouse offers excellent value near the
centre of town. Rooms share bathrooms, are
spotless, and need to be booked ahead during the festival. There's a kitchen you can use,
and breakfast is included. No wi-fi.

Hotelli Kainuu HOTEL €€
(☏655 1711; www.hotellikainuu.com; Kainuuntie 84;
s/d €64/80; P@) Right in the slow-beating
heart of Kuhmo, this family-run hotel offers
rooms that are comfortable without being
flashy; there's also a gym and sauna, a bar
with a terrace, and a restaurant, Eskobar,
serving uninspiring food. It's cheaper at
weekends; a little extra cash gets you a room
with private sauna.

Kalevala Camping CAMPGROUND €
(☏044-075 5500; www.kalevalaspirit.fi; Väinämöinen 13; tent sites €10, 2-/4-person cabins €40/50,
cottages €90/110; ☉Jun-Aug) Four kilometres from town, this has a most attractive
lakeside location among tall pines. Facilities aren't wonderful, but there are saunas,
boats and different cabins, some with their
own bathroom. Reception is at adjacent Kalevalakylä.

🍴 Eating

Try a *rönttönen* in the kauppatori; this open
pastry with potato and lingonberry mixes
sweet and savoury tastes.

The best restaurant is in the **Hotelli Kalevala**, but it's only reliably open in July; book
it ahead at other times. The cafe at the **Petola Luontokeskus** does a lunchtime buffet
at busy times. The cafe in the **Kuhmo-Talo**
is good for festival-time drinks and snacks,
while **Pohjolantalo**, a wooden hall in the
Kalevalakylä, functions as a cafe and also,
according to demand, as a restaurant serving traditional Karelian food; check with Kalevala Spirit for opening times.

TREKKING THE UKK

Pockets of the now-rare Finnish wilderness still exist – in pristine condition –
along the eastern border of Finland. They
are best seen and experienced
on a trek along the **Urho K Kekkonen
(UKK) route**. This 240km trail is the
nation's longest and greatest trekking
route, starting at Koli in Karelia, and
ending in Syöte.

There are numerous possible access
points, and alternative branches of the
route, but the Kuhmo area offers some
excellent portions of it: the Kuhmo
to Hiidenportti leg and the Kuhmo to
Lentiira leg. The trek east from Kuhmo
to Lentiira village via Iso-Palonen park
takes at least four days and offers superb scenery. It's well marked and has
laavu (simple log shelters) at regular
intervals: these have an established
campfire place, firewood and pit toilet.
Carry a sleeping bag and *plenty* of insect repellent, and pick up route maps
at the Petola nature centre in Kuhmo.

Neljä Kaesaa CAFE €
(www.neljakaesaa.fi; Koulukatu 3; lunches €7-9; ⊗8am-5pm Mon-Fri, to 1pm Sat) The best central option is only open at lunchtime, when it doles out portions of warming and traditional Finnish comfort food like stews (sometimes with elk), or fried *muikku* (vendace, or whitefish). It opens for extended hours during the festival.

Information

There's no tourist office as such. The Petola nature centre, museums, the **bookshop** (kirjakauppa; Kainuuntie 89) and both hotels give out limited info.

Public library (Pajakkakatu 2; ⊗10am-7pm Mon-Wed & Fri, 2-7pm Thu, plus 9am-3pm Sat Sep-May) Free internet.

Getting There & Around

Numerous daily buses head to/from Kajaani (€19, 1¾ hours), and a couple to Nurmes, usually requiring a change at Sotkamo. There's a bus Monday and Friday mornings in school time to Suomussalmi. For other destinations, you'll have to go via Kajaani. There's a direct connection between Kajaani's airport and Kuhmo.

Bicycles can be hired from **Kesport** (Kainuuntie 85; ⊗9am-6pm Mon-Fri, to 2pm Sat) on the kauppatori for €15 per day.

Kuusamo
◢08 / POP 16,491

An excellent base for the active, though neither handsome nor seductive in itself, Kuusamo, in the Koillismaa region, already feels like Lapland, with reindeer roaming the tarmac hereabouts and a frontier feel to the spread-out settlement. Russia's just down the road, and the border crossing is creating increasing tourism both ways. Wonderful canoeing, hiking and wildlife-watching is available in the surrounding area; nearby Ruka also draws the winter crowds.

◉ Sights

The factory shops of Bjarmia ceramics and Kuusamo fishing lures are also popular stops, while the sleek Kuusamotalo concert hall designed by Arto Sipinen is the pride of town.

TOP CHOICE Kuusamon
Suurpetokeskus WILDLIFE RESERVE
(www.kuusamon-suurpetokeskus.fi; Keronrannantie 31; adult/child €8/4; ⊗10am-5pm roughly Apr-Sep)

There's a great backstory to this bear sanctuary situated 33km south of Kuusamo on the Kajaani road. The bears were rescued as tiny, helpless orphans and nursed by their 'father', Sulo Karjalainen, who then refused to have them put down – they can't return to the wild – when the government research project wound up. He casually takes them fishing and walking in the forest, but you'll meet them in their cages here; the guide introduces you to all of them. It's a real thrill to see these impressive, intelligent animals up so close and appreciate their different personalities. There are also lynx, a wolverine, foxes and reindeer.

Hannun Luontokuvakeskus GALLERY
(www.hannuhautala.fi; adult/child €5/2; ⊗9am-5pm Mon-Fri, 10am-2pm Sat, plus noon-4pm Sun Jul-Sep) In the tourist-office building, this rotating exhibition displays the work of famous Finnish nature photographer Hannu Hautala with great information. There are some stunning shots; equally impressive is the patience that it required to get them.

Activities & Tours

The **fishing** season is from June to August; contact the Ruka or Kuusamo tourist information offices for permits and details.

There are many tour operators based in Kuusamo, Ruka and Juuma, offering a full range of winter and summer activities. The Ruka webpage, www.ruka.fi, is a good place to look for active ideas.

Sleeping

Numerous holiday cottages dot the area. Contact the tourist office, **FinFun** (☎030-650 2530; www.ruka.finfun.fi), which has a portfolio of hundreds, or **ProLoma** (☎020-792 9700; www.proloma.fi).

Hotelli Kuusanka HOTEL €€
(☎852 2240; www.kuusanka.fi; Ouluntie 2; s/d incl breakfast €63/80; P) A cordial welcome is guaranteed at this sweet main-street hotel, whose blue-shaded rooms are so clean you can smell them. They vary widely in size and sleep up to four; some have tables, chairs and a sofa, so if it's not busy ask for one with extra space. Good breakfast is included and there's a little gym, but the sauna costs extra. It also has big, well-equipped cottages 6km up the Ruka road.

Kuusamon Kansanopisto HOSTEL €
(☎050-444 1157; kuusamon.kansanopisto@koillismaa. fi; Kitkantie 35; s/d €30/50, with shared shower

EXPLORING NORTHERN KAINUU

Kainuu is a sizeable swath of largely unvisited territory. As you venture further north, rivers and lakes become steelier, you'll see traditional haystacks and farmsteads in the middle of nowhere, and might spot your first reindeer or hear the howling of sled-dogs impatient for snow.

There are buses to Suomussalmi from Kajaani. Minibuses run between Suomussalmi and Kuusamo via Hossa.

Suomussalmi & Around

Suomussalmi, which has a hotel, is northern Kainuu's hub. Near Suomussalmi was some of the bitterest fighting of the Winter War, along the Raate Rd. Rusted ordnance commemorates it, as does **Raatteen Portti exhibition** (www.raatteenportti.fi; adult/child €7/4; ☺mid-May–Sep), 20km east of town. Nearby, the moving **Avara Syli** monument is endowed with 105 bells, one for each day of the war, and surrounded by a field of stones, one for each dead soldier.

Thirty kilometres north of Suomussalmi, by the main Rd 5 to Kuusamo, another unearthly field confronts travellers; a thousand scarecrowlike figures with heads of peat and straw stand like mute witnesses to the triumphs and failures of humanity and also, inevitably, recall the war dead. A creation of local choreographer Reijo Kela, they are given a biannual change of look by locals donating clothes.

Hossa

This remote, strung-out settlement is wonderfully set up for fishing, hiking, snowmobiling and cross-country skiing: there are many marked trails and numerous lakes. A **reindeer park** (Poropuisto; www.hossanporopuisto.fi; ☺9am-9pm mid-Jun–Sep) offers the opportunity to get to know these gentle antlered beasts.

The settlement's centre is the **Luontokeskus** (www.outdoors.fi; ☺mid-Feb–Oct), a lakeside nature centre arranging fishing permits and hiring equipment including tackle, boats and skis. It also deals with bookings for the network of trail huts scattered around the area and runs the adjacent **Karhunkainalo** (tent sites €14 plus per person €4; ☺mid-Feb–Oct; P), which has tent sites and cottages.

Four kilometres south, **Hossan Lomakeskus** (☎08-732 322; www.hossanlomakeskus.com; Hossantie 278; s/d €30/60; P) has lake frontage and a selection of cabins, as well as a long hotel, whose rooms have decent bathrooms and exterior doors. Sauna and breakfast are included, and there's a bar and mediocre restaurant. It can organise transfers from Kuusamo or Kajaani.

€25/42; P) Around the corner from the bus station, this folk high school offers great budget accommodation in comfortable spacious rooms with ensuites (some share shower facilities) in a variety of buildings. There are kitchen and laundry facilities; the bad news is that you have to arrive during office hours (8am to 3.45pm Monday to Friday). There's still some availability during term-time.

Holiday Club Kuusamon Tropiikki　　　　SPA HOTEL, CAMPGROUND €€
(☎020-123 4906; www.holidayclub.fi; Kylpyläntie; s/d summer €60/90, winter €140/170, tent sites €10; P@≋) Six clicks north of Kuusamo centre, this hotel is built around a great-for-kids spa complex, whose fake palms make quite a contrast to the typically Finnish forest that surrounds the complex. The bedrooms have decent mattresses and curious bathrooms; superiors have a lot more space and a couple of extras. Rates are normally somewhere in between the summer minimum and winter maximum listed here. There's a pleasant adjacent camping ground, **Rantatropiikki Camping**, with cabins and cottages. Among several other facilities, you can rent bikes at the hotel (€7/9 for two/four hours).

✖ Eating & Drinking

Choices are limited. Near the tourist office are several giant supermarkets where you can stock up on trekking supplies.

Hiking

verse the wilderness along well-
ntained trails in Oulanka National
k (p262)

2. Bears

Meet furry locals in the bear
sanctuary at Kuusamo (p256)

3. Nature

Take in the peaceful scenery
surrounding Jyrävä waterfall in
Oulanka National Park (p262)

Martina FINNISH, ITALIAN €
(www.martina.fi; Ouluntie 3; mains €10-25) This chain place has a huge menu for the whole family, with a range of pizzas and pastas as well as fish, salad buffet, and grilled chicken, meat and vegetables. In the same place is **Wanha Mestari** (open from 6pm), the reliable town boozer.

Baari Martai FINNISH €
(Airotie; lunches €7-9; ⊙lunch Mon-Fri) In an unattractive industrial area not far from the tourist office (look behind the ABC service station), this place keeps lunching workers happy with excellent, very authentic hot dishes. Sautéed reindeer and fried vendace were the choices the day we last dropped in; there's also a plate for kids.

Vesitorni CAFE
(Joukamontie 32; ⊙10am-6pm Tue-Sun Jun-early Aug) The town's water tower makes a pleasant, unusual place for a drink. There's a licensed cafe up the top, with rather nice tables from which to appreciate the view.

ℹ Information

Karhuntassu (☑030-650 2540; www.kuusamo. fi; Torangintaival 2; ⊙9am-5pm Mon-Fri, plus weekends in high season) This large visitor

---

GETTING ACTIVE AROUND KUUSAMO

The Kuusamo/Ruka area is probably Finland's best equipped for outdoor activities. There are numerous operators offering year-round excursions:

Karhu-Kuusamo (☑040-021 0681; www.karhukuusamo.com; trips €120-140) Recommended bear-watching trips. You spend the evening at a comfortable hide overlooking a meadow where bears regularly stop by for a feed: most of the summer, you have a very high chance of seeing a honeypaw. You get back to town around midnight or the next morning. The guide Tuomo is very knowledgeable and can also arrange birdwatching.

NorthTrek (☑040-418 2832; www.northtrek.net; Erkkorannantie 1, Ruka) Offers family-friendly rafting, canoeing and hiking trips. In winter it's snowshoeing, cross-country skiing, huskies and snow ponies.

Ruka Safaris (☑852 1610; www.rukasafaris.fi; Rukarinteentie 1, Ruka) At the hairpin bend on the way up to Ruka fell. Wide range of summer and winter activities including reindeer safaris, fishing, canoeing and rafting, and has its own accommodation and restaurant.

Rukapalvelu (☑010-271 0510; www.rukapalvelu.fi; Rukakyläntie 13, Ruka) Comprehensive range from husky and snowmobile safaris to winter and summer fishing, canoeing in Oulanka, and rapids-floating. It also arranges trips to Russia to see breathtakingly pretty Karelian villages (visa required). Has an office at the Tropiikki hotel too.

Ruka Adventures (☑852 2007; www.rukaadventures.fi; Rukanriutta 7, Ruka) At the main-road turn-off. Canoeing, fishing, ATV trips and winter activities.

Basecamp Oulanka (☑040-050 9741; www.basecampoulanka.fi, Myllykoskentie 30, Juuma) These guys are great for rafting trips on the Kitkajoki. The family-friendly Käylä–Juuma trip lasts three hours (adults €36). The Wild Route (€56) lasts two hours and is for those aged 18 and over, as is the longer trip to the border zone (€85). Winter activities include snowshoeing and ice climbing. Conservation fee included.

Stella Polaris (☑040-843 3235; www.stellapolaris.fi; Sompatie 2, Ruka) Covers all the local rafting trips as well as fishing classes, canoeing and snowmobiling.

Kuusamon Lintumatkailu (☑0500-501 706; olli.lamminsalo@gmail.com) Specialist birdwatching guide.

Kota-Husky (☑040-718 7287; www.kota-husky.fi; Jaksamontie 58, Karjalaisenniemi) Excellent small-group husky excursions and picturesque kennels in an old barn. Based north of Posio.

Erä-Susi (☑huskies 040-570 0279, canoes 040-913 6652; www.erasusi.com) Rent canoes from the Oulanka visitor centre in the middle of the park. Prices depend on your route and include pick-up or drop-off and safety lesson. It also does guided trips. In winter, there are husky safaris from Ruka; in summer you can hike with huskies or visit their farm (€5).

centre is at the highway junction, 2km from the centre. There's comprehensive tourist information, free internet, a FinFun desk for booking rental cottages, and a cafe-shop. Open slightly different hours is a wildlife photography exhibition (see Hannun Luontokuvakeskus, p256) and national park information desk.

Public library (Kaiterantie 22; ☺Mon-Fri year-round, plus Sat Sep-May) Free internet.

❶ Getting There & Away

Finnair hits **Kuusamo airport**, 6km northeast of the town centre, from Helsinki. Blue1 also flies the route daily in winter. Buses meet flights (€7 to Kuusamo, €10 to Ruka), leaving Kuusamo bus station just over an hour before departure. Call ☎010-084 200 for a taxi.

Buses run daily from Kajaani (€40.70, 3½ hours), Oulu (€38.10, three hours) and Rovaniemi (€32.20, three hours). Several daily services run to Ruka (€6.30, 30 minutes).

Ruka

☎08

Ruka is one of Finland's major ski resorts and is buzzing during winter, when prices are at their highest. It's a great base for outdoors activities year-round though. In summer, it makes a useful base for hiking the Karhunkierros, and there's enough going on that it doesn't feel too spooky. You can nab some excellent accommodation deals at this time too.

The Ruka turn-off is 26km north of Kuusamo. Two kilometres down this road, you can turn right to the small centre of Itä-Ruka (another 3km), or continue up the hill to the pedestrianised main centre of the resort, where most facilities are.

🏃 Activities

See p260 for details of tour operators in Ruka and Kuusamo. In the centre of Ruka, **RukaStore** is open daily year-round and rents **mountain bikes** (€25 per day). **Ruka-Palvelu** does too, as well as fishing equipment and canoes.

Summer

There's plenty to do around Ruka in summer, with great walking and birdwatching on the doorstep and good mountain-biking trails. There are lots of free activities organised throughout summer, including some for kids if you fancy an afternoon off.

Skiing

Busy **Ruka fell** (www.ruka.fi) boasts 30 downhill ski slopes, dedicated snowboard areas, a vertical drop of 201m and a longest run of 1300m, as well as the bonus of well over 200 skiable days per year: the season normally runs from mid-October to early June. Ruka also boasts cross-country trails totalling an impressive 500km, with 40km illuminated.

🛏 Sleeping

Ruka's very busy in winter and it can be difficult to find a reasonably priced bed. In summer, it's great value.

There are numerous apartments available in Ruka itself, and hundreds of cabins and cottages throughout the surrounding area. See Kuusamo's Sleeping section, p256, for details of two of the biggest agencies. For rooms, apartments and chalets in Ruka, go for **RukaBooking** (☎8600 300; www.ski-inn.fi), which rents out most of the central ones, or **Ruka-ko** (☎866 0088; www.ruka-ko.fi; Rukanriutta 7), at the main-road turn-off to Ruka. There are links to more cabin and cottage providers on www.ruka.fi.

If you stay in Ruka in summer, you get a 'Summer Wristband', which gets you plenty of decent discounts on meals and activities in the area.

TOP CHOICE **Royal Hotel Ruka** HOTEL €€€
(☎040-0819 840; www.royalruka.fi; s/d €175/190, r Jul-Oct €90; ☺Jul-Apr; ☒) Down at the foot of the fell at the turn-off to Rukajärvi, this small and intimate hotel looks like a children's fort to be populated with toy soldiers. It's the most luxurious accommodation choice in the Kuusamo area; service is excellent here, and the classy restaurant offers delicacies such as roast hare. From July to November it only opens for bookings.

Hotel Rantasipi Rukahovi HOTEL €€€
(☎85910; www.rantasipi.fi; Rukatunturientie 16; s/d winter €133/173, summer r €82; ☒@) Right by the major slopes in the centre of town, this huge complex aims to please everyone from conferencing execs to snowball-lobbing families, and largely succeeds, thanks to plenty of facilities and a wide variety of rooms, from standard Nordic pads to more upmarket beds in the new extension, and capacious duplex apartments. Its restaurant, bars and nightclub are well patronised in the cold season.

Willi's West MOTEL €

(☑0400-242 992; www.wwsaloon.com; Rukanriutta 13; apt s/d summer €45/49, winter €59-89; P) At the Ruka turn-off on the main road is this friendly motel-style set-up offering good value. Rooms are small apartments sleeping up to five, and have spacious bathroom and a small, equipped kitchen. It's a steal in summer. The owners will take groups of walkers to the Karhunkierros trailheads.

Vuosselin Helmi APARTMENT €

(☑040-0241 795; www.vuosselinhelmi.com; Bistrontie 6; r summer/winter €45/79; P) At Itä-Ruka behind the Wings Bar (where reception is), these cheap rooms have a double bed plus a fold-out couch and are great value for families. There's a microwave and fridge; linen is extra. In summer you must prebook (two-night minimum).

✕ Eating & Drinking

Riipisen Riistaravintola FINNISH €€

(www.riistaravintolat.fi; Rukatunturintie 9; most mains €18-35; ⊘daily Nov-Apr, noon-9pm Mon-Fri May-Oct) At the Kelo ski-lift area, a five-minute walk from Ruka square, this friendly log cabin has an attractively rustic interior. It specialises in game dishes, and you'll find Rudolf, Bullwinkle and, yes, poor Yogi (€60) on the menu here in various guises, depending on availability and season. Arctic hare also features, while capercaillie in a creamy sauce will get bird-lovers twitching too.

Kalakeidas FISH €€

(☑0400-836 023; www.kalakeidas.fi; Rukatunturintie 2; mains €15-30; ⊘5-11pm Sep-Apr) In a *kota*-style building (traditional dwelling resembling a tepee or wigwam) near Riipisen Riistaravintola, this candlelit aquatic-oriented restaurant has a range of temptations created with locally caught fish. There are various shared platters that should be ordered the day before. Try the flavoured house schnapps.

Piste FINNISH €

(www.ruka.fi; mains €10-25; ⊘11am midnight daily Sep-May, noon-6pm Sun-Thu, to 8pm Fri-Sat Jun-Aug) At the base of the lifts on Ruka's main square, this cavernous wooden hall has several attractive dining areas and good service. Dishes range from burgers and fried fish to steaks and fish cooked on hot stones.

Zone BAR

(www.ravintolazone.fi; ⊘noon-4am) This central bar's big glassed-in terrace packs out at night in the ski season and has its own fast-food kiosk. There's karaoke nightly, regular live music, and a general vibe of pissed-up goodwill.

❶ Information

Ruka Info (☑860 0250; www.ruka.fi; ⊘9am-5pm early Jun & late Aug, 9.30am-7pm Sep & late Jun–mid-Aug, 10am-8pm Oct-May) In the Kumpare building in the main village square. Tourist information and accommodation booking. In the same building is pricey internet access (€1 per 10 minutes), a self-service laundry, supermarket, gym and more.

❶ Getting There & Away

Ruka is 30km north of Kuusamo on Rd 5 and served by bus a few times daily (€6.30, 30 minutes). Buses run between Kuusamo airport and Ruka (€10), and during the ski season there's a shuttle bus between Ruka and Kuusamo, stopping at major hotels.

Karhunkierros Trek & Oulanka National Park

The Karhunkierros (Bear's Ring), one of the oldest and best-established trekking routes in Finland, offers up some of the country's most breathtaking scenery. It is extremely popular in summer but it can be walked practically any time between late May and October.

Despite the name, it's not a circuit, rather a point-to-point walk of anything from 52km (Ristikallio to Juuma) to 80km (Hautajärvi to Ruka). There are four trailheads: the northern access point is from Hautajärvi visitor centre on the road to Salla; further south on Rd 950 is the Ristikallio parking area; in the south you can start the walk at Ruka ski resort; or further northeast at Juuma village. Also at Juuma there's a spectacular loop trail, the 12km Pieni Karhunkierros (Little Bear's Ring); see p267.

Most people choose to walk north to south for transport-connection reasons.

Much of the walk is through the Oulanka National Park, which is also a great destination for canoeing and rafting (see p266).

Trekking

The track's well marked with orange paint and regular signboards. If you're just on a day trip, you could do it in light shoes on dry summer days, but for the full route, you'll need proper hiking boots, particularly for the Juuma to Ruka section. Prior to mid-June the ground is too soggy to make hiking enjoyable. Even if you don't intend to walk the whole route, a day walk can take you from Ristikallio to Oulanka Canyon and back, for example. It's also possible to drive to within 1km of Oulanka Canyon along a signposted dirt road about 12km north of Ristikallio.

There are plenty of wilderness huts, so you can divide the route up according to your own pace. People tend to do Ristikallio to Juuma in two or three days, with a further long day to Ruka.

FROM RISTIKALLIO

Start at the parking area at Ristikallio; you'll soon enter the national park. There's a wilderness hut (of use if you're coming the other way) about an hour in. Less than an hour further gets you to Puikkokämppä hut at a small lake. Continue another kilometre and a bit past the lake to Taivalköngäs (9km from the start), near the wilderness hut of the same name), with two sets of rapids and three suspension bridges.

FROM HAUTAJÄRVI

Another starting point is further north at the Hautajärvi visitor centre – this adds an extra 10km to the hike. The landscape is unimpressive until the path reaches the Savinajoki. The deep Oulanka Canyon is a highlight of this part of the trek. A wilderness hut is at the Oulanka riverfront near Savilampi, a lake 15km south of Hautajärvi. The distance from Savilampi to Taivalköngäs – where you'll join the Ristikallio trail – is 4km.

TAIVALKÖNGÄS TO JUUMA

From Taivalköngäs the first stretch is through typical forest scenery enlivened by beautiful lakes. After 4km, you can camp at Lake Runsulampi; there's dry wood available. About 3.5km further east, there's Oulanka Camping; another kilometre brings you to the Oulanka Visitor Centre and its welcome cafe. The rugged cliffs and muscular waters of the Kiutaköngäs rapids are a short way further on. From Oulanka it's 7km to Ansakämppä cabin, and a further 8km to Jussinkämppä wilderness hut on Kulmakkajärvi.

From here the trail is a little tougher. A hike through ridges and forests takes you to the Kitkajoki in another deep gorge. When

EXPLORING RIISITUNTURI

Another worthwhile national park is Riisitunturi, 54km northwest of Kusamo, not far from the town of Posio. Consisting of fells and hillside bogs, it offers spectacular views and rewarding hiking: a 29km trail crosses the park from one side to the other. See www.outdoors.fi for details of huts and trails.

you meet the Pieni Karhunkierros trail, you can turn right to head directly to Juuma via the bridge at Myllykoski, or turn left for the more scenic route via the Jyrävä waterfall (where you'll find Siilastupa hut, 16km beyond Jussinkämppä). Three and a half kilometres beyond here is Juuma, where there are camp sites, and the Basecamp Oulanka lodge on the trail just outside it.

RUKA EXTENSION

Juuma is a convenient end to the trek, but you can also walk 24km further to Ruka, which has a big choice of accommodation and better road connections to Kuusamo. This is more strenuous than the previous sections, with many ascents and descents. There is one wilderness hut, Porontimajoki (often full), 8km down this trail, and several lean-to shelters.

🛏 Sleeping

There is a good network of **wilderness huts** along the Karhunkierros. All are pretty similar and tend to be crowded in high season. Although tradition says there's always room for the last to arrive, a tent's handy, as someone often ends up sleeping outside. Dry firewood is generally available, and there's a gas cooker in most, but carry a lightweight mattress. Your options north to south:

Savilampi On the Hautajärvi route, about 15km in, this hut sleeps 10.

Ristikallio Located 5km east of the main road, has a nice lakeside location. Accommodates 10 and has dry firewood.

Puikkokämppä Situated 2.5km further east, a basic lakeside hut sleeping 10 people.

Taivalköngäs Near the junction of the trails, accommodates 15 on two floors. This is 19km from Hautajärvi, 9km from Ristikallio, and 8.5km from Oulanka Visitor Centre.

OULU, KAINUU & KOILLISMAA KARHUNKIERROS TREK & OULANKA NATIONAL PARK

Karhunkierros Trek & Oulanka National Park

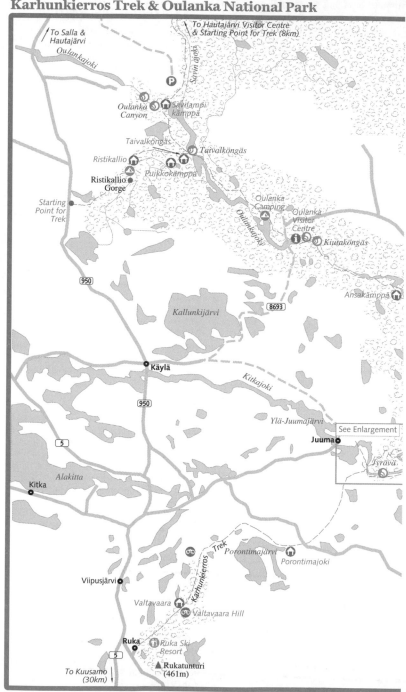

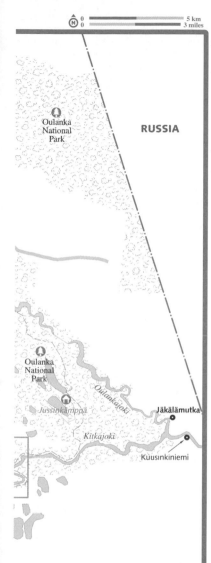

Ansakämppä Located 7km east of the visitor centre, sleeps 20.

Jussinkämppä Situated 8km further on, sleeps 20.

Siilastupa Positioned 3.5km from Juuma opposite the Jyrävä waterfall, sleeps 12. Often full. Once a fishing lodge for a Finnish general. This is also on the Pieni Karhunkierros loop trail.

Porontimajoki Located 8km south of Juuma, it sleeps eight in two huts. Popular last- or first-night stop, and often full.

Oulanka Camping CAMPGROUND €
(☑020-564 6855; www.outdoors.fi; Liikasenvaarantie 137; tent sites for 1 person/more €6/12, 4-person cabins €40; ☺Jun-Aug) The trail runs right through this place, 1km from the visitor centre. It rents canoes and rowing boats to use on the Oulankajoki, and has a kiosk and sauna. It will open in early September if you book ahead. A 5km circular walk leaves from here.

❶ Information

The 1:50,000 *Rukatunturi-Oulanka* map is useful for treks of any length. It costs €19 and is sold at both park visitor centres and the Kuusamo and Ruka tourist offices. The map-guide to the Karhunkierros costs €25. The trail is so well signposted that you can easily make do with the free map.

If you need gear, Rukapalvelu in Ruka rents tents, packs and other hiking equipment.

Hautajärvi Visitor Centre (www.outdoors.fi; ☺9am-4pm Mon-Fri Jan-May & Oct, to 5pm Jun-Sep) Helpful, at the northern trailhead, right on the Arctic Circle on the Kuusamo–Salla road, 1km north of Hautajärvi village. There's a cafe and exhibition on the ecosystem of the mires, dotted with apposite literary quotes.

Oulanka Visitor Centre (www.outdoors.fi; Liikasenvaarantie 132; ☺10am-4pm Oct-May, to 6pm Jun-Sep) In the middle of Oulanka National Park, accessible along a 13km un-sealed road from Käylä on Rd 950. There are several free audiovisuals, trekking supplies, a cafe, maps and fishing licences. An 8km round trip takes you along the Oulankajoki to the Kiutaköngäs rapids. You can also rent canoes here; the price includes pick-up or drop-off and a safety lesson.

❶ Getting There & Away

From early June to early August, a handy early-morning **bus** (☑020-1303 520; www.pohjolanmatka.fi) runs from Kuusamo to Salla via Ruka, Juuma, Ristikallio and Hautajärvi from Monday to Friday, and returns, arriving back in Kuusamo at 1.50pm. There's a connection from Käylä to the Oulanka Visitor Centre on Mondays, Wednesdays and Fridays during this period. Outside these dates, the bus runs a little later, doesn't go to Juuma, but still passes Ristikallio and Hautajärvi. There are no buses at weekends.

A **taxi** (☑868 1222) from Ruka can be a good option if shared between three or four people; it costs a fixed €35 to €40 to Juuma, and €65 to Hautajärvi.

River Routes Around Kuusamo

The Oulankajoki and Kitkajoki, which meet almost at the Russian border, offer wonderful canoeing and rafting opportunities in protected wilderness areas. You can do these trips as organised, guided adventures, or hire canoes or kayaks from operators, who can also arrange transport at either end. See p260 for operators.

OULANKAJOKI

Shadowing the Karhunkierros much of the way, the Oulankajoki gives you a chance to see mighty canyons from a canoe or kayak. You *must* carry your canoe at least four times. Take a river map.

The first leg, a 20km trip, starts from Rd 950, north of Ristikallio. The first 7km or so is relatively calm paddling, until you reach the impressive Oulanka Canyon. The safe section extends for about 1km, after which you should pull aside and carry your canoe twice past dangerous rapids. You can overnight at Savilampi hut, which is also a popular spot to start.

Some 3km after Savilampi are the Taivalköngäs rapids (carry your canoe), where there's a wilderness hut. The next 9km are quiet and pass a couple of camping grounds before reaching the Oulanka Visitor Centre, which has a cafe that rents canoes for this trip. Not far below here are the Kiutaköngäs rapids, where you'll need to carry your canoe again. Below them starts the Lower Oulankajoki stretch, 25km of easy paddling, suitable for beginners. You end up at the Jäkälämutka parking area just short of the Russian border.

KITKAJOKI

The spectacular Kitkajoki offers some of Finland's best canoeing and rafting. There are two main sections: the family-friendly section from Käylä to Juuma, and the challenging 'wild' section beyond Juuma, which includes plenty of tricky rapids, including the class IV, 900m Aallokkokoski.

The village of **Käylä**, on the Kuusamo–Salla road, is the starting point for the gentle first section. The starting point for the wild section is Juuma.

KÄYLÄ TO JUUMA

The first 14km leg of the journey is definitely the easier of the two, suitable for families with children, and does not involve any carrying at all. You start at the Käylänkoski, continue 3km to the easy Kiehtäjänniva, and a further kilometre to the Vähä-Käylänkoski. These are both class I rapids. After a bit more than 1km, there are three class II rapids spaced every 400m or so. A kilometre further, there's the trickiest one, the class III Harjakoski, which is 300m long. The rest of the journey, almost 7km, is mostly lakes. The road bridge between the lakes Ylä-Juumajärvi and Ala-Juumajärvi marks the end of the trip. It is 1km to Juuma from the bridge.

JUUMA TO THE RUSSIAN BORDER

This 20km journey is one of Finland's most challenging river routes: you should be an expert paddler, and you *must* carry your canoe at least once – around the 12m, class VI Jyrävä waterfall. Ask for local advice and inspect the tricky rapids before you let go. There's a minimum age of 18 to canoe this route.

The thrill starts just 300m after Juuma, with the class II Niskakoski. From here on, there is only 1km of quiet water. Myllykoski, with a watermill, is a tricky class IV waterfall. Right after Myllykoski, the 900m Aallokkokoski rapids mean quick paddling for quite some time. The Jyrävä waterfall comes right after this long section. Pull aside before Jyrävä, and carry your canoe. You might want to carry it from Myllykoski to well beyond the Jyrävä waterfall, skipping the Aallokkokoski rapids.

After Jyrävä things cool down considerably, although there are some class III rapids. When you meet the Oulankajoki, 13km further downriver, paddle upriver to Jäkälämutka or downriver to Kuusinkiniemi, 100m from the Russian border. At either spot you can access a forest road that will take you back to civilisation. You must arrange return transport from this point in advance, as traffic is nonexistent.

Juuma

☑08

The village of Juuma is a popular base for Karhunkierros treks and canoeing on the Kitkajoki. It's a convenient place to stock up on supplies

If you have a little time for trekking, take the **Pieni Karhunkierros** (Little Bear's Ring), an easy to moderate 12km loop trail taking in some fantastic scenery as it follows the river valley far below. It leaves from by the Retki-Etappi cafe and traverses varying terrain; the wet bits are all boardwalked, so this is less mushy in spring than most hikes. The walk takes three to four hours and is one of the most scenic short routes in Finland. There's a wilderness hut on this trail – Siilastupa (see p263) – and a day hut at Myllykoski. It's well signposted, and busy. You can do it with snowshoes in winter.

See p265 for details of getting to Juuma.

🛏 Sleeping & Eating

See p256 for details of rental cottages in this area.

TOP
CHOICE **Basecamp Oulanka**   LODGE €€
(☑040-050 9741; www.basecampoulanka.fi; Myllykoskentie 30; s/d/tw €99/115/125, summer €65/90/100; P) This excellent wilderness lodge is just the place to rest your weary legs, right on the Karhunkierros trail itself near Myllykoski, about 1km from Juuma (but 5.5km by car). The snug rustic rooms smell of pine: the larger ones are great for families and groups, with a roof-space that can sleep extra bodies, and a charming balcony looking over the forest. There's a convivial bar and restaurant (lunch always on, dinner by prior arrangement), sauna and jacuzzi. Friendly staff organise all sorts of daily activities; rafting, fishing and snowshoe-walking among others. It gets cheaper if you stay more than one night; in low season it's worth asking for discounted rates. There's no internet and no kitchen facilities, but you can rent skis, canoes, kayaks and more.

Lomakylä Retki-Etappi   CAMPGROUND €
(☑040-565 3474; www.retkietappi.fi; Juumantie 134; tent sites for 1 person/more €5/10, cabins from €30; ☺Jun-Sep; P) This place, at the start of the Little Bear's Ring and a Karhunkierros trailhead, is a convenient spot to stay. There are several cabins, a couple of them available in winter, and a cafe serving snacks and meals. There's also a sauna, and boats and bikes to rent.

Juuman Leirintäalue   CAMPGROUND €
(☑044-272 7872; www.juumanleirintaalue.fi; Riekamontie 1; tent sites €15, cabins/cottages €30/60; ☺Jun-Sep; P) This place has a lovely lakeside location in Juuma at the beginning of the Käylä road. There's a sauna, laundry and a cafe that can do evening meals if you book the day before. It also arranges fishing licences and rents boats.

Lapland

Includes »

Best Places to Stay

Best Places to Eat

Why Go?

Lapland casts a powerful spell and has an irresistible romance to it that haunts the imagination and memory. While you won't see polar bears or rocky fjords, there is something intangible here that makes it magic.

The midnight sun, the Sámi peoples, the aurora borealis (Northern Lights) and the wandering reindeer are all components of this, as is good old ho-ho-ho himself, who 'officially' resides here. Another part of the spell is in the awesome latitudes – at Nuorgam, the northernmost point, you have passed Iceland and nearly all of Canada and Alaska.

Lapland, which occupies 30% of Finland's land area but houses just 3% of its population, has vast and awesome wildernesses, ripe for exploring on foot, skis or sledge. The sense of space, pure air and big skies is what is memorable here, more than the towns.

Lapland's far north is known as Sápmi, home of the Sámi people. Their main communities are around Inari, Utsjoki and Hetta. Rovaniemi is the most popular gateway to the north.

When to Go
LAPLAND

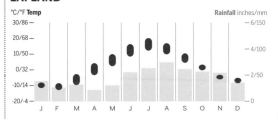

Apr The best month for sled treks and skiing, with plenty of light and not-so-scary temperatures.

Aug Plenty of light and sunshine, the trails are less crowded, and fewer biting insects.

Dec Reindeer, snow and Santa Claus himself guaranteed to inject Christmas spirit.

Lapland Highlights

1 Trekking the lonely wildernesses around **Saariselkä** (p298)

2 Dashing through the snow pulled by a team of **huskies** or **reindeer** (p287)

3 Lapping up wonderful winter experiences in **Kemi** (p277), where you can sail on an ice-breaker, swim in the frozen-over sea, then spend the night in the ethereally beautiful snow castle.

4 Panning for gold in beautiful **Lemmenjoki** and walking in the national park (p305)

5 Picnicking with views on top Saana Fell in **Kilpisjärvi** (p289)

6 Learning about its environments at Rovaniemi's **Arktikum museum** (p271)

7 Taking your first steps at exploring Sámi culture at **Siida** (p302) in Inari.

8 Skiing at Lapland's best-equipped resort at **Levi** (p282)

9 Gazing in awe at the **aurora borealis** (p295)

History

For information on Sámi and the history of Finland, see the History chapter, p314. See p311 for more detailed information on the Sámi. Sámi settlements were spread throughout the vast region but during the 1600s, Swedes increased their presence and in 1670 various cult sites and religious objects were destroyed by the Lutheran Church's Gabriel Tuderus (1638–1703). Churches were built throughout Lapland: Sodankylä's is one of the oldest left.

In the following centuries, more Finns filtered into the vast province, adopted reindeer-herding and were assimilated into Sámi communities (or vice versa), especially in southern Lapland.

The Petsamo area, northeast of Inari, was annexed to Finland in 1920 by the Treaty of Tartu; a nickel mine opened in 1937. The Soviet Union attacked the mineral-rich area during the Winter War (1939–40), annexed it in 1944, and has kept it ever since. The Skolt Sámi from Petsamo were resettled in Sevettijärvi, Nellim and Virtaniemi.

The German army's retreat in 1944–45 was a scorched-earth affair; they burned all buildings in their path to hold off pursuit. Only a few churches, villages and houses in Lapland date from the period before WWII.

Activities

Lapland's joy is the outdoors and range of exciting things to do year-round. There's good downhill skiing for almost six months of the year at several spots; Levi is Finland's most popular resort, while smaller Pyhä-

---

LAPLAND SEASONS

It's important to pick your time in Lapland carefully. In the far north there's no sun for 50 days of the year, and no night for 70-odd days. In June it's very muddy, and in July insects can be hard to deal with. If you're here to walk, August is great and in September the *ruska* (colour of the leaves in Autumn) can be seen. There's thick snow cover from mid-October to May; December draws charter flights looking for Santa, real reindeer and guaranteed snow, but the best time for skiing and husky/reindeer/snowmobile safaris is March and April, when you get a decent amount of daylight and less extreme temperatures.

Luosto and Ylläs are more family- than party-oriented. All these spots also have extensive cross-country trails.

Most memorable are sleigh safaris. Pulled by a team of huskies or reindeer, you cross the snowy wilderness, overnighting in log cabins with a relaxing wood sauna and eating meals cooked over a fire. You can organise trips of up to a week or more, or just head out for a jaunt of a couple of hours. Similar trips can be arranged on snowmobiles; Muonio and Saariselkä are particularly good places for all these excursions.

Once the snow melts, there are some fabulous multiday treks and shorter walks. The national parks network offers everything from wheelchair-accessible nature trails to demanding wilderness routes for experienced hikers, but there are good walks almost everywhere, including around Kilpisjärvi, in the far northwest, and Sevettijärvi, in the remote northeast.

Lapland's rivers are frisky, and there are several excellent canoeing routes and spots for whitewater rafting. The Ounasjoki offers perhaps the best paddling. Fishing is popular year-round: ice-fishing is a memorable and sociable experience, and the beautiful Teno Valley offers superb salmon-fishing.

Major settlements have plenty of tour operators offering all these activities. Rovaniemi, Lapland's capital, is a popular base, but Saariselkä, Levi and Muonio are equally good and are closer to genuine wilderness.

Self-Catering Accommodation

There is a huge quantity of self-catering apartments, cottages and cabins throughout the region. Out of season, ski resorts are particularly fertile ground; fully furnished places with their own sauna can be great value in summer.

Local tourist offices often double as booking agents for these accommodation options; see the Information sections of the relevant towns. **Villi Pohjola/Wild North** (www.villipohjola.fi), an arm of the Forest and Park Service, has a large selection of cabins available throughout the region.

Language

Three Sámi languages are spoken in the region, and signs in Sámi areas are bilingual. See p323 for more on Sámi languages.

Dangers & Annoyances

From mid-June to early August, Lapland is home to millions of biting insects: at times there are quite literally clouds of them, and during this räkkä season, you'll need heavy-duty repellent. By early August, most squadrons have dispersed.

Parts of Lapland are real wildernesses; always speak to staff at national park centres before attempting unmarked routes.

Winter temperatures are seriously low; don't head outdoors without being properly equipped.

Driving in Lapland calls for particular caution due to the reindeer (see p347).

❶ Getting Around

Considering the remoteness, bus connections are good, although there may only be one service a day, and none on Sundays. Hiring a car is a good option, with plenty of choice in Rovaniemi, Levi and Saariselkä/Ivalo. Petrol stations are sparsely spread, and some are automatic: carry cash.

Rovaniemi

⟐016 / POP 60,112

Expanding rapidly on the back of a tourism boom, the 'official' terrestrial residence of Santa Claus is the capital of Finnish Lapland and a more-or-less obligatory northern stop. Its wonderful Arktikum museum is the perfect introduction to the mysteries of these latitudes, and Rovaniemi is a good place to organise activities from. It's also a transport hub, a convenient spot to hire a car, and has some of Lapland's best accommodation.

Thoroughly destroyed by the retreating Wehrmacht in 1944, the town was rebuilt to a plan by Alvar Aalto, with the major streets in the shape of a reindeer's head and antlers (don't worry, it took us years to work it out). Its unattractive buildings are compensated for by its marvellous location on the fast-flowing – when not frozen over – Kemijoki, spanned by a bridge dubbed the 'Lumberjack's Candle' for its light-topped pylons.

◎ Sights

Arktikum   MUSEUM

(www.arktikum.fi; Pohjoisranta 4; adult/student/child/family €12/8/5/25; ⊙9am-6pm mid-Jun-Aug, 10am-6pm early Jun & Dec, 10am-6pm Tue-Sun Sep-Nov & Jan-May) With its beautifully designed glass tunnel stretching out to the Ounasjoki, this is one of Finland's best museums and well worth the admission fee if you are interested in the north. There are two main exhibitions; one side deals with Lapland, with some information on Sámi culture, including both traditional and mod-

ern music, and a variety of costumes. There's a display of canoes, dwellings and fishing materials, as well as a room devoted to the history of Rovaniemi itself.

The highlight, though, is the other side, with a wide-ranging display on the Arctic, with superb static and interactive displays focusing on flora and fauna, as well as on the peoples of Arctic Europe, Asia and North America. There's a research library here if you want to learn more, as well as a good restaurant. There's an audiovisual show in the auditorium three times daily; it's basically a pretty slide show, so don't stress should you miss it.

Pilke   MUSEUM

(www.sciencecentre-pilke.fi; Ounasjoentie 6; adult/child €7/5; ⊙9am-6pm Mon-Fri, 10am-6pm Sat & Sun) This new building by the Arktikum is run by the Forest and Park Service. It has permanent displays and changing summer exhibitions on sustainable forestry in Finland, as well as a national parks information point. It closes Mondays in autumn and spring.

Lappia-talo   THEATRE

(⟐040-028 2484; www.rovaniementeatteri.fi; Hallituskatu 11) Rovaniemi's concert hall is one of several buildings in Rovaniemi designed by Alvar Aalto (others include the adjacent library and town hall).

Rovaniemen Taidemuseo   GALLERY

(www.korundi.fi; Lapinkävijäntie 4; adult/child €4/free; ⊙11am-6pm Tue-Sun) This gallery has a wide collection of contemporary Finnish art that it rotates in its clean white exhibition space. Admission's free on Saturday and it's also open Monday from December to early January and from June to August.

Rovaniemen Kirkko   CHURCH

(Rauhankatu 79; ⊙9am-9pm mid-May–Aug) Completed in 1950, this church replaced the one destroyed during WWII. The impressively large fresco behind the altar depicts a Christ figure emerging from Lappish scenery. A work of Lennart Segerstråle, it has two sides, one populated by the faithful, the other by brawling drunkards and ravening wolves.

🏃 Activities

See p274 for more activities. Bicycles can be rented from **Lapland Safaris** (⟐331 1200; Koskikatu 1; per 3/24 hr €16/26) and from **Europcar** (⟐040-306 2870; Pohjanpuistikko 2; per 3/24 hr €10/20).

Rovaniemi

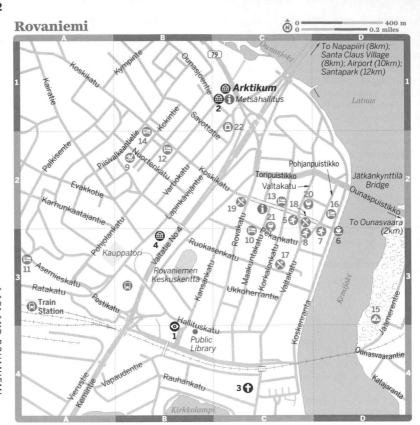

Ounasvaara
SKIING

This long fell across the river to the east of town is a place to get active. In winter, there's a **ski centre** (www.ounasvaara.fi). There are also three ski-jumps here, plus more than 100km of cross-country tracks.

ARCTIC ANIMALS

Places to visit animals include **Napapiirin Porofarmi** (📞384 150; www.porofarmi.fi; Iamsintie 7b), a reindeer farm 8km north of town. **Huskypoint** (📞040-079 0096; www.huskypoint.fi) at Sinettä offers guided kennel visits and sled rides in both summer and winter with optional transport from Rovaniemi. **Arctic Circle Husky Park** (📞040-824 7503; www.huskypark.fi) is near Santa's grotto and allows you to meet dogs. Don't forget the **zoo** at Ranua, an easy day trip from Rovaniemi.

In summer, one ski-lift and a **toboggan run** (1/3/5 rounds €6/15/20; ⊙11am-7pm mid-Jun–mid-Aug) are working if it's not raining. Walkers can take advantage of the cross-country tracks, which are well signposted. You can walk to Napapiiri (12km) as well as other places.

Bus 9 gets you to the bottom of the ski slope from town.

Vesihiisi
SWIMMING, SAUNA

(Nuortenkatu 11; admission €6; ⊙6.30am-8.30pm Mon-Fri, 9am-4.30pm Sat & Sun) Outdoor and indoor pool as well as saunas. It's cheaper in summer (€4).

👉 Tours

Kemijoen Helmi
CRUISES

(📞0400-292 132; www.kemijoenhelmi.fi; cruises €15) Two-hour jaunts on the river, some with live music or karaoke.

Rovaniemi

LAPLAND ROVANIEMI

★ Festivals & Events

With the Arctic Circle – and Santa Claus – close by, Christmas is a big time of the year and there are plenty of festive activities in December. In March, Rovaniemi hosts the **Napapiirinhiihto** (www.napapiirinhiihto.fi) with skiing and ski-jumping competitions as well as a reindeer race in the centre of town. **Jutajaiset** (www.jutajaiset.fi), in late June, is a celebration of Lapland folklore by various youth ensembles.

🛏 Sleeping

TOP CHOICE Santasport   HOTEL €€
(☏020-798 4200; www.santasport.fi; Ounasvaara; s/d/f in Sep-Apr €95/140/230, in May-Aug €60/80/110; P@⛄) A 15-minute stroll from the centre at the base of Ounasvaara, this sports complex offers great value. Brand-new rooms – including excellent family suites – offer heaps of space, fridge, microwave and drying cupboard. On site is a full-size swimming pool, spa facilities, bowling, gym, an indoor playpark for kids, and rental of bikes and cross-country skis. It also has good cottages (€195 summer, €400 winter) that sleep six, and some older, cheaper student-style rooms.

City Hotel   HOTEL €€
(☏330 0111; www.cityhotel.fi; Pekankatu 9; s/d €107/120, in Jun-Sep €75/82; P@) There's something pleasing about this warm and welcoming place a block off the main drag and cheerfully tucked between the convivial ambience of its own restaurant and bar. It retains an intimate feel, with excellent service and plenty of extras included free of charge. All the rooms are functional and compact; it's worth the small upgrade to the recently refurbished 'comfort' rooms with their new beds and plush maroon and brown fabrics.

Hotel Santa Claus   HOTEL €€€
(☏321 321; www.hotelsantaclaus.fi; Korkalonkatu 29; s/d €149/179, r weekend & summer €99; P@) Thankfully this excellent hotel is devoid of sleighbells and 'ho-ho-ho' kitsch. It's right in the heart of town and very upbeat and busy, with helpful staff and a great bar and restaurant. The rooms have all the trimmings and are spacious, with a sofa and good-sized beds; a small supplement gets you a superior room, which is slightly bigger but not really worth the upgrade.

Rantasipi Pohjanhovi   HOTEL €€
(☏33711; www.rantasipi.fi; Pohjanpuistikko 2; s/d €124/146, in summer €75/92; P@⛄) By the river, this is the historic hotel of Rovaniemi. There are two grades of room (as well as lovely suites); the standards are comfortable, though a little stuffy in summer. Superiors, which don't cost too much more, are classier and much more spacious, with

ROVANIEMI ADVENTURES

Rovaniemi is Lapland's most popular base for winter and summer activities, offering the convenience of frequent departures and professional trips with multilingual guides.

In summer, activities offered by most operators include guided walks, mountain biking (€55 to €60), river cruises (€25), visits to a reindeer farm (€50 to €60) or huskies (€80), rafting, canoeing and wilderness camping. Winter activities are snowmobiling (€97 to €155 for a two- to six-hour trip), snowshoe-walking (€49), reindeer-sledding (€104 to €111), husky-sledding (€68 to €240), cross-country skiing (€50 to €60) or a combination of activities. These can include ice-fishing, a sauna, a shot at seeing aurora borealis or an overnight trip to a wilderness cottage (€350 to €450). Longer safaris might take you to the Arctic Ocean or across central Lapland (€300 to €500 per day). All prices are based on two people sharing a snowmobile/sled; you'll pay up to 50% more if you want one all to yourself. You need a driving licence to operate a snowmobile.

Some recommended operators (most offices unstaffed in summer so call or book via the tourist office):

Lapland Safaris (☏331 1200; www.laplandsafaris.fi; Koskikatu 1) Reliable and well-established outfit for most of the above activities.

Eräsetti Wild North (☏020-564 6980; www.erasetiwildnorth.fi; Ounasjoentie 6, Pilke) Experienced operator with another office at Santa's village.

Husky Point (☏040-079 0096; www.huskypoint.fi; Koskikatu 9) From short rides to multi-day treks. They also do summer dog-trips and reindeer visits.

Safartica (☏311 485; www.safartica.com; Valtakatu 18) One of the best for snowmobiling and river activities.

dark floorboards, Lapp shaman motifs and a flatscreen TV. Most face the river. Summer prices represent real value, though they don't always appear on the website; contact the hotel directly. The restaurant has regular live Finnish golden-oldie music and hosts the local dance scene.

Arctic Snow Hotel
ICE HOTEL €€€
(☏040-769 0395; www.arcticsnowhotel.fi; Lehtoahontie 27, Sinettä; s/d/ste €160/240/320; ☉Jan-Mar; P) On the shore of a lake, this friendly place offers the complete snow hotel experience and also has a snow restaurant as well as warmer eating choices. It's 26km northwest of Rovaniemi, but they'll collect you for not much more. You can get a tour of the complex even if you're not a guest.

Hostel Rudolf
HOSTEL €
(☏321 321; www.rudolf.fi; Koskikatu 41; dm/s/d in winter €46/60/85, summer €35/44/56; P) Run by Hotel Santa Claus, where you inconveniently have to go to check in, this staffless hostel is Rovaniemi's only one and can fill up fast. Private rooms are good for the price, with spotless bathrooms, solid desks and bedside lamps; dorm rates get you the same deal. There's also a kitchen available and free wi-fi. HI discount.

Guesthouse Borealis
GUESTHOUSE €
(☏342 0130; www.guesthouseborealis.com; Asemieskatu 1; s/d/tr €47/58/81; P@) The cordial hospitality and proximity to the train station make this family-run spot a winner. The rooms have no frills but are bright and clean; some have a balcony. The airy dining room is the venue for breakfast, which features Finnish porridge; there's also a sauna for a small extra charge. A couple of apartments (€182) sleep up to seven. Prices rise slightly in winter.

Hotelli Aakenus
HOTEL €€
(☏342 2051; www.hotelliaakenus.net; Koskikatu 47; s/d €70/80; P@) Offering excellent summer value right from mid-May to the end of August (s/d €60/65), this friendly, efficient little hotel is a short distance west of the centre and a quick stroll from the Arktikum. The rooms are simple and spacious, with narrow beds. A sauna (with large timer-window) and buffet breakfast are included.

Sky Ounasvaara
HOTEL €€
(☏323 400; www.laplandhotels.com; Ounasvaarantie; s/d in Sep-Apr €128/154, Dec €159/194; P@) Atop the Ounasvaara fell by the ski runs, this offers great summer value, when not much extra cash gets you a room with a sauna.

The rooms have huge windows and are very spacious with a Nordic feel; ask for one with views down the hill. There's also a good restaurant here with fine perspectives.

Ounaskoski Camping　CAMPGROUND €
(☏345 304; ounaskoski-camping@windowslive.com; Jäämerentie 1; tent sites €13 plus per adult/child €7.50/3; ☺late May–mid-Sep) Just across the elegant bridge from the town centre, this camp site is perfectly situated on the riverbank. There are no cabins, but plenty of grassy tent and van sites, with great views over the Ounaskoski.

✕ Eating

The cafe at the Arktikum is a decent choice for lunch.

Gaissa　FINNISH €€
(☏321 321; www.hotelsantaclaus.fi; Korkalonkatu 29; mains €23-28; ☺dinner Mon-Sat, also Sun Dec & Jan) One of the two adjoining restaurants at the Hotel Santa Claus, this elegant place offers petite, reindeer-heavy cuisine including slow-roasted lamb that falls off the bone.

ZoomUp　BISTRO €€
(☏321 321; www.hotelsantaclaus.fi; Korkalonkatu 29; mains €14-20; ☺lunch Mon-Fri, dinner daily) Upstairs at the Hotel Santa Claus, this bar serves excellent salads, pastas, grilled meats, and succulent tuna and salmon steaks in a casual atmosphere aimed at pulling a local crowd. You can mix and match by ordering dishes from Gaissa's menu, too.

Nili　FINNISH €€
(☏0400-369 669; www.nili.fi; Valtakatu 20; mains €17-28; ☺dinner Tue-Sat, also Mon in winter) There's much more English than Finnish heard at this popular central restaurant, with an attractive interior and a Lapland theme. There are a few glitches – the staff, who wear 'Lapp' smocks, are obviously instructed to sell as much as they can – but the meals are very tasty, with wild mushroom sauces garnishing fish, reindeer and even sometimes bear dishes.

Mariza　FINNISH €
(www.ruokahuonemariza.fi; Ruokasenkatu 2; lunch €8.20; ☺lunch Mon-Fri) A couple of blocks from the centre in untouristed territory, this simple lunch place is a real find, and offers a buffet of home-cooked Finnish food, including daily changing hot dishes, soup and salad. Authentic and excellent.

Monte Rosa　FINNISH €€
(www.cityhotel.fi; Pekankatu 9; mains €15-28; ☺lunch & dinner Mon-Sat, 3-9pm Sun) Attached to the City Hotel, this bistro goes for the romance vote with a low-candlelit interior and chummy booth seating. The house salad topped with a slab of salmon is worth a go. Friendly service and generous portions make this a reliable standby.

Xiang Long　CHINESE €
(Koskikatu 21; mains €11-17; ☺lunch & dinner) This main-street Chinese is family run and a level above your typical Finnish example of the genre. Friendly service, tasty steamed prawn dim sum, a salad bar and several reindeer dishes, including one served on a sizzling platter, are the highlights, and the lunch buffet (€8.90, Monday to Friday) is great value.

♥ Drinking & Entertainment

Excluding ski resorts, Rovaniemi is the only place north of Oulu with a half-decent nightlife.

TOP CHOICE ❯ Kauppayhtiö　CAFE, BAR €
(www.myspace.com/kauppayhtio; Valtakatu 24; light meals €5-10; ☺10.30am-8pm Mon-Thu, 10.30am-late Fri & Sat) Rovaniemi's most personable cafe, this is an oddball collection of retro curios with a coffee and gasoline theme and colourful plastic tables. All the knick-knacks are purportedly for sale here, but it's the espresso machine, outdoor seating, salads, sundaes and bohemian Lapland crowd that keep the place ticking. There are often bands at weekends. The coffee is bottomless.

ZoomIt　BAR, CAFE
(www.hotelsantaclaus.fi; Koskikatu 14; ☺11am-midnight Mon-Thu, 11am-2am Fri & Sat, noon-11pm Sun) Large, light, modern ZoomIt is a popular, buzzy central bar and cafe, and a good place for a drink or coffee while you scope out Rovaniemi. Right in the heart of town, its terrace is the spot to be on a sunny afternoon and its spacious interior gives room to stretch out with a book if it's raining or snowing.

Roy Club　BAR, CLUB
(www.royclub.fi; Maakuntakatu 24; ☺9pm-4am) This friendly bar has a sedate, comfortable top half with cosy seating, cheap and long happy hours, and regular karaoke. There's also a downstairs nightclub that gets cheerily boisterous with students and stays open late.

Shopping

Sámi handicrafts made from reindeer skin and horn, or birch, are popular souvenirs; colourful Sámi hats, mittens and shoes are also top sellers.

The widest selection of souvenirs can be found in shops at Napapiiri (see Around Rovaniemi), where you'll also find branches of Marttiini knife shop, Marimekko, Iittala/Arabia and Taigakoru, a Lapland jeweller.

Marttiini   KNIVES
(www.marttiini.fi; Vartiokatu 32; ⊘10am-6pm Mon-Fri, 10am-4pm Sat, also noon-4pm Sun mid-Jun–Aug) This former factory of Finland's famous knife manufacturer is now a shop open to visitors with a small knife exhibition, and cheaper prices than you can get elsewhere. It's near the Arktikum. They've another shop at Napapiiri.

Information

There are lockers (€2) at both train and bus stations, and a storage counter at the train station.
Metsähallitus (✆020-564 7820; pilke@metsa.fi; Ounasjoentie 6, Pilke; ⊘8am-4pm Mon-Fri) Information centre for the national parks, with information on hiking and fishing in Lapland and an exhibition on sustainable forestry. The office sells maps and fishing permits, and books cottages.
Public library (Hallituskatu 9; ⊘11am-7pm Mon-Thu, to 6pm Fri, to 3pm Sat) Aalto-designed; has free internet. Opens longer hours in winter.
Tourist Information (✆346 270; www.visit rovaniemi.fi; Maakuntakatu 29; ⊘9am-5pm Mon-Fri) On the square in the middle of town. Free internet. They open until 6pm from mid-June to mid-August, when they also open weekends from 9am to 1pm. They use the same extended opening hours over the Christmas high season.

Getting There & Away
Air
Rovaniemi's airport is a major winter destination for charter flights from all over Europe and it's the 'official airport of Santa Claus' – does he hangar his sleigh here? Finnair flies daily from Helsinki. The budget carrier Norwegian also flies to Helsinki, as does Blue1 on weekends in winter, while Air Baltic connects with Tampere and Riga, Latvia.

Bus
Rovaniemi is Lapland's transport hub. Frequent express buses go south to Kemi (€15 to €24, 1½ hours), Oulu (€41, 3½ hours), and there are night buses to Helsinki (€121.50, 12½ hours). Daily connections serve just about everywhere else in Lapland: see destination sections for details. Some buses head on north into Norway.

Train
The train between Helsinki and Rovaniemi (€80 to €84, 10 to 12 hours) is quicker and cheaper than the bus. There are three daily direct services (via Oulu), including overnighters (high-season total prices go from €126 for a berth up to €195 for a smart modern cabin with en suite) with car transport. There's one train daily to Kemijärvi, further northeast (€14.90, 1½ hours).

Getting Around
Rovaniemi airport is 10km northeast of town. Minibuses meet arriving flights, dropping off at hotels in the centre (€7, 15 minutes). They pick up along the same route about an hour before flight departures.

Car-rental agencies have offices in the centre and at the airport. These include **Budget** (✆020-746 6620; www.budget.fi; Rovakatu 21), and **Europcar** (✆040-306 2870; www.europcar.fi; Pohjanpuistikko 2) at the Rantasipi Pohjanhovi hotel.

Call ✆106 410 for a cab.

Around Rovaniemi

NAPAPIIRI & SANTA CLAUS VILLAGE

The southernmost line at which the sun doesn't set at least one day a year, the Arctic Circle, is called **Napapiiri** in Finland and crosses the Sodankylä road about 8km north of Rovaniemi (although the Arctic Circle can actually shift several metres daily). There's an **Arctic Circle marker** here, conveniently painted on the roadside – and built right on top of it is the 'official' **Santa Claus Village** (www.santaclausvillage.info; Valtatie 4; admission free; ⊘10am-5pm Sep-Nov & early Jan-May, 9am-6pm Jun-Aug, 9am-7pm Dec-early Jan). There's a mixture of humdrum souvenir stands and classier shops, and it's just about the best spot to buy Sámi handicrafts if you're not heading further north. Tour groups have great fun crossing the line painted on the asphalt in order to be awarded their Arctic Circle certificates (€4.20).

Here too is **Santa Claus Post Office** (www.santaclaus.posti.fi; FIN-96930 Arctic Circle), which receives over half a million letters each year from children all over the world (with kids from the UK, Romania, Italy, Poland, Japan and Finland the biggest correspondents). You can browse a selection of the letters, which range from rather mercenary requests for thousands of euros of electronic goods to heart-rending pleas for parents to recover from cancer. Your postcard sent from here will bear an official Santa stamp, and you can arrange to have it delivered at Christmas time. For €6, you can get Santa to send a Christmas card to you.

But the big attraction is, of course, Santa himself, who sees visitors year-round in a rather impressive grotto (www.santaclauslive. com; admission free; ⊙9am-6pm Jun-Aug, 9am-7pm Dec, 10am-5pm Sep-Nov & Jan-May), where a huge clock mechanism (it slows the earth's rotation so that Santa can visit the whole world's children on Christmas night) eerily surrounds those queuing for an audience. The portly saint is quite a linguist, and an old hand at chatting with kids and adults alike. A private chat with the man is absolutely free, but you can't photograph the moment, and official photos of your visit start at an outrageous €25.

Other things at the complex are Santamus; the 'Arctic Circle Experience', a 20-minute immersion into Lapp 'culture' with a tepee interior, nature sounds and a hot berry juice; a husky park; reindeer rides; ice sculpture; and varying Christmassy exhibitions in the Christmas House. There's also a cafe serving salmon smoked over a traditional fire and an office of Eräsetti Safaris.

Napapiiri is 8km north of Rovaniemi on the Sodankylä road. Bus 8 heads there from the train station, passing through the centre (adult/child €6.60/3.80 return).

SANTAPARK

This Christmas-theme amusement park (www.santapark.com; Tarvantie 1; adult/child €28/23 winter; ⊙10am-6pm late Nov–mid-Jan, 10am-6pm Tue-Sat mid-Jun–mid-Aug) is built inside a cavern in the mountain and features an army of elves baking gingerbread, a magic sleigh ride, a Christmas carousel, an ice-bar, a theatre, a restaurant and, of course, Santa Claus himself. The most intriguing section is the gallery of ice sculpture. It's great fun for kids in winter but lacks a bit of atmosphere in the summer season (though it's cheaper at €13/16 for kids/adults). Entrance tickets are also valid the next day.

Bus 8 heads on from Napapiiri to here (same fare from town, adult/child €3/1.60 to go from one to the other).

Ranua

🗺016

This small town is 82km south of Rovaniemi on Rd 78 and famous for its excellent zoo (Ranuan Eläinpuisto; www.ranuazoo.com; Rovaniementie 29; adult/child €14/11; ⊙9am-7pm Jun-Aug, 10am-4pm Sep-May), which focuses almost entirely on Finnish animals, although there are also polar bears and musk oxen from further north. A boardwalk takes you on a 2.5km circuit past all the creatures, which include minks and stoats, impressive owls and eagles, wild reindeer, elk, a big bear paddock (they hibernate from November to March), lynx and wolverines. Apart from the animals, there's plenty to do for kids, with horse rides, a minikart circuit, pettable domestic animals and little assault courses. Ice-cream stops dot the route, and there's a cafe and lunch restaurant. It's slightly cheaper in winter.

In Ranua itself, 3km south of the zoo, Hotelli Ilveslinna (☎0400-177 130; www.hotel liilveslinna.fi; Keskustie 10; s/d €76/94; Ⓟ) makes a good place to hole up, with light, clean rooms that are gradually being renovated. There are interconnecting rooms so you can keep an eye on the kids, and they offer various packages including meals and zoo entry for families.

The closest camp site is 2km south of town.

There are four to six daily buses from Rovaniemi to Ranua (€16.20, 1¼ hours) as well as connections from Kajaani and Oulu.

Kemi

🗺016 / POP 22,579

Kemi is an industrial town and important deepwater harbour. Although not hugely appealing (in summer only the gem museum and wide waterfront have any sort of appeal), Kemi is home to two of Finland's blockbuster winter attractions.

⊙ Sights & Activities

Sampo CRUISE

(☎258 878; www.sampotours.com; Kauppakatu 16, 4hr cruise adult/child €240/133) Kemi comes into its own in winter; *Sampo*, a retired ice-breaker built in 1960, runs memorable, though overpriced, excursions. The four-hour cruise includes lunch and ice-swimming in special drysuits. *Sampo* sails two to four times weekly from late December to mid-April. If you choose to approach and leave the ship on snowmobiles (reindeer visit included), the price is per adult/child €387/215. The best time to go is when the ice is thickest, usually March. Book well in advance. Note that kids under 12 aren't allowed to do the ice-swimming part.

Departures are from Ajos Harbour, 11km south of Kemi. Transport there costs extra. The *Sampo* is out to pasture here in summer and open as a **restaurant** (mains €11-15; ⊙10am-6pm early Jun–mid-Aug) serving OK sandwiches, soups, salads and a buffet lunch in the rather dark interior. You're free to clamber over the decks and explore the ship, but it's not that interesting without the eerie crunching of ice.

Lumilinna   CASTLE

(☑258 878; www.snowcastle.net; adult/child €8/4.50; ⊙10am-7pm end Jan–mid-Apr) Of all the marvels under the big sky, few things conjure the fairy-tale romance of a snow castle, and few can compete with Kemi's. First built in 1996 as a Unicef project, the castle is now one of Lapland's winter highlights and a favoured destination for weddings, honeymoons, or just general marvelling at the weird light and sumptuously realised decoration of the multistoreyed interior.

The castle is constructed over a four-week period after Christmas. The design changes every year but always includes an ethereally beautiful chapel (here's hoping the vows last longer than those ice wedding rings), a **snow hotel** (s/d/ste €180/280/330) and a **restaurant** (3-course menus from €35). Overnighting in the hotel is memorable: the interior temperature is -5°C, but a woolly sheepskin and sturdy sleeping bag keep you warm(ish) atop the ice bed. Sleep on top of your clothes or you'll struggle to get into them the next day. In the morning you can thaw out in the sauna of a nearby hotel.

EXPLORING THE ARCHIPELAGO

Off the Kemi/Tornio coast, the Perämeri National Park is an archipelago of small islands that's an important conservation area for seals and a richly populated bird habitat. You'll need a boat (or snowmobile) to explore; ask at the tourist office about renting one.

Jalokivigalleria   MUSEUM

(www.kemi.fi/gemstonegallery; Kauppakatu 29; adult/child €7/4.50; ⊙9am-4pm Mon-Fri Sep-Jan & Apr-Jun, 9am-5pm Tue-Sat Jul-Aug, 9am-5pm daily Feb-Mar) The Gemstone Gallery, in an old seaside customs house, has an internationally notable collection of more than 3000 beautiful, rare stones and jewellery, including a replica crown based on a design that was meant for the short-lived king of Finland. Sheets in various languages guide you in an offbeat manner around the exhibits, which include replicas of famous diamonds and a solid dose of Finnish humour.

🛏 Sleeping, Eating & Drinking

The snow castle Lumilinna is the most interesting place to sleep or eat until it melts. Apart from it, there are three hotels in the centre, and a hotel-campsite 4km south.

In summer, the best place for a drink and a snack is down by the water, where old wooden warehouses and a boat bar make lively and picturesque places to eat and drink.

Hotelli Palomestari   HOTEL €€

(☑257 117; www.hotellipalomestari.com; Valtakatu 12; r €82; P@) This likeable family place is a block south and one west of the train and bus stations on a pedestrian street, and offers friendly service and decent rooms with trademark Finnish furniture, including a desk and sofa. There's also a friendly bar downstairs with outside seating. Summer prices are great (double around €60).

Paussi   FINNISH €

(www.keminpaussi.fi; Kauppakatu 12; lunch €7-8; ⊙lunch Mon-Fri) Standard Finnish lunch stop with good-value soups and hot dishes.

Näköala Kahvio   CAFE €

(Valtakatu 26; ⊙9am-3pm Mon-Fri) If you like your morning coffee with a stunning view, and aren't superstitious by nature, this simple cafe on the 13th floor of the town hall, is the place to be. You can't go outside; the table down by the toilets has the best view.

Hemingway's   PUB

(www.hemingways.fi; ⊙2pm-late) Popular chain spot whose terrace overlooks, er, the supermarket car park.

❶ Information

Library (Marina Takalonkatu 3; ⊙11am-8pm Mon-Thu, 11am-6pm Fri, 10am-4pm Sat; @) At the kauppatori (market square), has free internet access.

Tourist Office (040-569 2069; www.kemi.fi/
matkailu; Kauppakatu 29) In the gemstone gallery, with the same hours. Sampo Tours (p277)
also has tourist information.

ⓘ Getting There & Away

Kemi-Tornio airport is 6km north, and FlyBe has
regular Helsinki flights and also serves other
Finnish cities. The airport taxi service costs €20.

Buses run to Tornio (€6.30, 45 minutes) more
than hourly (fewer at weekends), Rovaniemi (€15
to €24, two hours) and Oulu (€20.50, 1¾ hours),
among other places.

There are trains from Helsinki (€79.20, nine
hours), Oulu (€20.10, 1¼ hours) and Rovaniemi
(€21.30, 1½ hours).

Tornio

016 / POP 22,546

Right on the impressive Tornionjoki, the
longest free-flowing river in northern Europe, Tornio is joined to its Swedish counter-
part Haparanda (Finnish: Haaparanta) by
short bridges. Growing shopping complexes
tempt Finns across to Ikea, and Swedes into
the designer clothing stores. Don't forget
that Finland is an hour ahead of Sweden.

◉ Sights

Tornion Kirkko CHURCH
(Tornio Church; www.tornio.seurakunta.net; Semi-
naarinkatu) The town church was completed in
1686 and is one of the most beautiful wooden
churches in Finland. Ask at the tourist office
for opening hours as they are irregular.

Aineen Taidemuseo GALLERY
(www.tornio.fi/aine; Torikatu 2; adult/child €4/2;
⊙11am-6pm Tue-Thu, 11am-3pm Fri-Sun) The attractive modern Tornio gallery comprises
the private collection of Veli Aine, a local
business tycoon. It displays Finnish art from
the 19th and 20th centuries, and has decent
temporary exhibitions and a good cafe.

Tornionlaakson Maakuntamuseo MUSEUM
(www.tornio.fi/museo; Keskikatu 22; adult/child
€4/2; ⊙11am-5pm Tue-Fri, 11am-3pm Sat & Sun)
The local historical museum has a collection
of interesting old artefacts and costumes, although all displays are labelled in Finnish.
Temporary exhibitions spice it up in summer. Entry is valid for the art museum (and
vice versa) if you go on the same day.

Across the border in Haparanda, the huge
brick water tower built in 1919 is visible for
miles around.

Tornio

◉ **Sights**
1 Aineen Taidemuseo A2
2 Tornion Kirkko A2
3 Tornionlaakson Maakuntamuseo A2

⌂ **Sleeping**
4 E-City Matkakoti B1
5 Kaupunginhotelli B2

⊗ **Eating**
À La Carte ....(see 5)

⊖ **Drinking**
6 Umpitunneli B2

🏃 Activities

The tourist office can make bookings for
all trips and handles fishing permits; there
are several excellent spots along the Tornio
River.

River-rafting is popular in summer on the
Kukkolankoski rapids north of town.

Lapland Connection WINTER, RAFTING
(253 405; www.laplandconnection.com) Snowmobile, husky- and reindeer-safaris in winter, rafting on the Tornionjoki in summer.

LAPLAND TORNIO

Pohjolan Safarit/Nordic Safaris   RAFTING
(☏040-755 1858; www.nordicsafaris.com) Rafting
on the Tornionjoki from around €45 to €75
per person, using inflatable rubber rafts or
traditional wooden boats.

Arctic Iceroad Production   RALLY DRIVING
(☏040-555 8529; www.arctic-iceroad.com) Organises fishing, canoeing and winter adventures including ice-driving in rally cars.
They also hire bikes, canoes and skis.

Green Zone Golf Course   GOLF
(☏431 711; www.golf.fi/mlgk; Näräntie) This famous golf course straddles Finland and
Sweden, allowing you to fire shots into a different country and time zone. You'll need a
Green Card or handicap certificate to play.
There's also a driving range and pitch 'n'
putt course here.

🛏 Sleeping

Haparanda Stadshotell   HOTEL €€€
(☏+46 922-61490; www.haparandastadshotell.se;
Torget 7; s/d €147/178, summer & weekends €100/
119; P) Across the river in Sweden, this is the
most characterful spot to stay, a beautiful
old building that dignifies the centre of the
small town. The rooms are decorated in an
old-fashioned style and are most commodious. They sometimes offer bargain 'summer
rooms' that come without breakfast or linen
included.

Hostel Vandrarhem   HOSTEL €
(☏+46 922 61171; www.haparandavandrarhem.se;
Strandgatan 26; dm/s/d €22/37/52, s without bathroom €28; P) The cheapest accommodation
in the twin cities is this hostel just across the
bridge in Sweden. There's a variety of clean
rooms and a great riverside location. There's
a good kitchen, laundry facilities and high-
standard disabled access. Linen costs an
extra €5.50. Reception is open 4pm to 7pm
so ring ahead if you're going to arrive after
that time.

E-City Matkakoti   GUESTHOUSE €
(☏044-509 0358; www.ecitybedandbreakfast.com;
Saarenpäänkatu 39; s/d €45/65, d with bathroom
€75; P) Tornio's best budget option, this is
a friendly guesthouse north of the brewery,
and run by a welcoming young family. Cosy
rooms feature comfortable beds and colourful fabrics; the shared bathrooms are clean
and have good showers, and breakfast includes traditional Finnish porridge.

Kaupunginhotelli   HOTEL €€
(☏43311; www.tornionkaupunginhotelli.fi; Itäranta
4; s/d €116/131, r in Jul €96; P@☲) Tornio's
only real hotel has decent facilities, including a small pool, a restaurant, a bar, karaoke
and a nightclub. The rooms are attractive,
with colourful bedspreads and plenty of natural light (in summer at least), though closer
examination might have you calling for a pot
of varnish and a tin of paint to touch things
up.

Camping Tornio   CAMPGROUND €
(☏445 945; www.campingtornio.com; Matkailijantie; tent sites €12 plus per adult/child €4/2, cabins
€36-52; ☉May–mid-Dec; P) About 3km from
town, off the road to Kemi. Also boat and
bike hire, tennis and a beach.

🍴 Eating & Drinking

There is little eating choice in Tornio. In
Haparanda, the Stadshotell has a quality
restaurant (mains €28-33; ☉5-10pm Swedish
time).

Umpitunneli   TEX-MEX, PUB €
(www.umpitunneli.fi; Hallituskatu 15; mains €12-17;
☉food served 3-9.30pm Mon-Fri, 1-9.30pm Sat,
1-8pm Sun) The 'Dead-End Tunnel' may be
a road to nowhere but it's a most enjoyable
one, with a huge terrace, plenty of drunken
locals adding entertainment value at weekends, and large plates of food, from creamy
pastas to steaks and Tex-Mex. There are often live bands.

À La Carte   FINNISH €€
(www.tornionkaupunginhotelli.fi; Itäranta 4; mains
€10-22) Tornio's best restaurant is in the Kaupunginhotelli and its elegant decor, outdoor
tables, OK food and lack of other options
make it a decent choice. Dishes come generously proportioned and very fairly priced.
There are a few Lapp thematic plates alongside the expected pork, salmon and steaks.
Opening depends on how busy the hotel is.

🛈 Information

Green Line Centre (☏050-590 0562; www.
haparandatornio.com; Pakkahuoneenkatu 1; ☉7am-
7pm Mon-Fri, 10am-6pm Sat & Sun Jun–mid-Aug,
9am-6pm Mon-Fri mid-Aug–May; @) Acts as the
tourist office for both towns. Free internet
terminal.

Public library (Torikatu 2; ☉10am-7pm Mon-
Thu, 10am-5pm Fri, 10am-4pm Sat; @) Free
internet. Closed Saturday in summer.

❶ Getting There & Away

Kemi-Tornio Airport is 18km east of town, and there are regular flights to and from Helsinki. A shared taxi from Tornio to the airport costs €20.

There are a couple of bus services to Rovaniemi, but you usually have to change (to bus or train) in Kemi (€6.30, 45 minutes, more than hourly, less at weekends). Many Tornio-bound buses continue to Haparanda, although the distance is so short you can walk.

From Haparanda, there are buses to Luleå, from where buses and trains run to other Swedish destinations.

Ylläs

🗹 016

Ylläs (www.yllas.fi), 35km northeast of Kolari, is Finland's highest skiable fell. On either side of the mountain are the villages **Äkäslompolo**, prettily set by a lake, and smaller **Ylläsjärvi**. Both are typical ski-resort towns with top-end hotels and holiday cottages, and shut down substantially in summer, when reindeer roam with impunity. Both villages are about 5km from their respective ski slopes. The Ylläs area is at the southern boundary of Pallas-Yllästunturi National Park and a trailhead for the trek to Hetta.

◉ Sights & Activities

Äkäslompolo's remarkable modern wooden church is worth a look. See Sleeping & Eating for the Snow Village.

Kellokas   NATURE CENTRE
(www.outdoors.fi; Tunturintie 54; ⊘9am-4pm Mon-Fri Oct-May, plus weekends at busy times, 9am-5pm daily Jun-Sep) At the foot of the fell's western slopes, 2.5km from Äkäslompolo, this has a good downstairs exhibition on the local environment and way of life, as well as a cafe, maps, information and advice on hiking in the park. This also functions as the tourist information centre for the region.

Skiing

Ylläs has 37 downhill slopes and 17 lifts, plus special areas for snowboarders. The vertical drop is 463m and the longest run is 3km. Cross-country skiing trails total 250km. **Lift passes** cost €36/170 per day/week; equipment rental and ski lessons are available. The ski season usually runs from late November to early May.

Mountain Biking

In summer Ylläs is popular with mountain-biking enthusiasts, and you can take your bike up in the **gondola lift** (single/day €8/20; ⊘Mon-Sat late Jun-Sep) to the top of the downhill trails (430m vertical descent). **Sport-Store** (www.sportresortyllas.com; ⊘late Jun-Apr), in the Taiga building at the base of the lifts on the Ylläsjärvi side, rents bikes of all types (€15 to €30 per day).

Hiking

There are numerous nature trails and hiking possibilities. Check the Pallas-Yllästunturi pages on www.outdoors.fi for a list. A couple of long-distance treks head to Olos or Levi (50km to 54km); there are several shorter trails including the 3.5km **Varkaankuru nature trail**, and the 12km **Kiirunankieppi (Ptarmigan Trail)**, both of which start from the Kellokas Nature Centre. Longer routes lead all the way to Pallastunturi (72km) and from there to Hetta (see p289).

☞ Tours

Various tour operators cluster in Äkäslompolo along the road near the Ylläskaltio ho tel. Most are open only in winter, and offer snowmobiling, reindeer safaris, snowshoe walking and husky treks.

🍴 Sleeping & Eating

Most accommodation is shut in summer, but there are still plenty of empty cottages around. **Destination Lapland** (🗹510 3300; www.destinationlapland.com) is the major booker. The **Äkäshotelli** (www.laplandhotels.com) in Äkäslompolo stays open, as does the **Ylläs Saaga** (www.yllassaaga.com) spa hotel at the slopes on the Ylläsjärvi side. They offer summer rooms for around €80 a twin.

Hotel Ylläshumina   HOTEL €€
(🗹020-719 9820; www.yllashumina.com; Tiurajärventie; s/d €121/152; ⊘late Aug-Apr; 🅿) In Äkäslompolo, near the lake, this welcoming complex resembles a courting willow grouse with its flamboyant wooden architecture. There's full ski service here, and the sauna and outdoor hot tub are great after a day on the slopes. The rooms, set in separate raised buildings, are like apartments, and fit a whole family, with a loft sleeping area and kitchenette. They're considerably cheaper between August and mid-December. The restaurant (mains €21 to €34) serves upmarket fare including willow grouse and reindeer.

Lainio Snow Village   ICE HOTEL €€€
(🗹040-416 7227; www.snowvillage.fi; s/d/ste €180/240/320; ⊘mid-Dec–mid-Apr) Between

Ylläsjärvi and Kittilä, this ice hotel is built every winter. It's a spectacular complex of buildings including an ice bar in a huge igloo, and sumptuous rooms where you sleep in heavy-duty sleeping bags atop your icy bed. You can visit the complex for €10/5 per adult/child.

Getting There & Away

During the ski season, a shuttle heads from Kittilä airport to Ylläsjärvi (€19) and Äkäslompolo (€21). Book at www.yllasexpress.fi.

The nearest train station is in Kolari and there are connecting buses to Ylläsjärvi and Äkäslompolo in the ski season. There's also a weekly bus from Kittilä.

Kittilä

🕘 016 / POP 6193

One of the main service centres for northwestern Lapland, Kittilä is a jumping-off point for the ski resorts of Ylläs and Levi. Although Kittilä is the regional centre, Levi is now, in fact, so popular, that their roles have been effectively reversed.

Golden Goose Majatalo (🕘642 043; www.goldengoose.fi; Valtatie 42; s/d €55/60, s/d without bathroom €35/40; P) is a friendly B&B right in the village centre, with a variety of room options and free sauna. **Hotelli Kittilä** (🕘643 201; www.hotellikittila.fi; Valtatie 49; s/d in summer €65/75; P🏊) is on the main road: look for the red aeroplane mounted out the front. Rooms are spacious, and there's a sauna and a small pool. The restaurant serves a good buffet lunch and there's dancing and entertainment some evenings.

Daily flights operate between Helsinki and Kittilä, as do winter budget routes and charters from the UK and elsewhere. The airport is 4km north of town. Four to five daily buses run between Rovaniemi and Kittilä (€26, two hours). All continue to Levi.

Levi (Sirkka)

🕘 016

The phenomenal amount of construction that goes on here every summer attests to the boom of the Finnish ski business and Levi's place near the top of the pile. Its compact centre, top-shelf modern facilities and large accommodation capacity mean it hosts many high-profile winter events; it's also a very popular destination for *ruska* (Autumn leave) season

hiking. Though many places shut down, there's enough going on here in summer that it's not moribund, and the great deals on smart modern apartments make this a tempting base from which to explore western Lapland, particularly for families.

Levi is actually the name of the fell, while Sirkka is the village, but most people refer to the whole place as Levi. The ski season runs from November to May, with the busiest period in March and April, when snow is good, temperatures aren't extreme and there's a bit of daylight. In summer and autumn, trekking and mountain biking are the main outdoor activities, while in December overseas charter flights descend, bringing families in search of reindeer and a white Christmas.

Activities

Skiing & Snowboarding

The ski resort **Levitunturi** (www.levi.fi) has 45 downhill slopes and 26 lifts (two of which are gondola lifts and several are free children's lifts). Many of the slopes are lit, and stay open until 7pm. The vertical drop is approximately 325m, and the longest run is 2.5km. There are two half-pipes and a superpipe for snowboarders, a snow park and several ski runs for children.

Opportunities for cross-country skiing are also good, with hundreds of kilometres of trails, some of the shorter ones illuminated. On longer ski-treks, you can stay overnight in wilderness huts, which have supplies of firewood.

In the high season (February to early May), lift tickets cost €35/170 per day/week. Single tickets are €4. Rental and lessons are available.

Other Activities

In winter there's a full complement of snowy activities from husky, reindeer and snowmobile short trips or safaris to snowshoe walking and ice-fishing. In summer, **canoeing** on the long Ounasjoki that runs from Hetta in the north to Rovaniemi in the south is deservedly popular, as is the **mountainbiking park** (www.bikepark.fi; ☉early Jun-late Sep) on the ski slopes: there are decent rigs available for hire and you can take your bike up in the gondola lift; the gravity trails have a drop of 310m. There's also a **golf course** (green fee €30) and **horse riding**. The tourist office can book most activities. There's a free bike scheme in summer – just sign up and ride away.

Western Lapland

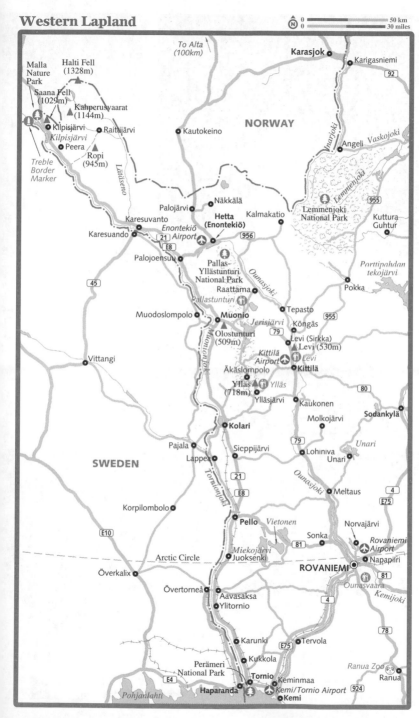

PAUL HARDING / LONELY PLANET IMAGES ©

GLOBAL WARMING IMAGES / ALAMY ©

Ho, ho, ho
et Santa know what you want for
hristmas in person at the Santa Claus
llage (p276) near Rovaniemi

Wilderness
ek through stunning arctic scenery in
ho Kekkonen National Park (p298)

Northern Lights
ake in nature's ethereal light show with the
esmerising colours of the aurora borealis
295), above the Arctic Circle

Winter Festivals
atch some high-speed action at a reindeer-
cing event (p303) in Inari

DAVID TIPLING /LONELY PLANET IMAGES ©

Kinos Safaris   SUMMER, WINTER
(☑050-403 2000; www.kinossafaris.com) Winter safaris plus summer canoeing and fishing.

Lapland Safaris   WINTER
(☑654 222; www.laplandsafaris.fi; Keskuskuja 2) A full range of winter excursions. Closed summer.

PerheSafarit   SUMMER, WINTER
(☑643 861; www.perhesafarit.fi) Snowmobile and motor-sled excursions in winter and Ounasjoki canoeing trips in summer.

Polar Speed   DOG-SLEDDING
(☑040-570 6572; www.polarspeed.fi) Single or multiday dog-sledding safaris with accommodation in wilderness huts. In summer you can visit the dogs at the Husky Park in Köngäs, 10km northeast of Levi.

🛏 Sleeping

Levi is one of Finland's most popular winter holiday centres and prices go through the roof in the peak season of December, and from February to May.

Virtually the whole town consists of holiday apartments and cottages, most of which are available for rent. They typically sleep four to six, have a sauna, a fully equipped kitchen and many other mod cons. In summer, they are a real bargain, costing €45 to €55 per night; in winter €1100 a week is average. **Levin Matkailu Keskusvaraamo** (☑639 3300; www.levi.fi), in the tourist office, is the place to book these.

Hotelli K5 Levi   HOTEL €€€
(☑639 1100; www.k5levi.fi; Kätkänrannantie 2; r high season €170-190, late summer €80; ⊘mid-Aug–Apr; P@) Right opposite the tourist office, this sleek, modern hotel has excellent rooms; most come with sauna and glassed-in balcony, or otherwise a jacuzzi. There are also good family rooms and classy holiday apartments. Despite the swish design, they haven't forgotten where they are: there's a laundry, mountain bikes and sets of skis free for guests to use, canoes to rent, and a drying cupboard in all the rooms. Nonguests can use the gym for a small charge.

Hotel Levi Panorama   HOTEL €€€
(☑336 3000; www.golevi.fi; Tunturitie 205; s/d winter €130/180, summer €60/80; P@) Halfway up the slopes, with a great ski-in-ski-out area downstairs, this stylish newcomer has great rooms with lots of space, modish furniture, big photos of Lapland wildlife and views over the pistes. Superiors add a balcony but most look the other way. You can nip up and down to town on the gondola. It's top value in summer.

Hullu Poro   HOTEL €€
(☑651 0100; www.hulluporo.fi; Rakkavaarantie 5; d with sauna €110-180, without sauna €90-122; P@) The friendly, informal 'Crazy Reindeer' keeps expanding, and now seems like a small city of its own. It has every kind of room you can imagine, with family suites, apartments and rooms with private sauna; there are various restaurants and a spa complex, though no pool. It's a lot cheaper in summer.

Golden Crown   IGLOO, SUITE €€€
(☑044-056 6334; www.leviniglut.fi; igloo €240-345, kammi €300-680; P) These perspex igloos with kitchenette and bathroom are on the side of the fell. The beds are motorised so you move around while skywatching. There are also more luxurious 'kammis', which are large apartment suites with floor-to-ceiling windows, saunas and jacuzzi. Great deals ara available in summer.

🍴 Eating & Drinking

Most eating and drinking options centre on the big hotels, which have multiple bars, restaurants and nightclubs. Most open only during the ski season and the autumn *ruska* period. There are also a couple of restaurants atop the fell.

Hullu Poro   RESTAURANTS
(☑651 0100; www.hulluporo.fi) Choices include **Pihvipirtti** (steaks €26 to €32, open September to April), down the road from the main complex, where the €42 steakhouse menu gets you a crack at the cold fish buffet followed by a sirloin, and the year-round **Wanha Hullu Poro** (mains €11 to €16) in the original wooden building, serving up OK food with loud music from the bar, which is the liveliest in town in summer. The **Areena**, down the hill, has live music almost every night in ski season, DJs, and dancing on two floors.

Panimo Pub   FINNISH, PUB €€
(www.levinpanimo.fi; Levinraitti 1) Pints of homebrew and, in summer, a terrace that catches the afternoon sun are reasons to visit this spot by the central supermarket. Downstairs, in the atmospheric **Kellari** (mains €13-27; 2-11pm), tasty Lappish meals are served year-round.

ℹ️ Information

Tourist office (☎639 3300; www.levi.fi; Myl-lyojantie 2; ⊙9am-7pm Mon-Fri, 11am-4.30pm Sat & Sun Jun-Sep, 9am-4.30pm Mon-Fri, 11am-4pm Sat & Sun Nov-May, closed Oct) Be-hind the tepeelike building on the roundabout in the centre of the resort. The main accom-modation booking agency is also here, and staff can book activities such as snowmobile safaris, dog-sled treks and reindeer rides.

ℹ️ Getting There & Away

Levi is on Rd 79, 170km north of Rovaniemi. All buses from Rovaniemi to Kittilä continue on to here, some continuing to Muonio. A bus meets all incoming flights at Kittilä Airport, 15km to the south.

Franchises of the major car hire companies are located at the airport; they will deliver cars to Levi or Kittilä free of charge.

Muonio

☑016

The village of Muonio is the last significant stop on Rd 21 before Kilpisjärvi and Norway. It sits on the scenic Muonionjoki that forms the border between Finland and Sweden and is a fine base for summer and winter activities. There are plenty of places to stay around here, and low key skiing in winter. Most of the town was razed during WWII, but the wooden church, dating from 1817, escaped that fate.

◎ Sights & Activities

Harriniva   ACTIVITY CENTRE
(☎530 0300; www.harriniva.fi; Valtatie 21) Three kilometres south of town, this excellent set-up has a vast program of summer and winter activities for individuals or small groups, ranging from short jaunts to multi-day adventures. In summer these include guided hikes, canoe and boat trips, horse trekking, quad bike safaris and fishing on the salmon-packed Muonionjoki. You can also rent bikes, boats and rods here.

In winter, there are wonderful dog-sledding safaris from 1½ hours (€70) to two days (€530), or trips of a week or longer, per-haps adding reindeer-sledding and snow-mobiling to the mix.

Harriniva has the **Arktinen Rekikoirake-skus** (Arctic sled-dog centre) with more than 400 lovable dogs, all with names and personalities. A great guided tour of their town is €7/4 per adult/child and teaches you plenty about the different breeds of huskies

and their characteristics. Prebook it; there are two departures daily. You can also go on summer hikes (€40/30 per adult/child, Tuesdays) with a posse of them.

Kiela Naturium   NATURE CENTRE
(www.muonio.fi; Valtatie 21; ⊙10am-6pm; @) This information centre has a gift shop, Thai cafe, slow free internet, local fish in a tank and a small nature display.

🛏️ Sleeping & Eating

Harriniva   HOTEL, CAMPGROUND €€
(☎530 0300; www.harriniva.fi; Valtatie 21; s/d summer €70/80, winter €120/140, cabins s/d/q €22/40/70, camping €10 plus per person €4; P@) Three kilometres south of town, this is a great place to stay, with a wide range of ac-commodation. The hotel rooms are attrac-tively done out in wood and have plenty of space – some come with their own sauna – and there are also apartments, cottages, cab-ins by the river and camping space. There's a good restaurant that's the best place to eat in the Muonio area.

Lomamaja Pekonen   CABIN, GUESTHOUSE €
(☎040-550 8436; www.lomamajapekonen.fi; La-henrannantie 10; s/d €45/60, cabins €35-45, apt s/d €60/80, cottages €70-90; P) In the cen-tre of town, this appealing spot has wee red wooden cabins running up a slope just across from the Muonionjoki, and more upmarket apartments and cottages behind them. There's space for vans but not tents. They hire canoes, fishing equipment and bikes as well as organising guided trips on the river in summer.

ℹ️ Getting There & Away

Muonio is at the junction of western Lapland's main two roads: Rd 21, which runs from Tornio to Kilpisjärvi, and Rd 79, which runs northwest from Rovaniemi via Kittilä.

There are three daily buses from Rovaniemi (€41, 3½ hours) via Kittilä, and services from Kemi/Tornio changing at Kolari.

Enontekiö (Hetta)

☑016 / POP 1879

The village of Hetta, usually signposted as Enontekiö (the name of the municipal dis-trict) is an important Sámi town and a good place to start trekking and exploring the area. Though a bit spread-out, it makes a good stop for a night or two. It's also the northern end of the popular Pallastunturi Trek.

LAPLAND MUONIO

🎿 Sights & Activities

Skierri (www.outdoors.fi; Peuratie 15; ☺9am-5pm Mar-Apr & mid-Jul–Sep, otherwise 9am-4pm Mon-Fri) nature centre at the eastern end of town provides information about Pallas-Yllästunturi National Park and the Enontekiö region. There's a smart exhibition on the Sámi and their nomadic history as well as nature displays on the park and a cafe.

In the centre of Hetta is the slender-spired **Enontekiö church** (Ounastie; ☺10am-4pm Jun-Sep), built in 1952 with the financial help of American churches. The organ was a gift from Germany. The church has an altar mosaic picturing Christ blessing Lapland and its people (and reindeer). Opening hours aren't reliable.

A less permanent building is the annual **snow castle** (www.sonsoma.fi; visits €8, d €110) built in mid-December and lasting until April.

At the junction of the westbound and northbound roads, 2km west of the centre, the market square has a couple of worthwhile shops, **Sámi Duodji Ry** (www.samiduodji.com; cnr Ounastie & Hwy 93; ☺10.30am-4.30pm Mon-Fri Aug-May), the Sámi handicrafts cooperative, and **Hetta Silver** (www.hettasilver.com; cnr Ounastie & Hwy 93), a local silversmith's workshop.

The biggest festival in Hetta is **Marianpäivä** (feast day of the Annunciation), usually celebrated in March; there are Sámi dances and parties, and the town buzzes with a lot of activity.

There's a small **ski resort** (www.hettahiihtomaa.fi) here in winter, and various guides offering husky, snowmobile, and ski-trekking excursions.

🛏 Sleeping & Eating

TOP CHOICE **Ounasloma** COTTAGE € (☎521 055; www.ounasloma.fi; Ounastie 1; cottage €55 plus €11 per person; P@) This friendly family-run place has a series of excellent wooden cottages in a well-kept area with a river and a lake beach. The standard cottages are great for families, and there are bigger ones suitable for large groups. Some have an open fireplace. Boats, bikes and sledges are free to use, and there's a discount if you stay longer. They also run ice-fishing, and winter trips in an unusual heated sledge-bus pulled by a snowmobile.

Hetan Majatalo HOTEL, GUESTHOUSE € (☎554 0400; www.hetan-majatalo.fi; Riekontie 8; s/d hotel €61/82, guesthouse €40/60; P@) In the centre of town, but set back in its own garden away from the road, this welcoming pad offers two types of accommodation in facing buildings: clean and simple guesthouse rooms sharing bathrooms, and very handsome and spacious wood-clad hotel rooms with good bathrooms and pyramid-shaped skylights. It's an excellent deal that includes good breakfast and sauna, and it's even a little cheaper in summer.

Hotelli Hetta HOTEL €€ (☎323 700; www.laplandhotels.com; Ounastie 281; hostel s/d €72/88, hotel s/d €105/120; P@≋) At the eastern end of town towards the visitor centre, Hetta has good facilities and bland but spacious renovated rooms – the ones facing the lake have a much nicer outlook. There are also 'hostel' rooms that have their own toilet but shared shower. The restaurant opens for dinner and offers perspectives over the water and good, generous meals, with plenty of reindeer and other Lapland staples. The hotel is closed October, November, and most of May. Summer prices are lower.

Hetan Lomakylä CAMPGROUND € (☎040-020 5408; www.hetanlomakyla.fi; Ounastie 23; sites €10 plus per adult/child €4/2, 2-person cabins €50, small/large cottages €60/80; ☺Mar-Oct) Just near the north/west road junction 2km from the centre, this has grassy tent pitches and smart painted wooden cabins and cottages. The latter come with kitchen, sauna and a loft sleeping area, and even a hanging flowerpot. There are various discounts and activities on offer.

ℹ Information

Tourist information (www.tosilappi.fi; Ounastie 165; ☺9am-3.45pm Mon-Thu, 9am-3pm Fri) In the municipal building on the main road.

ℹ Getting There & Away

FlyBe flies to Enontekiö from Helsinki daily from March to May only. The airport, mainly used for winter charters, is 7km west.

Buses from Hetta head out to the main road to Rovaniemi (€53.10, five hours) and Kilpisjärvi (€29, 3¼ hours) via a swap-over at Palojoensuu. There's a summer service from Rovaniemi to Tromsøin Norway via Hetta, Kautokeino and Alta. There are also buses to Hetta from Muonio.

Pallas-Yllästunturi National Park

🏃016

Finland's third-largest national park forms a long, thin area running from Hetta in the north to the Ylläs ski area in the south. The main attraction is the excellent 55km trekking route from the village of Hetta to Pallastunturi in the middle of the park, where there's a hotel, information centre and transport connections. You can continue from here to Ylläs, although there are few facilities on that section. In winter, Pallastunturi Fell is a small but popular place for both cross-country and downhill skiing.

Pallastunturi Luontokeskus   NATURE CENTRE
(www.outdoors.fi; Pallastunturintie; ⊗9am-4pm Mon-Fri Oct–mid-Feb & May, 9am-4pm or 5pm daily other times) This nature centre at Pallastunturi Fell sells trekking maps (€19.50), makes reservations for locked huts (per person €10) and provides information and advice about the region. The Hetta route leaves from here; good shorter walks include a 9km loop across the tops of Taivaskero and Laukukero.

Skierri in Hetta also has keys for the lockable huts.

Trekking Route

The 55km trek/ski from Hetta village to Pallastunturi (or vice versa) offers some of the best views in the country from the top of the fells. While there's plenty of up-and-down, it's not a difficult route; much of it is through pretty, flattish, light forest cover with sandy soil. It usually takes three to four days to complete. The route is well marked, and there are several wilderness huts along the way. The popularity of the trek means huts get pretty crowded at peak times. See www.outdoors.fi for the route and wilderness huts.

From Pallastunturi you can extend your trek a further 70km to the park's southernmost border, by the ski resorts at Ylläs.

🛏 Sleeping

Hotelli Pallas   HOTEL €€
(🏃323 355; www.laplandhotels.com; Pallastunturintie; s/d in summer €76/90; 🅿) This noble old wooden place is up in the fells by the national park information centre, and just what you want to see when you finish your trek. The first hotel in Lapland was built on this site in 1938. It's in need of a bit of a refit –

rooms are plain with lino floors – but the natural setting is wonderful. Cheaper rooms have their own toilet but share a shower (singles/doubles €61/80 in summer). It's got skiing right alongside in winter, and the room prices jump accordingly, but it's good value at other times. There's a nice lakeside sauna (with winter ice-hole) and walks on the doorstep. Hikers can pay for a shower here.

ℹ Getting There & Away

A morning bus runs Monday to Friday, plus Saturday in summer, from Muonio (€10.80, 40 minutes) to Kittilä via Pallastunturi. At other times, you'll have to hitch or call a local taxi on 🏃538 582 or 🏃040-039 3103.

Kilpisjärvi

🏃016

The remote village of **Kilpisjärvi** (www.kilpisjarvi.org), the northernmost settlement in the 'arm' of Finland, is in a memorable setting among lakes and snowy mountains on the doorstep of both Norway and Sweden. At 480m above sea level, this small border post, wedged between the lake of Kilpisjärvi and the magnificent surrounding fells, is also the highest village in Finland. Unless you're just passing through on your way to Tromsø or Narvik in Norway, the main reason to venture out here is for summer trekking or spring cross-country skiing. There are popular walks to the joint border post of Finland, Norway and Sweden, up spectacular Saana Fell, home to the rough-legged buzzard, and longer treks to Finland's highest fell, Halti (1328m).

Every Midsummer, the folk of Kilpisjärvi put on a ski race at Saana Fell, where the snow may not melt until mid-July. Across in Norway, you can see year-round patches of snow on the mountains.

Kilpisjärvi consists of two small settlements 5km apart – the main (southern) centre has the information office, hotel, petrol station and supermarket, and most of the accommodation. The northern knot, 2km shy of the border, has the Kilpisjärven Retkeilykeskus (Kilpisjärvi Hiking Centre) and trailheads.

🔱 Activities

Hiking

The Kilpisjärvi area offers fantastic long and short hikes.

From the Retkeilykeskus, the ascent to slate-capped **Saana Fell** (1029m) takes two to three hours return. A gentle climb through woodland ends abruptly in a thigh-straining 742 wooden steps up the steeper part of the fell. From the top, it's an easier gradient up the angled slate cap to the highest point. When you come down, you can continue right around the base of the fell to make a long loop trail (10km plus the ascent/descent of 3km each way). There's a day hut at Saanajärvi 4km from the Retkeilykeskus.

Another Kilpisjärvi classic is the route through **Malla Nature Park** to the Kolmen Valtakunnan Raja, a concrete block in a lake, suspiciously painted Swedish yellow, that marks the **treble border** of Finland, Sweden and Norway. Nearby is a free wilderness hut, where you can stay overnight. From the car park that's 2.5km north of the Retkeilykeskus, it is 11km to the treble border, with a climb through birch forest rewarded with a spectacular route along the Malla hillside, with great lake views below. Apart from a short section picking your way over rocks, it's an easy and rewarding walk in either direction. A side trip takes you up Pikku-Malla, the hill at the northern end of the lake.

A summer **boat service** (☎040-066 9392) leaves from just below the Retkeilykeskus at 10am, 2pm and 6pm, dropping you a light 3km stroll from the border marker (one-way/return €15/20, 30 minutes). This allows an easy visit, or to walk one way and cruise the other. The boat returns at 12.30pm, 4.30pm and 8.30pm.

For a longer trek, the 54km hike to **Halti Fell** (1328m), the highest point in Finland, is a rewarding, reasonably well-marked, trip. There are simple wilderness cabins along the route, but you should really take a tent. You can get close to it by road through Norway. **Kilpissafarit** (☎040-516 1952; www.kilpissafarit.fi) can arrange guided treks there and also runs winter snowmobile safaris.

All trekking routes and wilderness huts around the Kilpisjärvi area are clearly displayed on the 1:100,000 *Halti Kilpisjärvi* map (€19.50).

Scenic Flights

There's a heliport at the southern end of Kilpisjärvi. Sightseeing flights cost €180 for 10 minutes (usually up to three passengers) or €440 for a half-hour spin around Halti Fell. For information, call **Polar-Lento** (☎040-039 6087; www.harriniva.fi). **Heliflite** (www.heliflite.fi) offers a similar service.

Sleeping & Eating

Lining the main road are several camp sites with cabins. Many places are only open during the trekking season, which is June to September. As well as the hotel and Retkeilykeskus, several of the cabin complexes have their own cafe-restaurant, usually only open during the day.

Hotelli Kilpis HOTEL **€€**
(☎537 761; www.laplandhotels.com; Käsivarrentie 14206; s/d without bathroom €73/87, s/d €90/97, apt €121-260; ⊙Mar-Sep; P) This ageing hotel is on the main road in the centre of town, opposite the supermarket. Its rooms are simply appointed but comfortable enough; those that face the carpark can be noisy. There's one suite (€121) that's worth the upgrade for the view alone. The 'hostel' rooms share bathrooms, and there are also apartments, more modern and stylish than the main hotel. The restaurant (mains €13 to €26, 5pm to 11pm) is the best around, and serves smallish portions of Lapp-style food, such as a 'Northern Union' of reindeer and salmon. The bar is the town's weekend watering hole.

Kilpisjärven Lomakeskus CAMPGROUND, COTTAGE **€**
(☎537 801; www.kilpisjarvi.net; Käsivarrentie 14188; camping €14 plus per adult €4, cottages €70-200, apt €70-120; P) This is the best of the clutch of camping 'n' cabins sites in the centre of Kilpisjärvi. It has a cafe and excellent wooden cottages and apartments with their own sauna, loft bedroom, fully equipped kitchen, TV and video (films at reception). These are great value in summer.

Kilpisjärven Retkeilykeskus GUESTHOUSE, CABIN **€€**
(☎537 771; www.kilpisjarvi.info; Käsivarrentie 14663; s/d €70/80, 2/4-person cottages €90/100; ⊙mid-Mar–Sep; P) Close to the border but 5km north of the village, this is conveniently close to the trekking routes and the Malla boat. You'll find a range of rooms and cottages here, all with bathroom. There's camping too, but it's more appealing for vans than tents. The no-frills restaurant dishes up a good all-you-can-eat buffet lunch daily in the high season (€14, from noon to 8pm) as well as breakfasts (€8) and à la carte dishes.

Information

The petrol station also sells trekking maps.

Kilpisjärven Retkeilykeskus (Kilpisjärvi Hiking Centre; www.kilpisjarvi.info; Käsivarrentie

14663; ⊘8am-10pm mid-Mar–Sep) This is a central meeting place for all trekkers. They hire bikes, hiking and skiing equipment. There's also a shop and a cafe and accommodation close to the main walking routes.

Kilpisjärvi Visitor Centre (www.outdoors.fi; Käsivarrentie 14145; ⊘9am-5pm late Jun-late Sep, 9am-4pm Tue-Sat Mar–mid-May) At the southern end of the village, this national park centre is effectively the tourist information office. It has maps, advice on trekking and a nature display.

ⓘ Getting There & Away

Two daily buses connect Rovaniemi and Kilpis-järvi (€68, six to eight hours) via Kittilä, Levi and Muonio, with a connection to Hetta. In summer, one heads on to Tromsø in Norway.

It's a spectacular drive from Muonio to Kilpis-järvi (almost 200km). There are service stations at the small settlement of Kaaresuvanto (where there's a border crossing into Sweden) and in Kilpisjärvi itself. North of Kilpisjärvi, the road continues into Norway and a spectacular ascent through mountains before descending to the fjords.

Kemijärvi

🎵016 / POP 8426

Kemijärvi, situated on north–south Hwy 5, is many people's first glimpse of Lapland. Its location on a spectacular lake is the main attraction.

⊙ Sights & Activities

Hire a bike or canoe and explore the lake, for there's little to do in town apart from admire the 18th-century bell tower by the modern church and the legacies of the international wood-sculpting festivals.

Puustelli   ART CENTRE
(www.kemijarvi.fi; Pöyliöjärventie; admission €3; ⊘noon-6pm Tue-Sun mid-Jun–mid-Aug) On the western side of town (follow the path past the camp site and keep going), this noble old building displays many of the wooden sculptures from past years of the Kuvanveistoviikko festival.

⭐ Festivals & Events

The **Kuvanveistoviikko** (Woodsculpting Symposium; www.kemijarven-kuvanveistoviikot.fi) is held in late June or early July every odd-numbered year. It attracts artists from many countries, whom you can see about their work. In early September, Kemijärvi hosts **Ruska Swing**

(www.ruskaswing.fi), a festival of swing music and dancing.

🛏 Sleeping & Eating

Mestarin Kievari   HOTEL, RESTAURANT €€
(🎵322 7700; www.mestarinkievari.fi; Kirkkokatu 9; s/d €84/98, in summer €74/84; ⊘lunch & dinner Mon-Sat; Ⓟ 🅐) Kemijärvi's eating and drinking scene pretty much begins and ends here, and it's also the better of the town's two hotels. It's a welcoming spot that'll fortify you for your onward journey with a variety of comfortable, fairly unadorned rooms that differ only slightly in price. Some are in a newer wing, while others have private sauna; spacious family rooms with sloping ceilings sit at the top. The restaurant features mostly meaty fare (mains €13 to €28), though there is a vegetarian option, and the lunch buffet (€10) is very popular with passing traffic. The pub opens from 10pm.

Hietaniemi Camping   CAMPGROUND €
(🎵040-778 9106; Hietaniemenkatu 7; tent sites €13 plus per adult/child €5/2; ⊘late May–mid-Sep; Ⓟ) Very close to the centre on Pöyliöjärvi, a secondary part of the main lake, this is a friendly grassy camp site with not a great deal of privacy if it's full. There's a caravan you can bunk in if you don't have a tent.

Lohen Lomakeskus   HOSTEL, COTTAGE €
(🎵040-581 2007; www.lohenlomakeskus.fi; Lohe-lankatu 1; dm/s/d €30/50/65, cottages €70-120; Ⓟ) Just beyond the camp site, this complex offers a variety of sleeping choices. The cheerful red wooden, green-roofed cottages all come with bathroom, kitchen and sauna, while the lakefront apartments are even fancier. In the reception building, wooden bunk rooms offer plenty of space and value, and simple private rooms share the same kitchen and bathroom facilities. HI discount. Reception closed between 10am and 5pm. You can rent canoes and bikes here.

ⓘ Information

Mestarin Kievari has a public internet terminal.
Tourist office (🎵040-189 250; www.kemijarvi.fi; Vapaudenkatu 8; ⊘9am-3.30pm Mon-Fri, summer office 11am-6pm Mon-Sat, noon-6pm Sun mid-Jun–mid-Aug; 🅐) In a municipal building in the centre with free internet access. In summer it transfers to nearby Jaakonkatu 2 and opens longer hours.
Library (Hietaniemenkatu 3; 🅐) Free internet access.

LAPLAND KEMIJÄRVI

ℹ️ Getting There & Away

There are buses to Pyhä (€9.40, one hour), Rovaniemi (€16.20, 1¼ hours), Sodankylä (€19, 1¾ hours) and elsewhere. There's one daily train to Helsinki, via Rovaniemi (€14.90, 1½ hours).

Pyhä-Luosto

♪016

The area between the fells of Luosto (514m) and Pyhä (540m) forms a popular winter sports centre. Most of the area forms part of Pyhä-Luosto National Park, which is excellent for trekking. Pyhä and Luosto both have ski slopes and are fully serviced resort 'villages'. They make excellent value, if quiet, places to stay in summer with bargain modern apartments and log cottages available.

Pyhä is about 14km from the main Kemijärvi to Sodankylä road, while Luosto is the same distance east of the Rovaniemi–Sodankylä road. A good road connects the two resorts, which are 25km apart.

◉ Sights & Activities

Pyhä-Luosto National Park   WALKING, BIRDWATCHING

(www.outdoors.fi) The core of this park is the long line of fells stretching 35km from Pyhä itself to north of Luosto. It preserves old-growth forest with various endangered plant species, the southern reaches of the Lapland fell ecosystems, and *aapa* (open bog) areas that harbour snipe, bean geese, swans and the occasional golden eagle cruising for prey. There is a birdwatching tower at the southeastern corner of the park, about 2.5km from the Pyhätunturi Nature Centre. A circular nature trail of 5km takes you there.

Within the park are several marked trails, which, together with the network of cross-country skiing trails around the resorts, means that walkers are very well provided for. One of the nicest walks is the 35km trail between Pyhä and Luosto, involving plenty of ascents and descents as it climbs from fell to fell. From Pyhätunturi Nature Centre, a 10km loop trail runs to Pyhäkuru Gorge, while from Luosto, a hilly 15km nature trail loops to the top of the fell and around the flatlands and mires on the other side.

There are several huts where you can stay overnight in the national park.

Lampivaara   MINE

(www.amethystmine.fi; adult/child €14/8, in winter €17/10; ☉11am-5pm Jun–mid-Aug, 11am-4pm mid-Aug–Sep, 11am-3pm Tue-Sat Oct, noon & 2pm Tue, Thu & Sat late Nov-late Dec, noon & 2pm daily Jan-Apr, closed May) Five kilometres above Luosto, this amethyst mine focuses on small-scale production for jewellery, using low-impact mining methods. There are guided tours (in English by request) on the hour, and you get to have a dig around for your own piece of amethyst. The mine is a 30-minute walk from Ukko-Luosto parking; you're meant to get a cab there if you don't fancy the stroll. In winter, go on skis, or use the snow-train from Ukko-Luosto parking (adult/child including admission €32/20).

Kopara   REINDEER

(www.kopara.fi; Luostontie 1160; ☉11am-3pm Mon-Fri Jun-Sep, 11am-4pm Jan-Apr) More or less midway between Pyhä and Luosto, this is a good place to meet some reindeer. You can go on a short walk that has information boards on the creatures (€5 per person), and tempt them closer with a feed bucket. In winter, various sledge trips are on offer. The cafe here specialises in blueberry pie in summer and, er, reindeer soup in winter.

Arctic Husky Farm   HUSKIES

(www.huskysafaris.com; Luostontie; ☉noon-1pm Jun-Aug) Near Kopara, this is where dogs relax all summer gaining strength for winter sledge safaris. You can visit their enclosures at noon on weekdays (€5 per person).

Skiing

At Pyhä there are 10 ski-runs and seven lifts. The longest run is 1.8km, with a vertical drop of 280m. At Luosto there are seven runs and four lifts, plus a half-pipe and snowboard slopes. The longest run is 1.5km, with a vertical drop of 230m.

Between them, Pyhä and Luosto have over 150km of trails for cross-country skiers, some 40km of which are lit. You can rent equipment and get lessons at either location.

➔ Tours

Luontosafarit   QUAD BIKE

(624 336; www.luontosafarit.fi; Orresokantie 1, Luosto) In summer take trips on quad bikes to the amethyst mine or reindeer farm (€65 to €85 per person), or head to the river for canoeing and fishing. Winter has similar trips on snowmobiles (€100 to €200); there are also multiday trips to the Arctic Ocean.

Pyhä Safaris   SNOWMOBILE

(☎040-778 9106; www.pyhasafaris.com; Pyhäntie 2030, Pyhä) At the Pyhä roundabout, this offers reindeer, husky and snowmobile trips.

🛏 Sleeping & Eating

There are many designated camping areas within a short walk from the Pyhätunturi Nature Centre, and a site for vans by the Luosto ski slope.

TOP CHOICE Aurora Chalet   HOTEL €€€

(☑327 2700; www.aurorachalet.fi; Luppokeino 2, Luosto; d from €156; ☺Sep-Apr; [P]) At the Luosto slope, this is one of Lapland's most original and stylish hotels and a great winter hideaway. All rooms have their own sauna, and many a wood fire; the wide floorboards, warm colours and romantic design create a whole ambience of great creativity, with an old-fashioned rustic air combined with modern comforts. Reception will SMS you when the northern lights are visible, a nice touch that'll save a few shivers. Their activity company can arrange snowmobiling and more.

Hotelli Luostotunturi   HOTEL €€

(☑620 400; www.laplandhotels.com; Luostontie 1, Luosto; s/d €120/150, apt €175-230, r in summer €80; [P][@][≋]) The rounded design of this curious hotel is supposed to resemble a reindeer's earmark. Happily, the comforts and facilities on offer are much less difficult to perceive. Most of the spacious rooms have a log-girt balcony, and some have an extra loft-style sleeping space, ideal for families. A new wing has excellent apartments, with a kitchenette and sauna. There's a pretty indoor pool and various spa treatments. Visitors can use the facilities (adult/child €12/7), and also rents bikes.

Hotelli Pyhätunturi   HOTEL €€

(☑040-010 1695; www.pyha.fi; Kultakeronkatu 21, Pyhä; r €100-140; [P][@]) Pyhä's major hotel sits halfway up the chairlift at the top of the road. The big bright white double rooms have recycling bags, a drying cupboard and flatscreen TV, and the hotel's restaurant has a great view and is romantically candlelit at night. There are also self-contained chalets available. There's no pool, but a sauna, gym and jacuzzi will ease those ski-tired muscles. The hotel also rents bikes.

Kerttuli   FINNISH €€

(www.luoston-kerttuli.fi; Hartsutie 1, Luosto; mains €14-24; ☺2-9pm Oct-Aug, noon-11pm Sep) In the centre of Luosto, this is a cosy place that offers pizzas as well as more intriguing fare such as unusual cuts of reindeer, roast meats and risotto in its cosy interior.

Cottages and Cabins

Hundreds of cottages, cabins and apartments in the Pyhä-Luosto area make great places to stay. The three main agencies are the excellent **Keskusvaraamo Pyhähippu** (☑882 820; www.pyhahippu.fi; Käärmepolku 2, Pyhä; ☺roughly noon-8pm mid-Jun–mid-Aug & Nov-Apr, noon-5pm at other times) by the supermarket at the Pyhä roundabout; **Pyhä Booking** (☑860 0400; www.pyhabooking.fi; Käärmepolku 2, Pyhä) in the same complex; and **Pyhä-Luosto Matkailu** (☑020-730 3020; www.pyha-luostomatkailu.fi; Laukotie 1, Luosto; ☺9am-5pm Mon-Fri) on the main road in Luosto. These offer hundreds of cabins, apartments and cottages that you can book online; Pyhähippu has the advantage of convenient opening hours for on-spec arrivals. For around €50 in summer, you can nab a luxury cottage or apartment for two, complete with sofa, balcony, sauna and fireplace with free firewood, not to mention a fully equipped kitchen and a drying cupboard. Rates increase sharply in winter, and at peak periods there's a one-week minimum stay (from €600).

ℹ Information

Pyhätunturi Nature Centre (☑020-564 7302; www.outdoors.fi; Kultakeronkatu 22, Pyhä; ☺10am-4pm Mon-Fri Nov-Jan, 10am-4pm Tue-Sun Feb-Apr & Oct, 9am-4pm Mon-Fri May–mid-Jun, 9am-5pm Mon-Fri, 10am-4pm Sat & Sun mid-Jun–Sep) Opposite the Pyhätunturi hotel. Information on Pyhä-Luosto National Park and activities such as hiking and fishing.

ℹ Getting There & Away

Two daily buses (four in winter) run from Rovaniemi to Luosto (€23, one hour 40 minutes) and Pyhä (€26, two hours): one meets the morning Finnair flight from Helsinki en route. These are the only buses connecting Pyhä and Luosto (€6, 20 minutes).

There are also buses to Pyhä from Kemijärvi (€9.40, 50 minutes) and Sodankylä (€16.20, 1¼ hours), with extra buses put on for the Midnight Sun Film Festival. Call a local cab on ☑106 425. The fare between Pyhä and Luosto is €40.

Sodankylä

☑016 / POP 5540

Likeable Sodankylä is the main service centre for one of Europe's least populated areas, which has a population density of just 0.8 people per sq km. It's at the junction of the main two southbound highways and makes a decent staging post between Rovaniemi and the north; even if you're just passing through, stop to see the wooden church – humble but achingly beautiful. A contrast is provided by the high-tech observatory just outside town, an important collection point of data on the atmosphere and aurora.

◉ Sights & Activities

Vanha Kirkko
CHURCH

(Jäämerentie 1; ◎9am-6pm early Jun–mid-Aug, 9am-6pm Fri-Mon rest of Aug, by request [€20] rest of year) One of the few buildings in Lapland to survive the Germans' scorched-earth retreat in WWII is the church by the tourist office, near the Kitinen riverside. It is the region's oldest and dates back to 1689. The church stands in a graveyard encircled by a low wooden fence and is noteworthy for its decorative shingles and prominent prong-like standards. The interior is simple and charming, with gnarled wooden benches and pulpit, and a simple altar made from leftover beams. The stone church nearby was built in 1859.

Alariesto Galleria
GALLERY

(www.sodankyla.fi; Jäämerentie 3; adult/child €3/1.50; ◎10am-4pm Mon-Fri Jun-Sep, plus 10am-3pm Sat mid-Jun–Sep) Above the tourist office, this gallery displays paintings by the famous local artist Andreas Alariesto (1900–89), who depicted traditional Sámi life in an attractive naive style, and also has temporary exhibitions. There are good-value prints on sale.

Pohjan Kruunu
SHOW

(☎040-514 2858; www.arcticacademy.fi; Välisuvannontie; adult/child €11/6; ◎on the hour noon-4pm mid-Jun–mid-Jul) The Aurora House, 11km southeast of Sodankylä (take the Kemijärvi road, then turn right towards the airport and keep going) has a half-hour aurora borealis audiovisual show projected on the ceiling of a *kota*-style building (traditional dwelling resembling a tepee or wigwam).

Taiga Koru
JEWELLERY

(www.taigakoru.fi; Sompiontie 4; ◎Mon-Sat) In the centre of town, this jewellery shop is famous hereabouts for the gold and silver works of goldsmith Seppo Penttinen.

✦ Festivals

Midnight Sun Film Festival
FILM

(www.msfilmfestival.fi) Dubbed as the 'anti-Cannes', this festival in mid-June sees the village's population double with round-the-clock screenings in three venues, often with high-profile directors in attendance. If you can't find a bed, head for Luosto, less than 40km away.

🛏 Sleeping & Eating

TOP CHOICE Hotelli Karhu
HOTEL €€

(☎020-162 0610; www.hotel-bearinn.com; Lapintie 7; s/d May-Oct €70/90, Nov-Apr €80/104; P@) This central hotel is a great deal, offering buzzy staff, offbeat lobby decor and inviting chambers, with big fluffy beds, grey-wood floors and great modern bathrooms. Single travellers are in for a treat here, as the same rate gets a room with a cute minisauna to call your own. You can borrow bikes and ski gear, and the restaurant does evening mains and cheap lunch.

Camping Sodankylä Nilimella
CAMPGROUND, COTTAGE €

(☎612 181; www.nature-ventures.fi; Kelukoskentie 5; tent sites €6 plus per adult/child €4/2, 2-/4-person cabins €36/52, 2-/4-person cottage €65/95; ◎Jun-Aug; P) Across the river from the town, this camp site has a sauna and good showers as well as a riverside cafe-bar. The cabins, discreetly angled for privacy, are simple but spacious, with a fridge and camp stove; there are also cottage apartments with their own kitchen and sauna. You can hire bikes for €15 per day.

Majatalo Kolme Veljestä
GUESTHOUSE €

(☎040-053 9075; www.majatalokolmeveljesta.fi; Ivalontie 1; s/d/tr €46/64/75; P@) Five hundred metres north of the centre, this family-run guesthouse has small but spotless rooms with wire storage units and other comfortable Ikea-type furniture. Guests share decent bathrooms and have use of a lounge and kitchen facilities (there's a big supermarket across the road). Price includes breakfast, sauna, tea and coffee.

Päivin Kammari
CAFE €€

(www.paivinkammari.fi; Jäämerentie 11; mains €12-21; ◎10am-9pm Mon-Sat, noon-6pm Sun) Cosy and homelike, this is the best eating spot in town, with soups, quiches, cakes, good coffee and streetside seating. They do cheap lunches and tasty à la carte meals with local *muikku* (vendace, or whitefish) and reindeer. Behind is Rooperante, the town's best pub, though, like in any Lapland bar, there are always a few shamblers about.

THE NORTHERN LIGHTS

The Northern Lights, or aurora borealis, an utterly haunting and exhilarating sight, are often visible to observers standing at or above the Arctic Circle, which includes a large portion of Lapland. They're particularly striking during the dark winter; in summer, the sun more or less renders them invisible.

The aurora appears as curtains of greenish-white light stretching east to west across the sky for thousands of kilometres. At its lower edge, the aurora typically shades to a crimson-red glow. Hues of blue and violet can also be seen. The lights seem to dance and swirl in the night sky.

These auroral storms, however eerie, are quite natural. They're created when charged particles (protons and electrons) from the sun bombard the earth. These are deflected towards the North and South Poles by the earth's magnetic field. There they hit the earth's outer atmosphere, 100km to 1000km above ground, causing highly charged electrons to collide with molecules of nitrogen and oxygen. The excess energy from these collisions creates the colourful lights.

The ancient inhabitants of Lapland believed it was caused by a giant fox swishing its tail above the Arctic tundra. One of the Finnish words for the aurora borealis is *revontulet* (literally 'fires of the fox').

To see the lights, you'd best have a dark, clear night with high auroral activity. October, November and March are often optimal for this. Then it's a question of waiting patiently outside, preferably between the hours of 9pm and 2am, and seeing if things kick off. There are several useful websites for predicting auroral activity:

Geophysical Institute (www.gi.alaska.edu/AuroraForecast) Change the view to Europe and away you go.

University of Oulu (http://cc.oulu.fi/~thu/Aurora/forecast.html) Finland-based page with links so you can make your own prediction.

AuroraWatch (http://aurorawatch.lancs.ac.uk) UK-based but can send you alerts when high activity is predicted.

ℹ Information

Tourist office (☑040-746 9776; www.sodankyla.fi; Jäämerentie 3; ☉9am-5pm Mon-Fri, plus 10am-3pm Sat mid-Jun–mid-Aug) At the intersection of the Kemijärvi and Rovaniemi roads. Opposite is the library, with internet access.

ℹ Getting There & Away

Sodankylä is on the main Rovaniemi–Ivalo road (Rd 4), and Rd 5 from Kemijärvi and Karelia ends here. There are regular buses from Rovaniemi, Ivalo and Kemijärvi. The bus terminal is on the main road.

Saariselkä

☑016

The bustling, touristy village of Saariselkä (Sámi: Suolocielgi), 250km north of the Arctic Circle, makes a great spot to get active from. It's a major winter destination for Christmassy experiences, sled safaris and skiing, and in summer serves as the main base for trekkers heading into the awesome Saariselkä Wilderness. You could hike for weeks here; there's a good network of huts and marked trails. Saariselkä itself is basically a collection of enormous hotels and holiday cottages, more resort than community, but has plenty of accommodation and shops to stock up on trekking supplies and equipment, and high-quality souvenirs.

🏃 Activities & Tours

Saariselkä is bristling with things to do year-round. Things are most active in winter, with numerous snowy excursions organised by the many activity companies in town. Husky- and reindeer-sledding are understandably popular, with trips of a couple of hours starting at around €100. Snowmobiling is a little cheaper, and there are combination excursions, as well as multiday safaris. Snowshoe walks (€55), aurora borealis-watching trips and ice-fishing are other options.

In summer, things on offer include visits to Tankavaara (€75 to €95), reindeer farms (€60), canoeing on the Tankajoki (€124), fishing (€67), whitewater rafting in Inari

(€58), whole-day rafting on the Ivalojoki (€180), and various guided walks. All these can be booked at the tourist office or via the hotels. The best hiking is in the Saariselkä Wilderness (see p298).

Most operators (see www.saariselka.fi for a complete list) offer all these activities and also rent mountain bikes, skis and snowshoes. Some recommended providers include: **Eräsetti Wild North** (🖉668 345; www.erasettiwild north.fi; Holiday Club), **Husky & Co** (🖉050-413 1551; www.saariselka.fi/huskyco), **Lapland Safaris** (🖉668 901; www.laplandsafaris.fi; Riekonlinna hotel) which rents and sells camping gear, and **LuontoLoma/Pro Safaris** (🖉668 706; www.luontoloma.fi) based at the Tunturi hotel.

Skiing

There are 11 downhill **slopes** (www.skisaariselka .fi) served by five lifts; the longest run is 1300m and the vertical drop is 180m. There's also a freestyle park and some 240km of cross-country trails, some lit. Saariselkä is known for snow-kiting conditions, and you can have lessons.

🛏 Sleeping

Prices in Saariselkä's hotels are highest during the ski season and *ruska* (late August to mid-September). Here, as in other parts of Finland, the accommodation division of the Forest and Park Service has many rural cabins and cottages for rent. Ask at the Kiehinen information centre, or contact **Wild North** (🖉020-564 6990; www.villipohjola.fi) directly. **Saariselän Keskusvaraamo** (🖉554 0500; www.saariselka.com; Saariseläntie 1; ⊙to 8.30pm daily) is an accommodation service at the bottom of the Kuukkeli centre and can organise a wide range of cabins, cottages and apartments in and around the village.

Holiday Club Saariselkä
SPA HOTEL €€

(🖉020-123 4907; www.holidayclub.fi; Saariseläntie 7; d in winter €140-160, summer €80-100; 🅿@☒) In the centre of the village, this spa hotel is most family-friendly and a good choice in winter or summer. They're gradually renovating the rooms, so grab one of the new ones (same price) which have comfy chairs, trendy dark browns and magentas and a backlit photo of old Lapland. Nonguests can use the spa facilities (adult/child €15/9). Check before booking, as the pool's usually shut for a couple of weeks in May–June.

Santa's Hotel Tunturi
HOTEL €€

(🖉68111; www.tunturihotelli.fi; Lutontie 3; s/d standard €124/147, superior €174/208, 2-/4-person apt €185/236; 🅿@) Lapland's largest hotel, this complex sprawls across several buildings including the very appealing Gielas and the Dalmatian-like Paraspaikka but hasn't lost sight of its roots as a solid old place with a warm welcome and excellent service. We'd need the whole chapter to list the numerous grades of rooms and apartments (all but the standards come with their own sauna); the most modern are the enticing superiors and junior suites. Prices drop 20% or so in summer. Conveniently, it's right by the trailhead for the national park.

Saariselän Panimo
GUESTHOUSE €

(🖉675 6500; www.saariselanpanimo.fi; Saariseläntie 8; s/d €44/58, summer €34/48, peak winter €73/86; 🅿) The friendly village pub offers good accommodation in a variety of buildings around it, in the heart of Saariselkä. Rooms are spacious and warm, with bathroom and comfortable beds; they're an absolute steal in summer. A simple breakfast is served in winter only.

🍴 Eating & Drinking

Most restaurants are closed in summer, but the hotels all keep an eating option open. The Panimo brews its own beer and is a cosy, welcoming spot for a drink.

TOP CHOICE / Pirkon Pirtti
FINNISH €€

(🖉668 060; www.pirkonpirtti.fi; Honkapolku 2; mains €17-26; ⊙3-11pm Sun-Fri, 1-11pm Sat late Jun-Apr) This excellent place near the tourist office has a cosy wooden interior and welcoming service. They do well-presented and generous portions of fish (served on a plank of wood), reindeer, steaks, as well as tasty pizzas (€8 to €11).

Siberia
FINNISH, RUSSIAN €€€

(🖉040-502 0409; www.ravintolasiberia.fi; Saariseläntie 3; 5/7/10 courses €65/75/109; ⊙dinner late Nov-Apr) This smart spot sits behind the rainbow screen on the main street and offers quality glassware and various degustation menus with typical Lapland ingredients beautifully served, with the option of matching wines. There's a Russian touch to some of the dishes. During the day it opens as a cafe.

Rakka FINNISH €€
(Saariseläntie 7; mains €13-25; ⊙noon-10:30pm)
The Holiday Club's à la carte restaurant has
a few traditional Finnish plates like pepper
steak, alongside a few marked-up healthy
choices, with delicious salads and salmon
on roasted vegetables. They also offer pizzas
and burgers, though the adjacent buffet restaurant will be more to the kids' liking.

Huippu FINNISH, CAFE €€
(www.saariselka.fi/huippu; Kaunispääntie; mains
€10-24; ⊙10am-5pm) Situated at the summit
of Kaunispää fell at the top of the ski slopes,
this cafe is worth a visit for the great views.
It's touristy but serves a salad buffet, restaurant mains with Arctic char and reindeer,
and delicious lighter cafe snacks like fish
pie and cloudberry cheesecake. It's 2.5km by
road but a nice walk uphill from the village.
In winter just jump on the skilift.

Petronella FINNISH €€
(☑668 930; www.ravintolapetronella.fi; Honkapolku
5; mains €20-30; ⊙dinner Sep & late Nov-Apr)
Serves appetising portions of smart Lappish
food in a wood-and-stone decorated dining
room.

ⓘ Information

The Kuukkeli building, at the main entrance
to the village, has baggage lockers, post office, supermarket and the main accommodation agency.

Kiehinen (☑020-564 7200; www.outdoors.fi;
⊙9am-5pm Mon-Fri) In the Siula building, just
off the main road near the petrol station, this
is a national parks centre with hiking information, cabin reservations, fishing permits, maps
and a small nature display. It also contains
Saariselkä's **tourist information desk** (☑040-
168 7838; www.saariselka.fi). The office opens
weekends from high season summer to late
September and in peak skiing season.

ⓘ Getting There & Away

There are four or more daily buses from Rovaniemi (€46.90, 4½ hours), continuing to Ivalo
(€6.90, 30 minutes). Each incoming flight at
Ivalo is met by a shuttle bus to Saariselkä.

ⓘ Getting Around

In winter a ski-bus connects Ivalo and all the
major hotels with Saariselkä slopes, Kakslauttanen and Kiilopää several times a day. An all-
day pass is €4.

Around Saariselkä
KIILOPÄÄ

Kiilopää, 17km southeast of Saariselkä, is the
best launchpad for hiking in the national
park; marked trails head directly into the
wilderness from here. The Saariselkä-Kiilopää hiking map (€3) gives you a wealth of
day-walk options. Short walks from here include the boardwalked ascent of Kiilopää fell
(one hour return), rewarded by great views.

Suomen Latu Kiilopää (☑670 0700;
www.kiilopaa.fi; Kiilopääntie; s/d €79/88, 2 nights
€121/136; P@) is an excellent and very professional facility that takes care of all accommodation and services. It rents mountain
bikes, rucksacks, sleeping bags, skiing
equipment and more. It also sells fishing
permits and dispenses sound advice on trekking; guided treks are possible. There are
hotel rooms and a cafe-restaurant (packed
lunch €7, dinner €13 to €17), as well as a
variety of cottages and apartments starting
at €83/90 for a two-/four-person apartment
in summer, and the **Ahopää hostel** (dm sum-
mer/winter €34/37), a comfortable facility with
OK bunks and a small kitchen. HI discount
applies.

The centre has a traditional **smoke sauna** that's fired up on Tuesdays, Wednesdays
and Fridays from June to August. It's open
from 3pm to 8pm and costs €9 (free if you're
staying here).

Several daily buses do the one-hour trip
between Ivalo and Kiilopää; a bus meets
every incoming flight to Ivalo airport. If you
are travelling by bus from Rovaniemi, check
whether the bus runs to Kiilopää: some do,
some don't.

KAKSLAUTTANEN
On the main road at the Kiilopää turn-off,
Hotel Kakslauttanen (☑667 100; www.kak
slauttanen.fi; s/d cabins in winter from €198/242,
igloo €225/338, glass igloo €300/342; P@) is
a large accommodation complex that has
comfortable log cabins that are a decent deal
in summer (s/d €70/100).

In winter, Kakslauttanen becomes the site
of the **Snow Village** (⊙Nov-Apr), consisting
of igloos to bed down in, and a snow restaurant for your tucker. There are traditional
snow igloos (warm sleeping bag provided)
as well as rows of glass igloos, which are
by no means luxurious or spacious but are
heated and have a tiny toilet cubicle. The romance of them: you get the chance to watch
the aurora borealis from the luxury of your

own bed. The downside: you'd expect much more luxury and charm for the price, which seems to increase astronomically every year.

West of the hotel, the **Santa's Resort** (www.santasresort.fi) village appears in winter, with reindeer, elves and the old man himself in attendance.

Hotel Kakslauttanen is on Rd 4, 11km south of Saariselkä. Kiilopää is 6km east of it. All north- and southbound buses will stop here on request.

TANKAVAARA

Back in 1868, a cry went up and started a gold rush to this remote area on the Ivalojoki that saw a community of up to 500 panners seeking their fortune here after an arduous journey. Though people still work claims, Tankavaara these days sees more income from the tourist trade than from the bottom of the goldpans.

◉ Sights & Activities

Kultamuseo   MUSEUM
(www.kultamuseo.fi; Valtatie 4; adult/child €8/4; ☺9am-6pm Jun–mid-Aug, 9am-5pm mid-Aug–Sep, 10am-4pm Mon-Fri Oct-May) The main attraction is this gold museum, which has several parts. Nearest the entrance gate are replica buildings from American goldfields; the nearby smoke sauna and octagonal hut are less flashy but original. Rockhounds will enjoy the gemstone and mineral exhibition despite its neglected air, but the highlight is the main museum, with sections on the Finnish gold rush, and on gold production around the world. A cubic metre of sand is on display along with the sobering 2g of gold it normally contains here. In summer, try your luck and pan for gold (€5 for an hour, or €30 for a day's licence); indoor gold-panning is available in winter. Gold-related events and festivals are held in summer.

Koilliskaira   VISITOR CENTRE
(www.outdoors.fi; Valtatie 4; ☺9am-5pm Mon-Fri, 9am-4pm Sat & Sun Jun-Sep, 10am-4pm Wed-Fri Mar & Apr; @) Also in Tankavaara is this nature centre with advice on activities and trekking in Urho Kekkonen National Park. It has good exhibitions on the local environment, including a display on raptors upstairs, as well as a half-hour audiovisual, an internet terminal, a shop and a selection of maps. Various circular **nature trails** arc out from the centre (1km to 6km).

🍴 Sleeping & Eating

Wanha Waskoolimies   HOTEL, CAFE €
(✆626 158; www.tankavaara.fi; Valtatie 4; mains €10-20; ☺9am-9pm summer) By the entrance to the gold village, this is a kitsch but atmospheric cafe-restaurant that actually predates the museum and serves typical Lapland dishes. They have hotel rooms (doubles €65) and cabins (€55) and you can also camp here (€12).

ⓘ Getting There & Away

Tankavaara is on the main Rovaniemi–Ivalo road 30km south of Saariselkä and 100km north of Sodankylä. All buses pass the village, stopping on request; nonexpress buses actually enter.

Saariselkä Wilderness & Urho Kekkonen National Park

Saariselkä Wilderness, including the 2538-sq-km **Urho Kekkonen National Park** and also large tracts of protected forest, extends to the Russian border. It's a fabulous slice of Finland, home to bears, wolverines and golden eagles, as well as many thousands of free-grazing reindeer. This is a highly rated trekking area, partly because of the large network of wilderness huts, but also for the unspoilt beauty of the low fells. You certainly won't be alone in peak season on the most popular routes, but there are plenty of options in this huge and memorable expanse of forest, fell and marshland.

The park's divided into several zones, each with different rules. Check www.outdoors.fi for details. Although fires (using dead wood) are allowed in certain areas, take a camp stove, as fire bans are common in summer.

There are national park visitor centres in Saariselkä, Tankavaara and Savukoski villages; you can also pick up information at Kiilopää, although it isn't an official information centre. A map and compass are *essential* for the most remote areas of the park.

There are three Karttakeskus maps available for the area. The western part of the park is shown on the 1:50,000 *Saariselkä-Kiilopää* map; the 1:50,000 *Sokosti-Suomujoki* map will take you beyond Luirojärvi; the entire park is shown on the 1:100,000 *Koilliskaira* map. Each map costs €19.50. The visitor centres also sell a simpler map for day walks in the Saariselkä-Kiilopää area (€3).

Saariselkä Wilderness & Urho Kekkonen National Park

RUSSIA

To Ivalo (15km)

To Ivalo (15km)

Raja-Jooseppi

Kaunispää Fell

Saariselkä

Rumakuru Gorge
Suomen Latu
Kiilopää
Hotel
Kakslauttanen

Kuttamuseo (Gold Museum)
Sompio Strict Nature Reserve
Koilliskaira Visitor Centre

To Sodankylä (85km);
Rovaniemi (185km)

Vuotso
Tankavaara

Moitakuru
Vellinsärpimä
468m
Kivipää 438m
Taajostupa
Rumakuru
Luulampi
Niilanpää
546m
Portikoski
Lankojärvi
Rautulampi
431m
Luirojärvi
Luirojärvi
Luirojärvi
Suomunjoki
Suomunruoktu
Tammakkolampi
544m

Snelmanninhara
Skolt Sámi Settlements
91

Skolt Fields
Kiertämäjärvi
Jyrkkävaara

678m
Sarvioja
Paratiisikuru (Paradise Gorge)
Muotravaararakka
530m
Ukselmapää (698m)
627m
Lumikuru (Snow Gorge)
619m
Sokosti (718m)
691m
Anterinmukka
Vongoiva
Hammaskuru
Luiro
Tuiskukuru
Gorge
Karapuljy

Lokan tekojärvi

71½m

Juulinjoki

74m

Korvatunturi Fell (483m)
Vierharju
Mantoselkä
Manto-oja
352m
Karhuoja
Mettopalo
Nuortti
Naltiohoki
429m
Tikkasen Vierharju
Kemihaara
Peuraselkä
Keskihaara
Tahvontupa
Peskihaara
Härkävaara
Urho K Kekkonen National Park
Sulanruoktu
Gorge
Hammaskota
Protected Forestry Area

Nuortti Recreational Fishing Area
Marjarova
Sokli
Tulppio
Kärkekeoja
Nuortti
Reindeer Roundup Site

To Savukoski (60km)

Nuortti River

0   10 km
0   6 miles

◉ Sights

There are several natural attractions within the park boundaries, of which **Rumakuru Gorge**, near the hut of the same name, is closest to the main road. **Luirojärvi** is the most popular trekking destination, including a hike up the nearby **Sokosti summit** (718m), the highest in the park. **Paratiisikuru** (Paradise Gorge), a steep descent from the 698m **Ukselmapää summit**, and the nearby **Lumikuru** (Snow Gorge), are popular day trips between Sarvioja and Muorravaarakka huts.

Two historical **Skolt Sámi settlements**, with restored old houses, lie 2km south of Raja-Jooseppi, and 2km west of Snelmanninmaja hut, respectively.

Trekking

There's some great hiking to be done sticking to the well-defined trails in the Saariselkä-Kakslauttanen-Kiilopää area. Grab a map and plan your own day hikes. For longer adventures, use wilderness huts as bases and destinations, and create your own itinerary according to your ability: an experienced, fit trekker can cover up to 4km per hour, and up to 25km per day. You will need to carry all food, as wilderness huts in the park are not stocked with supplies; water in rivers is drinkable.

The four- to six-day loop from the main road to Luirojärvi is the most popular, and can be extended beyond the lake. To reach areas where few have been, take a one-week walk from Kiilopää to Kemihaara.

The most remote route follows old roads and walking routes through the fells all the way from Raja-Jooseppi in the north to Kemihaara or Tulppio in the southeast.

🛏 Sleeping

Within the park are 200 designated free camping areas as well as some 40 free wilderness huts. Some of these have locked areas with beds, and there are a few cabins, which must both be booked in advance. The charge is €10 per bed per night; this is on a shared basis. Book beds at any of the park visitor centres.

You'll need a sleeping bag and mat for the wilderness huts; bookable ones have mattresses. Visitor centres supply maps and details of huts, as does the www.outdoors.fi website.

➊ Getting There & Away

The easiest starting points for treks are Saariselkä or Kiilopää. From Savukoski you can catch a **post-taxi** (☑040-730 6484) to Kemihaara village (Wednesday and Friday), 1km from the park's boundary.

The Raja-Jooseppi border station is another starting point for treks, as it takes you directly into the real wilderness; you can get there by taxi-bus and Murmansk-bound buses from Ivalo.

Ivalo

☑016 / POP 4000

A small town by most standards, Ivalo (Sámi: Avvil) is a metropolis in these latitudes. With plenty of services and an air-

---

HUT-IQUETTE AND HIKING

Lonely Planet reader Andrew Pitt had this to say on a recent hiking adventure in the Urho Kekkonen National Park:

Huts are usually conveniently spaced a comfortable day's walk apart (four to six hours walking – 10km to 20km). In near proximity there are usually pit toilets, camp sites, established fire sites, a supply of dried firewood and occasionally a sauna. The huts have sleeping platforms and/or bunkbeds, and open access. However, should it be busy, etiquette has it that the walkers arriving *last* have first option on sleeping inside as they theoretically have less opportunity to set up camp outside. So carrying a tent is advised – you'll probably sleep better anyway given the high likelihood the hut will be full of mosquitoes by the end of the evening.

Trails are generally good and well marked, but not always. There are a variety of easy day walks accessible from the villages lining the western side of the park. For longer treks in the park, expect river crossings and be careful to choose the best place to cross. The landscape is undulating and mainly forested but not particularly difficult for confident walkers during the warmer months.

port busy with charters at Christmas, it's a useful service centre, but has little to detain the visitor, however Inari's Sámi culture and Saariselkä's plentiful activities are close by.

🏃 Activities

Several husky kennels around Ivalo offer dog-sledding trips in winter and pooch visits in summer.

Kamisak   DOG-SLEDDING
(☎050-570 7871; www.kamisak.com; Rovaniementie 915; ☺10am-5pm Tue-Sat) Kamisak is 8km south of Ivalo and open year-round. There's a cafe, knowledgeable canine chat, and you can prebook a guided tour of the husky enclosures and meet the dogs (adult/child €10/5). From November to April, they run safaris that range from a half-day trip to multiday adventures. They also have two double rooms (s/d €50/65 in summer) and a log cabin that sleeps two.

Arctic Rally Team   RALLY DRIVING
(☎663 456; www.arcticrallyteam.fi) If you've always fancied yourself as another Kimi Räikkönen or Marcus Grönholm, get onto these people. They organise crash courses (so to speak) in winter driving, rallying and even navigating.

🛏 Sleeping & Eating

Guesthouse Husky   GUESTHOUSE €
(☎663 377; www.guesthousehusky.fi; Hirviniementie 65; s/d €62/90; P) Five kilometres from Ivalo, this friendly family-run husky farm has more than 150 dogs and also offers cosy modern ensuite rooms with kitchen and laundry use. Breakfast is included and meals are available. HI discount. Slightly more expensive in winter.

Hotel Kultahippu   HOTEL €€
(☎320 8800; www.kultahippuhotel.fi; Petsamontie 1; s/d €70/85; P@) In the friendly 'Speck of Gold' you might still see the odd gold panner stooped pensively over their *tuoppi* (glass) of beer. The rooms are simple but decent, with big windows and original art on the walls; the riverside location appeals, especially in winter. The spacious restaurant does a €9.50 buffet lunch, and the pub and club are the main local nightspots (the noise isn't too bad from the rooms though).

Hotelli Ivalo   HOTEL €€
(☎688 111; www.hotelivalo.fi; Ivalontie 34; s/d €95/115; P@≋) Half a kilometre south of the centre on the main road, the town's main hotel has functional, comfortable rooms (some are newer than others so ask), saunas and an indoor pool. When things are quiet, rates come down to €68/85 for singles/doubles, which seems like much better value.

ℹ Information

Metsähallitus (☎020-564 7701; www.outdoors.fi; Ivalontie 10; ☺9am-4pm Mon-Fri) On the main road, this has local and national park information.

ℹ Getting There & Away

There are numerous winter charters to Ivalo Airport, and regular Finnair services from Helsinki. The airport is 12km south of Ivalo; a connecting bus meets each arriving flight.

There are a few daily buses from Rovaniemi (€49.90, 4¾ hours) to Ivalo. Major car-rental companies have offices at Ivalo Airport (and in town).

Three weekly buses (see p344) travel the 300km east to Murmansk, Russia.

Nellim

This tucked-away village with a population of under 200 is one of the major Skolt settlements and worth a visit for anyone interested in Sámi culture. There's also a significant Inari Sámi and Finnish population and Nellim likes to dub itself as the meeting point of three peoples. Situated on the shores of Inarijärvi 42km northeast of Ivalo, it has a beautiful wooden Orthodox church amid the forest, built in 1987.

You can head out in a boat on Inarijärvi with **Safari Service** (☎040-773 9142; www.safariservice.fi). Near the dock, there's a versatile summer-only shop that has internet access, a cafe, petrol, and a post office.

TOP CHOICE **Erähotelli Nellim** (☎040-041 5989; www.nellim.fi; Nellimintie 4230; s/d/apt €65/95/165; ☺mid-Jun–mid-Sep, Nov-Apr; P) is a great place to stay in remote Finland, with lovely modern rooms smelling of wood, beds with Sámi blankets in old timber buildings surrounding a courtyard. There are also excellent apartments sleeping up to eight, and meals served in a rustic wooden dining room. They organise winter packages with northern-lights watching, huskies and snowmobiles.

Three weekly buses run between Nellim and Ivalo in summer. During the school year, a bus runs the route Mondays to Fridays (50 minutes).

Inari

☑016 / POP 550

Though it's Finland's most significant Sámi centre, and one of Lapland's major visitor destinations, you might miss the tiny village of Inari (Sámi: Anár), if you're not paying attention. Don't, for this is the place to begin to learn something of Sámi culture: it has the wonderful Siida museum and the brand-new Sámi cultural centre, as well as excellent handicrafts shops. It's also a great base for locations like Lemmenjoki National Park and the Kevo Strict Nature Reserve.

The village sits on Lapland's largest lake, Inarijärvi, a spectacular body of water with more than 3000 islands in its 1153-sq-km area. Inari is the seat of the Finnish Sámi parliament, and the spectacular wood-and-glass Sámi cultural centre, Sajos, that will hold it, as well as a library and music archive, should have been completed in the centre of town by the time this book comes out. It will also have exhibitions and a craft shop.

◉ Sights

TOP CHOICE **Siida**   MUSEUM
(www.siida.fi; Inarintie 46; adult/child €9/5; ☺9am-8pm Jun-Sep, 10am-5pm Tue-Sun Oct-May) One of Finland's finest museums, Siida should not be missed. It's a comprehensive overview of the Sámi and their environment, and it's actually two museums skilfully interwoven. The main exhibition hall consists of a fabulous nature exhibition around the edge, detailing northern Lapland's ecology by season, with some wonderful photos and information panels. In the centre of the room is detailed information on the Sámi, from their former seminomadic existence to modern times. In an adjacent hall is a timeline framing Sámi prehistory and history, alongside other world events. Two other halls have excellent temporary exhibitions of Sámi crafts and traditions.

Outside is the original museum, a complex of **open-air buildings** that reflect postnomadic Sámi life. They are mostly original buildings brought here and include farmhouses, storage huts and a courthouse, where miscreants scratched their names on the wooden walls while awaiting a likely flogging.

Back inside, a theatrette shows pretty visuals of the aurora borealis and Inarijärvi a few times a day; there's also a fine craft shop and a good cafe for lunch.

Siida's website is itself worth a mention: via the 'web exhibitions' page you can access a series of excellent pages on the Inari and Skolt Sámi cultures.

Pielpajärven Kirkko   CHURCH
The *erämaakirkko* (wilderness church) of Pielpajärvi is accessible from Inari by a marked walking track (7.5km one way) from the parking area at Siida. If you have a vehicle there's another car park 2.5km beyond here, up Sarviniementie, from where it's a 4.3km walk to the church. In winter, you'll need snowshoes and a keen attitude. The church area has been an important marketplace for the Sámi over the centuries, with the first church erected here in 1646. The present church was built in 1760, and restored in the 1970s. It's always open. Open the shutters to get the full benefit of the interior, but close them again after your visit.

🏃 Activities & Tours

As well as the walk to the wilderness church above, there are other worthwhile trails, including one that leads 9km from Siida to the top of Otsamo fell, where you're rewarded with a great view. There's a day hut here for shelter and cooking.

Lake & Snow   CRUISE
(☑671 108; www.saariselka.fi/lakesnow; Inarintie 26; 2-hour cruise adult/child €19/10) These cruises sail on Inarijärvi from June (as soon as the ice melts) to September. Departures are at 2pm daily, with an additional departure in July at 6pm. Boats leave from the wharf at the Siida car park. The destination is **Ukko Island** (Sámi: Äjjih), which is sacred to the Sámi. During the brief (20-minute) stop, most people climb to the top of the island, but there are also cave formations at the island's northern end. The same company also organises fishing trips and snowmobile safaris, and in summer can organise quad-bike trips.

Inari Event   SUMMER, WINTER
(☑040-777 4339; www.visitinari.fi; Saarikoskentie 2) This excellent set-up is based at the Kulta-hovi hotel and organises all sorts of tours and programs from fishing to visits to Skolt Sámi villages, all with a deep knowledge of local culture. They also rent bikes for €20 per day and arrange transfers to Kirkenes for the Hurtigruten boat.

Northeastern Lapland

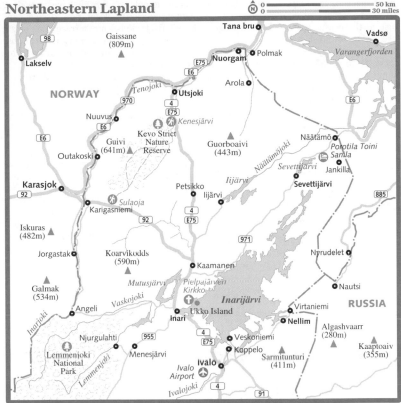

Villa Lanca
HORSEBACK RIDING

(☑040-748 0984; www.villalanca.com; Kittilän Ratsutie 2) Summer riding excursions and winter sledge trips with personable Norwegian fjording horses.

Ivalon Lentopalvelu
SCENIC FLIGHTS

(☑040-570 8369; www.lentopalvelu.fi) The seaplanes parked in the lake do scenic flights and chartered trips (one to three people €180) around Inarijärvi.

LuontoLoma/Pro Safaris
RAFTING

(☑668 706; www.luontoloma.fi) Organises daily one-hour rafting jaunts on the rapids from the Kultahovi hotel (€25) as well as other watery trips in the region.

Inarin Porofarmi
REINDEER

(☑050-066 6444; www.reindeerfarm.fi; Kittiläntie 1445) This spot 14km west of Inari runs sled-trips in winter and visits in summer (mid-June to mid-August), with plenty of

information on reindeer herding and Sámi culture. The two-hour visit costs €20, or €50 including transport from Inari.

Petri Mattus
REINDEER

(☑0400-193 950; www.petrimattus.com; Kittiläntie 3070) Offers the chance to head out in snowmobiles to feed the reindeer (one/two people €130/200, two to four hours) or, in May, to head out to watch calving and earmarking – depending on conditions, this could be an overnight trip.

✦ Festivals & Events

The third weekend of January is **Skábmagovat** (www.skabmagovat.fi) an indigenousthemed film festival that in recent years has seen collaborations with groups from northern Russia, Australia, Canada and Brazil. There's enough English content to make it worthwhile.

Held over the last weekend of March or first weekend of April, the King's Cup is the grand finale of Lapland's **reindeer-racing** (www.paliskunnat.fi) season and a great spectacle as the beasts race around the frozen lake, jockeys sliding like water-skiers behind them. The semifinals are on Saturday, the final on Sunday, and plenty of betting livens things up. There's also a race for visitors, which degenerates into comedy, as driving a reindeer is harder than it looks.

Inari Viikot (www.inariviikko.fi) is two weeks of cultural events in the second half of July. Over a weekend usually in August is **Ijahis Idja** (www.ijahisidja.fi), an excellent music festival that features groups from all spectra of Sámi music. The name means 'nightless night'.

🛏 Sleeping & Eating

TOP CHOICE **Kultahovi** HOTEL €€

(☎511 7100; www.hotelkultahovi.fi; Saarikoskentie 2; s/d €69/90; **P**@) Just behind the new Sámi cultural centre, this cosy family-run place overlooks the rapids and has spruce rooms, some with a great river view. An underwater camera beams the fishy depths to your TV screen. Chambers in the new wing (singles/doubles €109/125) have appealing light-wood Nordic decoration, drying cupboard, riverside balcony/terrace and (most) a sauna. The riverside sauna is great too, and there's a restaurant (⊘lunch and dinner) that serves well-presented, tasty Lappish specialities (mains €14 to €23) with great views of the Alakoski.

TOP CHOICE **Villa Lanca** GUESTHOUSE €€

(☎040-748 0984; www.villalanca.com; Kittilän Ratsutie 2; s/d €55/79, with kitchen €68/95; **P**) Near the supermarket on the main road through town, this is Inari's most characterful lodging, with original rooms that are full of atmosphere and decorated with Asian fabrics, feather charms and real artistic flair. The spacious apartments come with fully equipped kitchen, and the cosy upstairs dens have romantic sloping ceilings. Breakfast is great. Downstairs is a friendly licensed summer cafe.

Lomakylä Inari CABIN, CAMPGROUND €

(☎671 108; www.saariselka.fi/lomakylainari; Inarintie 26; 2-/4-person cabins €38/48, with bathroom €65/75, cottages with sauna €130-170, 1-/2-person

---

MODERN SÁMI LIFE *HEIKKI PALTTO*

Reindeer herder and member of the Sámi parliament

The reindeer year starts at the beginning of June because the calves that are born around May have to be earmarked. After that marking they are free in the fells for the summer. In autumn we start herding them and decide which are to be killed for meat. To herd them I use an ATV and after the snow falls, a snowmobile. It takes over two months to herd the reindeer and it's hopefully done by Christmas. During the winter we move the reindeer from one area to another because there's not enough food to last them in one place.

You should never ask a Sámi how many reindeer they have; it's like asking someone's salary. I wouldn't even tell a close friend. Some people have hundreds, some only have a few.

Our traditions are still important, even to young Sámi. We describe by yoiking (chanting) nature, people, all sorts of happenings, but one never yoiks about oneself. Traditional clothes are still important to us; we do wear them, mainly on special occasions. The locations of *seita* (holy site) places are still remembered by people, but they don't visit them. And if they do visit them, it's a secret that you wouldn't tell to anybody else.

The Sámi parliament deals with all aspects of Sámi life. We meet four times a year in Inari and are elected by the Sámi people. Our government does listen to us, though that doesn't mean that they do anything. If we want something it is our only channel so in that way it is important. The government asks our advice a lot if they want to know something. That is our main power I suppose. Of course, we'd like to have more!

Though some areas are protected, in parts of Lapland we have big battles with the forestry industry. Some are solved, and some are not. I think the question will never go away; there will always be people wanting to make money from the forest.

Tourism is a good thing for the Sámi people if Sámi people get the results, the benefits from it. That isn't always the case. Where I live, tourism directly benefits the Sámi community, but in other parts the money flows straight out to other places.

tent €10/15; ⊙Jun-Sep; P) The closest cabin accommodation to town, this is 500m south of the centre and a good option. There's a range of cabins and facilities that include a cafe and wi-fi. Lakeside cabins cost a little more but are worth it for the memorable sunsets.

Hotelli Inari HOTEL, PUB €€
(☑671 026; www.hotelliinari.fi; Inarintie 40; s/d €69/96, d with sauna €124; P) In the heart of the metropolis, this hotel has decent spacious rooms with nice private bathrooms. It's worth trying to get a room facing the lake rather than the road. The slightly cheaper 'small doubles' are cramped. The hotel's restaurant-bar is the heart of the village and serves reasonable burgers and pizzas (€6 to €10) as well as mediocre Lappish dishes (€12 to €20). Look out the windows and watch the amazing sun at these latitudes, low over the lake.

Uruniemi Camping CABIN, CAMPGROUND €
(☑050-371 8826; www.uruniemi.com; Uruniemientie; camp sites €14.50, rooms from €20, cabins €22-75; ⊙Jun-late Sep) This place, 2km south of town, is a well-equipped lakeside camping ground with rooms, cottages, a cafe, sauna and boats and bikes for hire. It's better for tents than the Lomakylä.

🛍 Shopping

Inari is the main centre for Sámi handicrafts and there are several studios and boutique shops in the village.

🖋 Sámi Duodji Ry HANDICRAFTS, MUSIC
(www.samiduodji.com; Inarintie 51; ⊙10am-4pm Mon-Fri) This place is the main shop of the Finnish association of Sámi craftspeople. It has a good range of Sámi books and CDs, as well as beautifully crafted silverware and handmade clothing. It should be in the new Sajos building by the time you read this.

🖋 Samekki JEWELLERY, HANDICRAFTS
(www.saariselka.fi/samekki; Lehtolantie; ⊙10am-4pm Mon-Fri, also weekends mid-Jun–mid-Aug) Down a small lane behind the library is the studio of Petteri Laiti, a famous Sámi artisan. The silverwork and handicrafts are very highly regarded; you'll often see the artist at work here.

🖋 Nativa HANDICRAFTS
(www.natureco.info; ⊙10am-4pm Mon-Sat) Original and excellent Sámi handicrafts next to Villa Lanca.

ℹ Information

Inari's **tourist office** (☑040-168 9668; www.inari.fi; @) is in the Siida museum and open the same hours. There's also a nature information point here. They have pricy internet access, too (€2 per 15 mins).

ℹ Getting There & Away

Inari is 38km north of Ivalo on Rd 4. Buses run here daily (€7.70, 30 minutes). Two daily buses hit Inari from Rovaniemi (€56.10, 5¼ hours) and continue to Norway, one to Karasjok and on to Nordkapp in summer, another to Tana bru.

Lemmenjoki National Park

At 2855 sq km, Lemmenjoki (Sámi: Leammi) is Finland's largest national park, covering a remote wilderness area between Inari and Norway. It is prime hiking territory, with desolate wilderness rivers, rough landscapes and the mystique of gold, with solitary prospectors sloshing away with their pans in the middle of nowhere. Boat trips on the river allow more leisurely exploration of the park.

The launch pad for the park is Njurgulahti, an Inari Sámi community by the river; it's often simply referred to as Lemmenjoki. It's 11km down a turn-off signposted 34km southwest of Inari on the Kittilä road. The village's main festival is the last weekend of July, when there's a gold-panning competition on the Saturday followed by a traditional village dance.

◉ Sights

Lemmenjoki Nature Information Hut NATURE CENTRE
(www.outdoors.fi; Lemmenjoentie 968; ⊙9am-5pm mid-Jun–mid-Sep) A small nature centre with displays on the river, maps, walking information, fishing permits and a powerful set of binoculars trained on a nearby fell. The entrance to the park itself is 1.5km away.

Sallivaara REINDEER, BIRDWATCHING
Within the park boundaries, and accessed off the Inari–Kittilä road, 70km southwest of Inari, this reindeer roundup site was used by Sámi reindeer herders twice yearly until 1964. Round-ups were an important social event for the people of northern Lapland, usually lasting several weeks and involving hundreds of people and animals. The corrals and cabins have been reconstructed, and you can overnight in one of the huts, which also

serves coffee in summer. Many come here in spring and summer for the top-quality bird-watching on nearby wetlands. To reach the site, park in the Repojoki parking area then follow the marked trail, 6km one way.

Kaapin Jouni MUSEUM
This historic farm on the other side of the river from Njurgulahti was once the home of the 'reindeer king' Jouni Aikio. You can visit it by organising boat trips from Ahkun Tupa and others.

Paltto GALLERY
(☑016-673 413; www.lemmenjoki.org; ⊙10am-7pm Jun-Aug, other times by appointment) Felt artworks and handicrafts of extraordinary quality in this artist's studio a kilometre from Njurgulahti.

Kammigalleria GALLERY
(www.kammigalleria.fi; Lemmenjoentie 650; ⊙noon-6pm Tue-Sat Jun-Sep) Male reindeer drop their heavy antlers in November: see beautiful jewellery and handicrafts that Kikka Laakso makes from them here on the Lemmenjoki road.

🏃 Activities & Tours

Hiking
Most trails start from Njurgulahti, including a 4km marked nature trail suitable for families. The marked trekking routes are in the relatively small 'basic area' between the rivers Lemmenjoki and Vaskojoki; a 20km loop between Kultahamina and Ravadas-järvi huts takes you to some of the most interesting gold-panning areas. Another route heads over Látnjoaivi Fell to Vaskojoki hut and back, taking you into the 'wilderness area', which has less restrictions on where to camp but no trail markings. For any serious trekking, you will need the 1:100,000 *Lemmenjoki* map (€19.50), available at the Lemmenjoki Nature Centre.

From Kultahamina, it's a 21.5km walk back to Njurgulahti along the river, via Ravadas, 6.5km closer. You can get the boat one-way and walk the other (see below).

Boat trips
In summer, there's a scheduled boat service on the Lemmenjoki, from Njurgulahti village to the Kultahamina wilderness hut at Kultasatama (Gold Harbour). You can also get on or off the boat at the Ravadas falls en route. There are departures at 10am and 5pm from mid-June to mid-August; in early June and from mid-August to mid-September, only the evening one goes (€18 one-way, 1½ hours to Kultasatama).

🛏 Sleeping & Eating
There are several places offering camping and/or cabin accommodation, food and boat trips. Inside the park, a dozen wilderness huts provide free accommodation (another three can be booked in advance for a fee). Several are along the river.

Korpikartano HOTEL €€
(☑040-456 0789; www.menesjarvi.fi; Menesjärvi; s/d €75/89, lake d €104, apt €115-150; P@) Three kilometres short of the Lemmenjoki turnoff, this wilderness hotel has a superb position on the shores of one of the region's most beautiful lakes. Spruce, colourful rooms, some with kitchenette, are complemented by excellent activities and a flexible attitude that makes staying here a delight. Bikes, canoes and kayaks are available, and there's a great wood-burning sauna with outdoor hot tub that's the place to be in winter.

Paltto CABIN €
(☑016-673 413; www.lemmenjoki.org; cabin €52-72; ⊙early Jun-late Sep; P) A kilometre from the centre of Njurgulahti, this home of an active Sámi family has a felt studio selling some extraordinary works of art, as well as comfortable cabin accommodation with sauna and boat. Excellent boat trips are on offer (€29 to €55): from half days to full day trips that can include reindeer-meeting, Sámi yoiks (chants), gold-panning and traditional lunch.

Ahkun Tupa CABIN, CAMPGROUND €
(☑016-673 435; www.ahkuntupa.fi; 2-person cottages €35, 4-person cottages €60-80, log cabins €50, d/q €25/40; ⊙mid-Jun–mid-Sep; P) By the water in Njurgulahti, this has rooms, cottages and some further-flung log cabins. They'll let you pitch a tent for pennies. They offer English-speaking river cruises (from €10 for a runabout, to €42 for a seven-hour day including gold-panning) and rent canoes. The restaurant does lunch specials and salmon and reindeer mains (€13 to €22), including reindeer tongue.

Valkeaporo COTTAGE, CAMPGROUND €
(☑040-039 4682; www.valkeaporo.fi; Lemmenjoentie 134; 4-person cottages €50-110) A kilometre down the Lemmenjoki turn-off from the main Inari–Kittilä road, with splendid water frontage on spectacular Menesjärvi, this

place has smart cottages, good facilities and boat and canoe hire. You can also camp here. It is another good base for river trips on the Lemmenjoki.

Lemmenliekki   COTTAGE €
(☑016-673 400; www.lemmenliekki.fi; Äivihjärventie 435; 1-/2-/4-person cottage €60/70/80; ℗) Perfectly positioned right by a spectacular part of the wide Lemmenjoki, 5km from the Njurgulahti road, this reindeer-herding family offers excellent cottages sleeping up to six, with sauna, fireplace, rowing boat and kitchenette. It's great value for groups or families.

❶ Getting There & Away

There is one **taxi-bus** on weekdays between Inari and Njurgulahti village; it currently leaves Inari at 3pm, returning at 7.15am (it's a school bus service). In school holidays (ie early June to early August) it leaves Lemmenjoki later, at 1.15pm, giving you time to take the morning boat trip. Check times in advance with the Inari tourist office. A local taxi service can be called on ☑040-039 6312.

Kevo Strict Nature Reserve

The 712-sq-km Kevo Strict Nature Reserve, northwest of Inari, has within its boundaries some of the most breathtaking scenery in Finland along the splendid 40km gorge of the Kevojoki (Sámi: Geävu).

Rules for visiting the Kevo reserve are stricter than those concerning national parks: hikers cannot hunt, fish or collect plants and berries, and *must* stay on marked trails. The gorge area is off limits from April to mid-June.

The main trail is 64km long and runs through the canyon, from the Sulaoja parking area 11km east of Karigasniemi on the road westbound from Kaamanen, to Kenesjärvi, on the Kaamanen–Utsjoki road. The trek is rough with several fords – ask about water levels before heading off – and takes about four days one way. The Guivi trail separates from the main trail and loops through fell scenery before rejoining further along: it's a 78km journey but has two extra huts en route. You can also walk a round-trip from Sulaoja. See www.outdoors.fi for more details and use the 1:100,000 *Utsjoki Kevo* outdoor map.

🛏 Sleeping

You will need a tent if you plan to hike the canyon, as there is only one wilderness hut on this route (there are another two on the Guivi leg). Camping is permitted within the reserve at 20 designated sites.

There are three free wilderness huts along the trail. Ruktajärvi is at the southern end of the gorge route near where the Guivi trail branches off, and Njávgoaivi and Kuivi are on the Guivi loop. There's also a simple turf hut between these two.

There are cabins on the main road 500m south of the eastern trailhead.

❶ Getting There & Away

The preferred route is from the southwest; catch the Karigasniemi-bound bus from Inari and ask the driver to drop you off at the clearly marked Sulaoja trailhead. From Kenestupa you can catch buses to Inari or Utsjoki/Nuorgam. The early afternoon southbound bus that passes Kenestupa has a convenient changeover at Kaamasen Kievari to the westbound bus for Sulaoja, allowing you to leave your car there.

Inari To Norway
☑016

Norway stretches right across the top of Finland, and there are three main routes north from Inari: to the west via Karigasniemi (the most common Nordkapp route); north to Utsjoki; and east to Sevettijärvi. From Utsjoki, you can turn east along the fabulous Tenojoki to Nuorgam, the EU's northernmost village. The Kevo Strict Nature reserve stretches between the western route and the northern one.

KAAMANEN
Kaamanen, 25km north of Inari, is the crossing point of the three northern roads. All buses – and most locals for that matter – call in at **Kaamasen Kievari** (☑672 713; www.kaamasenkievari.fi; tent site €6, s/d cabin €20/39, with shower €46/64, with sauna €65/80; mains €11-27; ⏰9am-midnight), a legendary roadhouse a few kilometres north of the Sevettijärvi turn-off and 5km south of the Karigasniemi crossing. It has a cafe, petrol station and hard-drinking bar with pool table, as well as a surprisingly good restaurant serving local dishes such as salmon, whitefish and tasty reindeer steak. They also have cheap rooms and cabins (HI-affiliated), but Jokitörmä, 1km to the south, is better.

LAPLAND KEVO STRICT NATURE RESERVE

TOP CHOICE Jokitörmä (☎672 725; www.jokitorma. net; camping €13 plus per adult/child €2/1, s/d €35/46, cabin/hostel dm €20/23, 2-/4-person cabins €35/55; P), on the highway about 24km north of Inari, is a great campsite and hostel. The cabins are small and cosy and look over the river (mosquito repellent is in order in summer). They have a simple stove but no fridge. The adjacent camp sites are grassy, there are good two- and four-person rooms in the main building, and a separate set of cottages, with full facilities (€112 for up to six people). HI discount. The friendly owners can sort out transport to trailheads in the area.

KARIGASNIEMI
The border village of Karigasniemi (Sámi: Gáregasnjárga) thrives on Norwegian trade, and has several supermarkets open seven days a week, bars and restaurants, and a couple of petrol stations, as well as plenty of accommodation catering to fishermen beating the Tenojoki. The locals speak Fell Sámi, the main Sámi language of northern Norway.

A few accommodation choices are in the centre of town, by the border crossing, while others are strung out along the Tenojoki north and south of town.

Kalastajan Majatalo (☎040-484 8171; www.hansabar.fi; d €70, apt €85-110, cabins €50) is in the centre, and offers comfortable rooms and apartments, and simple cabins. The restaurant (mains €15 to €24) serves tasty salmon and is popular with Norwegians fleeing high beer prices.

There's a daily bus from Ivalo to Karigasniemi via Inari and the Kaamasen Kievari. Another bus runs from Rovaniemi to Karasjok in Norway via here. In summer it continues to Nordkapp.

UTSJOKI
The border village of Utsjoki (Sámi: Ohcejohka) is strung out along the main road that crosses the Tenojoki into Norway over a handsome bridge. It's an important Sámi community. The river is the main attraction in these parts; head along its banks towards Nuorgam or Karigasniemi and you'll find several picturesque spots with cabins catering to fishing families.

The **tourist office** (☎040-181 0263; www. utsjoki.fi; ☉10am-8pm mid-Jun–mid-Sep, to 6pm late Sep) is in a hut on the left just before the bridge. It also serves as a Metsähallitus (www.outdoors.fi) point; they can give fishing information, as well as advice and maps

for the Kevo trail and the various less-used trails that fan out from Utsjoki – the best is a 35km circular route with a wilderness hut at Koahpelásjärvi to overnight in. There's also a small exhibition that'll let you sort out a Silver Doctor from a Flashabou-Garry.

🖊 **Kylätalo Giisá** (☉8am-5pm Mon-Fri Sep–mid-Jun, 9am-6pm Mon-Fri, 10am-3pm Sat mid-Jun–Aug; @), the village hall, has an excellent handicraft shop, a cafe and internet access (per hour). They also sort out bus tickets and fishing licences.

Opposite it is **Camping Lapinkylä** (☎040-559 1542; www.arctictravel.fi; cabins €50, tent sites €13; ☉Jun–mid-Sep), which has a grilli (fast-food outlet), sauna, neat wooden cabins and plenty of grass underfoot to pitch your tent. They also do fishing trips and rent boats and have heated apartments (two/four persons €95/115), which are available in winter.

A couple of hundred metres up the side road opposite the information hut, **Hotelli Luossajohka** (☎321 2100; www.luossajohka. fi; Luossatie 4; r €95, superior s/d €100/125; P) is the only hotel in the town itself and has decent rooms decked out in blue, smart superior rooms in a new wing, as well as a restaurant and bar; like most places around here, they can organise fishing on the Tenojoki. At quiet times, check in at the pub Rastigaisa on the main road.

NUORGAM & TENO VALLEY
The 44km road from Utsjoki northeast to Nuorgam (Sámi: Njuorggan), the northernmost village of Finland (N 70° 4'), is one of Lapland's most spectacular. It follows the Tenojoki, one of Europe's best **salmon-fishing** rivers, and a spectacular sight as its broad waters cut through the undulating dunelike landscape and across sandy spits and rocky banks. Most anglers gather near Boratbokcankoski and Alaköngäs Rapids (7km southwest of Nuorgam) But there are good spots right along this stretch, and the other way from Utsjoki, towards Karigasniemi, which is another beautiful drive following the Tenojoki and the Norwegian border.

Apart from fishing, there's not a great deal to do in Nuorgam, but it's a relaxing spot. Norwegians flock to the (comparatively) cheap supermarkets, Alko store and petrol stations in town, but the heart of village life is **Nuorgamin Lomakeskus** (☎678 312; www.nuorgaminlomakeskus.fi; tent sites €20, cabins/apt €50/100; ☉Jun-late Aug, plus Mar & Apr; P @), which offers camping, cabins and cottage apartments with the works. It sells fishing permits, has a cafe (☉noon to

7pm in summer), and sells the *Nuorgam: Top of EU* t-shirt. Book ahead for cabins, as fisherfolk fill them fast.

There are many camp sites and good-value cabin villages catering to fishing parties scattered by the river between Nuorgam and Utsjoki, and several more on the Karigasniemi road. The Utsjoki website (www.utsjoki.fi) has a full list: click on 'Majoituspalvelut' under the 'Matkailu' menu. One is **Alakönkään Lomamökit** (☑678 612; cabins €45-80; Ⓟ), perched above the Tenojoki 7km from Nuorgam. The spacious cabins are great for families and have simple kitchens. They share a camp toilet, sauna and showers, and offer wonderful river views and sounds. There's a grilli-cafe on the main road just below.

Nuorgam is the northern end of a great trekking route from Sevettijärvi (see below).

There's a daily bus from Ivalo to Nuorgam via Inari and Utsjoki. A late-evening bus travels from Rovaniemi and on to Tana bru in Norway.

SEVETTIJÄRVI

The road east from Kaamanen heads along the shore of spectacularly beautiful Inarijärvi to the village of Sevettijärvi (Skolt Sámi: Ce'vetjäu'rr), in the far northeast of Finland. It's a remote area: the road only got out here in the 1970s.

Sevettijärvi is a major village of the Skolt Sámi, who resettled here when Finland was forced to cede the Petsamo area to the USSR in 1944. About 300 Skolt live in and around Sevettijärvi, which has a church (Orthodox, as the Skolt were evangelised by the Russians back in the 15th century), a shop and bar (Sevetin Baari), and a school, whose dozen-odd pupils are taught in the Skolt language. There's also **Kolttien Perinnetalo** (☺9am-5pm Jun–mid-Sep), a delightful little museum with photos, crafts and memorabilia of the poignant Skolt history.

Sevettijärvi's namesake lake offers good fishing, as does the Näätämöjoki and, of course, Inarijärvi. Sevettijärvi also has some excellent, remote, long-distance hiking trails.

The Orthodox **festival** of St Triphon is celebrated by the Skolt Sámi on the last weekend of August. It starts in Nellim on the Friday, then moves to Sevettijärvi, with celebrations and dances on the Saturday evening and Sunday morning. Visitors are welcome. As far as the Skolt are concerned, Lapp-dancing is the *katrilli* (quadrille).

There are a couple of good cabin places in and near town but if you have transport

TOP CHOICE **Porotila Toini Sanila** (☑672 509; www.sanila.fi; Sanilantie 36; r €32-130; Ⓟ) is the area's most inviting place to stay. The owners have reindeer and teach at the local school, so it's a good place to learn about the Skolt way of life. A cafe does home-cooked meals, and they have accommodation ranging from simple rooms sleeping up to six, to comfortable separate cottages. It's 1km off the main road halfway between Sevettijärvi and the Norwegian border.

Between Sevettijärvi and Inari, at Partakko, **Hietajoen Leirintä** (☑0400-434 411; www.hietajoenleirinta.net; Partakko; cabins €32) has simple cabins in a wonderful position on Inarijärvi. There's a sauna on the lakeshore and boats for rent.

There is a bus connection between Ivalo and Sevettijärvi on weekdays. There is no petrol station in Sevettijärvi; the nearest is in the border village of Näätämö, 30km northeast.

TREKKING AROUND SEVETTIJÄRVI

There's excellent trekking in this remote lake-spangled wilderness. The **Sevettijärvi to Nuorgam** trek is an established route, and the most popular from Sevettijärvi. Though the trail is easily followed, this is a remote area, so you'll need a compass and the 1:50,000 trekking maps for the area, available at tourist offices throughout the region. You can do the trek in four or five days.

The better of two trailheads is just north of Sevettijärvi, at Saunaranta. You'll see a sign that reads 'Ahvenjärvi 5', and a trekking sign, '12km to Opukasjärvi, 69km to Pulmankijärvi'. There are six mountain huts along the route; after the last one, you emerge onto a road, along which you can walk 18km, or call ☑040-037 7665 for the Nuorgam taxi.

Other marked routes from Sevettijärvi include the **Saamenpolku** (Sámi trail), a circular trail of 87km that loops around to Näätämö and the Norwegian border and back (five to six days). The **Inarinpolku** is a 100km trek to the fjords of the Arctic Ocean in Norway: allow about five days for this one.

There's a shop in Sevettijärvi, but if you have transport you might want to stock up on supplies at the supermarket by the Norwegian border at Näätämö, which is much larger and open daily.

Understand
Finland

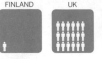

population per sq km

FINLAND   UK   SWEDEN

👤 ≈ 16 people

Finland Today

Century of Success

Remote, forested, cold, sparsely populated Finland has had a hell of a last hundred years. It's propelled itself from agricultural backwater of the Russian empire to one of the world's most prosperous nations, with great standards of living and education, low crime, a practical, deep-rooted sense of environmentalism and a booming technology industry.

In Europe only Iceland and Norway are more sparsely populated than Finland's 16 people per square kilometre. In much of Lapland, this falls to under one person per square kilometre.

Shadows Within

Devastating school and college shootings in 2007 and 2008 horrified peaceful Suomi. Always keen for a bit of introspection, Finns wondered if it revealed something rotten at their society's core, some hangover from the war years, or a dramatic manifestation of those seasonal depressive tendencies that seem to boost alcoholism and suicide stats. Did people feel alienated in the occasionally impersonal Nordic social democracy? Or was it just too easy for angry youths to buy a gun? As usual there were no clear answers.

External Relations

Ever since the 12th century, Russia has loomed large over Finland. Long experience with the Bear has stood Suomi in good stead, and the two countries have a strong relationship, with much exchange of commerce and tourism. Nevertheless, Finns on the street are understandably nervous of a nationalistic Moscow. Memories of the bitter fights for freedom are too painful for national service and the army not to be taken seriously here.

The 2011 parliamentary elections in Finland sent a shockwave through Europe as the nationalistic, populist True Finns party came from nowhere to seize 19% of the vote. Their absolute rejection of bailouts of other EU economies meant that rather than compromise their principles by entering a coalition government, they opted to become the major

Top Films

Man Without a Past (2002) One of Aki Kaurismäki's best.
Miesten Vuoro (Steam of Life; 2010) Documentary of men sharing their lives in the sauna.
Tuntematon Sotilas (1955) Considered Finland's greatest film a bout the Winter War.

Dos & Don'ts

» Do take shoes off in people's homes.

» Do shake hands with men and women.

» Don't wear a swimsuit in the sauna unless it's mixed.

» Don't wait for table service in cafes.

Top Books

Kalevala (Elias Lönnrot) Epic compiled from the songs of bards.
The Year of the Hare (Arto Paasilinna) Offbeat tale of hare-y travels.
Seven Brothers (Aleksis Kivi) A Finnish classic.

electricity generation
(% of power sources)

33 Nuclear
18 Hydro
16 Coal
14 Gas
12 Other renewable
7 Other

If Finland were 100 people

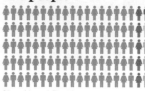

91 would speak Finnish
6 would speak Swedish
1 would speak Russian
3 would speak other languages

opposition party instead, establishing them as a serious political force. Meanwhile, the other MPs finally formed a six-party coalition under the prime ministership of centre-right Jyrki Katainen.

The True Finns' success reflected concerns about rising immigration and a feeling of frustration that Finnish taxpayers were being forced to pay for other countries' problems. It evoked a stereotype of the lonely Finn sitting at home and not caring much about the rest of the world.

Climate Change
Southern Finland has already noticed dramatically changed weather patterns, and the almost unthinkable prospect of a non-white Christmas in Helsinki looks ever likelier. Scientists in the Arctic are producing increasingly worrying data and it seems that northern nations like Finland may be some of the earliest to be seriously affected.

Society & Economy
Finns are rightly proud of the strong foundations of their society. The famously high tax rate means the nation is well equipped to look after its citizenry with some of the world's best healthcare and education. Though Finns grumble about the high excise on alcohol, they appreciate the reliable public transport and world-class universities and libraries these same taxes afford. Like much of the world, the country is holding its breath as aging baby boomers retire and it attempts to maintain high pensions.

Finland's economy, once dominated by forestry, is now more about Nokia. Economists have worried for some time that Finland is overly dependent on the company, especially now that Apple and Google have muscled into the intelligent phone market. In 2011 the company staked its future on an alliance with Microsoft.

Finns are the world's biggest coffee drinkers, downing 12kg of the black gold annually, well ahead of its Nordic counterparts, who fill the next few places.

Top Bands

HIM dark romantic 'love metal'.
Poets of the Fall Indie rockers.
The Rasmus Catchy platinum-selling pop-rock.
Nightwish Finland's most well-known metal band.
Apocalyptica Metal meets classical cellists.

Myths

» **Finns are silent.** This is broadly true, until they get a couple of pints of lager into them. Silence is acceptable in Finland when in other countries it would be considered awkward.

» **Finns beat themselves with tree branches.** Actually the *vihta* is a small bouquet of birch leaves lightly whisked over the skin during the sauna.

» **Finns have the highest rate of suicide in the world.** Not so. While undoubtedly a problem, it only comes in 9th in Europe, between Serbia and Belgium.

History

Finland's history is the story of a country which for centuries was used as a wrestling mat between two heavyweights, Sweden and Russia, and the nation's eventful emergence from their grip to become one of the world's most progressive and prosperous nations.

Early Days

What is now Finland was inhabited way back: pre-ice age remains have been found dating from some 120,000 years ago. But the big chill erased most traces and sent folk scurrying south to warmer climes. Only at the retreat of the formidable glaciers, which had blanketed the country 3km deep, was human presence re-established.

The first post thaw inhabitants had spread over most of Finland by about 9000 BC. The people used stone tools and hunted elk and beaver.

Pottery in the archaeological record shows that a new influence arrived from the east to southern Finland about 5000 years ago. Because Finland was the furthest point west that this culture reached, it's suggested that these new people brought a Finnic language with them from Russia. If so, those who lived in Finland at this time were the ancestors of the Finns and the Sámi.

One of the best places to learn about the Stone Age in Finland is the Kierikki museum near Oulu, p251.

In the 1st century AD, the Roman historian Tacitus mentioned a tribe called the Fenni, whom he described as wild savages who had neither homes nor horses. He might have been referring to the Sámi or their forebears, whose nomadic existence better fits this description. Studies indicate that today's Sámi are descended mostly from a small original group, and some claim that a divergence of pre-Finnish and Sámi cultures can be seen as far back as 700 BC. Nomadic cultures leave little archaeological evidence, but it seems the Sámi gradually migrated northwards, probably displaced by the southerners and the advance of agriculture into former hunting lands. Verses of the *Kalevala,* which is derived from ancient oral tradition, seem to refer to this conflictive relationship.

TIMELINE	120,000 BC	10,000 BC	3000 BC
	Present-day Finland is inhabited, as finds at Susiluola cave, near Kristinestad, indicate, but its residents, of whom we know little, are eventually evicted by the last ice age.	The retreat of the ice age's glaciers reopens the northern lands to human habitation. The forests and lakes that replace the ice provide tempting hunting and fishing grounds.	The appearance of distinctive 'Comb Ware' pottery indicates the presence of a new culture that seems to come from the Volga region to the east, perhaps bringing a pre-Finnish language with it.

Swedish Rule

The nascent kingdom of Sweden saw Finland as a natural direction for extending its influence in the Baltic and countering the growing power of Novgorod (later to become Russia) in the east. Missionary activity began in the 12th century, and legend tells of an Englishman, Bishop Henry, leading an expedition of baptism that ended stickily when he was murdered by Lalli, a disgruntled peasant.

Things started to heat up in the 13th century. The Pope called a crusade against the Häme tribe, which was increasingly influenced both religiously and politically from Novgorod, and Russian and Swedish forces clashed several times in the first battles of an ongoing saga.

Swedish settlement began in earnest around the middle of the century when Birger Jarl established fortifications at Häme and Turku, among other places. The cathedral at Turku was also under construction and this city was to be Finland's pre-eminent centre for most of its history. The Swedish knights and nobles in charge of these operations set a pattern for a Swedish-speaking bourgeoisie in Finland, which lasted well into the 20th century. Other Swedes, including farmers and fishers, gradually settled, mainly along Finland's Baltic coast. A number of incentives such as land grants and tax concessions were given to encourage new settlers, many of whom were veterans of the Swedish army.

Sweden's squabbles with Novgorod continued for two centuries. Treaties drawn up by the two powers defined the spheres of influence, with Sweden gaining control of southwest Finland and much of the west coast, while Novgorod controlled Karelia, spreading the Orthodox faith and Byzantine culture in the region.

In 1527 King Gustav Vasa of Sweden adopted the Lutheran faith and confiscated much of the property of the Catholic Church. The Finnish Reformation was ushered in by Mikael Agricola, who studied with Luther in Germany, and returned to Finland in 1539 to translate parts of the Bible into Finnish. His hard-line Protestant attitudes meant that most of the frescoes in medieval churches were whitewashed (to be rediscovered some 400 years later in relatively good condition).

Sweden started another chess game with Russia in Savo and Kainuu, using its Finnish subjects as pawns to settle areas well beyond the agreed boundaries. Russia retaliated, and most of the new settlements were razed in the bloody Kainuu War of the late 16th century.

The 17th century was Sweden's golden age, when it controlled much of the Baltic. Finland was put under the control of various governors.

During the Thirty Years' War in Europe, political power in Finland was exercised by Count Per Brahe, who travelled around the country and founded many towns. He was a larger-than-life figure who made his own

For more details on Finnish history, head to the website http://virtual.finland.fi, which has excellent essays written by experts on various periods.

HISTORY SWEDISH RULE

Duke Karl, regent of Finland, didn't care much for the family business. Campaigning against his nephew the king, he encouraged a peasant mutiny in 1596 and finally deposed him, exacting brutal revenge on his opponents.

AD 100	**1155**	**1323**	**1527**
The Roman historian Tacitus refers to the 'Fenni', most likely the Sámi, in the first known historical mention of the area. He isn't complimentary about their lack of permanent housing.	The first Christianising expedition is launched from Sweden against the pagan Finns. Further expeditions follow, and Finland is effectively under Swedish dominion for the next six centuries.	The Peace of Oreshek, signed by Sweden and Novgorod at Pähkinäsaari, establishes a frontier in the Karelian Isthmus, and delineates permitted spheres of influence still evident in present-day Finland.	King Gustav Vasa of Sweden adopts the Lutheran faith and confiscates much of the property of the Catholic Church. Finland's main Reformation figure, Mikael Agricola, returns from Germany in 1539.

rules: once censured for having illegally bagged an elk, he responded curtly that it had been on its last legs and he had killed it out of mercy.

Although Finland never experienced feudal serfdom to the extent seen in Russia, ethnic Finns were largely peasant farmers forced to lease land from Swedish landlords.

In 1697 the Swede Karl XII ascended the throne. Within three years he was drawn into the Great Northern War (1700–21), between Sweden and allied forces of Russia, Denmark and other Baltic powers, which marked the beginning of the end of the Swedish empire.

From Sweden to Russia

Peter the Great took advantage of Sweden's troubles and, though losing early engagements, soon stormed through Finland, which had been recently decimated by famine. From 1714 to 1721 Russia occupied Finland, a time still referred to as the Great Wrath, when several thousand Finns were killed and many more were taken into slavery. The 1721 Treaty of Uusikaupunki brought peace at a cost – Sweden lost south Karelia to Russia.

Finland again paid the price for thwarted Swedish ambitions in the war of 1741–43; Russia again occupied the country, a period called the Lesser Wrath.

Tsar Alexander I signed a treaty with Napoleon and then attacked Finland in 1808. Following a bloody war, Sweden ceded Finland to Russia in 1809. Alexander pledged to respect Finnish customs and institutions; Finland kept its legal system and its Lutheran faith, and became a semi-autonomous grand duchy. At first, Russia encouraged development, and Finland benefited from the annexation. The capital was transferred from Turku to Helsinki in 1812.

Finland was still very much an impoverished rural society in the 19th century, and travel to the interior, especially in Lapland, could be an arduous journey of weeks by riverboat and overland. The tar and paper industries produced revenue from the vast forests, but were controlled by magnates in Baltic and Bothnian ports such as Oulu, which flourished while the hinterland remained poor.

A Nation Born

Early stirrings of Finnish nationalism could be heard in the 19th century. Dissatisfaction with the Swedish administration came to a head with a letter written from officers of the Finnish army to the queen of Sweden questioning the legality of the war they were pursuing against Russia. Meanwhile, academic studies of Finnish cultural traditions were creating a base on which future nationalistic feelings could be founded.

As well as being the biggest land-owner in Sweden, Per Brahe was a gourmet and wrote his own cookbook, which he took with him on his travels and insisted was followed to the letter.

Though still part of Russia, Finland issued its first postage stamps in 1856 and its own currency, the markka, in 1860.

Tar, used to caulk sailing ships, was a major 19th-century Finnish export, produced by burning pine trees in a tar pit; bark had been removed from the trees four years earlier to stimulate resin production.

1637	1640	1700	1714
Per Brahe becomes governor of Finland and goes on to found many towns. Meanwhile, Finnish cavalry earn a fearsome reputation in the Thirty Years' War.	Finland's first university is founded in Turku, which is the country's principal city until Helsinki is made capital in 1812.	Karl XII of Sweden is drawn into the Great Northern War, which is to mark the beginning of the end for the Swedish empire.	Russia occupies Finland, marking the beginning of the seven years known as the Great Wrath. When peace is made, Russia retains southern Karelia.

The famous phrase 'Swedes we are not, Russians we will not become, so let us be Finns', though of uncertain origin, encapsulated the growing sense of Finnishness. Artistic achievements like Elias Lönnrot's *Kalevala* and Johan Ludvig Runeberg's poem *Our Land,* which became the national anthem, acted as standards to rally around. As Russia tightened its grip with a policy of Russification, workers, and artists such as Jean Sibelius, began to be inspired against the growing oppression, and the nation became emotionally ripe for independence.

In 1906 the Eduskunta parliament was introduced in Finland with universal and equal suffrage (Finland was the first country in Europe to grant women full political rights); however, Russian political oppression continued and poverty was endemic. In search of work and a better life, many Finns moved south to Helsinki or emigrated to North America in the first decades of the 20th century.

The Russian Revolution of October 1917 enabled the Finnish parliament to declare independence on 6 December of that year. Although Russia recognised the new nation, it hoped for a parallel workers' uprising; it fomented dissent and supplied arms to that end.

Following an attack by Russian-armed Finnish Reds on the civil guards in Vyborg, the Finnish Civil War flared in late January 1918. During 108 days of heavy fighting, approximately 30,000 Finns were killed.

In the first elections in 1907, 19 female members were elected to the Eduskunta, the first woman MPs in the world. Finland has been a trailblazer for equality in politics ever since.

LENIN IN FINLAND

One man who spent plenty of time in Finland was Vladimir Ilyich Lenin, father of the Russian Revolution. Having had a Finnish cellmate during his exile in Siberia, he then regularly visited the country for conferences of the Social Democratic Party, meeting Stalin for the first time at one of them. Lenin lived near Helsinki in 1907 before he was forced to flee the Russian Empire. In a Hollywood-style escape, he jumped off a moving train to avoid tsarist agents, and was then sheltered in Turku, before being moved to remote island communities in the southwest. Lenin found shelter on Parainen, but fearing capture, he walked across thin ice with a local guide to Nauvo (there's a famous painting of this in the Hermitage in St Petersburg), from where he finally jumped on a steamer to Stockholm.

Lenin entered Finland again via Tornio in 1917. After the abortive first revolution, he lived in a tent for a while in Iljitsevo, before going back to Russia and his date with destiny.

Lenin, even before having visited Finland, had agitated for Finnish independence, a conviction which he maintained. In December 1917, he signed the declaration of Finnish independence; without his support, it is doubtful that the nation would have been born at that time.

You can learn more about Lenin in Finland at the Lenin Museum in Tampere (p139).

1741–43	1808	1827	
Russian again occupies Finland. The Treaty of Turku ends what becomes known as the Lesser Wrath, but cedes parts of the Savo region of Finland to Russia.	Finland is invaded and occupied by Russia, becoming a grand duchy of the Russian Empire in 1809; Tsar Alexander I promises to respect its autonomy at the Diet of Porvoo.	Elias Lönnrot makes the first of his song-collecting journeys into remote Karelian forests, which culminate in the publication of *Kalevala,* the national epic.	

INTERFOTO / ALAMY ©

» Elias Lönnrot

MANNERHEIM

The Reds, comprising the rising working class, aspired to a Russian-style socialist revolution while retaining independence. The nationalist Whites, led by CGE Mannerheim, dreamed of monarchy and sought to emulate Germany.

The Whites, with substantial German help, eventually gained victory and the war ended in May 1918. Friedrich Karl, Prince of Hessen, was elected king of Finland by the Eduskunta on 9 October 1918, but the defeat of imperial Germany a month later made Finland choose a republican state model, under its first president, KJ Ståhlberg.

Though internal struggles continued, and despite the crushing blows of WWII, Finland gained fame internationally as a brave new nation. Significant events included Finland's Winter War heroics, Paavo Nurmi's distinguished career as a long-distance runner, Ester Toivonen's Miss Europe title in 1933, Artturi Virtanen's Nobel Prize for Chemistry in 1945, the Helsinki Olympics of 1952, and plaudits won by Finnish designers in international expositions. These achievements fostered national confidence, helped Finland to feel that it belonged at the table of nations, and gave it strength to survive the difficult Cold War period that followed.

The Cold War

The year of the Helsinki Olympics, 1952, was also the year that Finland completed paying its heavy war reparations to the Soviet Union. Mostly paid in machinery and ships, they in fact had a positive effect, as they established the heavy engineering industry that eventually stabilised the Finnish postwar economy.

Finnish society changed profoundly during this period. In the 1940s, the population was still predominantly agricultural, but the privations of the war, which sent people to the towns and cities in search of work, as well as the influx of nearly half a million Karelian refugees, sparked an acute housing crisis. Old wooden town centres were demolished to make way for apartment blocks, and new suburbs appeared almost overnight around Helsinki; conversely, areas in the north and east lost most of their young people (often half their population) to domestic emigration.

From the end of the war until the early 1990s, the overriding political issue was a familiar one: balance between east and west. Stalin's 'friendship and cooperation' treaty of 1948 was used by the USSR throughout the Cold War as coercion in an attempt to limit Finland's interaction with the West.

A savvy political head was needed to negotiate these choppy waters, and Finland found it in the astute if controversial figure of Urho K Kekkonen, president from 1956 to 1981 and a master of diplomacy.

Canny and unorthodox, Kekkonen realised that he was the devil the Kremlin knew, and he used this to his advantage. Similarly, he did so with the West's fear that Finland would fall completely under the sway

Mannerheim had a fascinating life divided into several distinct phases. Check out www.mannerheim.fi for an extremely comprehensive online biography.

1853	1899	1917	1920
As part of the Russian Empire, Finland is involved in the Crimean War, with British troops destroying fortifications at Loviisa, Helsinki and Bomarsund.	The Tsar implements a policy of Russification in Finland, and attempts to impose the Russian language on the country. Widespread protests result and campaigns for independence gain strength.	Finland declares independence from the Soviet Union. Shortly afterwards, the Finnish Civil War breaks out between the communist Reds and the establishment Whites.	Relations with the Soviets are normalised by the Treaty of Tartu, which sees Finnish territory expand to its largest point ever, including the Petsamo region in the far northeast.

of the USSR. He signed a free-trade agreement with the European Free Trade Association (EFTA) in 1961 which brought Finland closer to a European orbit, but also signed a parallel agreement for preferential trade with the Soviets.

Kekkonen and his government had a close relationship with many of the KGB's big men in Finland, and political nominations were submitted to Moscow for approval within a framework of 'friendly coexistence'. Many Finns regard his era with embarrassment, believing that Kekkonen abased the country by such close contact with the Bear, and that his grip on power and web of behind-the-scenes manoeuvrings were uncomfortably reminiscent of the Kremlin itself. Nevertheless, Kekkonen presided over a period in which the nation moved from an impoverished agricultural state to a modern European democracy with a watertight welfare system and healthy economy, all in the shadow of a great power whose actions in Eastern Europe had given ample reason for Finland to tread with extreme caution.

After Kekkonen's resignation due to ill health at 81, the Soviets continued to dabble in Finnish politics, mostly with the aim of reducing US influence and preventing Finland joining what is now the EU. That particular chapter of Finland's long and complicated relationship with its eastern neighbour came to a close with the collapse of the USSR.

A *kotiryssä*, or Russian contact, was crucial for politicians of ambition in Cold War Finland, when much career advancement was under Moscow's control. But those friendly dinners on the Kremlin's tab could look a little treasonous if the vodka loosened your tongue...

Modern Finland

Following the collapse of the Soviet Union, a load was lifted from Finland, but the early 1990s were not the easiest of times. The bubble of the 1980s had burst, the Soviet Union disappeared with debts unpaid, the markka was devalued, and unemployment jumped from 3% to 20%.

However, Finland could finally integrate itself fully with Europe. Since joining the EU in January 1995, Finland has prospered, and was a founder member of the euro in 2002.

Balancing power between the president and the parliament had long been on the agenda since Kekkonen's monarchlike presidency, and in 1999 a new constitution was approved limiting certain presidential powers. The first to take the wheel under the new order was Tarja Halonen of the Social Democratic Party, elected in 2000. Referred to affectionately as Muumimamma (Moominmummy), she was well loved by many Finns, and was re-elected for a second (and, by law, final) six-year term in 2006.

In the new millennium, Finland has boomed on the back of a strong technology sector, the traditionally important forestry industry, design and manufacturing, and, increasingly, tourism. It's a major success story of the new Europe with a strong economy, robust social values, and superlow crime and corruption. Finland consistently ranks highly in

1939	1948	1950	1952
The Winter War sees the Soviet Union invade Finland. After 15 weeks of fighting in subzero conditions, Finland is defeated and forced to cede a substantial amount of territory.	The 'friendship and cooperation' treaty is signed between Finland and the Soviet Union.	Urho K Kekkonen becomes prime minister for the first time. In 1956 he is elected to the position of president, which he holds for 25 years.	Helsinki hosts the summer Olympic Games. Finland completes war reparation payments of US$300 million to the USSR as decreed by the Peace of Paris in 1947.

THE WINTER WAR AND ITS CONTINUATION

Diplomatic manoeuvrings in Europe in the 1930s meant that Finland, inexperienced in the sinuous negotiations of Great Power politics, had a few difficult choices to make. The security threat posed by the Soviet Union meant that some factions were in favour of developing closer ties with Nazi Germany, while others favoured rapprochement with Moscow. On 23 August 1939, the Soviet and German foreign ministers, Molotov and Ribbentrop, signed a nonaggression pact, which gave the Soviet Union a free hand in Finland. The USSR argued that its security required a slice of southeastern Karelia and the right to build bases on Finnish soil. Finland refused, and on 30 November 1939 the Winter War between Finland and the Soviet Union began.

This was a harsh winter – temperatures reached -40°C and soldiers died in their thousands. Finland resisted the Red Army, with mobile skiing troops conducting successful guerrilla-style assaults in small groups. Stalin was forced to send more and more divisions to the front, with some 600,000 soldiers eventually being committed. Several Russian divisions were destroyed, with an estimated 130,000 dead as the Finns stopped the Russian advance by early January. But this was an unwinnable war; after 105 days of fighting in the harshest imaginable conditions, Finland conceded. In the Treaty of Moscow (March 1940), Finland was forced to cede the Karelian Isthmus, together with the eastern Salla and Kuusamo regions and some islands: in total nearly one-tenth of its territory. Over 400,000 Karelian refugees flooded across the new border into Finland.

In the following months, the Soviet Union attempted to persuade Finland to cede more territory. Isolated from the Western Allies, Finland turned to Germany for help and allowed the transit of German troops. When hostilities broke out between Germany and the Soviets in June 1941, German troops were already on Finnish soil, and the Continuation War between Finland and the Red Army followed. In the subsequent fighting, the Finns advanced, reaching their old borderline in December. Finns began to resettle Karelia. When Soviet forces staged a huge comeback in the summer of 1944, Finnish president Risto Ryti, who had promised Ribbentrop that Finland would not negotiate peace with Russia without German agreement, resigned, with Mannerheim taking his place. Mannerheim negotiated an armistice with the Russians, ceding Finland's 'other arm', the Petsamo area of the Kola Peninsula, and ordered the evacuation of German troops. Finland waged a bitter war in Lapland to oust the Germans, who staged a 'scorched earth' retreat from the country until the general peace in the spring of 1945.

Against the odds, Finland had remained independent, but at a heavy price: the territorial losses of 1940 and 1944 were ratified at the Peace of Paris in February 1947, and heavy war reparations were ordered to be paid to the Soviet Union. Many in Finland are still bitter about the loss of these territories. Nevertheless, the resistance against the might of the Red Army is something of which Finns are still proud.

1971	1973	1995	2000
For the first time, urban dwellers outnumber rural dwellers in Finland.	The Delegation for Sámi affairs, the beginnings of the Sámi parliament, convenes for the first time. Finland signs a trade agreement with the EEC despite Soviet pressure not to.	After a referendum with a 57% 'yes' vote in October 1994, Finland joins the EU.	Finland elects Tarja Halonen as its first female president. She proves a popular figure and holds the post for the maximum 12 years.

quality-of-life indices and has in recent years outperformed its traditionally superior neighbour Sweden in many areas.

Russia is, as ever, still high on the agenda. Finland's geographical proximity and close historical relationship with its neighbour gave it a head start in dealing with post-Soviet Moscow, and the trade relationship remains close between the two countries. Many Finnish companies contract much of their business to Russia, where wages and overheads are lower, while Russian labour and tourism both make important contributions to the Finnish economy. Nevertheless, many Finns are still suspicious of Russia and the Putin brand of nationalism. The Winter War has not been forgotten: national service and border patrols are taken seriously.

Though Finland has experienced far less immigration than most European countries, immigration has increased in recent years and is an issue that has raised headlines.

Finland's own indigenous people, the Sámi, have been afforded greater recognition in the last four decades

Finland's own indigenous people, the Sámi, have been afforded greater recognition in the last four decades, with the establishment of a Finnish Sámi parliament and the enshrinement of their languages in regional laws. However, disputes between reindeer herders and forestry firms in the north have ignited debate as to whether Sámi interests continue to come second to those of the country's timber industry.

Despite the challenges ahead, Finland can feel just a wee bit pleased with itself. For a cold and remote, sparsely populated forest nation, it's done rather well. Though there has been concern that Finland's powerful economy is overly reliant on the success of Nokia (p313), the rise of this humble manufacturer of rubber tyres and cable insulation to communications giant parallels the transformation of Finland from war-ravaged farming nation to wealthy technological innovator.

» Tarja Halonen

2002	2006	2011
Along with several other European countries, Finland adopts the euro, bidding farewell to the markka after 142 years.	The nation celebrates as outrageous horror metal band Lordi blow away the syrupy competition and win Finland the Eurovision Song Contest.	The rise of the anti-immigration True Finns party reflects increasingly ambivalent attitudes towards Finland's role in the EU.

The Sámi

Sámi are the indigenous inhabitants of Lapland and are today spread across four countries from the Kola Peninsula in Russia to the southern Norwegian mountains. More than half of the 70,000 Sámi population are in Norway, while around 8000 reside in Finland; there are close cross-border cultural ties. The Sámi region is called Sápmi, and about half of Finnish Sámi live in it.

According to archaeological evidence, this region was first settled soon after the last Ice Age around 10,000 years ago, but it wasn't until the beginning of the Christian era – the early Iron Age – that Finns and Sámi had become two distinct groups with diverging languages. The early inhabitants were nomadic people – hunters, fishers and food-gatherers – who migrated with the seasons.

Traditions & Beliefs

Early Sámi society was based on the *siida,* small groups comprising a number of families who controlled particular hunting, herding and fishing grounds. Families lived in a *kota,* a traditional dwelling resembling the tepee or wigwam of native North Americans. Smaller tents served as temporary shelters while following the migrating reindeer herds; a 'winter village' system also developed, where groups came together to help survive the harsh winter months. Mechanisation in the 1950s meant reindeer herders could go out on snowmobiles and return home every night. This ended the need for nomadism and the Sámi became a settled people.

The natural environment was essential to Sámi existence: they worshipped the sun (father), earth (mother) and wind and believed all things in nature had a soul. There were many gods, who dwelled in *seita* (holy sites): fells, lakes or sacred stones. The link with the gods was through the *noaidi* (shaman), the most important member of the community.

Traditional legends, rules of society and fairy tales were handed down through the generations by storytelling. A unique form of storytelling was the yoik, a chant in which the singer would use words, or imitate the sounds of animals and nature to describe experiences or people. It's still used by the Sámi today, sometimes accompanied by instruments.

For more information, visit the excellent Siida museum in Inari or the Arktikum in Rovaniemi. Via the 'web exhibitions' page on Siida's website (www.siida.fi) you can access a series of excellent pages on the Inari and Skolt Sámi cultures.

Groups

Five distinct Sámi groups with distinct cultural traditions live in Finland. Vuotso Sámi live around Saariselkä and are the southernmost group. Enontekiö Sámi dwell around Hetta in the west and, with Utsjoki Sámi, who settled from Finland's northernmost tip along the Norwegian border to Karigasniemi, have the strongest reindeer-herding heritage. Inari Sámi live around the shores of Inarijärvi, and have a strong fishing tradition. Skolt Sámi originally inhabited the Kola Peninsula around Petsamo, and fled to Finland when the Soviet Union took back control of that area. They number around 600, live around Sevettijärvi and Nellim, and are of Orthodox religion.

Role of the Reindeer

Reindeer have always been central to the Sámi existence. Sámi consumed the meat and milk, used the fur for clothing and bedding, and made fish hooks and harpoons from the bones and antlers. Today around 40% of Sámi living in Sápmi are involved in reindeer husbandry; tourism is another big employer.

Originally the Sámi hunted wild reindeer, usually trapping them in pitfalls. Hunting continued until around the 16th century, when the Sámi began to domesticate entire herds and migrate with them. Towards the end of the 19th century, Finland's reindeer herders were organised into *paliskunta* cooperatives, of which there are now 56 in northern Finland. Reindeer wander free around the large natural areas within each *paliskunta,* which are bordered by enormous fences that cross the Lapland wilderness. Each herder is responsible for his stock and identifies them by earmarks – a series of distinctive notches cut into the ear of each animal.

Never ask a Sámi how many reindeer he or she owns. It's a very personal matter, like someone's bank balance. It's something they wouldn't even necessarily reveal to their closest friends.

Handicrafts

The colourful Sámi costumes, featuring jackets, pants or skirts embroidered with bright red, blue and yellow patterns, are now mostly worn on special occasions and during Sámi festivals.

Sámi handicrafts (including bags and boots made from reindeer hide, knitted gloves and socks, textiles, shawls, strikingly colourful Sámi hats, jewellery and silverware) are recognised as indigenous art. Genuine handicrafts carry the name Sámi duodji. Inari is one of the best places to buy them.

Languages

Sámi languages are related to Finnish and other Finno-Ugric languages. There are three Sámi languages, not very mutually intelligible, used in Finland today. There are another seven Sámi languages in Norway, Sweden and Russia.

SATU NATUNEN, SÁMI ARTIST

'Sámi culture to me means the very act of staying and being alive – it's a life source. It's been my roots; what has bound me to something. When I was a child, I spent a lot of time in my grandmother's house in Karigasniemi. My grandfather showed me the flowers, nature, told me things. Later I understood how valuable it had been to have heard even short parts of the stories. I asked to tape them but he said no, there must be a possibility for mistakes. I fill the missing parts in. That's how these tales have always developed and grown.

» Do parents still maintain the oral tradition? Unfortunately not so much, but there's still something like that going on. Mostly you see it in attitude, the way of behaving in nature, respect for animals. Stories and beliefs have disappeared more, partly because of Christianity, partly because of the school system. People don't explain things in the same way these days.

» There'll never be a united Sámi people, but self-confidence is stronger all the time. Politically, we are weak: 7000 in Finland, divided in three groups. But Sámi people are respecting their roots more and are finding positives from their own culture. But we are somehow in danger of being hugged into destruction. So many subsidies are sort of destroying the culture. We have no real political power but at least you can study Sámi in school these days.

» Sámi women have always been strong women. They needed to run the home – the men were always somewhere else, away with the reindeer and so on. It's been quite a maternal culture and still is in most ways.'

Finnish Culture

Despite the magnificent lakescapes and outdoor activities, Finland's greatest highlight is the Finns. Isolated in this corner of Europe, they do their own thing and have developed a strongly independent, self-reliant streak, coloured by a seriously offbeat sense of humour.

Love of Nature

Finns have a deep and abiding love of their country's forests and lakes. In July, Finland is one of the world's most relaxing, joyful places to be – a reason they traditionally have not been big travellers. After the long winter, why miss the best their country has to offer? Finns head en-masse for the *mökki* from Midsummer until the end of the July holidays. Most Finns of any age could forage in a forest for an hour at the right time of year and emerge with a feast of fresh berries, wild mushrooms and probably a fish or two. City-dwelling Finns are far more in touch with nature than many of their European equivalents.

Sisu

Finland is not part of Scandinavia, nor is it a part of Russia; nevertheless, Finnish tradition owes something to both cultures. But the modern Finn is staunchly independent. The long struggle for emancipation, together with the battle to survive in a harsh environment, have engendered an ordered society which solves its own problems in its own way. They have also given birth to the Finnish trait of *sisu*, often translated as 'guts', or the resilience to survive prolonged hardship. Even if all looks lost, until

> Despite its proximity, Finland is generally considered not to be part of Scandinavia, neither culturally nor geographically. Finnish-speaking Finns are insistent on this point, and prefer the less specific term 'Nordic countries' to describe Finland and its western neighbours.

THE MÖKKI

Tucked away in Finland's forests and lakelands are half a million *kesämökkejä*, or summer cottages. Part holiday house, part sacred place, the *mökki* is the spiritual home of the Finn and you don't know the country until you've spent time in one. The average Finn spends less than two days in a hotel per year, but several weeks in a cottage.

These are places where people get back to nature. Amenities are often basic – the gloriously genuine ones have no electricity or running water – but even the highest-flying Nokia executives are in their element, chopping wood, DIY-ing, picking chanterelles and blueberries, rowing, and selecting young birch twigs for the *vihta*, or sauna whisk. There's no better sauna than a *mökki* one: the soft steam of the wood stove caresses rather than burns, and the nude dash for an invigorating spring into the chilly lake is a Finnish summer icon. As is the post-sauna can of beer, new potatoes with fresh dill, and sausages grilled over pine cones on the barbecue. It's hard not to feel at peace when gazing out at the silent lake, trees perfectly reflected in it by the midnight sun, and anything of consequence miles away.

The best way to experience a *mökki* is to be invited to one by a Finnish friend, but failing that, there are numerous ones that you can rent (see p339), particularly in the Lakeland area (see p171).

the final defeat, a Finn with *sisu* will fight – or swim, or run, or work – valiantly. This trait is valued highly, with the country's heroic resistance against the Red Army in the Winter War usually thought of as the ultimate example.

Saunas

No matter where you are in Finland, you'll never be far from a sauna (pronounced *sah*-oo-nah, not *saw*-nuh). With over two million in homes, hotels, summer cottages, camp sites and numerous other unlikely places, saunas are prescribed to cure almost every ailment, used to seal business deals or just socialise over a few beers.

Traditionally, saunas were used as a family bathhouse as well as a place to smoke meat and even give birth. The earliest references to the Finnish sauna date from chronicles of 1113 and there are numerous mentions of their use in the *Kalevala*.

Most saunas are private, in Finnish homes, but public saunas are common and almost every hotel has one. An invitation to a family's sauna is an honour, as it is to be invited to a person's home for a meal. The sauna is taken naked. While a Finnish family will often take the sauna together, in mixed gatherings it is usual for the men and women to go separately.

Public saunas are usually separated by gender and if there is just one sauna, the hours are different for men and women. In unisex saunas you will be given some sort of wrap or covering to wear. Finns strictly observe the nonsexual character of the sauna and this point should be respected. The sauna was originally a place to bathe and meditate.

The most common sauna is the electric sauna stove, which produces a fairly dry, harsh heat compared with the much-loved chimney sauna, driven by a log fire and the staple of life at summer cottages. Even rarer is the true *savusauna* (smoke sauna), without a chimney. The smoke is let out just before entry and the soot-blackened walls are part of the experience. Although the top of a sauna can reach over 120°C, many Finns consider the most satisfying temperature for a sauna to be around 80°C. At this temperature you'll sweat and, some Finns claim, feel the woodsmoke in your lungs.

Proper sauna etiquette dictates that you use a *kauha* (ladle) to throw water on the *kiuas* (sauna stove), which then gives off the *löyly* (sauna steam). At this point, at least in summer in the countryside, you might take the *vihta* or *vasta* (a bunch of fresh, leafy birch twigs) and lightly strike yourself. This improves circulation, has cleansing properties and gives your skin a pleasant smell. When you are sufficiently warmed, you'll jump in the sea, a lake, river or pool, then return to the sauna to warm up and repeat the cycle several times. If you're indoors, a cold shower will do. The swim and hot-cold aspect is such an integral part of the sauna experience that in the dead of winter Finns cut a hole in the ice and jump right in.

Sadness

There's a definite depressive streak in Finns, more so than in their western neighbours. While they aren't among Europe's biggest drinkers per capita, the incidence of alcoholism is high. The winter darkness can strain even the most optimistic soul – seasonal affective disorder (SAD) is significant here and suicide levels are higher than the comfortable standard of living would predict. The melancholic trend is reflected in Finns' love of darkly themed music and lyrics of lost love; even the cheeriest Suomi-pop hits sound like the singer's just backed over their dog, and Finnish tango (see p230) takes lugubriousness off the chart.

DANCING

FINNISH CULTURE

Traditional ballroom-style dancing is big in Finland in dedicated dance bar/restaurants or in summer dance pavilions. The website www.tanssi.net encourages visitors to participate in a night of Finnish dancing (no Finnish required) and has a detailed English page explaining the etiquette.

Finns love the weekend, when they head to the summer cottage, play sport or party in the evening. But the working week also has a high point. On Wednesday nights restaurants are busy, music is playing at all the nightspots, bars are full – Finns are celebrating *pikku lauantai:* 'little Saturday'.

DRIVIN' WHEELS

Few countries have such an obsession with cars as Finland. The interest goes right down the scale, from watching Formula One to changing the oil on the old Datsun parked outside.

You won't be in Finland for long before you'll hear a baritone bellow and see a glint of fins and whitewall tyres as some American classic car rolls by, immaculately polished and tuned. You probably never knew that so many Mustangs, Chargers or Firebirds existed this side of the Atlantic. Even non-classics long since dead elsewhere are kept alive here with loyal home maintenance.

Rally driving sends Finns wild; the exploits of legends like Tommi Mäkinen and Marcus Grönholm are the latest of a long line in a sport in which Finland has excelled. In Formula One, too, Suomi punches well above its weight, with Keke Rosberg, Mika Häkkinen and Kimi Räikkönen all former world champions. In small towns, often the only entertainment for the local young is trying to emulate them by doing blockies around the kauppatori...

Silence

In and around Helsinki, Cosy Finland (www. cosyfinland. com) offers an interesting chance to meet Finns in their own habitat. They'll set you up with a dinner invitation at a multilingual host's home, where you'll try local specialities and get to know Finland away from the tourist beat.

While the 'silent Finn' concept has been exaggerated over the years, it's certainly true that Finns believe in comfortable silences, so if a conversation dies off naturally there's no need to jump-start it with small talk. Finns quip that they invented text messaging so they didn't have to talk to each other, and sitting in the sauna for 20 minutes with your best friend, saying nothing, is perfectly normal. Finns generally have a quirky, dark, self-deprecating sense of humour and may just be saving their words for a well-timed jibe.

Not to say Finns don't talk. They do, and down the pub on a Friday night they certainly do – a lot.

Religion

The Lutheran church dominates the religious scene here, with some 78% describing themselves as such on a census form; the next religious group, Finnish Orthodox, is only 1.5%. Nevertheless, Finns have one of the lowest rates of church attendance in the Christian world.

Various Lutheran revivalist movements are seeking to combat this and are often in the news. The ultra-conservative Laestadian movement – many of whose members frown on such evils as dancing and earrings – has many adherents, as does the charismatic church Nokia-Missio. Almost one in 10 Finns belongs to a revivalist movement.

Finnish Design

The Roots of Creativity

Its inhabitants' almost mystical closeness to nature has always underpinned design in Finland, and it's rarely been a self-conscious art. However high Finland may climb on the lifestyle indexes these days, its design still has its roots in practicality. Indeed, it is a practicality originally born of poverty: the inventiveness of a hand-to-mouth rural population made life easier in very small steps.

Finland's location, and its historical role as a pawn in the figurative Russia-Sweden chess championship, have given it a variety of influences and a certain flexibility. As a meeting point between east and west, it has traditionally been a place of trade, a point of tension and, therefore, a point of change and innovation. Its climate, too, is a key factor, as it has meant that efficiency has always been the primary requisite for design of everyday objects. In bald terms, if that axe didn't chop enough wood for the winter, you wouldn't survive it.

For the forest is ever-present in Finnish life, so it's no surprise to find that nature is the dominant and enduring motif in the country's designs, from Lapland's sheath knives to the seasonal flower-and-forest colours of Marimekko's palette. Timber remains an important material, and reassuringly chunky wooden objects adorn almost every Finnish home and summer cottage.

Alvar Aalto

Alvar Aalto was for many the 20th century's number one architect. In an era of increasing urbanisation, postwar rebuilding and immense housing pressure, Aalto found elegant solutions for public and private edifices that embraced functionalism but never at the expense of humanity. Viewed from the next century, his work still more than holds its own, and his huge contributions in other areas of art and design make him a mighty figure indeed.

Aalto had a democratic, practical view of his field: he saw his task as 'a question of making architecture serve the wellbeing and prosperity of millions of citizens' where it had previously been the preserve of a wealthy few. But he was no utilitarian; beauty was always a concern, and he was adamant that a proper studio environment was essential for the creativity of the architect to flower.

Born in 1898 in Kuortane near Seinäjoki, Aalto worked in Jyväskylä, Turku and Helsinki before gaining an international reputation for his pavilions at the World Fairs of the late 1930s. His 1925 marriage to Aino Marsio created a dynamic team that pushed boundaries in several fields, including glassware and furniture design. Their work on bending and laminating wood revolutionised the furniture industry, and the classic forms they produced for their company, Artek, are still Finnish staples.

Top Aalto Buildings

» Finlandia Talo, Helsinki

» Otaniemi University, Espoo

» Workers' Club Building, Jyväskylä

» Aalto Centre, Seinäjoki

» Kolmen Ristin Kirkko, Imatra

Aalto's use of rod-shaped ceramic tiles, undulated wood, woven cane, brick and marble was particularly distinctive.

Aalto's notable buildings are dotted throughout Finland. A comparison of the Aalto Centre in Seinäjoki with the Kolmen Ristin Kirkko in Imatra highlights the range of his work. Charmingly, Aalto's favourite design was his own wooden boat (on show at his summer house near Jyväskylä), which he planned and built with great love, but little skill. It was barely seaworthy at the best of times, and regularly capsized and sank.

The Classics

ONLINE DESIGN

The website www. finnishdesign. com mostly sticks to the well-established names but it's a good introduction. Design Forum Finland's webpage www. designforum.fi has useful links; its awards are another good way to keep tabs on the scene.

If the early 21st century is a new golden age for Finnish design, the original one was in the 1950s and 1960s. The freelance designers producing marvels in glass for Iittala, ceramics for Arabia, cookware for Hackman and furniture for Artek won international recognition and numerous prestigious awards, particularly at the Triennale di Milano shows. Though times were still tough after the war, and the country was struggling to house refugees from occupied Karelia, the successes of these firms, together with the Helsinki Olympic Games of 1952, helped put a still-young nation on the map and build confidence and national pride, which were weakened after the gruelling battles with Russia and Germany.

The story of the Iittala glass company could be a metaphor for the story of Finnish design. Still producing to models imported from Sweden in the early 20th century, the company began to explore more homegrown options. Glass design competitions were an outward-looking source of ideas: from one of these came Alvar Aalto's famous Iittala vase, which he described as 'an Eskimo woman's leather trousers'. Then two giants of postwar design, Tapio Wirkkala (1915–85) and Timo Sarpaneva (1926–2006), began to explore textures and forms gleaned from Finnish lakescapes. Coloured glass fell from use and the classic Iittala ranges were born, with sand-scouring creating the appearance of cut ice, and Wirkkala's impossibly fluid forms seemingly melting away. The opaque look, which resembled ceramics, was a later creation as a new generation took to the field. Harri Koskinen (b 1970) and Annaleena Hakatie (b 1965) were among the leading lights, though the company has never been afraid to commission foreign designers. Iittala is today under the same ownership as Hackman, the long-established cutlery and cookware producers, and Arabia, who roughly paralleled Iittala's glassware trajectory with ceramics.

Clothing has been another area of success. Finland, unlike its Nordic neighbours, has tended to beat its own fashion path. It's traditionally been a place where teenagers can wear a jumper knitted by granny to

FINNISH DESIGN CLASSICS

» Artek's Aalto chairs. To think that we take bent wood for granted in our furniture these days.

» The Iittala vase. Yes, Aalto again. Whether or not it actually resembles an Inuit woman's leather pants, it's undeniably a classic.

» An Unikko bed sheet from Marimekko. Who doesn't dream better under those upbeat red poppies?

» 1930s ringed tumblers designed by Aino Aalto – you'll drink your breakfast juice out of one of them within a couple of days of your arrival.

» Marttiini knives, which are made way up north at Rovaniemi and are still first choice for outdoors folk 80 years after they were first produced.

NEW THINGS THAT'LL FIT IN YOUR CASE

» One of Sami Rinne's engagingly quirky ceramics – maybe that mug with a handle like a reindeer's antlers?

» A pair of Minna Parikka's shoes – 21st-century style straight from a smoky 1930s nightclub.

» One of Jani Martikainen's birch trivets (pot-plant bases) from his Majamoo company. The only trouble is that the plant hides it.

» Whatever the versatile Harri Koskinen has just designed – from lighting to glassware.

» The versatile Medusa lamp, produced by Saas and designed by Mikko Paakkanen.

school, and though new and exciting ideas are constantly created here, they tend to be built on solid, traditional foundations.

The godfather of Finnish design, Kaj Franck (1911–89) took ideas from traditional rustic clothing for his pared-back creations, but it was the birth and rapid rise to prominence of Marimekko, founded in 1951, that made an international impact. Optimistic, colourful and well-made, it bucked contemporary trends, focusing on a simple and unashamed beauty. Though the company went through a difficult period, it's back at the top these days, as the retro appeal of its classic shirts, bags, curtains and fabrics fills wardrobes with flowers once again.

Other well-established Finnish names include Aarikka, whose wooden jewellery and other accessories have always had a cheerily reassuring solidity and honesty, and Kalevala Koru, a byword for quality silver and gold jewellery. Pentik's wide range of interior design and homeware products includes the recent Saaga range, inspired by the designs of Sámi shaman drums.

The Newcomers

A strong design tradition tends to produce good young designers and Finland's education system is strong on fostering creativity, so Suomi is churning them out at a fair rate. New names, ranges and shops crop up in the Helsinki's design district like mushrooms overnight, and exciting contemporary design is being produced on all fronts. Fennofolk is the name for one broad movement that seeks, like the original giants of Finnish design, to take inspiration from Suomi's natural and cultural heritage, adding a typically Finnish injection of weirdness along the way.

There are exciting things continuing to happen across all fields of design. Paola Suhonen's IVANAhelsinki clothing label combines innovation with practicality and sustainability, while Hanna Sarén's clothing shot to fame after being referenced in *Sex and the City*. Julia Lundsten and Minna Parikka are head-turning young stars of the footwear world. In industrial design, Harri Koskinen is a giant; his clean-lined minimalism produces objects that are always reassuringly practical but quite unlike anything you've ever seen before. Graphic design studios like Agent Pekka or Underware are leading lights in their field.

One of the biggest and most versatile names on the Finnish design scene is Stefan Lindfors (www.stefan lindfors.com), whose reptile- and insect-inspired work has been described as a warped update of Aalto's own nature-influenced work.

The Arts

Literature

Finland had a rich oral tradition of folklore, but written Finnish was created by the Reformation figure Mikael Agricola (1510–57), who wrote the first alphabet. Although written Finnish was emerging in schools, the earliest fiction was written in Swedish.

As well as compiling and writing the *Kalevala,* Elias Lönnrot's work in creating a standard Finnish grammar and vocabulary by adopting words and expressions from various dialects was of great importance. Finnish has remained very much the same ever since, at least in written form.

All that changed in the early 19th century with the penning of the *Kalevala* (see p331) and the beginning of a nationalistic renaissance. Poet JL Runeberg wrote *Tales of the Ensign Stål,* capturing Finland at war with Russia, while Aleksis Kivi wrote *Seven Brothers,* the nation's first novel, about brothers escaping conventional life in the forest, allegorising the birth of Finnish national consciousness.

This theme continued in the 1970s' *The Year of the Hare,* looking at a journalist's escape into the wilds by the prolific, popular and bizarre Arto Paasilinna. Other 20th-century novelists include Mika Waltari who gained international fame with *The Egyptian,* and FE Sillanpää who received the Nobel Prize for Literature in 1939. The national bestseller during the postwar period was *The Unknown Soldier* by Väinö Linna. The seemingly endless series of autobiographical novels by Kalle Päätalo and the witty short stories by Veikko Huovinen are also very popular. Finland's most internationally famous author is the late Tove Jansson (see p93), whose books about the fantastic Moomin family have long captured the imagination.

Music

Finland's music scene is one of the world's richest and the output of quality musicians per capita is amazingly high, whether we're talking another polished symphony orchestra violinist or a headbanging bassist for the next big death metal band.

There's an excellent, detailed, though somewhat out-of-date, index of Finnish and other Nordic authors in English at www.kirjasto.sci.fi.

Summer here is all about music festivals of all conceivable types.

Classical Music

Composer Jean Sibelius' work dominates Finland's music (see p155). Partly thanks to Helsinki's Sibelius Academy, Finnish musical education is among the best in the world, with Finnish conductors, singers and musicians performing with some of the world's top orchestras. There are always some excellent classical music festivals in Finland (see p19).

Popular Music

In recent years, Finnish bands, mostly from the heavier side of the spectrum, have taken the world by storm, and indeed Finland has one of the liveliest metal scenes around. The biggest exports are HIM with their 'love metal' and darkly atmospheric Nightwish, whose former vocalist Tarja Turunen is also pursuing a solo career. Catchy light-metal rockers the Rasmus continue to be successful. All genres of metal, as well as a few made-up ones, are represented, including Finntroll's folk metal (blending metal and humppa), the 69 Eyes' gothic metal, Apocalyptica's classical metal, Children of Bodom's melodic death metal, Sonata Arctica's and Stratovarius' power metal, Eternal Tears of Sorrow's symphonic metal, and Impaled Nazarene's black metal. All great stuff.

But there is lighter music, such as the Von Hertzen Brothers, indie band Disco Ensemble, emo-punks Poets of the Fall and melodic Husky Rescue. Glam rockers Lovex were making waves with their third album *Watch Out* at last visit. Past legends (still going in some cases) include Hanoi Rocks, the Hurriganes and, of course, the unicorn-quiffed Leningrad Cowboys. While singing in English appeals to an international audience, several groups sing in Finnish including Zen Café, Kotiteollisuus, Apulanta and mellow folk rockers Scandinavian Music Group. There's also a huge number of staggeringly popular solo artists; you'll hear their lovelorn tunes at karaoke sessions in bars and pubs around the country.

Jazz is also very big in Finland, with huge festivals at Pori and Espoo among other places. Finns have created humppa, a jazz-based music that's synonymous with social dances. One of the biggest names in humppa are the Eläkeläiset, whose regular albums are dotted with tongue in cheek covers of famous rock songs. Less traditionally, Finnish rap and hip hop is a real growth industry that's receiving a lot of airplay these days.

Best Rock Festivals

» Ruisrock, Turku

» Provinssirock, Seinäjoki

» Ilosaari Rock Festival, Joensuu

» Tammerfest, Tampere

Painting & Sculpture

Modern Finnish art and sculpture plays with disaffection with technological society (think warped Nokias) and reinterprets the 'Finnishness' (expect parodies of sauna, birches and blonde stereotypes). It's a long way from the pagan prehistoric rock paintings found across Finland in places like Hossa. Medieval churches in Åland and southern Finland have enchanting frescoes that are well worth seeking out.

FINLAND'S NATIONAL EPIC

It's hard to overestimate the influence on Finland of the *Kalevala*, an epic tale compiled from the songs of bards that tells everything from the history of the world to how to make decent homebrew. Intrepid country doctor Elias Lönnrot trekked eastern Finland during the first half of the 19th century in order to collect traditional poems, oral runes, legends, lore and folk stories. Over 11 long tours, he compiled this material with his own writing to form what came to be regarded as the national epic of Finland.

The mythology of the book blends creation stories, wedding poems and classic struggles between good and evil. Although there are heroes and villains, there are also more nuanced characters that are not so simply described. The main storyline concentrates on the events in two imaginary countries, Kalevala (characterised as 'our country') and Pohjola ('the other place', or the north). Many commentators feel that the epic echoes ancient territorial conflicts between the Finns and the Sámi. Although impossible to accurately reproduce the Finnish original, the memorable characters are particularly well brought to life in poet Keith Bosley's English translation of the *Kalevala*, which is a fantastic, lyrical read.

The first version of *Kalevala* appeared in 1833, with another following in 1835 and yet another, the final version, *Uusi-Kalevala* (New Kalevala), in 1849. Its influence on generations of Finnish artists, writers and composers was and is immense, particularly on painter Akseli Gallen-Kallela and composer Jean Sibelius, who repeatedly returned to the work for inspiration.

Beyond Finland the epic has influenced the Estonian epic *Kalevipoeg* and American poet Henry Wadsworth Longfellow and JRR Tolkien based significant parts of his mythos on the *Kalevala*.

MODERN SÁMI MUSIC

Several Finnish Sámi groups and artists have created excellent modern music with the traditional yoik (chant; also *joiks* or *juoiggus*) form. The yoik is traditionally sung a capella, often invoking a person or place with immense spiritual importance in Sámi culture. Wimme is a big name in this sphere, and Angelit produce popular, dancefloor-style Sámi music. One of their former members, Ulla Pirttijärvi, releases particularly haunting solo albums, while Vilddas are on the trance-y side of Sámi music, combining it with other influences. Look out too for rockier offerings from SomBy and Tiina Sanila.

Although contemporary art enjoys a high profile in Finland, it is the work produced by painters and sculptors active during the National Romantic era that is thought of as Finland's 'Golden Age' of art. The main features of these artworks are virgin forests and pastoral landscapes. Following is a list of the most well-known artists of this era. The most comprehensive collections are displayed by the Ateneum and Kansallis-museo in Helsinki, and the Turun Taidemuseo in Turku.

Fanny Churberg (1845–92) One of the most famous female painters in Finland, created landscapes, self-portraits and still lifes.

Albert Edelfelt (1854–1905) Among the most appreciated of Finnish artists. Was educated in Paris, and a number of his paintings date from this period. Many paintings are photolike depictions of rural life.

Akseli Gallen-Kallela (1865–1931) An important figure in the National Romantic movement, drinking companion of composer Jean Sibelius and perhaps Finland's most famous painter. Had a distinguished and prolific career as creator of *Kalevala*-inspired paintings.

Pekka Halonen (1865–1933) A popular artist of the National Romantic era. Thought of as a 'nature mystic', his work, mostly devoted to typical winter scenery, is largely privately owned.

Eero Järnefelt (1863–1937) A keen visitor to Koli, where he created more than 50 paintings of the 'national landscape'. His sister married Sibelius.

Juho Rissanen (1873–1950) Depicted life among ordinary Finns, and his much-loved paintings are displayed at the Ateneum and at Turku art gallery.

Tyko Sallinen (1879–1955) The greatest of the Finnish expressionists, Sallinen is often considered the last of the Golden Age artists.

Helene Schjerfbeck (1862–1946) Probably the most famous female painter of her age, she is known for her self-portraits, which reflect the situation of Finnish women more than 100 years ago. Is considered Finland's greatest artist by many contemporary observers.

Hugo Simberg (1873–1917) Most famous for his haunting work in Tampere's cathedral, which employs his characteristic folk symbolism. Unusual and well worth investigating. Also well represented in Helsinki's Ateneum.

Ville Vallgren (1855–1940) A notable Golden Age sculptor, Vallgren is most famous for creating the Havis Amanda statue in Helsinki.

von Wright, Magnus (1805–68), Wilhelm (1810–87) and Ferdinand (1822–1902) The brothers von Wright are considered the first Finnish painters of the Golden Age, most famous for their paintings of birds. They worked in their home near Kuopio and in Porvoo.

Victor Westerholm (1860–1919) Most famous for his large Åland landscapes. He had his summer studio in Önningeby, but there are landscapes from other locations too.

Emil Wickström (1864–1942) Was to sculpture what Gallen-Kallela was to painting, and sculpted the memorial to Elias Lönnrot in Helsinki. Many of his works are at his studio in Visavuori.

Best Painted Churches

» Pyhän Ristin Kirkko, Hattula

» Keuruu church, Keuruu

» Pyhän Laurin Kirkko, Lohja

» Sankta Maria Kyrka, Kvarnbo

» Sankt Mikael Kyrka, Finström

» Haukipudas church, Haukipudas

» Paltaniemi church, Paltaniemi

Suomi Seasons

Finland's lofty latitudes make for a proper array of utterly contrasting seasons, and human, animal and plant life have all had to adapt accordingly. For the visitor it means that different times of year offer a wholly distinct experience of the country.

Spring

The short Finnish spring is like a blessing after the long months of winter. As the snow melts, life races to reassert itself; green shoots emerge through the white blanket, ice on the rivers cracks and washes away downstream, and birds and animals start busying themselves for summer. It's boggy on hiking trails, but a pleasurable time to visit Finland's towns and cities. The Finns themselves seem to be awaking from a winter slumber, and there's a palpable optimism in the air. In Lapland, there's still plenty of snow on the ground, and you can ski for most of May.

Summer

The sun makes up for its winter neglect by spending some quality time with the Finns in summer: right up north it hangs in the sky for 10 weeks without setting, bathing the land in fertility and festivity. Finland's sparkling waters reflect the birch and spruce forests and people revel in an escape back to nature by remote lakesides. But *kesä* (summer) is also party-time, with terraces packed, dance pavilions rocking as stately couples twirl about, marketplaces humming, midsummer celebrations emptying the breweries and festivals going off right across the land.

Back to Nature

It's almost compulsory to spend some downtime each summer at a *mökki*, or summer cottage. A wood-burning sauna, skinny dips in the shimmering lake, a rowing boat, darts and the smell of sausages on the grill: a pretty good definition of Nordic peace.

Tastes of Summer

Summer marketplaces burst with straight-from-the-garden vegetables, and berries and mushrooms foraged in the forests and fells. The glorious sweetness of tiny wild strawberries, the delicate pepperiness of chanterelles, melt-in-the-mouth new potatoes glorified with fresh dill, the tangy, creamy splendour of a Lapland cloudberry: tastes of nature that define the Finnish summer.

All Aboard!

With so much water, it'd be a crime not to get out on it. Hire a canoe and meet freshwater seals, go rafting on the frisky northern rivers, pull on the waders and cast for salmon, or cruise one of the classic lake routes aboard a steamer.

» Number of days of no sunrise in Nuorgam: 51

» Number of days of no sunset in Nuorgam: 72

» Lowest temperature recorded in Finland: -51.5°C

Freaky Festivals

However offbeat or classical your tastes, there's a festival for you in Finland. Music on offer ranges from marvellous opera in a castle setting and melancholic Finnish tango to the biggest names in heavy rock; wife-carrying, playing air guitar, and voting for the town's laziest resident then throwing them in the sea head up the more bizarre offerings.

Island-hopping

For nipping out for a crayfish lunch at a restaurant in the middle of Helsinki harbour, chugging across Inarijärvi to a Sámi holy place or exploring the Swedish-speaking semi-independent Åland archipelago by bike: one of Finland's nearly two hundred thousand islands will suit you.

Autumn

As bears look for somewhere to sleep out the winter and the last calls of migratory birds fade away in the south, Finland's billions of birch trees bathe the forests in a glow of gold, russet and bronze. It's a fairytale palette, a last artistic caprice of nature before the winter's harsh glory. The season of autumn colours is known as *ruska,* and it's a wonderful time to go hiking, especially in the north.

Best Ruska Hikes

» Kevo Strict Nature Reserve

» Urho Kekkonen National Park

» Pallas-Yllästunturi National Park

» Karhunkierros trail

Ruska Hiking

The insects have long since disappeared, and if there's a bit of a chill in the air in Lapland, all the better for ruddy-faced treks through the forests. The colours are magnificent and the facilities of the national park network are top-notch. This is some of Europe's best walking.

Northern Lights

Whether caused by the collision of charged particles high in the atmosphere, or, as the Sámi once believed, sparked by a giant snow fox running across the Arctic tundra, the haunting, humbling splendour of the aurora borealis never leaves those fortunate to have witnessed it. October and November tend to be the best months to maximise your chances of seeing something special. The further north you go, the better your chances.

Winter

It's cold – Finnish thermometers have more numbers below the line than above – and it's dark, but winter *(talvi)* in Finland is something quite magical. Sparkling summer lakes become snowmobile highways, and only the undaunted spruces and pines, poking above their snowy blankets, can be recognised. Though bears snuggle in dens to sleep through it, Finns are far from cowed by the climatic conditions; they bolt on the winter tyres, strap on the skis and skates, start up the snowmobiles, and head out to enjoy the subzero temperatures. There's enormous scope for activity, and a real magic in the air, especially in Lapland, where there's snow on the ground for seven months of the year.

Sledge Safaris

Fizzing over the snow behind a team of huskies under the low winter sun is tough to beat. Short jaunts are great, but overnight safaris give you time to feed and bond with your lovable dogs, and try out a wood-fired sauna in the middle of the winter wilderness. If you're more of a cat person, you can enjoy similar trips on a snowmobile or behind reindeer.

Christmas Spirit

Old, bearded Joulupukki – as Santa calls himself in Finland – makes his home here, there's guaranteed snow, reindeer wherever you care to look, plenty of local festive tradition, and the forests are full of Christmas trees. So where better to bring the family for a bit of December romance?

Ice-fishing

Finns love to fish, so when the lakes freeze over they have to find an angle. Taking their lead from the polar bear, they cut a hole in the ice, bring something warm (or warming...) to drink, and hope for a bite before getting frostbite.

Ice Hotels

Even reading the words can shoot a shiver up your spine, but spending a night in one of these ethereally beautiful, extravagantly artistic snow buildings is a marvellous experience. Heavy duty sleeping bags ensure a (relatively) cosy slumber, and a morning sauna banishes any lingering chills.

Survival Guide

Directory A–Z

Accommodation

Finland's not generally a nation of quirky boutique hotels. Solid Nordic comfort in standard rooms dominates rather than whimsical conversions or new-agey fabrics. Many accommodation choices open only in summer, usually camp sites or converted student residences.

Sleeping listings in this chapter are divided into three price categories based on the cost of a standard double room at its most expensive:

€ up to €70
€€ €70 to €160
€€€ €160 plus

In the budget category, expect shared bathrooms; midrange will have private bathroom, good facilities and breakfast buffet included; while top end has business-class or five-star facilities.

The double bed is a rare beast in Finnish accommodation; hotel rooms tend to have twin beds that can be pushed together. Family or group rooms are common, and extra beds can usually be added to a twin room at a low extra cost.

Camping

Finland's camp sites are a delight, and have much to offer to all types of travellers. Most camping grounds are open only from June to August (ie summer) and popular spots are crowded during July and the Midsummer weekend. Sites usually cost around €13 plus €4 per person. Almost all camping grounds have cabins or cottages for rent, which are usually excellent value; from €35 for a basic double cabin to €120 for a cottage with kitchen, bathroom and sauna.

The Camping Card Scandinavia offers useful discounts. You can buy it at most camp sites for €9. Finland's *jokamiehenoikeus* (everyman's right) allows access to most land and means you can pitch a tent almost anywhere on public land or at designated free camp sites in national parks.

Finnish Camping Association (www.camping.fi) Carries an extensive listing of camp sites across the country.

Guesthouses

A Finnish *matkakoti,* or guesthouse, is a no-frills spot offering simple but usually comfy accommodation with shared bathroom, typically for travelling salespeople. It can be pretty good value, usually includes breakfast, and sometimes rises well above the norm: check out places like Naantali and Hanko for some exceptional sleeps in this class.

Hostels & Summer Hotels

For solo travellers, hostels generally offer the cheapest bed, and can be good value for twin rooms. Finnish hostels are invariably clean, comfortable and very well equipped, though most are in somewhat institutional buildings.

Some Finnish hostels are run by the Finnish Youth Hostel Association (SRM), and many more are affiliated. It's worth being a member of **HI** (www.hihostels.com), as members save €2.50 per night at affiliated places. You'll save money with a sleep sheet or your own linen, as hostels tend to charge €4 to €8 for this.

From June to August, many student residences are made over as summer hostels and hotels. These are often great value, as you usually get your own room, with kitchen (bring your own utensils though) and bathroom either to yourself or shared between two.

BOOK YOUR STAY ONLINE

For more accommodation reviews by Lonely Planet authors, check out hotels.lonelyplanet.com. You'll find independent reviews, as well as recommendations on the best places to stay. Best of all, you can book online.

Hotels

Most hotels belong to one of a few major chains. These include:

Cumulus (www.cumulus.fi)

Scandic (www.scandichotels.com)

Sokos (www.sokoshotels.fi)

Finlandia (www.finlandiahotels.fi) is an association of independent hotels, while **Omenahotelli** (www.omena.com) offers great-value unstaffed hotels booked online.

Hotels in Finland are designed with the business traveller in mind and tend to charge robustly. But at weekends and during the summer holidays, prices in three- and four-star hotels tend to drop by 40% or so. Prices listed in this guide are weekday prices unless otherwise specified.

Superior rooms vary in value. In many places they are identical to the standard and your extra cash gets you only a bathrobe and a fancier shampoo. In others, an extra €10 can get you 50% more space, views over the town and a private sauna. It's worth asking. The discount for singles is marginal at all times, so you may prefer to pay the little extra for a twin room, which is usually much larger.

Most hotel rooms have tiny Nordic bathrooms; if you want a bathtub, this can usually be arranged. Many hotels have 'allergy rooms', which have no carpet and minimal fabric.

All Finnish hotels have a plentiful and delicious buffet breakfast included in the rate and most include a sauna session.

FARMSTAYS

A growing, and often ecologically sound, accommodation sector in Finland is that of farmstays. Many rural farms, particularly in the south, offer B&B accommodation, a unique opportunity to meet local people and experience their way of life. Plenty of activities are also usually on offer. **ECEAT** (www.eceat.fi) lists a number of organic, sustainable farms in Finland that offer accommodation. Local tourist offices keep lists of farmstay options in the surrounding area; the website www.visitfinland.com links to a few (click on accommodation), and **Lomarengas** (☑0306-502 502; www.lomarengas.fi) also has many listed on its website. In general, prices are good – from around €30 per person per night, country breakfast included. Evening meals are also usually available. Your hosts may not speak much English; if you have difficulties the local tourist office will be happy to help arrange the booking.

PRACTICALITIES

» *Helsingin Sanomat* (www.hs.fi/english) is the main daily paper in Finland. There's an English version online.

» The *Helsinki Times* (www.helsinkitimes.fi) is an English-language weekly; and foreign newspapers and magazines are widely available.

» The national radio broadcaster is YLE (www.yle.fi), which has a number of stations offering news and various types of music.

» National TV networks broadcast plenty of English-language programs, subtitled in Finnish.

» Cinemas show films in the original language, with subtitles in Finnish and Swedish.

» The electric current is 230V AC, 50Hz, and plugs are of the standard northern European type with two round pins that require no switch.

» Finland uses the metric system (see the conversion table in the inside front cover of this book). Decimals are indicated by commas.

Self-Catering Accommodation

One of Finland's joys is its plethora of cottages for rental, ranging from simple camping cabins to fully equipped bungalows with electric sauna and gleaming modern kitchen. These can be remarkably good value and are perfect for families. There are tens of thousands of cabins and cottages for rent in Finland, many in typical, romantic forest lakeside locations. Local booking agents are mentioned under individual destinations.

Lomarengas (☑0306-502 502; www.lomarengas.fi; Eteläesplanadi 22, Helsinki) By far the biggest national agent for cottage rentals.

Villi Pohjola (☑0205-646 980; www.wildnorth.fi) Another good choice. This arm of the Forests & Parks Service has cottages and cabins for rent all over Finland, but especially in Lapland and the north. It's substantially cheaper to book online. Local tourist offices and town websites also have lists.

Wilderness Huts

See p27 for details on huts, shelters and other options on trekking routes.

Business Hours

Many attractions in Finland, particularly of the outdoor variety, are only open for a short summer season, typically mid-June to late August or early September. Opening hours in general tend to be far longer in the summer months and shorter in winter.

Following are usual business hours in Finland. Opening hours are not given in the book unless they differ significantly from these:

Alko (state alcohol store) 9am to 8pm Monday to Friday, to 6pm Saturday

Banks 9am to 4.15pm Monday to Friday

Businesses & Shops 9am to 6pm Monday to Friday, to 3pm Saturday

Nightclubs As late as 4am

Post offices 9am to 6pm Monday to Friday

Pubs 11am to 1am (often later on Friday and Saturday)

Restaurants 11am to 10pm, lunch 11am to 3pm

Customs Regulations

Travellers arriving from outside the EU can bring duty-free goods up to the value of €430 without declaration. You can also bring in up to 16L of beer, 4L of wine, 2L of liquors not exceeding 22% vol and 1L of spirits, 200 cigarettes or 250g of tobacco.

If you're coming from another EU country, there is no restriction on the value of gifts or purchases for personal use.

Although technically part of the EU, arriving on or from the Åland archipelago carries the same import restrictions as arriving from a non-EU country.

Electricity

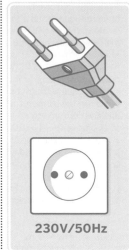

230V/50Hz

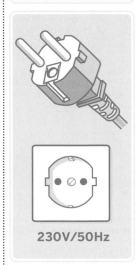

230V/50Hz

Embassies & Consulates

The following is a list of foreign government representatives in Helsinki. Use the Helsinki area telephone code (☎09) if calling from elsewhere.

Australia (☎4777 6640; australian.consulate@tradimex.fi; Museokatu 25B) This is the consulate; the nearest embassy is in Stockholm.

Canada (☎228 530; www.canada.fi; Pohjoisesplanadi 25B)

Denmark (☎684 1050; www.ambhelsingfors.um.dk; Mannerheimintie 8)

Estonia (☎622 028; www.estemb.fi; Kalliolinnantie 18)

France (☎618 780; www.ambafrance-fi.org; Itäinen Puistotie 13)

Germany (☎458 580; www.helsinki.diplo.de; Krogiuksentie 4)

Ireland (☎646 006; www.embassyofireland.fi; Erottajankatu 7A)

Japan (☎686 0200; www.fi.emb-japan.go.jp; Unioninkatu 20)

Latvia (☎4764 7266; www.mfa.gov.lv/en/helsinki; Armfeltintie 10)

Lithuania (☎684 4880; http://fi.mfa.lt; Rauhankatu 13A)

Netherlands (☎228 920; www.netherlands.fi; Erottajankatu 19B)

New Zealand (☎470 1818; paddais@paddais.net; Johanneksenrinne 2) This is the consulate-general; otherwise contact embassy in The Hague, Netherlands.

Norway (☎686 0180; www.norge.fi; Rehbinderintie 17)

Russia (☎661 877; http://helsinki.rusembassy.org; Tehtaankatu 1B)

Sweden (☎687 7660; www.sverige.fi; Pohjoisesplanadi 7B)

UK (☎2286 5100; http://ukinfinland.fco.gov.uk; Itäinen Puistotie 17)

USA (☎616 250; http://finland.usembassy.gov; Itäinen Puistotie 14A)

Food

Restaurants in this guide have been categorised as follows:

€ Average main course less than €15

€€ Average main course €15–25

€€€ Average main course over €25

Finnish Cuisine

Typically Finnish food is similar to the fare you get elsewhere in Scandinavia – lots of fish, such as Baltic herring, salmon and white-fish, along with heavy food such as potatoes, meatballs, sausages, soups, stews and dark rye bread. Finns tend to make lunch the main meal of the day. Breakfast can be anything from coffee and a bun (pulla) to a buffet of cold cuts, porridge, eggs, berries and pickled fish.

A new wave of Finnish cuisine has washed over Helsinki and is apparent elsewhere around the country. It seeks to reinvent the national cuisine, using traditional ingredients such as berries, wild mushrooms, reindeer and other seasonal produce in decidedly untraditional fashion. It makes an intriguing contrast to the heavier, sauce-laden staple platters.

STAPLES & SPECIALITIES

Simple hamburgers, hot dogs and kebabs are a cheap, common snack, served from grilli (fast food) kiosks. Fish is a mainstay of the Finnish diet. Fresh salmon, herring and Arctic char are common, and the tiny lake fish muikku are another treat. Elk and bear make occasional appearances, while in Lapland, reindeer is a staple on every menu.

Regional specialities from Karelia include vety, a sandwich made with ham, eggs and pickles, and the karjalanpiirakka, a savoury rice pastie folded in a thin, open crust. In Tampere, try mustamakkara, a thick sausage made from cow's blood. In Savo, especially Kuopio, a highlight is kalakukko, fish baked in a rye loaf. Åland is known for its fluffy semolina pancakes. Seasonal berries are a delight in Finland – look out for cloudberries and lingonberries from Lapland, and market stalls selling blueberries, strawberries and raspberries.

Finns drink plenty of beer and among the big local brews are Lapin Kulta and Karhu. Cider is also popular, as is lonkero, a ready-made mix of gin and fruity soft drink, usually grapefruit. Other uniquely Finnish drinks include salmiakkikossu, which combines dissolved liquorice sweets with the iconic Koskenkorva vodka (an acquired taste); fisu, which does the same but with Fisherman's Friend pastilles; sahti, a sweet, high-alcohol beer; and cloudberry or cranberry liqueurs.

Where to Eat & Drink

Big towns all have a kaupp-ahalli (market hall), the place to head for all sorts of Finnish specialities, breads, cheeses, fresh fish and cheap sandwiches and snacks. The summer kauppatori (market square) also has food stalls and market produce.

Meals in a restaurant (ravintola) can be expensive, particularly dinner, but Finns tend to eat their main meal in the middle of the day, so most restaurants and some cafes put on a generous lunch (lounas) buffet for between €7 and €10. These include all-you-can-eat salad, bread, coffee and dessert, plus big helpings of hearty fare – sausage and potatoes or fish and pasta are common.

Finns are big lovers of chain restaurants (Golden Rax Pizza Buffet, Rosso, Amarillo, Koti Pizza, Hesburger, Fransmanni and many more) which can be found in most towns. Quality isn't wonderful, but they can be cheap refuelling options and tend to open long hours.

Finns are the world's biggest coffee drinkers, so cafes are everywhere, ranging from 100-year-old imperial classics to trendy networking joints and simple country caffeine stops.

Beer, wine and spirits are sold by the state network, beautifully named Alko. There are stores in every town. The legal age for drinking is 18 for beer and wine, and 20 for spirits. Beer and cider with less than 4.7% alcohol can be bought easily at supermarkets, service stations and convenience stores.

Restaurants are pricey places to enjoy a drink, usually adding around €20 per bottle to the retail price of wine.

If you're buying bottles and cans, the price includes a small deposit (about €0.20) which is redeemed at recycling stations in supermarkets.

Vegetarians & Vegans

Most medium-sized towns in Finland will have a vegetarian restaurant (kasvisravintola), usually open weekday lunchtimes only. It's easy to self-cater at markets, or eat only the salad and vegetables at lunch buffets (which is usually cheaper). Many restaurants also have a salad buffet. The website www.veg aaniliitto.fi has a useful listing of vegetarian and vegan restaurants; follow 'ruoka' and 'kasvisravintoloita' (the Finnish list is more up-to-date than the English one).

Health

Travel in Finland presents very few health problems. The standard of care is extremely high and English is widely spoken by doctors and medical clinic staff, tap water is safe to drink, the level of hygiene is high and there are no endemic diseases.

The main health issues to be aware of are extreme climates (with the potential for such nasties like hypothermia, frostbite or viral infections such as influenza) and biting insects such as mosquitoes, though they're more of an annoyance than a real health risk.

Specific travel vaccinations are not required for visitors to Finland.

Citizens of the European Economic Area (EEA) are

covered for emergency medical treatment on presentation of a European Health Insurance Card (EHIC). Enquire about EHICs at your health centre, travel agency or (in some countries) post office well in advance of travel. Citizens from other countries should find out if there is a reciprocal arrangement for free medical care between their country and Finalnd. If not, health insurance is recommended (see below).

Insurance

A travel insurance policy to cover theft, personal liability, loss and medical problems is recommended. There's a variety of policies available and travel agencies will have recommendations. Travel insurance also usually covers cancellation or delays in travel arrangements; for example, if you fall seriously ill two days before departure.

Buy insurance as early as possible. If you buy it the week before you are due to fly, you may find that you're not covered for delays to your flight caused by strikes or other industrial actions that may have been in force before you took out the insurance.

Paying for your airline ticket with a credit card often provides limited travel accident insurance, and you may be able to reclaim the payment if the operator doesn't deliver.

Certain bank accounts offer their holders automatic travel insurance.

Make sure you get a policy that covers you for the worst possible health scenario if you aren't already covered. Make sure it covers you for any activities you plan to do, like skiing. Be sure to check the small print. Also find out in advance if your insurance plan will make payments directly to providers or reimburse you later for overseas health expenditures.

Worldwide travel insurance is available at www.lonely planet.com/travel_services. You can buy, extend and claim online anytime – even if you're already on the road.

For car insurance, see p344.

Internet Access

Public libraries always have at least one free internet terminal; there's usually a time limit. Many tourist offices have an internet terminal that you can use for free (usually 15 minutes).

Wireless internet access is very widespread; several cities have extensive networks and nearly all hotels, as well as many restaurants, cafes and bars, offer free access to customers and guests. So many, in fact, that we've decided not to clog up the text of this guide by mentioning them in reviews.

Money

Finland adopted the euro (€) in 2002. Euro notes come in five, 10, 20, 50, 100 and 500 denominations and coins in five, 10, 20, 50 cents and €1 and €2. The one- and two-cent coins used in other Eurozone nations are not accepted in Finland.

Cards

Credit cards are widely accepted and Finns are dedicated users of the plastic even to buy a beer or cup of coffee.

Using ATMs with a credit or debit card is by far the easiest way of getting cash in Finland. ATMs have a name, Otto, and can be found even in small villages.

Moneychangers

Travellers cheques and cash can be exchanged at banks and, in the big cities, independent exchange facilities such as **Forex** (www.forex. fi), which usually offer better rates.

Tipping

Service is considered to be included in bills, so there's no need to tip at all unless you want to reward exceptional service. Doormen in bars and restaurants expect a cloakroom tip if there's no mandatory coat charge.

Public Holidays

Finland grinds to a halt twice a year: around Christmas and New Year, and during the Midsummer weekend. National public holidays:

New Year's Day 1 January
Epiphany 6 January
Good Friday March/April
Easter Sunday & Monday
May Day 1 May
Ascension Day May
Whitsunday Late May or early June
Midsummer's Eve & Day Weekend in June closest to 24 June
All Saints Day First Saturday in November
Independence Day 6 December
Christmas Eve 24 December
Christmas Day 25 December
Boxing Day 26 December

Telephone

Public telephones no longer exist on the street in Finland, so if you don't have a mobile you're reduced to making expensive calls from your hotel room or talking over the internet.

The cheapest and most practical solution is to purchase a Finnish SIM card and pop it in your own phone. First make sure your phone isn't blocked from doing this by your home network. If coming from outside Europe, check that it will work in Europe's GSM 900/1800 network.

You can buy a prepaid SIM-card at any R-kioski. There are always several deals on offer, and you might be able to pick up a card for as little as €10, including some call credit. Top the credit up at the same outlets, online or at ATMs.

At the R-kioski you can also buy cut-rate phone cards that substantially lower the cost of making international calls.

The country code for Finland is ☑358. To dial abroad it's ☑00. The number for the international operator is ☑020208.

Time

Finland is on Eastern European Time (EET), an hour ahead of Sweden and Norway and two hours ahead of UTC/GMT (three hours from late March to late October).

Toilets

Public toilets are widespread in Finland but expensive – often €1 a time. On doors, 'M' is for men, while 'N' is for women.

Tourist Information

The main website of the Finnish Tourist Board is www.visitfinland.com. Local tourist offices and websites are mentioned throughout the regional chapters.

Travellers with Disabilities

Finland may be the best-equipped country in the world for the disabled traveller. By law, most institutions must provide ramps, lifts and special toilets for disabled persons; all new hotels and restaurants must install disabled facilities. Trains and city buses are also accessible by wheelchair. Some national parks offer accessible nature trails, and Helsinki and other cities have ongoing projects in place designed to maximise disabled access in all aspects of urban life.

The website www.finland forall.fi has a searchable database of accessible attractions, accommodation and restaurants.

Before leaving home, get in touch with your national support organisation – preferably the 'travel officer' if there is one. One such organisation in the UK is **Can Be Done** (www.canbedone.co.uk).

Visas

A valid passport or EU identity card is required to enter Finland. Most Western nationals don't need a tourist visa for stays of less than three months. South Africans, Indians and Chinese, however, are among those who need a Schengen visa. For more information contact the nearest Finnish embassy or consulate, or check the website www.formin.finland.fi.

Australian and New Zealand citizens aged between 18 and 30 can apply for a 12-month working holiday visa under a reciprocal agreement – contact the Finnish embassy in your home country.

Transport

GETTING THERE & AWAY

Finland is easily accessed from the rest of Europe and beyond. There are direct flights from numerous destinations, while Baltic ferries are another good option for arriving in the south of the country.

Flights, tours and rail tickets can be booked online at lonelyplanet.com/bookings.

Air

Finland is easily reached by air, with a growing number of direct flights to Helsinki from European, American and Asian destinations. It's also served by various budget carriers from several European countries, especially Ryanair, Air Baltic and Blue1; check www.whichbudget.com for a complete list. Most other flights are with Finnair or Scandinavian Airlines (SAS). Most flights to Finland land at **Helsinki-Vantaa airport** (HEL; www.helsinki-vantaa.fi), situated 19km north of the capital. Winter charters hit **Rovaniemi** (RVN; www.finavia.fi), Lapland's main airport, and other smaller airports in the region.

Other international airports include Tampere (TMP), Lappeenranta (LPP), Turku (TKU), Oulu (OUL) and Vaasa (VAA). The website www.finavia.fi includes contact details and other information for all Finnish airports.

Land

Border Crossings

There are several border crossings from northern Sweden and Norway to northern Finland, with no passport or customs formalities. There are nine main border crossings between Finland and Russia, including several in the southeast and two in Lapland. They are more serious frontiers; you must already have a Russian visa.

Bus

SWEDEN
The only bus route between Finland and Sweden is between the linked towns of Tornio (Finland) and Haparanda (Sweden), from where you can get onward transport into their respective countries. The other possible crossing point is the Lapland towns of Kaaresuvanto (Finland)

and Karesuando (Sweden), separated by a bridge and both served sporadically by domestic buses.

NORWAY
There are various daily routes linking Finnish Lapland with northern Norway, some running only in summer. These are operated by **Eskelisen Lapin Linjat** (www.eskelisen-lapinlinjat.com), whose website has detailed maps and timetables, as does the Finnish bus website for **Matkahuolto** (www.matkahuolto.fi).

All routes originate or pass through Rovaniemi; the three northeastern routes continue via Inari to Tana Bru/Vadsø or Karasjok. The Karasjok bus continues in summer to Nord-kapp (North Cape). On the western route, a Rovaniemi–Kilpisjärvi bus runs daily to Tromsø in summer, and a Rovaniemi-Hetta bus continues to Kautokeino and Alta.

RUSSIA
There are daily express buses to Vyborg and St Petersburg from Helsinki and Lappeenranta (one originates in Turku). These services appear on the website of **Matkahuolto** (www.matkahuolto.fi). There are also semi-official buses and minibuses that can be cheaper options (see p74). **Goldline** (www.goldline.fi) runs three weekly buses from Rovaniemi via Ivalo to Murmansk.

Car & Motorcycle

Vehicles can easily be brought into Finland on the Baltic ferries, provided you have registration papers and valid insurance (Green Card).

See p346 for information about driving in Finland.

Train

RUSSIA
The only international train links with Finland are to/from Moscow and St Petersburg in Russia.

There are two high-speed Allegro train services daily from Helsinki to the Finland

Station in St Petersburg (2nd/1st class €84/134, 3½ hours). The Tolstoi sleeper runs from Helsinki via St Petersburg (Ladozhki station) to Moscow (2nd/1st class €103/155, 13 hours). The fare includes a sleeper berth. There are a number of more upmarket sleepers costing up to €393.

All trains go via the Finnish towns of Lahti and Kouvola, and the Russian city of Vyborg. Tickets are sold at the international ticket counter at Helsinki station.

You must have a valid Russian visa; passport checks are carried out on board.

Return fares are double, and there are significant discounts for families and small groups. See www.vr.fi for details.

SWEDEN

There is no direct train service between Finland and Sweden, but train passes give significant discounts on ferry and bus connections.

Swedish trains travel no closer than Boden/Luleå, from there take connecting buses (train passes are valid) to Haparanda/Tornio, and on to the railway station at Kemi. International railpasses cover bus travel all the way from Boden to Kemi.

Sea

Arriving in Finland by ferry is a memorable way to begin your visit, especially if you dock in Helsinki. Baltic ferries are some of the world's most impressive seagoing craft; the big ferries are floating hotels-cum-shopping plazas, with duty-free shopping, restaurants, bars, karaoke, nightclubs and saunas. Many Scandinavians use them simply for boozy overnight cruises, so they can get pretty rowdy on Friday and Saturday nights.

Services are year-round between major cities: book ahead in summer, at weekends and if travelling with a vehicle. The boats are amazingly cheap if you travel deck class (without a cabin): they make their money from duty-free purchases. Many ferry lines offer 50% discounts for holders of Eurail, Scanrail and InterRail passes. Some offer discounts for seniors, and for ISIC and youth-card holders; enquire when purchasing your ticket. There are usually discounts for families and small groups travelling together.

Ferry companies have detailed timetables and fares on their websites. Fares vary according to season. Operators with their Finnish contact numbers:

Eckerö Line (☎060-004 300) Tallinn www.eckeroline. fi; Åland (www.eckerolinjen.fi)

Finnlines (☎010-343 4500; www.finnlines.com)

Linda Line (☎060-0066 8970; www.lindaliini.ee)

RG Line (☎020-771 6810; www.rgline.com)

St Peter Line (☎010-346 7820; www.stpeterline.com)

Tallink/Silja Line (☎060-015 700; www.tallinksilja.com)

Viking Line (☎060-041 577; www.vikingline.fi)

Sweden

The daily Stockholm to Helsinki, Stockholm to Turku and Kapellskär to Mariehamn (Åland) routes are dominated by Tallink/Silja and Viking Line. Viking Line is the cheaper, with a passenger ticket between Stockholm and Helsinki costing from €36 to €50 (up to €62 on Friday). You can doss down in chairs or on the floor; the cheapest berths start at €45 in peak season.

Tallink/Silja doesn't offer deck tickets on the Helsinki run: the cheapest cabins start at €122 for the crossing.

It's cheaper to cross to Turku (11 to 12 hours), with tickets costing €20 in summer on the day ferries. Note that Åbo is Swedish for Turku.

Eckerö Linjen sails from Grisslehamn, north of Stockholm, to Eckerö in Åland. It's by far the quickest, at just two hours, and, with prices around €6 to €10 return, and €10 for a car, it's an amazing bargain. There's a connecting bus from Stockholm and Uppsala.

RG Lines sails from Vaasa in Finland to Umeå, Sweden (€60 per person plus €65 per car, 4½ hours), almost daily year-round. Finnlines runs a cargo ferry, which connects Naantali, near Turku, with Kapellskär three times daily.

Estonia

Several ferry companies ply the Gulf of Finland between Helsinki and Tallinn in Estonia. Car ferries cross in 3½ hours, catamarans and hydrofoils in about 1½ hours, although in winter there are fewer departures and traffic is slower due to the ice.

See p71 for more details on this route.

Germany & Poland

Finnlines runs from Helsinki to Travemünde (from €196 June to August one way plus €100 per vehicle, 28 hours), with connecting bus service to Hamburg. Finnlines also runs to Gdynia in Poland (from 21 hours).

Tallink/Silja also runs a fast ferry from Helsinki to Rostock (27 hours), with seats costing from €73 to €98, and berths starting at €127. Vehicle places start at €115/196 one way/return.

Russia

St Peter Line connects Helsinki with St Petersburg three times weekly. A significant added benefit of arriving in Russia this way is a visa-free stay of up to three days in St Petersburg. See p71 for more details on this route.

GETTING AROUND

Both bus (www.matkahuolto.fi) and rail (www.vr.fi) services have excellent online timetables, and a useful combined journey planner for Finland's public transport network is online at www.journey.fi.

Air

Finnair runs a fairly comprehensive domestic service, mainly out of Helsinki. Standard prices are expensive, but check the website for offers. Budget carriers offer the cheapest fares for advance internet bookings.

Major airlines flying domestically:

AirBaltic (☎060-018 181; www.airbaltic.com) Offers several low-budget domestic routes.

Blue1 (☎060-002 5831; www.blue1.com) Budget flights from Helsinki to Kuopio, Oulu, Rovaniemi and Vaasa.

Finnair (☎81881; www.finnair.com) Extensive domestic network.

FlyBe (www.flybe.com) Runs the old Finncomm domestic routes; look out for new routes as this book goes to press.

Bicycle

Finland is largely flat and is as bicycle-friendly as any country you'll find, with plenty of paths that cyclists share with in-line skaters in summer. The only drawback to an extensive tour is distance, but bikes can be taken on most trains, buses and ferries. Åland is particularly good for cycling. Helmets are required by law.

For more information about cycling in Finland, see p29.

Hire

You can hire a bike in nearly every Finnish town, but it's important to bear in mind the type of bikes on offer. Most camp sites and many urban hotels offer bikes for a small fee or for free, but these are made for the job of cycling into or around town, not for ambitious road trips. Better bikes are available at dedicated outlets that we list in the text. Expect to pay around €20 per day or €100 per week for a good-quality road or mountain bike.

Boat

Lake and river passenger services were once important means of summer transport in Finland. These services are now largely kept on as cruises, and make a great, leisurely way to journey between towns. The most popular routes are Tampere–Hämeenlinna, Savonlinna–Kuopio, Lahti–Jyväskylä and Joensuu–Koli–Lieksa.

The main coastal routes are Turku–Naantali, Helsinki–Porvoo and the archipelago ferries to the Åland islands.

Bus

The main form of long-distance transport in Finland, especially in remote areas, is the bus. The network it covers is far more comprehensive than the train, taking in some 90% of the nation's road system. Buses are comfortable, run on time and are rarely full.

There are two types of intercity bus service: *vakiovuoro* (regular), which stops frequently at towns and villages; and *pikavuoro* (express), which travels swiftly between cities. Because there are few motorways in Finland, even express buses aren't that fast, averaging about 60km per hour. Express buses are pricier, but not much more so.

All long-distance bus ticketing is handled by **Matkahuolto** (☎0200 4000; www.matkahuolto.fi), whose excellent website has all the timetables. Matkahuolto offices tend to work normal business hours, but you can always just buy the ticket from the driver.

Each town and municipal centre has a *linja-autoasema* (bus terminal), with local timetables displayed (*lähtevät* is departures, *saapuvat* arrivals). Schedules change often so *always* double-check – particularly in rural areas where there may be only one weekly bus on some routes.

Departures between major towns are very frequent, but reduce substantially at weekends. In more remote areas, there may be no weekend buses at all. Schedules change during the summer holidays: buses that normally do the school run are struck off, so it can be much harder to move around isolated regions.

Costs

Prices in this guide refer to express services if they are available, or local services if not. Ticket prices are fixed and depend on the number of kilometres travelled; return tickets are 10% cheaper than two one-way fares, provided the trip is at least 80km each way. Children aged four to 11 always pay half fare, while there's a 30% reduction for those aged 12 to 16. For student discounts, you need to be studying full-time in Finland and buy a student coach discount card (€8) from any bus station. Proper student ID and a passport photo is required, and the card entitles you to a 50% discount on journeys more than 80km.

If booking three or more adult tickets together, a 25% discount applies, meaning good news for groups.

The one-way fare for a 100km trip is normal/express €16.90/19.90.

Car & Motorcycle

Finland's road network is excellent, although there are only a few motorways. When approaching a town or city, look for signs saying *keskusta* (town centre). There are no road tolls but lots of speed cameras.

Petrol is expensive in Finland. Many petrol stations are unstaffed, so have bank notes handy for the machine: they don't accept foreign cards. Change is not given.

Hire

Car rental is expensive, but between a group of three or

ROAD DISTANCES (KM)

	Helsinki	Jyväskylä	Kuopio	Kuusamo	Lappeenranta	Oulu	Rovaniemi	Savonlinna	Tampere	Turku
Jyväskylä	272									
Kuopio	383	144								
Kuusamo	804	553	419							
Lappeenranta	223	219	264	684						
Oulu	612	339	286	215	551					
Rovaniemi	837	563	511	191	776	224				
Savonlinna	338	206	160	579	155	446	671			
Tampere	174	148	293	702	275	491	712	355		
Turku	166	304	448	848	361	633	858	446	155	
Vaasa	419	282	377	533	501	318	543	488	241	348

four it can work out at a reasonable cost. From the major rental companies a small car starts at €60/280 per day/week with 300km free per day. As ever, the cheapest deals are online.

While the daily rate is high, the weekly rate offers some respite. Best of all, though, are the weekend rates. These can cost little more than the rate for a single day, and you can pick up the car early afternoon on Friday, and return it late Sunday or early Monday.

Car-rental franchises with offices in many Finnish cities include **Budget** (☎020-746 6600; www.budget.fi), **Hertz** (☎020-011 2233; www.hertz. fi), **Europcar** (☎020-012 154; www.europcar.fi) and **Avis** (☎098-598 356; www.avis.fi). One of the cheapest is **Sixt** (☎020-011 1222; www.sixt.fi).

Road Conditions & Hazards

Beware of elk and reindeer, which don't respect vehicles and can dash onto the road unexpectedly. This sounds comical, but elks especially constitute a deadly danger. Notify the police if there is an accident involving these animals. Reindeer are very common in Lapland; slow

right down if you see one, as there will be more nearby.

Snow and ice on the roads, potentially from September to April, and as late as June in Lapland, make driving a serious undertaking. Snow chains are illegal: instead, people use either snow tyres, which have metal studs, or special all-weather tyres. The website http://alk.tiehallinto. fi has road webcams around Finland, good for checking conditions on your prospective route.

Road Rules

Finns drive on the right; the speed limit is 50km/h in built-up areas, from 80km/h to 100km/h on highways, and 120km/h on motorways. You must use headlights at all times, and seat belts are compulsory for all. The blood alcohol limit is 0.05%.

An important feature of Finland is that there are fewer give-way signs than in many countries. Traffic entering an intersection from the right has right of way. While this doesn't apply to highways or main roads, you'll find that in towns cars will nip out from the right without looking: you must give way, so be careful at every intersection.

Hitching

Hitching in Finland is possible but not an activity for the impatient: expect long waits and pack waterproofs. It's more common in remote areas where bus services are fewer, but it's still unusual. Your greatest friend as a hitchhiker in Finland will be your insect repellent. Mosquitoes can't believe their luck that such a large juicy mammal will stand in one place for such a very long time.

Local Transport

The only tram and metro networks are in Helsinki. There is a bus service in all Finnish cities and towns, with departures every 10 to 15 minutes in Helsinki and other large towns, and every 30 to 60 minutes in smaller towns. Fares are usually around €2.50 to €3, payable to the driver. See individual towns for details of local public transport.

Taxi

The taxi (taksi) in Finland is an expensive creature, particularly for short rides. There's a flag fall of €5.50 in Helsinki, and typically €8 to €10 in other places, and a per-kilometre charge of €1.30. These increase if there are more than two passengers, and there's a surcharge for night and weekend service.

Hail taxis at bus and train stations or pick up the phone; they are listed in the phone book under 'Taksi'. Shared taxis often cover airport routes, and are a common mode of transport in Karelia, Kainuu and, to a lesser extent, Lapland.

Train

Finnish trains are run by the state-owned **Valtion Rautatiet** (VR; ☎060-041 900; www. vr.fi) and are a fast, efficient service, with prices roughly

Major Railway Routes

equivalent to buses on the same route.

VR's website has comprehensive timetable information and some ticket sales. Major stations have a VR office: this is where to buy your ticket, as the automated machines only accept Finnish bankcards. You can pay for tickets over the phone, then pick them up at any R-Kioski newsstand. You can also board and pay the conductor, but if the ticket office was open, you'll be charged a small penalty fee (€3 to €6).

Classes

The main classes of trains are the high-speed Pendolino (the fastest and most expensive class), fast Intercity (IC), Express and Regional trains. The first three have both 1st- and 2nd-class sections, while regional trains ('H' on the timetable) are the cheapest and slowest services, and only have 2nd-class carriages.

On longer routes there are two types of sleeping carriage currently in operation. The traditional blue ones offer berths in one-/two-/three-bed cabins; the newer sleeping cars offer single and double compartments in a double-decker carriage. There are cabins equipped for wheelchair use, and ones with bathroom. Berths cost from €19 to €82 in high season. Sleeper trains transport cars, handy if you've brought your own vehicle.

Costs

Fares vary slightly according to the class of train, with Pendolino the most expensive. A one-way ticket for a 100km express train journey costs approximately €15.50 in 2nd

class. First-class tickets cost 50% more than a 2nd-class ticket. A return fare is about 10% less than two one-way tickets.

Children under 17 pay half fare and children aged under six travel free (but without a seat). A child travels free with every adult on long-distance trips, and there are also discounts for seniors, local students and any group of three or more adults travelling together.

Bicycles

See p29 for details on transporting bikes.

Train Passes

There are various passes available for rail travel within Finland, or in various European countries including Finland. There are cheaper passes for students, people under 26, and seniors. Supplements (eg for high-speed services) and reservation costs are not covered by passes, and terms and conditions change – check carefully before buying. Pass-holders must always carry their passport on the train for identification purposes.

EURAIL PASSES
Eurail (www.eurail.com) offers a good selection of different passes available to residents of non-European countries, which should be purchased before arriving in Europe. Most of the passes offer discounts of around 25% for under-26s, or 15% for two people travelling together.

The Eurail Scandinavia pass gives a number of days in a two-month period, and is valid for travel in Denmark, Sweden, Norway and Finland. It costs €241 for four days,

and up to €375 for 10 days. A similar but cheaper pass includes just Sweden and Finland. The Finland Eurail Pass costs €131/172/234 for three/five/10 days' 2nd-class travel in a one-month period within Finland.

Eurail Global Passes offer travel in 22 European countries, either 10 or 15 days in a two-month period, or unlimited travel from 15 days up to three months. The Global Passes are much better value for under-26s, as those older have to buy a 1st-class pass.

On most Eurail passes, children aged between four and 11 get a 50% discount on the full adult fare.

Eurail passes give a 30% to 50% discount on several ferry lines in the region; check the website for details.

INTERRAIL PASSES
If you've lived in Europe for more than six months, you're eligible for an InterRail (www. interrailnet.com) pass. The InterRail Finland pass offers travel only in Finland for three/four/six/eight days in a one-month period, costing €112/139/189/229 in 2nd class. The Global Pass offers travel in 30 European countries and costs from €259 for five days' travel in any 10 countries, to €619 for a month's unlimited train travel. On both these passes, there's a 33% discount for under-26s.

InterRail passes give a 30% to 50% discount on several ferry lines in the region; check the website for details.

FINNRAIL PASS
The Finnrail Pass (www.vr.fi) is available to travellers residing outside Finland, and offers a similar deal to the Finland Eurail pass at a similar price.

Language

WANT MORE?

For in-depth language information and handy phrases, check out Lonely Planet's *Scandinavian Phrasebook*. You'll find it at **shop.lonelyplanet.com**, or you can buy Lonely Planet's iPhone phrasebooks at the Apple App Store.

Finnish is a distinct national icon that sets Finland apart from its Scandinavian neighbours. It belongs to the exclusive Finno-Ugric language family, of which Estonian and Hungarian are the only other members. There are around six million Finnish speakers in Finland, Sweden, Norway and Russian Karelia. In Finnish, Finland is known as *Suomi* and the language itself as *suomi*.

If you read our coloured pronunciation guides as if they were English, you shouldn't have problems being understood. Note that a is pronounced as in 'act', ai as in 'aisle', eu as the 'u' in 'nurse', ew as the 'ee' in 'see' with rounded lips, oh as the 'o' in 'note', ow as in 'how', uh as the 'u' in 'run', and the r sound is rolled. The stressed syllables are indicated with italics in our pronunciation guides.

BASICS

Hello.	*Hei.*	hayn
Goodbye.	*Näkemiin.*	na·ke·meen
Yes.	*Kyllä.*	kewl·la
No.	*Ei.*	ay
Please.	*Ole hyvä.*	o·le hew·va
Thank you (very much).	*Kiitos (paljon).*	kee·tos (puhl·yon)
You're welcome.	*Ole hyvä.*	o·le hew·va
Excuse me.	*Anteeksi.*	uhn·tayk·si
Sorry.	*Anteeksi.*	uhn·tayk·si

How are you?
Mitä kuuluu?　　　　　mi·ta koo·loo

Fine. And you?
Hyvää. Entä itsellesi?　hew·va en·ta it·sel·le·si

What's your name?
Mikä sinun nimesi on?　mi·ka si·nun ni·me·si on

My name is ...
Minun nimeni on ...　　mi·nun ni·me·ni on ...

Do you speak English?
Puhutko englantia?　　pu·hut·ko en·gluhn·ti·uh

I don't understand.
En ymmärrä.　　　　　en ewm·mar·ra

ACCOMMODATION

Where's a cheap/nearby hotel?
Missä olisi halpa/　　　mis·sa o·li·si huhl·puh/
lähin hotelli?　　　　　la·hin ho·tel·li

I'd like a single/double room.
Haluaisin yhden/　　　huh·lu·ai·sin ewh·den/
kahden hengen　　　　kuh·den hen·gen
huoneen.　　　　　　　hu·o·nayn

How much is it per night/person?
Paljonko se on　　　　puhl·yon·ko se on
yöltä/hengeltä?　　　ew·eul·ta/hen·gel·ta

I want a room with a ...	*Minä haluan huoneen ...*	mi·na huh·lu·uhn hu·o·nayn ...
bathroom	*kylpy-huoneella*	kewl·pew-hu·o·nayl·luh
window	*jossa on ikkuna*	yos·suh on ik·ku·nuh

DIRECTIONS

Where's the ...?	*Missä on ...?*	mis·sa on ...
bank	*pankki*	puhnk·ki
market	*kauppatori*	kowp·pa·to·ri
post office	*postitoi-misto*	pos·ti·toy-mis·to

Signs

Sisään	Entrance
Ulos	Exit
Avoinna	Open
Suljettu	Closed
Kielletty	Prohibited
WC	Toilets

Can you show me (on the map)?
Voitko näyttää sen   voyt·ko na·ewt·ta sen
minulle (kartalta)?   mi·nul·le (kar·tuhl·tuh)

EATING & DRINKING

I'd like ..., please.   *Saisinko ...*   sai·sin·ko ...

a table for (four)	*pöydän (neljälle)*	peu·ew·dan (nel·yal·le)
the non-smoking section	*savutto-malta puolelta*	suh·vut·to·muhl·tuh pu·o·lel·tuh

Do you have vegetarian food?
Onko teillä   on·ko teyl·la
kasvisruokia?   kuhs·vis·ru·o·ki·uh

What would you recommend?
Mitä voit suositella?   mi·ta voyt su·o·si·tel·luh

I'll have a ...
Tilaan ...   ti·laan ...

Cheers!
Kippis!   kip·pis

I'd like (the) ..., please.   *Saisinko ...*   sai·sin·ko ...

bill	*laskun*	luhs·kun
drink list	*juoma-listan*	yu·o·muh·lis·tuhn
menu	*ruokalistan*	ru·o·kuh·lis·tuhn
that dish	*tuon ruokalajin*	tu·on ru·o·kuh·luh·yin

breakfast	*aamiaisen*	aa·mi·ai·sen
lunch	*lounaan*	loh·naan
dinner	*illallisen*	il·luhl·li·sen

bottle of (beer)	*pullon (olutta)*	pul·lon (o·lut·tuh)
(cup of) coffee	*(kupin) kahvia*	(ku·pin) kuh·vi·uh
glass of (wine)	*lasillisen (viiniä)*	luh·sil·li·sen (vee·ni·a)
(cup of) tea	*(kupin) teetä*	(ku·pin) tay·ta
(mineral) water	*(kivennäis-) vettä*	(ki·ven·na·is·) vet·ta

EMERGENCIES

Help!   *Apua!*   uh·pu·uh
Go away!   *Mene pois!*   me·ne poys

Call ...!   *Soittakaa paikalle ...!*   soyt·tuh·kaa pai·kuhl·le ...

a doctor	*lääkäri*	la·ka·ri
the police	*poliisi*	po·lee·si

I'm lost.
Olen eksynyt.   o·len ek·sew·newt

Where are the toilets?
Missä on vessa?   mis·sa on ves·suh

SHOPPING & SERVICES

I'm looking for ...
Etsin ...   et·sin ...

How much is it?
Mitä se maksaa?   mi·ta se muhk·saa

Can you write down the price?
Voitko kirjoittaa   voyt·ko kir·yoyt·taa
hinnan lapulle?   hin·nuhn luh·pul·le

That's too expensive.
Se on liian kallis.   se on lee·uhn kuhl·lis

It's faulty.
Se on viallinen.   se on vi·uhl·li·nen

There's a mistake in the bill.
Laskussa on virhe.   luhs·kus·suh on vir·he

Do you accept ...?   *Voinko maksaa ...?*   voyn·ko muhk·saa ...

credit cards	*luotto-kortilla*	lu·ot·to·kor·til·luh
travellers cheques	*matka-sekillä*	muht·kuh·se·kil·la

I'd like ..., please.   *Saisinko ...*   sai·sin·ko ...

a receipt	*kuitin*	ku·i·tin
my change	*vaihto-rahat*	vaih·to·ruh·huht

I'd like ..., please.   *Haluaisin ...*   huh·lu·ai·sin ...

a refund	*vaihtaa tämän*	vaih·taa ta·man
to return this	*palauttaa tämän*	puh·lowt·taa ta·man

TIME, DATES & WEATHER

What time is it?
Paljonko   puhl·yon·ko
kello on?   kel·lo on

It's in the ...	Kello on ...	kel·lo on ...
morning	aamulla	aa·mul·luh
afternoon	iltapäivällä	il·tuh·pa·i·val·la
evening	illalla	il·luhl·luh

Monday	maanantai	maa·nuhn·tai
Tuesday	tiistai	tees·tai
Wednesday	keskiviikko	kes·ki·veek·ko
Thursday	torstai	tors·tai
Friday	perjantai	per·yuhn·tai
Saturday	lauantai	low·uhn·tai
Sunday	sunnuntai	sun·nun·tai

What's the weather like?
Millainen ilma   *mil·lai·nen il·muh*
siellä on?   *si·el·la on*

It's ...	Siellä ...	si·el·la ...
cold	on kylmä	on kewl·ma
hot	on kuuma	on koo·ma
raining	sataa	suh·taa
snowing	sataa	suh·taa
	lunta	lun·tuh

Numbers

1	yksi	ewk·si
2	kaksi	kuhk·si
3	kolme	kol·me
4	neljä	nel·ya
5	viisi	vee·si
6	kuusi	koo·si
7	seitsemän	sayt·se·man
8	kahdeksan	kuhk·dek·suhn
9	yhdeksän	ewh·dek·san
10	kymmenen	kewm·me·nen
20	kaksi-kymmentä	kuhk·si·kewm·men·ta
30	kolme-kymmentä	kol·me·kewm·men·ta
40	neljäkymmentä	nel·ya·kewm·men·ta
50	viisikymmentä	vee·si·kewm·men·ta
60	kuusikymmentä	koo·si·kewm·men·ta
70	seitsemän-kymmentä	sayt·se·man·kewm·men·ta
80	kahdeksan-kymmentä	kuhk·dek·suhn·kewm·men·ta
90	yhdeksän-kymmentä	ewh·dek·san·kewm·men·ta
100	sata	suh·tuh
1000	tuhat	tu·huht

TRANSPORT

Can we get there by public transport?
Pääseekö sinne   *paa·see·keu sin·ne*
julkisella   *yul·ki·sel·luh*
liikenteellä?   *lee·ken·teel·la*

Where can I buy a ticket?
Mistä voin ostaa lipun?   *mis·ta voyn os·taa li·pun*

One ... ticket, please.	Saisinko yhden ... lipun.	sai·sin·ko ewh·den ... li·pun
one-way	yksi-suuntaisen	ewk·si·soon·tai·sen
return	meno-paluu	me·no·pa·loo

My luggage has been ...	Matkata-varani ...	muht·kuh·tuh·vuh·ruh·ni ...
lost	ovat kadonneet	o·vuht kuh·don·nayt
stolen	on varastettu	on vuh·ruhs·tet·tu

Where does this ... go?	Minne tämä ... menee?	min·ne ta·ma ... me·nay
boat	laiva	lai·vuh
bus	bussi	bus·si
plane	lentokone	len·to·ko·ne
train	juna	yu·nuh

What time's the ... bus?	Mihin aikaan lähtee ... bussi?	mi·hin ai·kaan lah·tay ... bus·si
first	ensimmäinen	en·sim·mai·nen
last	viimeinen	vee·may·nen
next	seuraava	se·u·raa·vuh

I'd like a taxi ...	Haluaisin tilata taksin ...	huh·lu·ai·sin ti·luh·tuh tuhk·sin ...
at (9am)	kello (yhdeksäksi aamulla)	kel·lo (ewh·dek·sak·si aa·mul·luh)
tomorrow	huomiseksi	hu·o·mi·sek·si

How much is it to ...?
Miten paljon maksaa   *mi·ten puhl·yon muhk·saa*
matka ...?   *muht·kuh ...*

Please take me to (this address).
Voitko viedä minut   *voyt·ko vi·e·da mi·nut*
(tähän osoitteeseen). *(ta·han o·soyt·tay·sayn)*

Please stop here.
Pysähdy tässä.   *pew·sah·dew tas·sa*

GLOSSARY

You may meet many of the following terms and abbreviations during your travels in Finland. Throughout the country you will often hear the words *järvi* (lake), *lampi* (pond), *saari* (island), *ranta* (shore), *niemi* (cape), *lahti* (bay), *koski* (rapids), *virta* (stream) and *joki* (river). Unless otherwise noted, all entries are Finnish. Note that **å**, **ä** and **ö** fall at the end of the Finnish alphabet.

ala- – lower, eg in place names; see also *yli*, *ylä-*
apteekki – pharmacy
asema – station, eg *linja autoasema* (bus station), *rautatieasema* (train station) or *lentoasema* (airport terminal)

baari – simple restaurant serving light lager and some snacks (also called *kapakka*)
bruk – early ironworks precinct (Swedish)
-by – village (Swedish); as in Godby (in Åland) or Nykarleby (in Pohjanmaa)

etelä – south

gamla – old (Swedish)
grilli – stand or kiosk selling burgers, grilled sausages and other greasy snacks

hamn – harbour (Swedish)
huone – room

itä – east; *itään* means 'to the east'

jokamiehenoikeus – literally 'everyman's right'; every person's right to wilderness access
joki – river
joulu – Christmas
juna – train
järvi – lake
jää – ice
kahvila – cafe

kahvio – cafeteria-style cafe, usually more basic than a *kahvila*
kala – fish; *kalastus* means 'fishing'
Kalevala – the national epic of Finland; *Kalevala* is Elias Lönnrot's 19th-century literary creation, which combines old poetry, runes and folk tales with creation myths and ethical teaching
kantele – Karelian stringed instrument similar to a zither
kapakka – see *baari*
karhu – bear
Karjala – Karelia
karjalanpiirakka – rice-filled savoury pastry
katu – street
kauppa – shop
kauppahalli – market hall
kauppatori – market square (usually just referred to as *tori*)
kaupungintalo – city hall
kesä – summer
kioski – small stand that sells sweets, newspapers, phonecards, food items and beer
kirjakauppa – bookshop
kirjasto – library
kirkko – church
koski – rapids
kota – Sámi hut, resembling a teepee or wigwam (from the Finnish word *koti*)
koti – home
kuja – lane
kylpylä – spa
kylä – village
kyrka – church (Swedish)

laavu – Sámi permanent or temporary open-air shelter, also used by trekkers
lahti – bay
laituri – platform (for buses or trains); wharf or pier
lakka – cloudberry
lampi – pond, small lake
laiva – ship
Lappi – Lapland, a province

and a popular term, usually applied to the land north of Oulu; it's better understood as roughly the area between Rovaniemi and Sodankylä; north of this is the Sámi region called Sápmi, which many consider the 'true Lapland'; see also Sápmi
leirintäalue – camping ground
linja-auto – bus (informally called *bussi*)
linna – castle
linnoitus – fortification
lippu – ticket
lounas – lunch
länsi – west

maatila – farm
Matkahuolto – national umbrella company managing the long-distance bus system
matkakoti – guesthouse, inn; also called *matkustaja-koti* (traveller home)
Midsummer – (or Juhannus) longest day of the year, celebrated at the end of June, beginning on Friday evening (Juhannusaatto). Saturday, Sunday and Monday following are also serious holidays when Finland is basically closed.
muikku – vendace, or whitefish, a common lake fish
museo – museum
mustamakkara – mild sausage made with cow's blood, black-pudding style
mäki – hill
mökki – cottage

Napapiiri – Arctic Circle
niemi – cape

olut – beer

pirtti – the living area of a Finnish farmhouse; a word that is often affixed to a rustic restaurant or tourist attraction

pitkospuu – boardwalk constructed over wetlands or swamps

pohjoinen – north; also *pohjois*

polku – path

poro – reindeer, a generic term for the common, domesticated variety

Praasniekka – also *Prazniek*; Orthodox religious festival that sometimes includes a *ristinsaatto* to a lake, where a sermon takes place

puisto – park

pulla – cardamom-flavoured bun, the classic Finnish pastry

raatihuone – town hall; see also *kaupungintalo*

raatihuoneentori – *town square*

raja – border

ranta – shore

rautatie – railway

ravintola – restaurant, but also a bar

retkeilymaja – hostel

ruska – gorgeous but brief period in autumn (fall) when leaves turn red and yellow

saari – island

sahti – traditional ale flavoured with juniper berries

Sámi – the term for most indigenous people in the north of Finland; see also *lappalainen*

Sápmi – the area where Sámi culture and customs are still active; it is a quasi-legal territory covering the far north of Finland as well as parts of northern Sweden, Norway and Russia

satama – harbour

savusauna – 'smoke sauna'; these have no chimney but a small outlet for smoke

seita – holy site

seurahuone – literally, 'club room'

stad – city or town (Swedish)

Suomi – Finland

susi – wolf

taksi – taxi

talo – house or building

talvi – winter

tie – road

torget – market square (Swedish)

tori – market square; also called kauppatori

tsasouna – small chapel or prayer hall used by the Orthodox faith

tunturi – a northern fell, or large hill, that is treeless on top (as opposed to the less dramatic, tree-covered *vaara*); most of Finland's fells are in the Sápmi area, where many are sacred to the Sámi

tuomiokirkko – cathedral

tuoppi – beer-glass

vaara – danger; low, broad hill (typical in Lapland Province and North Karelia)

valtio – State or government

vandrarhem – hostel (Swedish)

vene – boat

vesi – water (generic form: *vettä*)

vihta – a bunch of fresh, leafy birch twigs used to beat/spank oneself in a sauna-type situation

vägen – road (Swedish)

yli, ylä- – upper; see also *ala-*

behind the scenes

SEND US YOUR FEEDBACK

We love to hear from travellers – your comments keep us on our toes and help make our books better. Our well-travelled team reads every word on what you loved or loathed about this book. Although we cannot reply individually to postal submissions, we always guarantee that your feedback goes straight to the appropriate authors, in time for the next edition. Each person who sends us information is thanked in the next edition – the most useful submissions are rewarded with a selection of digital PDF chapters.

Visit **lonelyplanet.com/contact** to submit your updates and suggestions or to ask for help. Our award-winning website also features inspirational travel stories, news and discussions.

Note: We may edit, reproduce and incorporate your comments in Lonely Planet products such as guidebooks, websites and digital products, so let us know if you don't want your comments reproduced or your name acknowledged. For a copy of our privacy policy visit lonelyplanet.com/privacy.

OUR READERS

Many thanks to the travellers who used the last edition and wrote to us with helpful hints, useful advice and interesting anecdotes:

Luke Anderson, Robert Basford, Betty Buldan, Alexandra Cadick, Jane Duckett, Laurence Dunn, Francis, Jim Hawkins, Benzi Kahana, Katell Le Guen, Richard Lemon, Renato Losio, Marcin Makowski, Takis Markopoulos, Alan Matthews, Tim McGrath, Dean Meservy, Mark Moloney, David Montgomery, Tom Moore, Ignacio Morejon, Jim O'Donnell, Ulrike Pellner, Torsten Reichardt, Gladys Rousseau, Michal Rudziecki, Juha Saarinen, Jarkko Salonen, Helena Savolainen, Felix Scholtes, Mike Scott, Jenni Stenman, Janne Toivonen, Hans van der Veeke, Indiya Whitehead, Edward Williams, Sekeun Yu

AUTHOR THANKS

Andy Symington

Research was brightened for a few days by the excellent company of my parents: many thanks! As ever, a large *kiitos* to Gustav, Marja, Mirjam and recent arrival Meri Schulman for unfailingly generous Helsinki hospitality; and to Fran Parnell great co-writing and for an excellent authors' evening in the capital. For various helpful deeds thanks to Iain, Teija, Jonah and Alex Campbell, Riika Åkerlind, Jenni Vähäsöyrinki, Alexis Kouros, Anne Harju, Heikki Paltto, and Satu Natunen. Lastly, much love and thanks for constant support to Elena Vázquez Rodríguez – *a por los veinte mil.*

Fran Parnell

A huge thank you to Andy Symington for being such a star coordinating author. I experienced so much kindness in Finland – if only I could thank everyone. Tourist-office staff were generous with their time and expertise, particularly Heli Hulkko, Leena Varpiola, Max Lindström, Tomi Karjalainen, Pirjo Taurula and Henna Arvela. Special thanks are due to Ami Ahlgren; wildlife guide and translator Esa Muikku; traveller Kate Brown; and the bus driver who rescued my car near Vuonislahti – I wish I knew your name.

ACKNOWLEDGMENTS

Climate map data adapted from Peel MC, Finlayson BL & McMahon TA (2007) 'Updated World Map of the Köppen-Geiger Climate Classification', *Hydrology and Earth System Sciences*, 11, 163344.

Bestselling guide to Finland – source: Nielsen BookScan, Australia, UK and USA, January 2011 to December 2011.

Cover photograph: Winter landscape at Kuusamo. Franz Christoph Robiller/Imagebroker.

Many of the images in this guide are available for licensing from Lonely Planet Images: www.lonelyplanetimages.com.

THIS BOOK

This 7th edition of Lonely Planet's Finland guidebook was researched and written by Andy Symington and Fran Parnell. The previous edition was written by Andy Symington and George Dunford.

This guidebook was commissioned in Lonely Planet's London office, and produced by the following:

Commissioning Editors Katie O'Connell, Glenn van der Knijff

Coordinating Editors Trent Holden, Briohny Hooper

Coordinating Cartographer Eve Kelly

Coordinating Layout Designer Virginia Moreno

Managing Editors Barbara Delissen, Angela Tinson

Senior Editor Martine Power

Managing Cartographer Shahara Ahmed

Managing Layout Designer Jane Hart

Assisting Editors Janet Austin, Kim Hutchins, Anne Mulvaney, Catherine Naghten, Sophie Splatt, Ross Taylor, Saralinda Turner

Assisting Cartographers Valeska Canas, Valentina Kremenchutskaya, Alex Leung

Cover Research Naomi Jennings

Internal Image Research Aude Vauconsant

Language Content Branislava Vladisavljevic

Thanks to Imogen Bannister, Xavier Di Toro, Ryan Evans, Martin Heng, Heather Howard, Yvonne Kirk, Ali Lemer, Alison Lyall, Kathleen Munnelly, Trent Paton, Adrian Persoglia, Anthony Phelan, Kirsten Rawlings, Amanda Sierp, Gerard Walker, Juan Winata

NOTES

index

The Finnish language places the letters å, ä and ö at the end of the alphabet.

OUR STORY

A beat-up old car, a few dollars in the pocket and a sense of adventure. In 1972 that's all Tony and Maureen Wheeler needed for the trip of a lifetime – across Europe and Asia overland to Australia. It took several months, and at the end – broke but inspired – they sat at their kitchen table writing and stapling together their first travel guide, *Across Asia on the Cheap*. Within a week they'd sold 1500 copies. Lonely Planet was born. Today, Lonely Planet has offices in Melbourne, London and Oakland, with more than 600 staff and writers. We share Tony's belief that 'a great guidebook should do three things: inform, educate and amuse'.

OUR WRITERS

Andy Symington

Coordinating Author; Helsinki; Tampere & Häme; The Lakeland; Oulu, Kainuu & Koillismaa; Lapland Andy has covered Finland for Lonely Planet several times, having first visited Helsinki many years ago more or less by accident. Walking on frozen lakes with the midday sun low in the sky made a quick and deep impression on him, even as fingers froze in the -30°C temperatures. Since then they can't keep him away from the country, fuelled by a love of the Kalevala, huskies, saunas, Finnish mustard, moody Suomi rock and metal, but above all of Finnish people and their beautiful country.

DISCARD

Fran Parnell

Turku & the South Coast; Åland Archipelago; Karelia; West Coast Fran's passion for northern Europe began while studying for a masters degree in Anglo-Saxon, Norse and Celtic, and any opportunity to visit the region is taken with glee. Particular highlights of this research trip were wandering the Bomarsund ruins eating wild strawberries; seeing bears in Karelia; rowing at midnight on Lake Pielinen; and coming across so much Finnish warmth and generosity while on the road. Fran has worked on other Lonely Planet guides, including *Scandinavian Europe, Iceland, Sweden, Denmark* and *Reykjavík*.

Published by Lonely Planet Publications Pty Ltd

ABN 36 005 607 983
7th edition – May 2012
ISBN 978 1 74179 582 0
© Lonely Planet 2012   Photographs © as indicated 2012
10 9 8 7 6 5 4 3 2 1
Printed in Singapore

Although the authors and Lonely Planet have taken all reasonable care in preparing this book, we make no warranty about the accuracy or completeness of its content and, to the maximum extent permitted, disclaim all liability arising from its use.

how to use this book

These symbols will help you find the listings you want:

- 👁 Sights
- 🏃 Beaches
- 🏃 Activities
- 🤝 Courses
- 👉 Tours
- 🎉 Festivals & Events
- 🛏 Sleeping
- ✕ Eating
- 🍷 Drinking
- ☆ Entertainment
- 🔒 Shopping
- ℹ Information/Transport

These symbols give you the vital information for each listing:

- 📞 Telephone Numbers
- ⊙ Opening Hours
- P Parking
- ⊖ Nonsmoking
- ✳ Air-Conditioning
- @ Internet Access
- 📶 Wi-Fi Access
- 🏊 Swimming Pool
- 🥗 Vegetarian Selection
- 📋 English-Language Menu
- 👪 Family-Friendly
- 🐾 Pet-Friendly
- 🚌 Bus
- ⛴ Ferry
- Ⓜ Metro
- Ⓢ Subway
- ⊖ London Tube
- 🚊 Tram
- 🚆 Train

Reviews are organised by author preference.

Look out for these icons:

- **TOP CHOICE** Our author's recommendation
- **FREE** No payment required
- 🌱 A green or sustainable option

Our authors have nominated these places as demonstrating a strong commitment to sustainability – for example by supporting local communities and producers, operating in an environmentally friendly way, or supporting conservation projects.

Map Legend

Sights
- 🏖 Beach
- 🛕 Buddhist
- 🏰 Castle
- ✝ Christian
- ☪ Hindu
- ☪ Islamic
- ✡ Jewish
- 🗿 Monument
- 🏛 Museum/Gallery
- 🏛 Ruin
- 🍷 Winery/Vineyard
- 🐾 Zoo
- 👁 Other Sight

Activities, Courses & Tours
- 🤿 Diving/Snorkelling
- 🛶 Canoeing/Kayaking
- ⛷ Skiing
- 🏄 Surfing
- 🏊 Swimming/Pool
- 🚶 Walking
- 🏄 Windsurfing
- ➕ Other Activity/Course/Tour

Sleeping
- 🛏 Sleeping
- ⛺ Camping

Eating
- ✕ Eating

Drinking
- ☕ Drinking
- ☕ Cafe

Entertainment
- ☆ Entertainment

Shopping
- 🔒 Shopping

Information
- ✉ Post Office
- ℹ Tourist Information

Transport
- ✈ Airport
- ⊗ Border Crossing
- 🚌 Bus
- Cable Car/Funicular
- Cycling
- Ferry
- Ⓜ Metro
- Monorail
- P Parking
- Ⓢ S-Bahn
- Taxi
- Train/Railway
- Tram
- Tube Station
- Ⓤ U-Bahn
- ● Other Transport

Routes
- Tollway
- Freeway
- Primary
- Secondary
- Tertiary
- Lane
- Unsealed Road
- Plaza/Mall
- Steps
- Tunnel
- Pedestrian Overpass
- Walking Tour
- Walking Tour Detour
- Path

Boundaries
- International
- State/Province
- Disputed
- Regional/Suburb
- Marine Park
- Cliff
- Wall

Population
- ● Capital (National)
- ◉ Capital (State/Province)
- ● City/Large Town
- ● Town/Village

Geographic
- 🏠 Hut/Shelter
- 🚡 Lighthouse
- 👓 Lookout
- ▲ Mountain/Volcano
- 🌴 Oasis
- 🌳 Park
-)(Pass
- 🧺 Picnic Area
- 💧 Waterfall

Hydrography
- River/Creek
- Intermittent River
- Swamp/Mangrove
- Reef
- Canal
- Water
- Dry/Salt/Intermittent Lake
- Glacier

Areas
- Beach/Desert
- + + + Cemetery (Christian)
- × × × Cemetery (Other)
- Park/Forest
- Sportsground
- Sight (Building)
- Top Sight (Building)